The Beard

Written and illustrated by
JO LAWRENCE

HODDER AND STOUGHTON
LONDON SYDNEY AUCKLAND TORONTO

This book is dedicated
to Collin Bates, the jazz
pianist, who told this
story to his daughters,
twenty years ago.

British Library Cataloguing in Publication Data

Lawrence, Jo
  The beard.
  I. Title
  823'.914 [J]   PZ7
    ISBN 0-340-39785-3

Text and illustrations copyright © Jo Lawrence 1986

First published 1986

Published by Hodder and Stoughton Children's Books,
a division of Hodder and Stoughton Ltd,
Mill Road, Dunton Green, Sevenoaks, Kent TN13 2YJ

Printed in Great Britain by Cambus Litho,
East Kilbride, Glasgow

Once upon a time there was a Beard.
He lived on a man's face. He was a reddish
brown Beard and the man took good care of
him, brushing him night and morning until he
shone, and cutting his edges neatly on Sundays.

The Beard was very contented with the man and the man was well pleased with the Beard, which kept him as warm as toast in winter.

On cold, dark nights, he would pull the

blankets right up to his chin which would have
been very cold indeed without the Beard.

Then summer came,
and one hot day, when
the man woke up, the
Beard had a very
strange feeling in the pit
of his middle
that something terrible
was about to
happen.

Sure enough the man went to the bathroom and peered into his shaving mirror.

"Hum," said the man to himself, tugging gently and affectionately at the Beard.

"This is really far too hot . . . I've had this beard for a long time now."

The man stared into the mirror for a minute or two. "I think I will have to shave it off," he said sadly. The Beard flinched in terror and bristled at the edges. "I have nowhere to go," he thought unhappily.

"No, no, please," said the Beard aloud.
"I am sorry, my old friend," said the man,
"but I am going abroad tomorrow where it will
be far too hot for a beautiful warm beard like
you."

"No, no," pleaded the Beard, but no sound came out.

Then the man shaved off the Beard very carefully, all in one piece.

When it was over the Beard lay on the edge of the sink, utterly exhausted.

When the man looked in the mirror he was
so pleased with himself. His chin was very pink
and shiny underneath. Then he dressed in a
new suit, and left his home to board the ship
which would take him far, far away.

The Beard, lonely and homeless, wandered all over the town and then went down to the sea to watch the man leave on his ship. He felt so sad, he had nowhere to go. He knew of no one who needed a beard. So he watched from the cliff as the ship took the man off into the distance, until it became a dot on the edge of the sea and disappeared.

"Hello," said a voice.
The Beard didn't even look round.
   "Nice evening."
   "Yes," said the Beard but he didn't mean it.
   "You're a fine looking beard. I'd like a beard, but I've never been able to grow one. I've never managed anything more than a few bristles."

The Beard looked at the man.
He began to feel a little better.
    "Tell you what, why don't you come
and live on my chin? You
look a bit lost." The Beard
couldn't believe his
luck. He jumped up
on to the man's chin,
shouting for joy.

"Well, you fit very well," said the man. "We'll go home now and see my wife, she'll be very pleased."

So the man took his new beard home, stopping every now and then to look at himself in a shop window.

When the man's wife saw his new beard, she hardly recognised him.

The man said "Hello," and kissed her, but she frowned and pulled away.

"Where did you find that beard? It tickles horribly." The man stroked the Beard. "You'll get used to it."

"I won't – it's itchy and untidy, and anyway, I don't like it," said his wife.

The Beard looked at her and waited, resigned to his fate.

Once again that day he was shaved off and forced to leave his new-found home.

He was alone once more.

The man watched him go very sadly. His wife began to feel sorry that she had been so harsh with the Beard, (she had had a bad day at work).

"Oh, what can we do?" said the woman. She was thinking that the Beard had nowhere to go that night and already it was late.

"I just don't know," said the man.

"I've had an idea." She brightened suddenly. "He . . . he could live on your head!"

It was true enough the man WAS bald. His head got cold in winter and he had to wear a warm hat.

"Quickly," she said, "he may have gone."

The man rushed out of the house and round the corner and down the street and up the hill.

There was no sign of the Beard, and it was getting dark, and large, cold drops of rain began to fall from the sky.

The man could hardly see, but just as he was about to give up, he saw the Beard, standing shivering on a doorstep.

The man was so out of breath he could hardly speak. "Wh . . . why don't you come and live on my head? I'm bald, as you can see."

"Whoever heard of a beard living on a man's head?" said the Beard.

But he had nowhere to go.

So he leapt on to the bald shiny head of the man, where to his great surprise he felt very comfortable.

Now the man had glossy, reddish brown hair, which kept him warm in winter, and the man's wife was pleased because she wouldn't need to knit any more hats for the man's head.

And all three of them lived happily for the rest of their days.

A New Geography of Britain

Rex Beddis

Oxford University Press 1985

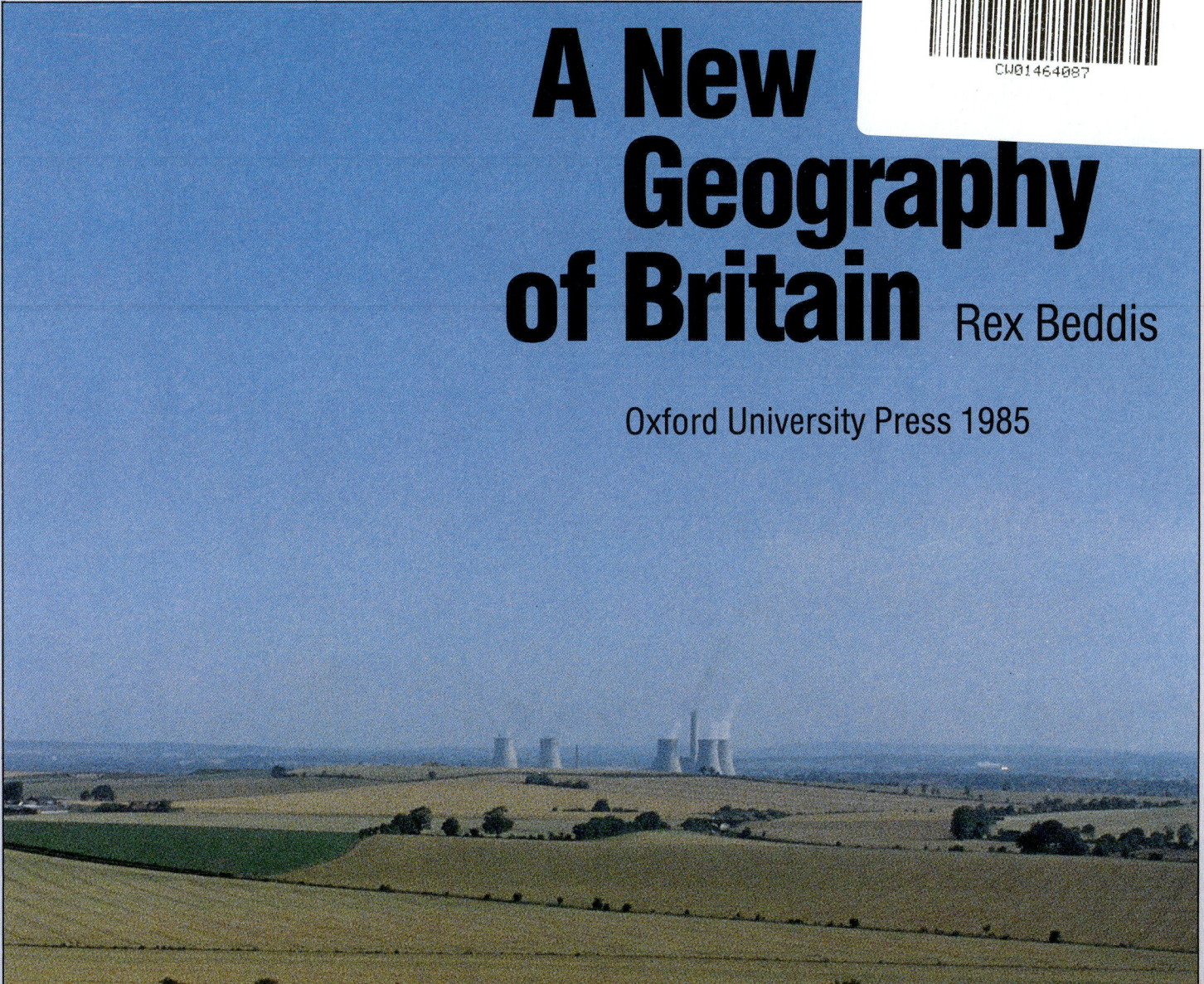

Oxford University Press, Walton Street, Oxford OX2 6DP

Oxford London
New York Toronto Melbourne Auckland
Kuala Lumpur Singapore Hong Kong Tokyo
Delhi Bombay Calcutta Madras Karachi
Nairobi Dar es Salaam Cape Town
and associated companies in
Beirut Berlin Ibadan Mexico City Nicosia
Oxford is a trade mark of Oxford University Press

ISBN 0 19 913293 3

Phototypeset by Tradespools Ltd., Frome, Somerset
Printed in Hong Kong

Introduction

The aim of the book is to present an accurate picture of Britain in the mid 1980s. All places change and nowadays the pace of change can be rapid and dramatic. This applies not only to the appearance of cities and the country-side, but also to types of work available and social conditions.

Because of this, 'facts' and statistics soon become dated and care has to be taken not to give a wrong impression about places and people.

Every effort has been made to give a balanced view of Britain, but every author, given the limited extent of the book, has to choose which features to include, emphasize or omit.

Many features described in the book are found in other parts of Britain and it is useful and interesting to compare the local area and its issues with these other places.

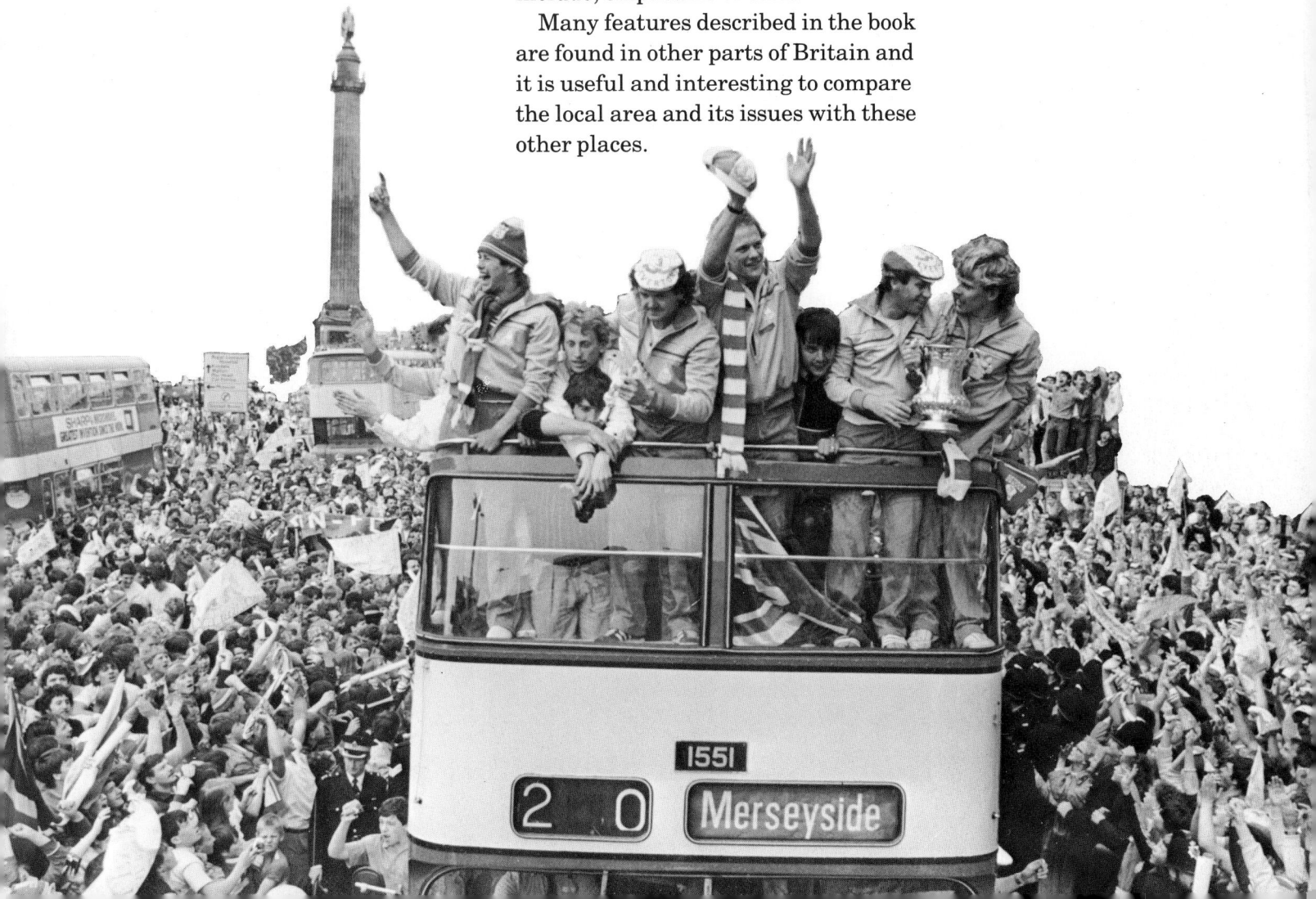

Contents

Acknowledgements

The Publishers would like to thank the following for permission to reproduce photographic material:

Aerofilms Ltd: 15, 21 (bottom), 23, 24 (bottom right), 27, 50, 51, 55, 118 (top), 145, 149, 165, 202, 208 (right), 210, 247; Airviews (M/C) Ltd: 109, 218, 229 (top); Asda Stores: 118 (bottom); Associated British Foods plc: 88, 89 (both), 91, 117; Austin Rover Group: 102 (bottom); Australian Information Service: 263; BACO plc: 216; Patrick Bailey: 16 (right), 20, 29 (top left), 44, 45 (top), 56 (top), 136, 138 (left), 140 (top), 161, 232 (bottom left), 252 (left); Barbican Centre: 245, 246 (all three); Balfour, Beatty Fairclough Keilder Joint Venture: 188; John Bartholomew & Son Ltd 48; Barnaby's Picture Library: 28, 139 (both), 144, 148 (top), 204 (both), 229 (bottom); Basildon Development Corporation: 126; BBC Hulton Picture Library: 114 (top); B.L. Heritage Ltd: 102 (top); The Board of Deputies of British Jews: 225 (top); BOC Group plc: 250 (left); Martin Bond: 206 (top); British Airports Authority: 209; The British Council: 261; British Petroleum: 174; British Rail: 155, 160; British Steel Corporation: 99; Cable & Wireless plc: 255; Romano Cagnoni: 67; Camera Press Ltd: 57, 142 (right), 219, 228 (bottom right), 248 (top); Paul Campbell: 7; J. Allan Cash Ltd: 18, 71, 182; Derek Cattani: 68 (top); CEGB: 176, 177 (top); Centre for Remote Sensing (Imperial College, London): 32 (top both); COI: 250 (centre), 251; Clarks Ltd: 217 (top):
D. Constance Ltd: 49 (bottom); Gerry Cranham: 127; Tony Dale: 49 (top & centre); The Daily Telegraph Colour Library: 116, 129, 185 (top), 208 (top left), 241 (top left); EEC Commission: 256; Eros Data Center: 9, 17 (bottom); Keith Evans: 146 (top left); Farmer's Weekly: 77, 82 (top, bottom left, right); Sam Farr: 73, 74, 75 (all three); Ferranti: 87; Colin A. Fletcher: 207 (both); Nick Fogden: 122 (all); Jenny Matthews/Format Photographers: 111; Ford Motor Company Ltd: 4 (right), 100 (left); Sally & Richard Greenhill: 5 (left), 255 (bottom), 243 (both); GLC: 205 (bottom), 213; Nick Hedges: 215; David Higgs: 12 (top & centre), 16 (left), 17 (top), 137 (centre), 198; Ian Berry/John Hillelson Agency Ltd: 40 (bottom); Georg Gerster/John Hillelson Agency Ltd: 137 (top), 239; J.P. Laffont/John Hillelson Agency Ltd: 128 (both); Michael Hardy/John Hillelson Agency Ltd: 132 (top); Brian Seed/John Hillelson Agency Ltd: 153 (top); David Hurn/John Hillelson Agency Ltd: 200 (top & bottom left); John Hillelson Agency Ltd: 248 (bottom); Mike Howarth: 61 (both), 72 (bottom), 81 (top right), 154, 233; Peter Holdgate: 260; IBM UK Ltd: 104 (bottom right); ICI plc: 93, 94; Donald I. Innes: 151; Interfoto Archives Ltd: 46 (top), 125 (bottom right); Terry Jennings: 42 (bottom right); Jean Guy Jules: 84; Keystone Press Agency: 230 (top); Lansing Ltd: 221 (left); Leeds Utd Association Football Club Ltd: 134 (bottom left); Liverpool Daily Post & Echo: 3, 235 (bottom), 236 (right); London Express News & Feature Service: 38; Lotus Cars Ltd: 100 (right); The Mansell Collection Ltd: 42 (bottom left), 56 (bottom); Christopher Mares: 48; Merseyside Development Corporation: 232 (top); Milton Keynes Development

Corporation: 64 (bottom); Richard Morris: 195; National Coal Board: 153 (bottom), 168 (both), 169; National Monuments Record: 214 (top); New Scientist: 205 (top); Laurie Sparham/Network: 46 (bottom left); John Sturrock/Network 60, 221 (right), 222 (bottom), 230 (bottom), 232 (bottom right), 235 (top); Steve Benbow/Network: 96, 97, 224 (left), 228 (left); Barry Lewis/Network: 137 (bottom), 200 (right); Mike Abrams/Network: 2, 177 (bottom), 179, 254 (centre); Chris Davies/Network: 178; Mike Goldwater/Network: 262 (left); North East Regional Airport Authority/Airfotos Newcastle: 164; The Observer: 85 (right), 98; Ordnance Survey: 47, 93; Prof. J.A. Patmore: 196 (bottom); Photo Library International: 125 (bottom left), 141, 180 (right); Picturepoint: 79; Port of Felixstowe, Suffolk: 166 (bottom); Press Association: 34; Stewart Ramsden: 197 (top); Rex Features Ltd: 68 (bottom), 132 (bottom left & right), 180 (left), 224 (right), 226 (top right); RSPB: 203; Sefton Photo Library: 212 (right), 237 (right); Gatton/Selfridges: 113 (right); Shell UK Ltd: 80 (top); Arthur Shepherd: 80 (bottom); K.B. Shone, F.R.Met.S: 29 (bottom three); Adrian Smith: 12 (bottom), 24 (top); The Sunday Times: 82 (bottom centre); Alison Souster: 13, 65 (left), 212 (top left), 237 (left); Space Frontiers Ltd: 8; Spectrum Colour Library: 140 (bottom); South Yorkshire P.T.E: 158 (bottom right); R. Stephenson: 113 (left); Jeffrey Tabberner: 4 (left), 5 (right), 21 (top), 32 (centre left, bottom left), 37, 39, 46 (right), 53 (both), 58 (three left), 64 (top), 66, 72 (bottom), 85 (left), 86, 101, 104 (top), 112, 120, 124, 125 (top), 130 (both), 133 (both), 146 (top right, bottom), 148 (bottom), 152, 156 (both), 157 (both), 158 (top left), 193 (all), 196 (top), 212 (bottom), 244 (both), 252 (right), 253; Thames Water: 186 (top), 189: The Times: 36, 78, 81 (top left), 107, 114 (bottom), 142 (left), 162, 183, 187, 194, 211, 214 (bottom), 222 (top), 226 (left & bottom) 236 (left), 258, 262 (right); John Topham Picture Library: 166 (top), 241 (top right), 250 (right); Tyne & Wear P.T.E: 159; UKAEA: 206 (bottom left & right); Understanding Electricity Education Service: 167; Universal Pictorial Press & Agency Ltd: 106; Andrew Varley: 186 (bottom); Vickers Defence Systems: 110 (both); Wales Tourist Board: 41, 143; Wessex Newspapers/Bath Evening Chronicle: 138 (right); Derek West: 158 (top right, bottom left), 254 (right); West Air Photography: 24 (bottom left), 25, 40 (top), 45 (bottom), 46 (centre), 52, 65 (right), 76, 81 (bottom), 119, 121, 173, 181, 184, 192 (both), 217 (bottom); Wilcon Homes: 241 (bottom); Wimpey Homes Holdings Ltd: 254 (left); Yorkshire Museum: 42 (top three); Yorkshire Post Newspapers Ltd: 134 (bottom left and right); Tom Young: 58 (right). Cover Photographs: (*front*) Jeffrey Tabberner/Adrian Smith, (*back*) John Hillelson Agency/Georg Gerster.

All newspaper articles in this book are from *The Times* newspaper except for pp 230 and 224 (*The Town and Country Planning Magazine*) and pp 43 and 203 (*The Geographical Magazine*). The diagrams on pp 113 and 115 are by permission of the editor of *Teaching Geography*.

Chapter 1 The physical environment

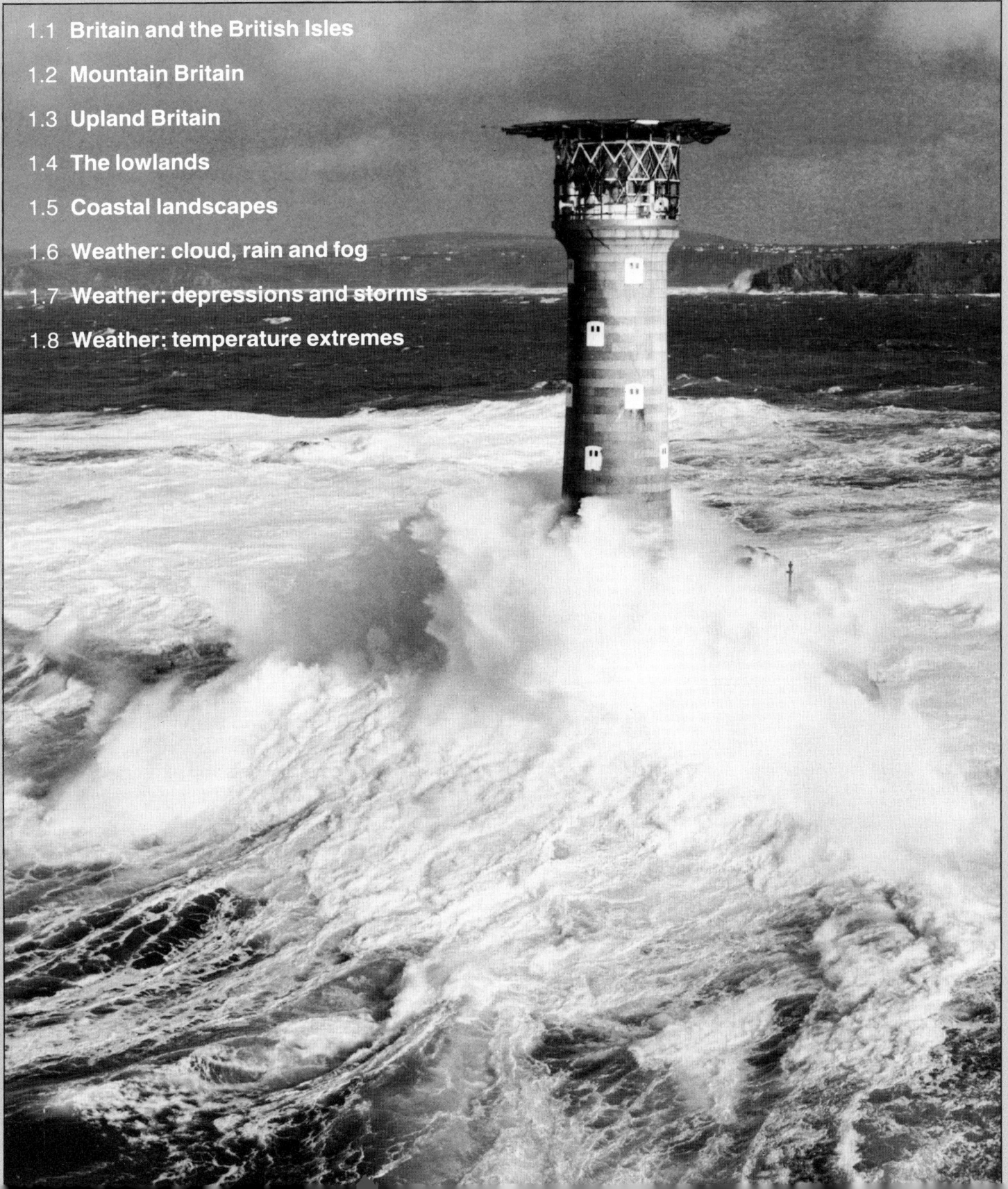

Britain and the British Isles

Britain is part of the United Kingdom of Great Britain and Northern Ireland. The United Kingdom is part of the British Isles

United Kingdom (England, Wales, Scotland and Northern Ireland)

Irish Republic

SCOTLAND

N. IRELAND

Dublin

WALES

ENGLAND

London

NORTH SEA

English Channel

N

0 100 200 300 km

Picture, taken from a weather satellite, of cloud cover over the British Isles and part of mainland Europe

Satellite pictures and images

Two of these views of Britain were obtained from satellites orbiting the earth at different heights. Some satellite pictures are taken by high quality cameras and nowadays these can show remarkable details of large areas of land. Others carry instruments that continually scan the earth and sense the brightness of reflected sunlight. This information is sent back to earth stations where computers turn it into false colour prints. The picture of South-East England showing London and the estuary of the River Thames was made in this way. The different colours tell us a great deal about this part of Britain, as can be seen on pages 10 and 11. It is only recently that such images have been available. In the past, pictures had to be drawn by surveyors and map makers. More recently they have been taken by 'ordinary' cameras from balloons, aeroplanes and space-craft. The area of the earth that can be seen and the amount of detail will clearly vary with the height from which the picture has been taken and with the kinds of instrument used.

Pictures and maps

The map of the British Isles, the surrounding seas, and part of mainland Europe shows the same area of the earth's surface as the satellite photograph below it, and the similarity of the coastlines should be easy to see. But there are great differences between the picture and the map. The picture shows all that could be seen (within the limits of the instruments) at a particular instant on a particular day. It includes cloud cover, and will never be exactly the same again. The map, on the other hand, is an artificial picture. The map makers have decided what to put in and what to leave out. Some of the information on the map, such as the words or the national boundaries, could not be seen on the picture no matter how great the detail provided by the instruments. Photographs, images and maps all have advantages and disadvantages in describing places and storing information about them.

The British Isles and Britain

If it had been possible to produce a satellite picture from this same position about two million years ago, before the Ice Age, it would have looked very different from this one. The British Isles are part of mainland Europe, and the North Sea and English Channel are shallow and very recent in terms of earth history. If the sea level were to fall about 200 metres, the British Isles would be once again a part of mainland Europe.

As the map shows, the British Isles consist of two states, The United Kingdom of Great Britain and Northern Ireland and The Irish Republic. Each state has its own government and laws. The boundary between the Irish Republic and the Province of Northern Ireland may be clearly defined on the map, though in places much less so on the ground. There is a great deal of argument about whether Northern Ireland should really be a part of the United Kingdom or the Irish Republic, but at the moment it is legally and in fact a part of the United Kingdom.

Great Britain is a term for the large island (and many smaller ones) which consists of the three 'countries' of England, Scotland and Wales. These are separate but not independent of each other. There is disagreement about how far each of these places should have their own government and laws. It is important to understand the differences between these three terms: The British Isles; The United Kingdom of Great Britain and Northern Ireland; and Great Britain. (Note that the 'Great' in 'Great Britain' is used in the sense of 'large', to distinguish it from 'Little Britain' or Brittany in France.)

1 **a**) Name four islands or groups of islands that have not been named on the map. Describe their location. **b**) Name an island group that is part of the United Kingdom that is not shown on the map or visible on the picture.

2 **a**) What is the name of the area that would become dry land if the sea level around the British Isles fell by about 200 metres? What is the shortest distance between Britain and the mainland of Europe?

3 **a**) Which areas on the photograph opposite were covered by cloud when the picture was taken? **b**) which parts of Britain were in clear sunlight?

4 Compare the photographs on pages 8, 9, and 247 in terms of **a**) the amount of area shown, **b**) the amount of detail given and **c**) what it tells us about the place.

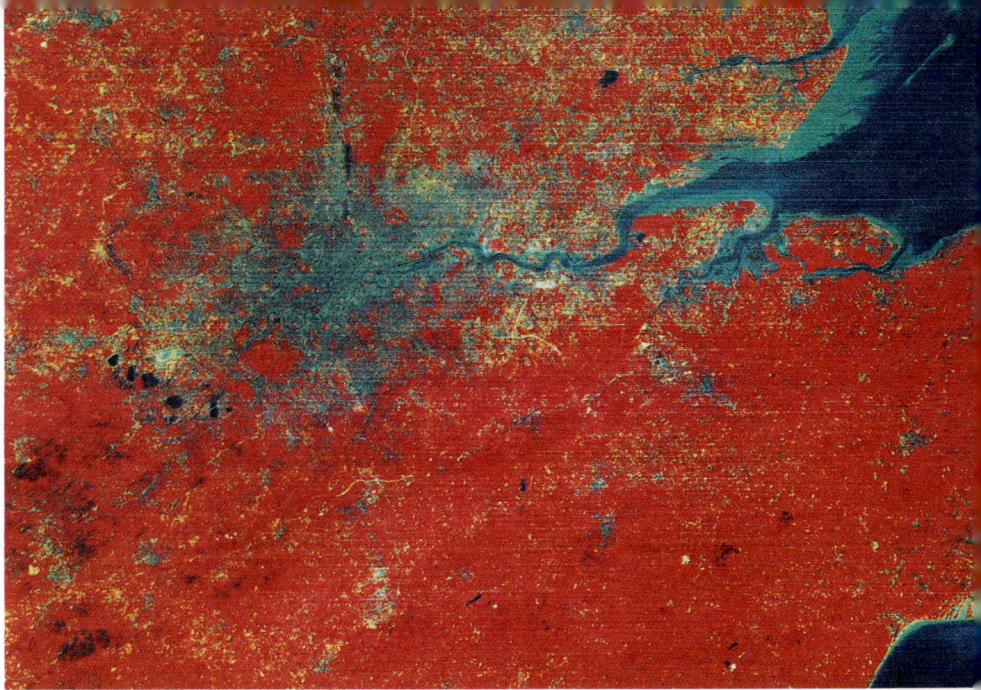

Landsat image of London and South-East England obtained on 29 July 1975 (see page 11)

Section across the British Isles, The North Sea and mainland Europe

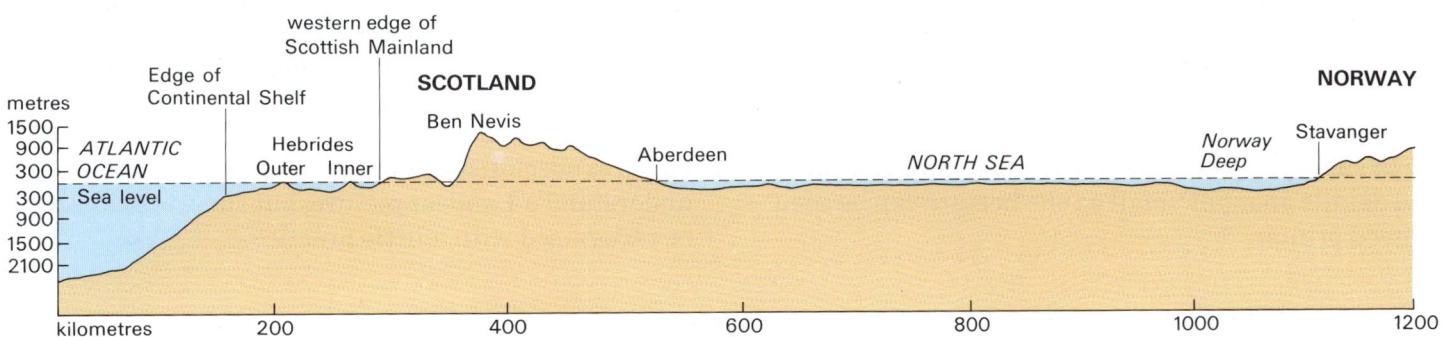

Landsat images

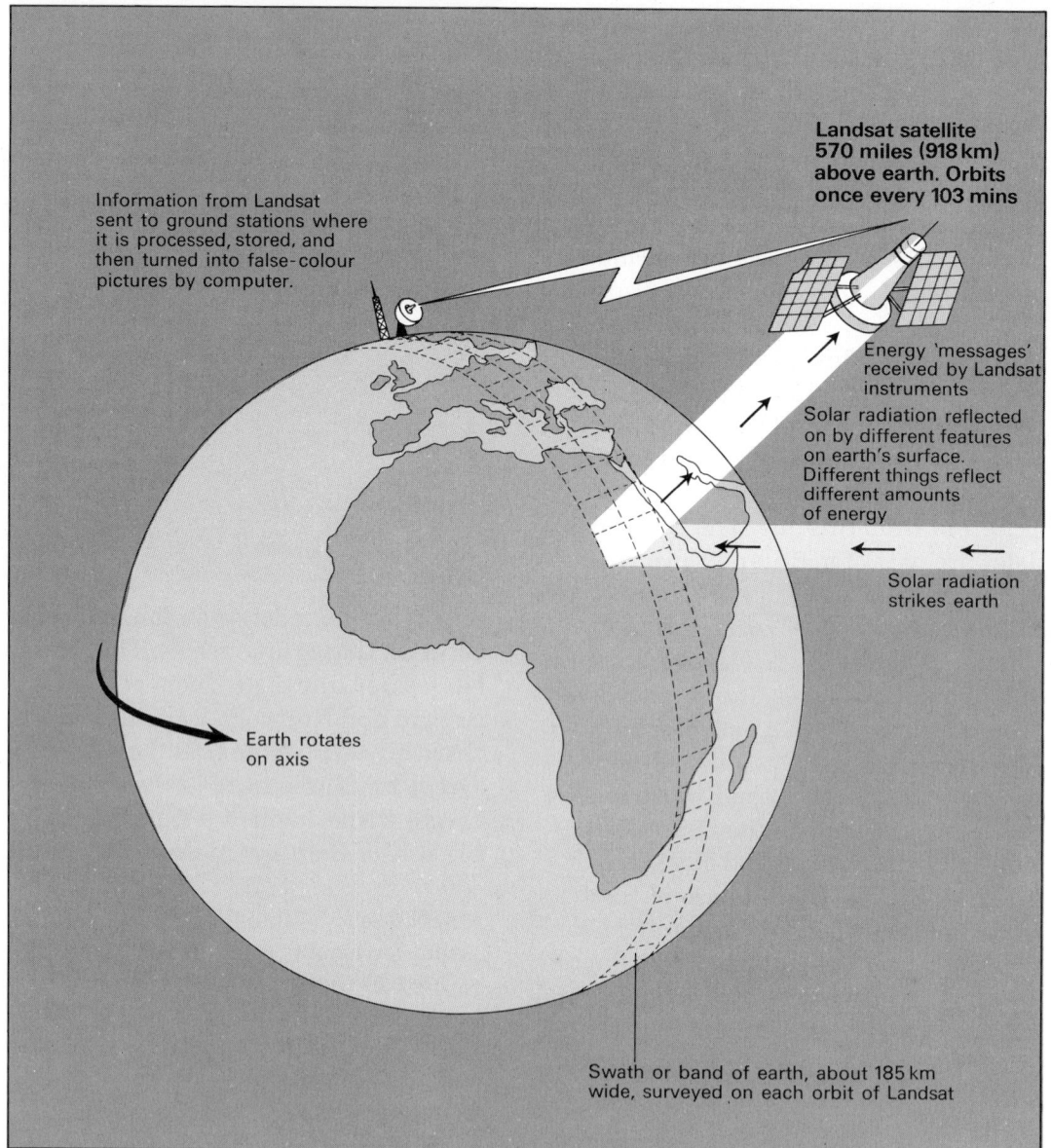

Information from Landsat sent to ground stations where it is processed, stored, and then turned into false-colour pictures by computer.

Landsat satellite 570 miles (918 km) above earth. Orbits once every 103 mins

Energy 'messages' received by Landsat instruments

Solar radiation reflected on by different features on earth's surface. Different things reflect different amounts of energy

Solar radiation strikes earth

Earth rotates on axis

Swath or band of earth, about 185 km wide, surveyed on each orbit of Landsat

How Landsat images are made

As it became more and more important to map the resources of the earth, scientists began to use satellites to observe and record the earth repeatedly from directly above. The first Landsat was launched in 1972 and continued until 1979. Landsat-2 and Landsat-3 were launched in 1975 and 1978.

The Landsat travels around the earth in an almost circular north-to-south orbit every 103 minutes. As the earth rotates beneath the orbiting satellite a slightly different swath or band of earth is sensed each time. Because of this rotation it is 18 days before the Landsat passes exactly over the same spot again. In other words Landsat will sense conditions in South-East England every 18 days, and each picture will be slightly different – quite apart from any cloud cover. The swath or band of earth surveyed by Landsat is about 115 miles wide, and details about as small as one hectare can be seen in good prints.

The pictures are not like photographs – they are made up from electric signals sent by the instruments in Landsat. These are based on the different amounts of energy reflected from the band of earth over which it is travelling. The signals are then made into false-colour prints that can be 'read' by anyone who knows what the colours represent.

Generally speaking, in the false-colour picture any green growing vegetation appears a red colour. Variation in the redness may show different sorts of plants, their stages of growth, or variations in the height of the vegetation. Cities and roads with their mixture of concrete, asphalt roofing materials and so on are bright and usually appear light blue. Deep clear water is black, while shallow water or water with silt or sand in it appears light blue to white. It requires specialist knowledge to be able to fully understand a Landsat picture, but some features can be recognised with a little practice.

Exercise 1 Landsat image of South East England

The map below is based on the Landsat picture of South East England on page 9. Copy or trace the map.

1 Print the names of the three towns shown by the circles. They are Chelmsford, Crawley and Maidstone.

2 What features can be seen at A, B, C, D, and E? What colour are they on the Landsat map?

3 The areas numbered 1–3 are two well-known London Parks and a Garden. What are they called?

4 What very large feature is shown by the light-blue patch at 4? What clue is given by the colour?

5 Give the names of the physical features at X, Y and Z.

6 Suggest how Landsat pictures taken earlier or later in the year of this area might be different and say why. What are the advantages of having a regular series of pictures of a part of the earth's surface as provided by Landsat?

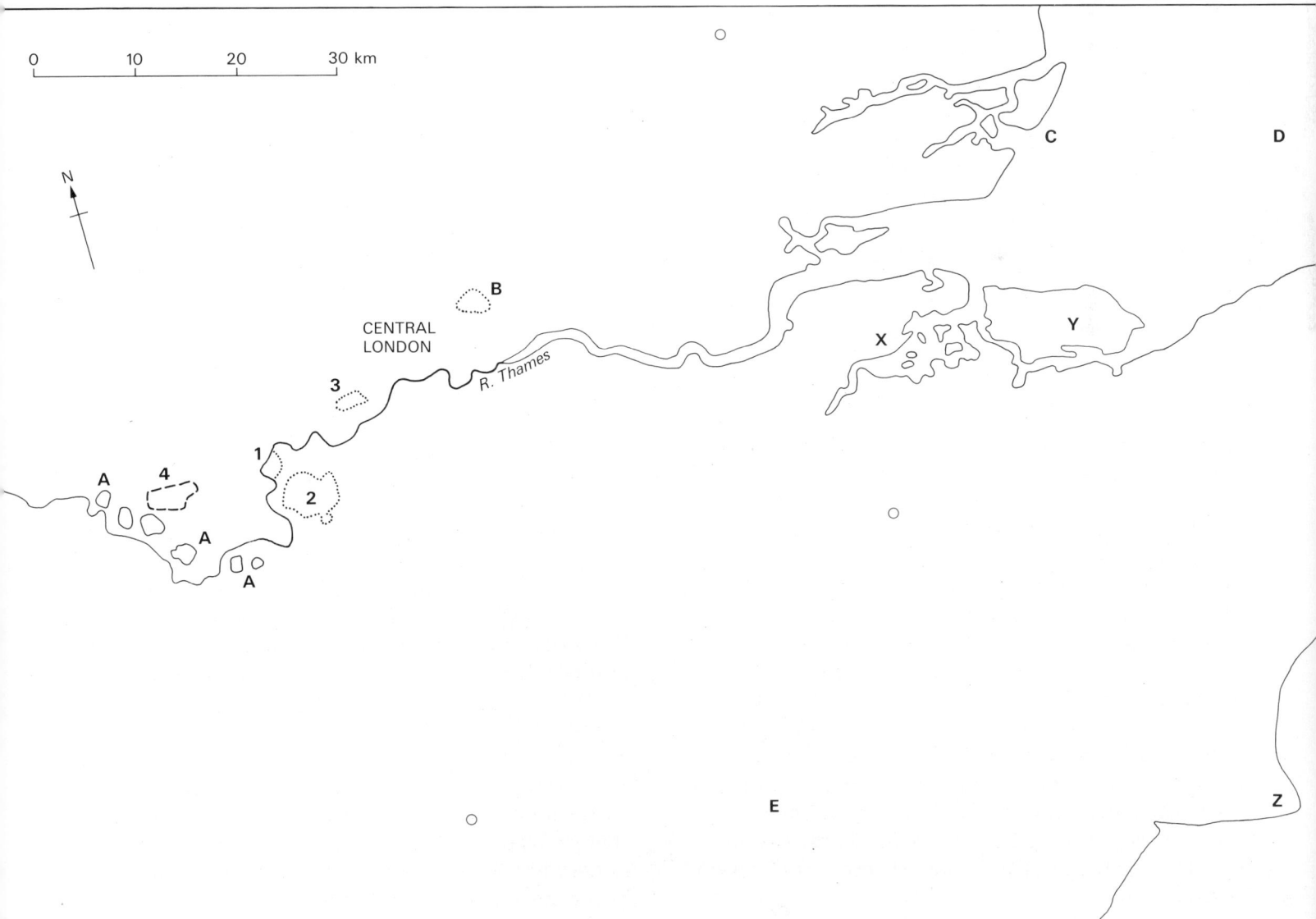

Mountain Britain

Crib Goch in the mountains of North Wales

Rescue by helicopter from the slopes of Tryton in North Wales

A view north along Borrowdale in the Lake District

In view of its fairly small size, Britain has a remarkable variety of landscapes. The appearance of some of these and the way in which they have been formed will be seen in the next few pages. The ways in which these environments have been used and affected by people will be considered throughout the book.

Mountain landscapes

The Cairngorm Mountains in Scotland (page 15), with four summits or peaks over 4000 feet (1220 metres) above sea level, provide the largest area of mountain landscape in Britain. The peaks rise above a high barren plateau that is carved and cut up by gullies, long narrow valleys and hollows known as corries. The corries and valleys sometimes contain lakes, their round or narrow ribbon-like shapes reflecting the shape of the land. Many of these features were formed by the action of ice sheets and valley glaciers during the bitterly cold conditions of the Ice Age. Nowadays the process of wearing down the mountains continues by the action of streams and rivers, and by the 'shattering' effects of freezing and thawing. Large quantities of broken rock or scree fragments are strewn across the lower margins of the steep slopes. The ways in which ice shapes mountain landscapes are shown on page 14.

The view of Ben Nevis, the highest point in Britain at 4406 feet (1349 metres) and about seventy kilometres from the Cairngorms, shows some of these features. The peak, knife-like ridge (arête) and the steep, sides of the corrie wall can be easily seen on this clear, calm day. Similar features can be recognised in the photograph of Crib Goch in the mountains of North Wales. These peaks are much lower than those in the Cairngorms, and suggest that a mountain landscape is the result of rugged and varied relief as much as sheer height or altitude.

The map on the right shows the areas of mountain landscape in Britain. These contain some of the oldest rocks in the world. Some have been formed from igneous activity, others are sedimentary rocks while many others were sedimentaries that have been changed into metamorphic rocks by the intense pressure and heat they have experienced over millions of years of upheaval and wearing down. It is hard to realise that some of these spectacular mountain peaks are made of rocks once laid down at the bottom of the sea.

The use of mountain areas

Mountains are spectacular and exciting places, but usually very dangerous. The average February temperature on Ben Nevis is − 4.6°C and the coldest temperatures fall well below this. Heavy rainfall, gale-force winds, and a thick cloud or mist are frequent and for much of the year there is a cover of snow. It is hardly surprising that only thin soils and a sparse cover of mountain or moorland vegetation are found under such conditions.

12

Ben Nevis, the highest point in Britain

The mountain, upland and lowland areas of Britain

The combination of rugged landscape and harsh weather is not very useful for most types of farming, but the areas are far from economically useless. Mountain areas also attract many visitors and tourists. The impact of these, in fact, can be so severe that the environment is threatened, and attempts have been made to solve the problem by setting up National Parks, Forest Parks and Nature Reserves.

1 What are the names and locations of the different areas of 'Mountain Britain'?

2 Draw a simple sketch map of Britain and on it locate the four mountain areas illustrated or mentioned on these pages.

3 Give some reasons why the weather (temperature, rain, snowfall and winds) are more extreme near the tops of mountains than on lower ground.

4 List some of the reasons why people are attracted to mountain environments. What are some of the dangers of such environments, and in what way may visitors and tourists be a threat?

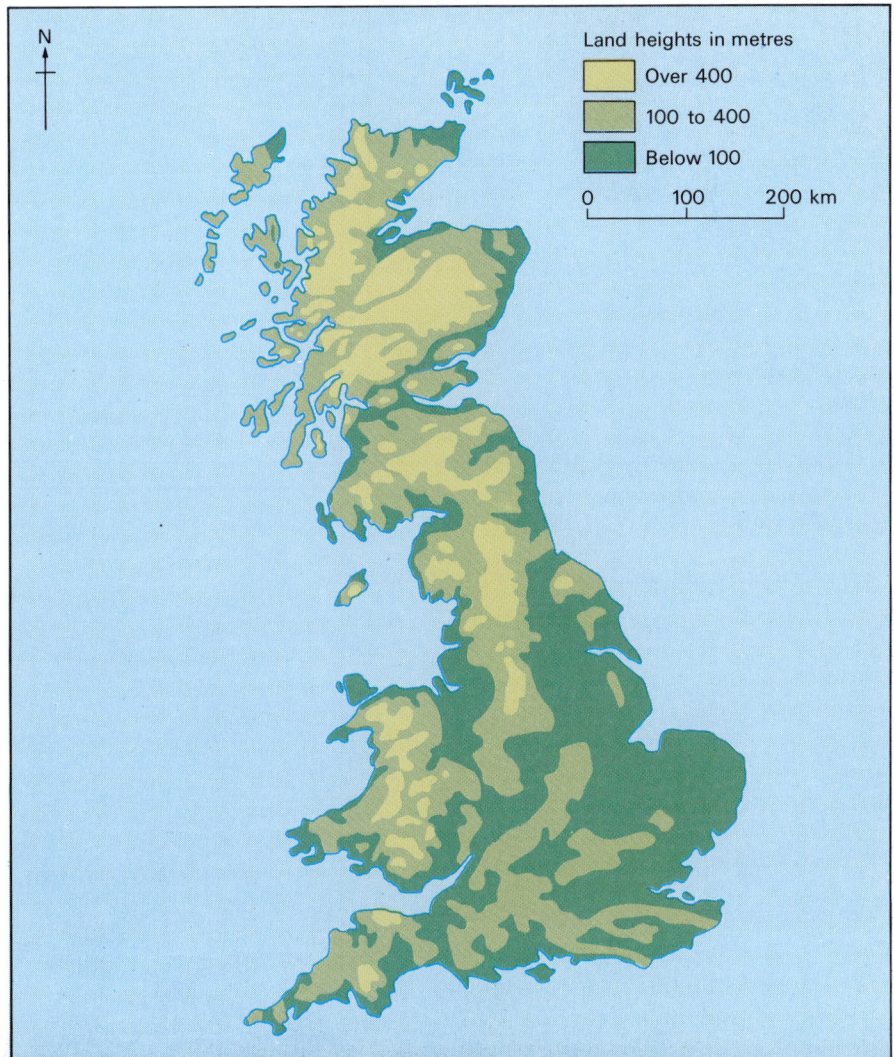

Land heights in metres

Over 400

100 to 400

Below 100

0   100   200 km

The work of ice in mountains

Most parts of Britain covered by ice sheets during the Ice Age have been affected by the action of the ice. In the mountains this has produced the sorts of landscapes shown here. The smoothed but scarred plateaux, the steep-sided corries and the long, deep, U-shaped valleys show the eroding power of ice and embedded rocks.

The moraines are the deposits of rocks and other smaller materials carried by the ice as it moved over the landscape and down the valleys. A great deal of ice-carried deposits is also found in lowland areas of Britain.

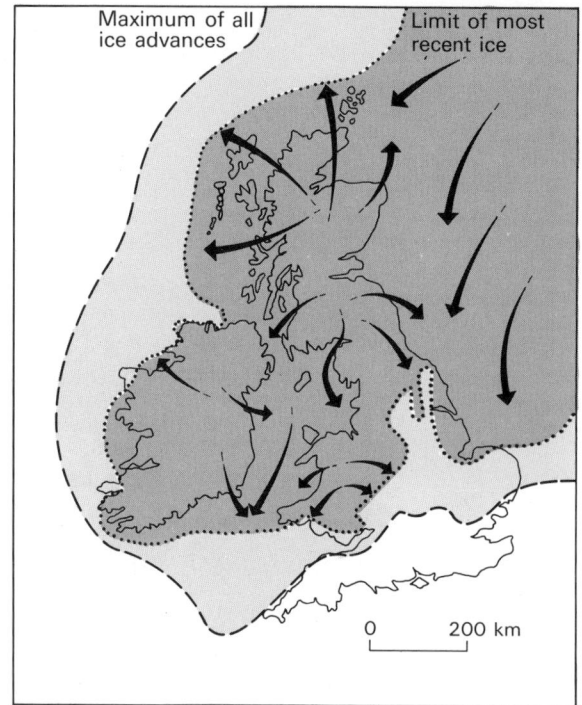

The parts of Britain covered by ice sheets during the ice age

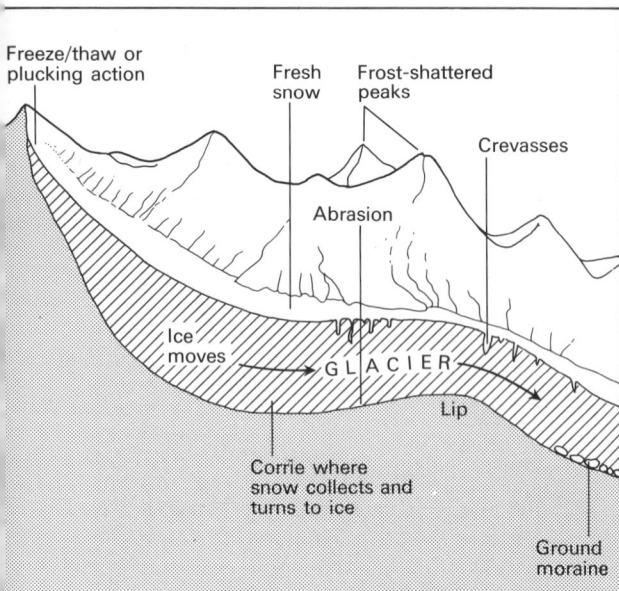

The formation and action of ice in the upper part of a valley

Above, right: Mountain landscape with glaciers

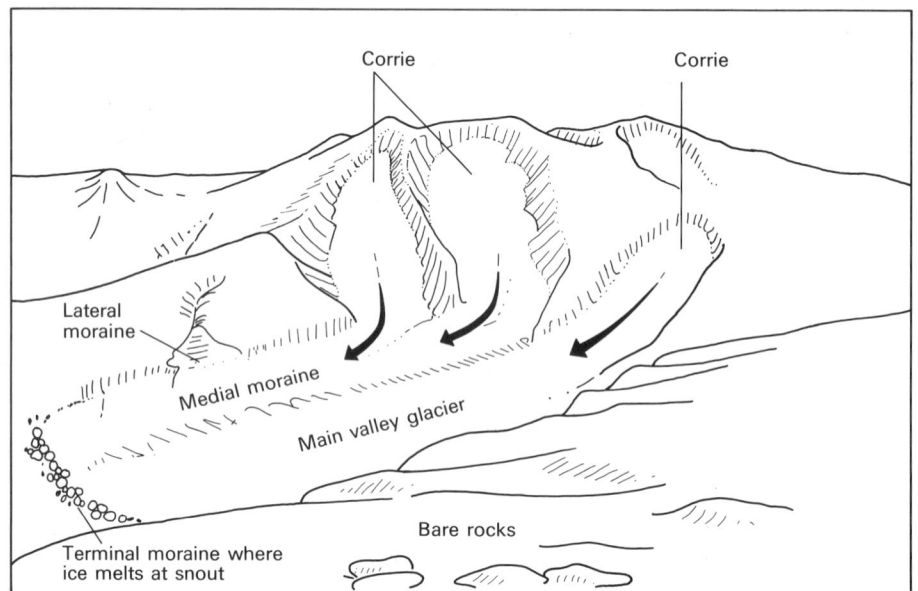

The same landscape after glaciers have melted

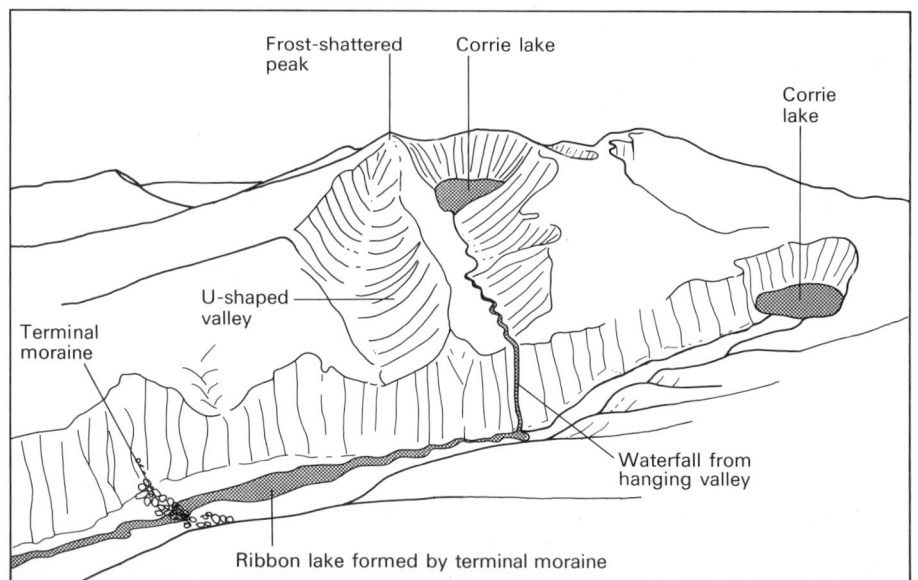

14

Exercise 2 **Ice-carved mountain landscapes**

1 Make an outline drawing from this photograph of the Cairngorm Mountains. Complete your sketch adding labels to show: mountain peak; barren plateau surface; U-shaped valley; scree; ribbon lake; stream; hanging valley.

2 Draw a sketch of the area shown in the photo-graph as it might have looked when the ice sheets were melting and valleys were filled with gla-ciers.

3 Describe the scene in a few words as you see it. Now describe what you feel about such a place. Do you like it or not, and why?

Upland Britain

The Pennines

Some parts of Britain can hardly be described as mountainous, but their hilly landscapes and sometimes severe weather make them very different from lowland Britain. The Pennine hills that run in a north-south direction through Northern England are a good example. At the time of the year when the Landsat picture was taken (February) the tops of the hills were covered in snow and these appear white. The richer vegetation of the river valleys and dales is in red and the urban areas are blue.

As can be seen from the maps and diagrams on page 18, the Pennines consist largely of limestone and sandstone rocks. These were originally laid down as almost horizontal beds of sedimentary rock with the sandstone overlying the limestone. They were later folded into a relatively gentle arch or anticline, with some breaking or faulting in places. Since then various types of erosion have stripped off much of the newer rocks and in the Northern Pennines and the southern part known as The Peak District much of the sandstone as well, exposing the limestone. The result is that the Pennine hills consist of two very different landscapes – the limestone and the sandstone.

The Millstone Grit areas

The sandstones consist of thick beds known as the Millstone Grit. They form broad rolling moorlands with dark brown rocks exposed here and there as edges, crags or tors. The rock is impervious, so drainage is poor and there are large areas of boggy peat covered with vegetation called cotton grass. Although there is some sheep farming on these hills the damp, acid soil does not encourage farming. The streams that rise in the hills, however, provide an important source of water for many of the towns in the nearby lowlands.

Below: Climbers and walkers on Froggat Edge, an outcrop of Millstone Grit

Right: The swallow-hole entrance to the vertical chamber of Gaping Gill in the limestone area of Ingleborough (see page 19)

Exit from underground caves in limestone, near Dovedale in the Peak District

The Carboniferous limestone areas

There are many different types of limestone rock in Britain, and this particular sort was deposited in the Carboniferous geological period some time before the Millstone Grit sandstones. Limestone rock is well jointed, and will slowly dissolve as rainwater eats away at the cracks and joints. The diagram on page 19 shows how there may be a network of underground tunnels and caves in the limestone. Surface water enters these through sink holes or swallow holes. The water eventually will reach an impervious layer of rock and find its way out of the limestone, sometimes miles away from its starting point. In places there are 'dry' valleys in this massive limestone. These may have been formed when the roof of an underground system collapsed, or they may have been formed under different climatic conditions in the past when water flowed over the surface of the limestone and carved a valley.

Unlike the Millstone Grit, there is very little surface water. The thin and dry soils are not very suitable for cultivation, but sheep are reared. The limestone is used as a building stone, and the grey stone farmhouses and walls between fields instead of hedges are a good sign of limestone country.

1 Draw a map showing the same area of northern England as shown in the Landsat picture (use map on page 18 to help). From this map and the geology sections label your map to show, **a)** two areas with different rock outcrop; name the rocks, **b)** two upland areas; give their names, **c)** two major rivers; give their names.

2 Describe the landscapes on pages 16 and 17, saying what clues there are about the underlying rock types.

3 What are some of the economic uses of these Pennine landscapes and rocks?

Landsat image of the snow-covered Pennines and North York Moors in Northern England, 26 February 1977

Exercise 3 **Pennine landscapes**

Pen-y-Ghent shows how in some places the Millstone Grit rocks still 'cap' the underlying limestone

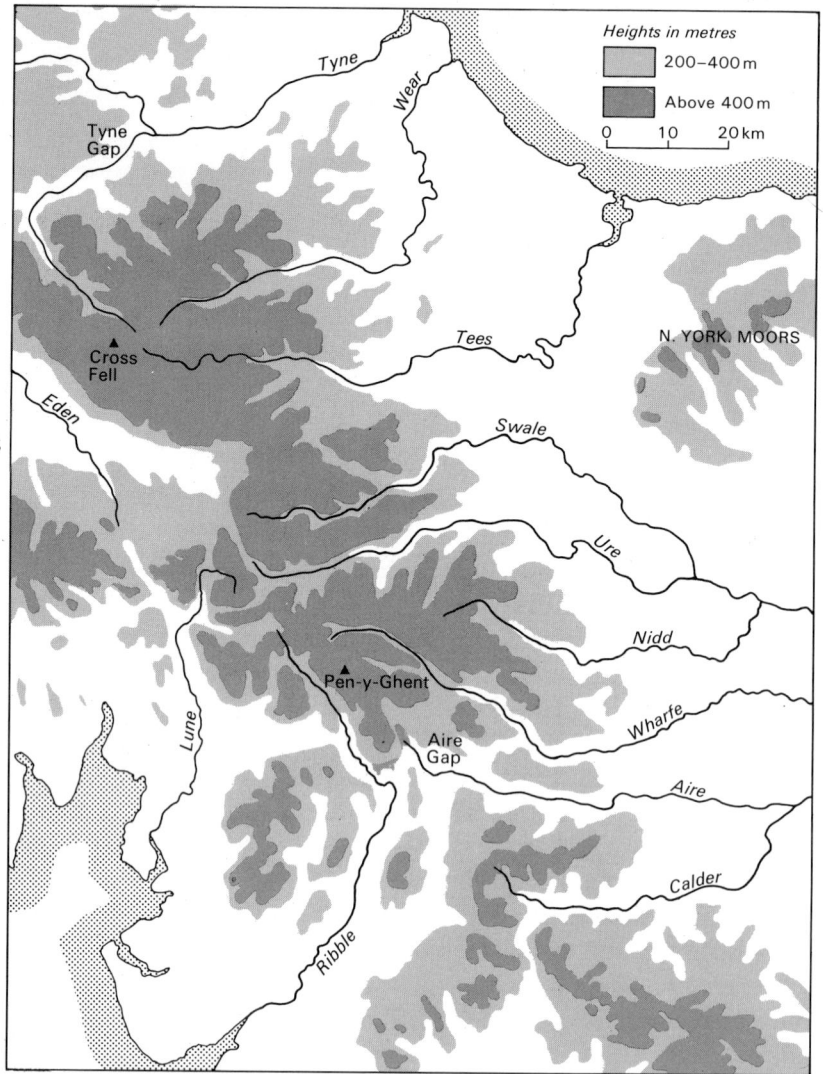

Map of Pennines and Northern England showing exactly the same area as the Landsat image, page 17

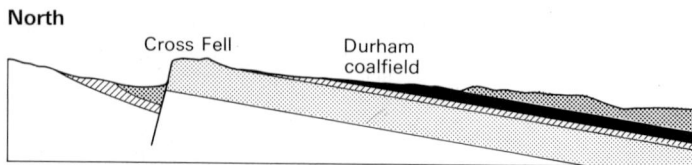

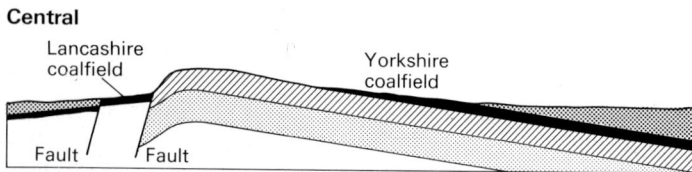

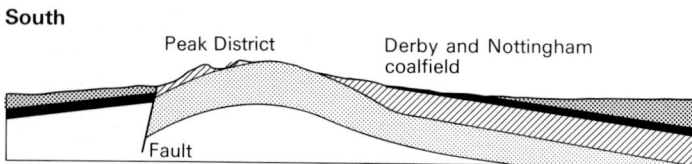

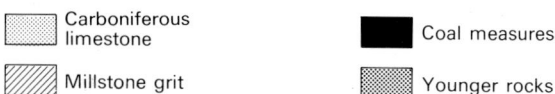

Three geological sections across Northern England

▨ Carboniferous limestone	■ Coal measures
▨ Millstone grit	▨ Younger rocks

1 Ingleborough is a short distance from Pen-y-Ghent in the Pennines, and is formed in a similar way. Trace or draw the map of Ingleborough and print the words Millstone Grit and Carboniferous Limestone in the appropriate places. Shade in the approximate area of Millstone Grit. How can you estimate roughly where the margin of the sandstones and limestones is?

2 What is the distance from the bottom of Gaping Gill (there is a sheer drop from the surface of over 100 metres) to the exit of the cave system at Clapham Beck Head? What is the name of the stream that flows from Clapham Beck Head?

3 From the map on page 13 and from your atlas locate and name some of the other upland areas of Britain.

One of these upland areas in Devon is made of an igneous rock called granite. What is the name of the upland?

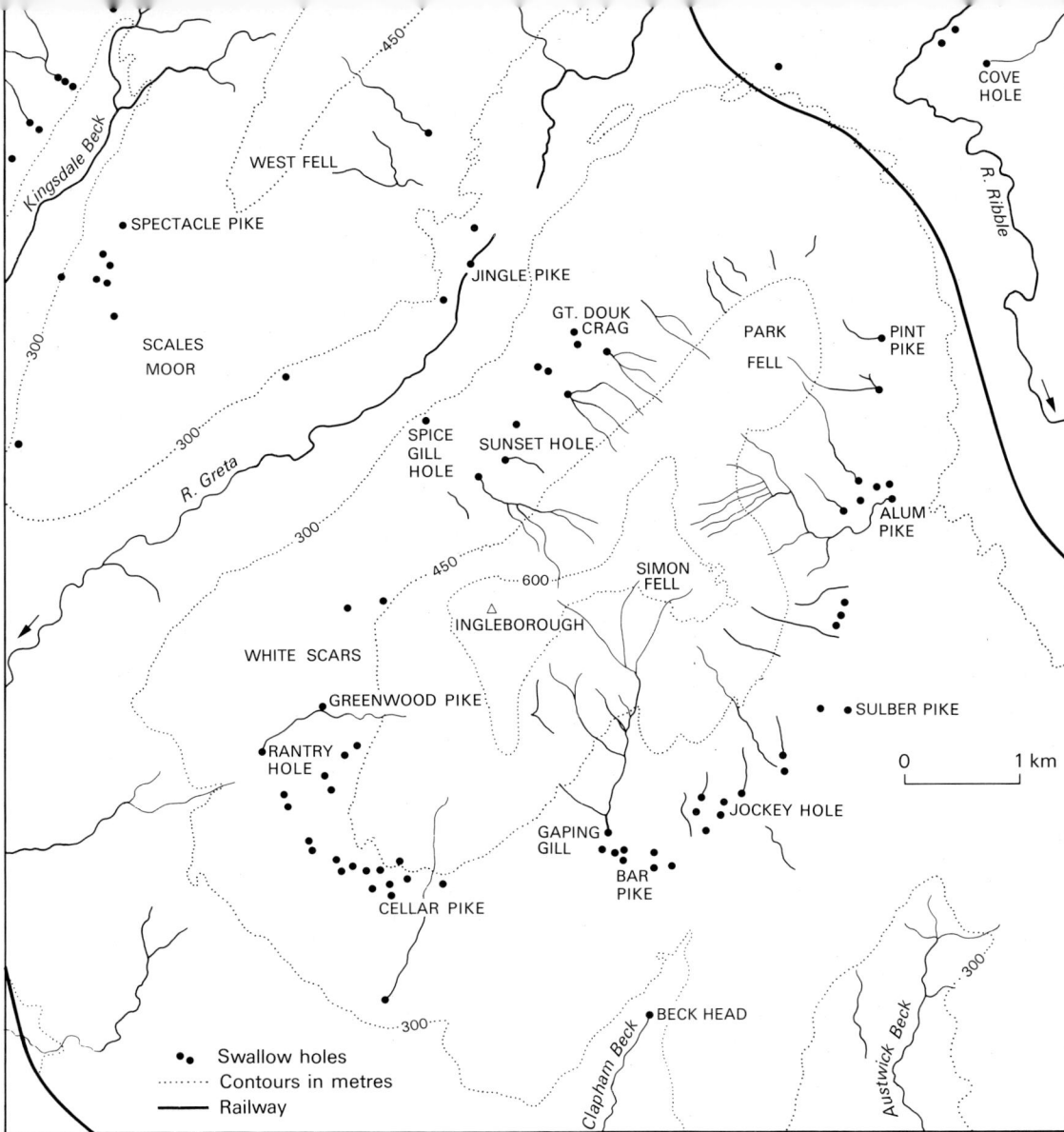

Map of the Ingleborough area where both Millstone Grit and carboniferous limestone rocks are exposed

Key (map):
- Swallow holes
- Contours in metres
- Railway

Map labels: Kingsdale Beck, WEST FELL, COVE HOLE, R. Ribble, SPECTACLE PIKE, JINGLE PIKE, SCALES MOOR, GT. DOUK CRAG, PARK FELL, PINT PIKE, SPICE GILL HOLE, SUNSET HOLE, R. Greta, ALUM PIKE, SIMON FELL, INGLEBOROUGH, WHITE SCARS, GREENWOOD PIKE, SULBER PIKE, RANTRY HOLE, JOCKEY HOLE, GAPING GILL, BAR PIKE, CELLAR PIKE, BECK HEAD, Clapham Beck, Austwick Beck

Diagram showing the nature of swallow holes and underground drainage in limestone areas

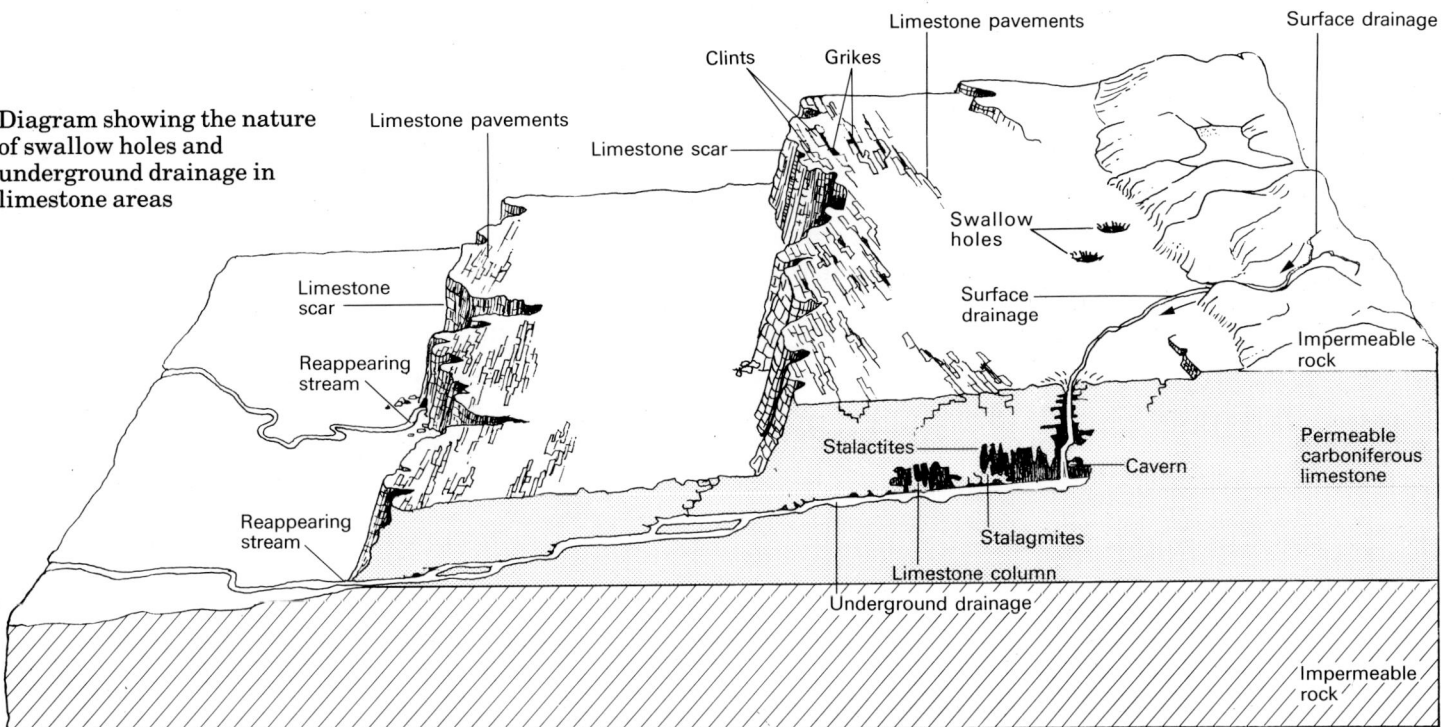

Diagram labels: Limestone pavements, Clints, Grikes, Surface drainage, Limestone scar, Swallow holes, Surface drainage, Impermeable rock, Reappearing stream, Stalactites, Cavern, Permeable carboniferous limestone, Reappearing stream, Stalagmites, Limestone column, Underground drainage, Impermeable rock

The lowlands

The steep scarp face of chalk hills. The top of the scarp is about 180 m above sea level

After the period of mountain building that created the Pennines, most of the area shown on this map was covered by a shallow sea. Vast amounts of material were carried from the land to the sea by winds and rivers, and these, along with the skeletons and remains of dead sea creatures were deposited on the sea floor. These deposits hardened to form beds of rock such as clay, shale, sandstone, limestone and chalk. These were later raised above sea level to form what is now southern Britain.

The scarplands

As these rocks were raised above sea level they were tilted and in places gently folded into dome or basin shapes. Because the rocks are made of materials that are affected by river erosion in different ways, some beds have been worn down much less than others. In particular the pervious chalk and limestone beds have resisted river erosion better than the impervious clays, and so form lines of hills. Due to the ways in which the beds were tilted and folded, these hills usually have a steeper 'scarp' and a gentler 'dip' slope, and the hills produce the pattern shown in the section. The map and section on this page show how these scarplands were formed and produce their distinctive landscapes.

Chalk is sufficiently permeable (it allows rainwater to pass through small pores and fractures) to have little surface drainage. Chalk hills have a

smooth, rounded relief. Their appearance and land use can be seen on the pictures of the Berkshire and South Downs on this page and page 50. The limestone is older, harder and more jointed than the chalk, and the limestone hills tend to be more rugged than the Downs. Although limestone is also permeable, the surface does carry some streams, especially if covered with clays. Many of the streams that go to form the River Thames, for example, rise on the dip slope of the Cotswolds. The limestone is a useful building stone in Cotswold villages and small towns and is also used in the dry-stone walls that mark the boundaries of fields.

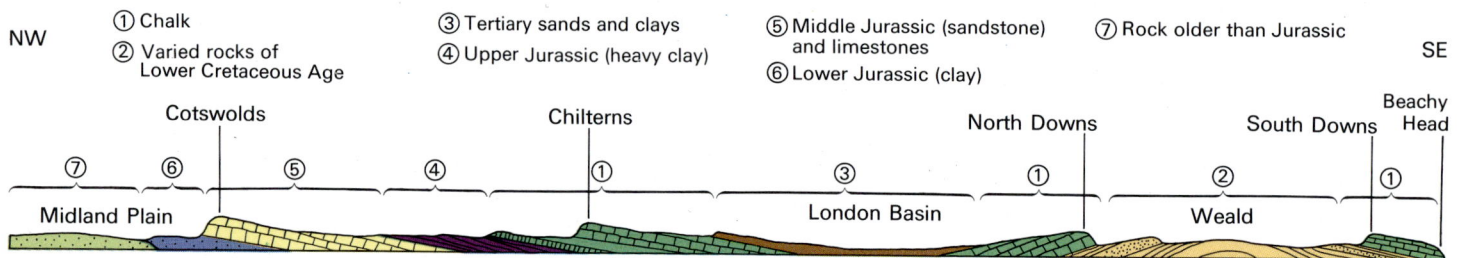

The scarplands of England showing the pattern of outcrop of the different sorts of rock

Triassic lowlands

Line of section shown below

	Edge of highland Britain
	Scarp slopes
	Major areas of alluvial deposits
	Tertiary sands and clays
	Chalk
	Varied rocks of Lower Cretaceous Age
	Upper Jurassic (heavy clay)
	Middle Jurassic (sandstones) and limestones
	Lower Jurassic (clay)
	Rock older than Jurassic

1 North York Moors
2 Lincoln Edge
3 Northampton Uplands
4 Cotswolds
5 Oxford Clay Vale
6 Vale of Pickering
7 Yorkshire Wolds
8 Lincoln Wolds
9 East Anglian Heights
10 Chiltern Hills
11 Salisbury Plain
12 North Downs
13 South Downs
14 The Weald
15 Hampshire Basin
16 London Basin
17 Fens
18 Somerset Levels

0   100 km

A geological section through the scarplands. The line of the section is shown on the map above

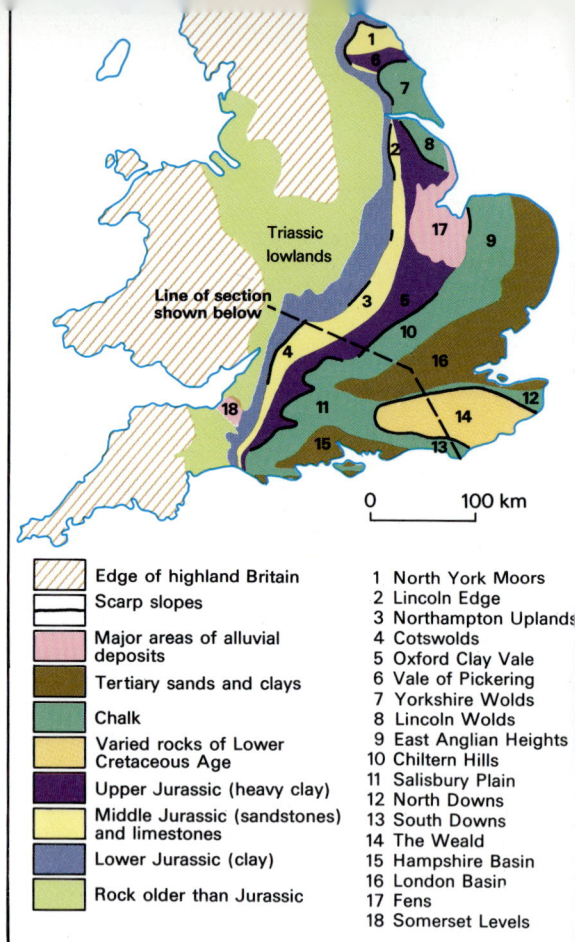

NW

① Chalk
② Varied rocks of Lower Cretaceous Age
③ Tertiary sands and clays
④ Upper Jurassic (heavy clay)
⑤ Middle Jurassic (sandstone) and limestones
⑥ Lower Jurassic (clay)
⑦ Rock older than Jurassic

SE

Cotswolds   Chilterns   North Downs   South Downs   Beachy Head

Midland Plain   London Basin   Weald

The lowland vales

Between the limestone Cotswold and chalk Chiltern hills there is a broad lowland vale. It is by no means flat as the section shows, and there may be gentle undulations in the surface as shown above. The clays are impervious, and there is a great deal of surface drainage. These rivers have covered the underlying clay beds with layers of river-carried alluvium and silt in many areas. The vales were once heavily wooded, but nowadays much of the land is used for farming. There is an emphasis on grassland farming and the fattening of animals. By contrast, the emphasis on the lighter, drier limestone and chalk soils is on the growing of cereals. The trees in the hedges and the scatter of small clumps of trees often give the vales a wooded appearance from ground level.

The Fens

The clay vales extend in a widening zone north-eastwards from Wiltshire and Oxfordshire. In the area near the great sea inlet of The Wash these lowlands are known as The Fens. Once again there are low hills formed of patches of gravel or clay, usually the site of villages and small towns, but much of the Fens is very flat indeed. The soils are made up of decayed vegetation and peat on the inner margins and of alluvium and silt closer to the Wash. These lands have been carefully drained and reclaimed, as can be seen on the right, and now form an extremely rich farming area.

All these lowlands are liable to flooding with considerable damage to property and farmland. The way in which attempts are being made to manage the flow of rivers in the lowlands will be considered in Chapter 9.

1 What rocks form the landscapes shown in this section? Describe as accurately as you can the location of these three landscapes.

2 From the cross-section name one scarp landscape, one vale, one syncline or downfold forming a basin and one upfold or anticline forming low hills.

3 Name two resources obtained from the chalk and limestone scarplands and two from the rocks and deposits of the vales. In each case say what the resource or material is used for.

21

Exercise 4 **The Upper Thames Valley**

The way in which gently tilted limestone, clay and chalk rocks erode to form scarplands is well illustrated in the Upper Thames Valley area. The Thames rises on the dip slopes of the Cotswolds and gathers water from a network of tributaries draining the Vale of Oxford. Between Oxford and Reading the river flows through a gap in the Chilterns known as the Goring Gap – shown in an exaggerated way in the block diagram. It is interesting to try and work out how this gap in the chalk hills was formed.

Block diagram of the Upper Thames Valley

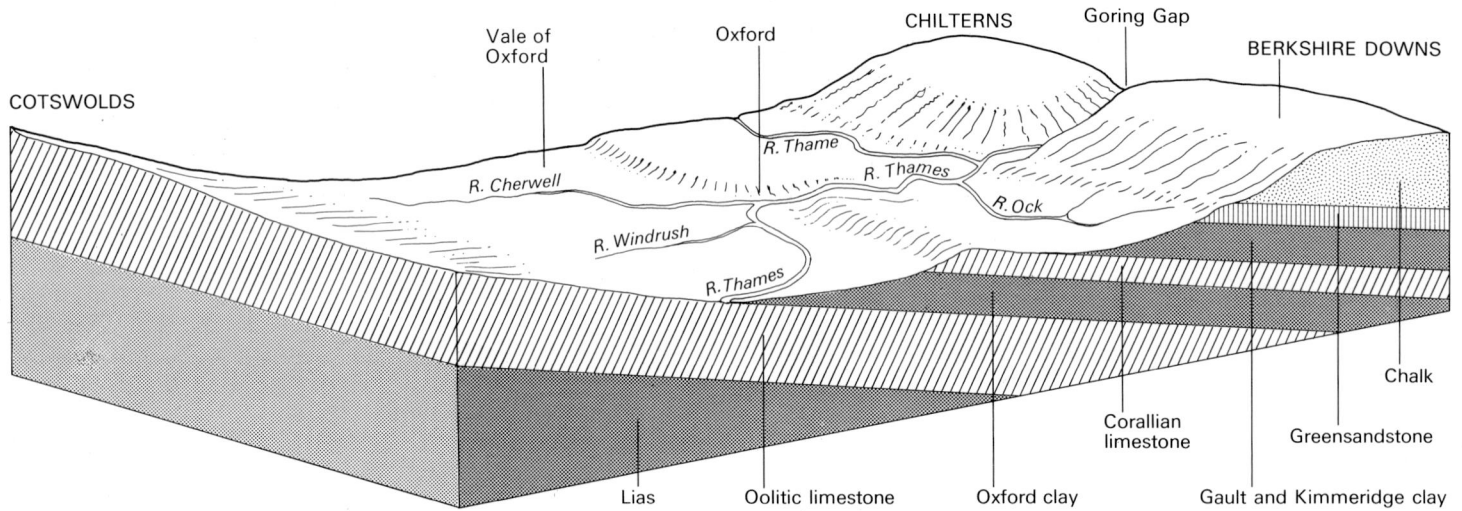

The pattern of erosion and deposition in a meandering river causes the river channel to move slowly downstream

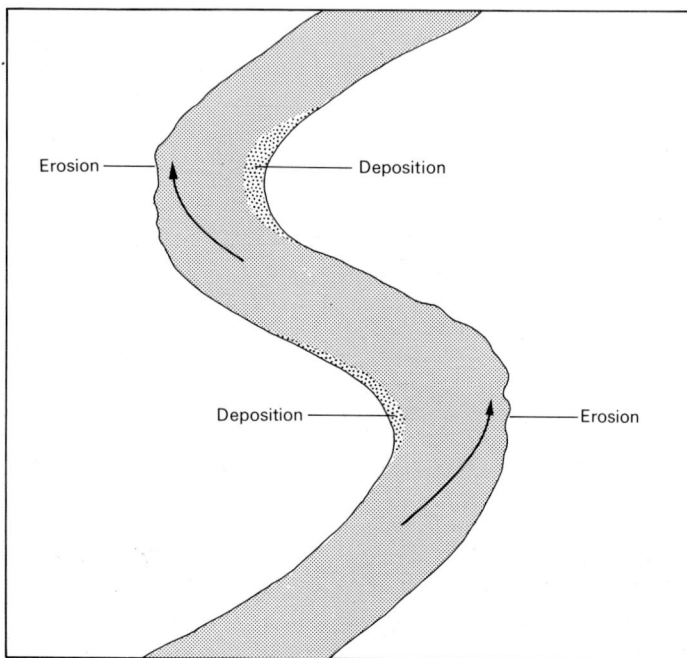

As meanders move slowly downstream they form a wide flood-plain. In some cases the river flows across the narrow neck of a meander leaving an abandoned 'ox-bow lake'

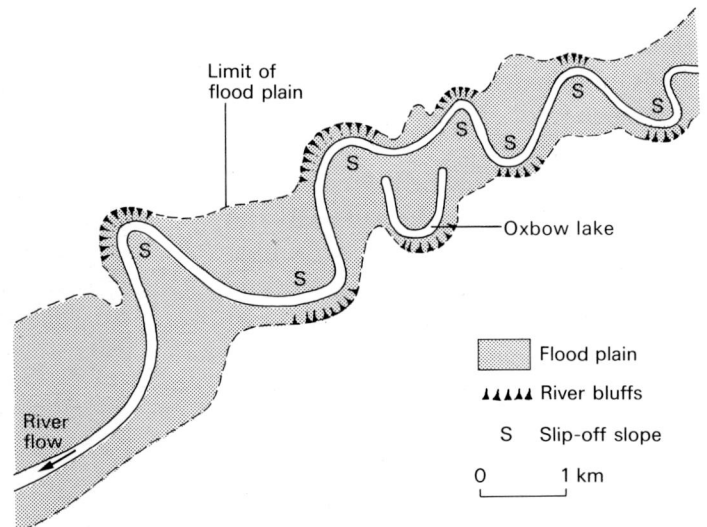

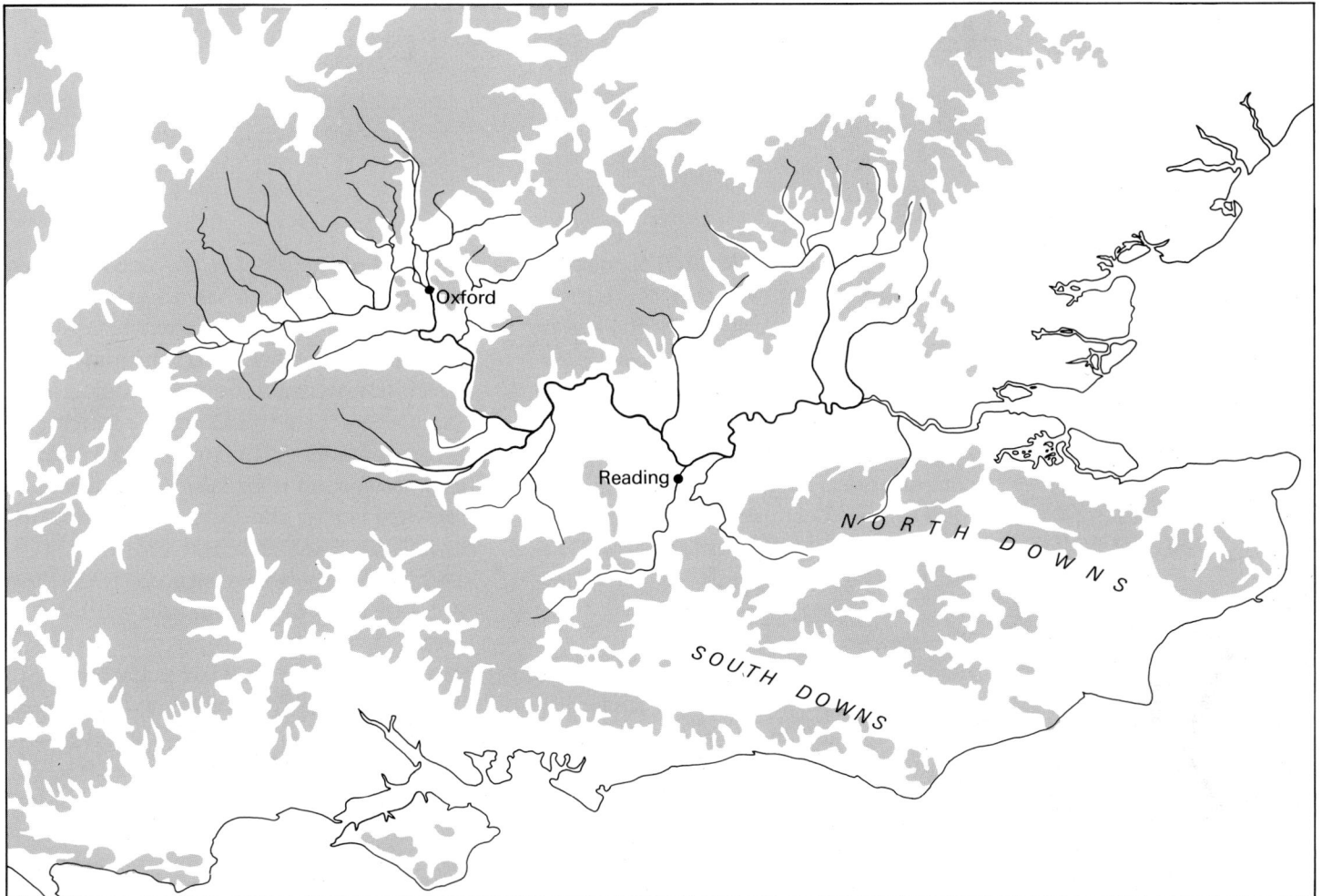

The drainage basin of the River Thames

This view of the River Thame near Aylesbury shows a complicated pattern of meanders as the river winds over its flood-plain towards the Thames

1 Copy or trace the pattern of the River Thames and its tributaries. With the help of the block diagram print in the names; Cotswolds, Vale of Oxford, Berkshire Downs, Chilterns, Goring Gap and the River Thames. Draw in approximately the line of the top of the scarp slopes.

2 Study the air photograph. Make a sketch to show the pattern made by the River Thame. Label **a**) a meander, **b**) the flood plain, **c**) land use in an unflooded area. Show a meander where the stream will soon cut across the neck to form an ox-bow lake.

3 Suggest how the River Thames has managed to cut a valley through the chalk hills (the Goring gap). Did the river carve it, or was it formed in some other way?

Coastal landscapes

Waves loaded with rock and stone crash against a cliff face, causing erosion and retreat of the cliff

Waves breaking gently on low coastline and island, Worms Head, West Wales

The appearance of a stretch of coastline depends partly on whether there has been a relative rise or fall of the sea in recent geological time. It also depends on the rocks and rock structures of the area and the ways they have been shaped by waves. From day to day it depends partly on whether the tide is high or low. Because of these influences there are many different types of coastal landscape in Britain.

Waves and beaches

Beaches are the gently sloping areas of sand or shingle between the water line at low tide and the highest point reached by storm waves. These are sometimes a line of sand dunes on the landward side and then an area of sand and shingle. Sometimes there may be seaweed-covered rocks near the low-tide mark.

Out in the ocean the water is always on the move, and the surface forms a series of wave crests and troughs. The size and pattern of the waves is affected by winds, and these are often blowing towards the land. As the waves approach shallow seas near the shore the friction between water and land causes the wave action to change. First a crest is formed and as this moves forward over the beach it 'breaks' and spills forward across the shingle or sand. This swash carries beach material with it, and finally the wave becomes a shallow flat sheet of water at rest for a brief moment. The water then either sinks into the sand, or flows directly back down the line of the beach as backwash. In both the Wales and the Dorset photographs waves can be seen breaking gently on curved beaches.

The picture is very different during storms. The waves are now large and powerful. They thunder up the beach, hurling sand, pebbles and salt spray high in the air and sometimes even over coastal defenses, in built-up areas. If these storms coincide with the outgoing

Essex mud flats are regularly flooded by salt sea water

ebb tide, the breaking waves may scoop out great quantities of sand and shingle and change the shape of the beach.

Waves and cliffs

Just as rivers can erode some types of rocks more easily than others, so can waves. Some types of rock such as limestone, chalk, sandstone and granite produce great headlands that present near vertical cliffs to the oncoming waves. When storm waves hit a cliff they give it an enormous pounding. The sheer weight of water hurled at the rock can be imagined by the mass of spray hurled into the air. Apart from this there are masses of stones and boulders pounding the base of the cliff. Most rocks are full of cracks and joints, and the air gets trapped in these under enormous pressure when the water surges forward. This again helps to weaken the rocks at the base of the cliff so that they eventually crumble away.

After a while caves may be formed as the rock collapses and the debris carried away by the wave action. Caves may be eroded right through a narrow headland to form an arch. When the roof of the arch finally collapses, the isolated rock is called a stack – it is rather like a small island. These in turn get worn down so that they may be hardly visible at high tide. In this way the whole headland or cliff face will be worn back. It may not be very visible, unless the sea level falls, but the retreat of the cliff face leaves a wave-cut platform at about sea level. There are many types of cliff features around Britain, and two of the varieties can be seen here.

1 Draw a picture of either the Durdle Door or Worms Head landscape and label to show a) a beach, b) waves gently breaking c) rocks forming a headland, d) an island or arch.

2 Study the diagram of cliff erosion. Imagine the sea level fell after the wave-cut platform had been formed. Draw a new diagram showing what the coastline might now look like with its old cliffs, a raised beach and new cliffs being formed.

3 What happens to the material that gets eroded from cliffs and headlands?

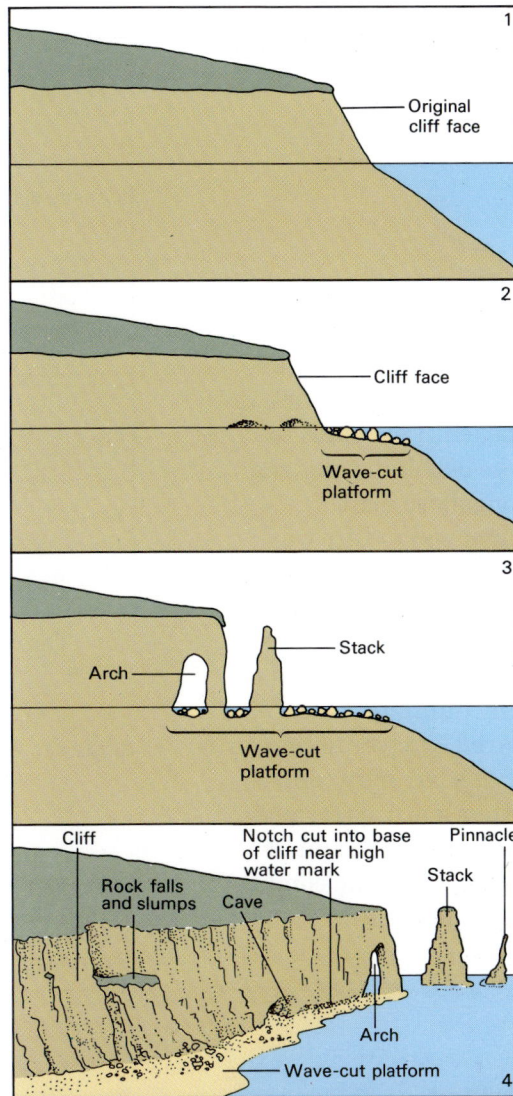

25

Erosion features in coastal limestone, Durdle Door, Dorset. Note the patterns on the beach made by the gently breaking waves

Stages in the formation of coastal features where cliffs meet the sea. First wave-cut platforms are formed, then caves followed by arches and then stacks

Longshore drift

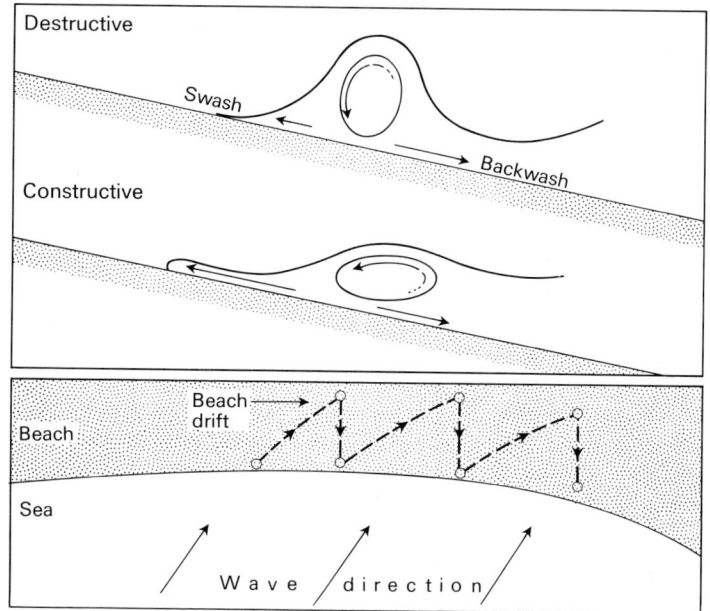

When waves reach the coast they usually approach at an angle. As the waves break, the swash pushes material across the beach at the same angle. The backwash, however, always drains straight back down the steepest line of the beach. This leads to material being moved along the beach in a zig-zag fashion, a process known as longshore drift.

Sooner or later the material moved in this way is stopped by a natural feature such as a headland or a man-made one such as a groyne. Sometimes the material is carried across a headland or mouth of a river estuary. The beach materials get deposited in the deeper water, and gradually build up a sand or shingle bar. Unless this is cleared by river action or tidal ebb and flow (or dredged) the bar may completely seal off the estuary. Other features formed by longshore drift are tombolos, where the spit or bar joins the mainland to an island, and the complicated wave-shaped structure of Dungeness.

Top: The destructive and constructive action of breaking waves

Above: Material is moved along a beach according to the angle the waves strike the beach

Four types of coastal features caused by deposition: a) Chesil Beach; b) Hurst Castle Spit; c) Loe Bar; d) Dungeness. The differences are due to different types of beach materials and contrasting wave patterns and strengths

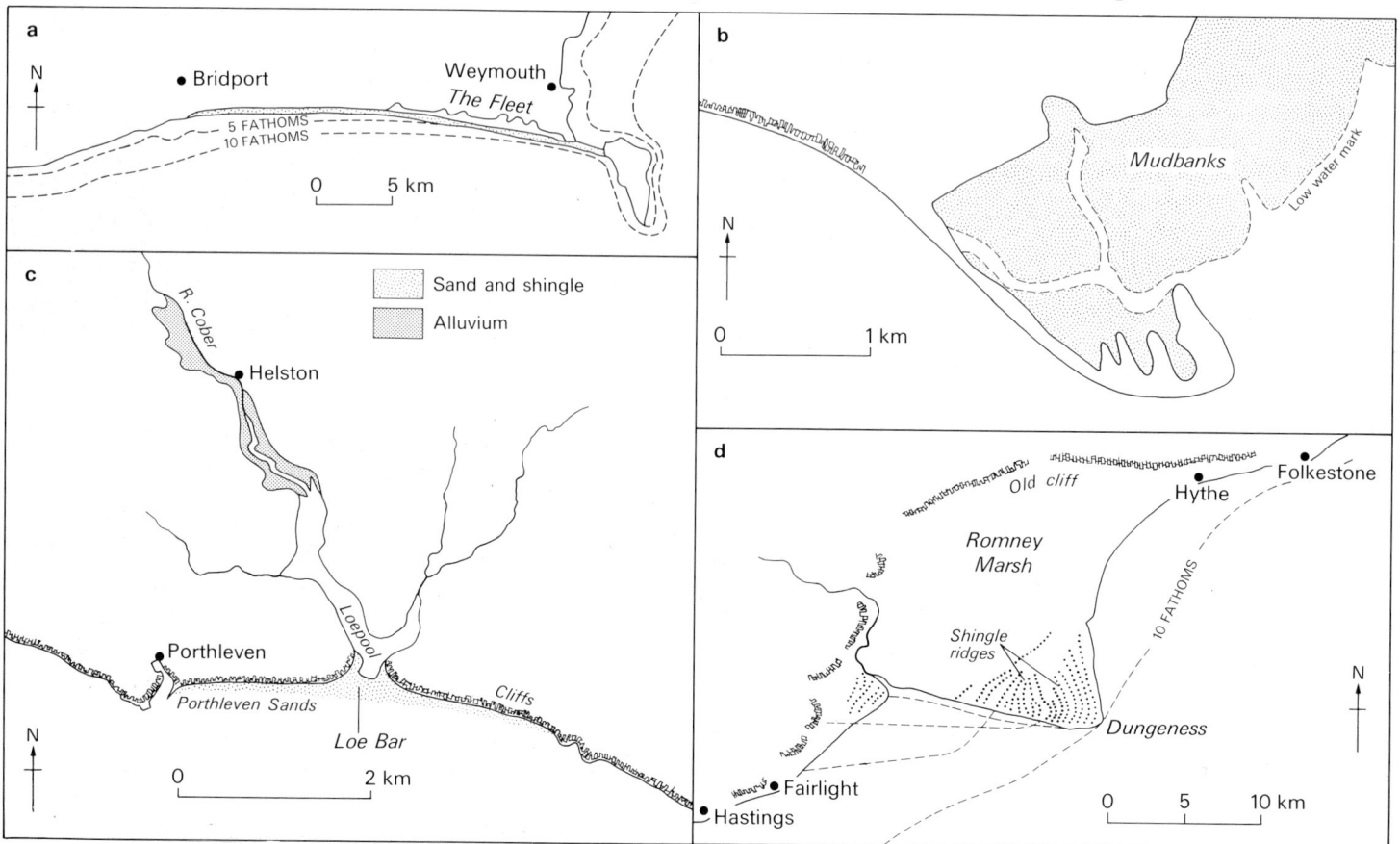

Exercise 5 **Rias: drowned river valleys**

The estuary of the River Looe and its tributary

Rias are river valleys that have been drowned with a rise in sea level (not to be confused with fjords which are drowned glacier-carved valleys). Amongst the characteristic feature of rias are:

a) Relatively gentle valley-side slopes.

b) Valley sides are often wooded or grass covered rather than of bare rock.

c) Unlike glacial valleys the tributaries are not 'hanging' but join the main stream without an abrupt change of level.

d) Produce good sheltered harbours.

e) Lead to difficulties of river-crossing.

f) There may be signs of river carried material being deposited in the river channel when river flow is checked.

1 Draw a simple sketch of the ria above and label to show the features of a 'model' ria described above.

2 Draw a simple map of the ria and stretch of coastline. Shade in the water areas. Now imagine that the sea level fell so that at high tide it only reached the mouth of the estuary. Draw another plan or map showing the area covered by sea and new river channel, and marking in the valley sides. Give suitable titles.

3 From an atlas check the locations of all the features shown on these two pages. Give their counties and any other location details.

Weather: cloud, rain and fog

Storm clouds approaching the village of Teversham, near Cambridge

The three main conditions for the formation of rain, sleet, hail or snow (precipitation)

a Relief: moist air is cooled on rising to cross hills or mountains

Water in the atmosphere

The weather we experience at any time is very much affected by the water in the atmosphere. This is often invisible and known as water vapour. The amount of vapour in the air, known as its humidity, will depend largely on where the air has come from. Air from over the sea, for example, is likely to contain a great deal of water vapour and have a high humidity. When the humidity is very high it can feel very warm and sticky, and it often leads to thunder and heavy rainfall.

A given amount of air can only hold a certain amount of water vapour. If that maximum is exceeded, the vapour will condense into something else. Cold air can hold less vapour than an equivalent mass of warm air. Put in another way, this means that if a mass of warm air containing vapour is cooled enough, a point will be reached when the air mass is saturated and condensation will begin. This is the main reason why mists, fogs and clouds form, and why the vapour in your warm breath condenses when it hits the icy air on a winter's day. The cooling of warm air

b Convectional: moist air rises vertically or strong heating

and the formation of clouds and rain can take place under three main conditions, as shown in the diagram.

Clouds and precipitation

Under normal circumstances, temperatures fall with height. Even on still, windless days the air temperature on mountain tops will be lower than in the lowlands. It is not surprising, then, that air being forced to rise to cross mountains should cool. If the rising air contains much vapour (if it has recently crossed a sea area, for example) this cooling will result in the formation of clouds as condensation occurs. These clouds are tiny droplets of visible water particles that can float in the atmosphere. If they form larger drops of water, however, usually around specks of dust or other material, then this will fall as rain. Under some conditions the drops may freeze and fall as hailstones. In others the temperature may be so low the vapour immediately turns into tiny ice crystals that make up snowflakes, and precipitation may be in the form of snow.

c Frontal or cyclonic: moist air cools as it is pushed over denser colder air in the 'front' of a depression

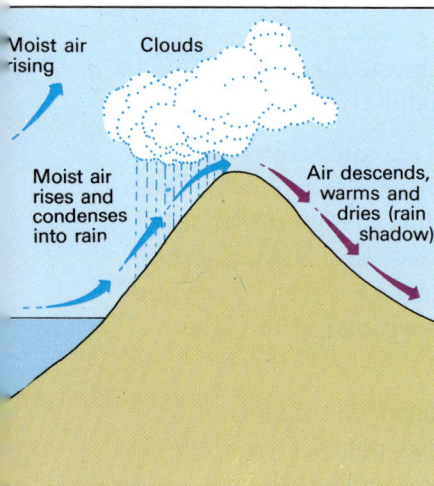

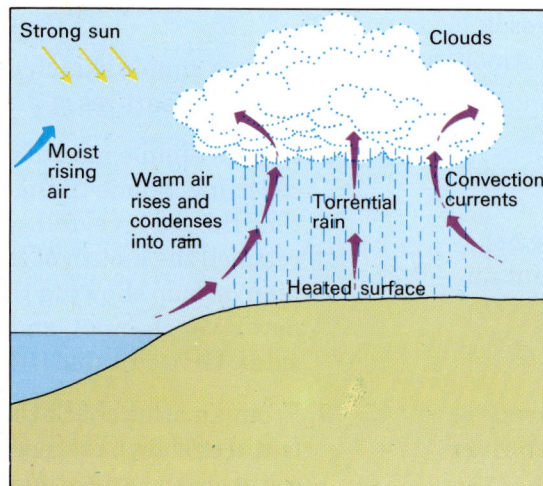

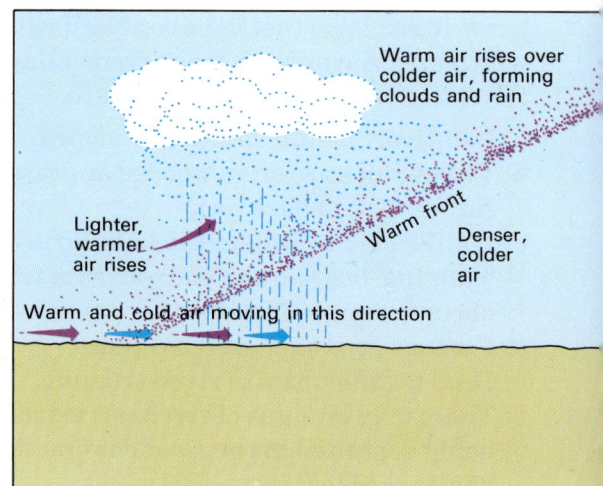

Early morning fog in October, clearing from hills but remaining in the low-lying depressions

If this were the only way air was cooled, then there would be little rainfall over lowland Britain. Another type of cooling is quite common in lowland areas, however, especially in summer months. As the summer sun heats the ground, so the air also gets warm. Warm air is less dense than cold air, and tends to rise. So the warm air with its load of water vapour rises vertically, expands, cools and produces clouds. These are the heaped cumulus variety, and may develop into towering cumulonimbus clouds with an enormous vertical range. There is often high humidity followed by thunder, hail or heavy rainfall. Lightning is caused when electrical charges are formed within these towering cloud masses and discharge takes place between parts of the clouds or the clouds and the ground.

A third type of cooling, cloud formation and precipitation takes place when warm and cold air masses meet in what is called a 'front'. These fronts and depressions are described more fully in the next section.

Mist and fog

Mist and fog are layers of condensed water vapour very close to the ground. The main difference is that mist is less dense and visibility not quite so limited as with fog. They are formed in a variety of ways. When warm moist air moves horizontally across a colder surface (not vertically, as in convectional movement) then the mists and fogs result from the condensation over the colder surface. Another cause is when rapid cooling of the land takes place on clear, cloud-free evenings and nights. The air in contact with the ground also cools and especially if there is a valley or hollow this denser, heavier air gathers in its floor. The water vapour in the cooled air condenses to form a mist or fog. When the sun rises in the morning the mist or fog soon clears over the higher ground, leaving the valley floor or hollow shrouded in mist until the sun heats the air sufficiently to absorb the droplets back into vapour. In spring and summer this may happen quite quickly, but with the weaker sun in autumn and winter the mist and fog may hang around for much of the day. In these conditions there is a rise in temperature with height at first (known as a temperature inversion), which is different from the normal pattern.

1 **a)** What are some of the signs that there is normally a decrease in air temperature with height? **b)** Give examples from home or school of condensation occurring when warm, moist air is cooled down.

2 Use the symbols for cloud cover and precipitation to describe the weather **a)** in the photographs, **b)** on the day you are doing the exercise. Describe and name the type of cloud cover, if there is any.

3 **a)** What are the problems to farmers of
   i) too much or too little rainfall,
   ii) hailstorms?
   b) What occupations, other than farming, are affected by mists and fogs?

Three types of cloud

Top: Fog near the ground lifting into low stratus cloud, as the sun begins to heat the ground
Middle: High level altocumulus at about 4–5 kilometres altitude
Bottom: Cumulus clouds caused by rapidly rising air currents

Symbols used on official weather maps to show precipitation and cloud cover

Precipitation	
꞊	Mist
≡	Fog
ꙇ	Drizzle
●	Rain
△	Hail
⋇	Sleet
✳	Snow
▽	Rain shower
⋇▽	Snow shower
⊼	Thunderstorm

Cloud cover	
○	0 (clear sky)
◍	1/8
◐	2/8 (1/4)
◑	3/8
◑	4/8 (1/2)
◒	5/8
◕	6/8 (3/4)
◖	7/8
●	8/8 (full cloud cover)
⊗	Sky obscured by mist, fog, etc.

29

Exercise 6 Rainfall: averages and extremes

Map showing average annual rainfall in Britain

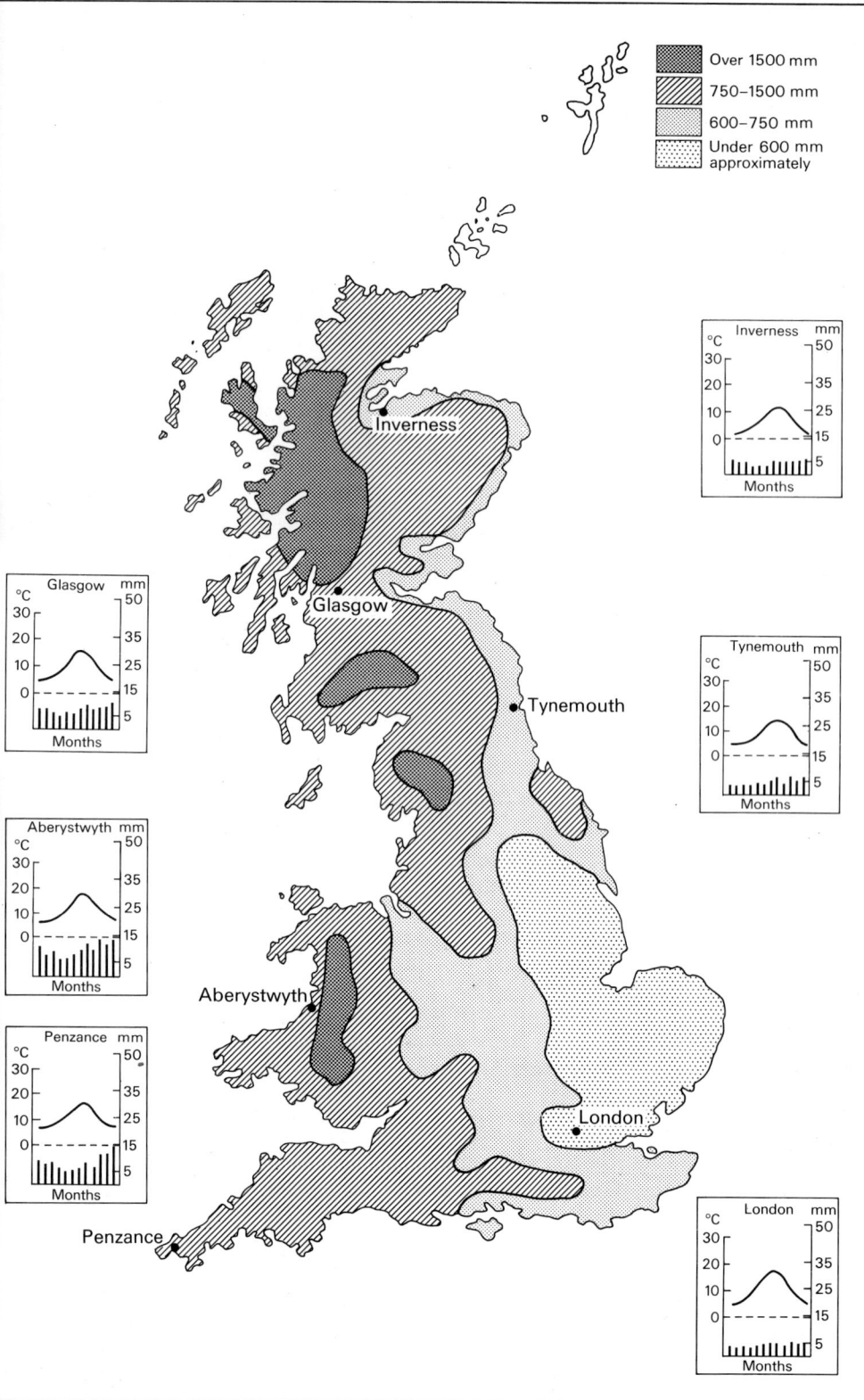

Over 1500 mm
750–1500 mm
600–750 mm
Under 600 mm approximately

It is very useful to have average rainfall figures (based on a number of years), in order to compare one place with another. The effect of mountains on rainfall can be easily seen in the map of average rainfall, for example. Actual rainfall for one year can also be mapped. This may be very different from the average figure as the map on the right shows. Actual precipitation affects daily life in many ways.

Annual total rainfall 1981 for representative weather stations

	mm	Per cent of average 1941–1970
London (St James's)	689	113
Margate	578	100
Worthing	901	126
Bristol	966	119
Cambridge	589	106
Plymouth	1126	114
Penzance	1308	119
Walsall	806	109
Carlisle	833	96
York	716	117
Stockton-on-Tees	561	100
Lowestoft	629	104
Cardiff	1153	105
Anglesey (Valley)	901	104
Llandrindod Wells	1124	115
Eskdalemuir	1630	108
Edinburgh	629	93
Glasgow	1159	111
Islay (Eallabus)	1357	106
Pitlochry	843	96
Inverness	677	102
Skye (Prabost)	2039	113
Stornoway	1347	123
Lerwick	1404	120

1 a) Which parts of Britain had below average rainfall in this year when rainfall in general was above average? b) Did your area have above or below average rainfall in 1981?
c) Which of the weather stations had the highest above average, which the furthest below average and which had exactly the average rainfall?

2 Choose one of the numbered paragraphs and describe the type of rainfall referred to, giving it its correct name.

3 From the extracts describe some of the damage caused by various types of precipitation throughout the year.

The Times, 4 February 1982

1981 was the third year in succession to be wetter than average

Total rainfall in 1981 over the United Kingdom exceeded the average for the third consecutive year, by about 10 per cent over England and Wales, and by about 6 per cent over Scotland. As is often the case, marked departures from normal were apparent in the seasonal trend.

1 January and February were in the main uneventful months with respect to rainfall, although even in uneventful months, hilly western districts may experience rainfall, with moist westerly winds, which, for persistence and amount, would astonish many inhabitants of lowland Britain. At the notoriously wet Honister Pass in the Lake District, for example, 134 mm was recorded on 2 January and 145 mm on 2 February.

A severe wintry spell occurred towards the end of April 1981 which was short lived but brought extensive disruption to traffic over most of the country.

2 Perhaps the outstanding rainfall event of the year occurred on 5–6 August when, following a short heatwave, severe thunderstorms broke out quite widely over England in a very complex distribution. The first of the storms appeared in the evening of 5 August in the Shropshire-Greater Manchester area and extended across the Pennines to West Yorkshire. At Eaton, Cheshire, 132 mm was recorded and at Manchester airport about 100 mm fell in 11 hours.

Meanwhile, in separate thundery systems, heavy rain was falling in the Midlands from Gloucestershire to the Lincoln Edge and rainfall in that area continued for much of 6 August. A third area of heavy thunderstorms crossed the Sussex coast in the early hours of 6 August and moved northwards over London towards the Wash; as much as 60 mm was recorded in that storm which was also remarkable for spectacular lightning displays and complete darkness at midday.

3 The three severe wintry weeks began on about 8 December in southern England and South Wales. Rain in the South-west quickly turned to snow as a waving front passed across the south of the country. A few days of extremely cold, foggy weather was followed by further snowfall on 10–11 December which again mainly affected southern Britain.

The worst blizzard in the wintry spell occurred on 13 December when snow spread from the South to all but the extreme north of Scotland and gale force winds caused deep drifting. The snowfall was followed by rainfall and flooding in the extreme south of Britain. Further rain fell in south-west England on 15–16 December but most of the country had a drier spell from 15 to 18 December.

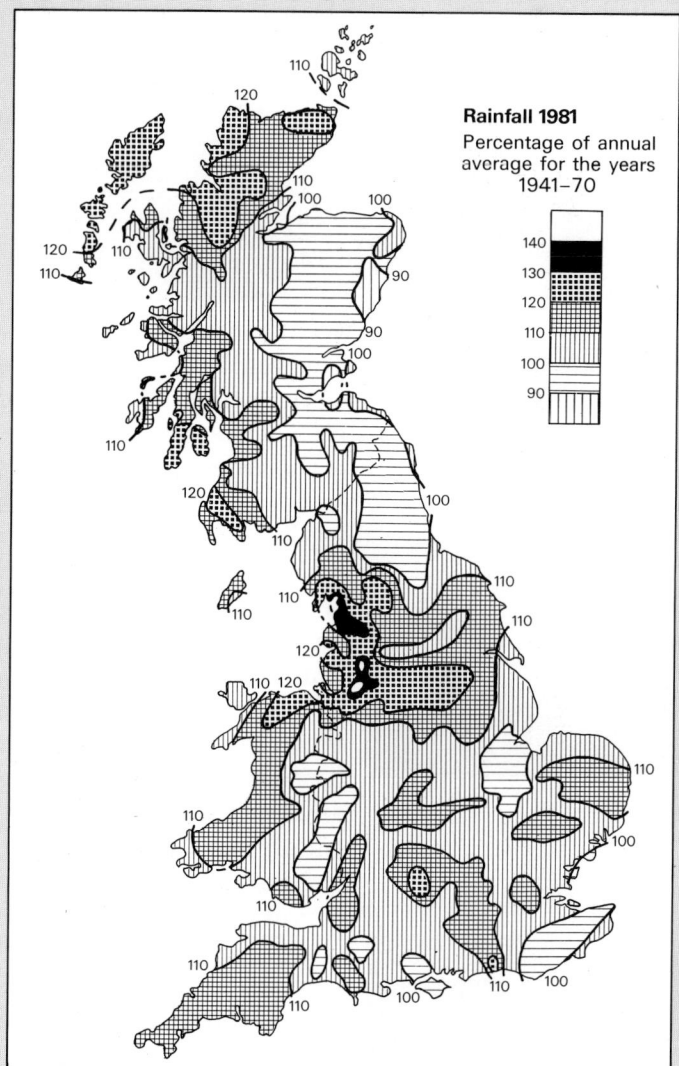

Rainfall 1981
Percentage of annual average for the years 1941–70

140
130
120
110
100
90

Weather: depressions and storms

Satellite pictures of weather conditions over Britain (*left*) under a depression and (*right*) after a depression has crossed

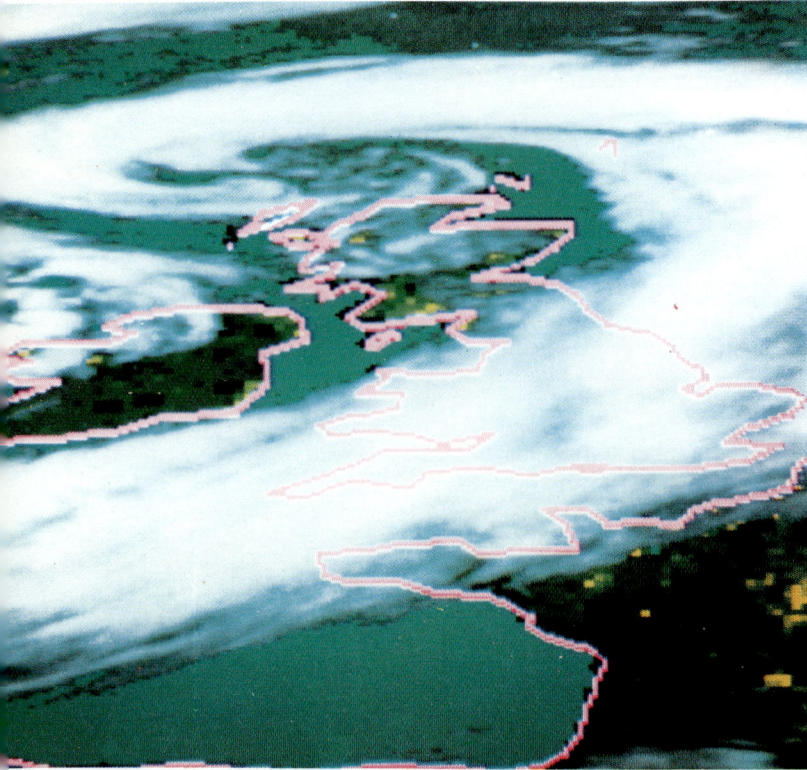

Weather conditions are affected by the passage of a depression, as shown in these two photographs

Weather and air masses

The weather at any place is dependent on the nature of the mass of air over the area at that particular time. The nature of the air mass will very much depend on where it has come from. It can be warm or cold, dry or full of moisture, with or without clouds, moving gently or windily and can be travelling in any direction. A great deal of our weather is caused by air masses that have come from over the Atlantic Ocean. That is an area where cold air from Polar latitudes meets and mixes with warm air from the Tropics. When these different air masses are drawn together and swirl around an area of low pressure, a depression is formed.

Depression and their tracks

The features of a depression or cyclone are shown in the map and diagram, and the cloud patterns associated with one seen from a satellite are shown in the photographs. Where there is low pressure, winds blow into the area from places with high pressure. Due to the rotation of the earth, however, the path followed by the wind is not a direct straight line. The winds move around the low pressure area in an anti-clockwise direction. As this happens the lighter warm air rises up and over the denser cold air, forming what is known as a warm front. There is a regular pattern of cloud, precipitation and temperature change as a warm front crosses a place. At the same time the dense cold air forces itself under the warm air from behind, forming a cold front. This too has certain characteristics that differ from those of the warm front. The wedge of warm air, known as the warm sector, in between the fronts gradually gets pushed higher and higher until it is no longer in contact with the ground.

The two fronts merge, and are then known as an occluded front.

It is important to realise that the depression does not stay over the same area while the winds merely swirl around the centre of low pressure. The depression as a whole moves along a path or track. This means that a place will have a sequence of weather as first the warm front, then the warm sector and finally the cold front pass over it. The paths followed by depressions are not fixed and vary considerably with the seasons. They tend to cross Britain in the winter but pass further north in the summer months. Often a whole series of depressions will cross Britain from over the Atlantic, one after the other. At times, of course, the pressure systems are different, and our weather is not affected by the passage of depressions at all. This different situation will be considered in the next section.

Storms

In general language the word 'storm' is used to describe any severe disturbance of the lower atmosphere. We talk of thunder storms, snow storms, rain storms and so on. It is also used in a more particular way to describe winds of considerable force. From the table on page 34 we see that storms are winds of Force 11 on the Beaufort scale, with only hurricanes being more powerful. These very strong winds are often caused by the passage of a depression. When they are associated with high tides, the effect on coastal areas can be devastating. The storm surges hitting the coast of Eastern England described on the next page were due to intense or deep depressions crossing the North Sea at the same time as very high tides occurred.

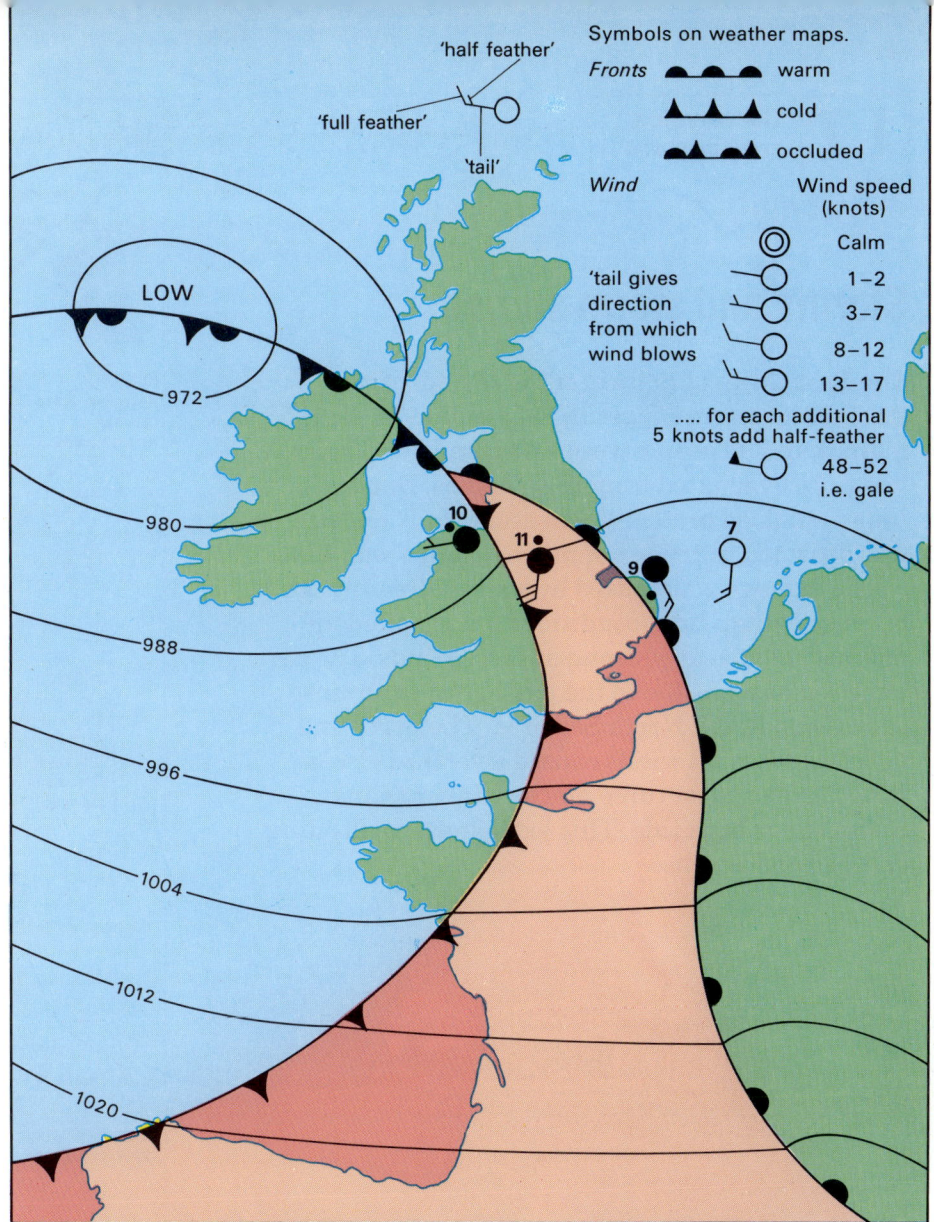

Symbols on weather maps.

Map showing different weather conditions at four places as a depression moves eastwards across Britain

1 Describe the cloud cover over Britain on the two days shown in the photographs.

2 The conditions in one of the photographs show the passage of a front. Say which it is and why you think so.

3 Describe the weather conditions at the four places shown on the weather map.

4 How do weather satellites help in forecasting weather conditions? Why can weather forecasting for a particular place never be absolutely accurate more than a day or so in advance?

Section through a depression, showing the weather usually experienced at each of the 'fronts', and the area between them

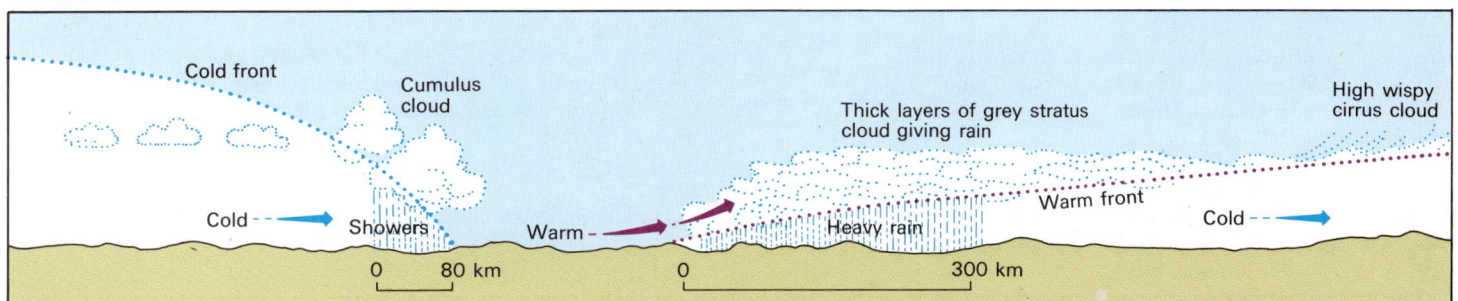

33

Storms and storm surges

The East Coast of Britain suffered badly from storms and storm surges in 1953 and 1978. In 1953 more than 300 people were killed and 30 000 people had to be evacuated from their homes. Due to improved flood protection measures only one person was drowned in 1978, but much damage was done.

The damage was caused by water, already high because of high tidal conditions, being 'piled up' against the coast by strong onshore winds. The gale-force winds were due to the passage of an intense depression in the North Sea area. The north and north-north-west winds caused a vertical rise in water level almost three metres higher than a normal very high tide. This led to massive flooding, damage and deaths.

Margate's 150-year-old pier was wrecked in the 1978 storms

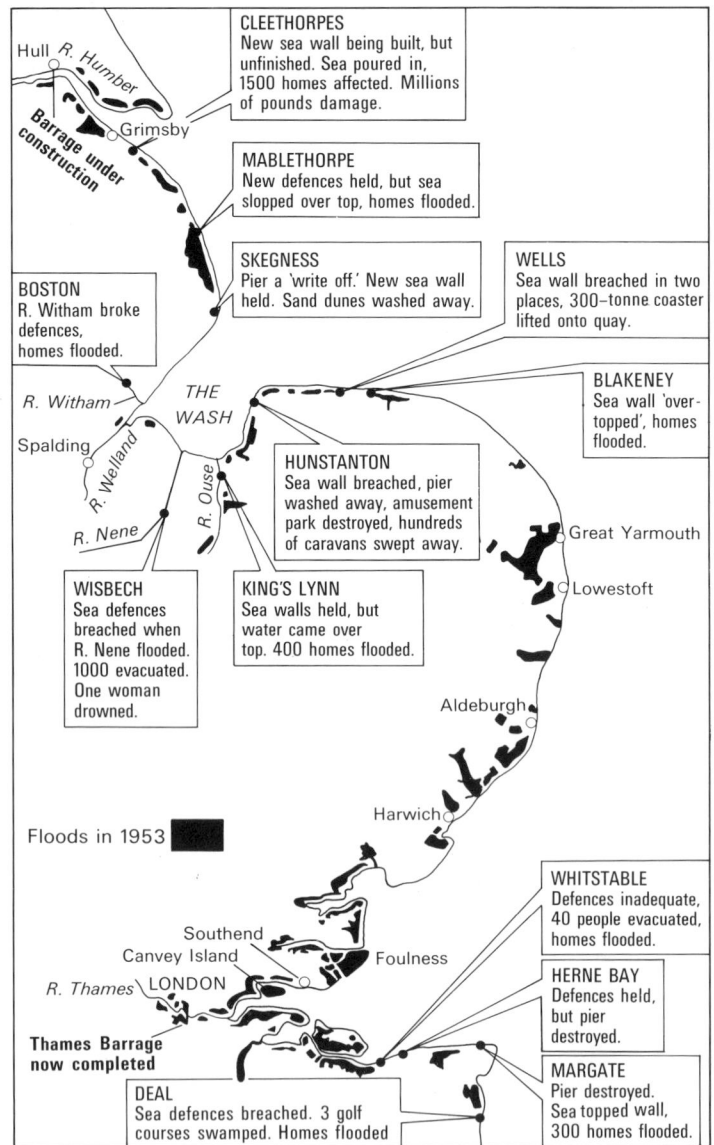

CLEETHORPES
New sea wall being built, but unfinished. Sea poured in, 1500 homes affected. Millions of pounds damage.

MABLETHORPE
New defences held, but sea slopped over top, homes flooded.

SKEGNESS
Pier a 'write off.' New sea wall held. Sand dunes washed away.

WELLS
Sea wall breached in two places, 300-tonne coaster lifted onto quay.

BOSTON
R. Witham broke defences, homes flooded.

BLAKENEY
Sea wall 'over-topped', homes flooded.

HUNSTANTON
Sea wall breached, pier washed away, amusement park destroyed, hundreds of caravans swept away.

WISBECH
Sea defences breached when R. Nene flooded. 1000 evacuated. One woman drowned.

KING'S LYNN
Sea walls held, but water came over top. 400 homes flooded.

Floods in 1953 ▆

WHITSTABLE
Defences inadequate, 40 people evacuated, homes flooded.

HERNE BAY
Defences held, but pier destroyed.

MARGATE
Pier destroyed. Sea topped wall, 300 homes flooded.

DEAL
Sea defences breached. 3 golf courses swamped. Homes flooded.

Thames Barrage now completed

Barrage under construction

Areas affected by the 1978 storms on the East Coast of Britain

The Beaufort scale: a measurement of the speed of winds

Beaufort number	Speed		Description	Effects on land
	Knots	Km/hour		
0	0	0–1	Calm	Smoke rises vertically
1	1–3	1–6	Light air	Direction shown by smoke but not by wind vane
2	4–6	7–11	Light breeze	Wind felt on face; leaves rustle; ordinary vane moved by wind
3	7–10	12–18	Gentle breeze	Leaves and small twigs in constant motion; wind extends a light flag
4	11–16	19–30	Moderate breeze	Raises dust and loose paper; small branches moved
5	17–21	31–39	Fresh breeze	Small trees in leaf begin to sway; crested wavelets form on inland waters
6	22–27	40–50	Strong breeze	Large branches in motion; whistling heard in telegraph wires; umbrellas used with difficulty
7	28–33	51–61	Moderate gale	Whole trees in motion; inconvenience felt when walking against wind
8	34–40	62–74	Fresh gale	Breaks twigs off trees; generally impedes progress
9	41–47	75–87	Strong gale	Slight structural damage occurs (chimney pots and slates removed; fences blown down)
10	48–55	88–102	Whole gale	Seldom experienced inland; trees uprooted; considerable structural damage
11	56–63	103–116	Storm	Very rarely experienced inland; accompanied by widespread damage
12	Above 63	Above 116	Hurricane	

Exercise 7 The passage of depressions

Newspaper maps and statistics for 11 June 1982

Weather Forecast

Troughs of low pressure will clear S districts of England but remain over the N.

6 am to midnight

London, SE, Central N and S and SW England, Midlands, Channel Islands, Wales: Cloudy, rain at first, becoming brighter with showers; max temp 17 to 20C (63 to 68F).

E Anglia, E and NE England, Borders, Edinburgh and Dundee: Outbreaks of thundery rain, becoming brighter later; SE, light to moderate; max temp 17 to 20C (63 to 68F).

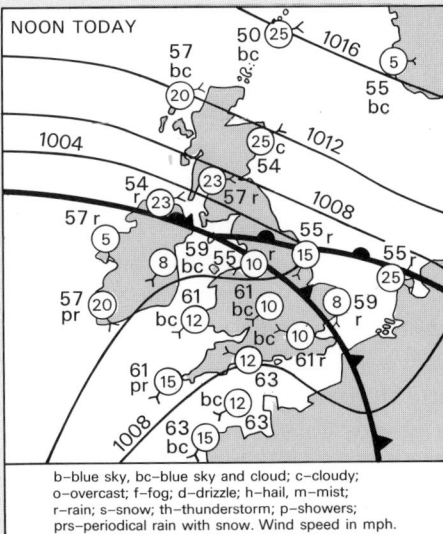

NOON TODAY Pressure is shown in millibars   FRONTS   Warm   Cold   Occluded
(Symbols are on advancing edge)

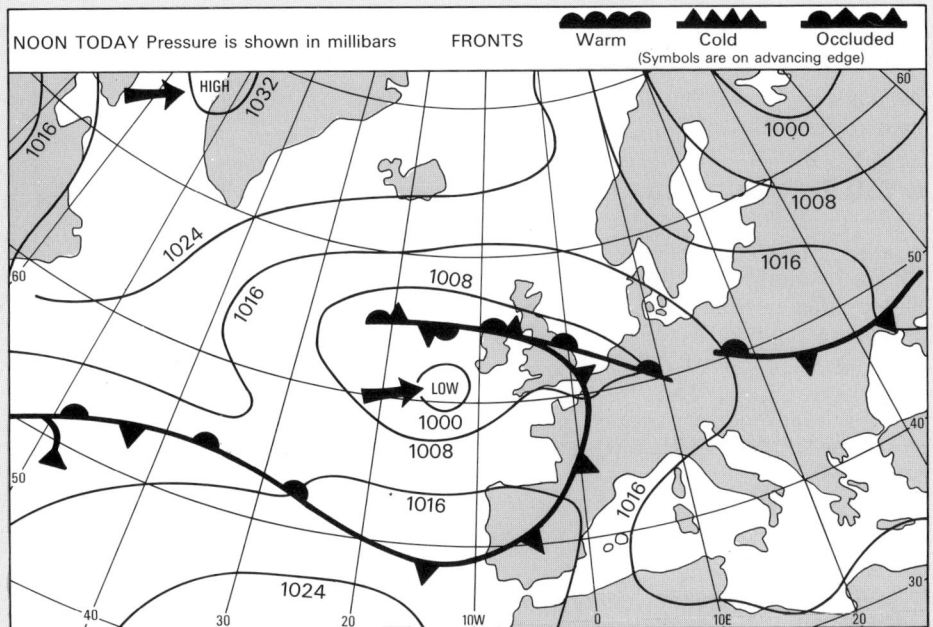

NOON TODAY

b–blue sky; bc–blue sky and cloud; c–cloudy; o–overcast; f–fog; d–drizzle; h–hail; m–mist; r–rain; s–snow; th–thunderstorm; p–showers; prs–periodical rain with snow. Wind speed in mph.

NW England, Lake District, Isle of Man, Scotland, Glasgow, Argyll, Northern Ireland: Mostly cloudy, rain at times, some bright intervals: wind SE, light to moderate: max temp 16 to 18C (61 to 64F).

Aberdeen, Moray Firth, NE Scotland, Orkney, Shetland: Mostly dry, sunny intervals: wind E, moderate, max temp 13 to 16C (55 to 61F).

Central Highlands, NW Scotland: Showers, wind E, moderate; max temp 15 to 17C (59 to 63F).

Outlook for tomorrow and Sunday: Bright intervals, occasional showers.

Yesterday

Temperatures at midday yesterday: c, cloud; r, rain; s, sun.

	C	F		C	F
Belfast	c 14	57	Guernsey	c 17	63
Birmingham	r 17	63	Inverness	s 13	55
Blackpool	c 17	63	Jersey	c 20	68
Bristol	r 17	63	London	c 17	63
Cardiff	c 18	64	Manchester	c 17	63
Edinburgh	c 13	55	Newcastle	c 13	55
Glasgow	c 13	55	Ronaldsway	c 15	50

1 Make a rough sketch of the North Atlantic/Europe map. Shade in the areas with pressures over 1 024 millibars and those below 1 008 millibars. Print the words High and Low in appropriate places.

2 What four pieces of weather information are given for each 'station' shown on the British Isles map? (Note that this is a newspaper map and the symbols differ from the 'official' symbols.)

3 Compare the weather in East Anglia, North Yorkshire and Merseyside as shown on the British Isles map. Explain these differences.

4 For the area in which you live explain the weather changes between 6 am and midnight on 11 June 1982.

35

Weather: temperature extremes and averages

Newspaper maps and statistics for 12 January 1982

Weather Forecast

An anticyclone will move slowly SE over central areas.

6 am to midnight

London, SE, Central S, SW England, Channel Islands: Dry, bright or sunny periods after early mist; wind E, moderate; max temp 0 to 3C (32 to 37F).

Midlands, Wales, NW, Central N England, Lake District: Dry, freezing fog patches, sunny periods in most parts; wind E or SE, light; max temp −2 to 1C (28 to 34F).

Yesterday

Temperatures at midday yesterday: c, cloud; s, sun.

		C	F			C	F
Belfast	s	−5	23	Guernsey	c	3	37
Birmingham	s	−5	23	Inverness	c	−1	30
Blackpool	s	−2	28	Jersey	c	3	37
Bristol	s	−3	27	London	s	1	34
Cardiff	s	−3	27	Manchester	s	−1	30
Edinburgh	c	−7	19	Newcastle	s	−6	21
Glasgow	s	−8	18	Ronaldsway	s	1	34

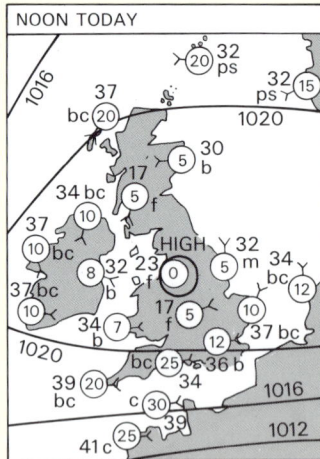

NOON TODAY

b–blue sky, bc–blue sky and cloud; c–cloudy; o–overcast; f–fog; d–drizzle; h–hail; m–mist; r–rain; s–snow; th–thunderstorm; p–showers; prs–periodical rain with snow. Wind speed in mph.

Highest and lowest

Highest day temp: Benbecula, 6C (43F); Lowest day max: Shawbury, −9C (16F); Highest rainfall: Guernsey, 0.31 in; Highest sunshine: Ilfracombe, 7.6 hr.

Blizzards put Welsh food supplies in danger

As freezing temperatures gripped Britain again last night, Wales, after 37 hours of continuous snowfall, was almost isolated by snow and ice and the Welsh Office was urged to use troops and tracked vehicles to deliver supplies. The South-west was also badly hit, with many roads blocked.

A new record low temperature for England was claimed at Newport, Shropshire, where −26.1°C was recorded. A temperature of −27.2°C was recorded at Braemar in Scotland on Saturday night, equalling the lowest recorded in Britain, also at Braemar on 11 February 1895.

Severe weather conditions in January 1982

Weather and climate

In the early weeks of 1982 much of Britain experienced remarkably cold weather with temperatures lower than were being recorded at the South Pole! At one period there had been very heavy snow and strong winds that brought down many electricity power lines. Some idea of the severity of the conditions can be obtained from the newspaper extract and photographs. For almost a week the country was brought to a virtual standstill. We usually use the term 'climate' to describe average conditions, and 'weather' for the conditions that actually existed at a particular time. The winter climate of Britain is cold and icy, although it does vary considerably from one place to another. This weather, though, was particularly extreme. Extremes can also be experienced in the summer months, and temperatures can be above or below average. During the summer the country may experience very high temperatures and strong sunshine during a 'heat wave'. It is worth remembering that rainfall can be described by averages or actual precipitation.

Anticyclones

There are a number of conditions of the atmosphere that produce weather such as that in January 1982. We have seen that Britain is sometimes crossed by a series of low-pressure systems or depressions. These bring a particular pattern of disturbed weather in both winter and summer. At other times, however, an area of high pressure may cross or be fairly stationary over Britain. These are known as anticyclones. The conditions are usually very cold and dry in the winter, with fogs or mists of the sort described earlier. If the temperatures are below freezing point the water vapour may freeze into tiny ice particles on the ground, forming a covering of frost. The air is still and the sky may be cloudless. Sometimes, though there may be a low layer of clouds that provide cold and dull conditions for days on end.

In the summer an anticyclone, with its clear skies and either calm conditions or winds moving gently in a clockwise direction around the centre of the high pressure area, will produce hot sunny weather. The weather may be ideal for those on holiday or in certain types of jobs, but farmers and water authorities soon get anxious about the lack of rainfall and possibilities of drought. It is often after days of this anticyclonic weather that summer thunderstorms occur as the atmosphere becomes unstable again.

Averages and extremes

The diagram shows how each day has a maximum and minimum temperature at any particular place or weather station. If these are collected over a number of years, the mean or average, maximum or minimum for that day of the year can be calculated. The highest ever maximum and minimum can also be recorded – though the record is likely to be exceeded sooner or later.

If the average maximum for each day of a month is known, then the average maximum for a month may be calculated. The same can be done for the minimum temperatures. The absolute or record maximum and minimum for the month (and also from this the year) can be recorded. So there are many average and absolute daily, monthly and annual data for climate available for most places. The average climate of a place often influences such things as type of farming practiced, building and transport construction and so on, but it is the actual weather that has to be enjoyed or endured – until the next inevitable change occurs.

1 What were the differences between the anticyclonic weather of 12 January 1982 (opposite) and cyclonic weather of 11 June

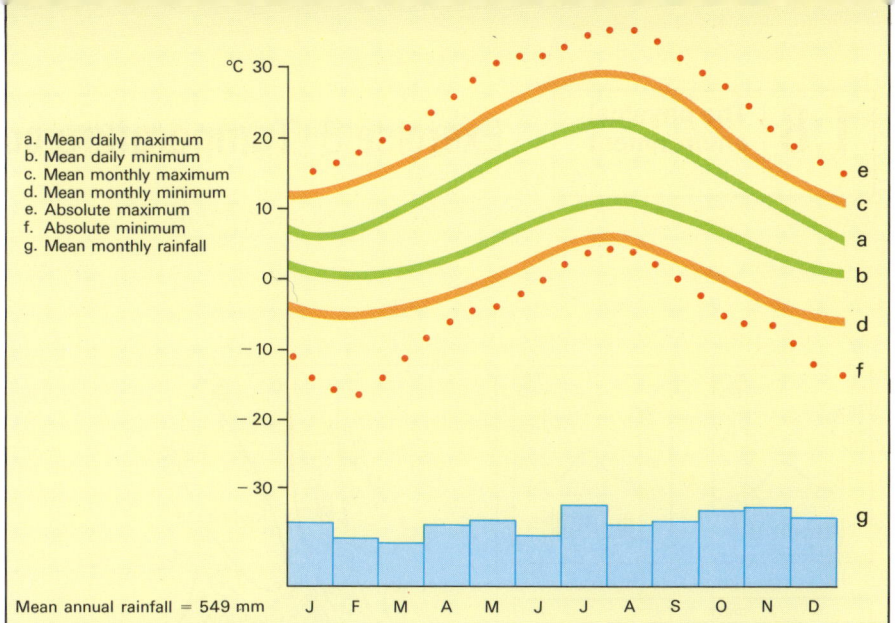

a. Mean daily maximum
b. Mean daily minimum
c. Mean monthly maximum
d. Mean monthly minimum
e. Absolute maximum
f. Absolute minimum
g. Mean monthly rainfall

Mean annual rainfall = 549 mm

1982 (see page 35) at London, East Anglia and Merseyside?

2 **a**) Which were the two coldest and which the two warmest places at midday on 11 January as given in the table? **b**) What was the lowest temperature recorded in England on 11 January? Why is the figure so much lower than those shown on the map? **c**) What are the indications that the snowstorms had stopped by 12 January over Britain?

3 What is the air temperature at the time you are doing this exercise? What and when was the hottest and the coldest temperature you have ever experienced?

4 What are some of the problems and hazards caused by **a**) extreme cold, **b**) heavy snowfall, **c**) very hot and dry weather conditions?

Many different sorts of weather information are available for places in Britain, as for Cambridge shown in this example

There can be striking contrasts between winter and summer conditions in Britain (*below and opposite*)

Exercise 8 **Temperature contrasts**

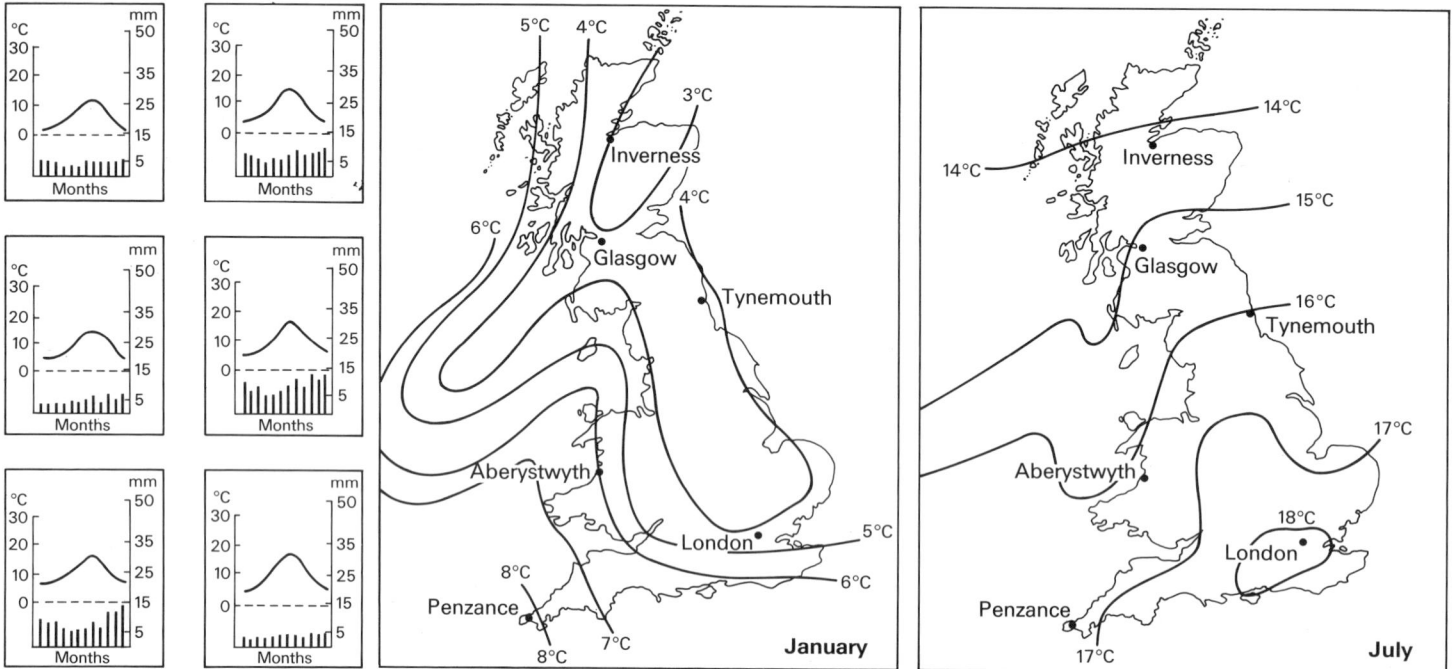

Maps and graphs showing the average temperature conditions in January and July in Britain. The graphs also show the variation in rainfall throughout the year

Heavy snowfall in January 1982 caused severe disruption to transport. Lorries on the M4 in Wales

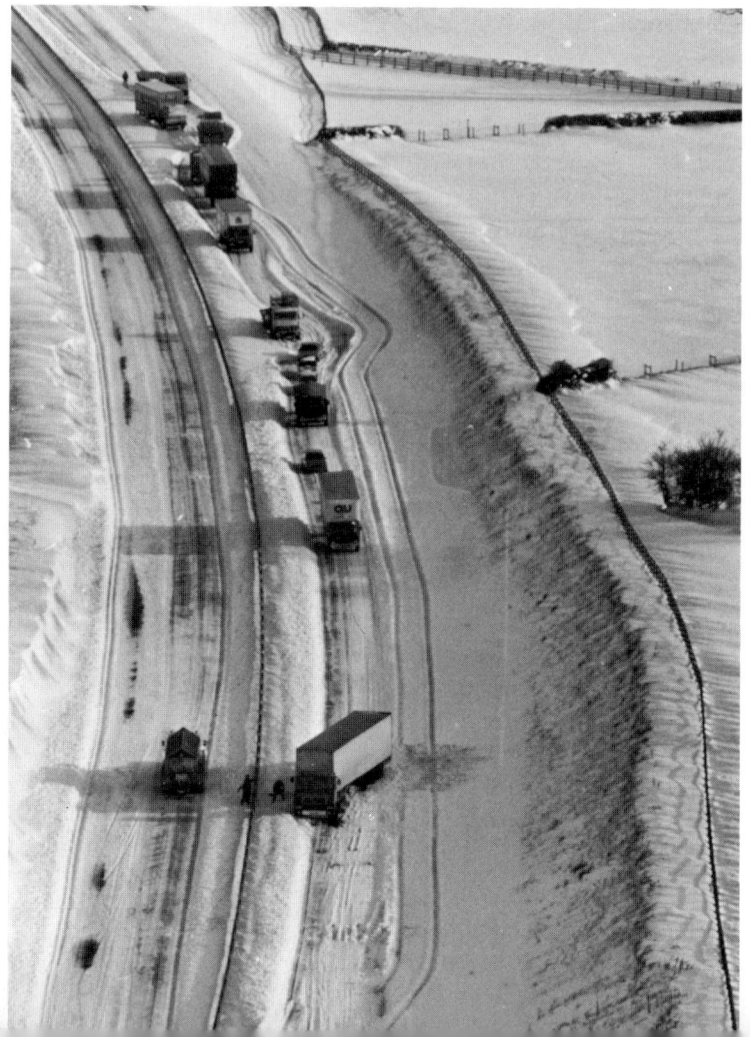

1 Describe the location of the warmest and coldest parts of Britain *on average* in **a**) January, **b**) July. Why is it helpful to have temperatures 'reduced to what they would be at sea-level' for this purpose?

2 How is the average or mean temperature for a month obtained? Why is it important to be careful about using this figure to describe the temperature of any place?

3 The two top temperature graphs are for Inverness and Glasgow; the second for Aberystwyth and Tynemouth and the lower for Penzance and London. Say which graphs are which, based on temperatures and rainfall.

Chapter 2 **People, population and settlement**

SOLD SUBJECT TO CONTRACT
ALLEN &HARRIS
THE ESTATE AGENTS
OXFORD 67414

A long-settled land

This white horse on the downs near Uffington, Oxfordshire, was first cut out of the chalk by prehistoric people

Part of the wall built by the Romans under Hadrian, which marked and protected the area of Britain they controlled from the marauding Scots

Pre-history

People have lived in Britain for many thousands of years. There are, of course, no written records from those earliest days, but other sorts of evidence have been found. For example, about twenty caves have been located in limestone areas that contain animal bones of creatures such as the mammoth and utensils and equipment that are estimated to be more than 10 000 years old! That means some human beings lived in what is now Britain during the last stages of the Ice Age.

These people survived by hunting, fishing and gathering foods that grew wild. Later groups kept animals and began to cultivate the land, and over thousands of years the land was slowly cleared and settled. Much of the lowland was heavily forested and difficult to clear, so settlement tended to be on the upland areas such as Dartmoor and the chalk and limestone hills, or around the coasts. There are many sites with signs of field boundaries, simple dwellings, more elaborate burial chambers or stone circles such as those at Avebury or Stonehenge, that go back to those days.

Many of these peoples, perhaps all, had migrated into the islands from mainland Europe. Some were from the Mediterranean area, others from Spain and the Western Alps. Some of these latter formed the Celtic peoples that occupied much of Britain when the Roman army arrived in A.D.43.

From Romans to Normans

By the time the Romans appeared the Celts had established villages and farms, surrounded by cultivated fields in many areas. But the Roman armies were superior and the Celts living in what is now England and Wales were conquered. The Romans built garrison towns and linking roads, and had a big impact on the life of the Celts. After about four hundred years the Romans left Britain, and soon afterwards German immigrants arrived and over-ran much of the country. The area that they occupied became known as Angle-land or England. These Anglo-Saxons once again affected the way of life of the peoples of Britain, but in ways very different to the Romans. They clashed with the Celts who were driven further west into Wales, Cumbria and Corn-wall. Christianity became firmly estab-lished, only to be challenged by another wave of pagan invaders – the Vikings from Norway, Denmark and Sweden. The Vikings in turn imposed many of their own beliefs and customs, language and social structure on the Anglo-Saxons, especially in the northern and eastern area known as the Danelaw. The end of Anglo-Saxon rule came dra-matically in 1066 at the Battle of Hast-ings when the Norman invaders from France defeated their army. The Nor-mans set out to control the whole of Britain and introduce their language, architecture, church and way of life.

Population growth after the Normans

Britain became one of the most prosper-ous countries in the world. It traded first in wool and cloth, then in iron, steel and manufactured goods. Raw materials were needed for these indus-tries, food for the growing population and markets for the products. The result of this wealth and power was that Britain spread its influence throughout the world and British people migrated to North America, Africa, Asia and Australia and New Zealand. Britain developed a remarkable Empire, con-trolling the lives and well-being of mil-lions of people.

Since the Norman Conquest many millions of people have also migrated to Britain. Groups have come from many places, over the centuries – from France and the Netherlands, Italy, Germany, Ireland and Poland and other eastern European countries. In recent decades people have migrated from many coun-tries that were once part of the British Empire.

Britain, then, consists of people of very different origins and backgrounds. The country has always received immi-grants, either as invaders, as people seeking refuge or as jobseekers. The nature of multicultural Britain will be looked at later. But first we can con-sider where these people live and the types of settlement and dwelling found in Britain today.

1 How do we know how prehistoric people lived?

2 Which of the Roman towns are now large cities, and which are quite small towns? Which parts of Britain were least under the control of the Roman armies?

3 **a)** In which part of Britain were the Vikings most powerful? **b)** Many place names introduced by the Danes end in '-by' and '-thorpe'. Name two present-day settlements with these name endings.

The remains of a castle built by the Normans in South Wales to protect their newly-taken lands (see page 43)

A map showing how Celtic Britain was settled and developed first by the Romans, then by the Saxons and the Vikings

Evidence of past migration

From the earliest days it seems that people have moved from place to place. For thousands of years Britain has been invaded or settled by people from other parts of the world. Until recently they were mostly from mainland Europe. The pattern and nature of these movements has been worked out from many different sorts of evidence. There are buildings, or the remains of buildings, reflecting the styles found in the homelands of the newcomers. There are 'artefacts' or objects such as weapons, clothes, ornaments, utensils, money, statues or any of the things people made and used at the time. From more recent times there is often written evidence, while place names and language often give a clue about the people who lived in a place in the past. From these different pieces of evidence it has proved possible to work out a fairly clear picture of life in Britain in the past.

Memorial stone set up in Britain by Gaius Aeresius Saenus, a veteran of the Roman Sixth Legion, for his wife and two children

Left: This stone cross from Yorkshire is typical of Celtic Christian art

This house in Norwich is of the sort built by Dutch settlers in Britain in the late sixteenth and seventeenth centuries. Its style reflects the architecture found in their homeland. These settlers came to Britain to escape religious persecution

A Viking silver armlet found near Flaxton, Yorkshire

The Bayeaux Tapestry, made by the French, records in picture form the story of the Norman invasion and the defeat of Britain. Stories and records, of course, may not be a completely true version of what happened

Exercise 9

Two cultures claim one Wales

There are great differences between Wales and the rest of Britain. When the territory we now know as Wales emerged as an independent unit in Western Britain in the Dark Ages it was a land with Celtic culture from the Iron Age which had survived the Roman occupation. From the sixth century onwards the Welsh faced persistent military pressure from the newly arrived Anglo-Saxon settlers in what was to become England or, more accurately, the Kingdom of Mercia. It was against the Saxon menace that the Celts of Wales became generally aware of their national identity.

From the fifth century until the coming of the Normans, Wales was virtually an independent country with its own institutions, laws, literature and economy. The whole area was held together by a common language. In the eighth century Offa, King of Mercia, built his great Dyke. This marked a compromise frontier with the Celts of Wales, while the Dyke provided the Welsh with an eastern boundary line stretching from sea to sea.

The physical nature of the country was unsuited to central government. While Wales remained a country with an intense feeling of national consciousness, there was no progress towards the establishment of a national centre. There was no capital, no national parliament or national church.

Following the Norman conquest of England, William I planted his powerful earldoms along the English Borderland of Wales at Chester, Shrewsbury, Hereford and Gloucester, and within a few years the barons began to thrust forward through the wide-open eastern facing valleys of Wales into the heart of the country. Because of the local physical geography this thrust forward was not so marked on the northern coastal plain as on the southern. The Normans took quick possession of much of eastern and southern Wales. Lands to the north and west, sheltered as they were by the uplands of central Wales, remained in native hands until the final conquest of Edward I in 1282. The location of Norman manors in Wales and the Borderland in the 14th century makes the resulting overall situation perfectly clear. There was a great contrast between Inner and Outer Wales, which the Norman penetration brought about. This has remained a feature of Wales. We must think of two Wales; Inner Wales, which retains its traditional Welsh life and culture and where more than 80 per cent of the people in most parts are able to speak the Welsh language, and Outer Wales, which is much more mixed ethnically and culturally and where for obvious reasons English is the spoken language.

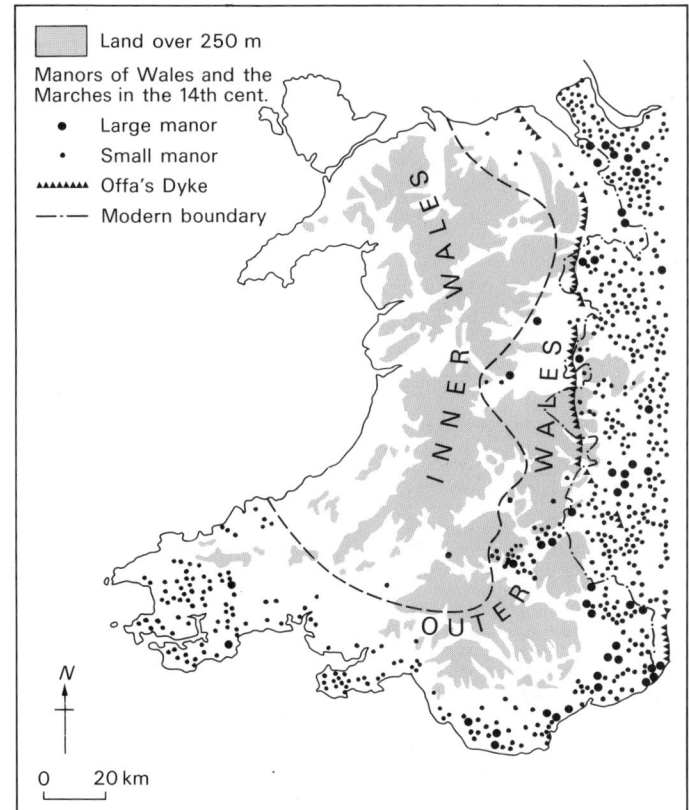

Legend:
- Land over 250 m
- Manors of Wales and the Marches in the 14th cent.
  - Large manor
  - Small manor
- Offa's Dyke
- Modern boundary

N

0   20 km

1 Describe some of the ways in which pre-Norman Wales and its history was different from the rest of Britain. What marked the boundary between Wales and England in the 8th century?

2 What was it about the 'physical nature' of Wales that made it difficult to have a 'national centre'?

3 Copy the map of Wales and on it a) mark Chester, Shrewsbury, Hereford and Gloucester, naming each, b) draw arrows showing the routes by which the barons and their people 'thrust forward through the wide-open eastern facing valleys'. Name the rivers that formed the valleys, c) shade in 'Inner Wales'.

4 What are some of the contrasts in the way of life of people in Inner and Outer Wales?

Population distribution

Distribution and density of population in Britain. This gives only a general impression: there are considerable variations within each of the coloured areas

Different homes for different needs
Although there are homeless people in Britain, and many more have to live in overcrowded or poor quality accommodation, the majority have a reasonable home of some sort. Housing in Britain varies greatly in size and shape, age and quality, type of ownership and cost to rent or buy. The housing needs of people vary. Some people live alone, and some in a family or as one of a group. Needs also vary according to such things as age, the number in the family or group and sometimes the type of work done. A single person, for example, is likely to want a different kind of accommodation from a young couple with small children or from an elderly retired couple. The sort of housing people actually own or rent varies a great deal according to their wealth and income.

Density of housing
Anyone who has travelled across Britain by road or rail is bound to have noticed that the density of housing, the number of houses and flats within a given area, changes a great deal from place to place. There is a close link between density of housing and density of population, and population density in Britain ranges from 0 to over 5000 people (in some urban areas) within a square kilometre (per km^2). The main reasons for the low densities in many areas, are because they offer little opportunity for large-scale employment and are not suitable locations for commuter, holiday or retirement settle-

Population per km^2

- Over 200
- 100–200
- 50–100
- 12–50
- Under 12

0   50   100   150 km

N

Helwith and Holgate, Yorkshire. Small settlements, made up of a cluster of three or four buildings, are known as hamlets

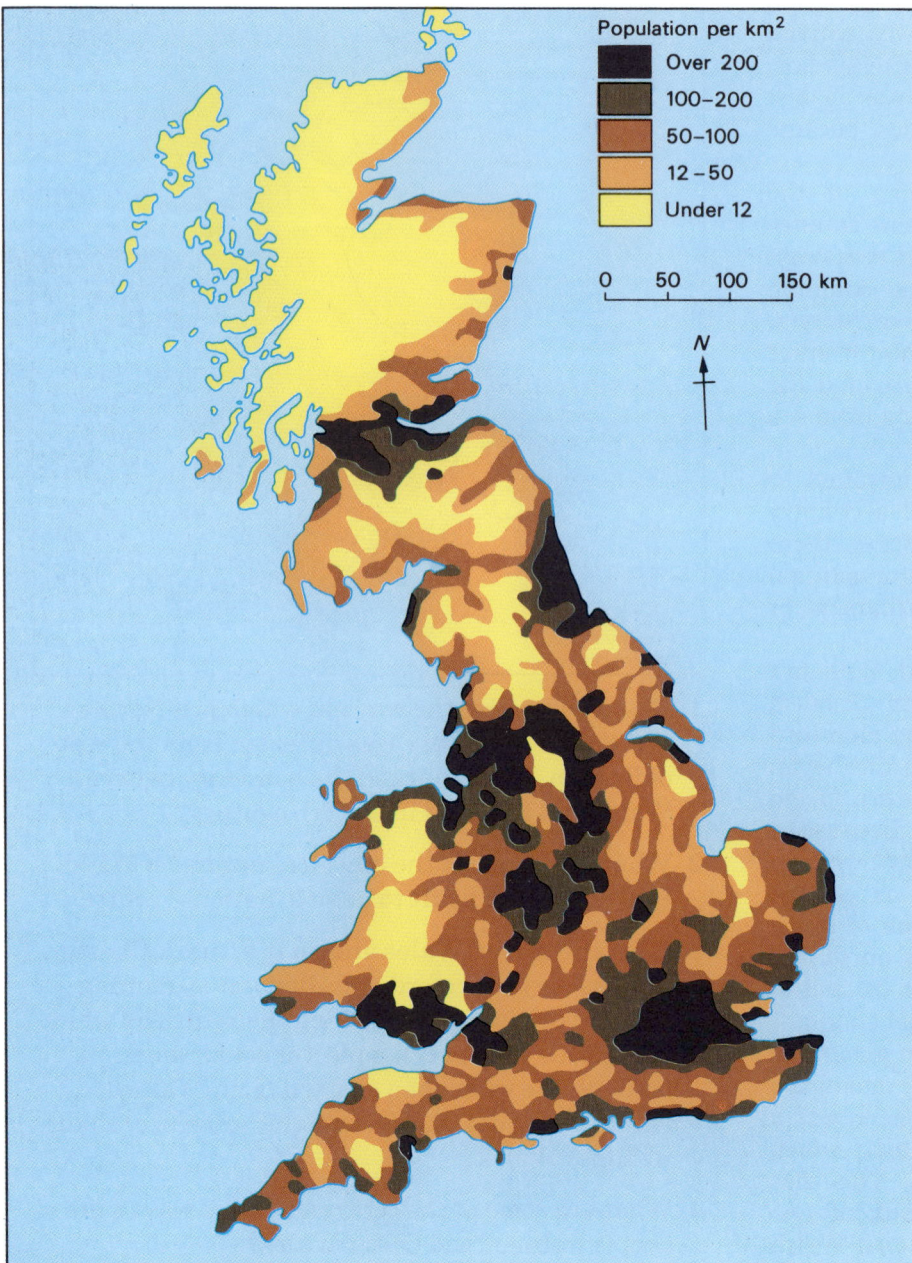

ments. By contrast some areas have a very high density of housing and population. These are usually where there is, or has been, plenty of employment or where it is available nearby. Low density areas are often referred to as 'rural', and the more built-up ones as 'urban'. The margins between rural and urban areas, however, are often blurred. There are sizeable towns within the countryside and areas of large open space within towns. It is also important to remember that the pattern is continually changing as people move from area to area and as new homes, even new towns, are built where there were none before.

Density and housing quality

It is a mistake to confuse density of housing with quality of homes, and wrong to think that high density means poor quality. It is true that some of the worst housing conditions consist of densely packed terraced houses and high-rise flats, but these types of housing can also be very attractive and expensive. It is also true that some appalling housing can be found in rural areas and in low-density suburbs and estates. More important than density is the quality of design and construction of the building and the amenities that are available. Some people enjoy living in towns while others prefer the countryside, but no one wants poor quality housing.

1 On census night in April 1981 there were 54 129 000 people in Britain. The area of Britain is 230 000 square kilometres. What was the average density of population?

2 Suggest why there was a low density of population in northern Scotland and the Fens and a high density in central London and South Wales.

3 Name one place you know that has a low density of population and another with a very high density. Suggest why.

4 Look at the illustrations on these pages: a) compare the density of housing; b) comment on the quality of the houses, c) comment on the quality of the surrounding environment.

Plockton, in the Highland Region of Scotland. Villages in Britain vary greatly in size, form and function. This is a good example of a small fishing village. The main type of activity in a village may change over time

St Paul's, Bristol. An example of housing in an old inner city area, with evidence of redevelopment in the foreground

Contrasts in housing

A single cottage with other derelict buildings, in a remote mountain area of Scotland

There are enormous differences in housing in Britain. Some of the contrasts in the size, nature and quality of individual dwellings are shown here. The costs of these will obviously vary. Some will be privately owned, some rented from other private owners and some rented from local authorities – often known as council houses.

Quite apart from individual dwellings, there are often marked differences in residential areas as a whole. These may range from individual homes standing alone in very large grounds to high density dwellings in packed terraces or to high-rise flats. It is important not to confuse density with quality or cost, as these pictures show.

These contrasting residential areas help make up the land use and social patterns of towns and cities.

Expensive detached housing with large grounds in north Bristol

Local authority high-rise flats and derelict terraced houses, Birkenhead

Expensive high density housing in London

Exercise 10 **Density of housing in Bristol**

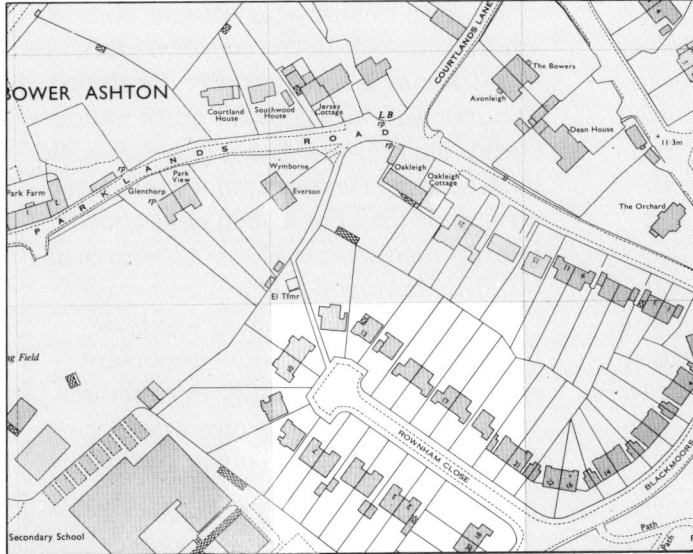

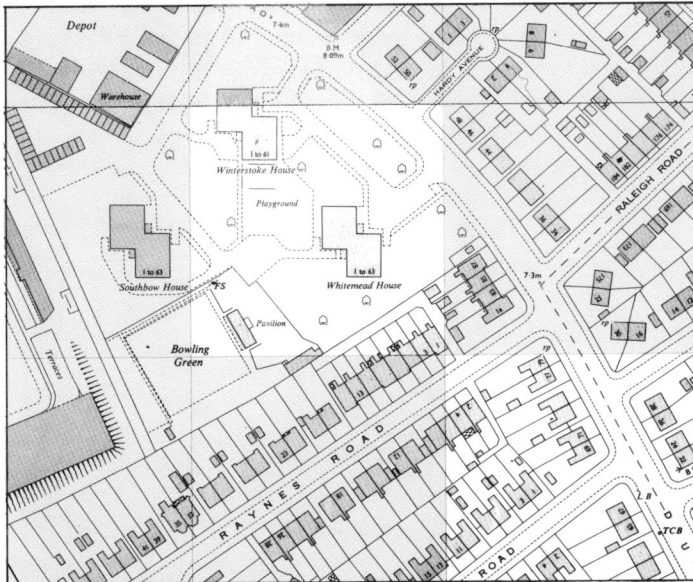

The wards of Bristol, with squares showing the location of the map extracts on the left

1 The areas outlined on the map are within a short distance of each other on the outskirts of Bristol. From the map evidence try to describe the type of housing in each area.

2 Each area is approximately 1 hectare. What is the approximate density of dwellings per hectare in each case. (In one case in particular it is impossible to give an accurate answer – which is it, and why?). Why would it be unwise to use these four extracts to calculate the overall density of population of each area?

Villages and towns

Kingston, near Brighton. A 'dormitory' village for people working in Brighton, Lewes, or even London

The size and location of settlement
Few people live on isolated farms deep in the countryside, and even fewer in large country houses set in their own grounds. The great majority live in settlements where buildings are clustered together. There is no hard and fast definition based on size, but the smaller settlements are usually called hamlets or villages and the larger ones towns or cities. In present-day Britain far more people live in large towns and cities than in hamlets, villages and small towns set in the countryside.

Settlements have usually developed at particular locations for quite understandable reasons. A site may have had good access to water from a well or a stream. It may have been near good quality farmland or close to a source of building materials. The site may have been free from flooding, or easily defended from attack. Some important sites were route crossings or junctions. Whatever the reasons once were for deciding to develop a settlement where

Settlements in East Sussex. Map scale 1:100 000

it is, they may no longer be of any importance. Most of these early settlements have grown in size as new housing and jobs have been provided, although some have disappeared altogether. Others have grown and then declined as jobs have been lost, services closed down and people have moved out.

Settlement patterns

Villages and towns are unevenly distributed in Britain. Large areas of upland have no settlements whatsoever. In lowland areas of gentler relief the density of rural settlement is usually much higher, although both the shapes of villages and the pattern made by their distribution varies a great deal from place to place.

A village may have a few shops, a post office, a church or chapel and perhaps a primary school, but villagers will probably have to go to the nearest town for such things as supermarket shopping, a bank, a doctor or for secondary schooling. As well as having more dwellings, towns provide more places of work and more services than villages. It is not so much the sheer numbers of houses as this variety of jobs, services, places of recreation and entertainment that leads to a settlement being thought of as a town rather than a village. Wherever the area and whatever the pattern of distribution of settlements, towns will be fewer and more widely spaced than villages.

The function of towns

Villages and towns can also be described by the main job or service they provide. We refer to a 'fishing' village, a 'market' or 'mining' town or a 'holiday resort'. Some have one principal function provided by a university or a single large factory (can you think of examples?). Each country or district has its administrative town where local authority offices are located. But most towns have a variety of functions. Villages and towns can be described in many ways, then, according to their shape, size, site and location, where they fit into the local pattern of settlements, and what functions they perform.

49

1 Lewes, Ditchling, Brighton, Kingston and Newhaven are five settlements in East Sussex. From the evidence provided here say something about their size shape, appearance, site, location and functions. What other evidence would be useful to do this task more fully?

2 Looking at the pattern of settlement as a whole, what features of the physical environment seem to have been of some significance?

3 Name and give the location of examples of the following settlements that you know: A seaside holiday resort, an industrial town, a commuter village or town, an administrative town. Think of two other sorts of village or town nearby and add to the list.

The town of Lewes, taken from the battlements of the castle

Ditchling, with the Downs in the background

Brighton, with a population of about 146 000, is the largest settlement in the area

Exercise 11 Villages and towns in Sussex

The illustrations on the last two pages showed the pattern of settlements in Sussex, from the clay weald, over the chalk Downs to the south coast. There is one major city, Brighton, several medium sized towns, and a scatter of smaller towns and villages. This pattern is found in most parts of Britain, other than the huge built-up conurbations (page 52) and the more remote mountain and upland zones.

What makes these Sussex settlements different from those in other areas is a combination of the particular landscape of chalk hills close to the English Channel, the distribution of features such as valleys, river estuaries and beaches, the local materials used in the older buildings, their past history and their position in relation to London and the rest of the country.

Most places show some features that are found elsewhere, and some that are unique to that area.

1 Photograph A shows a part of the South Downs and adjoining lowland to the north-west of Brighton. Compare the settlement pattern on the Downs with that on the lowland. Use a labelled sketch or written description. Try to explain the contrast.

2 Photograph B is of Central Lewes. Write out this list of land uses and by the side of each give the letter from the photograph where it can be seen.

3 Quite a few people commute from Lewes to London. How does the railway timetable (and air photograph) help confirm this fact?

4 What do you think is helpful and what is confusing about the use of picture symbols on the map of 'Historic' Lewes?

A A view looking westwards along the South Downs north-west of Brighton. The village of Fulking is on the lower land to the north of the chalk escarpment

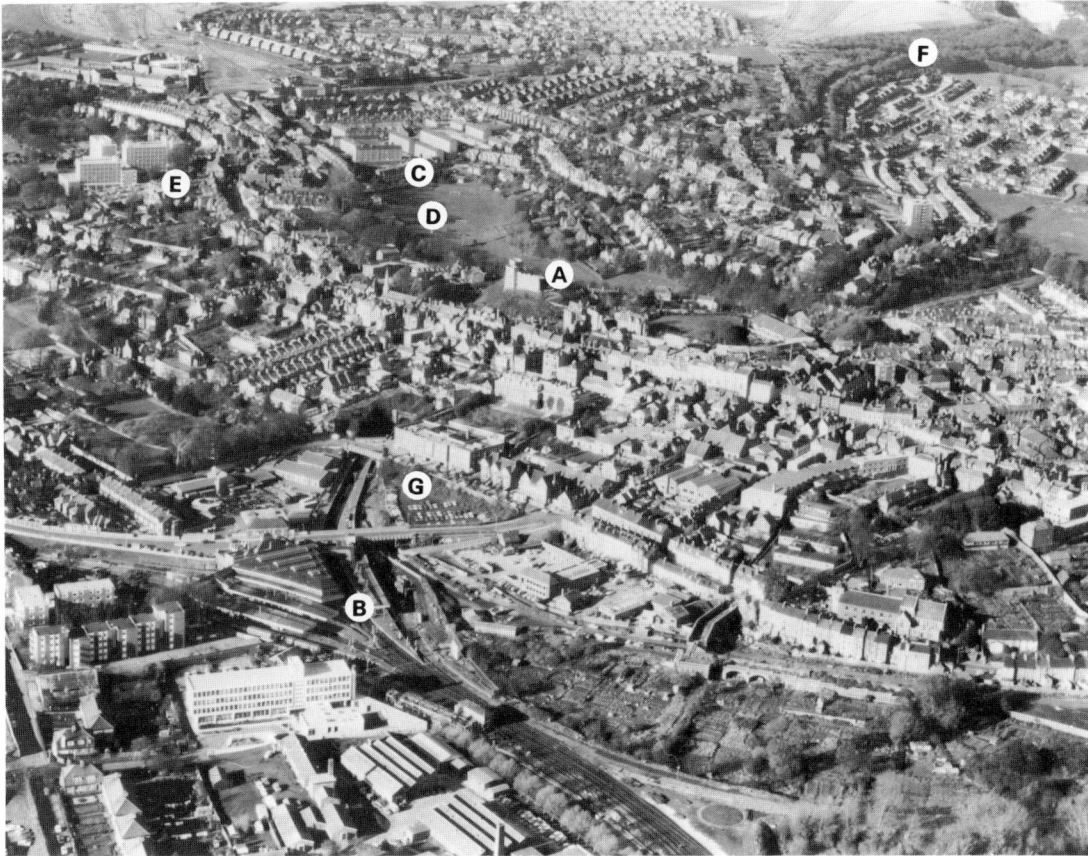

B Lewes, the county town of East Sussex

Office blocks
New blocks of houses
Woodland
Playing fields
Car Park
Castle
Railway Station

An adaptation of a town map of Lewes, designed for visitors and tourists

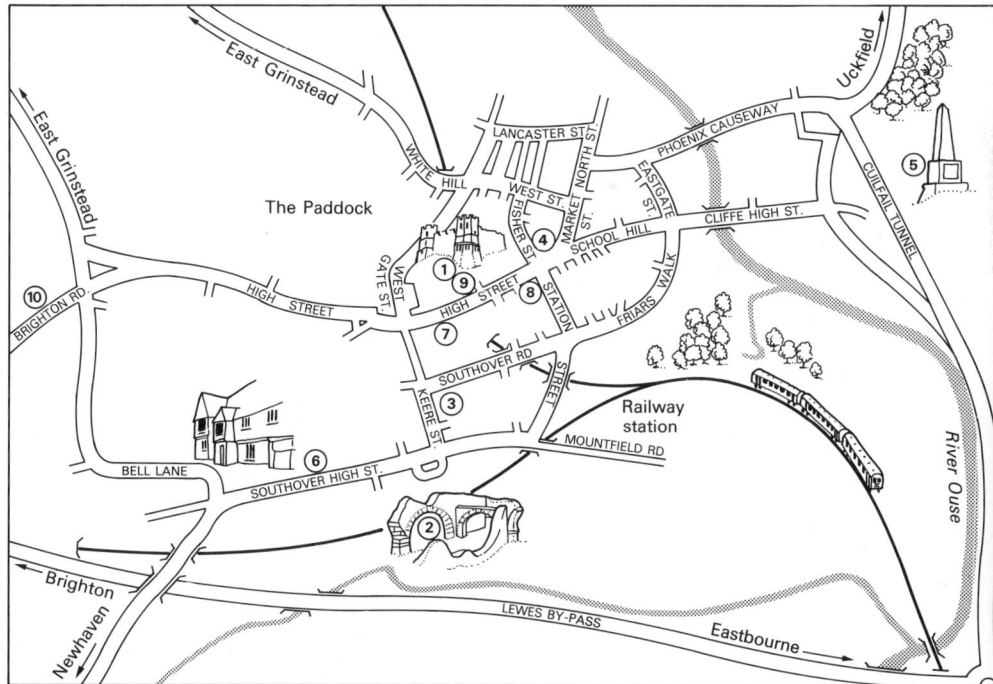

Mondays to Fridays

Lewes→London		London→Lewes	
Lewes	London Victoria	London Victoria	Lewes
dep	arr	dep	arr
05.54	07.12	F 03.30	04.45
06.38	07.53	05.18	06.40
07.02	08.11	06.18	07.46
07.22	08.34	06.55	08.16
07.36	08.41	07.18	08.46
07.52	09.04	07.59	09.26
08.07	09.11	08.53	09.58
08.22	09.30	09.53	10.58
08.55	10.05	10.53	11.58
09.22	10.27	11.53	12.58
10.21	11.27	12.53	13.58
11.21	12.27	13.53	14.58
12.21	13.27	14.53	15.58
13.21	14.27	15.53	16.58
14.21	15.27	16.40	17.42
15.21	16.27	17.02B	18.04
15.50	17.21	17.10	18.12
16.21	17.27	17.32B	18.34
17.21	18.27	17.40	18.42
18.21	19.27	18.10	19.15
19.21	20.27	18.53	19.58
20.21	21.27	19.53	20.58
21.21	22.27	20.53	21.58
22.21	23.27	21.53	22.58
22.54	00.33	22.53	23.58
23.49	02.10	23.52	01.21

1   The Castle.
2   The Priory of St. Pancras; destroyed during the Reformation.
3   Southover Grange; built 1572 from the ruins of the Priory.
4   The Town Hall; site of an Inn where the Protestant Martyrs were held before being burnt to death in the High Street.
5   The Obelisk; erected to the memory of the Martyrs in 1901.
6   Anne of Cleves' house; once owned by the fourth wife of Henry VIII.
7   Bull House; once the home of Thomas Paine.
8   The White Hart Inn; an old coaching inn, now with Georgian front.
9   166 Castle Place; the home of the Victorian scientist Gideon Mantell.
10 The Prison.

51

Cities and conurbations

The seven conurbations include six of the largest cities of Britain

The growth of towns and conurbations

During the nineteenth and twentieth centuries, when there was a dramatic growth of manufacturing industry, many towns expanded greatly in size. This was made possible by the development of tram, bus and rail transport. People were able to live further and further out from the town centres and factory areas, and travel to and from work each day. In time, factories, offices and shops were built in these suburbs as well, providing more jobs and the opportunity for yet further growth. In some areas, especially where a number of manufacturing towns had developed close to each other, so much expansion took place that the towns began to merge into one another. Although they remain separate towns and cities, they appear as an almost continuous built-up area. Seven areas in particular have grown in this way, and these are known as 'conurbations'.

Local Government was reorganised in 1974. The six conurbations in England became Metropolitan Counties and Greater London. The seventh conurbation, Clydeside in Scotland, became a part of the Strathclyde District. Another Metropolitan County was created that did not contain one of the seven big conurbations (see p. 54). Over a third of Britain's population lives in these seven areas though, as we shall see, their populations are declining. By 1984 the future of the Metropolitan Counties was in doubt.

The West Midlands conurbation

The towns and cities of Walsall, Wolverhampton, Dudley, Solihull and Birmingham have grown and merged to become the West Midlands conurbation. The city of Coventry is not part of the conurbation, but falls within the West Midlands Metropolitan County. Most of the West Midlands towns developed with the growth of manufacturing. In the early years this was based on coal, ore mining and smelting and a wide range of metal making (and using) industries. Because of the heavy, noisy, dirty nature of these activities for many decades a large part of the area was known as 'The Black Country', and evidence of this past can still be seen in much of the industrial townscape. With its skilled metal-working labour force and its central location with good transport links to the rest of Britain and its ports, the West Midlands attracted the motor car and lorry industry. The vast car plants at Longbridge and Coventry are a contrast to the older factories on

Air view of central Birmingham, the second largest city in Britain

52

congested sites near the centre of Birmingham. So are the associated factories of companies such as Dunlop, Goodyear and Lucas that make components and parts for cars and other vehicles.

Birmingham

Birmingham is the second largest city in Britain, and lies in the centre of the West Midlands conurbation. It is a regional centre for administration, commerce and entertainment, as its redeveloped Central Business District suggests. The slogan 'Birmingham: city at the heart of the nation' also indicates how local people see its importance. As with most parts of Britain, Birmingham experienced a big increase in unemployment during the late 1970s and early 1980s. In spite of this it remains a leading industrial city, providing over 580 000 jobs in its factories, offices and shops. About 150 000 of these employees live outside the city boundary, and their daily commuting puts considerable strain on the city's transport system.

Birmingham shows many of the features of the older centres within the conurbations. Poor quality housing and unattractive residential environments need to be improved by rehabilitation or redevelopment. New jobs are needed to replace those lost by closure of older factories if population decline is to be halted. The provision of decent homes, secure jobs, efficient transport and attractive surroundings are major tasks facing most older centres in the conurbations.

1 List the seven conurbations according to size.

2 Name one large city that is not part of a bigger conurbation. Name one conurbation that contains no city of over 450 000 people.

3 Compare and contrast the three townscapes in the West Midlands conurbation shown here.

4 Name one activity that is the responsibility of the Districts and one that is the responsibility of the County within a Metropolitan County.

53

Top: Residential area in Solihull. *Above*: Shopping centre in West Bromwich

Urban areas and the West Midlands Metropolitan County in 1984

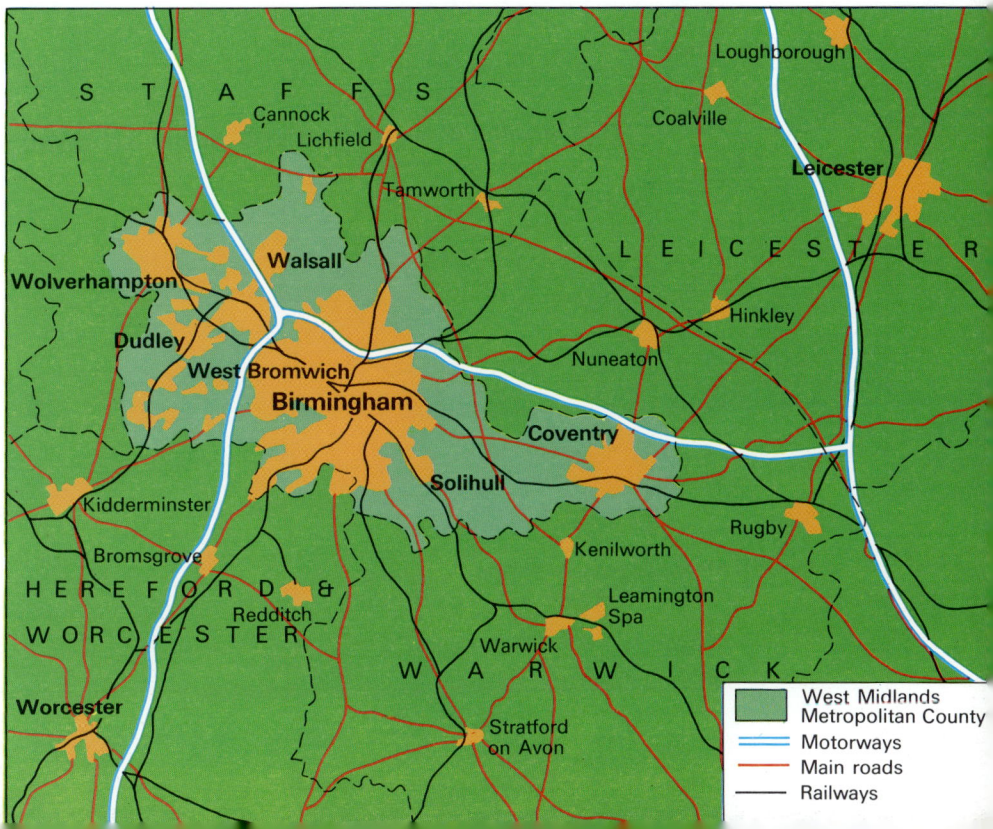

The counties of Britain in 1984

In 1974 many of the old county and other local authority boundaries were changed. The new pattern is shown on the map below. Apart from the Counties of England and Wales and the Regions of Scotland, there are the seven Metropolitan counties and Greater London. These include the conurbations and large built-up areas.

The Counties, Metropolitan Counties and Greater London are sub-divided into Districts and Boroughs. Councillors are elected to decide how things such as education, housing, roads, refuse collection and so on should be arranged and run in their areas, in collaboration with the central Government. In 1984 Central Government was proposing to disband the Metropolitan Counties and to hand their responsibilities over to the Districts and Boroughs.

Tyne and Wear
NEWCASTLE UPON TYNE — N. TYNESIDE — GATESHEAD — S. TYNESIDE — SUNDERLAND

West Yorkshire
BRADFORD — LEEDS — CALDERDALE — KIRKLEES — WAKEFIELD

South Yorkshire
BARNSLEY — DONCASTER — SHEFFIELD — ROTHERHAM

Greater Manchester
BOLTON — ROCHDALE — BURY — OLDHAM — WIGAN — SALFORD — TAMESIDE — MANCHESTER — TRAFFORD — STOCKPORT

Merseyside
SEFTON — KNOWSLEY — ST. HELENS — WIRRAL — LIVERPOOL

West Midlands
WOLVERHAMPTON — WALSALL — SANDWELL — DUDLEY — BIRMINGHAM — SOLIHULL — COVENTRY

For Greater London Boroughs see p.59

Exercise 12
Towns, conurbations and administrative areas in West and South Yorkshire in 1984

Urban areas in the Yorkshire and Greater Manchester Regions

The Districts of the Metropolitan Counties of West and South Yorkshire

1 Copy or trace the outline map of the districts in West and South Yorkshire. Draw the outlines of the urban areas within the two counties. (Barnsley has been done for you).

2 **a**) Which Districts are not named after a town or city? **b**) Which of the Districts have the three biggest cities in the region? **c**) Why is South Yorkshire, unlike West Yorkshire, not considered a conurbation?

3 What are the signs from the photograph that Sheffield is a major city in Britain?

Central Sheffield, one of the seven largest cities in Britain

55

London: capital city

Early beginnings

By far the largest conurbation is London. The administrative area, covered by the Greater London Council, is shown on the map opposite, but the built up area extends beyond this boundary. Some idea of its size within south-east England can be gained from the Landsat picture on page 9. This huge urban area, one of the largest in the world, grew from a small settlement that can be traced back to pre-Roman times.

In those distant days most routes in the area were along the chalk uplands now known as the North Downs. This gave a dry and more open landscape than the marshy lowlands along the margins of the River Thames to the north and the densely forested clay lowlands of the south. At one point near present-day London Bridge low gravel terraces rose above the badly drained flood plain. On the north side of the river, where a small tributary, known later as the Walbrook, joined the Thames the gravel formed two low hills.

The Romans built their settlement of Londinium on these low hills, surrounding it with a defensive wall, and established a small port. The important water supply was obtainable from wells sunk into the soil and bedrock. From that time onwards the city grew. Some idea of the extent and character of the city by the middle of the sixteenth century can be seen on the map drawn in 1572. By then the administrative and commercial city of London was linked along the north bank to the royal city of Westminster, while the settlement of Southwark was well established on the south side of the bridge. The urban area was now well outside the boundary of the Roman walls, but the really spectacular growth took place much later, mostly in the nineteenth and twentieth centuries with the development of the railway, tram, bus and underground networks.

Present-day functions

One of the major functions of modern London is to act as a centre for national affairs. In the hierarchy of settlements leading from small villages through towns, cities and conurbations, London stands at the top. It is the centre of national government in the sense that the Houses of Parliament are there, together with the major offices of the Civil Service. The commercial heart of London lies further east in the area known as The City – not to be confused with London as a whole. Here are the head offices of many banks, as well as the Bank of England, the Stock Exchange, Lloyds the insurers and many other financial institutions. Many argue that this is where the real power of Britain lies, in its financial institutions, rather than in the elected government. Whatever the balance, the cen-

View from the top of a new office block in 'the City', over St Paul's Cathedral and the River Thames

A map of Tudor London 1572

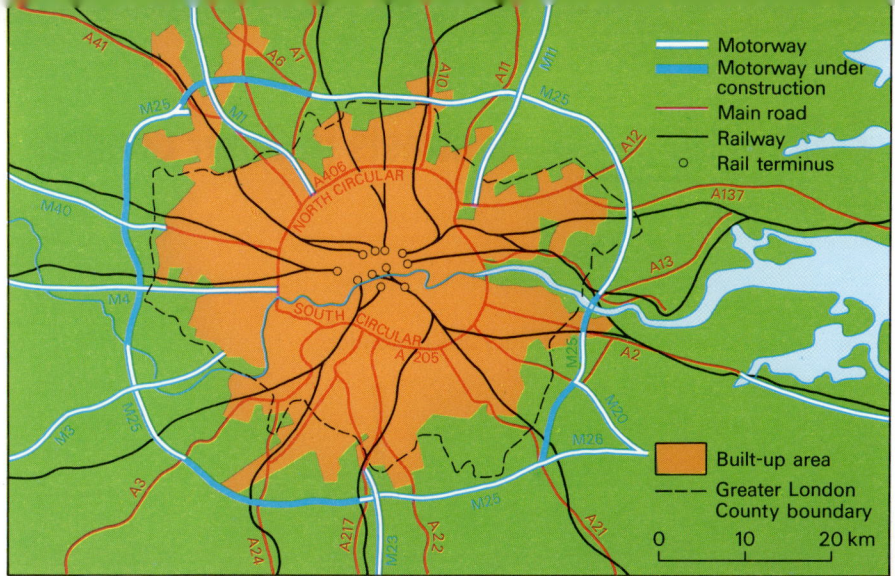

Motorway
Motorway under construction
Main road
Railway
Rail terminus

Built-up area
Greater London County boundary

0   10   20 km

1 Tower of London
2 Lloyds
3 Stock Exchange
4 Bank of England
5 Guildhall
6 St. Paul's Cathedral
7 Lincoln's Inn
8 Law Courts
9 Temple
10 British Museum
11 National Gallery
12 St. James's Palace
13 Buckingham Palace
14 Westminster Cathedral
15 Westminster Abbey
16 Houses of Parliament
17 County Hall
18 Festival Hall
19 National Theatre
20 Barbican Centre
21 Victoria Coach Station

- - - - Boundary of City of London
Park
Main line railway station
Main through route
Theatre

tral government at Westminster and the commercial centre of the City between then qualify London to be regarded as the capital of Britain.

There is a great deal of manufacturing within Greater London. This takes place in a few particular areas which are often on large industrial estates. In most cases the appearance of the industrial zone is not as spectacular as, say, the huge steelmaking, oil refining or shipbuilding areas, but in total the output of factories in London as well as the number of employees is very important to the economy as a whole.

What is striking about employment, however, is the high proportion of people (about seven out of ten workers) in the service industries (chapter five). These include workers in offices and shops, banking, insurance and finance, professional and service industries and in the various forms of transport and communication that link them all together. Much of this activity is located in particular parts of London, often the central area, and this results in a massive inwards and outwards flow of commuters each working day. London is also a national centre for recreation and tourism. This also results in large passenger flows, but the patterns are different from those associated with commuting. The tourist and recreation business revolves around central London with its rich architectural and historical heritage and its many theatres, cinemas, clubs and restaurants. Millions of people are also attracted by the many large shops and stores and by the galleries and museums that are amongst the best in the world.

Most of London's national functions are performed in this central area of Westminster, the West End and the City

1 a) Draw a rough sketch from the map of Central London above putting in only the river and boundary of the City. Now shade in the parts of London that existed when the map was drawn in 1572.
b) Draw an outline of the GLC area from the map above. Now shade in the area covered by the 1572 map.

2 a) Suggest why most of the railway terminals are north of the River Thames.
b) What methods are used to link up with the terminals across London?

3 London badly needs more than one coach station (Victoria). Where would you locate a second major coach station?

4 Some people argue that London is too much at the centre of power and events in Britain. What are some of the advantages and disadvantages of centralising so many functions in one big capital city?

Oxford Street, one of London's busiest thoroughfares. Note the absence of private cars in this section

Contrasts in Outer London

There are many industrial areas like this in London

Visitors may get the impression that all of London is like the central area and the City, unless they have been observant when travelling in by road or rail. All routes into London pass through various zones of residential suburbs. These vary very much from the outer suburbs of new, lower density housing to the old, densely-packed, inner city zones. Within each of these are new estates of high-rise flats, that give further variety. The view of Croydon is a reminder of the fact that Greater London consists of many once separate settlements, and that some of these are larger than distinct towns elsewhere in the country. They are regional centres, and many people who live in them may rarely visit central London. London, in fact, consists of a wide range of urban environments and ways of life, bound together partly by belonging to one continuous built-up area, and partly, at the time of writing, by a shared local government, the Greater London Council.

Left: Many people live in the outer suburbs and commute by rail to their work in central London

Below, left: Low density housing on the outskirts of London

Croydon has one of the more spectacular Central Business Districts in the outer suburbs

Exercise 13 **Greater London**

1 What is the maximum distance across Greater London? Name a place that is the same distance from your home or school.

2 Draw a line representing a section across London through Sutton, Merton, Lambeth, City of London, Islington, Haringey and Enfield. Draw a diagram representing the change in population density across the conurbation. Explain the various changes.

3 Draw the outline of Greater London. On your map shade in two ways the Boroughs where over 2.5 per cent are without an inside w.c. and where over 15 per cent of the households have to share a bath or shower. What do you notice about the distribution of these Boroughs? What are some possible explanations of this pattern?

Greater London, 1984

Housing conditions in Greater London, early 1980s

		Percentage of households	
	Persons per hectare 1982	lacking inside w.c.	not having sole use of bath or shower
Greater London	42.8	2.2	9.7
Barking and Dagenham	44.2	1.2	0.9
Barnet	32.9	0.7	6.9
Bexley	35.9	1.5	2.1
Brent	57.5	0.7	14.4
Bromley	19.6	1.2	4.3
City of London	19.0	0.1	1.4
Camden	81.0	0.8	16.0
Croydon	37.1	1.9	7.2
Ealing	50.8	1.9	10.5
Enfield	32.3	2.2	5.6
Greenwich	45.5	3.4	6.6
Hackney	94.1	2.4	16.8
Hammersmith and Fulham	92.4	3.2	22.3
Haringey	67.5	2.5	16.7
Harrow	39.1	0.6	3.8
Havering	20.6	0.9	1.9
Hillingdon	21.1	0.7	2.3
Hounslow	34.9	2.1	7.7
Islington	109.4	1.2	18.1
Kensington and Chelsea	114.5	0.8	18.2
Kingston upon Thames	35.6	1.5	6.3
Lambeth	90.8	—	18.4
Lewisham	67.3	2.1	10.4
Merton	43.9	1.7	6.4
Newham	58.4	11.0	16.0
Redbridge	40.3	1.9	5.8
Richmond upon Thames	29.0	2.6	9.1
Southwark	74.5	2.3	9.7
Sutton	39.2	1.1	3.3
Tower Hamlets	73.2	2.8	9.3
Waltham Forest	54.4	6.8	10.8
Wandsworth	74.0	3.3	13.3
Westminster, City of	86.1	0.8	17.2

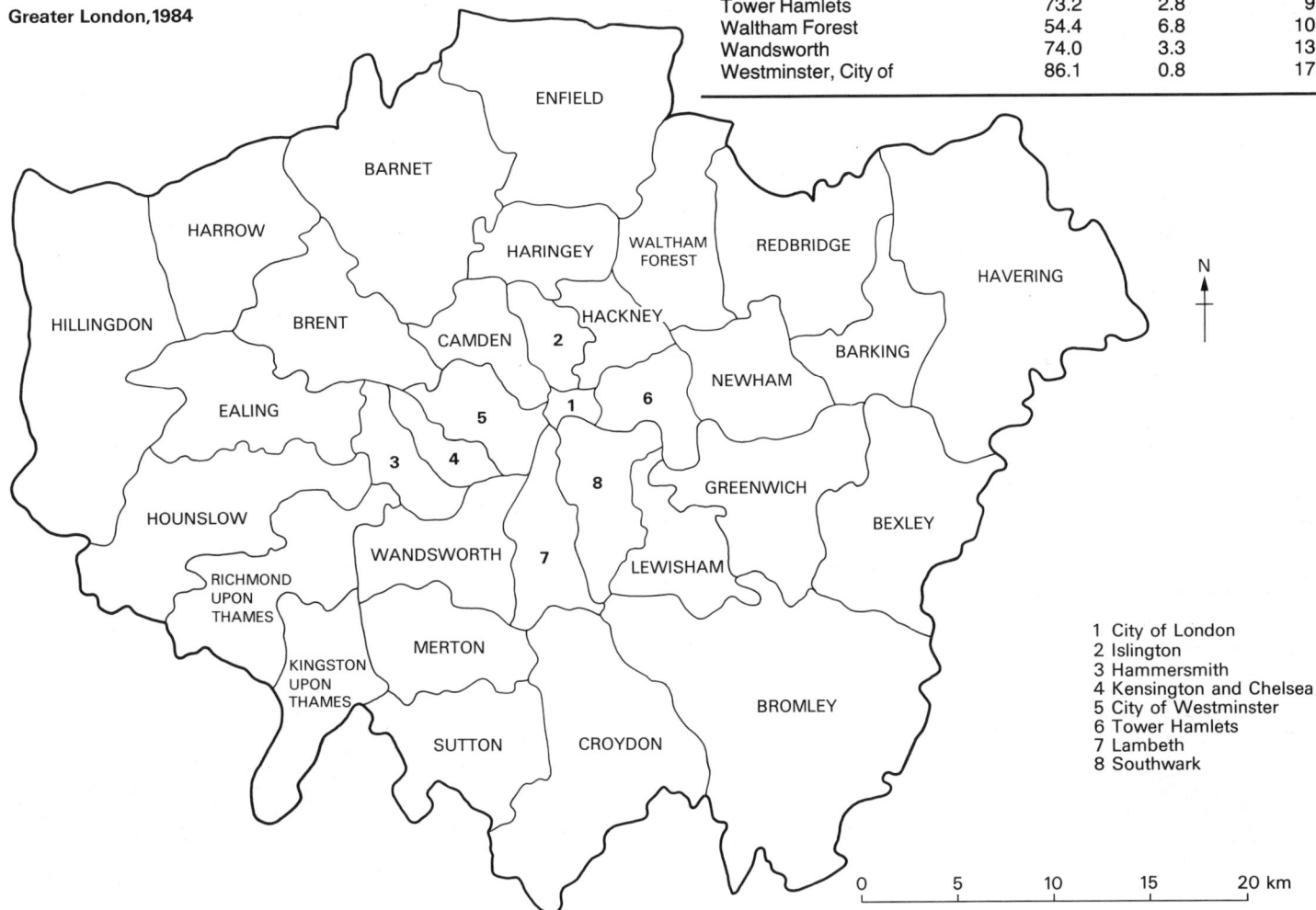

1 City of London
2 Islington
3 Hammersmith
4 Kensington and Chelsea
5 City of Westminster
6 Tower Hamlets
7 Lambeth
8 Southwark

0 5 10 15 20 km

Population change 1971–81

Changing opportunities for employment is one important cause of local or regional population change

The 1981 Census of Population

An accurate census of the population of Britain is taken every ten years, and the last one took place in April 1981. On census night there were 54 129 000 people in Britain, consisting of 26 286 000 males and 27 843 000 females. This showed a growth of about 150 000 or 0.3 per cent over the 1971 figure. This meant that population growth during the 1970s was much smaller than during the previous two decades, when for each of the ten year periods it had been about 5 per cent. This is thought to be due to a declining birth rate rather than to changes in international migration.

National and regional change

As the table and map show, the change was not the same everywhere. Population in England increased by a mere 0.4 per cent while Wales showed an increase of 2.2 per cent and Scotland a fall of an almost equal percentage. For many statistical reasons Britain is divided up into the regions shown on the

map. On this regional scale growth was greatest in East Anglia, with large gains also in the South-West and South East outside Greater London. By contrast there were considerable losses in Greater London, the North of England and Scotland. These are quite large areas, however, and there were marked differences within them.

Areas of population decline

One of the most striking changes during the 1970s was the continuing decline of population in the centres of the very big cities of London, Birmingham, Glasgow, Liverpool and Manchester. Inner London, for example, lost over half a million people during the

Contrasts in population change, by region. There are big local contrasts within each of these regions

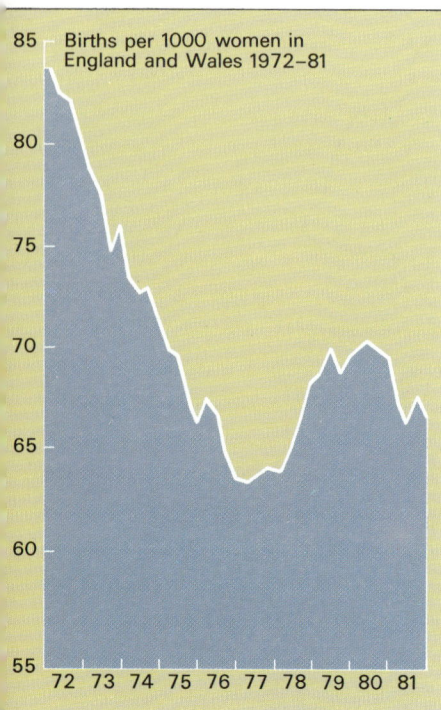

Births per 1000 women in England and Wales 1972–81

A changing birth or death rate affects the total population figures

Contrasts in population change, by region

Area	Population 1981 thousands	Population change 1971–81 thousands	%
England	46 221	203	0.4
North	3 097	−45	−1.4
Yorkshire and Humberside	4 854	−2	−0.1
East Midlands	3 807	174	4.8
East Anglia	1 856	196	11.7
South-East	16 729	−202	−1.2
Greater London	6 696	−756	−10.1
Remainder of South-East	10 033	555	5.9
South-West	4 326	246	6.0
West Midlands	5 136	27	0.5
North-West	6 406	−191	−2.9
Wales	2 790	59	2.2
Scotland	5 117	−112	−2.1

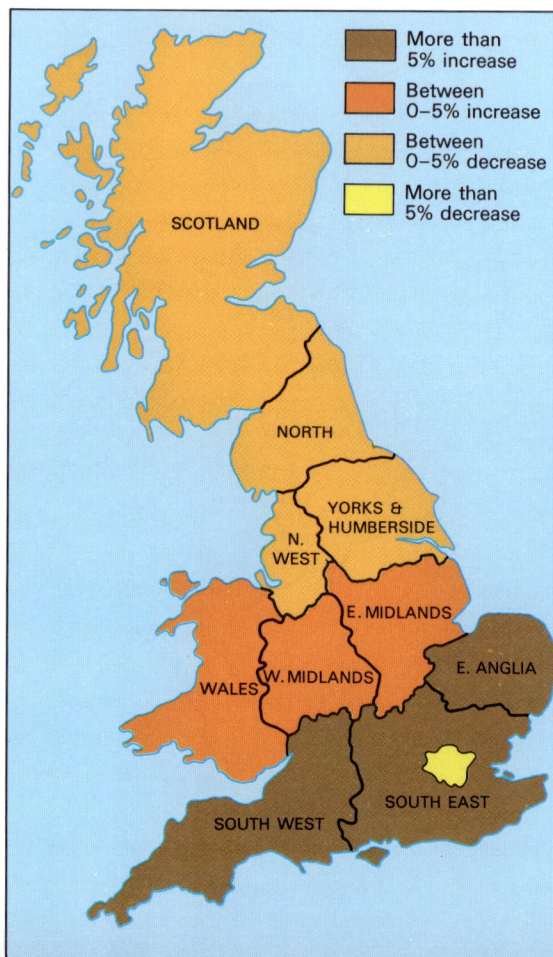

More than 5% increase	
Between 0–5% increase	
Between 0–5% decrease	
More than 5% decrease	

SCOTLAND
NORTH
YORKS & HUMBERSIDE
N. WEST
E. MIDLANDS
WALES
W. MIDLANDS
E. ANGLIA
SOUTH EAST
SOUTH WEST

ten years, with the loss in some boroughs being over 20 per cent. For the first time, though, some of the outer boroughs began to share this decline. Some of the outer boroughs of London (page 59) and places such as Wolverhampton in the West Midlands and Trafford in South-East Lancashire, that had shown an increase of population during the 1960s now began to show a loss. Quite apart from the conurbations, however, many large and medium-sized cities and towns showed the same trend, and added to the picture of decline in most of the established urban areas.

Selective migration

If local decline of population is due to people leaving the area, it is important to know what sort of people are leaving and who are staying. In the past there were many signs that the younger, more active and more skilled left the cities leaving behind a high proportion of elderly, unskilled and unemployed. If that process is continued long enough it throws great strains on the local authorities and leads to an unbalanced community. This trend may be changed by efforts to get new jobs back in the inner city areas and by any increase in employment. Another feature of inner cities has been that as some people have been compelled to move out, others with higher income have been able to buy the houses and rehabilitate them. These inner city areas have lost some of their population but have become 'gentrified' in the process.

1 Suggest different reasons for population change within a country over a given period of time.

2 Put the Regions of Britain into rank order of population change during the 1970s, with largest growth at the top and largest decline at the bottom of the list.

3 From the map opposite copy or trace the Region in which you live. With the help of the map on page 62 identify and explain one district of population growth and one of decline during the 1970s.

4 Explain the features and causes of either 'selective out-migration' or 'gentrification' in inner city areas.

Above: The beginnings of 'gentrification' in an old, run-down, inner city area

Left: Many inner city areas lost population as older, high-density housing was demolished

This population 'pyramid' shows how quickly birth rates can change. Note the 'booms' in the post-war years, the steady increase to a peak in the mid 1960s, and a striking decline in the late 1970s

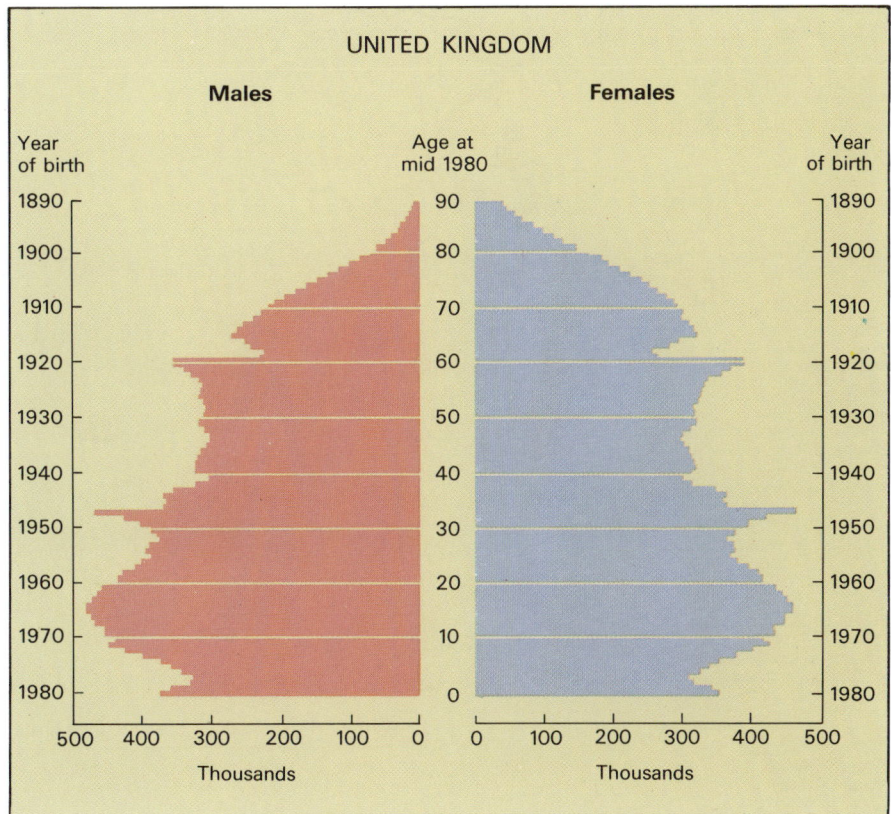

Population pyramid: UNITED KINGDOM. Males (left) and Females (right). Year of birth from 1890 to 1980. Age at mid 1980 from 0 to 90. Horizontal axis in Thousands, 0 to 500 on each side.

Population change 1971-81

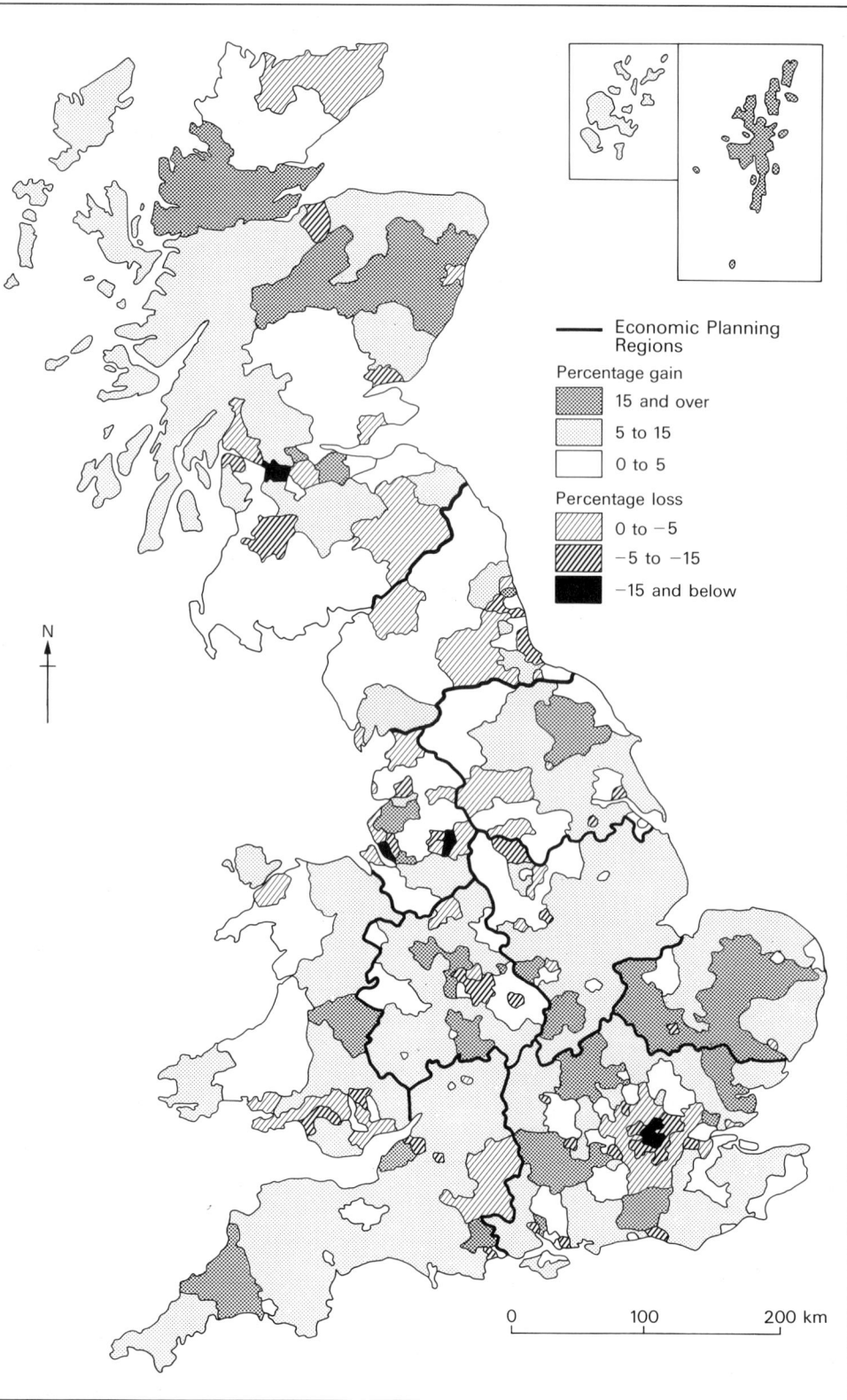

This map shows population changes between 1971–1981 in more detail than the one on page 60. The regions are still shown, but districts within them with similar population change have been grouped together. On the regional map the South-West, for example, is shown to have had an increase of over 5 per cent during the period. This map, however, shows that within the south-west some places such as Bristol and Bath showed a loss while others such as east Cornwall and the part of Avon south-west of Bristol had gains of 15 per cent and over. Even this map is generalised. Small areas of Bristol and Bath, for example, had increases of population as new housing areas were built. These maps are a reminder that we must look carefully at the scale of maps, and the ways in which the information shown is grouped, if we are to properly 'read' what they show.

Economic Planning Regions

Percentage gain

15 and over

5 to 15

0 to 5

Percentage loss

0 to −5

−5 to −15

−15 and below

N

0   100   200 km

Exercise 14 **Population change in the West Midlands 1971-81**

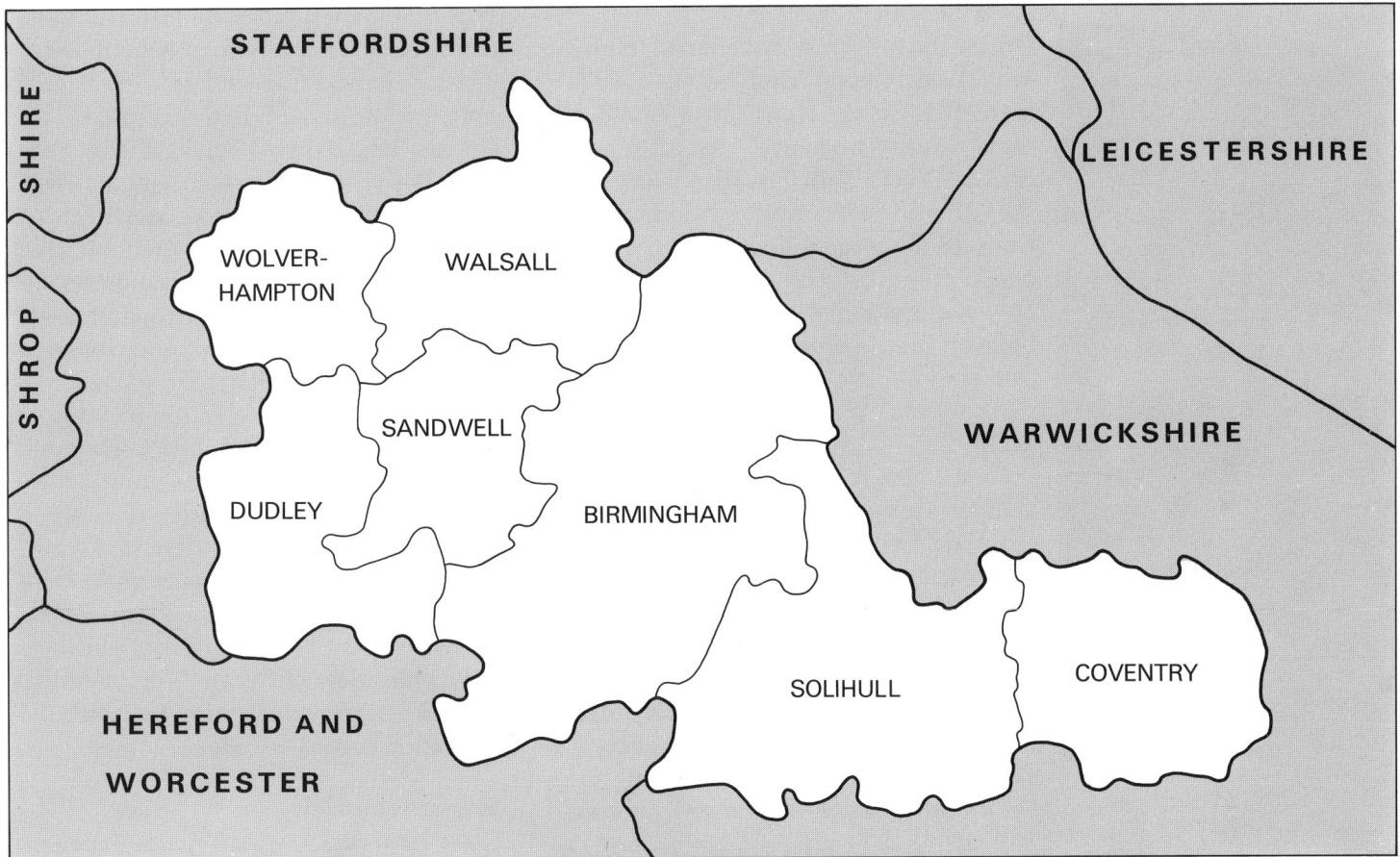

Map of the West Midlands conurbation and its seven Districts. Compare this with the map on page 53

1 Copy or trace the map of the seven Districts in the West Midlands Metropolitan County. On your map use different forms of shading to show the projected population change between 1979 and 1986.

2 Choose the two extremes of change and explain the possible reasons for the difference. Use the density figures and pages 52 and 53 to help.

3 Compare the projected population changes of the West Midlands Metropolitan County and the rest of the West Midlands Region for the same period. Suggest reasons for the difference.

Actual and expected population change in the West Midlands Metropolitan County, 1982

Districts	Density of population (persons per hectare)	Population (thousands)	Projected Population
Birmingham	38.5	1017	987.3
Coventry	32.9	317	326.1
Dudley	30.7	301	289.2
Sandwell	36.1	309	290.7
Solihull	11.1	199	206.7
Walsall	25.2	267	256.1
Wolverhampton	37.1	255	245.6
West Midlands Metropolitan County	29.7 (average)	2667 (total)	2601.7 (total)
Rest of West Midlands Region (Shropshire, Staffs, Warwicks, Hereford and Worcs.)	2.1 (average)	2515 (total)	2545.9 (total)

Areas of growth 1971-81

New Towns

One of the few types of urban settlement to gain population between 1971 and 1981 was the New Town. These were planned and developed after the Second World War. The idea was that they should be overspill settlements from the then growing cities where people from the decayed and overcrowded inner city areas could be rehoused. In some cases it was intended that they should give fresh life to regions where older industries were in decline.

Most of the New Towns were developed around small existing villages or towns. Unlike most earlier settlements they were planned as a whole. Although each is unique, they have many features in common. The houses to rent or buy are more or less of the same age and style over considerable areas, and this can make parts of New Towns look monotonous. The same can be said, of course, of many new estates built in other urban areas. Most have been planned on a neighbourhood basis, with the town divided up into smaller parts, each with its shops, schools, and other amenities, as well as with a central shopping and business area. Since the aim was to provide jobs within the New Town, areas are also set aside for manufacturing and trade. Many more people now own motor cars than in the past, so there is plenty of garage accommodation and parking space, and the road network is planned for a great deal of private and public traffic. Three towns in particular – Milton Keynes, Telford and Skelmersdale/Chorley in Central Lancashire – were planned to have a far bigger population than the others, and could be better called New Cities. Population targets have in most cases now been lowered, and in many ways the New Towns have not worked out as planned. Nevertheless they have made a major contribution to urban growth in recent decades.

Rural Wales

For over a century Mid-Wales experienced population decline, and traditional Welsh rural life was under threat. The 1970s saw a surprising change, and this is well illustrated by the District of Ceredigion in the County of Dyfed. The area includes a part of the Welsh Mountains, rural farmland and villages and a few towns such as Lampeter, Cardigan and Aberystwyth. During the decade its population increased by 11 per cent, well above the national average. This was largely due to inward migration. It is estimated that over 10 000 people, including children born in Ceredigion to parents who settle there, moved into the District during the decade.

Their reasons for settling there varied a great deal. The single most important reason was for employment.

Part of the New Town of Bracknell

Below: The central area of the New City of Milton Keynes, the most rapidly growing *District* in Britain between 1971–1981

Rural areas such as this in Ceredigion have seen a considerable increase in population over the past decade

The age structure of the migrants was 'younger' than that of the population of the District as a whole, and they included a high proportion of professionals, employers, managers and people in 'non-manual' jobs. Other motives for settling included 'because they liked the area', 'to get away from the stresses of urban living', 'for personal links such as family or friends', to try and find better housing, and in a few cases for retirement.

In the ten years some 3 400 houses were built, of which 70 per cent were for private owners. Only one-fifth of these were in the towns. Industrial estates had already been created in Aberystwyth, Cardigan and Lampeter to try to stop the drift of young people from the area, but during the decade only 120 new factory jobs and about 1 000 jobs in the 'service' industries were provided. As a result, unemployment is quite high, especially amongst the local Welsh people, many of whom are not as qualified as the newcomers. Apart from these pressures on housing and jobs, many local people feel that their Welsh language and way of life will be swamped by this migration. As with other rural areas experiencing population growth by migration, the District of Ceredigion is finding it brings problems as well as benefits.

Aberystwyth, port and University town on the west coast of Ceredigion

1 Many of the New Towns are located near one of the conurbations. Name the conurbations and next to each make a list of the New Towns they are likely to be linked with. Refer to the map on page 66.

2 What are some of the advantages and disadvantages of living in New Towns (or similar large estates in other urban areas) compared with older inner city areas?

3 Copy the map of Wales and show the following information in diagram form: Migrants to Ceredigion: from Wales 30 per cent; from England 60 per cent; elsewhere 10 per cent: For those from England 40 per cent came from the South-East Region and 25 per cent from the West Midlands.

4 Imagine you are each of the following people. Write a few comments that each person might make about the in-migration to Ceredigion described above: a) a local school-leaver, b) an elderly couple retiring there from Birmingham, c) a local shopkeeper, d) a Welsh-language supporter, e) a local builder.

The District of Ceredigion is in the County of Dyfed

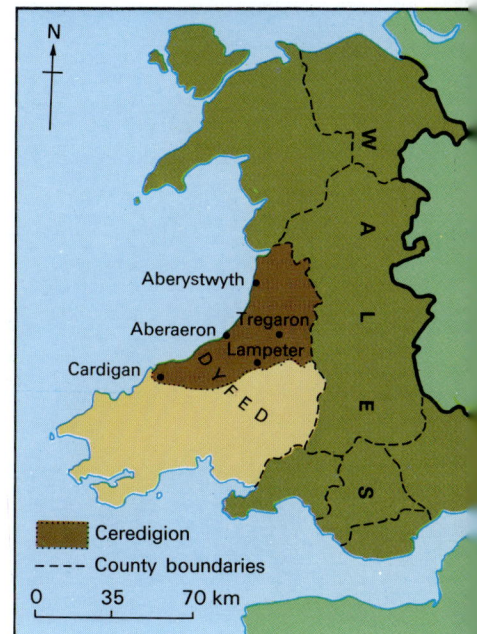

Aberystwyth
Aberaeron
Tregaron
Lampeter
Cardigan

Ceredigion
- - - - County boundaries
0   35   70 km

65

New Towns

The New Towns of Britain

New towns	Population 1981	% Population change 1961–71	% Population change 1971–81
Glenrothes	32700	114.4	19.6
Cumbernauld	47702	545.5	35.3
Livingston	38594	902.0	184.5
East Kilbride	70259	98.6	10.6
Irvine	32852	36.1	42.7
Washington	50899	25.3	102.6
Newton Aycliffe	36826	28.4	9.5
Peterlee	22756	63.9	4.2
Chorley	54775	12.9	22.0
Skelmersdale	43464	121.0	42.1
Runcorn	64117	26.6	78.1
Telford	103786	30.0	30.4
Redditch	66854	19.0	63.1
Corby	47773	32.9	−0.5
Milton Keynes	106974	42.5	102.0
Stevenage	74381	56.0	10.9
Welwyn	40496	15.0	0.1
Harlow	79276	45.4	1.5
Basildon	152301	45.9	17.7
Hatfield	25160	23.6	−0.8
Hemel Hempstead	76695	27.2	10.0
Bracknell	48752	65.9	27.7
Crawley	73081	25.1	6.9
Cwmbran	44876	32.2	7.6

Part of the covered central shopping centre in Milton Keynes

The New Towns of Britain, showing their relationship to old-established urban centres

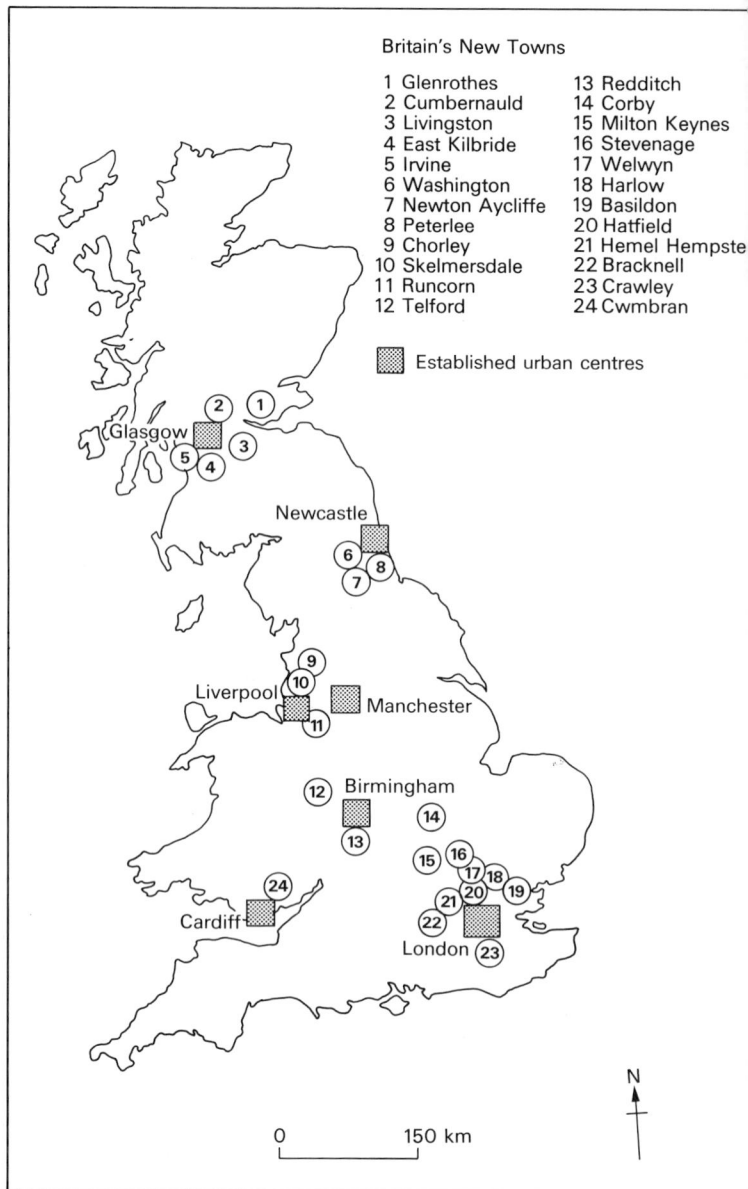

Britain's New Towns

1 Glenrothes
2 Cumbernauld
3 Livingston
4 East Kilbride
5 Irvine
6 Washington
7 Newton Aycliffe
8 Peterlee
9 Chorley
10 Skelmersdale
11 Runcorn
12 Telford
13 Redditch
14 Corby
15 Milton Keynes
16 Stevenage
17 Welwyn
18 Harlow
19 Basildon
20 Hatfield
21 Hemel Hempstead
22 Bracknell
23 Crawley
24 Cwmbran

Established urban centres

Some of the most rapidly growing parts of Britain are the New Towns. The reasons for their establishment, and some of their features, were described on page 64. The location of the New Towns is shown on the map, and the links with nearby large cities are often clear to see. These links may exist even where the New Town is located some distance from the city.

There have been many other major developments outside the New Towns, of course.

Exercise 15 Areas of growth

Population change, 1971–81

District	Increase	%
Milton Keynes	56 933	102.0
Redditch	25 754	63.1
Tamworth (Staffordshire)	24 030	59.6
Shetland Islands Area	9 387	54.2
City of London (London)	1 648	38.8
Gordon (Grampian)*	17 178	38.2
Ross and Cromarty (Highland)*	12 446	35.7
Cumbernauld and Kilsyth (Strathclyde)	16 113	35.3
Badenoch and Strathspey (Highland)*	3 048	32.7
Wimborne Minster (Dorset)	16 660	32.4
Forest Heath (Suffolk)	12 307	31.1
Bracknell (Berkshire)	17 705	27.7
Huntingdon (Cambridgeshire)	26 445	27.3

*Administrative Districts

1 Does there appear to be any correlation or link between population totals and percentage change for these thirteen places? Give evidence or draw a simple scatter graph to justify your opinion.

2 Choose three places from the thirteen showing large percentage increases of population during the 1970s. For each, describe its location and the general type of environment and suggest why population growth has been so great over this short period of time.

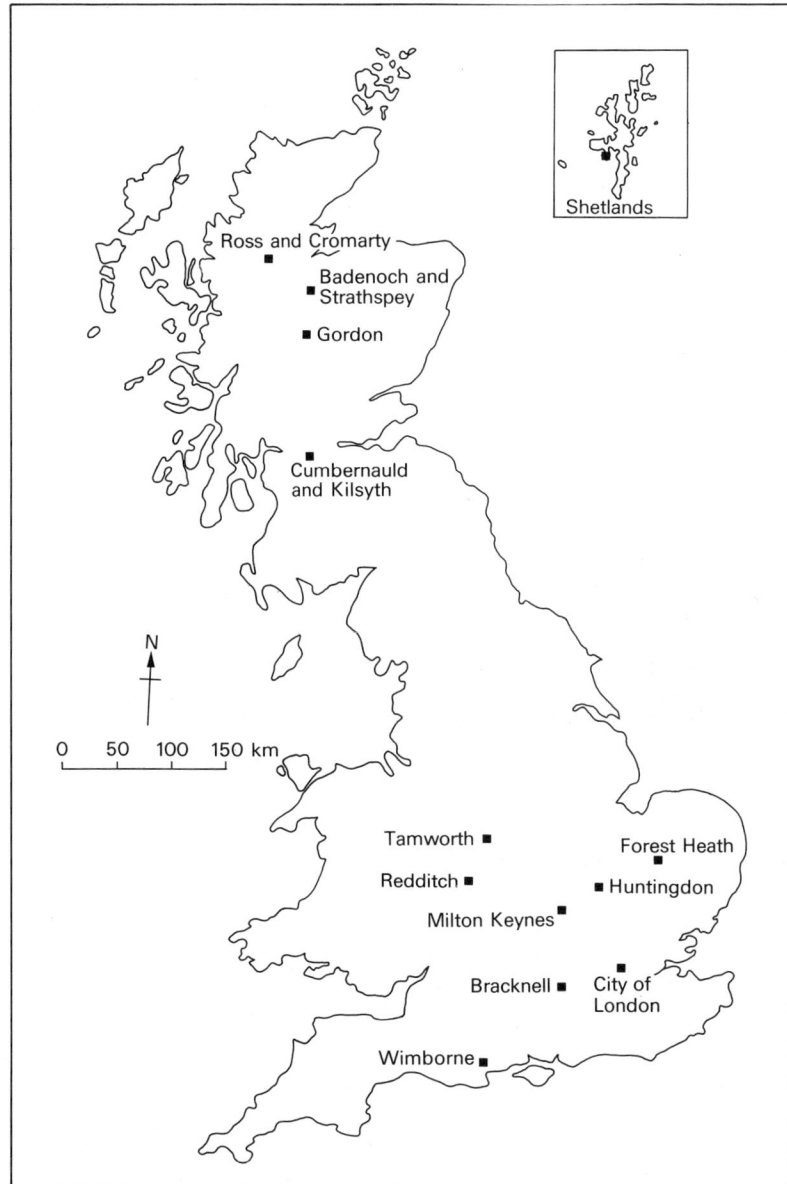

Districts showing greatest population growth, 1971–81

New houses contrast with the old in the Shetland Isles

Multicultural Britain

Migration and settlement

'To the outsider Coventry seems an unlikely cockpit for racial violence. For most of this century the city has absorbed wave upon wave of newcomers, from Tyneside, Merseyside, Scotland, Wales, Ireland, Poland and Hungary. Apart from the colour of their skins, those from the West Indies and the Punjab are merely the latest wave of those attracted by what were until recently an abundance of jobs and reputedly the highest wages in Britain.'

The balance between the proportion of black and white people in Britain is roughly reflected in this photograph of male employees in a factory

This extract from *The Times* and Unit 2.1 are reminders that people have always migrated, and that Britain has received migrants from all parts of the world since recorded time. A feature of recent migration into Britain is that many of the migrants are from non-European countries. Black and brown migrants mostly came from countries that were once a part of the British Empire and ruled from Britain. On gaining their independence, most of these countries were persuaded to join the Commonwealth and retain close and friendly links with Britain. The extract is also a reminder that many of these migrants were encouraged to come to Britain to take jobs, when there was a shortage of workers in the decades before the rapid rise in unemployment. These people settled in Britain and had families. In most cases their children, and those of the Irish,

Chinese New Year Festival in Soho, London. There are about 100 000 Chinese in Britain, most having migrated from Hong Kong and other parts of South East Asia. A large majority are involved in catering of some sort or other; often in small family businesses. London has the largest concentration of around 15 000 people

Polish and Hungarian migrants referred to in the extract are British citizens. They are not 'immigrants'.

Patterns of cultural groups

Similarities of language, religion, social habits and all those things that go to make up the 'culture' of a group tend to draw people together. This is reinforced if the majority of other people show prejudice or intolerance towards the group. The group will then want to be together for mutual support and enjoyment and security. In extreme cases, groups are forced to live in particular areas not out of choice, but because they are the only areas that are available, or where they will be tolerated by the other citizens.

Some of the more distant cultural groups are the result of recent migration. Recently-arrived migrants understandably want to live close to people that they know or who are like them and speak their language, or who are from their country of origin.

The concentration of one particular group, people with a West Indian cultural background in London, is shown on the map.

People disagree over whether a society is better off for having a mixture of cultural groups or whether everyone should have the same beliefs, attitudes and ways of behaving.

A multicultural society

Britain is a multicultural society in the sense that there are people from many different cultures living in it. But few people would claim that it is multicultural in the sense given in the definitions. For a great variety of unfortunate

reasons there is, sadly, suspicion, hostility and even hatred between individuals of all groups. Racism, for example, is a sad fact although it is important to realise that it is not an attitude held only by white people. On the other hand there are many people who enjoy genuine friendship and collaboration with those from other cultures. The aim of a genuine multicultural society in Britain is the only one that makes sense.

1 List some of the reasons why people choose to, or are forced to, migrate.
2 Why were many West Indian and Asian people invited and encouraged to migrate to Britain by the British? Why was it a natural country for these men and women to migrate to?
3 What do you understand by the word 'creed'? What is your creed?
4 Argue the case for and against the 'integration' or 'dispersal' of distinct migrant cultural groups in Britain.

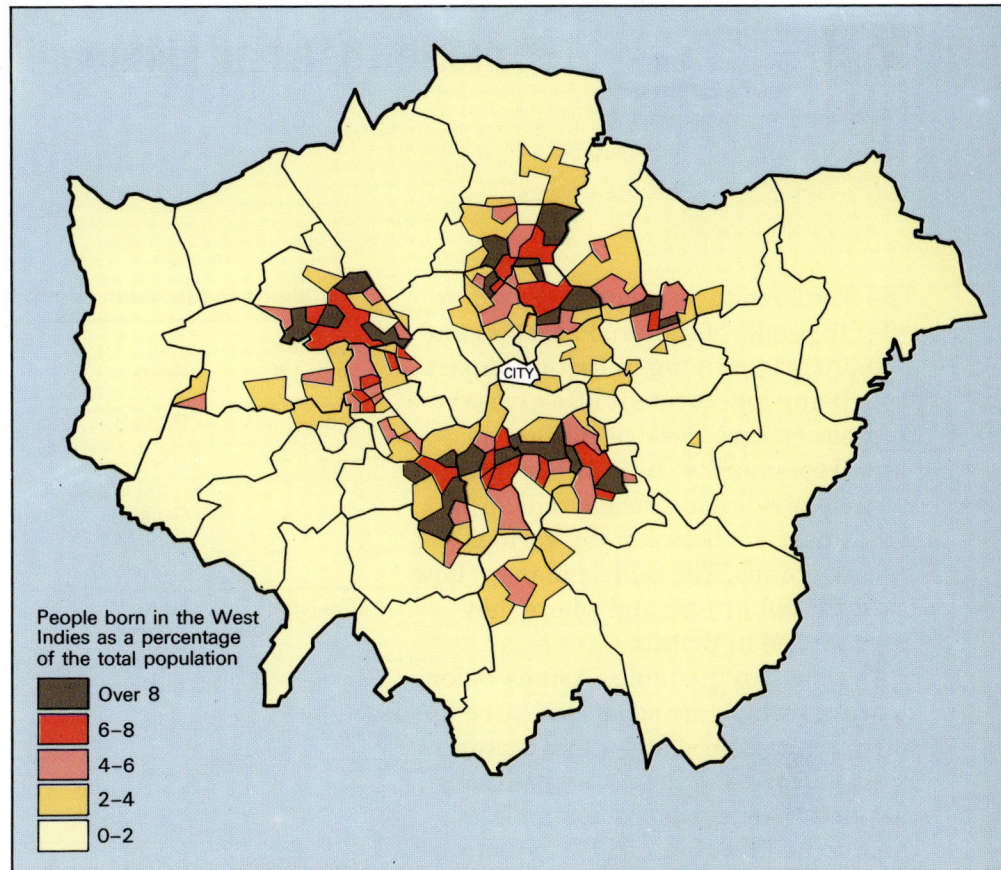

People born in the West Indies as a percentage of the total population

Over 8
6–8
4–6
2–4
0–2

Map of London, showing the percentage of the population in each area that was born in the West Indies

Definitions of a multicultural society

A society 'based on mutual understanding and respect'.

In which 'everyone is treated according to their own merits. A society in which individual customs and traditions are respected'.

In which 'all individuals whatsoever their race, colour or creed have equal rights, responsibilities and opportunities'.

Exercise 16 **Asian communities in Britain**

The word 'Asian' is commonly used to refer to people of Indian, Pakistani and Bengali origin living in Britain. Apart from being inaccurate it also gives the impression that these people are a united community. In fact there are very clear religious, social and language barriers between the various 'Asian' groups. The table and map show the different groups and where they have settled in Britain.

As shown in the table, 'Asians' belong to groups which are separated by religion, language, food and social customs. Even within each community old social distinctions survive. For example, among the first generations in Britain marriage between different communities would be unthinkable. This is breaking down, and more 'mixed' marriages are taking place, but often against strong opposition.

Variations in the Asian communities in Britain

Country of origin	Area	Religion	Language	Main areas settled in UK	Numbers
India	Punjab	1) Hindu 2) Sikh	Punjabi Punjabi	Southall/ Birmingham (Handsworth)	719 000
	Gujerat	1) Hindu 2) Muslim	Gujerati/ Kutchi ditto	Wembley/ Leicester	
Pakistan	North Western Frontier Province (Pathan)	Muslim	Pushto	Bradford (Hanover Square)	283 000
	Mirpur	Muslim	Mirpuri	Bradford	
	Punjab	Muslim	Punjabi	Manchester/ Birmingham (Sparkbrook)	
Bangladesh	Sylhet	Muslim	Bengali	London (Camden and Brick lane) Bradford	52 000
East Africa	Kenya	1) Hindu	Punjabi/ Gujerati	Southall/ Leicester	not available
	Uganda Tanzania Malawi Zambia	2) Sikh 3) Muslim	Punjabi Punjabi/ Gujerati	Southall/ Birmingham Leicester/ London	

Main centres of Indian/Pakistani/Bangladeshi ethnic groups in England

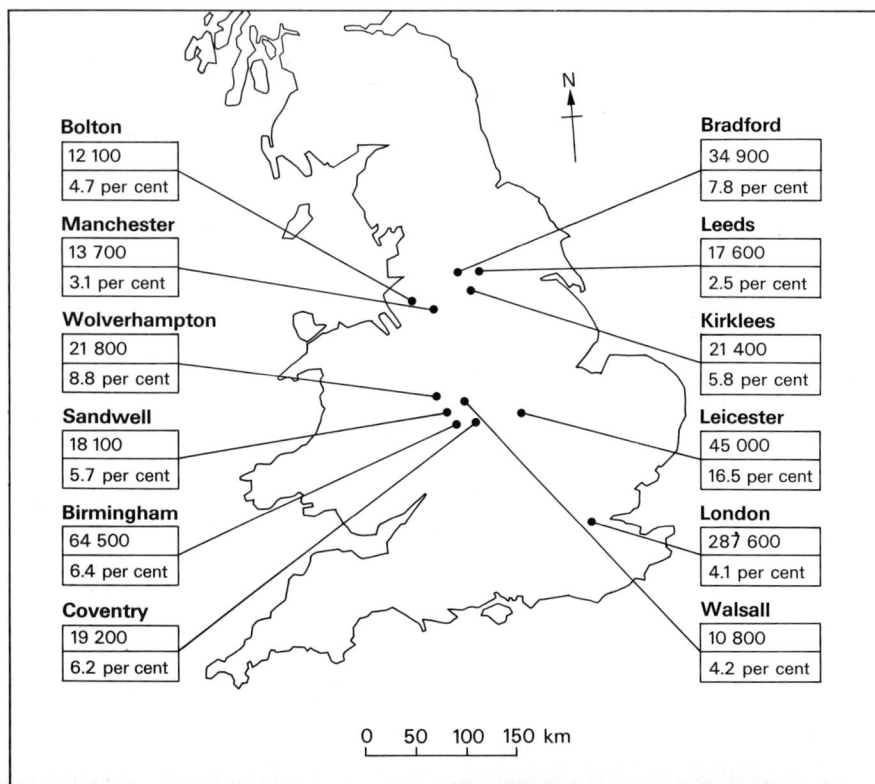

Bolton
12 100
4.7 per cent

Manchester
13 700
3.1 per cent

Wolverhampton
21 800
8.8 per cent

Sandwell
18 100
5.7 per cent

Birmingham
64 500
6.4 per cent

Coventry
19 200
6.2 per cent

Bradford
34 900
7.8 per cent

Leeds
17 600
2.5 per cent

Kirklees
21 400
5.8 per cent

Leicester
45 000
16.5 per cent

London
287 600
4.1 per cent

Walsall
10 800
4.2 per cent

N

0   50   100   150 km

1 Draw a map of Britain and show the location of the concentrations of two of the Asian communities. Use a key to show their different origins, languages and religions.

2 What particular difficulties might Asian families first settling in Britain face that would be different from **a)** East European, **b)** West Indian and **c)** Irish families?

3 Why are second and third generation Asians likely to have different attitudes than their parents to their traditional culture?

70

Chapter 3 **Farming in Britain**

Farms and farming

Large, hedgeless fields of wheat and barley are a feature of modern arable farming

The nature of farming

Although there are many different types of farming in Britain, they all have one thing in common; they are concerned with the growth of plants or animals. The farmer manages the environment (the soil, temperatures, rainfall, drainage, vegetation cover and so on) to obtain high yields and quality of product. As will be seen on the following pages, the different environments of Britain offer different possibilities for farmers. The type of farming practised will depend partly on the opportunities provided by the environment and partly on what products the farmer believes he will have a market for. It is quite a chancy business, for no one can say exactly what the weather will be like, for example, nor exactly what the demand will be. By careful planning, good managment and efficient farming methods, and with a

Dairy cattle are grazed mostly on lowland pastures. Dairy and cereal farmers receive large subsidies and grants from the government to encourage production

The importance of farming in Britain

Most people know that much of the countryside consists of farmland where crops are grown and animals reared, but few have any idea how important farming is to the country. Over 340 000 men and women are employed directly on farms doing a wide range of jobs. Apart from these there are many more providing the farms and farmers with their needs or 'inputs' and transporting, marketing or processing their 'outputs'. The total value of farm produce is far greater than that from the motor vehicle industry, for example. While a large proportion of our needs are provided by British farms, a lot of foreign farm produce is sold and consumed in Britain. One reason is because the items could never be produced here. Another is because they can be produced more cheaply elsewhere either because of better growing conditions or because of better government support.

Farming facts: early 80s

- 340 000 employed in agriculture (compared with 300 000 in the vehicle industry and 240 000 in railways).
- Agriculture produces about two-thirds of Britain's food needs.
- Agricultural exports equal the value of BL, BSC and British Shipbuilders exports combined.
- Agriculture receives more aid from the Government than BL, BSC, the National Coal Board and British Shipbuilders combined.
- Average productivity increases on the same area of land (1954–81)

wheat	98%
barley	60%
livestock	50%

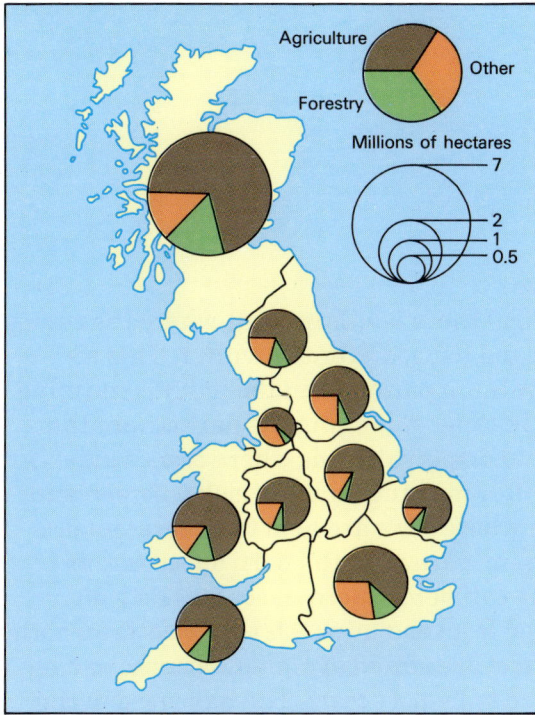

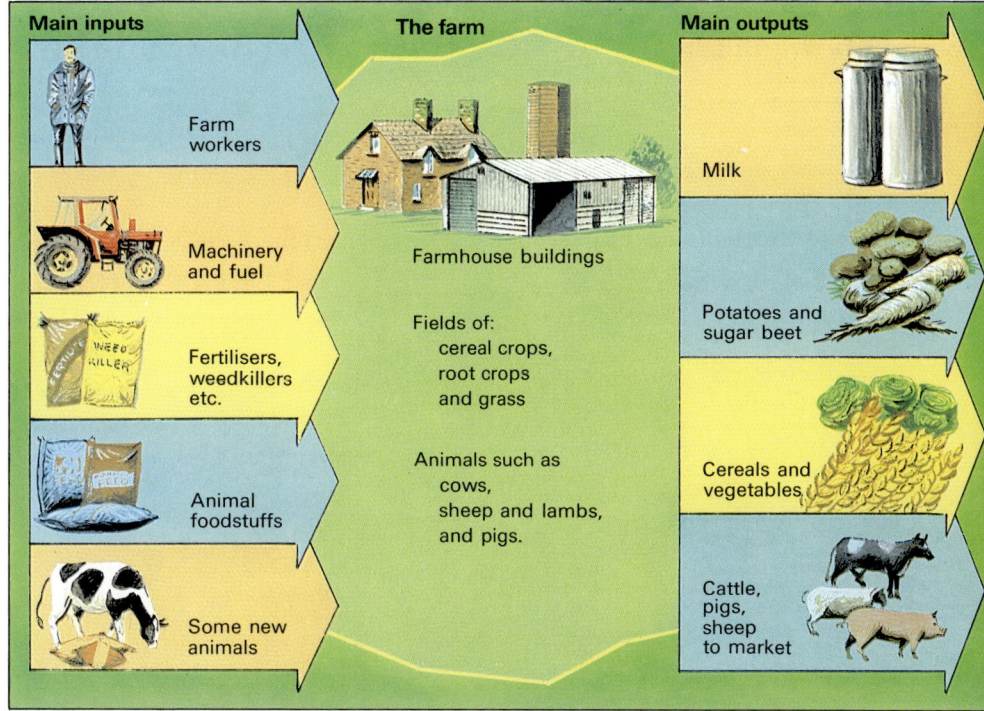

Farm workers

Machinery and fuel

Fertilisers, weedkillers etc.

Animal foodstuffs

Some new animals

The farm

Farmhouse buildings

Fields of:
cereal crops,
root crops
and grass

Animals such as
cows,
sheep and lambs,
and pigs.

Main outputs

Milk

Potatoes and sugar beet

Cereals and vegetables

Cattle, pigs, sheep to market

measure of good luck, the farmer hopes that the value of his outputs will be well above the cost of his inputs; which means a profit!

A good example of a mixed farm is the unit made up of Home Farm and Claysend Farm near Bath in the County of Avon. The two farms were once separate, but they are now run as one enterprise. The farm is part of the Newton Park Estate which is owned by the Duchy of Cornwall. Mr John Hughes, whose grandfather had been a tenant of Home Farm, took over the tenancy of Home Farm in 1960 and Claysend in 1973. It is often the case that farmers have come from farming families, and in many cases it is regarded as a way of life as well as just a business. The two parts together total about 140 hectares (346 acres), of which about 80 are arable. Claysend houses the farm machinery, workshop and grain stores. There is a herd of about 100 Ayrshire dairy cows, and these are centred on Home Farm. Mr Hughes has two full-time employees, one a dairyman, and the other a tractor driver. Extra help is taken on at busy times such as harvest, or for doing other seasonal jobs like hedge-laying.

1 What are some of the ways in which the importance of an industry can be judged? On this basis, do you think British farming is important?

2 a) Which regions of Britain have three-quarters or more of the total area in 'agricultural' land use? b) What does 'agricultural land' include? c) What does 'other' include?

3 Name two products available only from foreign farms, two that are almost entirely from British farms and two that might be from either British or foreign producers.

A farm can be thought of as a 'system' where inputs are converted into outputs

Above, left: The pattern and areas of land use in different parts of Britain. Agricultural use includes many different sorts of farming

Buildings and fields of *Home Farm*, on the outskirts of Bath

Exercise 17 **A mixed farm**

Typical farm buildings include a grain store and machinery sheds

The farm, covering about 140 acres, is part of one of the many estates in the south-west of England owned by the Prince of Wales

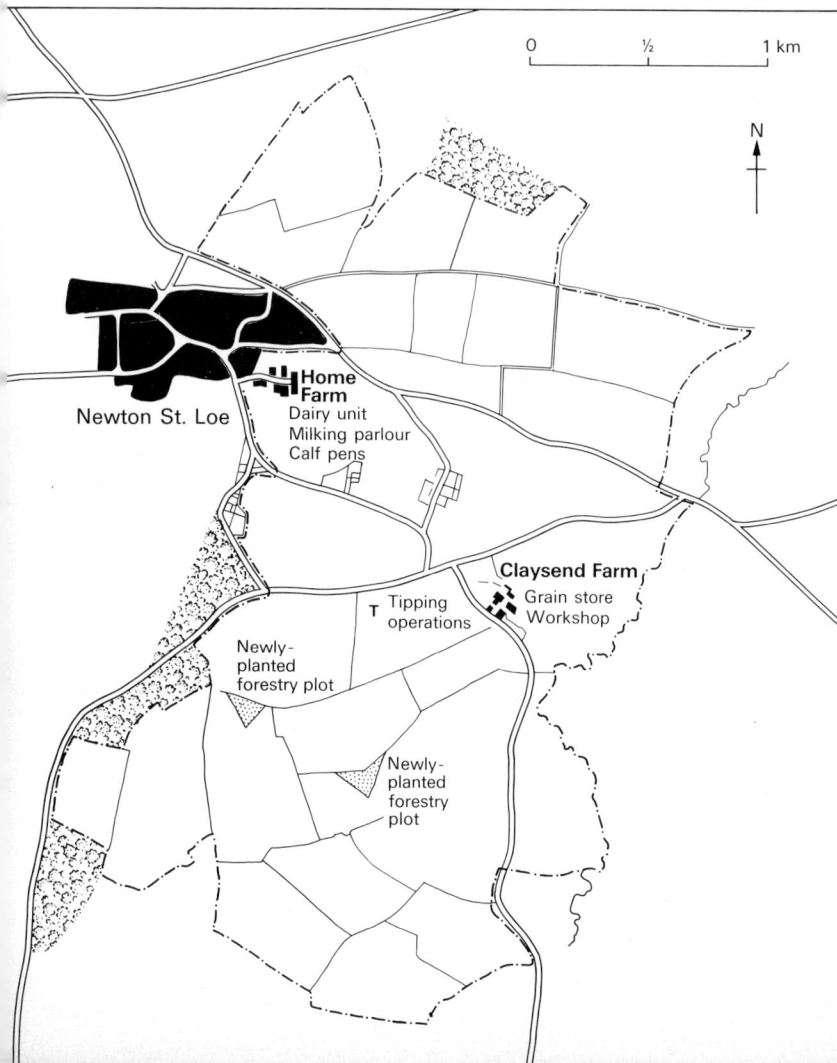

Home Farm

At Home Farm there is a dairy unit where the cows are milked, and housed over the winter. This includes the milking parlour and the dairy containing the bulk milk tank. Adjoining the parlour are the collecting and dispersal yards where cows wait before and after milking, and the isolating pen and cattle crush where cows are held for treatment or artificial insemination. In the barn opposite the dairy are the calf pens where the calves stay after being weaned from the cows. All the grass feed, both hay and silage, are stored at Home Farm, so saving on labour and transport costs. The hay is fed to the cows in their winter sheds while they can also feed off the silage clamp in the adjoining barn. At the back of the cattle sheds or 'kennels' is the slurry pit where manure from the stalls and yard is pushed and scraped by tractor. This is spread on the fields during summer, so reducing the need for expensive fertilizers.

Claysend Farm

Claysend was once a dairy farm also, but the old milking parlour and dairy are now used only for storage. The old barn is now used for tractor repairs. The grain store was converted from a covered yard in 1973. Here a cereal harvest can be dried to prevent mould, and cleaned by removing the chaff and small grains. During the winter, after the cereal crop has been sold, it is used as a fertilizer store. A workshop extension was added in 1975 so that all the expensive machinery could be kept in good working order. So that the milking herd can be made bigger a new covered yard is being built at Claysend to house the dry cows and young stock in winter.

The field marked (T) on the map was once an old orchard on fairly steep, uneven ground. It was not very valuable, being used only for rough grazing. The ground was partly levelled by tipping earth in the field, and grassed over to improve the quality of the soil. Eventually it will be ploughed and used for crop growing.

Another recent improvement has been the planting of several plots of land with trees. Dutch Elm disease led to the loss of many trees in the

74

hedgerows. These new plantings add to the attractiveness of the farmland, provide valuable timber, and are a home for wildlife. Most of the hedges have been 'laid' to form strong cattle-proof barriers, but, with the field margins and road verges, are important habitats for birds, flowers, insects and small mammals. Good farming means not only producing food as cheaply as possible, but caring for the landscape and environment.

The livestock and their produce

The dairy unit at Home Farm is close to grazing land within easy reach of the milking parlour. The fields near Claysend are too distant for the twice-daily walk by the cows for milking, so they are grazed by the young cattle or dry cows not being milked. Most of the cows are crossed with a Charolais bull to give calves that can be reared for beef. The best cows are put to an Ayreshire bull to give pure-bred heifer calves for replacement in the dairy herd. The average length of milking life of a cow is about eight years. The maximum workable size for one dairyman to handle is about 120 cows, most of which will be in milk at any one time. The dairy farmer gets a regular income from the Milk Marketing Board.

The crops and arable produce

The soils on the farm are well suited to cereal crops. Wheat gets the highest prices, but it needs rich soil and is liable to get diseased. It is best if only grown

in a particular field for two consecutive years, so in the following two years that field will be planted with barley. This is followed by three years in which grass is grown to enable the soil fertility to increase again, ready for more wheat and then barley. The grass is grazed by cattle and cut for silage two or three times a year. This provides valuable winter feed for the cattle. This grassland should not be confused with 'permanent pasture' on land too steep to be cultivated with large machinery. Cattle also graze on turnips in the arable fields near the dairy unit. These are seeded by aeroplane into the barley just before it is harvested. After the harvest the turnips grow rapidly and are grazed by cattle when ripe.

1 Read the description about the farm carefully. Give a brief explanation of the following terms: tenant; silage; slurry pit; hedgerow; heifer; permanent pasture.

2 Draw the outline of a field in the arable part of the farm. Complete a diagram that shows the pattern of crop-rotation over a period of seven years in that field. Say why the changes are necessary.

3 Make a flow-diagram showing the inputs and outputs of the combined Home and Claysend Farms.

4 What are the signs that this is a modern and reasonably prosperous farm?

Farm activities: (*far left*) preparing for drilling: (*left*) in the milking parlour; (*below*) tractor seed drilling

The influence of environment

Farming landscape, Gower Peninsula, South Wales

Crop growing areas in Britain. Different environments favour different crops

Barley and wheat
Barley and oats
Oats
Few or no crops

In order to make a profit, a farmer cannot produce just anything he chooses. He must try to work out what the likely demands will be, and what grants or financial support the government will give. But most of all he must make the best of what the environment offers. Some places are more suitable for certain sorts of farming than for others, and as the maps on these pages show, a certain type of farming tends to be found in an area with a particular balance of altitude, relief, soil pattern and climate. Before looking at these environmental influences in more detail it is worth remembering that farmers can change or control these environments to a certain degree and, as the demands for products or government subsidies change, so does the pattern of farming. Parts of the chalk Downs, for example, that were traditionally sheep rearing lands are now important for cereal growing (see pages 50 and 79).

Relief and altitude

In Chapter 1 it was shown that parts of Britain are very rugged and quite high above sea level. The altitude of a place has a considerable effect on its climate, while the steepness of the slopes can greatly affect the depth and stability of the soil. These things apart, rugged relief makes it difficult to use heavy and bulky machinery. So there is not likely to be a great deal of arable farming in upland areas. It is also difficult to walk cattle over rough ground to and from the farm twice a day for milking, so these areas are not very suitable for dairy farming. Of course some crops are grown and some dairy cows kept in quite hilly areas, but not as a major commercial activity. These high and rugged mountain and upland areas are also sparsely settled, with large towns some distance away. This means that transport of produce, which is important with commercial crop and dairy farming, is difficult and expensive. It is not surprising that rugged, hilly areas are used largely for rearing sheep and cattle, for sale to lowland farmers.

Flat and undulating land, on the other hand, is usually well-suited for farm machinery. But not all of it is ideal. Badly drained land, for example, will be no good for arable farming with heavy ploughs and combines.

Soils

We have already seen that different rocks such as limestones, clays, sandstones and granite break and weather down to form soils. If these stay where they are formed they will strongly reflect the nature of the parent rock. Soils on limestone or chalk tend to be alkaline, for example, while those on granite or sandstone are more acid. These chemical qualities affect what crops are most likely to grow, unless the character of the soil is changed by adding chemicals. Soils also contain plant food. Those containing decayed remains of leaf, grass or vegetable matter, known as humus, are usually quite rich. Farmers can increase the richness of the soil by adding fertilizers and other chemicals.

Other important qualities of the soil are its texture and drainage. Quite apart from the stones and boulders found in some soils there are differences in size of particles. Sandy soils have quite large particles while at the other extreme are the clays and silts. It is this fine texture of clays that lead to them becoming easily waterlogged. Sandy soils, by contrast, are fairly porous. Soils with a texture between these extremes, usually formed by a mixture of both, are known as loams. The thickness or depth of soil can also vary a great deal. Soils on steep slopes are often very thin, while they tend to be thicker on flat or gentle slopes.

Peat soils contain plenty of decayed vegetation. On flat-topped moorland where there is heavy rainfall they are acid, spongy and form peat bogs suitable for little more than sheep or cattle grazing. The lowland peats of the Fens and similar areas are much less acid. When drained these lowland peats provide deep, rich black fertile soils ideal for arable farming, particularly market gardening.

Climate and weather

Crops need a certain length of time with temperatures above a minimum level in order to grow and ripen. They also need rain, since it is through moisture in the soil that plants get their food. The amount of rainfall, length of the growing season and probability of frosts are some of the climate features which affect whether a place is suitable for crop or grassland farming. In the south-west of England, for example, the winters are mild and the growing season starts much earlier than further east. In places sheltered from the strong winds and occasional storms flowers

The population distribution of cattle and sheep in Britain (in thousands) 1982

	Cattle	Sheep
England	7976	15345
North	1016	3716
Yorkshire and Humberside	759	2058
East Midlands	771	1350
East Anglia	274	201
South-East	1076	1768
South-West	2357	3279
West Midlands	1080	2265
North-West	643	708
Wales	1432	8416
Scotland	2333	7961

and vegetables are grown so that they are ready for market well before those grown elsewhere in Britain. Dartmoor and Exmoor are in the southwest of England, but their height above sea level and poor soils make them unsuitable for the growing of early crops.

1 Compare the landscapes and farming types in the Gower and the Welsh uplands photographs.

2 Draw or trace a map showing the agricultural regions of Britain (see page 73 for the boundaries of the regions). Show the distribution of **a**) cattle **b**) sheep using the data in the table. Explain the contrasts in distribution shown by your map.

3 Study the map of crop areas and length of growing season. Describe and explain **a**) the areas of longest and shortest growing season, **b**) why any one area (name it) has little arable land, **c**) the distribution of the main barley and wheat growing areas.

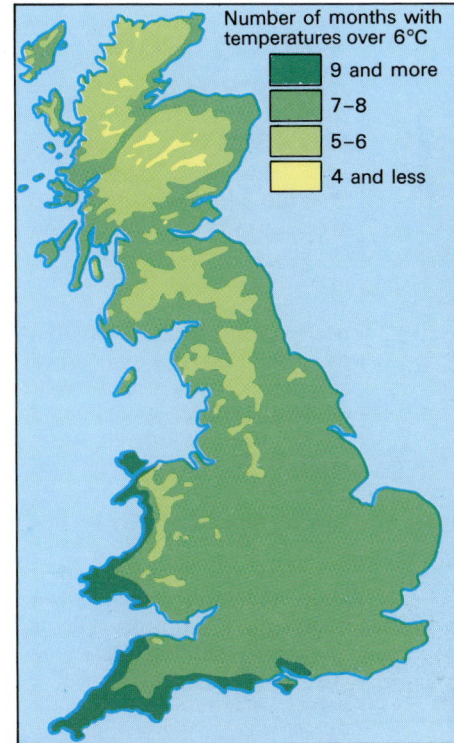

Number of months with temperatures over 6°C

- 9 and more
- 7–8
- 5–6
- 4 and less

Length of growing season is an important environmental influence

Sheep farming in upland areas shows a great contrast with cereal cultivation and lowland mixed farming

Weather and the farmer in 1982

The Times, 27 September 1982

Timely rain cheers up farmers

The recent rainy spell, however unwelcome to tennis and cricket enthusiasts, came at just the right time for farmers, according to the first of this year's crop surveys compiled by *The Times*. From grave concern over the near drought in April and May, the mood has changed to one of widespread joy, with crops in generally excellent conditions and no reports of serious diseases.

The change in the weather made all the difference. 'I can honestly say that prospects for the cereal harvest look the best that I have ever known', a correspondent in Suffolk writes. 'Again I am tempting providence by referring to near-perfect crops of wheat', a neighbour in Norfolk says.

In many areas grass appeared to suffer more from the dry weather than cereals. But a farmer in Worcestershire reports that 'the sun has kept grass growth going nicely, and a feature of the year is the marvellous way that sheep have thrived. I have never seen sheep in better condition, and lamb quality is absolutely top class.'

A report from Cornwall says: 'We had the best spring growing conditions for years.' Farmers as far apart as Lancashire, Gloucestershire and Cornwall say they cannot remember a better year for silage making.

Soft fruit farmers also benefited from the ideal weather conditions in 1982

The Times, June 1982. 1982 was a particularly good year for farms from the point of view of weather, output and profits

Crop survey, 1982

Reports of exceptionally high crop yields in many parts of the country, almost certainly without precedent, are confirmed by the third and final 1982 survey compiled by *The Times*.

Replies from more than 200 farmers in England, Wales and Scotland indicate an average wheat yield of 6.1 tonnes a hectare, an increase of more than 35 per cent on last year's figure of 4.5 tonnes, which was also the 10-year average.

The average yield for barley was 5.1 tonnes, more than 27 per cent above the 10-year average; for oats, 4.9 tonnes (22 per cent up); for potatoes 34.9 tonnes (24 per cent up); and for sugar beet, 39.8 tonnes (28 per cent up).

The table below shows the expected yield in tonnes a hectare of the principal crops in Britain compared with the previous 5 years and the 10 year average (72–82) at the same date.

	Wheat	Barley	Oats	Potatoes	Sugar Beet
1977	5.0	4.5	4.3	30.1	35.0
1978	4.4	3.9	4.0	26.8	32.3
1979	5.1	4.1	4.2	35.9	32.9
1980	4.5	3.9	4.0	28.0	31.7
1981	4.5	4.0	4.0	28.1	31.5
1982	6.1	5.1	4.9	34.9	39.8
10-year average	4.5	4.0	4.0	28.0	31.1

The variations of the climate around Britain, together with contrasts of relief and soils have led to certain patterns of farming. But the environment has a further impact. The weather in Britain can never be predicted with any certainty, and the fortunes of the farmer depend a great deal on the actual weather in particular months. Farmers may have planned as carefully and worked as hard in two consecutive years, yet had success in one and disaster in the other largely because of the chance of weather. In the next Unit we shall see how some farmers try to control the environment or create an artificial one, but for most farmers the weather remains a critical factor.

Exercise 18 Varieties of farming in a scarpland area

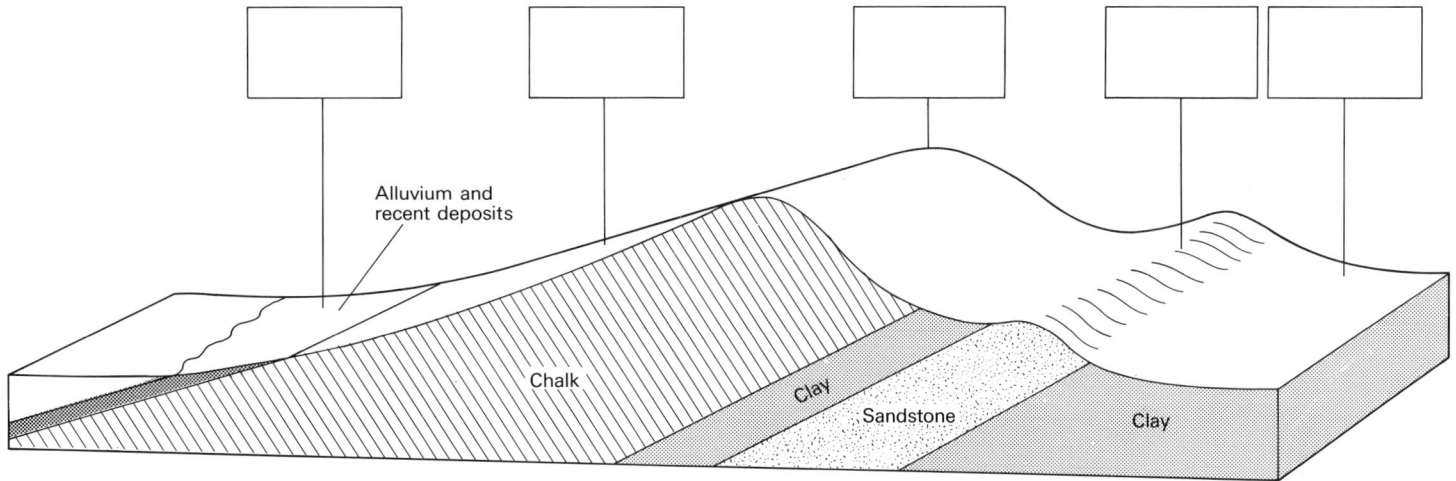

Alluvium and recent deposits

Chalk

Clay

Sandstone

Clay

1 Porous rock, little surface drainage
2 Impermeable rocks, lots of surface water
3 Thin soils, fertilizers needed
4 Heavy soils, naturally fertile

a Market gardening
b Cereal growing
c Sheep grazing
d Woodland / forestry
e Dairy farming

1 Copy the block diagram of the scarpland area. Add the names of land use in the boxes above the diagram in the appropriate place.

2 Label your diagram to show some of the characteristics of soil and drainage. Use the four phrases provided.

3 Add a short note explaining how your labelled diagram illustrates the effect of environment on farming. Give at least two reasons why your diagram might not give a full or accurate impressions of this relationship.

4 Which types of land use shown in the diagram can be seen in the photograph below?

Scarpland land use in the South Downs. Compare with the earlier photograph on page 50. What major change in land use can you see?

Higher yields, less land

Chemicals are used in many ways on the farm to increase production and reduce losses

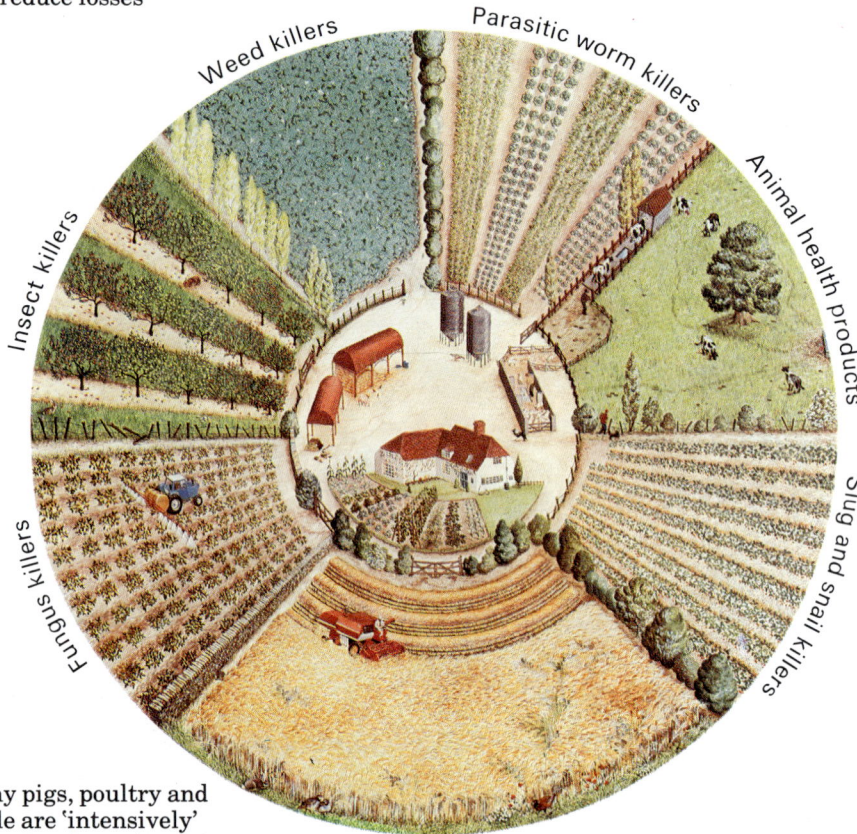

Weed killers
Parasitic worm killers
Insect killers
Animal health products
Fungus killers
Slug and snail killers

Many pigs, poultry and cattle are 'intensively' farmed, to keep down the costs of production

Bigger is better?

For many decades it has been argued that in farming as in any other form of production 'big is best'. At the simplest level this is why many farms that once consisted of many small fields separated by hedges may now contain only a few very large ones. This is not just to save the waste of space taken up by the hedges and corners of the fields. It means that giant machines can be used to plough, harrow and harvest the crops. For a given area of land these methods should lead to higher yields and output per worker. In animal farming there are examples of similar 'economies of scale'. There are huge poultry sheds where many thousands of birds are kept under intensive conditions. Pigs are also reared on this scale, rather than in traditional pigsties.

There are also many examples of separate farms being combined together and owned and managed as one big unit. We saw an example of this with Home and Claysend farms. A result of this is that many farms are so large that it is difficult for one person to have enough money or capital to own one. Another result is that more and more of these farm units are owned by companies and financial businesses. Sometimes these are food processing companies that need the farm produce for their factories. Sometimes the companies have nothing to do with food or farming but merely want to invest their money in land to make a profit. Farming nowadays is big business, and while there are still many family-owned farms, an increasing number are owned and managed rather like a factory.

Scientific methods and artificial environments

One important aim of British farmers is to be as efficient as possible, and to produce high productivity per worker and high yields per animal and per acre. Farmers have always tried to improve the quality of soils by such activities as ploughing, draining and adding manures. They have also improved the quality of their animals by controlling their grazing and breeding. All that is happening now is that these age-old practices are being continued in a more carefully researched and scientific method.

As the diagram shows, chemicals can be used for many purposes. Vast amounts are used nowadays to improve the plant food in the soil. More is used to kill unwanted weeds and pests and diseases that might damage the growing crop. Animal farmers also benefit from a wide range of drugs for control-

ling diseases. They also gain a lot from advice about breeding, feeding patterns, housing and managing stock. Modern farming depends heavily on the agri-chemical industry and scientific research. All this costs a great deal of money, but if it leads to higher yields and greater sales, then it should lead to increased profits.

Artificial climates are provided in several ways. One good example is the use of irrigation methods to provide water in areas of low rainfall or in periods of drought. Temperatures, humidity and water supply can be very carefully monitored and controlled in glasshouses. In a very real sense some crops now grow in completely artificial environments. Once again, the costs can be great. But if there is a demand for the product, then it is worth the farmer spending money to provide it.

The loss of farmland
There is a continual loss of farmland to other uses such as houses, quarries, roads and airports. Some people fear that there will be a serious shortage of land for farming in the near future. Others argue that while the fact of loss of farmland cannot be denied, it is not yet a serious problem. It is mostly restricted to a belt running south-east to north-west across England; elsewhere the loss of land is quite small. While there are plenty of examples of loss of high quality land, some of Britain's best farmland areas are relatively untouched.

Recent researchers claim that loss of farmland to urban uses is not a big

threat to the food supply of Britain. It is more important to improve productivity on existing farmland by changing the way it is managed and used.

1 What are some of the disadvantages of large-scale farming methods?
2 List some of the applications of science and technology to farming under the headings a) crop production, b) animal production.
3 What are some of the disadvantages and some of the advantages of owning farmland on the 'urban fringe'?
4 Between 1975 and 1980 an average of 45 000 acres of farmland *a year* were lost to urban and industrial development. How many farms the size of Home/Clay-send farm would cover this area?

Greenhouses provide an artificial, controllable environment, often on a big scale

Left: This Yorkshire farmer owns land worth over £2 million. British farmers like him are among the most efficient in the world. With the help of Common Market subsidies they increased their earnings by 45 per cent in 1982

One threat to farming. Between 1975 and 1980 over 45 000 acres of farmland was lost to urban, transport and industrial use each year.

81

Scientific farming

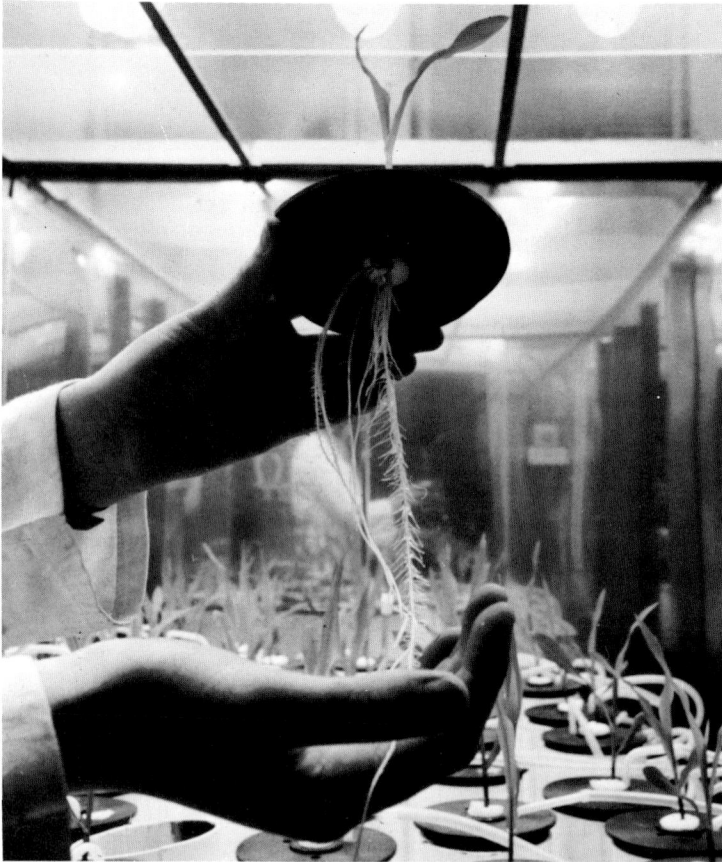

Research into plant root development

False teeth for sheep!

This cow has been fitted with a microchip paging device which enables it to feed and be milked on demand

Many of the ways in which scientists help the farmer were mentioned on the previous pages. A few more examples of scientific research and technology being applied to farming problems are shown here. By using these improved methods, materials and equipment production can be made more efficient and much waste avoided. Farming nowadays relies a great deal on research science, agricultural engineering and the agri-chemical industry.

Not all these improvements are without their dangers. Using huge modern machinery may be efficient, for example, but some people argue that it is slowly damaging the countryside. There are also anxieties about the effect of some chemicals on soils and plant and animal life, as well as on farm produce itself. Improved efficiency has to be matched against possible damage to the environment.

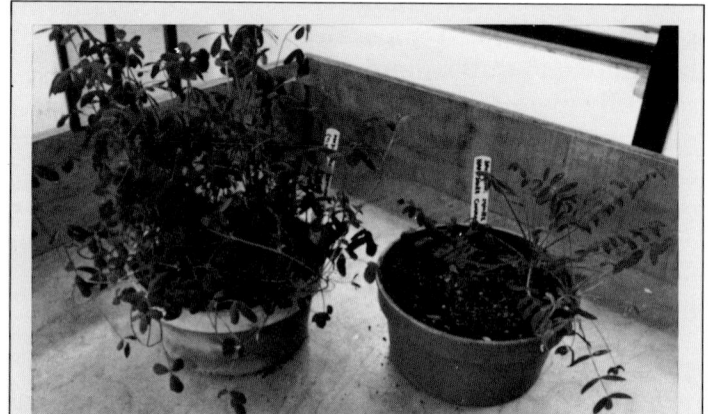

Genetic manipulation

'Genetic manipulation' is a technological breakthrough, developed at Nottingham University, which means that within 5 to 10 years UK farmers will be growing forage crops that have never been seen before. Normal plant breeding is within species but by this method unrelated species can be crossed to create 'instant' hybrids.

One forage crop that would be an ideal parent of a new hybrid is sainfoin. Sainfoin is an ideal crop for sheep because it fixes its own nitrogen and because the protein in its leaves is thoroughly digested by the sheep. The problem is that it does not yield well, is easily killed by overgrazing and only seems to do well on alkaline and light soils. Scientists now hope to marry the best features of sainfoin with the best of lucerne in the hope that the drawbacks will not come through to the offspring and can be selected out. In the picture the larger plant on the left is lucerne, and the one on the right is sainfoin.

Exercise 19
Variations in farm production

1 Use the map of production of four crops in 1979. For each crop rank the regions in order of importance. What do you notice about the difference? Explain these regional differences.

2 What are the dangers of using such a map to describe farming in a particular place?

3 Take two of the regions shown in the table and compare the differences in the sizes of agricultural holdings. How do you account for these differences?

4 Study the table of changing yields of five crops on page 78. Suggest why there was not a continuing increase in yield during this 6-year period, giving reasons for your answer.

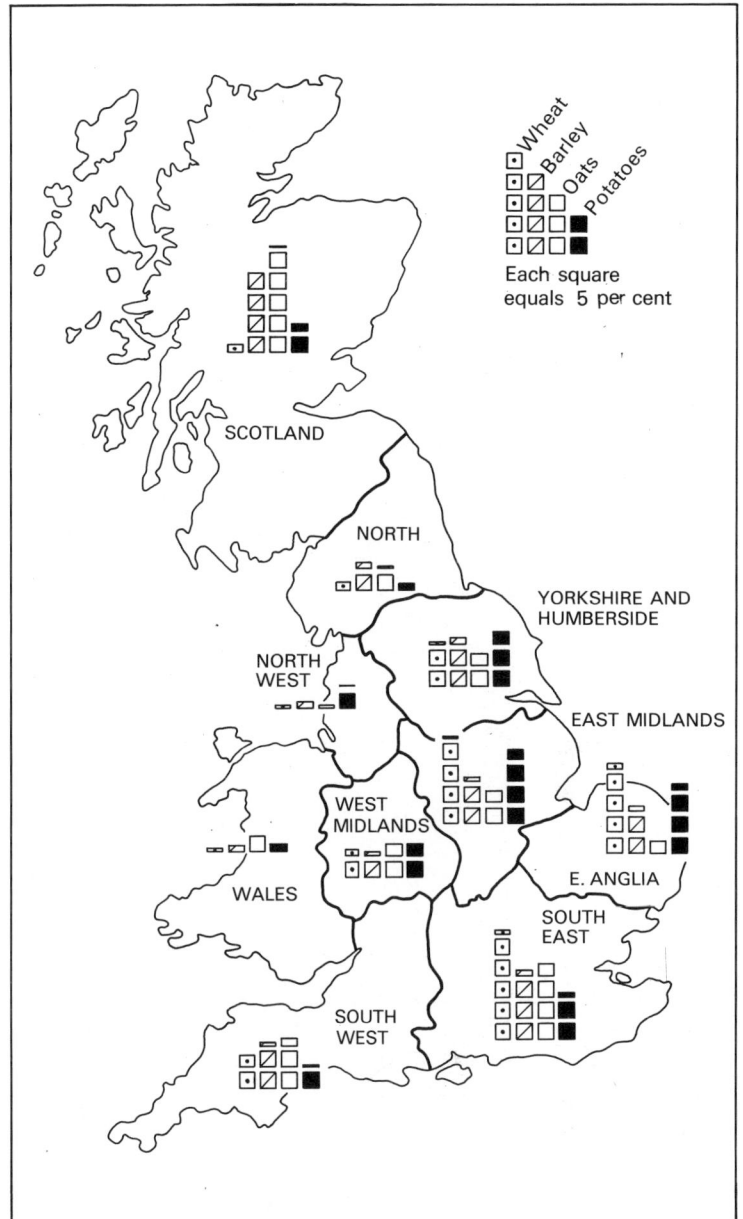

Each square equals 5 per cent

Percentages of size of farmholding by region

Region	Total	Nil*	Under 2	2– 4.9	5– 9.9	10– 19.9	20– 29.9	30– 39.9	40– 49.9	50– 99.9	100– 199.9	200 and over
England	100.0	3.2	8.3	10.4	11.0	13.0	10.2	7.7	6.3	16.3	9.2	4.4
North	100.0	2.6	3.4	6.5	8.0	10.9	10.8	10.1	8.5	23.5	11.8	3.9
Yorkshire and Humberside	100.0	3.0	5.9	8.9	10.5	13.2	10.4	8.0	6.8	19.1	10.2	4.0
East Midlands	100.0	2.6	6.9	9.6	10.5	13.0	10.6	7.0	5.8	16.6	10.8	6.6
East Anglia	100.0	3.1	11.6	11.7	9.9	10.3	9.5	6.9	4.8	13.2	10.7	8.3
South-East	100.0	4.8	12.3	12.0	11.1	11.5	7.6	5.7	4.5	12.9	10.6	7.0
South-West	100.0	2.5	7.4	10.4	11.3	13.5	11.0	8.9	7.4	17.4	7.5	2.7
West Midlands	100.0	2.9	6.2	11.6	12.9	14.2	10.2	7.4	5.9	16.6	9.2	2.9
North-West	100.0	3.8	11.5	10.3	11.6	17.1	12.6	8.4	6.8	14.1	3.3	0.5
Wales	100.0	2.7	2.7	9.4	13.5	17.4	13.9	10.6	8.1	16.2	4.6	0.9
Scotland	100.0	5.3	6.7	9.4	7.7	9.9	8.6	7.5	7.3	21.5	12.2	3.9

*'Nil' means holdings without crops or grass

Production and profits

One result of EEC subsidies, with guaranteed market and guaranteed prices for farmers, is the over-production of cereals, dairy produce, wine and vegetables. Some is stored in huge warehouses, some sold very cheaply to other countries. The rest is destroyed (such as these tomatoes)! In 1984 EEC laws were passed to greatly reduce the production of milk

The price of farm produce is affected by its availability (shortage or glut). Shortages may be due to low production, or to increased demand

Bad weather raises vegetable prices

The winter of 1981/82 was unusually severe. As a result the prices of many vegetables in the shops roughly doubled between December and January (as shown in the table).

Successive frosts, floods and snow prevented farmers from harvesting crops of winter greens and root vegetables, and blocked roads prevented retailers from getting to markets to collect supplies.

Home-grown vegetables reaching the shops, particularly brussels sprouts, cauliflowers and potatoes, showed signs of frost damage. Supplies had to be supplemented by expensive imports from Holland, France and Germany.

Average retail vegetable prices (in p.):

	Mid Jan 1982 per/lb	Early Dec 1981 per/lb
Sprouts	32–45	20–24
Cabbage	18–20	12–14
Cauliflower	55–70	45–60
Potatoes	9–12	8–10
Parsnips	25–35	14–20
Carrots	22–25	8–12
Leeks (scarce)	40–60	28–32
Swedes	12–18	8–12

Demand, income and profit

The profit a farmer makes in any year depends partly on the cost of production and partly on the income received from the sale of crops and animals. Farmers cannot avoid spending money. We have already seen that a great deal goes on fertilizers, drugs, machinery, animal food and so on. What matters is getting very high yields with as low a cost as possible. This is usually achieved by careful planning, good management and efficient methods, but we know that the weather, for example, can reduce yields on the best run farm.

Even if a farmer has obtained high yields in relation to the money spent, someone still has to buy the products! Firms buy produce from farmers in order to convert it into something else. Slaughterhouses and food processors are examples of these. Or people may buy from the farmer to improve the product yet further. Farmers will buy young lambs or cattle at a market from other farmers either to fatten up or to add to their own dairy herd. Other people will buy produce directly from the farmer to sell in their shops or sometimes at 'pick your own' centres. All these various people have a 'demand' for the farm produce, and will pay for what they want. There may be times when too much of a particular crop or too many animals have been produced. If there is a 'glut' then people will pay less, prices will fall, and the farmer make less money. It is to try to protect farmers from this that the government has guaranteed prices for certain items. No matter what the 'real' price of these goods, the farmer will get an agreed amount. Another problem is that foreign farmers sometimes sell their produce in Britain at a very low price, and this competition may force the British farmer to lower his prices or get no income at all. To protect British farmers the Government places certain quotas or taxes on some imported foods from some overseas countries to control the quantity and cost of imported foods in the shops.

Farming as an investment

In the past farms were usually worked by their owners or by tenants of the local landowner. Recently, much farmland has been bought by large companies as an investment. Their sole interest is in making a profit and they have less concern for the rural environment as a whole, compared with the traditional farmer.

The European Economic Community

The countries of the EEC have agreed to have a Common Agricultural Policy (CAP) and each year the various prices for products such as wheat or lamb, milk or wine are fixed at a common level for farmers in all EEC countries. Because each country has its own unit of money such as pounds, liras, or francs, a rate of exchange is fixed between them. To even things out a complicated set of regulations decide what the 'agricultural' value of money will be, and this is known as 'green' money.

Farmers are either given money as a subsidy if the sale of goods does not reach the agreed price, or pay extra taxes if they get more. If more of certain items are produced than is needed, the surplus is bought and put into store by the EEC. This leads to what is called butter or cereal 'mountains' and wine 'lakes'. All these price controls seem hard for most people to understand, but their aim is to provide farmers with a steady market and income on the one hand and the consumers with good quality and reliable food at a low price on the other. One problem is that often the interests of consumers and farmers do not match. Another is that each government tends to look after the needs of its own farmers in order to continue to receive their support.

1 What are some of the reasons why food can rapidly increase in price?

2 What is the difference between: a) *tax* (or *levy*) and *quota controls* on imported foods? b) *subsidies* and *guaranteed prices* for produce from British farms?

3 Why does the British consumer suffer from high tax/levy on imported foods, or from the existence of quotas on imported farm produce? How does the British farmer benefit from these taxes and quotas?

4 How does a) the British farmer, b) the British consumer, benefit from the payment of subsidies and guaranteed prices?

Most milk is sold through the Milk Marketing Board. This farmer however, sells his milk directly to local shops and customers, and so avoids large payments to the MMB

The growth in investment in farmland by institutions. In recent years land has also been bought as a financial investment by many companies and run by farm managers. The farming community is concerned that the prices paid are beyond those that farmers can afford

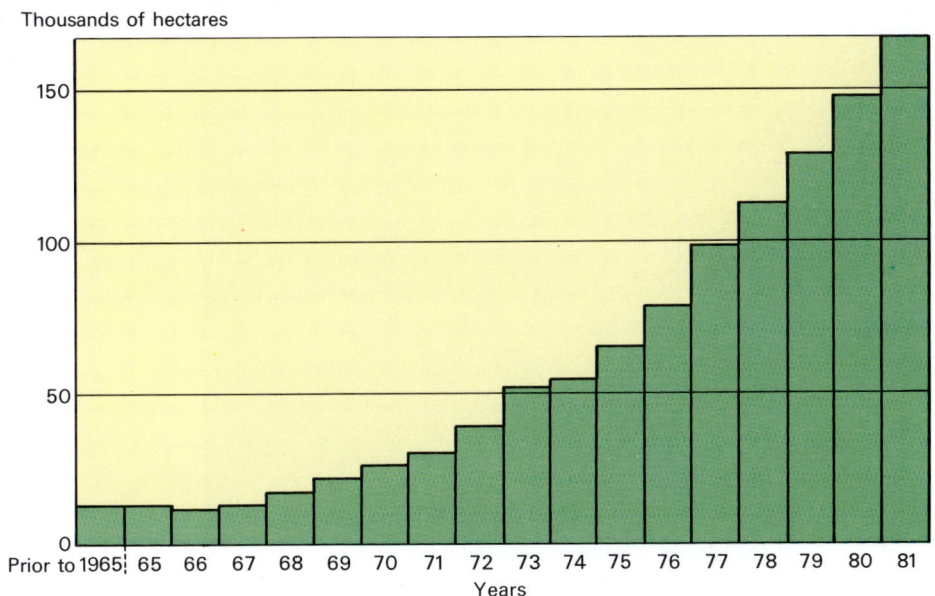

Thousands of hectares

Years

85

Exercise 20 Crop and land use patterns

Area of land under agriculture for selected crops, by region

Region	Agricultural area (thousands ha)					Total land area (including inland water)
	Wheat	Sugar Beet	Horti-culture	Grass	Grazing	
England	1338	213	263	4239	757	13041
North	25	—	1	537	321	1540
Yorks	134	29	27	406	138	1542
E Midlands	285	50	54	422	43	1563
W Midlands	105	19	19	571	24	1301
E Anglia	287	105	70	134	22	1257
S-East	375	8	70	639	44	2722
S-West	119	1	12	1230	108	2383
N-West	8	1	10	300	57	733
Scotland	24	—	13	1061	3779	7717
Wales	7	—	2	979	371	2077

1 Copy the map of the agricultural regions, omitting the symbols for the distribution of wheat. For one of the other crops or types of land use given in the table, complete the map showing the distribution.

2 Explain the pattern of the map you have drawn.

3 Give examples from this book of cereal growing, hill sheep farming, dairying, market gardening and intensive animal rearing, giving the page on which each is illustrated.

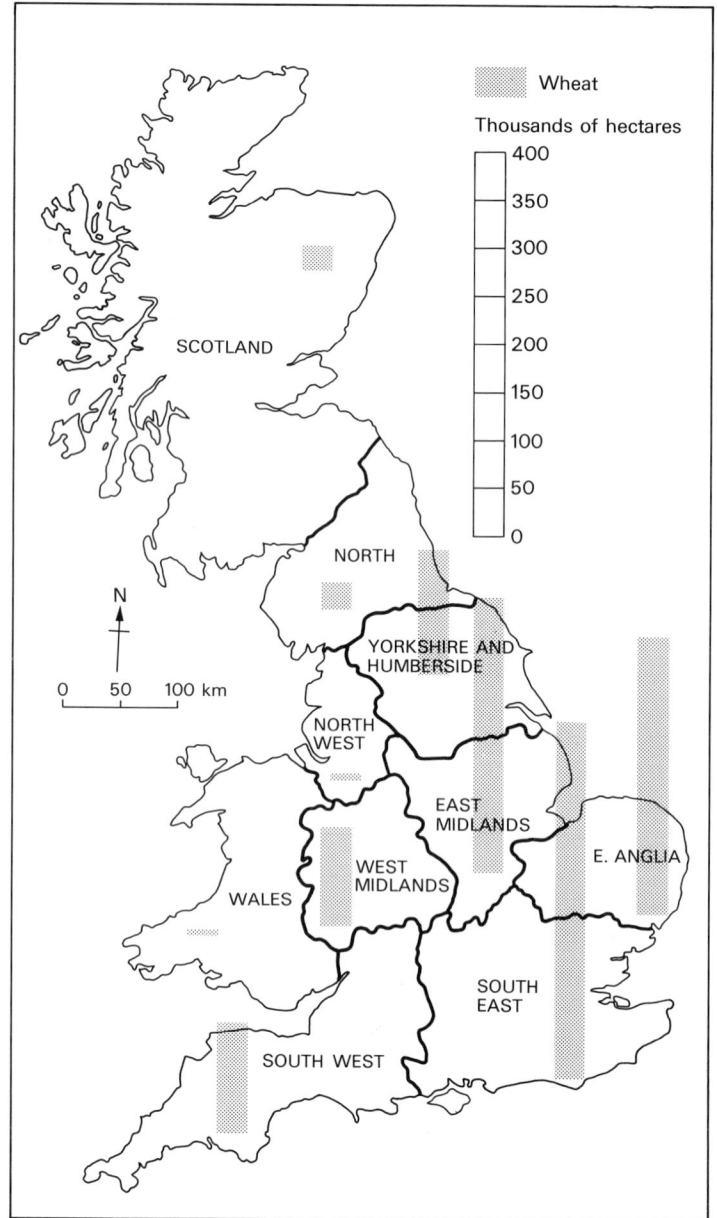

Map to show the area of land devoted to wheat in the early 1980s in each of the standard regions of Britain

Oil-seed rape is a recently introduced cash crop that has become very popular in Britain. It can be combine-harvested

Chapter 4 Manufacturing industries

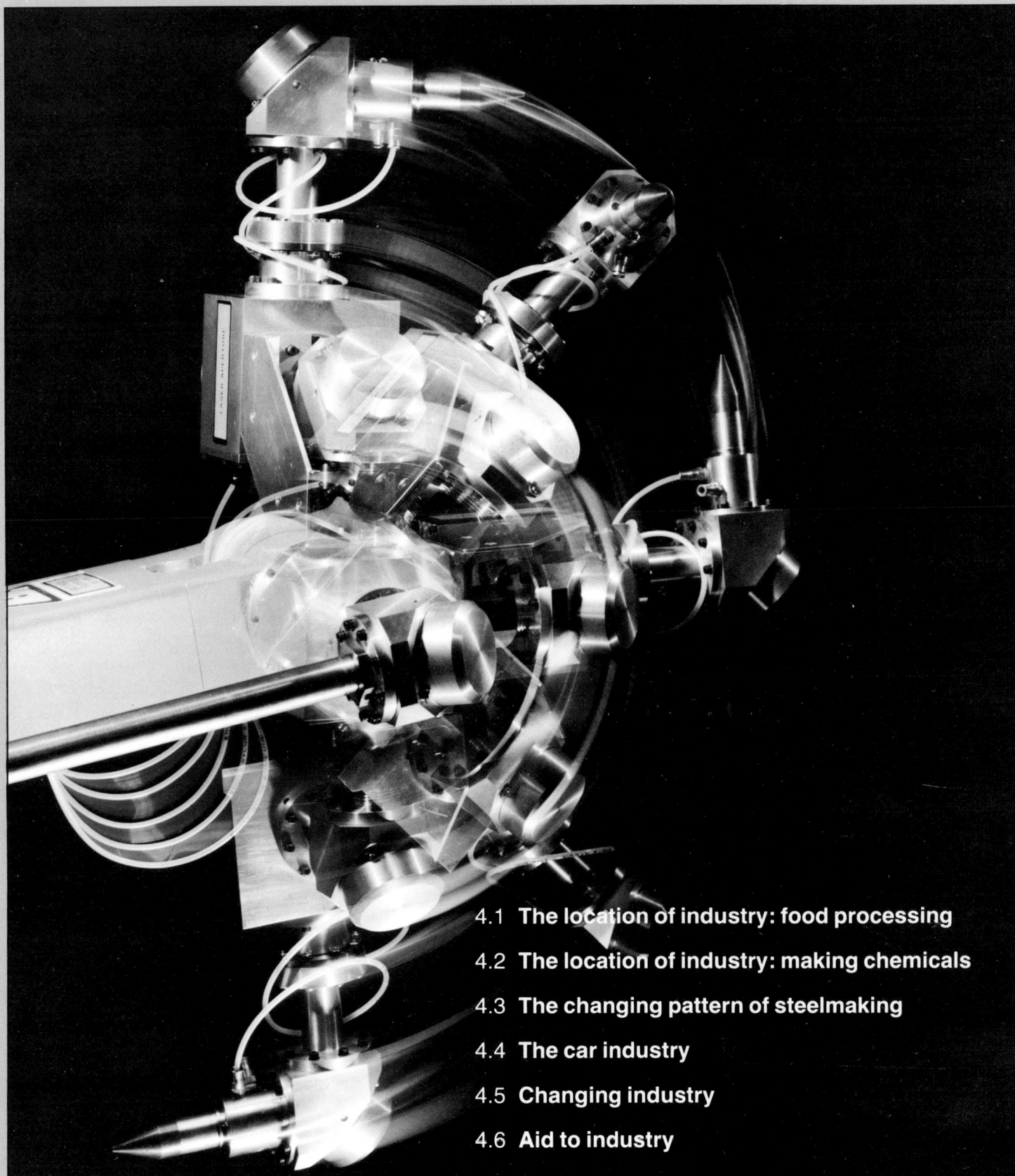

The location of industry: food processing

Bread, one of the basic products of the food processing industry

The location of the factories and units in the Associated British Foods Group

Associated British Foods Group

Allied Bakeries
Operating 49 bakeries and 1990 shops and restaurants including 445 Hot-Bread shops

Allied Mills Group
20 flour mills in Britain

Fine Fare Group
627 stores, including 37 superstores, and 180 Shoppers Paradise discount stores

Food Securities Group
10 factories 2 warehouses

Power Supermarket Group
S. Ireland, N. Ireland and 11 stores in Britain

Twining Crosfield Group
11 tea and coffee factories

Weston Food Group
6 factories - biscuits, desserts

Other companies
14 varied companies e.g. Ryvita, furniture, soft drinks etc.

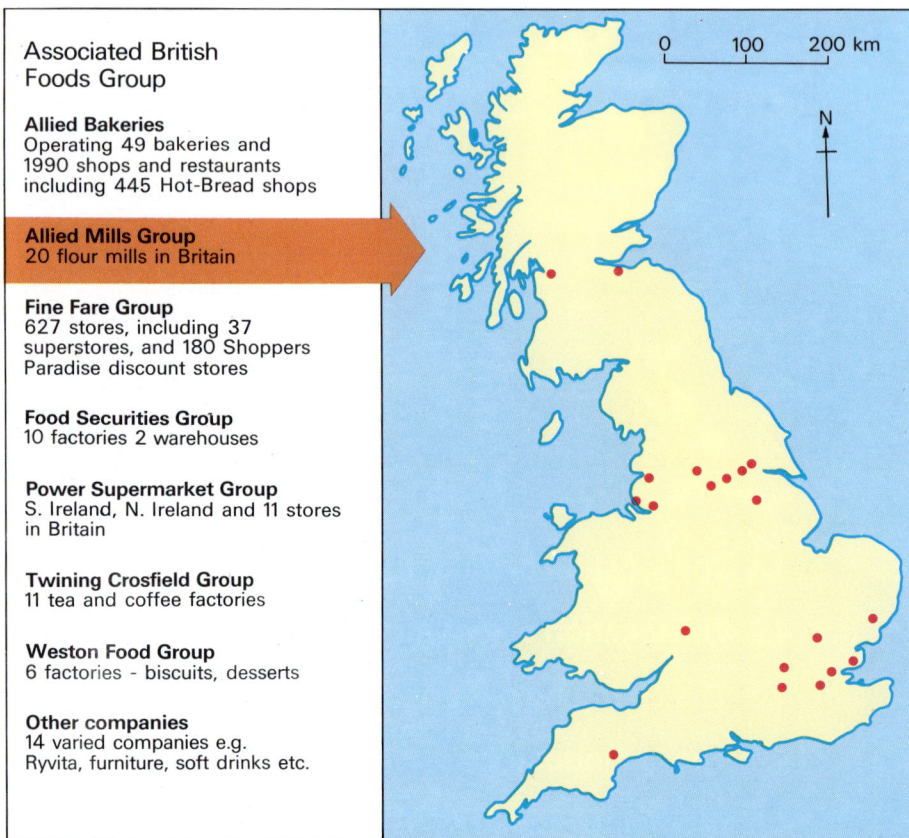

The food processing industry

The table on page 90 shows the number of people employed in different sorts of jobs in Britain in 1982, while the diagram illustrates the number of men and women working in the various branches of manufacturing. It can be seen that one of the biggest employers is the 'food, drink and tobacco' industry. In this branch of manufacturing a wide range of raw materials, usually crops, animals or fish, are processed into different forms of food or drink. Many products are preserved by freezing, dehydrating or putting into cans or other sorts of container.

Some manufactured foods and drinks are imported into Britain, but many more are made in British factories from either home produced or imported raw materials. Quite apart from the men and women working in the factories, there are many others transporting the raw materials and products, advertising the goods and selling them in stores and shops.

The location of food processing factories

Factories are usually located in particular places for very good reasons. Manufacturing involves taking raw materials or semi-processed goods and making them into something more valuable. Not surprisingly, many factories are located near the source of raw material, or at ports where raw materials are imported, or where they can be transported at not too great a cost. Large amounts of power and other resources such as water are often needed, and these may affect the location of the factory. Some factories are quite small and employ only a few workers, but very many are huge and employ a large labour force of workers, managers and clerical staff. In these cases the factory has to be in a town or where people can easily get to the works each day. Since the main aim of most manufacturing is to produce goods at a profit, factories are likely to be located where the costs of raw materials, power, transport of goods to the consumer, and wages and salaries are as low as possible. It takes a great deal of money to build and run a large factory, and firms are sometimes persuaded to locate their works in a particular area because financial advantages are being offered by the government or by the local authority.

Food processing factories using imported raw materials such as grain, cocoa or sugar, tend to be at or near ports. Those using raw materials from British farms are usually in the areas of production, such as the sugar factories that are found in the sugar beet growing areas of Eastern England. Those that produce large quantities of quickly consumed goods, such as bakeries and dairies, tend to be widely scattered wherever there are large concentrations of population.

1 Draw a diagram, based on the table on page 90, to stress the percentage of employees in manufacturing in the total workforce. Give the date of the statistics.

2 In terms of numbers of employees, where does 'food, drink and tobacco' come in the rank order of types of manufacturing? What is the difference in the proportion of men and women employed in this branch of manufacturing compared with the larger employers? Why is this?

3 Name a) two food or drink products made in British factories from British raw materials, b) two made in British factories from imported raw materials and c) two already manufactured imported products. Compile a class list from all the answers.

4 Draw a flow diagram like the one opposite to show the stages in the process 'From cocoa pod to buying a bar of chocolate'.

5 Describe and explain the features and location of the flour mill shown in the photograph.

Primary, secondary and tertiary activities are involved in the manufacture and sale of bread and confectionery

An ABF ice cream production line

An ABF flour mill

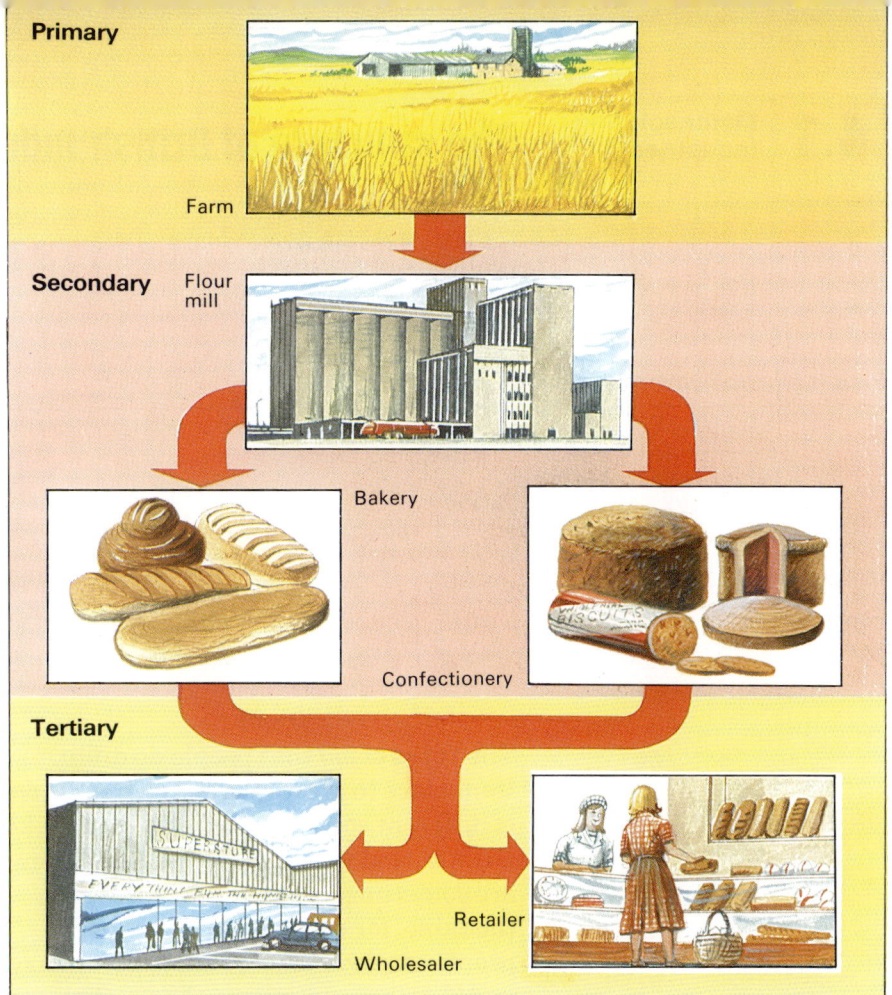

The structure of British industry

People in employment (thousands) 1982

| | Primary | | Secondary | | | Tertiary | |
	Agriculture forestry and fishing	Mining and quarrying	Manu- facturing	Con- struction	Gas electricity and water	Services	Total
Males	265	308	4107	934	272	6103	11989
Females	88	18	1645	116	68	7179	9114
All	354	326	5752	1049	340	13282	21103

The types of job that people do differ from place to place. There are hundreds of different sorts of jobs in a country like Britain, and to help describe them they are sometimes divided into groups. In the table, for example, the number of people employed in Primary, Secondary and Tertiary groups are shown. The first includes farming, mining, quarrying, forestry work, fishing and so on; activities producing raw materials and resources that usually need further treatment before use. The second group includes manufacturing, which can be sub-divided into many smaller parts, as the diagram shows. Most of the service

or professional activities, such as jobs in shops, offices, transport, finance, schools and so on are grouped in the Tertiary Sector.

When the proportion of men and women engaged in these three sectors in Britain is compared with other countries, the low proportion in Primary and the high in Tertiary is very noticeable. This is the pattern found in many West European, North American and 'developed' countries, and is unlike that found in many so-called 'developing' countries. It is important to remember that these proportions change, and in Britain in the past there was a far higher proportion in Primary and Secondary sectors than in the early 1980s. It is likely that the proportion in the Tertiary sector will be even bigger in the future.

This diagram shows the relative sizes of the different areas of British manufacturing industry, and proportion of men and women employed

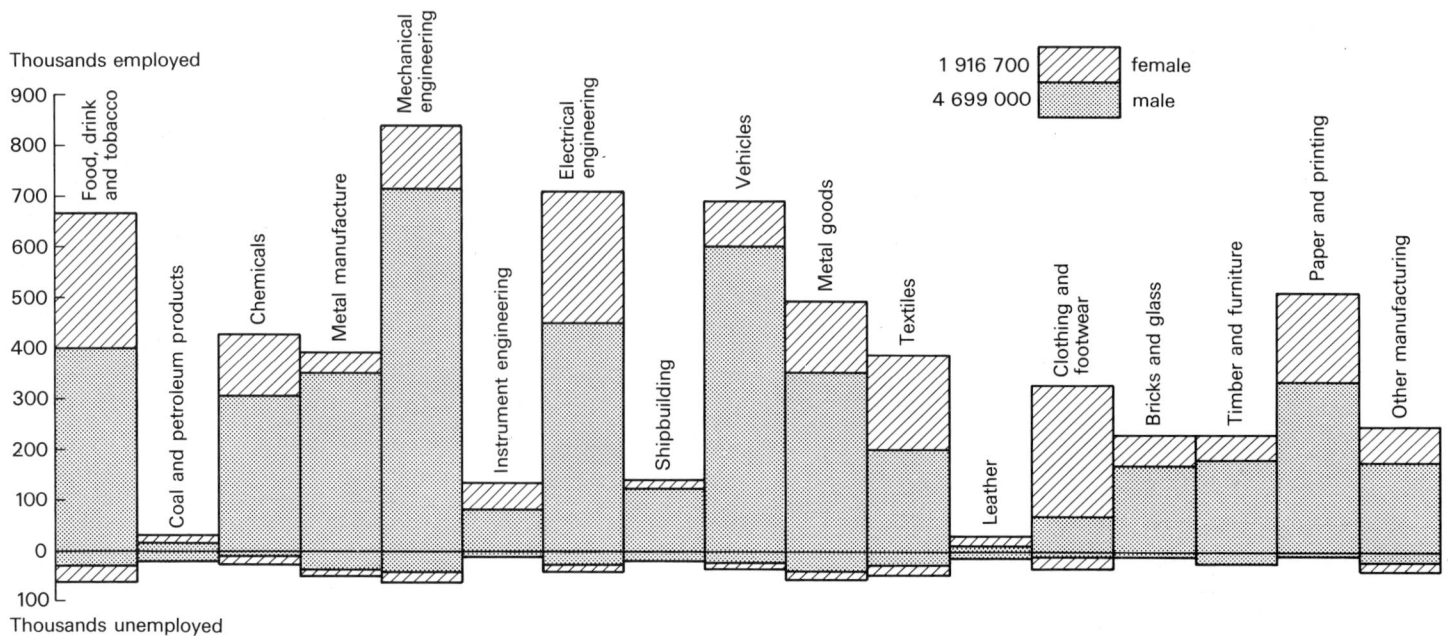

Exercise 21 A new food processing location at Corby

Mr Garry Weston announces
New major investment programme

New major investments for ABF
£30 million capital expenditure programme to commence at once in the field of grain processing and handling to back ABF Group skills and to take advantage of new technologies and market opportunities.

New major investments for Corby
The major part of this investment will be at Corby where it will create jobs and, we believe, confidence; and bring new skills to a location ideally situated near England's wheat growing heart land. Capital expenditure will include £15 million for a new bread flour mill designed to use the maximum of home grown wheat. Additionally at Corby will be a £10 million factory to produce gluten and starch for use in the food industry and for other industrial uses, providing an outlet for some 100,000 tonnes of home grown wheat.

New major investments for British farmers
In backing our skills we are backing the expanding cereal growing industry in this country for British farmers. The wheat these new investments will use, and the products they produce will replace cereals grown overseas and products manufactured outside this country.

In addition, the better to service the British farmer, our Group will be building a new major grain storage and shipping terminal in East Anglia to be operated by our international grain trading subsidiary. Through this terminal we expect to condition and export over half-a-million tonnes of grain a year – a facility that will help open up wider overseas markets for British grain, and help the products of the British farmer to compete abroad.

Associated British Foods

£25m grain mill boost for Corby

Investment of £30m in a new plant by Associated British Foods will lead to the creation of two automated grain factories and more than 100 jobs at the former steel town of Corby, Northamptonshire. Some of the money will be spent on a grain export terminal near Ipswich which will handle part of the growing British sale of grain to deficit countries such as Poland.

The projects mark a new stage in the steady conversion of Britain from being a leading importer of grain to a moderate exporter in the wake of record harvests and support for farmers through the Common Agricultural Policy.

ABF's chairman said that the group's £15m flour mill at Corby would be 'the first inland mill built in Britain in living memory'. Existing mills in ports reflected the country's long dependence on grain imports from North America.

The group is to build a £10m plant at Corby for the production of gluten and starch from home-grown wheat using technology made available through a partnership with its Finnish developers. Gluten is used in breakfast cereals. For the Corby development the group received regional development aid and a training grant of £125000 from the British Steel Corporation.

Read the advertisement and newspaper extract about new investments by Associated British Foods.

1 Draw a rough sketch map showing the location of Corby and Ipswich.

2 What two types of factory are being built at Corby? What raw materials will be used and what will be the products? What is unusual about this location for such manufacturing? Give three reasons for the choice of Corby as a location for new factories.

3 What type of 'factory' will be built at Ipswich? What raw materials will be sent there, and where will the products go? In what sense will the Ipswich development mark 'a new stage...'?

The location of industry: making chemicals

The location of Imperial Chemical Industries (ICI) works in Britain, 1984

The chemical industry

The chemical industry is very wide-ranging and complicated, with many different raw materials and a great variety of products. Some of these such as medicines, paints, soaps and fertilizers are sold directly to the consumer. Other chemical products are themselves raw materials for further processing. Examples of these include acids and alkalis used in steelmaking and explosives, man-made fibres and dyes used in the manufacture of textiles, and the many sorts of plastics used in thousands of different products.

The main raw materials are petroleum, natural gas, coal, salt and sulphur. Most chemical factories are where these are 'refined' or split up into their more useful separate chemical parts, and these parts are then re-combined or made into other products. Not surprisingly, chemical factories tend to be located near the source of the raw material since vast quantities are usually needed and this reduces the costs of transport. Alternatively, they may be found at coastal or estuary sites where raw materials can be transported by bulk carriers. Some chemical raw materials and products are transported by pipeline. There is often a need for a large area of flat land for a big chemical works, and this can be provided by the estuary site. Another important factor in location is the need to get rid of unpleasant and dangerous waste products and, in some cases, to be away from built-up areas for safety reasons. As a result of these various influences the chemical industry in Britain has become concentrated in Cheshire and Teeside where deposits of salt and other mineral deposits occur, and at Merseyside, Severnside, and parts of central Scotland where suitable coastal sites

The main products of the British chemical industry

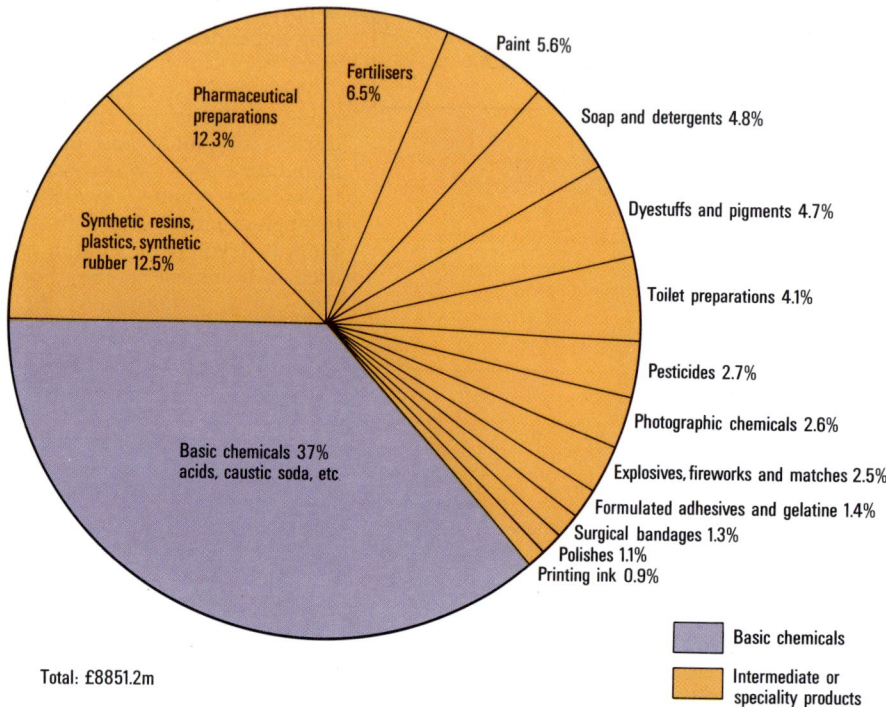

Paint 5.6%
Fertilisers 6.5%
Pharmaceutical preparations 12.3%
Soap and detergents 4.8%
Synthetic resins, plastics, synthetic rubber 12.5%
Dyestuffs and pigments 4.7%
Toilet preparations 4.1%
Pesticides 2.7%
Photographic chemicals 2.6%
Basic chemicals 37% acids, caustic soda, etc
Explosives, fireworks and matches 2.5%
Formulated adhesives and gelatine 1.4%
Surgical bandages 1.3%
Polishes 1.1%
Printing ink 0.9%

Total: £8851.2m

Basic chemicals
Intermediate or speciality products

are found. Apart from these main centres, of course, there are dozens of other refineries and factories scattered around the country and linked by a network of rail, road, canal, pipeline and coastal routes.

Imperial Chemical Industries (ICI)

One feature of the chemical industry is the way in which production is in the control of a few giant companies, usually multinationals. This is quite understandable in view of the huge costs of building a chemical plant (it is 'capital intensive'), and the large amounts of money needed for research and development. Imperial Chemical Industries (ICI) is a good example of a British chemical firm. It was formed in 1926 by the amalgamation of four existing companies. It has factories in most industrial areas, but especially in Cheshire and Teeside. About 40 per cent of the value of its factories are abroad, and about 60 per cent of the value of its sales are to overseas customers. In spite of a decline in profits, closure of some plants and a reduction of the workforce in the early 1980s, ICI remains a very large organisation employing about 70 000 men and women in Britain.

1 **a**) Name four chemical products used by you or your family during the past month. **b**) Describe two TV or newspaper advertisements for chemical products.

2 From the diagram on page 90 give the number and percentage of the workforce in the chemical industry in the early 1980s. What is its rank order in terms of number of employees?

3 Chemical manufacturing is sometimes described as a 'noxious' industry, and should therefore be kept away from residential areas. Describe two different sorts of dangers resulting from chemical manufacturing.

4 With the help of the photograph and O.S. map extract, describe the location and site of the ICI Chemical Works at Wilton. Calculate the area occupied by the chemical plant.

A photo of the chemical plant at Wilton, Teeside. How can you tell that it was taken after the map was made?

1:50 000 OS map extract of the Teeside area

Chemicals in the home

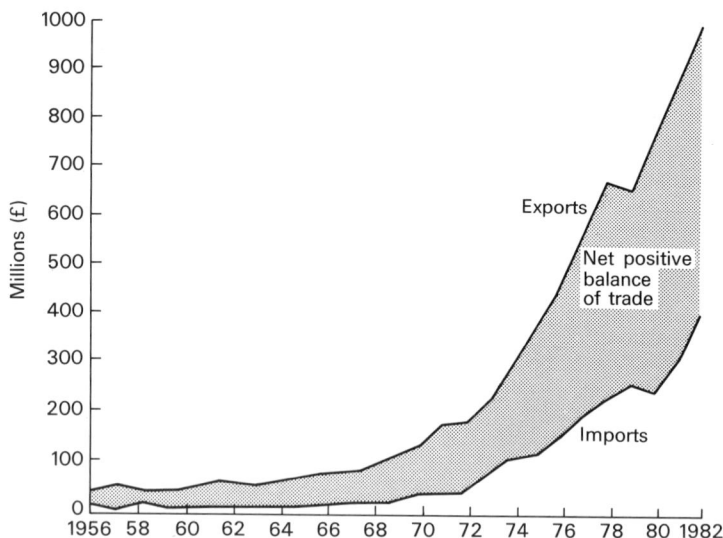

The graph shows the rise in exports of British pharmaceutical products from £100 million in the late 60s to £1 000 million in 1982. As companies competed for a larger share of this growing market, the marketing costs also grew – to £120 million in 1982. This resulted in more expensive drugs. But members of the industry point out that high marketing costs are necessary to increase sales and to release money for research.

The importance of the chemical industry is shown in this table of major advertisers

The top 20 advertisers: Expenditure in £000s

		1981	1980
1	Procter & Gamble	24897	17279
2	Mars	20791	13357
3	Cadbury	19164	11448
4	Rowntree/Mackintosh	18895	10991
5	Lever Bros	14042	8668
6	Nestlé	13652	7331
7	Kelloggs	13556	9789
8	Electricity Council	13040	9791
9	Van den Burghs	12995	9891
10	John Player	12404	14879
11	Pedigree Petfoods	12292	8573
12	Gallaher	11689	11135
13	H J Heinz	11602	8637
14	British Rail	11330	8172
15	Austin/Rover	11132	8389
16	Brooke Bond/Oxo	10929	11201
17	Ford	10850	10914
18	Birds Eye/Walls	10734	7514
19	General Foods	10715	6906
20	Cadbury/Typhoo	10186	6668

Products of the chemical industry have so many uses in the home, and are so familiar, that they are usually taken for granted. However, it is only necessary to imagine daily life without medicines, soaps and washing powders, cleaning materials, plastics, materials made from chemicals and so on, to realise the dependence most people have on the chemical industry. Apart from these direct uses, most foods we eat have chemicals added to them, while oils and petrol are used for domestic heating or to drive cars and motorcycles. For most people life would be very different and probably far less satisfactory without these products, although dependence on such things may bring its own problems.

Many products of the chemical industry are in everyday use

Exercise 22 **ICI/Teeside**

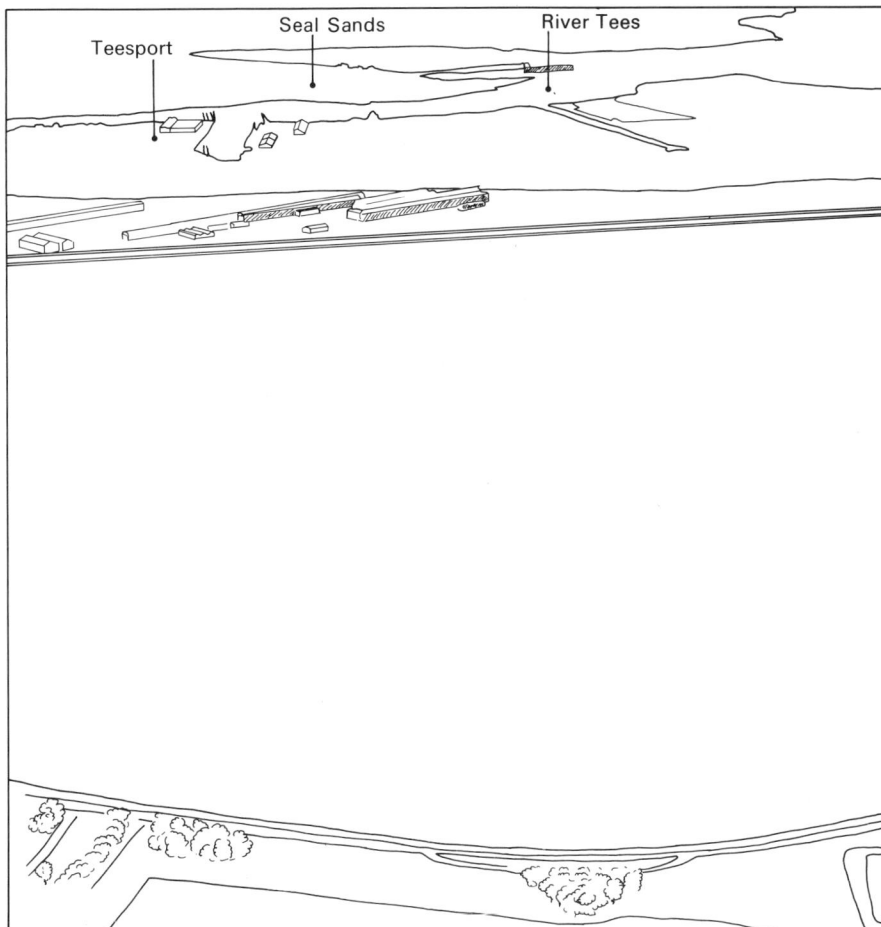

Outline sketch of the photograph of Wilton on page 93

The photograph, sketch and O.S. map extract show the location and appearance of the large chemical works at Wilton, owned by ICI, and the North Tees oil refinery that is jointly owned by the company. The Billingham works nearby was built in 1916 as an explosives factory, but was converted to produce fertilizers and cement. The raw materials were local deposits of the chemicals, salt and anhydrite, and imported oil. The Wilton works were built much later, in 1946, and since then it has expanded and like most chemical works is being continually modernised. The oil refinery was opened in 1964, and gave further value to the site and location for chemical produciton. In 1982 ICI sold the Wilton plant to BP.

1 Copy the sketch and using the photograph on page 93 as a guide, add the major features of the Wilton chemical plant.

2 Give the grid reference of each of the points shown on the sketch.

3 Draw an outline of the area shown on the OS extract. Add and label three different sorts of industrial activity and three indications of transport systems found in the area.

4 What are some of the advantages of the site for **a)** chemical manufacturing, **b)** steel making?

An article describing the change of ownership of the ICI Wilton plant in 1983

BP and ICI announce a plan to swap plants and shed 1800 jobs

The massive reorganisation of the British plastics and petrochemicals industry, announced yesterday by BP and ICI, is one of the most significant developments in the sector since the war. It may also herald more far-reaching changes throughout Europe, where there is a plastics and petrochemicals overcapacity. In spite of the loss of 1800 jobs it makes sense that BP should get out of PVC manufacture by selling its plants to ICI which in turn is getting out of polyethylene by selling its plants to BP. The effect may well be to prevent further job losses, as ICI have claimed.

The advantage to BP in getting rid of its two loss-making PVC plants in South Wales is obvious. To expand production of polyethylene at Wilton makes reasonable sense in view of the ready supply of ethylene from Grangemouth. It is more difficult to see precisely what is in it for ICI, although ICI has clearly decided that its PVC technology gives it a potential competitive edge. It is therefore worth persevering with so that the company can outdo the opposition when the upturn comes. ICI's purchase of BP's PVC business increases its British capacity by 90000 tonnes, so that with a total European capacity of 570000 tonnes ICI becomes Europe's second-largest PVC producer.

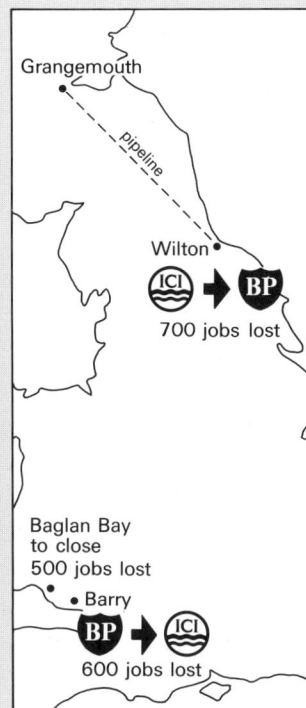

95

The changing pattern of steelmaking

Ebbw Vale was once a major steel-making town

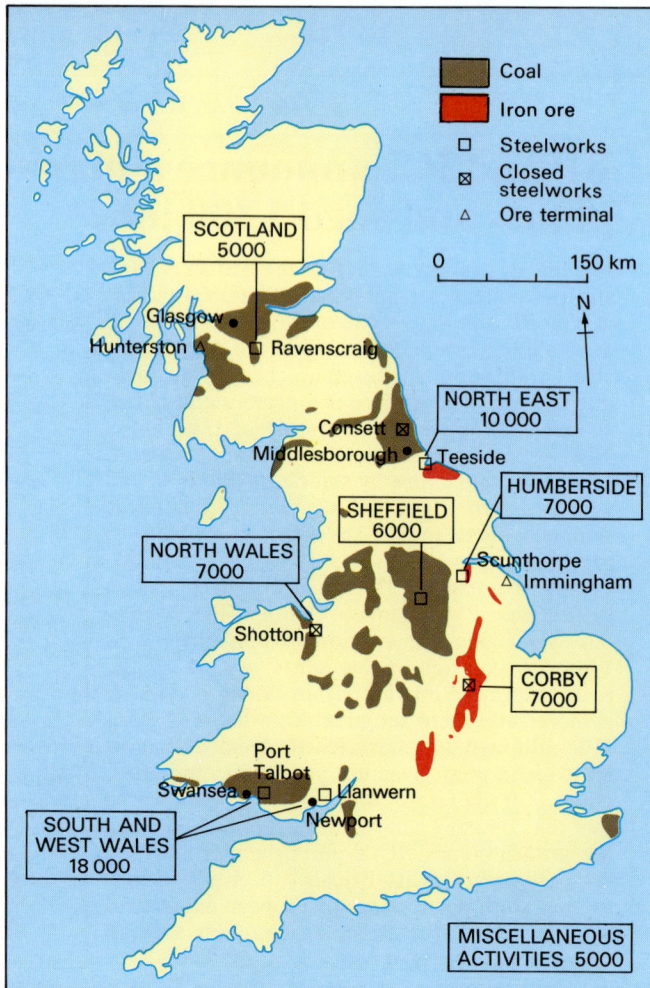

The numbers of jobs lost in steel making centres between January 1980 and May 1981

Map legend and labels:

- Coal
- Iron ore
- □ Steelworks
- ⊠ Closed steelworks
- △ Ore terminal

SCOTLAND 5000

Glasgow
Hunterston △ □ Ravenscraig

NORTH EAST 10 000

Consett ⊠
Middlesborough ●
□ Teeside

HUMBERSIDE 7000

SHEFFIELD 6000

NORTH WALES 7000

Scunthorpe
□ △ Immingham

Shotton ⊠

CORBY 7000 ⊠

Port Talbot
Swansea ●
□ Llanwern
Newport

SOUTH AND WEST WALES 18 000

MISCELLANEOUS ACTIVITIES 5000

0 ————— 150 km

The principle in manufacturing steel is the same as milling flour or making chemicals; raw or semi-processed materials are made into something more useful or valuable. The actual process is different, of course, as is shown in the diagram. Nowadays most steel is made in very large works, and the map shows that there are fewer of these huge integrated steelworks and steel-making towns than there are flour mills or chemical factories.

The changing location of steelmaking

Vast quantities of bulky ore, coking coal, steel products and steel scrap have to be brought to, and dispatched from, steelworks. Transport costs can be very high, and efforts are made to keep these to a minimum by using bulk carriers and special railway trucks, and by careful location of the works. The best type of location has changed with the development of new technology, and with the increase in size of the works.

In the earliest days, when ore was smelted with charcoal, wooded areas such as those of central Kent and the Forest of Dean were iron-making areas. When ways of using coke to smelt the iron ore had been developed, the coalfields where iron ore also existed became the main smelting centres. Towns such as Merthyr Tydfil and Ebbw Vale in the northern part of the South Wales coalfield are examples of these early steel-making centres. Then new ore fields were discovered in eastern and central England, and when new methods of using this low-grade and phosphorous-contaminated ore were found large steelworks were built at places such as Scunthorpe and Corby on the orefields. At first the blast furnaces converting iron ore to iron and the furnaces converting the iron to steel were often on different sites and in different areas, but a few decades ago large new integrated iron and steelworks were built so that steel could be made from iron ore and scrap in one continuous process. This meant that large areas of flat land were needed. Another trend was to build these large works at the coast, near the ports where foreign ore and coal were imported. By the 1950s many of the oldest works had been closed down, but there remained a large number of plants of varying age and size in different locations, all owned by different companies.

The British Steel Corporation

In 1967 about a dozen of the largest steel companies were nationalised and merged to become the British Steel Corporation (BSC). Since then the corporation and the remaining private firms have tried to increase productivity by closing down older inefficient works and introducing new equipment and methods in the remaining ones. Due to the worldwide overproduction of steel and the difficulty of selling steel in competition with many foreign companies, BSC was losing enormous sums of money in the early 1980s. This led to closure or part-closure of some of the large and once-famous steelworks, and whole towns, such as Corby, were affected by the loss of their major employer. There was a big reduction in the workforce, and BSC collaborated with some of the remaining private firms to make special items such as engineering steels. Throughout the early years of the 1980s, steelmaking jobs continued to be lost in most areas and by mid-1984 there were fears that at least one of the five big integrated works might have to close down. Further difficulties were caused by an EEC decision (p. 259) that British steel production should be cut again as part of its total reduction. The first three years of the 1980s saw a drop in the BSC labour force of over 35 000!

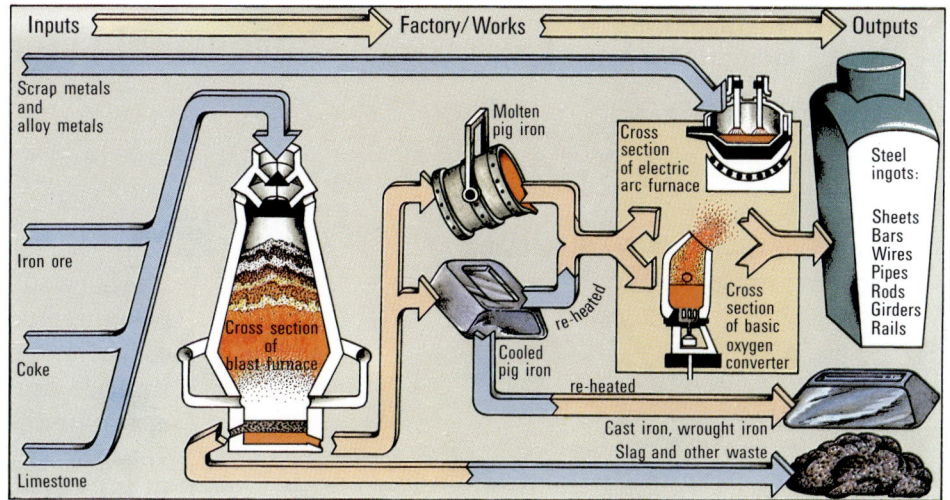

This diagram of the steel-making process shows that factories, like farms, can be seen as a system involving inputs and outputs

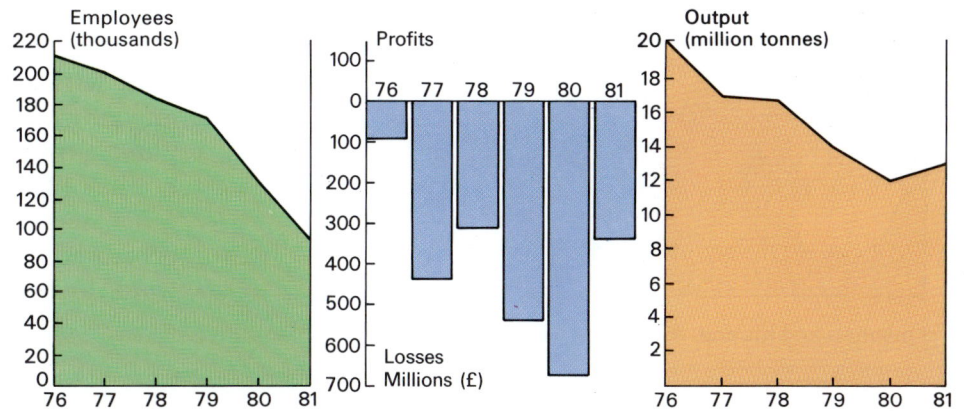

The changing nature of steel making in Britain

Port Talbot is one of the few remaining integrated steelworks in Britain

1 Copy the outline of Britain from the map. On it locate and name: **a)** One large integrated steelworks in England, one in Wales and one in Scotland, **b)** One ore terminal where iron and steel are *not* made, **c)** One large city in England that makes a lot of steel but no iron – (the iron is brought in from other integrated works), **d)** One iron and steelmaking town in England and one in Wales where the steelworks has recently closed down.

2 Draw two diagrams to show these facts about steelmaking in the early 1980s in Britain. Imported ores 75 per cent; home ores 25 per cent; home sales of steel 70 per cent; sales of steel abroad 30 per cent.

3 List some of the uses to which the steel products listed in the diagram will be put.

4 Give some reasons why there has been a big drop in demand for British steel.

5 What are the arguments for and against closing down loss-making steelworks?

Exercise 23 **Ravenscraig steelworks; will it die?**

The location of Ravenscraig and Hunterston

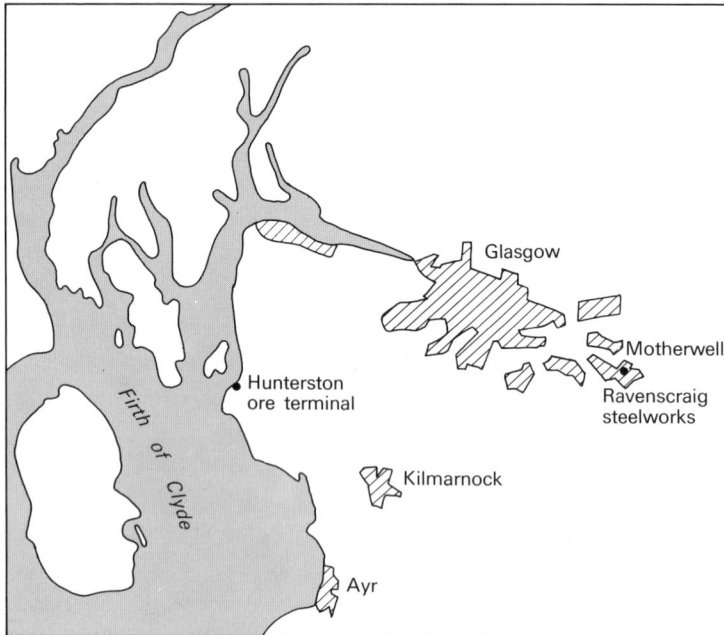

Motherwell and other towns near Glasgow have been involved with iron and steel making for several centuries. At first the works used local coking coal, iron ore and limestone. When local ore was no longer adequate the blast furnaces used imported ore. The 'big mill' at Ravenscraig at Motherwell was opened in 1962 and is now one of the leading producers of sheet steel in Britain. The iron ore is imported from the fairly new ore terminal at Hunterston, the coking coal from the north of England and limestone from quarries in the Pennines.

In 1982 suggestions were made to close Ravenscraig with a loss of over 12 000 jobs in the steelworks and many more in the 4 000 firms supplying the plant. Strong opposition from Scotland delayed this, but in 1983 new plans were made to close the slab mills, making 2000 unemployed, and send the semi-processed steel to a works in the United States. This would avoid closing the whole steelworks down.

One man and his dog. A thriving community has grown up around the steelworks

Big five steel plants saved

British Steel, which last week announced soaring losses and 6000 job cuts, is to axe a further 14000 steel jobs in coming months. But none of the big five steel plants in Scotland, South Wales and Teesside is to be shut before the general election. Ian MacGregor, British Steel's chairman and chief executive, has had his plan to close Ravenscraig, the heart of Scottish steelmaking, rejected by Industry Secretary Patrick Jenkin and Scottish Secretary George Younger.

The big five will be kept going, though thousands of jobs will go at each site in the round of 14000 redundancies for which MacGregor is

aiming, in order to get his workforce down to 78000 from 92000 today. Losses are now running at over £1 million a day and BSC is operating at barely half its 14.4 million tonnes a year capacity.

MacGregor sees no future in steel making at Ravenscraig, which long ago lost its biggest customer when the Linwood car factory closed. Ministers have been forced to recognise the commercial weight of his case for closure, but they do not think the political cost is worthwhile. 'Ravenscraig is different,' says Bill Sirs, the ISTC's moderate general secretary, 'if the Government closed it, Scotland would erupt'.

The Ravenscraig steelworks is a major employer in the area

In 1982/3 the future of Ravenscraig was in doubt, as this article shows, and again in 1984 when a miners' strike threatened its vital coal supplies

1 Describe the location and site of the steelworks at Ravenscraig.

2 Sketch or describe the main features of the steelworks.

3 In what sense is this a very poor site to locate a modern steelworks?

4 If the site is so poor, why does it continue to produce steel when many works in other parts of the country are being closed down?

5 Many people in other industries would lose their jobs if Ravenscraig steelworks was closed. Name some of the types of firms likely to be affected.

The car industry

Ford Sierra cars being assembled by robot

Assembling Lotus cars by hand

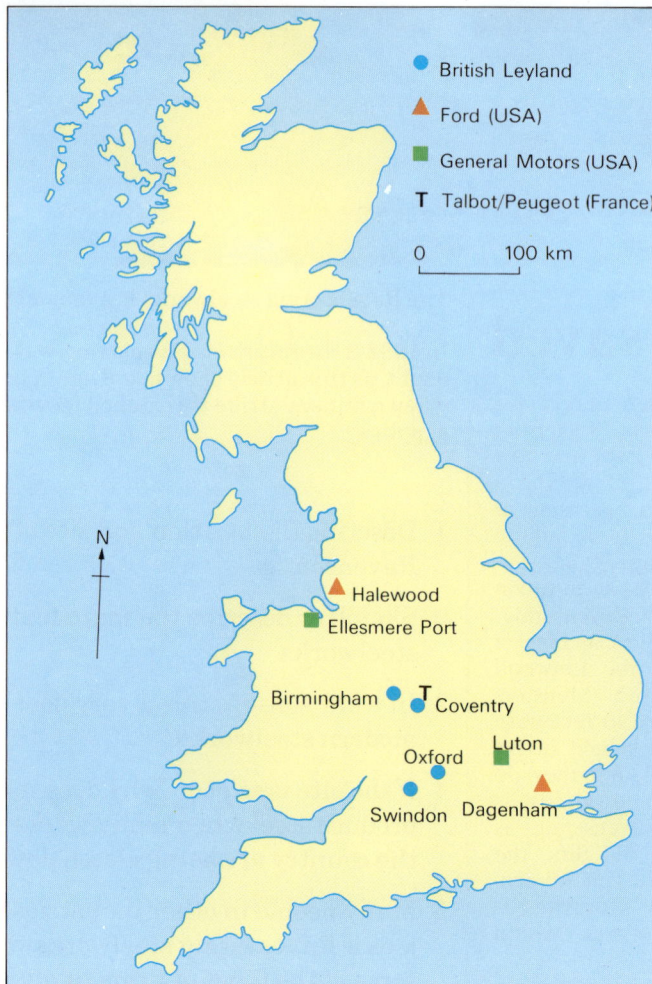

British Leyland
Ford (USA)
General Motors (USA)
T Talbot/Peugeot (France)

0   100 km

N

Halewood
Ellesmere Port
Birmingham T Coventry
Oxford Luton
Swindon Dagenham

The main factories of the 'big four' car-making companies

The history of car making in Britain

One of the largest of modern manufacturing industries is the making of cars and other vehicles. The main features are the large scale of operations, the use of mass production and assembly line techniques with specialisation of jobs, the growth of automation and the merging of companies worldwide.

The industry began in very different circumstances. Firms such as Vauxhall, Wolseley, Riley, Rover and Humber grew out of general engineering or bicycle and motor cycle manufacturing. In those days most of the parts were made on the spot or in near-by works, and the engineering skill of local workers was a main locating factor. Many of the earliest car making firms were based in London, the West Midlands and central Scotland where metal working was already important. At the beginning of this century there were about a dozen major firms and many smaller ones. As the mass production techniques devised by Henry Ford, the American car manufacturer, were developed in Britain, new factories were built and smaller firms found it hard to compete.

Towns such as Dagenham, Luton, Oxford, Linwood near Glasgow, Halewood and Ellesmere Port on Merseyside acquired large car-making factories. By the early 1980s most British cars were made by four companies; British Leyland, Ford, Talbot and General Motors (Vauxhall).

The structure of the car industry

Many semi-processed materials and components are used in making cars. British Leyland (BL), for example, has about 7 000 component suppliers. These range from huge firms such as BSC, ICI, Lucas and Dunlop that supply sheet steel, paints and plastics, electrical components and tyres to many smaller firms employing only a dozen or so people. The assembly line method has to be efficiently organised to ensure a steady flow of components to the assembly plants. These may be brought from other factories within the BL group, as the map on page 102 shows, or from other companies in Britain or abroad. Providing new machine tools for the assembly lines to make new models is very expensive, as is the introduction and use of automated machinery and robots managed by micro-computer. This is one reason why mass production firms are getter larger as mergers take place such as Talbot with Peugeot and Citröen (France).

International markets

British car makers try to sell their products in Britain and abroad, but foreign firms also try hard to sell their cars in Britain. The diagram shows how the British and foreign car manufacturers share of the British market changed between 1970 and 1980. At the end of the decade British car makers were selling fewer and fewer cars and losing money, in spite of financial help from the Government. In an effort to make and sell more cars against foreign competition, many factories were closed or reorganised, the workforce was cut, modern techniques introduced, financial mergers arranged and new models designed and produced. In spite of all its

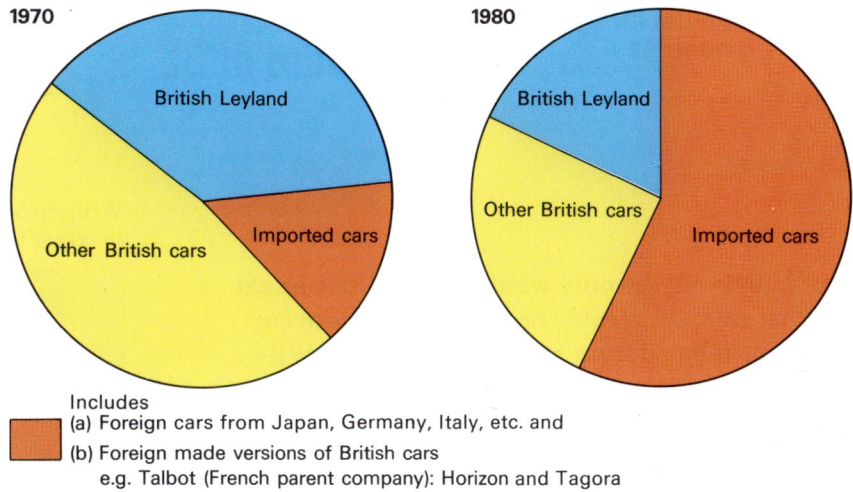

Includes
(a) Foreign cars from Japan, Germany, Italy, etc. and
(b) Foreign made versions of British cars
e.g. Talbot (French parent company): Horizon and Tagora

difficulties, British Leyland, the only one of the big four companies to be wholly British owned, began to improve its production and sales in the early 1980s, and launched the high selling Metro, Maestro and Montego models.

Changing shares of the British car market

1 Name four models of car made by British based companies and four models imported from other countries.

2 Suggest some of the reasons why the British-made share of the British market dropped so dramatically during the 1970s.

3 What are the advantages of one company making most of its own components? Why do even large firms such as BL choose to buy many of its components from other firms such as Lucas, Dunlop and BSC?

4 What are some of the advantages and disadvantages of a) automation of the assembly line, b) firms becoming part of a huge world-wide multinational company?

A BL Maestro being driven past advertisements for two of the foreign cars it hopes to beat

The structure of BL

British Leyland, the only wholly-owned British car manufacturer, illustrates how a large modern car firm has developed from many smaller ones. William Morris, later to become Lord Nuffield, was the first British car maker to adapt the main production techniques of Henry Ford. He built up the important Morris works at Cowley in Oxford. Later on, this company amalgamated with others such as Austin, Rover, Leyland, Wolseley and Riley to become the giant state-controlled British Leyland. In the early 1980s it developed international links by undertaking joint projects with the Japanese Honda company.

The activities of some 45 BL plants and over 500 BL dealers are supported by the computer centre of British Leyland Systems Ltd. in the Worcestershire countryside. £14m. of computer hardware processes some of the thousand million characters of company data, without which most of BL would rapidly come to a halt. BL is a very important British industrial company and its future matters not only to its employees, but also taxpayers, the government, and many other related industries.

The Longbridge assembly plant of British Leyland, Birmingham

William Morris, founder of Morris Motors, in one of the company's early models

British Leyland's main factories and workforces in 1983

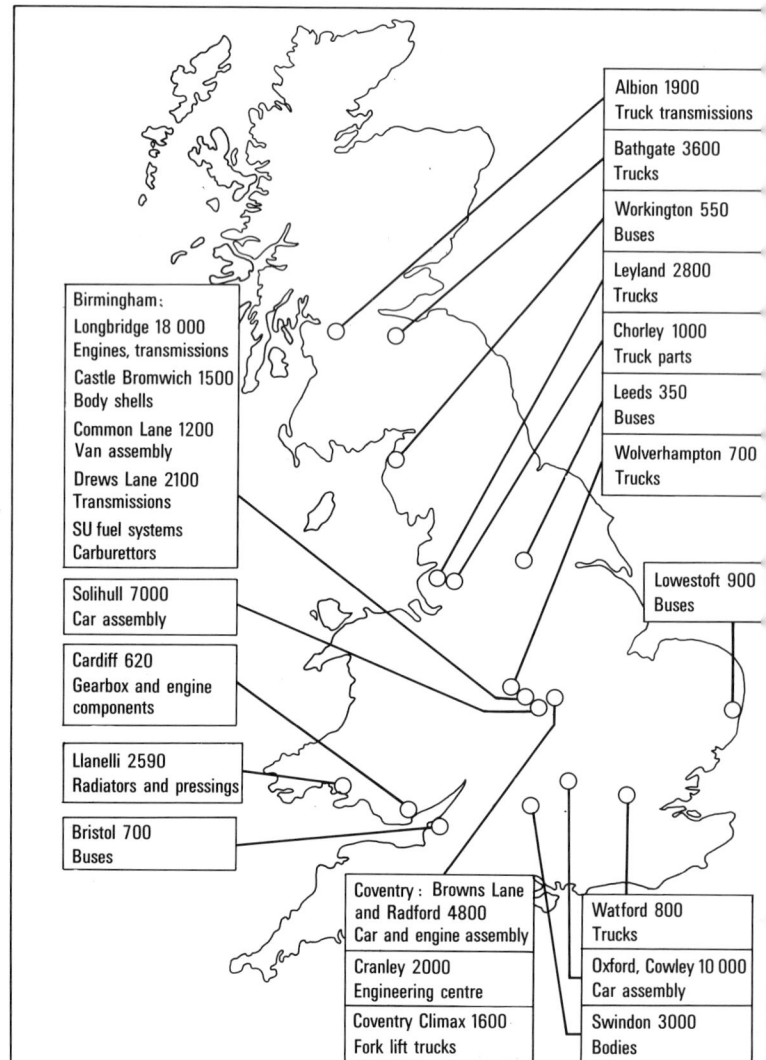

Albion 1900
Truck transmissions

Bathgate 3600
Trucks

Workington 550
Buses

Leyland 2800
Trucks

Chorley 1000
Truck parts

Leeds 350
Buses

Wolverhampton 700
Trucks

Lowestoft 900
Buses

Birmingham:
Longbridge 18 000
Engines, transmissions

Castle Bromwich 1500
Body shells

Common Lane 1200
Van assembly

Drews Lane 2100
Transmissions

SU fuel systems
Carburettors

Solihull 7000
Car assembly

Cardiff 620
Gearbox and engine components

Llanelli 2590
Radiators and pressings

Bristol 700
Buses

Coventry : Browns Lane and Radford 4800
Car and engine assembly

Cranley 2000
Engineering centre

Coventry Climax 1600
Fork lift trucks

Watford 800
Trucks

Oxford, Cowley 10 000
Car assembly

Swindon 3000
Bodies

Exercise 24 **The car industry**

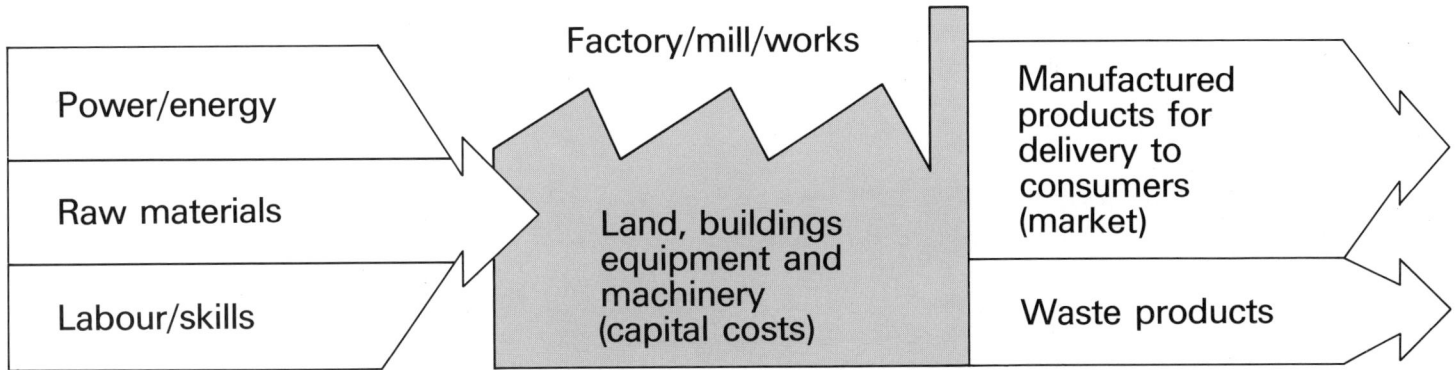

Factory/mill/works

Power/energy		Manufactured products for delivery to consumers (market)
Raw materials	Land, buildings equipment and machinery (capital costs)	
Labour/skills		Waste products

Input	Manufacture	Outputs
Aims To minimise cost of imports Example: reduce cost of transport by choice of location	**Aims** To produce efficiently/ at low cost Example: a good site, modern buildings, equipment, techniques and efficient/skilled work-force	**Aims** To maximise volume/ quality of products leading to high sales Example: high quality and reliable products at a competitive cost

Car sales slide

British-made cars continue to decline in the sales charts, capturing 41.83 per cent in the nine months against 44.24 per cent a year earlier. Meanwhile, cars produced elsewhere in the European Community are increasing their penetration, up from 35.86 to 39.32 per cent.

Ford, the market leader with just under 30 per cent, sold 371140 cars in the nine months but only 190059 were made at British plants. The Japanese importers, still constrained by the voluntary restrictions on shipments imposed by the manufacturers, took 14.19 per cent of the September market but in the nine months remained at just over 11 per cent with combined sales of 138561.

BL, which sold almost 56000 cars in August, managed only 18496 last month to give it a market share of 16.22 per cent against 23.9 per cent a year ago.

Top Ten car sales September 1982

1	Ford Escort	13361
2	Ford Cortina	10348
3	Austin Metro	7196
4	Vauxhall Cavalier	7204
5	Ford Fiesta	5525
6	Datsun Sunny	3296
7	Volvo 300 series	2589
8	Vauxhall Astra	2569
9	Triumph Acclaim	2539
10	VW Polo	2314

There is fierce competition between manufacturers to capture bigger shares of the British market

1 Draw a flow diagram similar to that shown above, but designed and labelled to show what happens at a car assembly plant like the one in the photograph on the opposite page.

2 What are some of the ways in which **a)** transport costs of raw materials could be minimised, **b)** production at the plant be made more efficient, **c)** demand for the product could be increased?

3 Name four towns with BL factories where different sorts of vehicle or component parts are manufactured.

4 What advertising and sales techniques are used by car manufacturers to increase their share of the market?

Changing industry

New factories themselves reflect the use of new materials and building techniques

High technology follows the motorway

This map shows the 'western corridor' which stretches out of London along the M4 motorway. The towns of Bracknell, Reading, Newbury and Swindon lie in this corridor and have attracted many High Technology companies like 3M Ferranti and Hewlett Packard to set up factories. In return these towns are able to offer an established skilled workforce.

American companies are also attracted to the western corridor because it is close to Heathrow Airport and London.

The new buildings that are springing up on the greenfield sites on the edges of these towns combine both factory and offices. They often have to be especially clean and air-conditioned. This new technology may be 'clean' but there will still be a great effect on the environment. Many new houses will have to be built and a lot more traffic will move along the country roads.

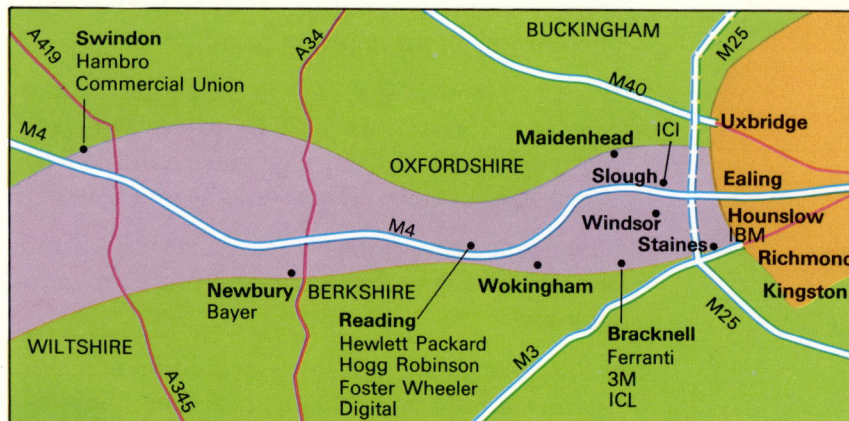

The nature and location of 'light' industry

Most people would agree that when the word 'industry' is used, they think of huge steel-making works, large car and lorry factories or shipyards or the spectacular oil refineries and petro-chemical plants. It should be realised, though, that a great deal of manufacturing takes place in small factories employing a small number of workers. They still perform the same process of converting raw or semi-finished materials into more useful products as the giant factories do, but because the amount of raw materials used and the space needed for the factory is far less they can be located in a wider range of places. Owners usually have more choice in selecting a site and location, and the firms are therefore often said to be 'footloose'. Most towns of any size have a scatter of factories.

In the past these tended to be concentrated around the inner city areas or along rivers, canals and main roads where transport was easy. Many of the small factory areas in inner cities have

Micro-electronics is one of the newer growth-industries. It is factories like the one below that are being attracted to the 'Western Corridor'

been cleared and redeveloped for other uses. In other cases the necessary changes in production methods and scale of operation have meant the owners have been forced to move to better sites in order to survive. Some firms have been able to relocate their works in brand new factories on new sites of their own choice, but many have been unable to afford this and have taken advantage of opportunities provided by industrial estates.

Industrial estates and 'greenfield' sites

Industrial estates are areas where factory buildings, road and sometimes rail links, power supplies and other industrial 'infrastructure' are provided ready for firms to occupy and use. The estates are normally used for manufacturing or warehousing and rarely include shops or houses. They are suitable for the sort of manufacturing where basic components are fairly inexpensive to assemble and products to dispatch – in other words where transport costs are relatively low. They are often found where there is an available workforce. In fact availability of workers is often used as a means of attracting firms to areas of high unemployment. Other locations are likely to prove attractive where there are financial advantages, where there is a pleasant working environment, or where there is easy access to the market. If the market is world-wide, then easy access to international airports and sea ports is an important consideration.

Industrial estates are sometimes provided by private developers, although in recent decades local authorities and the Government have used them to bring new jobs to areas of high unemployment. There are also planned estates on the New Towns which from the beginning are seen as part of the whole new community. Many regions attract manufacturing industries, especially those involved in new technology, by their natural advantages and without government help.

Scotland's 'Silicon Glen'

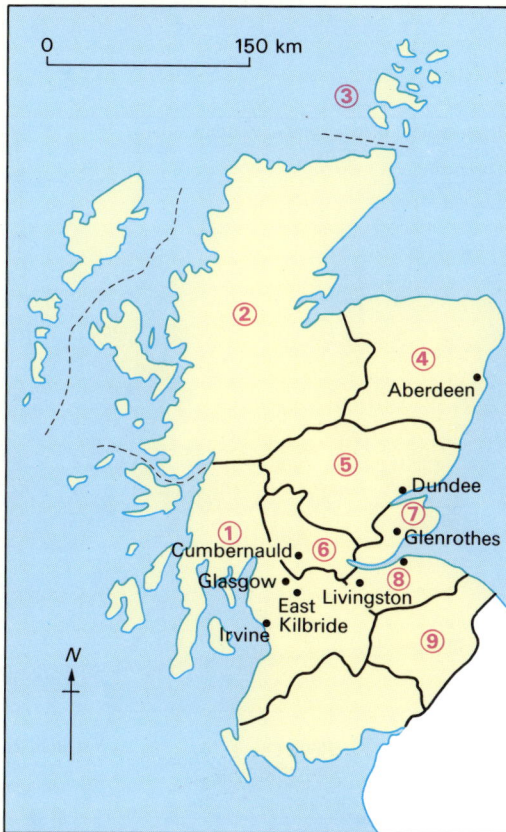

Electronics companies in Scotland

1 **Strathclyde**
   Glasgow 24
   East Kilbride 12
   Cumbernauld 6
   Irvine 2
   Rest of Strathclyde 62

2 **Highland** 9

3 **Islands** 1

4 **Grampian**
   Aberdeen 12
   Rest of Grampian 5

5 **Tayside**
   Dundee 7
   Rest of Tayside 7

6 **Central** 1

7 **Fife**
   Glenrothes 21
   Rest of Fife 16

8 **Lothian**
   Edinburgh 10
   Livingston 14
   Rest of Lothian 13

9 **Borders** 13

Total number of electronics companies in Scotland 235

By 1983 about 40000 people were employed in the electronics industry in Scotland, which is more than shipbuilding and more than steel. It is second only to California as a concentration of high technology industry.

While government grants and loans help to attract foreign companies to Scotland, they are also attracted by the environment, training and university links. One problem with having big multi-nationals set up factories in Scotland is that they are always likely to move out during a recession as part of an overall cut back.

Many parts of Scotland have proved attractive to the electronics industry

1 How do the location needs of newer industries differ from those of more traditional 'heavy' industries?

2 What advantages are offered by 'The Western Corridor' to firms seeking a new factory location and site?

3 What are the attractions of Scotland for factory location? What are some of the dangers of these developments?

The defence industry

Torpedoes
M.S.D.S.,
Portsmouth

Surveillance, tracking and navigation radar
Marconi/Kelvin Hughes,
Chelmsford,
Leicester,
London

Galley
Henry Nuttall,
Rochdale

Furniture
Maine Engineering/
LGR Plastics,
Kings Langley,
Bristol

Air conditioning
Hall Thermotank,
Dartford

Non-ferrous piping
Imperial Metal
Industries,
various locations

Helicopter
Westland,
Yeovil

Computers
Ferranti,
Manchester

Propellers
Stone Manganese
Deptford

Seawolf
British Aerospace,
Bristol, Stevenage

Missile launcher
Vickers, Barrow

Turbines
Rolls-Royce,
Coventry

Also:
Steel for hull
British Steel.
Paint, timber, cable, stores, insulation, fire-fighting equipment
etc.

Gearing
David Brown,
Huddersfield

Bearings
Vickers,
Newcastle

Generators
Paxman/GEC,
various locations

Pumps
Worthing Simpson/Weirs,
Lincoln, Glasgow

Hydraulics
McTaggart Scott,
Edinburgh

Electrical
Alsh,
Poole

Sonar
Plessey,
London

The British companies that benefited from the Royal Navy's order of a new class of frigate in 1982

Most people are unaware of the size of the armaments industry. Making weapons is a major industry employing thousands of people and earning millions of pounds for the armaments companies. Guns, missiles, tanks, planes, ships, communications systems and all the technology of modern warfare are manufactured for sale to the British Government or to other countries.

Arms suppliers to the Third World
(1977–80 in $ Million)

Soviet Union	36138
United States	26522
France	17775
Britain	7084
Italy	5570
West Germany	8307
Other Western Countries	8003
Other Eastern Countries	4478
Total	113877

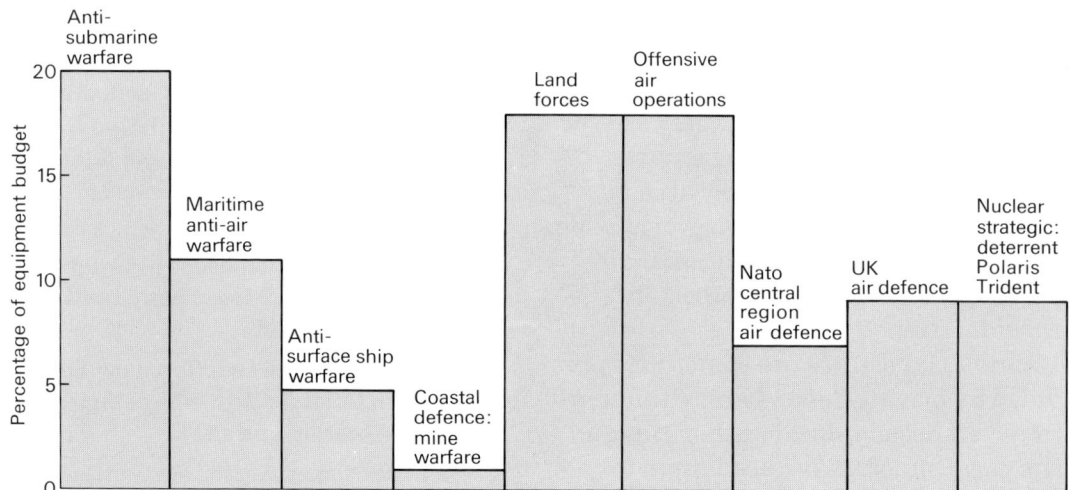

Likely spending on the different parts of the armaments and defence programme, 1980–95

Exercise 25 **Light industry**

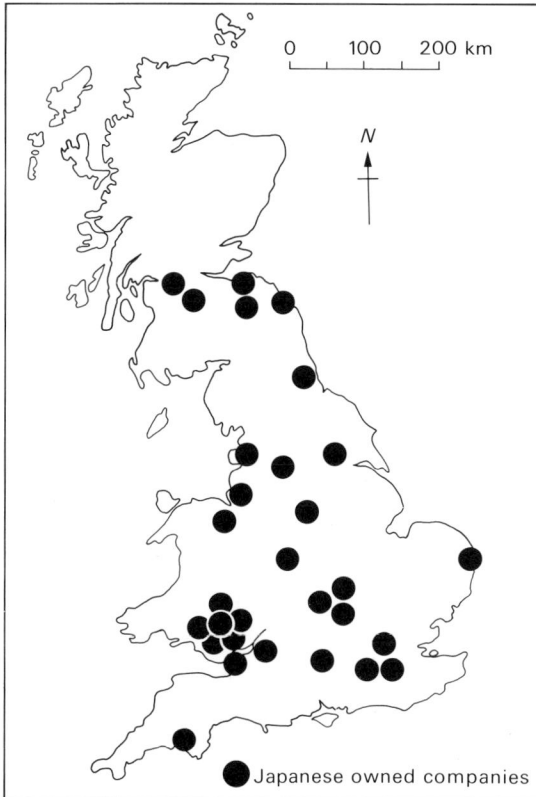

The names, type and location of Japanese-financed companies in Britain

Japanese-financed companies in Britain 1978–81

Name of firm and year commenced	Japanese shareholder (100% except where shown)	Product	Location
1978			
1 Daiwa Sports	Daiwa Seiko Inc (50%)	Fishing rods	Wishaw
2 No Fuse Circuit Breakers	Terasaki Denki (50%)	Circuit breakers	Cowlairs, Glasgow
3 Paddock Fine Worsted	Daido Worsted Mills	Fine worsted	Huddersfield
4 Kubota Tractors	Kubota	Tractor assembly	Selby
5 Sekisui	Sekisui Chemical	Polyethelene	South Wales
1979			
6 GEC-Hitachi	Hitachi (50%)	Colour TVs;	South Wales
7 Mitsubishi Tandberg	Mitsubishi Electric	Colour TVs	Haddington
1980			
8 George Ellison	Mitsubishi Electric (20%)	Electrical equipment	Birmingham
9 Aiwa	Aiwa	Music centres	South Wales
10 Hoya Lens	Hoya	Spectacle lens	Wrexham
11 Tamura Kaken	Tamura Kaken	Printing ink	Northants
1981			
12 Toshiba	Toshiba	Colour TVs	Plymouth
13 NEC Semiconductors	NEC	Integrated circuits	Livingston
14 Yuasa	Yuasa Battery	Lead batteries	South Wales
15 Dainichi/Sykes	Dainichi (50%)	Industrial robots	Lancashire
16 Sanyo	Sanyo	TV sets	Lowestoft

Japanese workers inside a factory at Peterlee

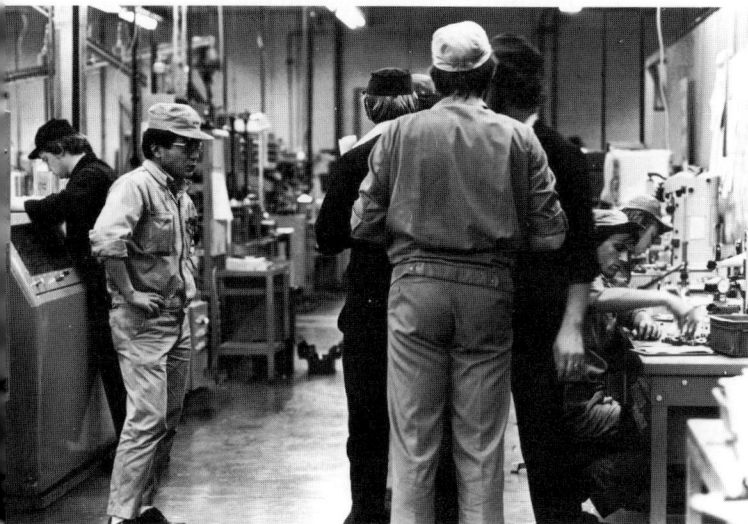

One feature of light industry in the past few decades has been the increased investment of money in British firms by foreign companies. The map shows the location of 30 firms with Japanese ownership or part ownership. The table lists 16 of these firms that were set up between 1978 and 1981. These manufacturing or assembly plants employed about 15 000 workers.

1 Put into your own words the general distribution of these Japanese owned or part owned companies. Where is the largest cluster?

2 What might attract Japanese firms to invest in British factories?

3 Describe two of the most common *types* of product from the factories in the list.

Aid to industry

Steel closure and Development Areas

The British Government and Local Authorities try in various ways to influence where industries are located. It is difficult for firms to get permission to open new factories in some areas where

An advertisement describing some of the help available for new factory development

A unique chance to get your factory project on the map.

If you're relocating or expanding, British Steel Corporation (Industry) Ltd, will help set up your business in any of these locations. All you need is a viable project that will create new jobs, and an eye for a unique incentive package.

LOANS UNDER 10%
Special arrangements with the European Coal and Steel Community means you can receive loans way below Bank Rate.

NEW FACTORIES RENT-FREE INITIALLY
Ready-built or custom-made factories, rent-free for up to two years on fully serviced sites.

HEAVILY SUBSIDISED WORKFORCE TRAINING
Grants can cover at least ⅔rds. of in-house training costs.

FREE FEASIBILITY STUDY
The viability of your project is vital, so we're prepared to pay for an independent assessment.

SUBSTANTIAL GOVERNMENT GRANTS
We know the system and we'll help you receive the maximum support available.

SPECIALIST TEAM TO CUT FORMALITIES
Our team of experts will help you cut through red tape and speed up your project implementation.
For details, ring our Action Desk on **01-235 1212** Ext. 200, or post the coupon.

• CAMBUSLANG
• MOTHERWELL
• GARNOCK VALLEY
DERWENTSIDE •
HARTLEPOOL/TEESSIDE •
• DEESIDE
CORBY •
BLAENAU GWENT
PORT TALBOT
NEWPORT
CARDIFF

BSCindustry
42 Grosvenor Gardens, London SW1W 0EB.
I want the above and more. Send me the details.
Name _____
Position _____
Company _____
Address _____
Tel. No: _____ CST/1

It pays to get moving.

there is no severe unemployment. On the other hand, where unemployment is high and many industries have closed down, local and national government may provide a lot of financial and other aid to persuade firms to locate there. Since industries pay high rates, many local authorities also try to encourage firms to locate in their areas. We have seen how the provision of industrial estates are often an attraction. In the so-called Development and Special Development Areas, (which are more or less those places where employment used to be provided by heavy industries such as mining, steelmaking and ship-building) financial aid is provided by the Government. Sometimes money is given or loaned directly to particular industries, both private and national-ised. But, in spite of this aid, it does not always result in secure and permanent production and employment. The BSC industry map and advertisement shows that areas that have lost jobs through closure of steelworks can get aid from other sources such as the EEC. In all these cases the aim is to try to get new jobs and fresh economic life back into hard-hit areas since under normal circumstances firms do not want to or cannot afford to locate there.

Enterprise Zones

Eleven Enterprise Zones were established in the early 1980s to give even more help to particularly needy areas. They are quite small and range in character from Dudley in the West Midlands, an area scattered with disused mineshafts where unemployment was about 15 per cent, to Speke in Liverpool where 2500 jobs had just been lost by the transfer of the TR7 British Leyland car to the Midlands factories, and Clydebank that had seen the loss of over 40 000 jobs in the previous 20 years.

The incentives include tax relief on factory buildings, exemption from paying rates for 10 years (the Government pay these instead to the Local Authorities concerned), exemption from land development taxes, freedom from some planning controls and so on. Some critics of the scheme think that the areas are so rundown because of poor housing, transport and shortage of skilled labour, that firms will not be attracted in spite of the aid they could get. The signs are however that some firms are moving in and considerable interest is being shown by others.

Another complaint is that the zones merely attract firms that would have gone somewhere else anyway. They are not creating new jobs, but just shifting them from other places whose needs might be almost as great. With all the aid they get, firms in the zones can compete easily with those outside.

Yet another criticism is that the zones attract the wrong sort of firms – warehouses and hypermarkets rather than factories. Against this, it is argued that modern automated factories provide no more jobs than warehouses, hypermarkets and offices. Further enterprise zones have been identified even though many people doubt their value to the regions concerned.

Tyneside, one of the original Enterprise Zones

1 Compare the two maps. Which Enterprise Zones include a BSC Industry Aid area? Why should BSC be involved in providing aid to other firms in these particular places shown on the map?

2 List the Enterprise Zones in rank order according to their size. Which zone is nearest to your school area?

3 Government aid comes from taxes paid by most working people. Do you think it right that such money should be given to help a particular small area? Explain your reasons for agreeing or disagreeing. Do you think aid should be restricted to certain sorts of work or types of product? If so, say why, and what you think the restrictions should include.

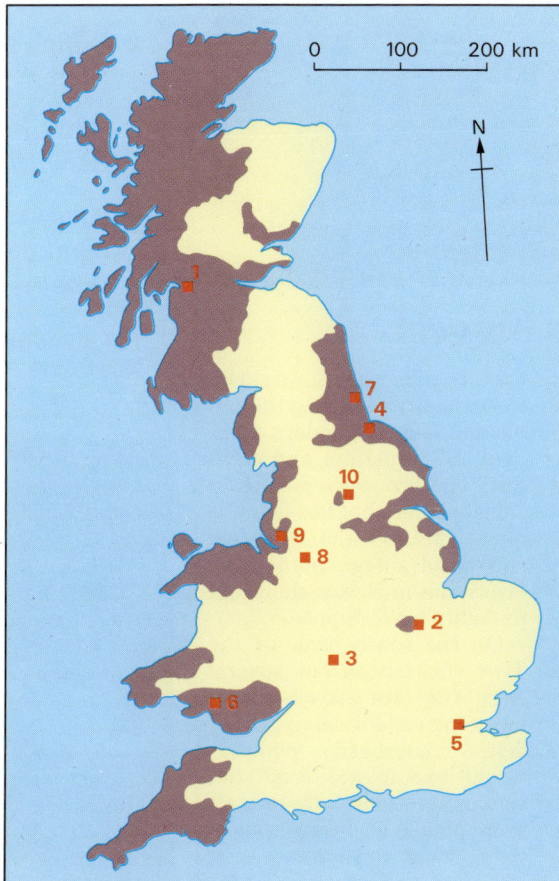

The location of the original ten Enterprise Zones in Britain

Development areas
a) Grants for buildings, machinery and equipment
b) Assistance with training
c) Other assistance with relocation

Enterprise Zones
a) No rates till 1991
b) Simplified planning procedures
c) Other allowances and tax reductions

The first ten Enterprise Zones in Britain (one in Belfast)

		Land areas in acres
1	Clydebank	570
2	Corby	280
3	Dudley	538
4	Hartlepool	270
5	Isle of Dogs	360
6	Lower Swansea Valley	735
7	Newcastle/Gateshead	1100
8	Salford/Trafford	870
9	Speke	328
10	Wakefield	140

Exercise 26 Aid to industry: Tyneside

Tyneside lies within a development area as well as having an Enterprise Zone

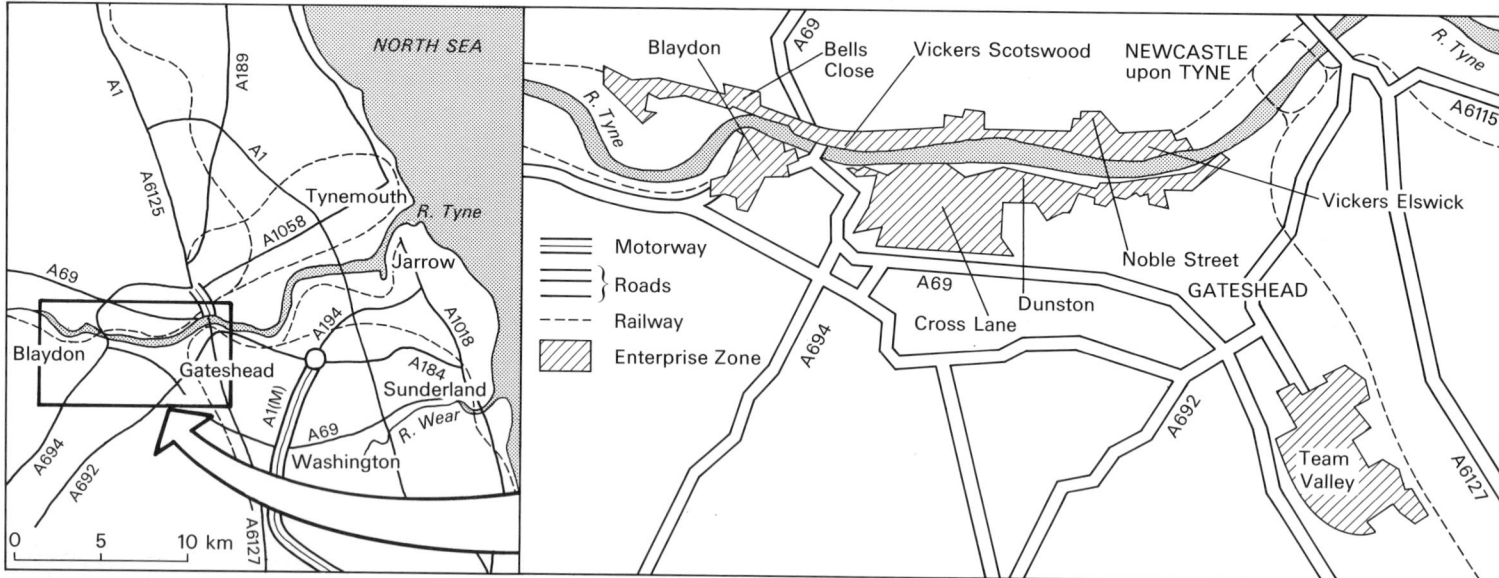

Legend:
- Motorway
- Roads
- Railway
- Enterprise Zone

This is Britain's biggest

Tyneside has Britain's biggest Enterprise Zone. Its 1100 acres are scattered along both banks of the heavily-industrialized river. There is also a 'detached place in the country' offering greenfield sites a mile and a half away, part of Team Valley estate.

North of the Tyne, the Enterprise Zone has encouraged Vickers Engineering to build a £7.5m factory on a 22-acre site at Scotswood. At the same time the company is releasing about 70 acres at Elswick, the end of the zone nearest to the city centre. The works there are to be demolished. Vickers has moved because it would be too expensive to bring the old buildings up to modern standards of insulation and comfort. The firm once employed 20 000 people, but this figure is now 1 200 and without the rate and tax advantages of the zone operations in Newcastle would probably have stopped.

On the south bank of the Tyne, Gateshead has several large sites for development, but some need to be upgraded first. Gateshead planners would like to see retail development there to attract some people who travel out of the borough to shop.

1 Describe the traditional industries located **a)** along the banks of the lower River Tyne, **b)** in the Team Valley Industrial Estate.

2 Which are the two local authorities with a share in the Tyneside Enterprise Zone?

3 What is the advantage of the Scotswood over the Elswick site for the new Vickers factory?

4 Apart from factories, what other sort of development do the Gateshead planners hope to attract. What is their reason for wanting this?

The giant new Vickers armaments factory at Scotswood in Newcastle

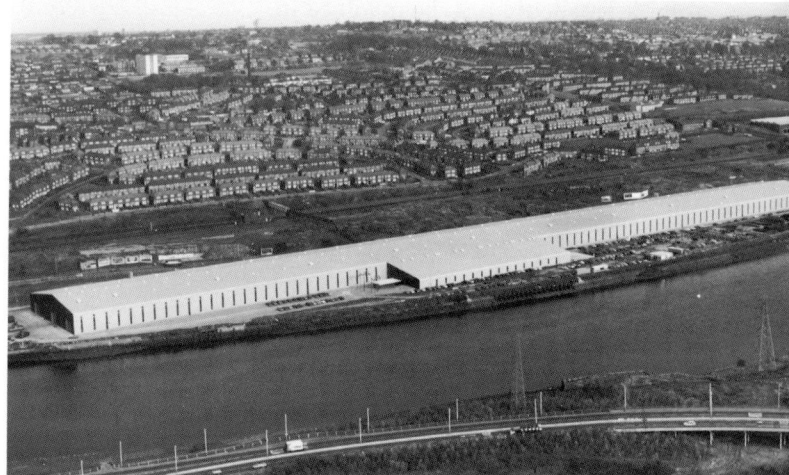

Chapter 5 The service industries

Shops and services

A typical High Street scene

The service industries

There are many ways of describing and classifying the jobs people do, and one used by the government was shown on page 90. A part of it is shown again below, and it is a reminder that very many people work in the 'service' industries. Some idea of the wide range of activities included are given in the diagram, and each of these main groups can be further sub-divided.

Many men and women are employed in transport, either carrying the raw materials and products to and from farms, mines and factories or carrying people from place to place. Others work in warehouses, wholesale markets and shops handling and selling these products. Yet another group handles the accounting and financial sides of business and trade. As the table shows there are other types of 'services' provided by people such as solicitors, doctors, entertainers, research workers, civil servants and so on. The list of jobs is enormous, and it is not really surprising that the total number of people working in the service industries is greater than in all the other jobs put together. Agriculture, mining, fishing and forestry is sometimes called the 'primary sector' and manufacturing the 'secondary sector' of the economy. In a similar way the service industries are grouped into the 'tertiary sector', or third major group of jobs. This high proportion of people in the service industries is a feature of most industrialised countries.

Shops and shopping

Some things can be bought directly from a producer or owner, such as pick-your-own fruit or vegetables. Others such as mail-order goods or milk may be delivered directly to the consumer. But the vast majority of items that are bought and sold are handled by some sort of market, store or shop. This is usually because it is more efficient for buyer and seller to have goods gathered together in this way, or because the sellers have some particular expertise or skill in selling.

The nature and size of markets and shops varies enormously. Some are places where goods are sold by auction, such as a livestock markets in some country towns, or auction rooms in the largest cities, that handle expensive luxury goods. Others are wholesale markets where producers sell their goods to merchants and traders, who then take them to their own retail shops for final sale to the customer. Smithfield, and the new Covent Garden and Billingsgate, are good examples of wholesale markets. They are all in London, though others can be found in most large towns and cities.

Some shops, ranging from very small to very large, sell a wide variety of goods. Examples include the small corner shop and the big department

People in employment in the United Kingdom 1982 (thousands)

Agriculture, forestry and fishing	354
Mining	326
Manufacturing	5752
Construction	1049
Gas, water, electricity	340
Services	13282
Total	21103

The tertiary sector, which includes the service industries, is a bigger employer than the primary or secondary sectors

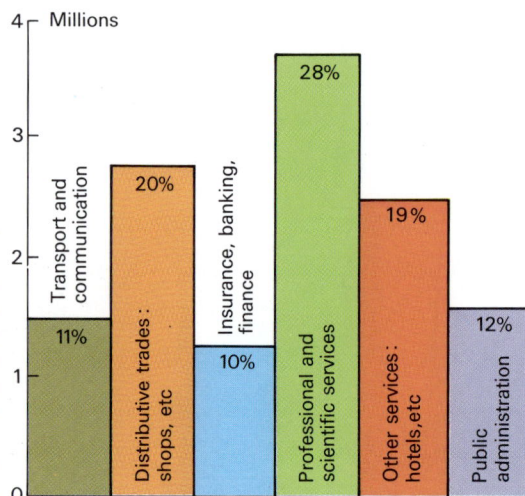

store. Others specialise in a particular range of goods such as clothes, groceries, cameras and cars. These also come in all shapes and sizes. The family-owned shop is still quite common, but more and more shops are now part of larger organisations with branches in many different parts of the country.

Shopping patterns

The diagram illustrates several important facts about shopping habits and patterns. The first is that the average person or family is likely to make many more shopping trips for some items than for others. Even with the growth of shopping by car it is likely that many more trips for food will be made than for, say, furniture or clothes. Generally speaking, people like to look around more for the expensive items that they buy only now and then. They are prepared to go further to get exactly what they need at a price they can afford. In any case it may be that some expensive goods are only obtainable in a large or specialist store in a nearby town or city. On the other hand, people are likely to go to their corner shop or local grocers many times a month, and apart from situations described in the next section, they will not want to travel too far to buy everyday items. Put in another way, this means that the 'catchment area' or 'sphere of influence' of a corner shop or small grocers is likely to be small. People will shop there frequently because it is nearby. On the other hand the catchment area of a large store can be very large, but customers will only visit the store a few times a year.

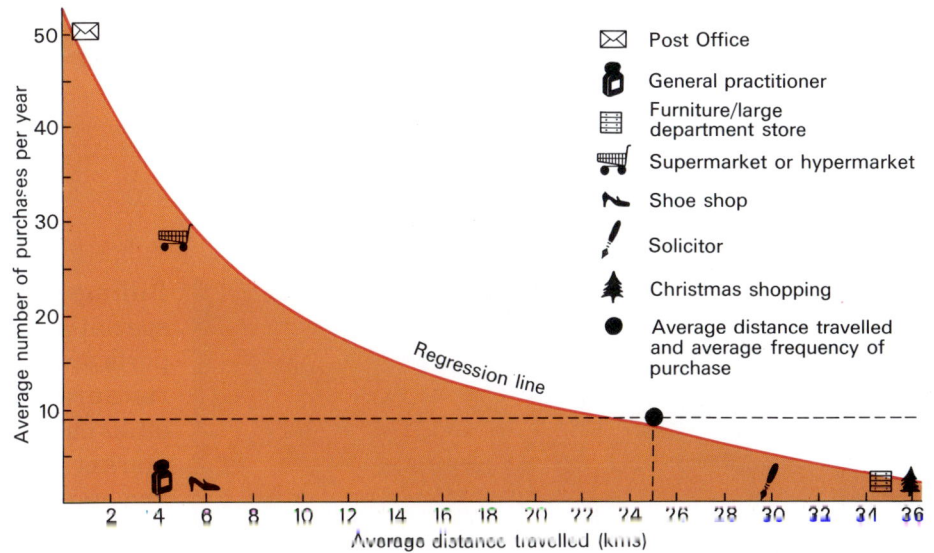

Post Office
General practitioner
Furniture/large department store
Supermarket or hypermarket
Shoe shop
Solicitor
Christmas shopping
Average distance travelled and average frequency of purchase

The shopping habits of a small sample of people in Clitheroe, Lancs

Not all shops and services visited or used only infrequently need be distant ones. People may only visit a doctor once or twice a year, but most live within reasonable distance of a surgery. What happens of course is that some people will be visiting it to consult the doctor every day, so it is important that a surgery is accessible. The varied use of shops and services has a big influence on their location, as we shall see.

1 List the sorts of shop used by you and your family a) about once a week or more, b) only once or twice a year. Account for the difference.

2 Name (if possible) a shop and its products that you have used a) less than 0.5 kilometres, b) between 1 and 2 kilometres, c) more than 5 kilometres away from your home in the past year.

3 What was the average distance travelled by Clitheroe people to a) a doctor b) a solicitor? Suggest reasons for the difference.

Left: This corner shop uses colour and interesting displays to attract shoppers

Large stores such as Selfridges use lavish displays and advertising to increase sales

Billingsgate: A wholesale market

This view gives a scene of working conditions in the old Billingsgate market

The new market overlooking the old West India Dock was opened in January 1982. It includes a display area, offices, a new cold store and sheltered off-loading bays for over 600 lorries

The location of the old and new Billingsgate markets

Billingsgate is an example of a wholesale market. It specialises in the sale of fish brought in from fishing ports around the coast of Britain. Fishmongers, restaurant owners, fish-and-chip sellers and many other customers buy their daily supplies from the market. It handles about 200 tonnes of fish a day and employs 500 people.

The old and new sites

Billingsgate market is very old indeed, and for many centuries it was located at Lower Thames Street in the City of London. The quarters were cramped, and fish had to be left stored on lorries, until customers loaded it onto their own transport. The surrounding roads were heavily congested and the ancient basement cold store was not really adequate.

The new market is about 5 kilometres downstream on the Isles of Dogs and was opened in 1982. Rates are higher than on the old site and merchants have to pay for all the services. But there are considerable advantages. There is far more space for the hundreds of lorries, and the working conditions are better. Most lorries delivering to the market come in from the east, early in the morning, so a location in East London is helpful. Many of the porters and market workers also live in the East End and are nearer their work than before. West London buyers, however, have to drive their vans back from the market during the early morning rush-hour. On balance though, the new site and location should be more efficient than the old one.

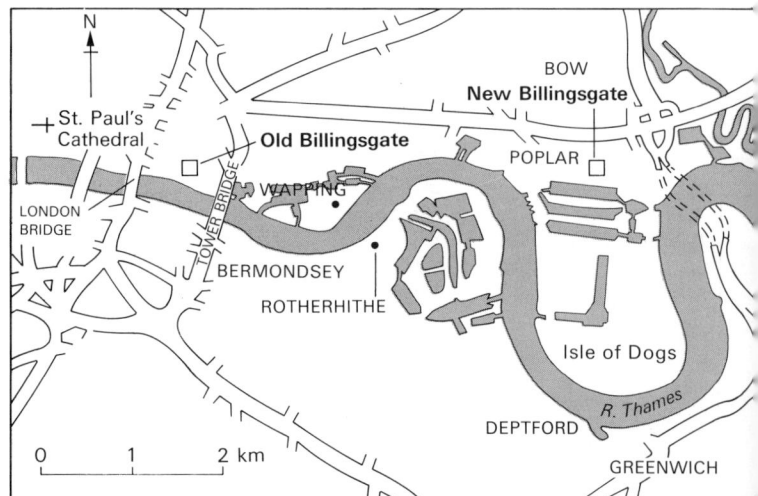

Exercise 27 **Hierarchy of settlements, shops and services**

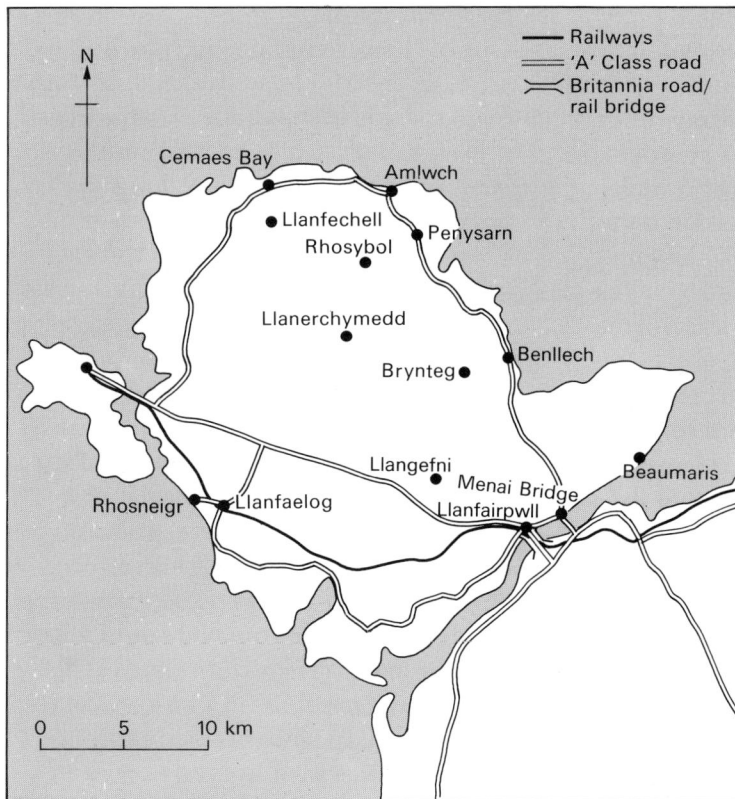

Anglesey, showing the location of the settlements studied in the survey

1 In the table, Llangefini and Rhosneigr have unexpected numbers of shops and services for their populations. What is the unusual feature in each case? Try to give a possible explanation.

2 Apart from the unusual settlements just mentioned, does there seem to be any general link or correlation between settlement population and total number of services? If there is, what do you notice about it?

3 Indicate Llangefini and Rhosneigr on the graph. Does the graph confirm the answer given in question 2? How can you tell?

4 If the settlements were to be grouped into three 'orders' of importance for total services, where would you draw the two horizontal lines on your graph? When you have made your decision, colour in the symbols on the map in one of three colours according to its order. What do you notice about the location of the different orders? Try to explain the general pattern and any unexpected ones.

A table and scattergraph to show information on the settlements in Anglesey

	Occupied houses	Total no. of services	Shops	Professional services
Llangefini	1 000	37	27	10
Beaumaris	908	58	49	9
Benllech	800	43	36	7
Amlwch	756	41	31	10
Llanfiarpwll	688	10	6	4
Menai Bridge	578	37	27	10
Camaes Bay	371	23	17	4
Llanerchymedd	265	10	7	3
Llanfechel	242	2	1	1
Rhosybol	200	2	2	0
Penysarn	126	7	7	0
Llanfaelog	96	3	3	0
Rhosneigr	95	23	21	2
Brynteg	66	2	2	0
Llanfaes	82	1	1	0

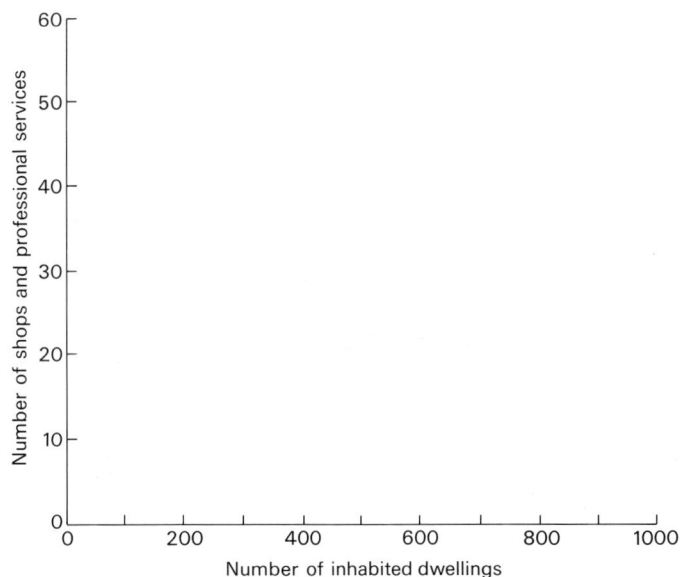

115

Supermarkets and superstores

The check-out point at a supermarket

Chain and multiple stores

In the past most shops were owned by individuals or families. Some successful owners used their profits to buy other shops or to increase the size and range of goods sold in their first one. Large companies grew up which nowadays own most shops. Frequently they are part of even larger organisations. The table shows the leading grocery firms, though the trend to large group ownership applies just as much to other commodities such as clothing, shoes, furniture and electrical items. Grocery shops belonging to some of the firms in the list are found in almost every large town in Britain. There is often fierce competition between them to attract customers by such things as price cutting, discount schemes, time of opening and convenience of paying for goods. Nearness to transport facilities is also important. The methods of retailing and the location of retail shops is always changing.

The distribution and growth of superstores in Britain

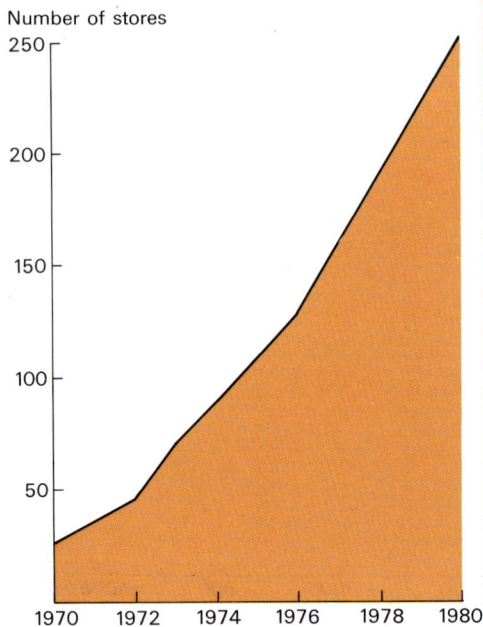

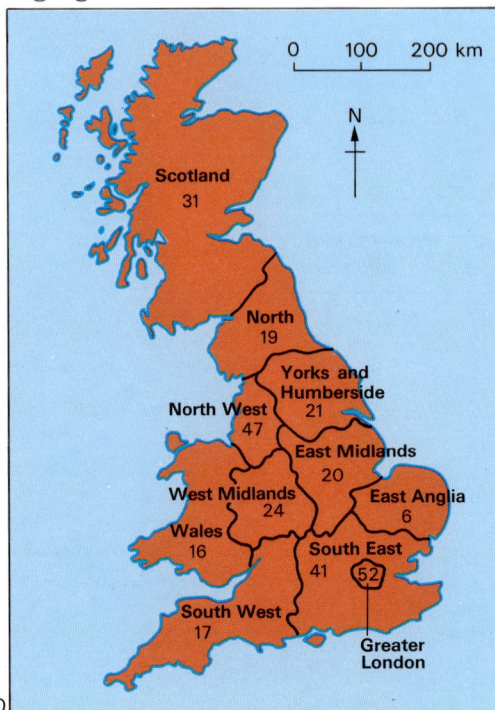

Supermarkets

One of the big changes in retailing took place in the 1960s, with the shift from over-the-counter sales by shopkeepers and their assistants, to a system where customers took what they wanted from open shelves and paid at a cash point. Staff were employed to keep the shelves stocked from the storerooms and serve at the cash-points, rather than to serve customers. There were still many shops where goods could only be bought from shop assistants, of course, but this was not the style of the supermarket. Because the supermarket could buy in bulk from the wholesalers, and cut costs of wages it could be more efficient. Profits came from the rapid turnover of goods, so the supermarket could afford to offer lower prices than those at the more traditional family grocer. On the other hand, in spite of its greater efficiency, some people even now prefer the personal attention provided by the older selling methods. Nevertheless, most 'high streets' have their scatter of supermarkets reflecting the changed pattern of retailing.

The growth of superstores

Most people will be familiar with the crowded conditions of many shopping areas and the difficulty of carrying the shopping to the bus stop or car park – if parking is available, that is! At certain times road traffic can get extremely congested, and this adds to the wear and tear of shopping. The costs of land, as well as of rent or rates in central areas are usually very high. Sometimes all these problems outweigh the advantages of being located at the centre, with its many potential customers. As a result, some firms have moved to completely new locations in the suburbs or on the fringes of the cities, and built

very much larger shops, known as superstores.

A superstore has been defined as having at least 25 000 square feet (2367 sq. m.) of sales area. This means it is much bigger than the average supermarket. Some are much bigger than this because they carry many non-food lines such as gardening and do-it-yourself items. They are spacious, often rather garish in design, with comfortable and wide shopping aisles and long rows of check-out points. Above all, they have huge car parks. People travel to them from long distances, and do a lot of their shopping in one go. (This is apart from the regular items bought from small local shops, and major items which are bought infrequently, such as furniture or clothes.) Because most people travel to the superstore by car once or twice a week, and get most of their needs there, this is sometimes known as 'one-stop shopping'.

The superstore trend in Britain started in earnest with Asda (part of the Leeds-based Associated Dairies Group) in the north of England. The graph shows how numbers increased during the 1970s. There were about 300 superstores in Britain in 1982, and it was thought these would double in number by 1986. Over thirty were opened in 1980 providing employment for more than 6000 people. Most of the companies listed in the table are increasing their number of superstores, though some have a concentration in certain parts of the country. Asda for example, have concentrated their developments outside the South. A rough idea of the distribution of supermarkets is given in the map.

Not everyone benefits from the growth of supermarkets and superstores. People without cars may find access to the superstores very difficult, while carrying large amounts of shopping from the supermarket in the town centre by bus is often troublesome, especially during rush hour or if the service is poor. The superstores have provided some new jobs in a time of growing unemployment but, as the caption about Fine Fare suggests, they may have led to loss of trade or closure of small independent shops and smaller stores in the older shopping areas. There is also the fear that as fewer and fewer large outlets become the only place to buy things, prices may go up and there may be less choice for the customer.

1 Give the names of several non-grocery chain stores in your town. What are their main 'lines' or items for sale?

2 Describe a) why you like or dislike supermarkets, b) the benefits and disadvantages of superstores.

3 Compare the map with the table on page 60. Is there any correlation between the population of a Standard Region and the number of superstores and hypermarkets? Suggest reasons for any unexpectedly high or low figures of superstore growth.

Fine Fare opens superstore in Warrington

Fine Fare is part of Associated British Foods (see page 88). There are 627 stores in the Fine Fare Group in Britain – 38 superstores, 180 shoppers paradise discount stores, 10 distribution and two cash-and-carry warehouses.

Fine Fare, through a combination of strong marketing and competitive pricing policies, has maintained a good rate of growth, and in 1981 all three of its operating divisions, superstores, supermarkets and Shopper's Paradise showed increases in sales volume. Fine Fare increased its share of the United Kingdom grocery market by about 5.4 per cent.

New superstores were opened at Redcar, Hartlepool, Elgin and Warrington, whilst a separate do-it-yourself branch was opened at Welwyn Garden City. By the end of the year Fine Fare was operating 37 superstores with the 38th opened at Bishopbriggs, Glasgow in April. The Warrington superstore is of particular interest as not only is it Fine Fare's largest selling area, but is the first to be opened featuring a new concept in interior decor and design.

Leaders in the grocery league table (January 1980)

	%
Co-op grocers	17.4
Tesco	13.6
Sainsbury	11.9
Asda	7.3
Independent grocers	7.2
International Stores	5.2
Fine Fare	5.0
Kwiksave	4.9
Allied Suppliers	4.8
Spar	3.2
Marks & Spencer	1.9
Key Markets	1.8
VG	1.6
Mace	1.5
Waitrose	1.3
Safeway	1.2
Boots	0.8
Woolworth	0.7

Hypermarkets and superstores

The hypermarket at Washington, near Newcastle-on-Tyne

A typical newspaper advertisement for a new superstore

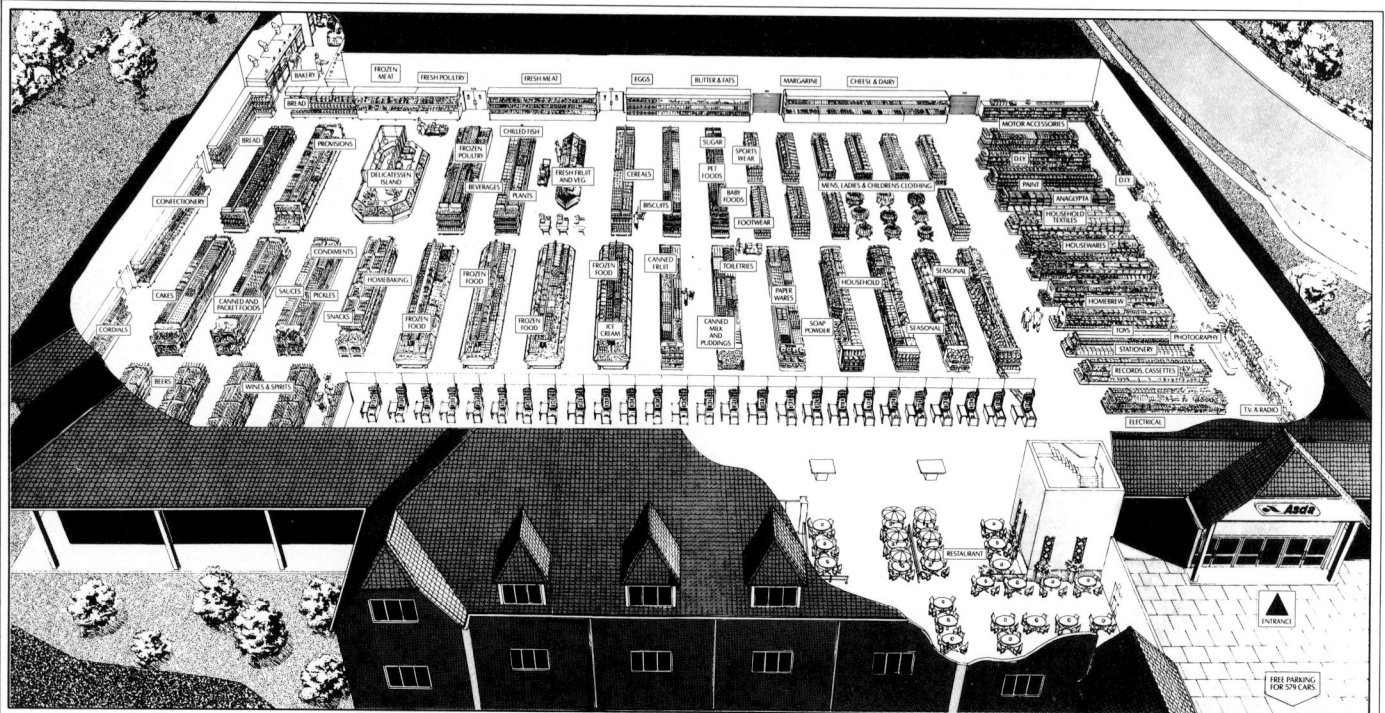

There is no strict distinction between superstores and hypermarkets, though the hypermarket is the larger of the two types of 'shop' and sells many more 'luxury' goods. There are not many true hypermarkets in Britain. Those at Caerphilly in South Wales, Bristol, Telford, Eastleigh in Hampshire and Swindon are probably the best known. As with supermarkets, they have large floor space and huge car-parking areas. They tend to be in locations more distant from the city and town centres than superstores, but they are very accessible by road. This is essential to enable large amounts of goods to be regularly delivered and collected by customers. The superstore advertised below could equally well be considered a hypermarket. Other superstores are big enough but do not qualify because they are in a district centre development. Whatever the details and names given to them, these huge superstores and hypermarkets have revolutionised shopping during the past decade.

ASDA HIGH WYCOMBE OPENS TUESDAY OCTOBER 25th.

TAKE A LOOK AROUND BEFORE EVERYONE ELSE DOES.

If you've never been to an Asda Superstore before, then now's the time to put yourself well and truly in the picture.

Take a look around the store plan above. Impressive don't you think?

Did you count the number of different departments? There are 21 of them. And each and every one offers a choice that we'd be hard pushed to better. (In our groceries department, for example, we have so many biscuits you could have 'elevenses' every day for the next six months and never taste the same variety twice.)

Mind you, there would be little point in spoiling you for choice if you weren't also assured of value. Which is where Asda Price comes in. Because, right throughout the store, you'll find Asda Price to be both remarkably low and (more importantly) consistently low.

We like to believe that shopping at Asda is an experience that the whole family can enjoy. And, thanks to Asda Price and free parking for 579 cars, one that every family can afford.

And after having had a quick look around your brand new Asda Superstore aren't you looking forward to the real thing?

ALL TOGETHER, BETTER.

Asda SUPERSTORES

ASDA HIGH WYCOMBE OPENS 9AM NEXT TUESDAY.

CREST ROAD, CRESSEX.

OPENING HOURS: MONDAY, TUESDAY, WEDNESDAY, THURSDAY, SATURDAY 8.30AM-8PM AND FRIDAY 8.30AM-9PM.

Exercise 28 **Hypermarket at Bristol**

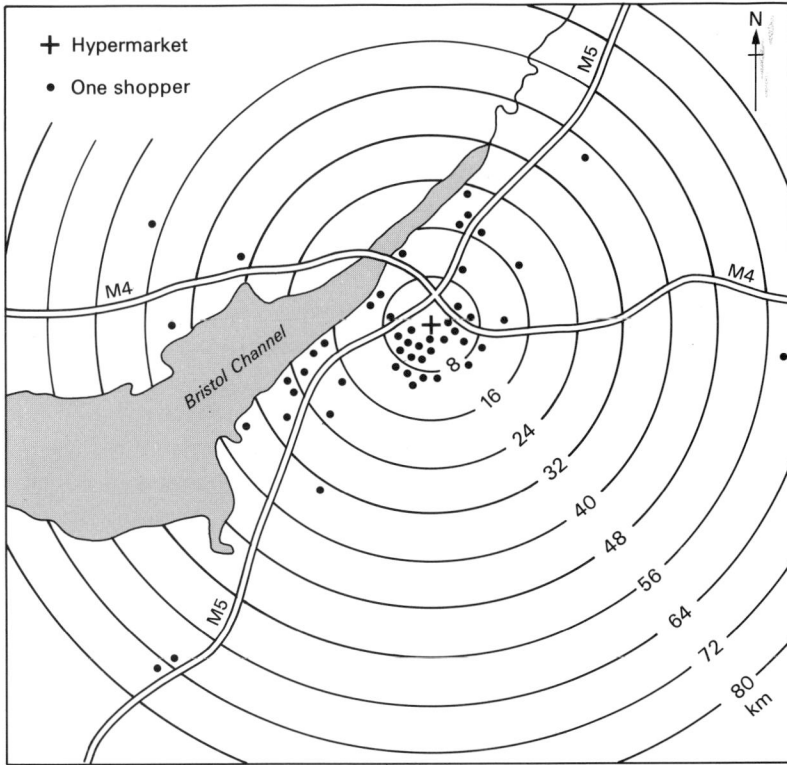

The distances a sample of shoppers travelled to the Carrefour hypermarket, near Bristol

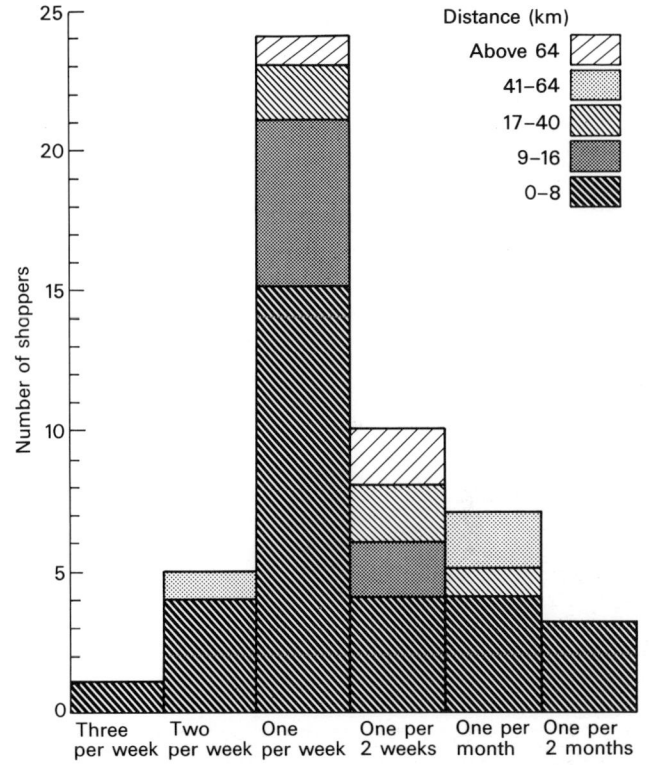

Frequency of shopping trips to the Carrefour hypermarket

1 From this map and the one on page 123, describe the location of the Carrefour hypermarket at Bristol. From the photograph here describe the site.

2 Describe the location of the homes of the shoppers that travelled more than 32 kilometres. What seems to be the important influence determining their journey? Why is *distance* a poor indicator of accessibility? Describe at least two other indicators of accessibility.

3 Which were the two most usual frequency of visits? Which distances were least represented in the three per week category? Why is this hardly surprising?

The Carrefour hypermarket, with its large car parking area, is adjacent to the M5 motorway

The location of offices

The old civic local authority offices contrast with new commercial high-rise offices in central Birmingham

A typical advertisement for a new office development on a 'greenfield' site

Offices and office workers

The wide variety of retail and wholesale shops are an important part of the urban landscape and contribute a great deal to the service or tertiary sector of industry. Very similar comments could be made about offices and the jobs that office workers do.

Many offices are parts of other buildings and service the activities that go on in them. Examples range from small offices with one or two secretaries as found in schools, doctor's surgeries or small businesses to the much larger ones that are part of large manufacturing companies or hospitals. In some cases the office work is very general, in others very specialised, dealing with such things as design, accounts, wages and salaries or public relations. Nowadays most towns of any size contain special office buildings. These may be in older buildings converted from an earlier use or, more often in modern, architect designed structures (see Basildon, page 126). Sometimes thousands of office workers are employed in one specialised building, and all work for one company. One of the more spectacular of these is the Head Office of The National Westminster Bank in the City of London, shown on page 56. Then there are other specialised offices such as Post Offices and those where Local Authority and Central Government work is done. The size, type of building, and nature of work performed in offices in Britain is enormously varied.

Location of offices

Quite obviously offices that are part of other activities are located where the main activity is found. So some will be found in or near factories, shops and schools. Many offices, however, tend to concentrate in certain parts of a town or city. This is because of the economic advantages of being in an 'office area'. This is particularly so in central areas or important suburban centres. Traffic routes usually focus on these places, and this means that workers can get to and from work relatively easily. On the other hand, the movement of large numbers of office workers to one place at one time means there is often enormous traffic congestion during the so-called 'rush hours'. Because these central areas are desirable locations, the cost of land is very high. One of the few ways of reducing costs is to build high, hence the growth of massive high-rise office blocks. This results in huge amounts of office space in small ground areas. This saves on some costs, but rates and rents can still be very high, while the increased numbers of workers in high rise offices adds to the travel problems. As will be seen in the next

To Let   EUROPA HOUSE Basingstoke

160 000 sq. ft
Possession summer 1985
40 000 sq. ft
available now

This award-winning office building is close to the M3 motorway, 50 miles west of London and 34 miles from Heathrow Airport.

You pay *one quarter less* in rent and rates compared with a city location.

For details, contact sole agents:
Smith and Jones 01–234–5678

section, offices are major land users in the Central Business Districts of most towns and cities.

New office locations

Office design and location is changing in the same way as the pattern and location of retailing is changing. These two examples suggest the main features of the changes. The advertisement for Europa House suggests many of the features of a modern office building and the attractions of the location.

The Aztec West development is very new. It is the first true 'greenfield' development, including both office and industrial space on the American model, to be built in Britain. It will eventually comprise about two million square feet of warehouse, office and industrial space on a landscaped site of 170 acres, and include shops, banks and leisure facilities. The aim is to create a 'village centre' atmosphere for the skilled staff who will work there. There is a special demand from companies in the micro-electronics industry for factories, laboratories and newly designed offices in locations such as Aztec West. Money for the development is provided by pension funds, and the investors hope to get a return on their money from rents for the factories, warehouses and offices.

Among the advantages of the location are the lower rents and rates, while the good car parking facilities and attractive environmental features such as landscaping and tree planting make it a pleasant place for the employees.

1 Give some of the advantages and disadvantages of a central town location for **a)** the company owning an office, **b)** an office worker, **c)** the Local Authority.

2 Describe some of the reasons why rush hour office journeys to and from work are likely to be different in the future.

3 From the advertisement and extract list the advantages claimed for Basingstoke as a location for offices.

The location of towns dealt with in this chapter

Aztec West Office Park on the outskirts of Bristol, near the junction of the M5 and M4 motorways

Basingstoke ideal site for office park

In the latest issue of *Savills' Property Trends Bulletin* Basingstoke is cited as a place where a purpose-built office/business estate was developed from green fields outside the town itself. As a location, Basingstoke fits the bill as far as communications are concerned, with good rail and road links and easy access to Heathrow Airport, coupled with delightful countryside on its doorstep.

If the office park concept is to take off in this country these will be the essential requirements, so it is likely to be in the Thames Valley or roughly along the routes of the M3 and M4 motorways as far south as Southampton and as far west as Bristol, that most attention will be focused.

121

Office environments

People are as much affected by the interior design of the building in which they work as by its location and siting. There are great variations in office interiors – the size of rooms, the number of people working in them, the nature of the work, lay-out of furniture and equipment, and so on. Many office workers have to share small rooms or

A variety of offices; the managerial, the open-plan, the corridor, the high technology and the customer service (in this case, a bank)

larger open-plan offices while people in senior positions often have their own well-furnished room. The degree of privacy and sense of 'personal space' varies a great deal. The well-being and efficiency of people who work in offices (and other types of buildings) can be greatly affected by these different aspects of the office environment.

Exercise 29
Aztec West office park

1 Copy the outline sketch of the Aztec West Office Park, and with the help of the photograph on page 121 label it to describe important features about site and location.

2 Who is likely to benefit from the development, and in what ways?

3 What are some of the disadvantages of such a development, and who is likely to suffer from them?

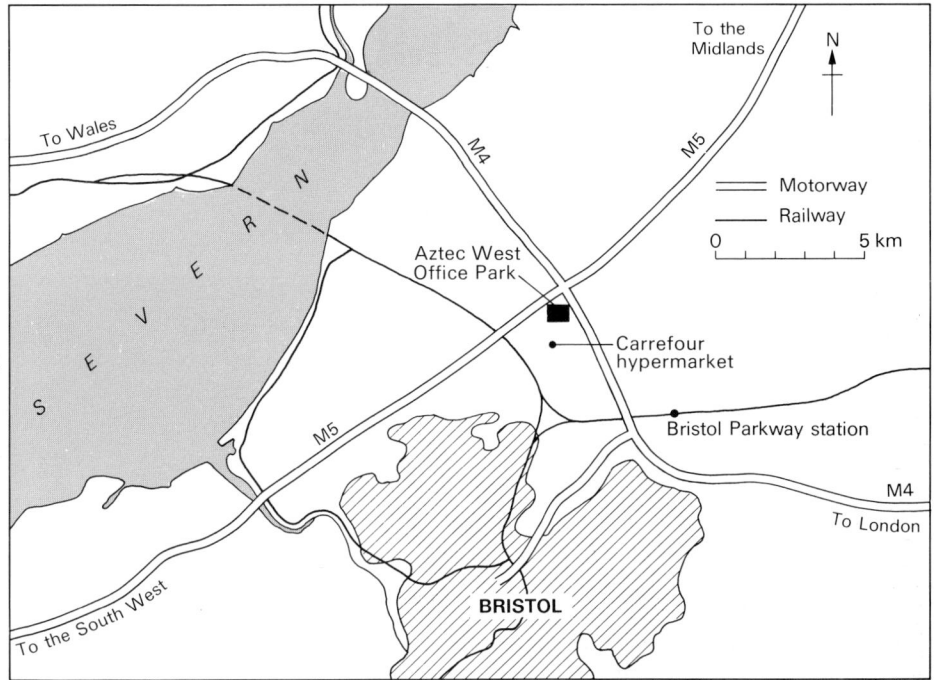

The location of the Aztec West development

Outline sketch of the Aztec West development

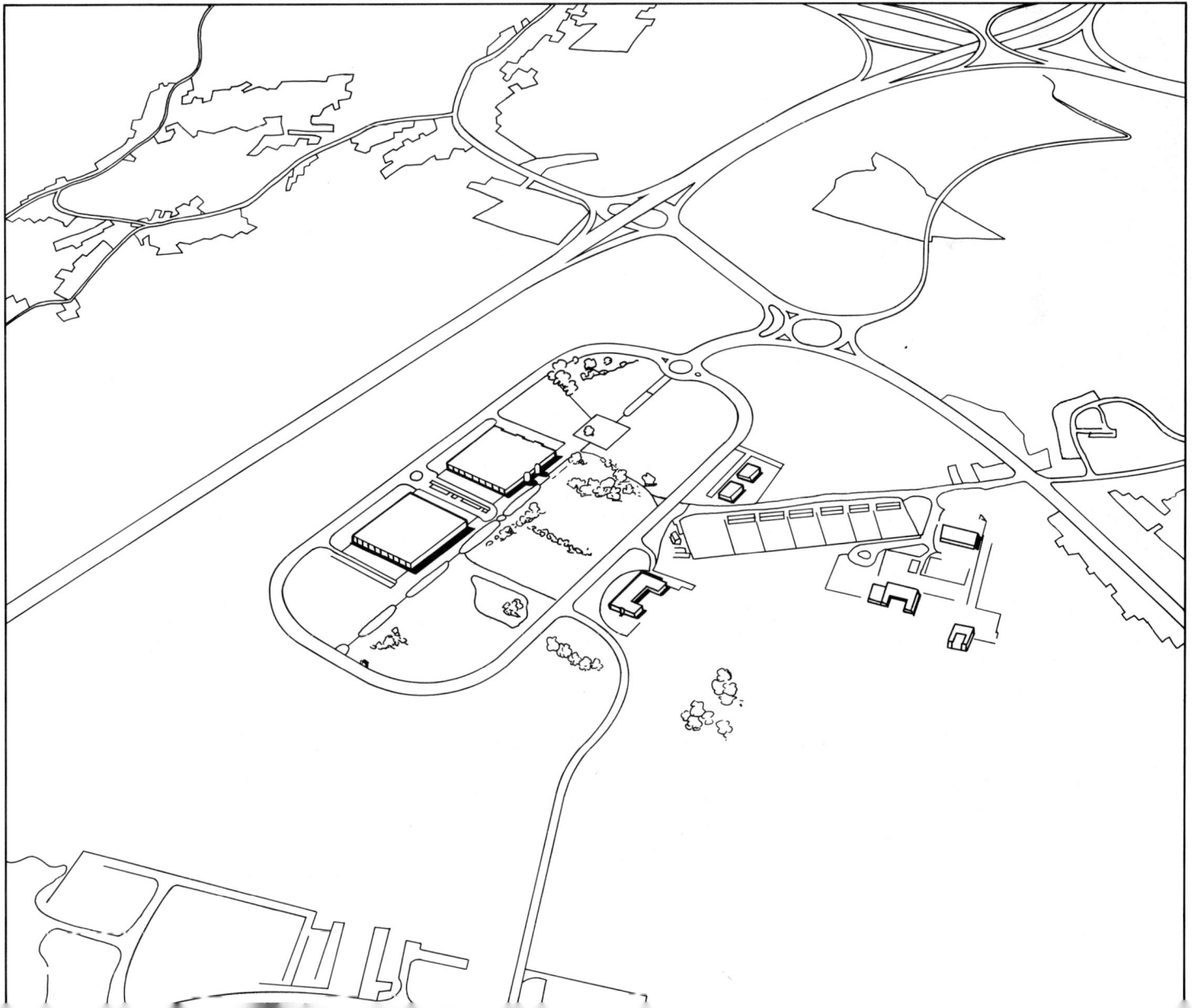

Central business areas

Shops and services in the High Street, Burton-on-Trent

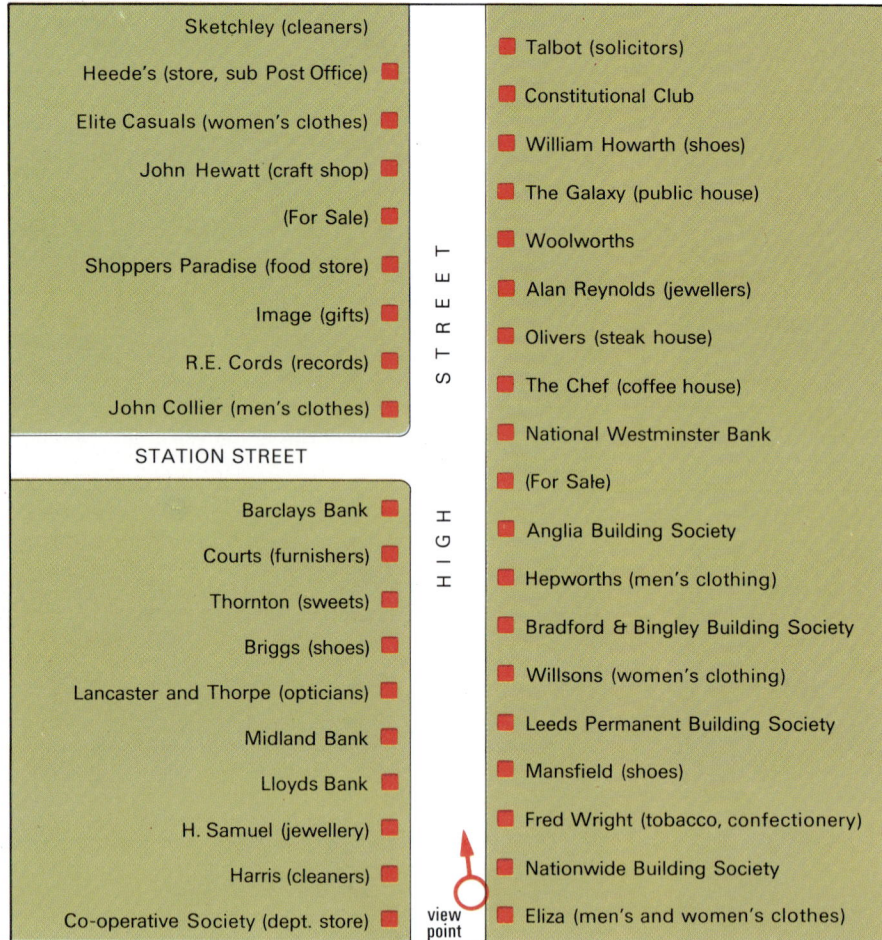

Sketchley (cleaners)	▮ Talbot (solicitors)
▮ Heede's (store, sub Post Office)	▮ Constitutional Club
▮ Elite Casuals (women's clothes)	▮ William Howarth (shoes)
▮ John Hewatt (craft shop)	▮ The Galaxy (public house)
▮ (For Sale)	▮ Woolworths
▮ Shoppers Paradise (food store)	▮ Alan Reynolds (jewellers)
▮ Image (gifts)	▮ Olivers (steak house)
▮ R.E. Cords (records)	▮ The Chef (coffee house)
▮ John Collier (men's clothes)	▮ National Westminster Bank

STATION STREET

Barclays Bank ▮	▮ (For Sale)
Courts (furnishers) ▮	▮ Anglia Building Society
Thornton (sweets) ▮	▮ Hepworths (men's clothing)
Briggs (shoes) ▮	▮ Bradford & Bingley Building Society
Lancaster and Thorpe (opticians) ▮	▮ Willsons (women's clothing)
Midland Bank ▮	▮ Leeds Permanent Building Society
Lloyds Bank ▮	▮ Mansfield (shoes)
H. Samuel (jewellery) ▮	▮ Fred Wright (tobacco, confectionery)
Harris (cleaners) ▮	▮ Nationwide Building Society
Co-operative Society (dept. store) ▮	view point — ▮ Eliza (men's and women's clothes)

STREET (left), HIGH (right) — HIGH STREET

A classification of types of shop and service in a central business area

Professional service

Entertainment

Financial service

Commercial service

Department store

Furniture and household

Retail food

Non-food retail

Retail clothing

High Street

Many of the service activities described in the past few pages are concentrated together in particular parts of the town. The photograph and street plan show how shops, offices, banks and restaurants are clustered together in one particular town. But every small and medium-sized town has a similar pattern. Some people may live on the upper floors, but these are often also used for office or storage purposes. Very little ground floor space is used for residential purposes in most town centres; the location is too valuable and expensive for such a use. In large towns there may be a scatter of business and service areas in the suburbs and a central

View along the High Street towards the junction with Station Street, Burton-on-Trent

business area extending over a number of adjacent streets.

Customers of these shops, offices and other services may come from considerable distances. Generally speaking, the larger and more varied the provision of services the larger the 'catchment area' served. As was shown on page 113, this area varies considerably according to the type of product of service offered. During the day the streets of the central area are busy with cars and buses, with pavements and shops crowded with customers. Most of these shops and offices close down at about 5 pm, when customers and workers leave. The place can then become almost deserted, unless there is a restaurant or two, bingo hall, public house, cinema or club to provide recreation or entertainment services during the evening. Apart from these activities the central 'high street' areas virtually close down during the evenings and on Sundays.

The Central Business District

In large towns and cities the concentration of these service activities is even more marked, and can cover a large central area. Central locations can be so desirable that firms that can afford it are prepared to pay big rents and rates for a central site. These are favourite and prestige locations for big shops, local authority offices, stores, banks and other services. There are exceptions, of course, and the trend to out-of-centre locations for shops and offices has been described. Nevertheless, the centres of most large towns and cities are dominated by service and business activities. Hence the name Central Business District, or CBD.

The name isn't entirely accurate, since the centre is often the place where cinemas, concert halls, museums, galleries, theatres and so on are also located. In spite of the high value of land in the centre, there are usually some gardens or public open spaces which contrast with the intense land use, and where people can walk, or sit and relax. Central areas also often contain bus or rail terminals, since so many people want to travel to and from the centre each day. Another characteristic is the large number of high-rise buildings. This is not surprising, in view of the high value of land. This concentration of taller buildings in the central area is a feature of almost every large town and city nowadays. In the largest of CBDs there may even be a sub-division into specialist areas such as entertainment, finance, legal, administrative and shopping areas.

The pattern of activity in the CBD is similar to that in the smaller 'high street' central areas, only on a bigger scale. People come from long distances to shop in the large stores, to see a solicitor or specialist doctor, to visit the regional or head office of a bank or financial company or to visit the concert hall or museum. But the daily rhythm is very much the same as in a small town, with a surge of people into the area in the morning, and out at the end of the working day. There may be a secondary flow in and out in the evenings, but on nothing like the scale of the journey to and from work.

1 Copy the classification of service activities from the table. How many of each of these are shown on the street plan? Are any on the street plan difficult to fit into the classification?

2 Compare the CBD of York with that of Birmingham here and on page 52. What are the contrasts and similarities?

3 a) List the six shops/services you used or visited in the local 'high street' or CBD in recent times, and b) make a similar list for your parents. Do they differ very much, and if so what does this suggest about the value of the central area to different age groups?

4 Survey and draw a land-use street plan for a street in your local central area. What are the problems of mapping when a building has several storeys? At the same time make another survey of where people have come from to use the central area, the main purposes of their visit and how often a visit is made. Map the findings of this survey.

The Bull Ring, Birmingham

The central business district of York, from the air (*left*), and on the ground (*below*)

Exercise 30 **A new town centre for Basildon**

1 From this map and those on pages 66 and 121 describe the location of Basildon and something of the nature of the town.

2 From the extract give the claimed 'market'; the potential number of users of the centre.

3 Why is it a little misleading to call the project a 'shopping' mall or area?

4 Why are some existing shops and companies keen to be included in the project?

5 Compare the proposed new centre with one that you know, mentioning the similarities and differences between your named example and the Basildon scheme.

The 1983 extract describes the proposed new town centre for Basildon. The map (*right*) shows the location of Basildon

Model of the proposed new town centre for Basildon

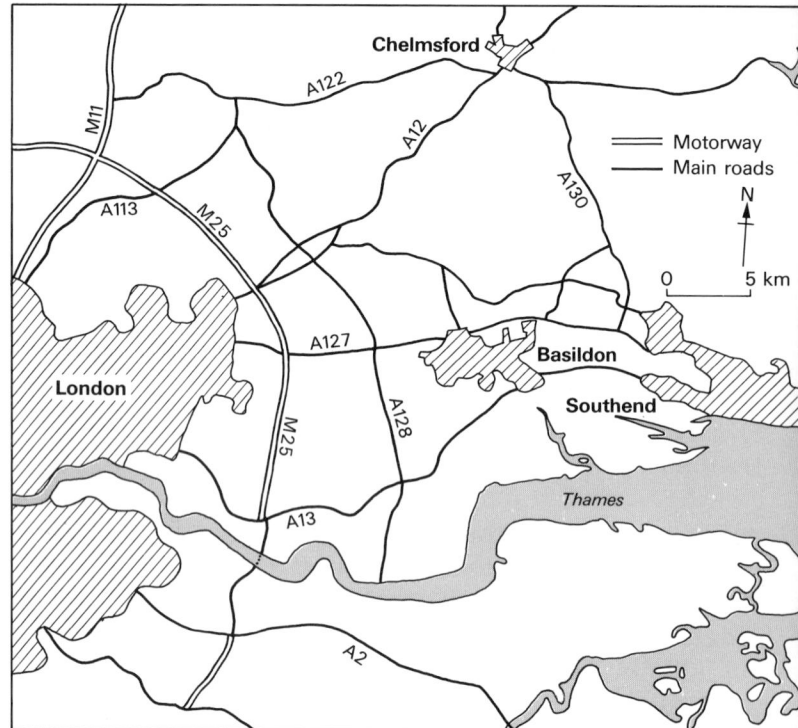

£50m shopping mall for Basildon

Norwich Union Insurance Group is partnering Basildon Development Corporation in a £50m enclosed shopping mall project. It will cover 6.75 acres and include a department store and two office blocks. An additional scheme could also bring the older part of the town centre under cover at a cost of up to £12m. The two ventures, due to be completed by 1984 or 1985, would create Britain's largest covered shopping area, it was claimed yesterday.

A 30 000 sq ft fashion store is included in the development with 75 smaller retail outlets. Applications for these have already oversubscribed the development twice over. This should allow a mix of shops that would provide the maximum attraction to shoppers – one million are estimated to be within 30 minutes travel of Basildon centre.

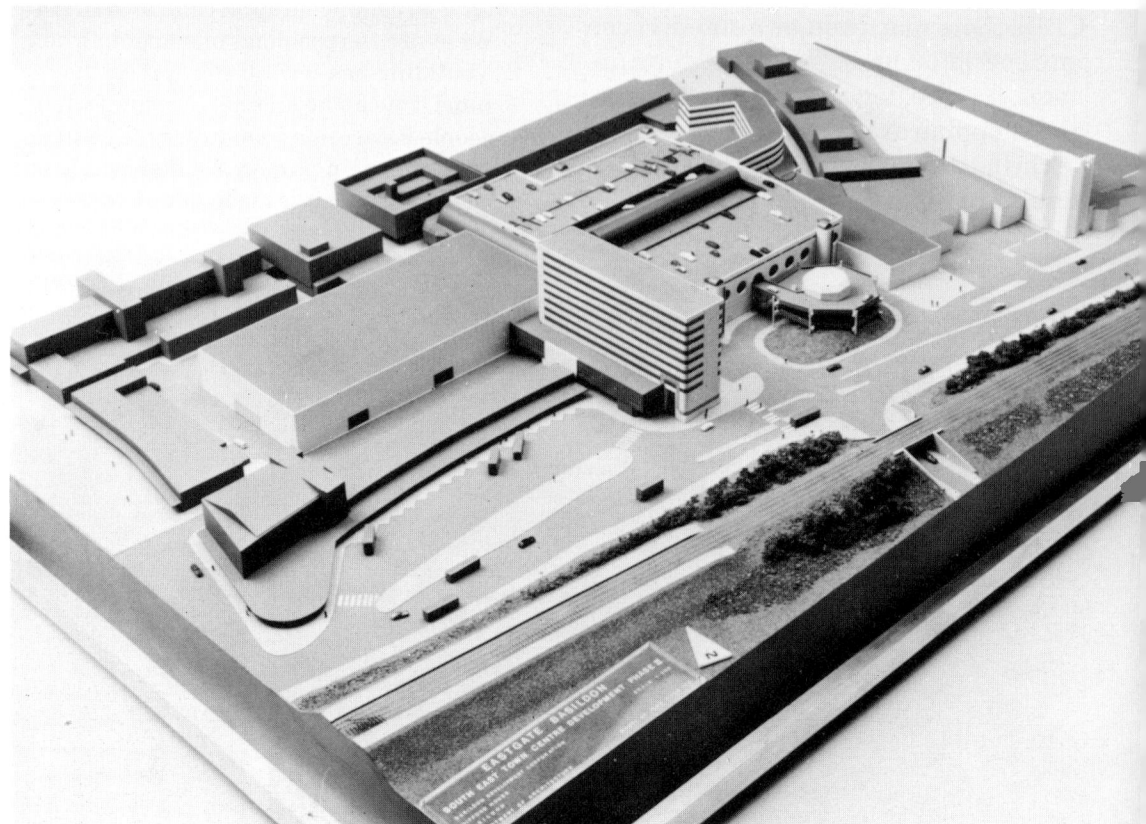

Chapter 6 Leisure, recreation and tourism

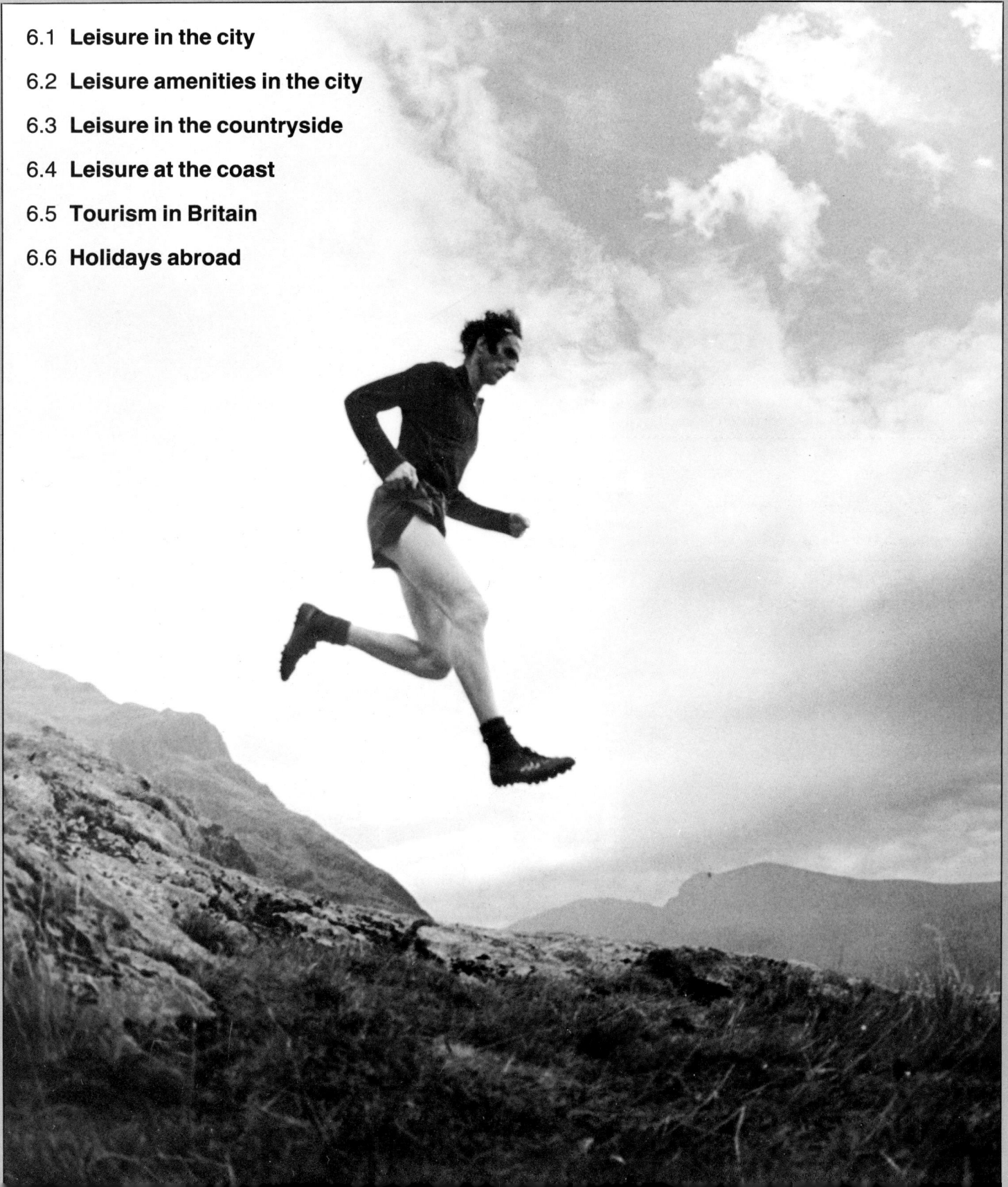

Leisure in the city

Many adults spend their leisure time in clubs and public houses

The local street is often the nearest play area

Figures from a survey on the use of leisure time, showing the percentage of each group which indulged regularly in each activity

Type of activity	Men				All men	All women
	Professional and managerial	Inter-mediate	Skilled manual	Semi-skilled and unskilled		
Open air outings						
Seaside	9	8	6	5	7	7
Country	7	5	4	2	4	4
Entertainment, social, and cultural activities						
Going to the cinema	10	13	10	8	11	10
Visiting historic buildings	15	12	7	4	9	9
Going to the theatre/opera/ballet	9	5	2	1	4	5
Going to museums/art galleries	5	5	2	2	3	3
Attending leisure classes	2	2	—	—	1	2
Going to fairs/amusement arcades	2	2	2	2	2	2
Going out for a meal	60	47	35	25	40	40
Going out for a drink	61	63	68	63	64	45
Home-based activities						
Listening to records/tapes	69	69	64	57	66	62
Gardening	62	54	47	41	49	38
Games of skill	21	21	20	17	20	15
Needlework/knitting	2	3	2	2	2	51
House repairs/DIY	64	58	55	40	53	23
Hobbies	12	15	10	7	11	3
Reading books	67	65	43	39	52	61
Total sample size (=100%) (numbers)	2089	1717	4107	2093	10478	12116

Contrasts in leisure activity

People of all ages enjoy leisure activities of some sort or other, but the interests, needs and time available vary a great deal. Very young children and the retired have a lot of time at their disposal. So, unfortunately, have several million unemployed adults. Young people at school and many students have long holidays, while people at work have evenings, weekends and annual holidays when they can relax and do something different.

The table, based on a survey made in 1981, shows how a sample of adults spent their leisure or non-working time in the early 1980s. There were some marked differences between men and women, and between people in the different socio-economic groups. Although it is not shown, some of the replies depended on the month in which the survey was taken. For example, the percentage taking 'outings to the seaside' was much higher in the sample taken during the summer three months. The table doesn't give variations according to age, but these would certainly have been marked if younger people had been included. The sort of leisure activities people enjoy and are able to afford or get to vary with age, occupation, sex and time of year.

Facilities and amenities for leisure

In the table, one group of activities is headed 'home-based'. It is a reminder that many leisure and recreation activities take place at home. Watching TV and listening to the radio were not included, but the diagram opposite shows that these are ways in which many hours of leisure are spent. For example, if a map were drawn showing where people were spending their leisure time in an evening, there would be several concentrations in places such as clubs or public houses, but a dense scatter in residential areas.

Leisure time spent outside the home may involve 'informal' activities such as playing in the street, going for a walk with friends or just wandering about and watching people who are themselves at work or play. More formal activities usually require special facilities. These may be indoors, as in the case of cinemas, pubs or restaurants where the activities are fairly 'passive', or clubs and sports centres where activities such as dancing or swimming are more 'active'.

Leisure and recreation out of doors may also need special facilities. They may be active, such as playing football and cricket. They may also be passive, such as watching those football or cricket matches, or listening to an open air concert. Some of these facilities use up a lot of space. Sports centres or leisure centres, particularly if they have car parks, can use up much land, while facilities such as golf courses cover very large areas.

The distinction between active and passive leisure is sometimes not all that clear. Many board games, for example, are very active in their way, while spectators at some outdoor events are far from passive! It is also sometimes misleading to talk of outdoor and indoor facilities, since many activities need both. Golf courses and sports fields, for

example, need their club houses, pavilions and changing rooms.

A large number of people are involved in the leisure and recreation business. They may be shopkeepers selling sports equipment or home entertainments. Then there are the pub and club owners and managers, and employees in the sports and leisure clubs dotted about the city. There are the staff employed in the museums, galleries and parks. Leisure and recreation in the city are important for the enjoyment and well-being of the users and participants. But they are also an important form of economic activity.

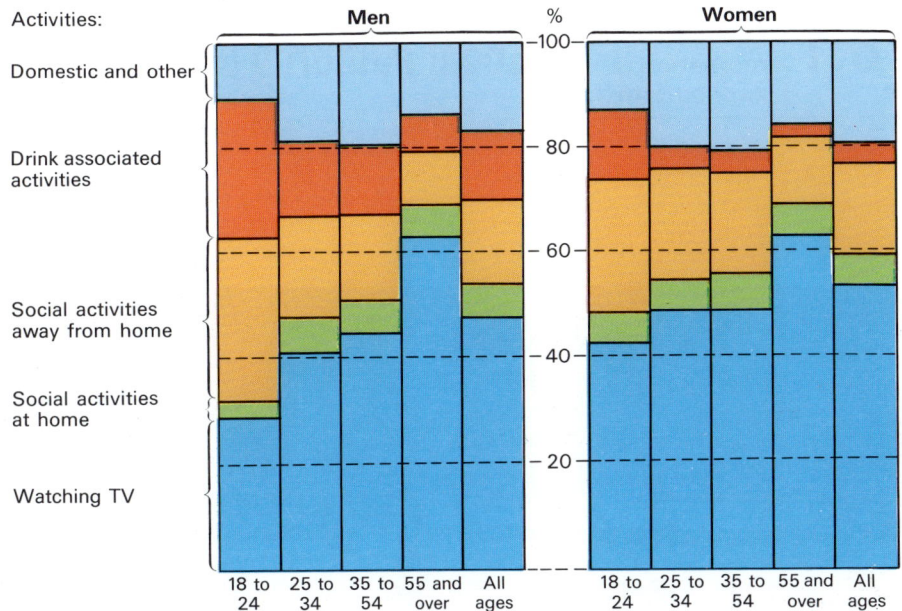

This diagram shows the different uses of leisure time from one age group to another

1 Consider the information given in the diagram above and the table opposite. **a)** Name and explain two marked male- and female-dominated activities, **b)** name three activities with a marked seasonal occurrence, **c)** for one of the activities listed, describe the differences between three of the age groups.

2 **a)** Do a similar survey for the members of your class. How do the results differ from the national survey? **b)** What are the dangers of using information from surveys of this sort?

3 What age groups of people are most likely to use sports centres? Which are not likely to want to use them? Which might like to use them but cannot afford to do so? What arrangements are made to help the latter groups?

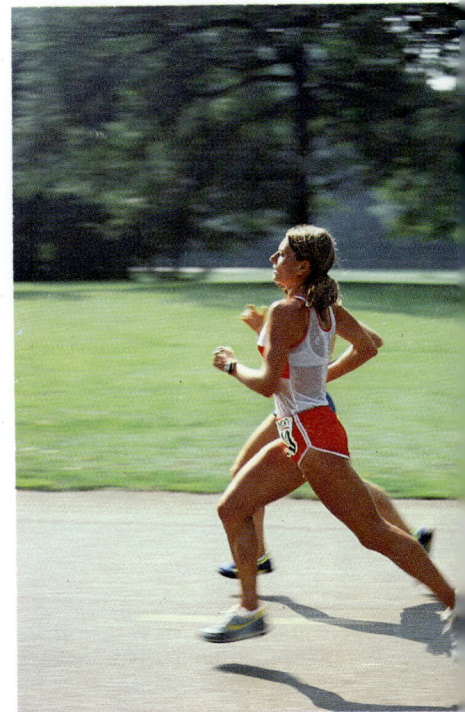

Taking exercise and 'keeping fit' is a popular way of spending leisure time

129

Local authority provision

Leisure facilities like these are a feature of most British towns

The use of a sports centre or other leisure amenity usually depends on the ability to pay

Expenditure and income from leisure facilities in England and Wales, 1983 (£ thousand)

	Expenditure	Income
Urban parks and open spaces	309 601	44 517
Indoor sports halls and leisure centres	173 045	77 222
Swimming pools	138 810	40 152
Theatres, performances, entertainment	60 423	30 040
Art galleries and museums	59 057	7 760
Community halls, public halls	46 481	13 188
Arts centre, hall mainly used for arts purposes	37 466	5 288
Central or departmental catering	30 308	32 070
Outdoor sports facilities	29 404	6 946
Country parks, amenity areas, picnic sites, and nature reserves	22 591	5 272
Promotion of tourism	14 390	3 598
Golf courses	11 393	9 797
Allotments	4 372	3 272
Others and central administration[3]	173 056	—
Total	1 110 397	279 122

Not all people have the same access to leisure facilities in towns and cities. This is partly due to where they live, and partly to what they can afford. Travel, entrance fees and costs of equipment must be considered. The mere presence of a club, sports centre or golf course does not mean they are 'accessible' in membership or cost terms. Some facilities are privately owned and others are provided and run by the local authority. In both cases there are likely to be limits and conditions on their use, and some charge to the user.

Another important feature is that there may be very heavy demand for the use of the facilities at certain times, while at other times they may be underused. Some school grounds and playing fields, for example, are used only during the school terms. By contrast, however, there may be times when a local swimming pool is too full for enjoyable use during the summer months.

130

Exercise 31 **Accessibility to leisure amenities**

The map shows the location of a house where there is a family of two parents a son and two daughters. There is a family car, but no bicycles. The parents don't swim, but do enjoy a game of tennis.

1 Copy the circular diagram and plot the locations of the four amenities from the house in terms of **a**) direct **b**) road distances. One example has been given.

2 Draw two circles similar to that in question 1. Work out suitable scales. On one circle plot the time from the house to the four amenities and on the other the cost. Describe and account for any unexpected differences between the distance time and cost to the four amenities.

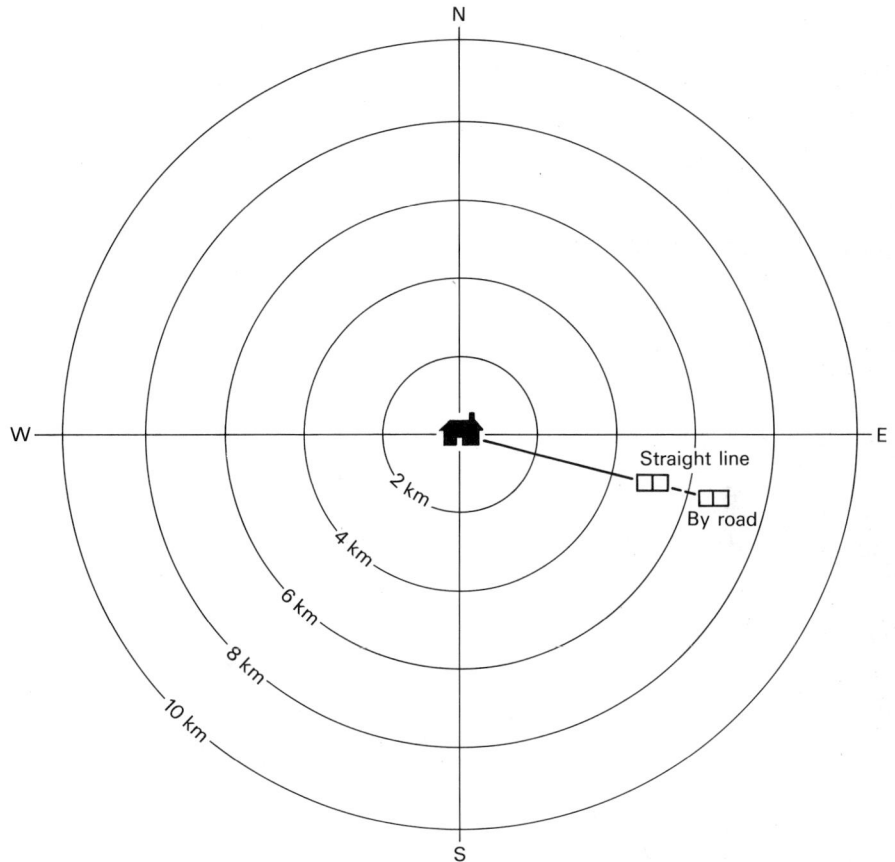

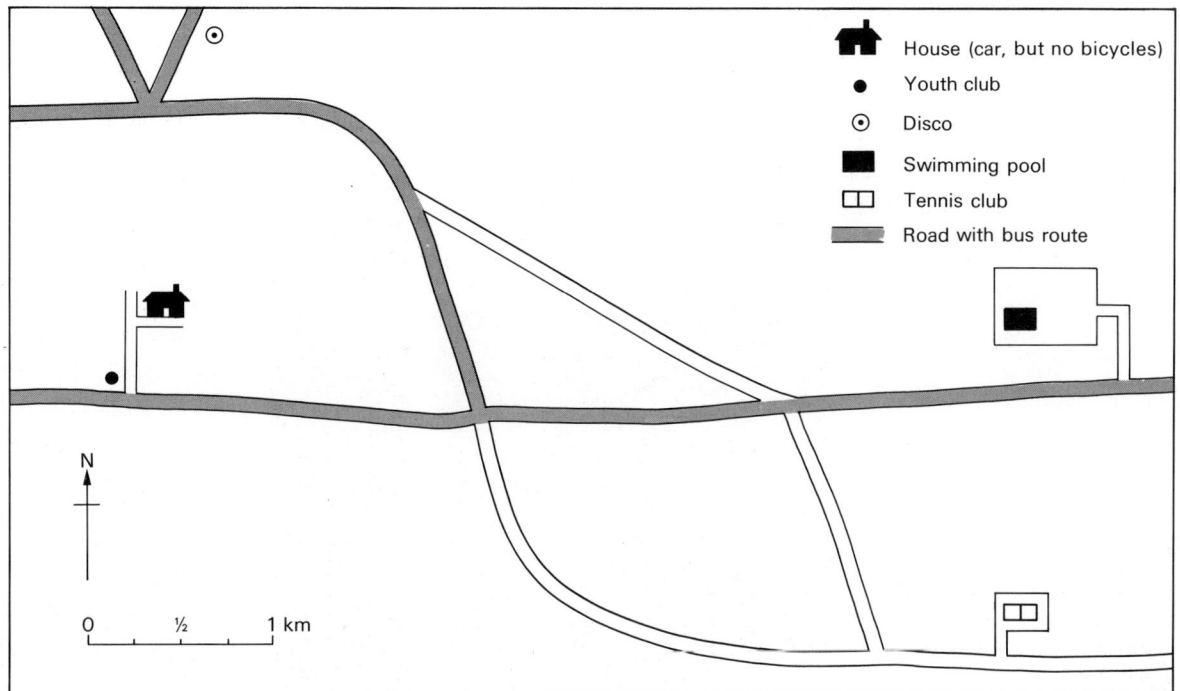

Time to get from home to 4 amenities

●	10 mins.
☉	40 mins.
■	20 mins.
▭▭	15 mins.

Cost of getting to 4 amenities

●	0
☉	60 p
■	60 p
▭▭	0

🏠	House (car, but no bicycles)
●	Youth club
☉	Disco
■	Swimming pool
▭▭	Tennis club
▬▬	Road with bus route

0   ½   1 km

Leisure amenities in the city

Most children like some excitement and adventure in their play areas

A fair at Hampstead Heath. A temporary but regular source of fun for all ages

Below, right: Discos are popular places of entertainment for the younger age groups

Inner city and suburbs

In any area, the numbers of different leisure amenities will vary. For example, there will be a considerable number of play areas for young children, but far fewer swimming pools. This is partly because the catchment areas of users are quite different. Young children, often of pre-school age, are the main users of small local play areas with their swings, climbing frames and sand pits. They are frequently taken to the play area by parents for a few hours during the day. Their parents will not want nor be able to travel far to get there. Ideally there should be some sort of communal play area within walking distance of young children or parents with pushchairs or prams. By contrast full-sized swimming pools need to attract large numbers of users of all ages if they are to justify the costs of building and running them. Public pools are likely to be near the city centre where they can be reached by public transport, or on a more extensive site in the suburbs where they can be reached by public transport or car. Quite apart from use, the cost of build-

ing and maintaining play areas and swimming pools puts a limit on their numbers.

Another factor to influence availability is the amount of space required. There have been several references in this book so far to the gradient of land values in towns, with space being most expensive near the centre. While many types of leisure and recreation are found in the central area, they tend to be small users of space unless they are big money earners. They may be a central park where office and shop workers can take their breaks, and where visitors to the city centre can get away from the noise and bustle, but on the whole the big space users such as parks, sports fields or golf courses tend to be in the suburbs, where the density of housing and cost of land is lower.

Inner city zones, on the margins of the Central Business District, are often lacking in leisure and recreation amenities. There may well be a lot of open space, but it is frequently derelict land waiting to be 'developed' into offices or houses or urban motorways. These areas, because of their age, may

have considerable amounts of high density, poor quality buildings. Unemployment is often very high, since many workshops and factories have been closed down or relocated elsewhere. This means there may not be enough income available to spend on leisure in other parts of the city, and there may be a reluctance of the local authority or private investors to put money into amenities in the area.

Some suburban areas, especially large housing estates, also lack places where people can relax and enjoy their leisure time. Others are better provided. There are quite often considerable contrasts in the provision of leisure amenities within cities.

The city centre

You read about the commercial activities of the Central Business District on page 124. The name is misleading because there are many recreational and leisure amenities located there which serve people from all over the city and the surrounding areas. The main emphasis is on indoor activities in theatres, cinemas, clubs, galleries, restaurants and museums. There may be some indoor sports facilities in the central area, and occasionally a league football ground is located near-by. Unlike the playing fields in parks these football grounds are a form of entertainment, like a cinema, and are run on a commercial basis.

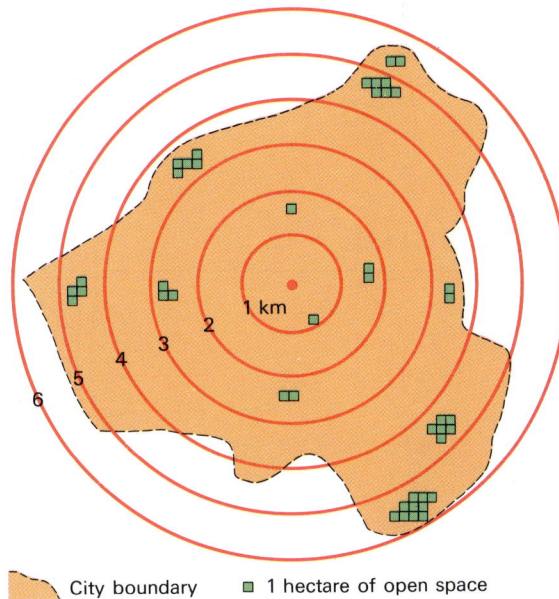

City boundary   ■ 1 hectare of open space

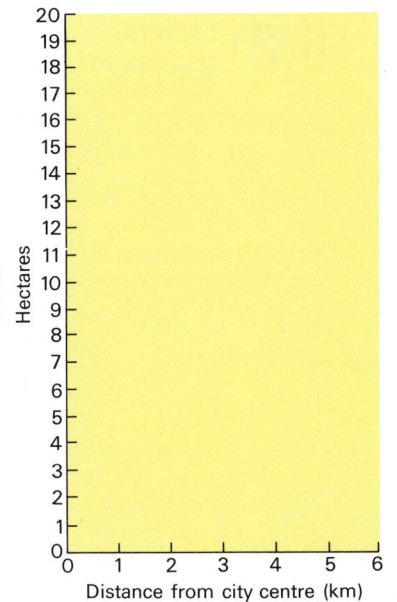

1 Why is the need for communal play areas greater in some residential areas than in others? Name a neighbourhood that you know that is well provided with toddler play areas and one that is not.

2 Make a list of **a**) what is well provided, and **b**) what is lacking in your home area in the way of leisure amenities for each of the following age groups: the very young; 14–18 year olds; young adults; the elderly.

3 Copy the graph coordinates above. Plot the variation of open recreational space with the distance from the city centre. Do this by calculating the rough area of open space in each zone. Comment on what you notice, explaining the pattern. Does your town or city show a similar or different pattern?

Most towns show a recognizable pattern in the distribution of open space

Left and below: Other leisure activities for different age groups

133

Leeds: a local, regional and national centre

The location of important leisure amenities in Leeds

Open spaces

1. International swimming pool
2. Concert hall
3. Art gallery
4.5.6. Theatres
7. Industrial museum
8. Folk museum
9. Test and county cricket
10. Rugby League
11. Model farm
12. Golf course
13. Leeds United Football Club
14. Greyhound stadium

Some larger cities have recreational and leisure centres of regional or national importance. People will travel long distances to hear a visiting musical group or entertainer, or listen to a city orchestra. Supporters will travel from all over the city or country to watch local teams or international events. As with shops and services, so with recreation and leisure, there is a hierarchy of demand and provision. Examples of local, regional and national provision can be seen in Leeds.

Below and right: Leeds is a centre for test and county cricket, as well as first class football and rugby league

Exercise 32 The location of major football grounds and sporting events

The map shows the location of the English First Division League Football clubs and the Scottish Premier Division clubs in the 1982/83 season. The tables give the names of the Fourth Division Football Clubs and Clubs in the Football League in the first year of its formation, 1888/9.

1 Draw or trace an outline of Britain. Plot the locations of Fourth Division clubs. How does this differ from the map of First Division clubs? Explain the differences.

2 **a**) Describe the distribution of clubs in the 1888/9 season and compare with those in the 1982 First Division. **b**) Describe and explain the distribution of Scottish Premier Division clubs.

3 On your map show the location of six places where six different international sporting events take place (not more than three in London). Name the place and the sporting event.

4 Locate the clubs of the 1983 England Women's Hockey team. What do you notice about their distribution?

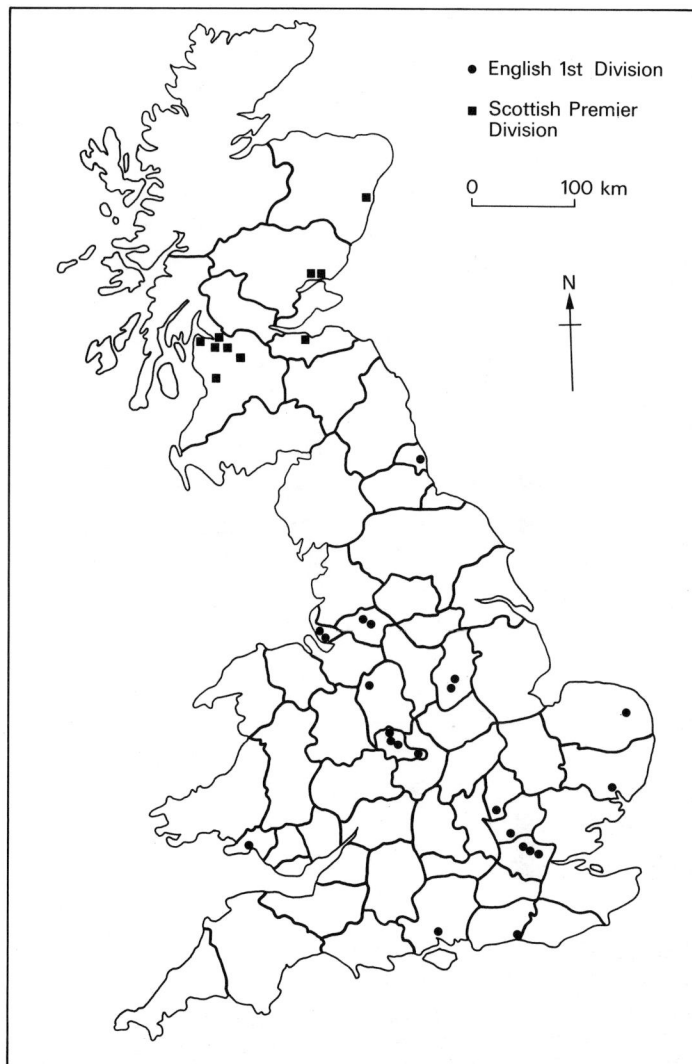

The Football League 1982–83

Division 4

Aldershot	Mansfield
Blackpool	Northampton
Bristol City	Peterborough
Bury	Port Vale
Chester	Rochdale
Colchester	Scunthorpe
Crewe	Stockport
Darlington	Swindon
Halifax	Torquay
Hartlepool	Tranmere
Hereford	Wimbledon
Hull	York

The Football League 1888–89

Preston North End (Champions)	West Bromwich Albion
Blackburn Rovers	Stoke City
Bolton Wanderers	Derby County
Everton	Notts County
Burnley	Aston Villa
Wolverhampton Wanderers	

England Women's Hockey Team, 1982–83 season

	Club	
Mary Allen		Bedford Town
Jane Swinnerton		Sutton Coldfield
Rosemary Goodridge		Exmouth
Pauline Gibbon		Tamworth
Vicky Dixon		Saffron Walden
Linda Carr		Hightown (Bradford)
Rosie Sykes		Ashford
Karen Lobb		Northampton
Barbara Hambly		Sutton Coldfield
Margaret Souyave		Hightown (Bradford)
Valerie Robinson		Great Harwood (Burnley)
Kim Gordon		Loughborough
Sandra Lister		Chelsea College of Physical Education
Mary Eckersall		Almskirk
Julie Cook		Harwich and Dovercourt
Ruth Hine		Wimbledon

Leisure in the countryside

SCOTLAND

NORTH SEA

IRISH SEA

ENGLAND

0   100 km

The Pennine Way, showing National Parks and 'highest points'

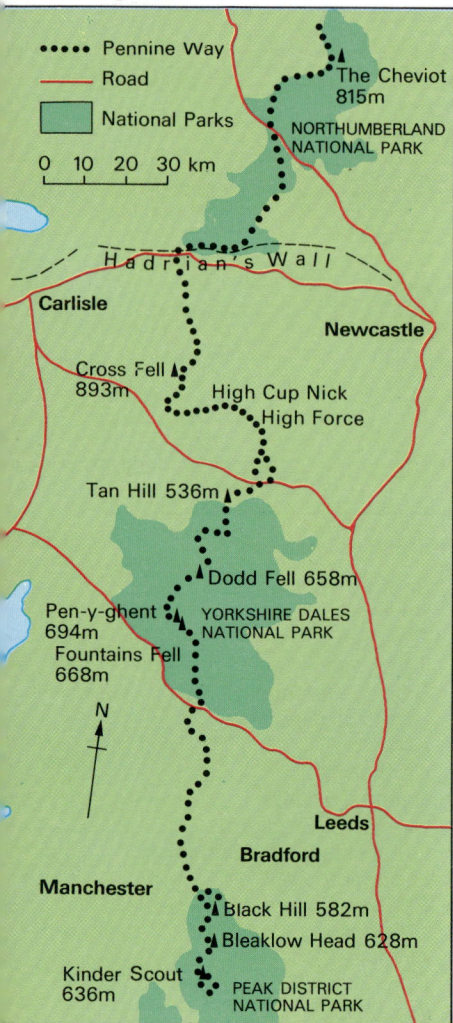

•••• Pennine Way
— Road
National Parks

0 10 20 30 km

The Cheviot 815m
NORTHUMBERLAND NATIONAL PARK

Hadrian's Wall

Carlisle

Newcastle

Cross Fell 893m
High Cup Nick
High Force

Tan Hill 536m

Dodd Fell 658m

Pen-y-ghent 694m   YORKSHIRE DALES NATIONAL PARK
Fountains Fell 668m

N

Leeds

Bradford

Manchester

Black Hill 582m
Bleaklow Head 628m
Kinder Scout 636m
PEAK DISTRICT NATIONAL PARK

Walkers on the High Cup Nick section of the Pennine Way

Leisure in the countryside

Britain has a remarkably varied countryside considering its small size. It is used for many purposes such as growing food, forestry and quarrying or mining. A further use is as an amenity for recreation and leisure, not just for landowners or those who live in villages, but also for those who live in towns and cities. The difficulties of managing the countryside for all these users is dealt with in Chapter 9, while the special attractions of the sea and coast are considered in the next section.

Different people seek different sorts of recreation in the countryside, just as they do within the city. This will depend on their age, interests and income. Some people like crowded places such as those found at well-known beauty spots, picnic areas or country parks. Others prefer more solitude and deliberately try to get away from crowds. The attraction may be the fresh air, the scenery or an interest in

animals (including those in safari parks!), or old country houses. A large number of people are more active than this, and visit the countryside to walk, climb, explore caves, fish or take part in sporting events, such as hang gliding or water-skiing.

Different sorts of landscapes provide different opportunities for activities. Caving, for example, is a sport practiced largely in limestone areas. People also have different views about landscapes. What appeals to one person leaves another quite unmoved. In extreme cases people may feel anxious or frightened when they find themselves in high places or in enclosed spaces. Again there are limits to what elderly people or very young children can do. Some people can walk long distances, but many are restricted to car or coach trips. The urge of many people to stay with crowds can be seen by the large numbers who stay near their cars at crowded sites.

Ownership of leisure areas

A great deal of the countryside is owned by private individuals. Those who own large estates frequently allow people to visit their country homes or parks as a business activity. In a number of cases they provide additional attractions such as safari parks or specialist museums. On the whole, farmers are not so involved in the leisure business, although in some places a good income can be had from letting cottages to holiday visitors. Because of the fear of damage to their property, farmers are sometimes reluctant to allow visitors to use even the public footpaths and rights-of-way across their farmland. Many large country houses and estates, and other attractive pieces of land are owned by the National Trust, and millions of people visit their property each year. Another body that encourages visitors is the Forestry Commission (page 198). It manages many sites where people can park cars, camp and take walks along marked routes.

There are other types of countryside amenity provided and managed by local and national authorities. Perhaps the best known of these are the National Parks (page 199).

The West Pennines Moors Plan

The area of the Pennines between Bolton and Blackburn is popular with the people living in the many towns of southern Lancashire and Greater Manchester. The aim of the plan is to try to channel informal recreation such as casual walking, picnicking, sightseeing and ball games into four Recreation Management Zones. This will be done by careful traffic control, siting of car parks and picnic areas and the development of three country parks. Active sports such as rock climbing, hang-gliding and water sports will also be encouraged in particular areas. Outside the RMZs the emphasis will be placed on the protection of farming, forestry and water provision from too much visitor pressure. In these ways those valuable sites and activities in danger of being spoilt by over-use or misuse can be partly protected while the area can still provide for the leisure needs of local people.

1 **a)** Measure the length of the Pennine Way. How long would it take you to walk at the rate of 20 kilometres a day.
b) Describe what you like or dislike about the landscape.

2 **a)** Compare the recreational amenities available in the West Pennine Plan area with those along the Pennine Way.
b) Why is stricter management necessary in the West Pennine area than along the Pennine Way?

3 **a)** What are the dangers to the countryside created by visitors and tourists?
b) Do you think that any authority should have the right to prevent visitors to the countryside doing whatever they feel like?

Above: Britain's historic houses attract millions of visitors. *Below*: Climbing in North Wales. *Bottom*: Fox hunting is still a popular country pastime

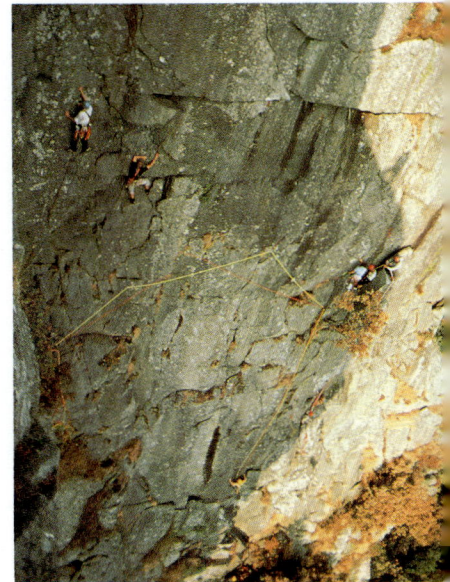

The West Pennines Moors Plan

Legend:
- Recreation management zones (RMZ)
- Country park
- Picnic area with car park
- Conservation management area
- Area covered by West Pennine Moors Plan
- Reservoir with recreational use
- A Rivington
- B Darwen Tower-Roddlesworth
- C Jumbles-Wayoh-Entwistle
- D Haslington Greene-Pickup Bank
- Educational training in water sports
- Hang gliding and model soaring
- Club sailing
- Rock climbing

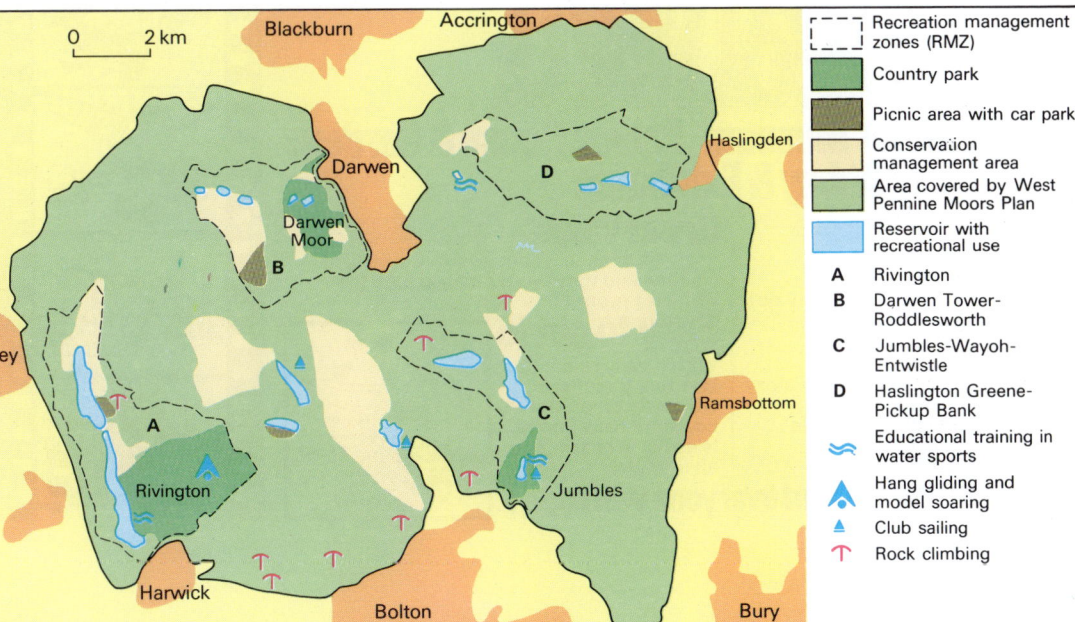

The Countryside leisure industry

People enjoy the countryside in very different ways. Some use the various landscapes for active recreation, such as walking, caving, car rallying or hang gliding. Others follow gentler pursuits such as visiting beauty spots or country homes and their gardens. In most cases the pleasure can be improved by the provision of amenities such as car parks, lavatories and places to rest and eat; although if badly planned they can be an eyesore and a nuisance.

Owners of houses or land in the countryside, whether private, local authority or national government, often invest money in these amenities and charge for their use. Profits may be used either for the upkeep of the site, to provide new or better amenities, or for financial gain. Catering for leisure needs in the countryside can be big business.

A car park at Cheddar. Proper arrangements are needed to make the visit enjoyable and to protect the site

Moto-cross is a countryside sport enjoyed by motorcyclists and spectators

The owners of many amenities encourage visitors by advertising; leisure is an important and profitable business

Beaulieu
The National Motor Museum Palace House & Gardens
Abbey & Exhibition

Enjoyable
There is so much to see and do – whatever your age. Past and present intermingle to give you a delightful day out.

Unforgettable
The charm of Palace House, the nostalgia of the Motor Museum, the history of the Abbey and Exhibition, all make Beaulieu an exciting and unforgettable experience!

Great value
Last year, in a special survey, 96% of visitors said they were pleased with the value for money!

Easy to get to
Within easy reach of London, Beaulieu, situated in the South's beautiful New Forest, is easily accessible to all tourists.

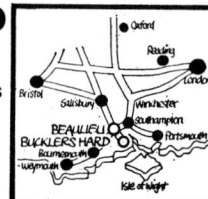

The great value Holiday day out that everyone will enjoy!

Exercise 33
The Aviemore Centre

The Aviemore Centre opened in 1966. It consists of luxury hotels, chalet accommodation, shops, a theatre, a dance hall and discotheque, a swimming pool, skittle alley, skating rink and restaurant. It is a private investment. Over a million people visited the Centre in its first year and a half.

1   Describe the site and the location of the Aviemore Centre.

2   Use the large-scale map and the photographs on these pages and page 15 to describe some of the attractions of the local environment for visitors.

3   **a**) What has been provided (by private investment) to create all-year-round tourism in the area? **b**) What benefits have been gained, and by whom, from the development? **c**) What are the problems caused by such a development?

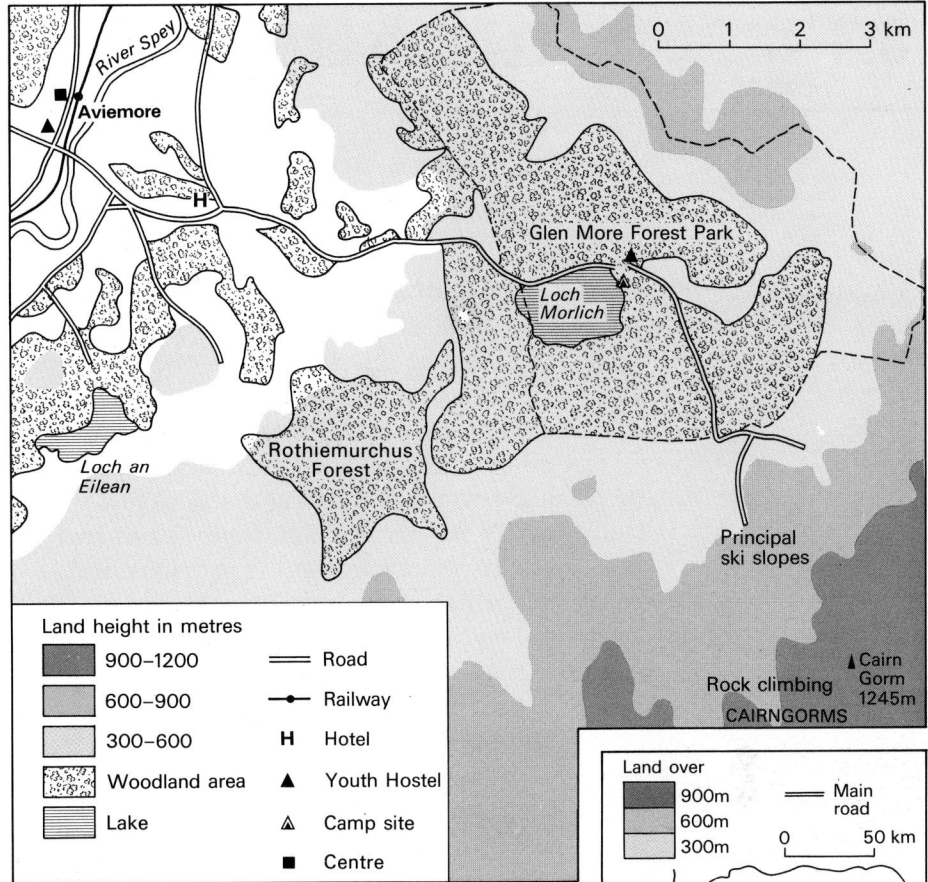

Right: Skiers at Aviemore

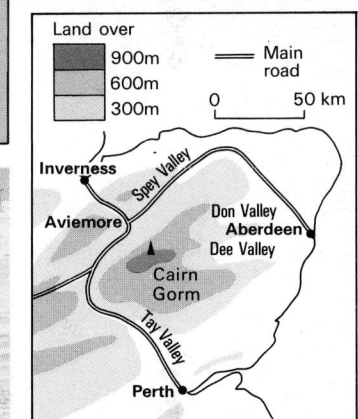

The Aviemore Centre

Land height in metres

▨	900–1200	═══	Road
▨	600–900	●─●	Railway
▨	300–600	H	Hotel
▨	Woodland area	▲	Youth Hostel
▤	Lake	△	Camp site
		■	Centre

Location map of Aviemore, and the surrounding area

Leisure at the coast

Walkers enjoying a quiet sandy beach and rocky coastline

Right: Chichester Harbour

Many different types of boat are found in Chichester Harbour

Attractions and uses

The attractions and leisure amenities provided by the sea and the coast are as varied as in the countryside and the city. Many people enjoy the peace and quiet of the sea and the coastal scenery, and several of the long-distance footpaths and areas of outstanding natural beauty mentioned in the previous unit are situated around our coasts.

The list of things to do is enormous. Many elderly people retire to coastal towns, and places such as Eastbourne and Bournemouth have a very high proportion of elderly and retired people. More vigorous activities include sea swimming, surfing, rock climbing and sailing while less energetic but equally enjoyable ones include wandering about the beach or coastline, lying in the sun or 'messing about in boats'. Some idea of this variety can be seen in the area around Chichester harbour.

Chichester harbour water park

Chichester harbour is on the south coast to the east of Portsmouth and the Isle of Wight. As the map shows, a number of inlets and creeks lead into the English Channel through the narrow entrance between Hayling

Island and East Head. The strong tide sweeps sand and shingle around the inlets, but the ebb tide keeps the channel free of sediment. The opportunities for leisure activities are well described in these extracts.

'The pressure on the harbour and its surroundings for the development of leisure activities (including second homes, holiday camps, caravan sites, yacht marinas, and dinghy parks) is very great. Fortunately this pressure has been resisted with some success ... helped by the formation in 1971 of the Chichester Harbour Conservancy which administers the whole harbour as one area ...

More than 1 500 yachts of up to twenty metres in length and each worth thousands of pounds are accommodated in the harbour at the four marinas of Chichester Yacht Basin, Birdham Pool, Emsworth Yacht Harbour and Northney Marina; and a further 3 000 are moored in the four channels. A surprisingly small proportion of these actually go to sea outside the harbour ... The harbour also provides accommodation and use for day boats, most of which are on moorings, and for sailing dinghies

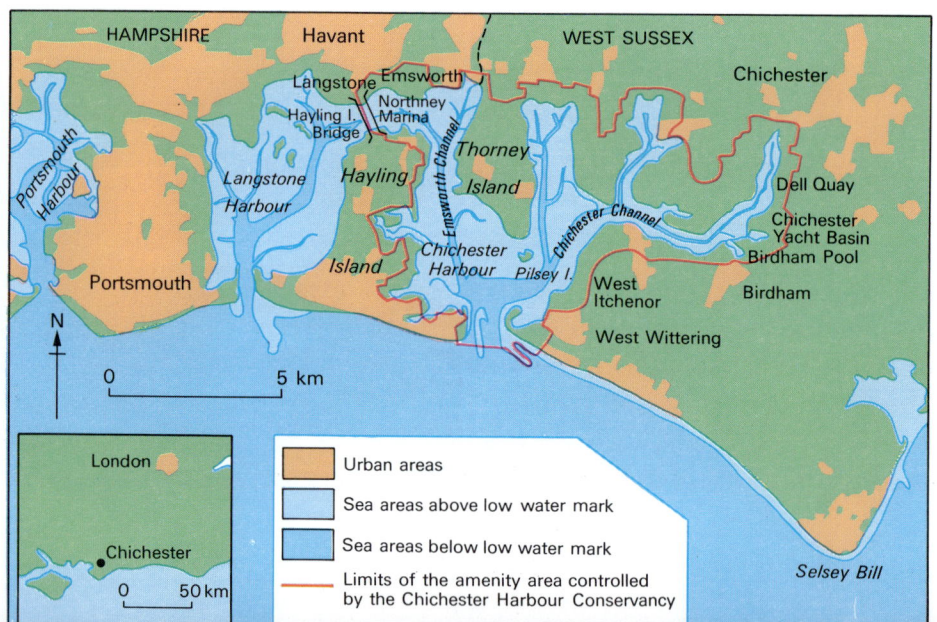

| Urban areas |
| Sea areas above low water mark |
| Sea areas below low water mark |
| Limits of the amenity area controlled by the Chichester Harbour Conservancy |

Blackpool
Bournemouth

Brighton and Hove
Dover
Eastbourne
Great Yarmouth
Hastings
Morecambe
Scarborough
Skegness
Southend
Southport
Torbay
Weston-super-Mare
Worthing

Most popular holiday coasts

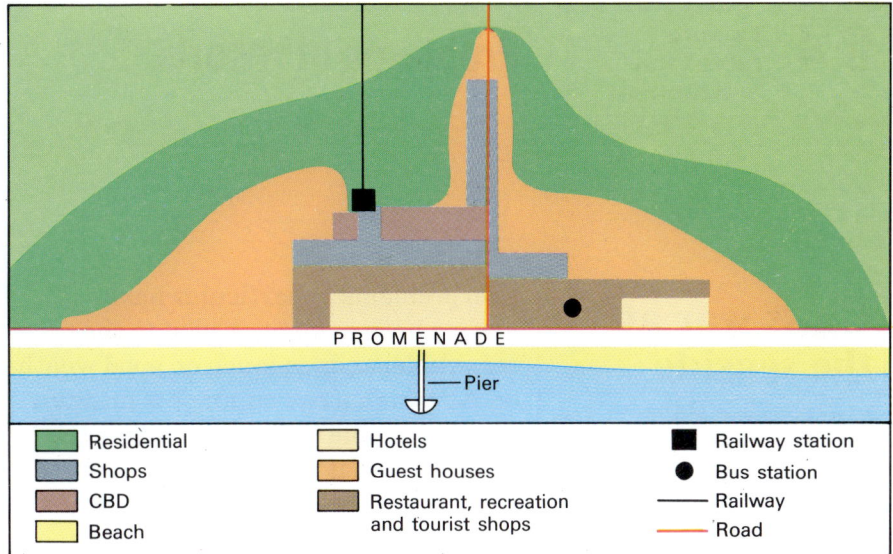

NORTH WALES
WEST WALES
SOUTH WEST WALES
NORTH DEVON
SOUTH DEVON
CORNWALL
DORSET
ISLE OF WIGHT
NORFOLK
SUFFOLK
ESSEX
KENT

0   100   200 km

Left: Coastal resorts and holiday areas

A generalised map of land use in a coastal resort

PROMENADE — Pier

Residential
Shops
CBD
Beach

Hotels
Guest houses
Restaurant, recreation and tourist shops

Railway station
Bus station
Railway
Road

less than five metres in length and which are light enough to be kept in dinghy parks on land and launched from trollies when required. There are a thousand craft in each of these two classes as well as many small rowing boats. These are intensively used. An unrecorded number of dinghies and lighter craft, including the recently popular sail board, are brought down by trailer or on car roof racks during the summer...'

Seaside resorts

The many seaside resorts around the coast are very different. Originally these coastal resorts were built for the wealthy and visited for reasons of health. Then during the last century, with the development of railways and coaches and the growth of annual holidays, they became very popular with people from the industrial towns. With the growth of car ownership during the 1950s people were able to travel further

for their holidays, and the day trip or longer holiday to the seaside was a major form of recreation.

The attractions are partly provided by the physical environment. Apart from the sea itself there is a beach, usually of sand but sometimes shingle or pebble. Then there is 'the bracing sea breeze', although most visitors hope for long hours of sunshine in a cloudless sky. There may also be attractive coastal scenery nearby. To these natural features have been added others such as hotels and boarding houses where visitors can stay, piers with amusement arcades and fun fairs, and usually a wide promenade running alongside the front and the beach. This is backed by theatres, cinemas, clubs, restaurants – a whole area devoted to catering for the recreation and leisure of the visitors. While each resort is unique, most have a land use pattern similar to that shown in the plan.

1 Describe the leisure activities around Chichester harbour under the headings **a)** sailing, **b)** other activities. What pressures do these place on the environment?

2 **a)** Compare the land use of a Seaside Resort with the CBD of an inland town. **b)** What are the main differences between a Holiday Camp and Seaside Resort?

3 Copy the map above and add the names of the top 15 English resorts in their correct locations.

Blackpool seafront

141

Problems of resorts

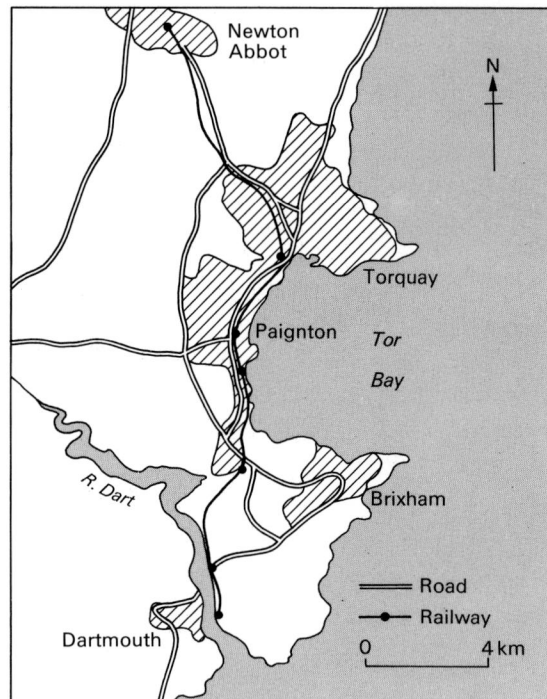

Torbay is the name of the bay and the district in Devon shown on the map

Class war at the seaside

Something was sizzling at Torbay's Sea View and Dun Roamin guest houses today – and it wasn't the breakfast bacon. It was the resentment of seaside landladies at the resort's attempts to go up-market. The local tourist board has decided to spend £100000 with a London advertising agency to try to attract a different class of holidaymaker to the area – and bring back the Edwardian gentility for which it was once famous.

But the landladies don't like the idea of the resort becoming a living experiment in social mobility. 'If we try and push Torbay as an upper-class resort we could be done under the Trades Description Act,' a council meeting was told.

Two problems in particular have always been evident. A visit to the seaside depends so much on good weather. Although a bad summer is unlikely to cause people to cancel holidays they have booked, it will definitely keep away day trippers. A bad summer can have a disastrous effect on the income of people who work in holiday resorts. The other problem is the seasonal pattern of holidaytaking. This means much casual labour has to be taken on during the height of the season, while there may be considerable unemployment during the winter. It was to counteract this that some of the larger resorts have built conference centres to even out their business throughout the year, as well as to make up for the continuing general decline in seaside holidays.

This decline had been largely due to the growth of foreign 'package' holidays, although changing interests and habits of those taking holidays in Britain have also contributed. Whatever the cause, many resorts face a bleak future and are trying various ways of increasing business.

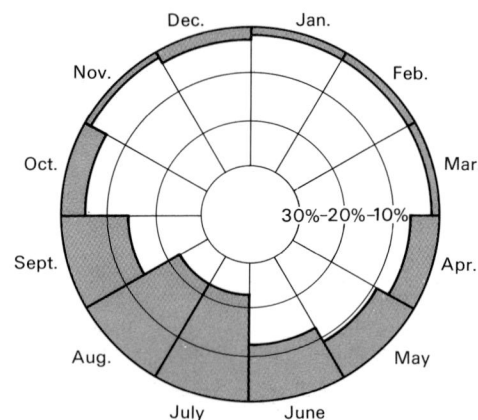

The monthly pattern of British holidaymaking

Below, Left: Poor weather can have a big impact on the number of visitors to seaside resorts. *Below, right*: Liberal MP, Cyril Smith, taking time off from the party's annual conference at Scarborough

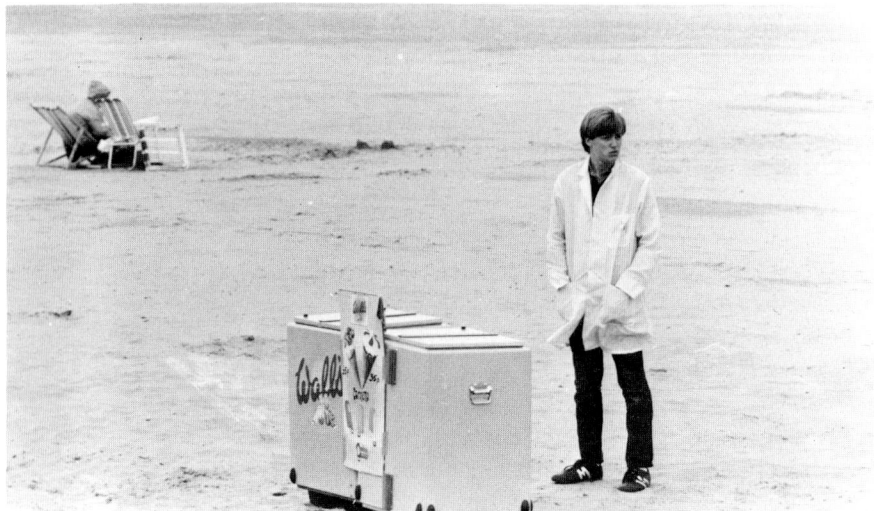

Exercise 34
Holiday in Tenby

This advertisement appeared in a Bath newspaper.

1 Make a sketch of the scene and label to show some of the visible attractions for the holiday maker.

2 What features are mentioned in the text to attract holiday makers to the resort. Which are within the town, and which beyond?

3 Which phrases used to emphasise the attractions of Tenby and its region are opinions rather than facts?

4 What advantages might be offered by Weston-super-Mare or the holiday camp at Minehead, for a resident of Bath wanting a seaside holiday?

Right: Advertisement describing the attraction of Tenby and its surrounding area

Location of three seaside resorts and holiday camps

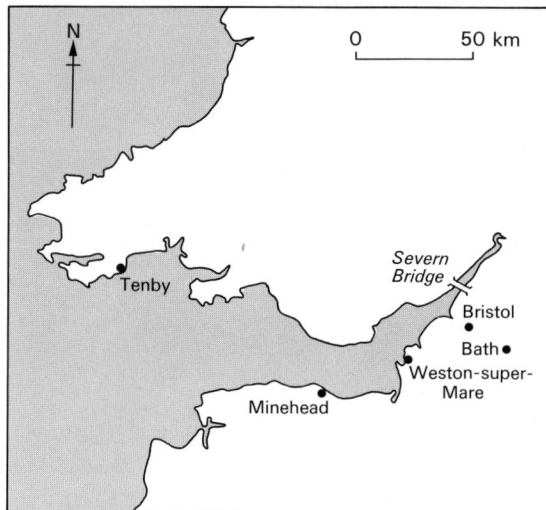

Spend Autumn in Wales

A one week holiday in Tenby for only £109

For all its proximity, Southern Wales is distinctly different. You will see it in the signposts, hear it in the language, and find it in its scenic splendour, natural charm and historic beauty. For those readers who wish to spend a duty free shopping day in Ireland, we have arranged an optional tour. With the best sunshine record in Wales, Dyfed is its warmest corner. We have planned this unique holiday to give you the maximum enjoyment, entertainment and comfort.

Tenby is a real jewel set within one of Europe's most magnificent coastlines, which forms the Pembrokeshire Coast National Park. We have chosen Tenby, a highly individual resort with four superb golden beaches, as the ideal centre at which to base our tour. The distinctive character of the ancient walled town is preserved by medieval narrow streets. Tenby has an indoor heated swimming pool, a museum, a wildlife and leisure park, zoo, two cinemas, 18-hole golf course, numerous restaurants and entertainment centres, and a discotheque. It is an ideal centre for walking or fishing.

Your accommodation

Set in heart of Tenby is the Royal Gatehouse Hotel, which is listed among the 100 best independent hotels in Great Britain. All modern amenities are available and guests may be assured of excellent cuisine, comfort and personal attention. From an elevated position on Tenby's sea front, it commands a superb view of the coastline and harbour. There are literally a few steps to the golden sands of the north beach. The hotel has modern bedrooms with radio, two restaurants, four bars, a colour television lounge and automatic lift.

Tourism in Britain

The historic Tower of London is always a leading tourist attraction

Changes in types of accommodation used by holiday-makers over a decade

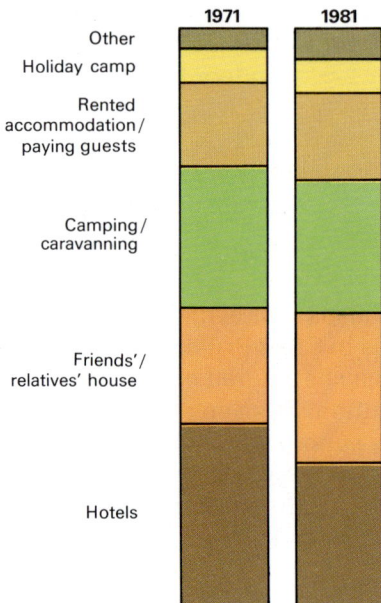

	1971	1981
Other		
Holiday camp		
Rented accommodation/ paying guests		
Camping/ caravanning		
Friends'/ relatives' house		
Hotels		

Changes in holidays taken between 1971 and 1980

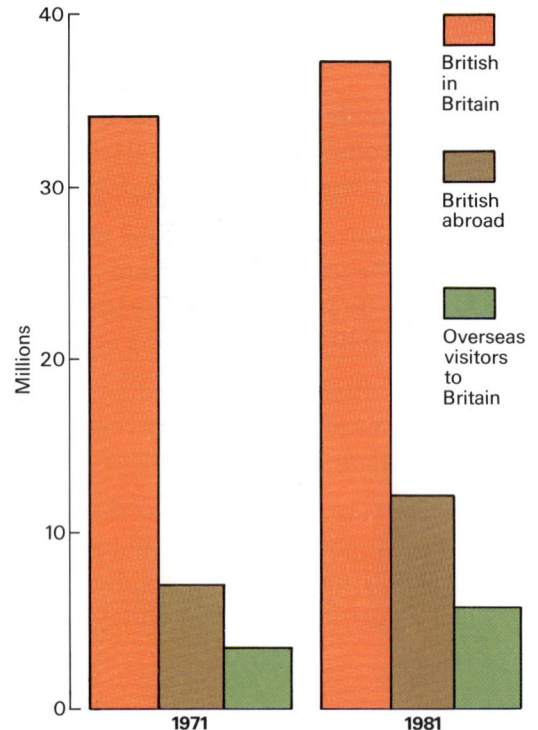

British in Britain

British abroad

Overseas visitors to Britain

Leisure, holidays and tourism

We have already seen that many leisure activities occur during the evenings and weekends, either at home or during visits to nearby places or events. We have also mentioned longer holidays in the sections on seaside resorts and the Aviemore Centre. In official statistics, a 'holiday' is a period of four or more nights spent away from home when the purpose is mainly for leisure and recreation, not work or just visiting people.

The diagrams show how holiday patterns have changed over recent years. The numbers of holidays taken by British residents at home, and the number of holidays taken by foreigners in Britain, have changed quite considerably. The type of holiday accommodation used has also changed. During 1981, for example, less costly accommodation, particularly guest houses, attracted more customers than the year before while there was a reduction in holidays at hotels.

It should be noted that about five and a half million foreign holidays were taken each year in Britain during the 1970s, earning a great deal of money. Tourism and the holiday industry is big business, with an annual turnover of about £8500 million.

The diagram on page 142 shows the months when holidays are taken in Britain. It is not surprising that about eighty per cent of holidaymaking is during the five warm and sunny months from May to September. This has a big effect on the price of accommodation, on congestion and crowding in the resorts, and on the traffic flow between resorts in many areas.

Tourist attractions

Apart from seaside resorts and areas of outstanding natural beauty already mentioned, there are a number of key tourist sites that attract millions of visitors during the year. Some of these are named on page 147. They attract day trippers as well as holidaymakers who may be making a day visit or a longer stay in the area. Some sites are an attraction because of their historic buildings, others because of their picturesque landscape. Another factor is accessibility from large cities and holiday towns and resorts.

Ludlow: historic town

Ludlow is a small town very popular with tourists. It is sited on a low hill within a loop of the River Teme, a tributary of the River Severn. It lies about half way between Hereford and Shrewsbury on the A49 trunk road in Shropshire. It has a rich history which is evident in its buildings and streets.

It has a population of only about 7500, and is an agricultural centre. Development can be traced back to the times of William the Conqueror who gave land to his supporters in return for defending these border areas against the unconquered Welsh (page 43). About 1090 the baron owning this manor began building the castle. Within a hundred years the outer walls were completed and a small town laid out near the castle, which still gives the older part of the town its present street pattern. Town walls were built at the end of the thirteenth century and the town prospered as a centre of the wool trade and clothing industry. The Ludford bridge was built soon after in the fourteenth century.

Ludlow was a place used by Royalty, and was a centre of the Yorkist side during the Wars of the Roses. It was captured and 'sacked' in 1459, and many buildings destroyed. Later on, though, it was rewarded for its loyalty. Ludlow merchants became wealthy as many of the buildings show. For a time Ludlow was virtually regional capital of Wales and the five border counties. It is small wonder with this history evident in its buildings that many tourists, including foreign visitors, enjoy the town.

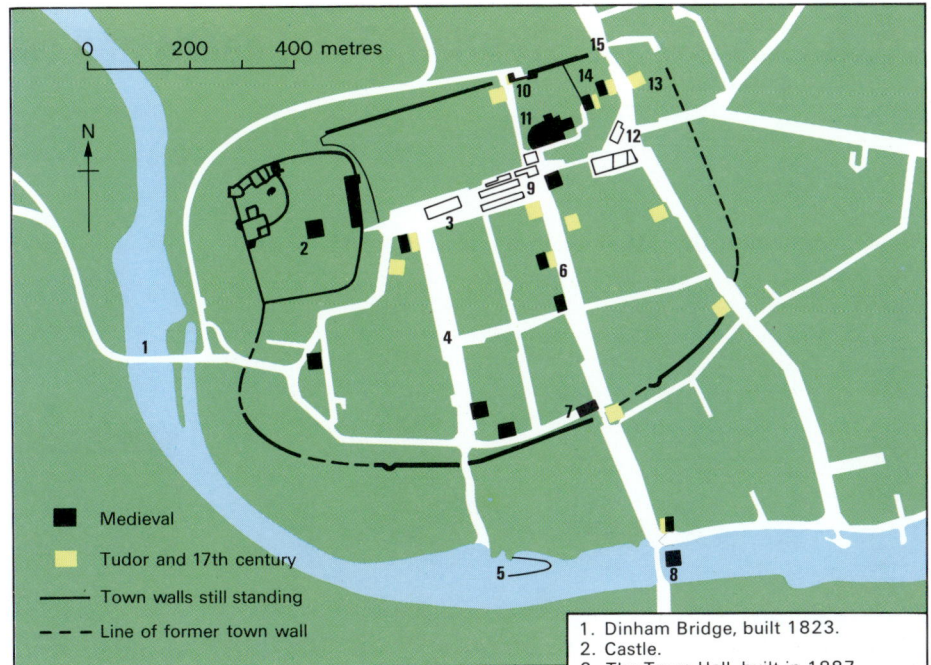

Plan of central Ludlow with main tourist attractions

1 Describe the changes in holidaymaking during the 1970s shown in the diagrams.

2 What is the effect of the seasonal nature of holidaymaking on **a**) prices, **b**) congestion, **c**) traffic flows?

3 How might the feelings towards Ludlow or a similar site vary between **a**) a young resident, **b**) a local shopkeeper **c**) a local builder and developer, **d**) a tourist?

4 Name an historic site or town near your home.

View over central Ludlow

1. Dinham Bridge, built 1823.
2. Castle.
3. The Town Hall, built in 1887.
4. Mill Street.
5. Site of medieval corn and fulling mills.
6. Broad Street, described in 1540 as 'the fayrest part of the town'.
7. The Broad Gate. A sixteenth and seventeenth century house is built over and round the medieval gatehouse.
8. Ludford Bridge. (fourteenth century).
9. The Butter Cross, built in 1743, replacing the medieval High Cross.
10. Site of Linney Gate. Ditch to east and west used for archery practice in 15th century.
11. St. Lawrence's Parish Church.
12. The Bull Ring, once called 'the Beastmarket'.
13. The Feathers, once a town house for local gentry and officials, later an inn.
14. The Bull, an inn since before 1600. Street widens at site of Corve Gate.
15. A few half-timbered buildings still stand in Corve Street.

Medieval
Tudor and 17th century
Town walls still standing
Line of former town wall

145

Stonehenge before the introduction of tourist control barriers

Attempts have been made to control visitors' access to the Stonehenge site, for its protection and for greater enjoyment

Stonehenge setting

From the Director-General of The National Trust

Sir, Launching the National Trust's appeal for the purchase of some 1400 acres of downland surrounding Stonehenge in 1927, the Prime Minister, Stanley Baldwin, wrote that 'The solitude of Stonehenge should be restored, and precautions taken to ensure that our posterity will see it against the sky in the lonely majesty before which our ancestors have stood in awe throughout all our recorded history.' This cardinal principle has been and is still the Trust policy at Stonehenge.

At Stonehenge today there is a threat whose effect could not have been fully anticipated in 1927. This is the great volume of traffic using the roads passing close to the monument. This is why the Trust wholeheartedly supports calls for the closure of the A344 where it passes beside the monument . . .

Yours faithfully
J. D. BOLES

Tourism provides an important source of income and many jobs to the people of Ludlow. Yet the older, historic town centre creates an inefficient traffic flow, and many of the older buildings are unsuitable for present-day uses. The problem of many heritage towns is how to develop them to meet the needs of residents, while conserving that evidence of the past that gives pleasure to both local people and thousands of tourists.

A similar problem exists with historic sites such as Stonehenge. The large stone circle, of great age and uncertain origin, has attracted millions of people over the decades. In fact the pressure from tourists – greater now that so many people have cars and motorcycles – is likely to damage the site and the stone circles themselves. Various means of controlling the visitors and sightseers have been tried, not always with success. It is difficult to know how to allow access to such a site to a lot of people with different, and sometimes conflicting interests, without their swamping the site and causing physical damage.

The car park at Stonehenge. Access to the site is by tunnel under the A344 road

The location of Stonehenge

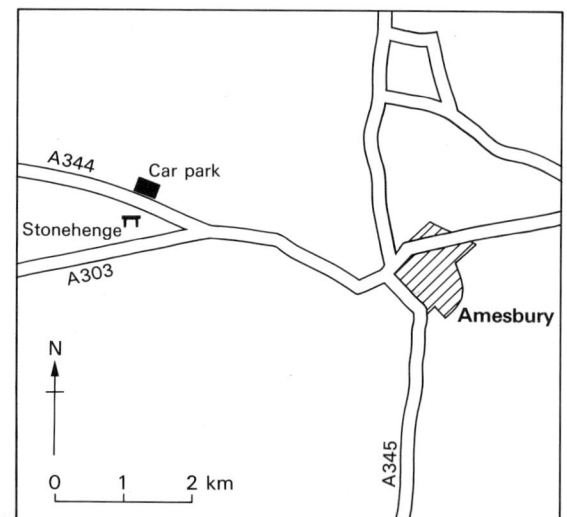

Exercise 35 Tourist sites

1 Imagine you are a foreign visitor to Britain. Choose one of the five routes on the map that you would like to follow. Draw a map of Britain, show the route and name the five places. For each place describe one of its tourist attractions.

2 Describe six different types of tourist attraction from the list below.

3 a) List the six top sites from the list. What do you notice about their location? **b**) Is there any relationship between the price of admission and the popularity of the attraction?

4 List the six top countries of origin of foreign tourists to Britain in 1980 in rank order.

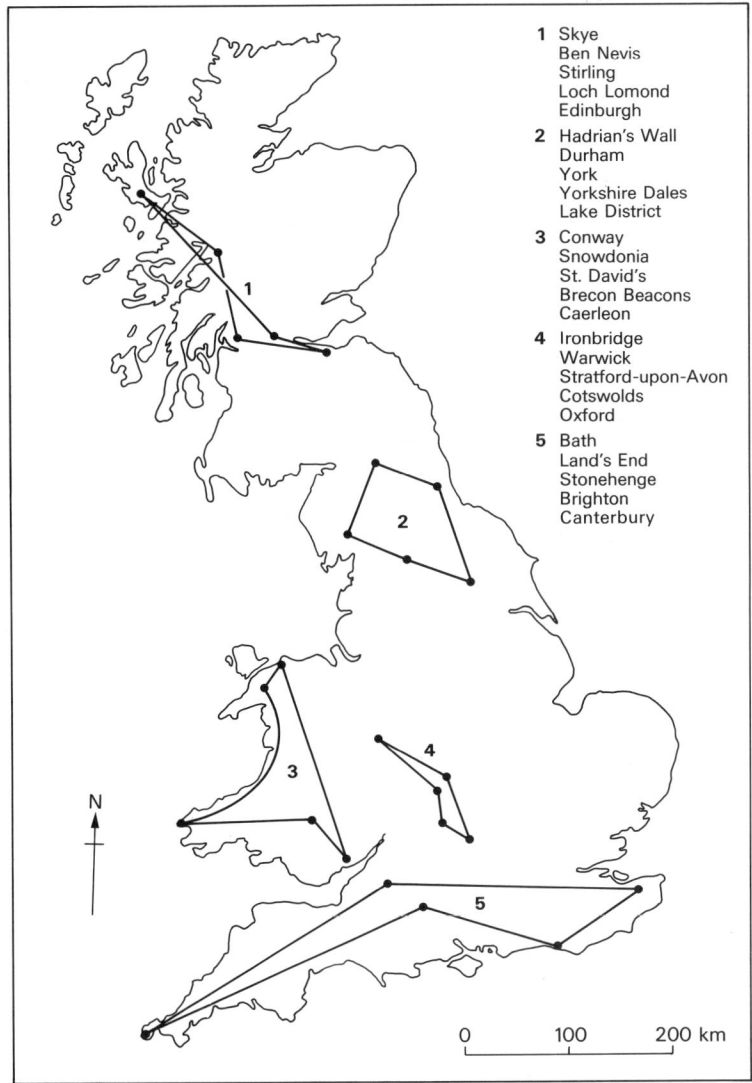

1 Skye
  Ben Nevis
  Stirling
  Loch Lomond
  Edinburgh
2 Hadrian's Wall
  Durham
  York
  Yorkshire Dales
  Lake District
3 Conway
  Snowdonia
  St. David's
  Brecon Beacons
  Caerleon
4 Ironbridge
  Warwick
  Stratford-upon-Avon
  Cotswolds
  Oxford
5 Bath
  Land's End
  Stonehenge
  Brighton
  Canterbury

Five different possible tourist routes

Popular English tourist attractions (number of visitors)

	1981	1982	Admission
Tower of London	2 088 000	1 895 000	£3.00
Roman Baths & Pump Room, Bath	657 000	675 000	£1.40
State Apartments, Windsor	727 000	659 000	£1.20
Stonehenge	546 000	531 000	60p
Beaulieu Abbey	477 000	502 000	£3.00
Hampton Court Palace	524 000	467 000	£1.80
Shakespeare's birthplace, Stratford-on-Avon	460 000	441 000	£1.00
Leeds Castle, Kent	340 000	300 000	£2.95
Blenheim Palace	340 000	312 000	£2.50
Salisbury Cathedral	300 000	300 000	Free
Royal Pavilion, Brighton	318 000	291 000	£1.00
Croxteth Hall, Merseyside	201 000	219 000	£1.20
Dickens' House	17 403	21 680	75p
Keats' House	23 814	23 485	Free
St Paul's Cathedral	2–3 million		Free
Westminster Abbey	1 900 000	1 700 000	Free
British Museum	2 603 022	2 966 244	Free
Tate Gallery	885 168	1 219 102	Free
Victoria and Albert Museum	1 368 460	1 667 071	Free
London Zoo	1 053 000	1 026 000	£2.75
Madame Tussaud's	1 991 995	1 875 315	£2.95

Overseas visitors to Britain, 1980

Area of residence of visitors	Thousands
Belgium and Luxembourg	307
Denmark	110
France.	660
West Germany	692
Irish Republic	343
Italy	148
Netherlands	440
Norway, Sweden, Finland	229
Spain	127
Switzerland	151
Australia	208
Canada	130
Commonwealth Africa	117
Commonwealth Asia	88
Japan	83
Latin America	166
Middle East	249
North Africa	57
South Africa	76
USA	806
Other countries	304
Total	5491

Holidays abroad

The tourist industry is big business, and very competitive

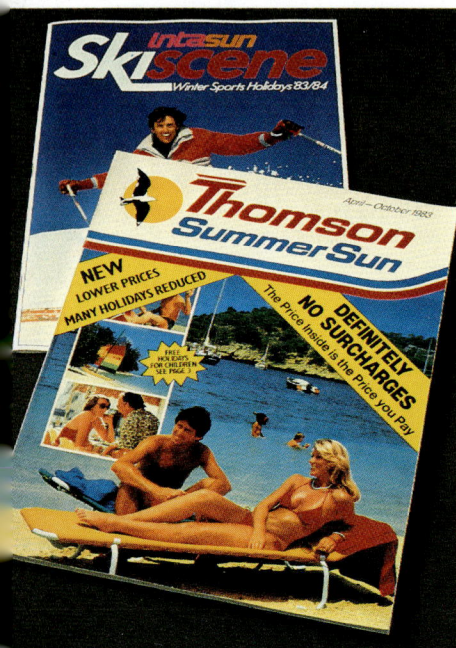

Holidays abroad

There has been an enormous increase in the number of British people taking holidays abroad in recent decades, and as the graph on page 144 shows the trend continued during the 1970s. This has been partly due to the increase in holiday time available and to increased income. Most significant has been the growth of the 'package' tour, where tour operators offer a complete package of travel, accommodation and sometimes entertainment. This has meant that the costs of some overseas holidays to selected places are as cheap as any in Britain. This could well offset the effect of high unemployment in the early 1980s on the number of people taking overseas holidays.

There have been increases in other sorts of holidays. Some people are able to afford luxury cruises on liners such as the QE2. By contrast many thousands go walking or camping all over Europe. Another variation is skiing or winter holidaying in the Alps or at other winter resorts, or winter tours to North Africa or the USA. One striking fact is that while less than 20 per cent of holidays in Britain start outside the

Corfu, Greece, attracts tourists with sun, beaches, and modern amenities

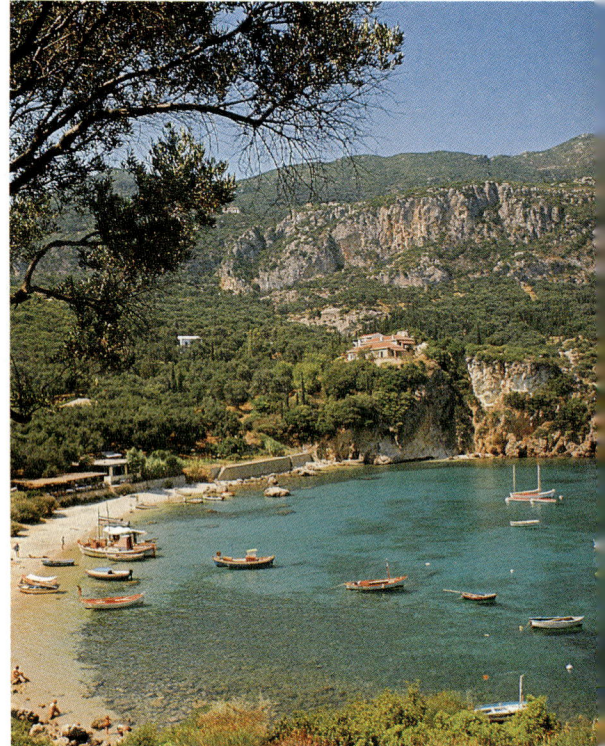

peak season between May and September, the figure for overseas holidays taken outside the peak season is over 30 per cent. The favourite package tourist centres in 1983 are given above, while the percentage of all tourists going to various countries in 1980 is given on page 150.

The seasonal variations in air traffic at Gatwick show the seasonal nature of tourism

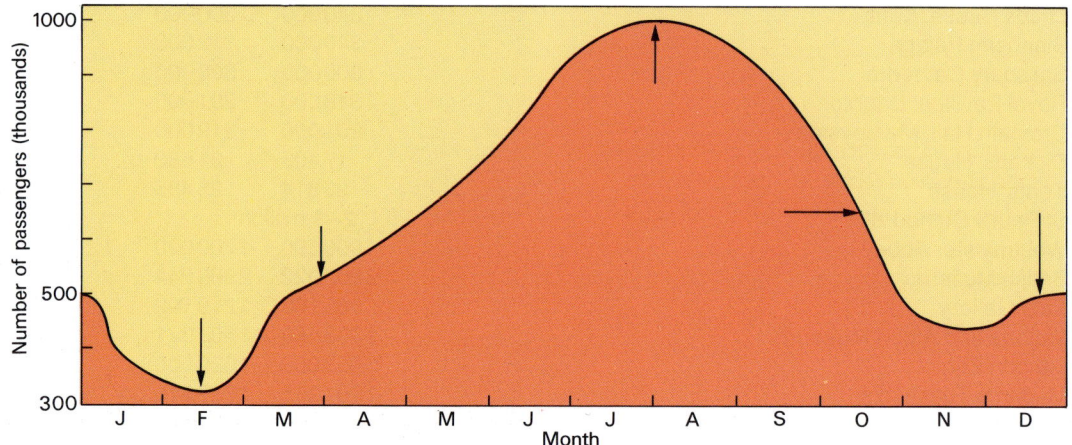

Holiday passenger ports

Many package tours leave and return from airports such as Gatwick, Luton and Heathrow. The seasonal nature of traffic at airports is suggested by the graph. Luxury liners need large harbour and dock facilities, and the main point of departure is Southampton. Dover is less spectacular to look at, but most impressive when passenger traffic is considered. Dover is one of the cross-Channel ferry ports that handle millions of tourists each year. It is particularly suited for travel to France, though its distance from some homes and destinations may make tourists prefer one of the other ferry ports. While there has been a decline in ocean passenger travel in the face of competition from faster air travel, there has been a big growth in cross-Channel passenger traffic.

Dover is an artificial harbour, with shelter being provided by various breakwaters. Ferry ships and Hovercraft operate from the port, each needing its own type of dockside facilities and equipment. Other features are the docks where railway coaches can be loaded directly on to ferries, and special road and dock facilities where cars, coaches (and transport lorries) can drive onto the special ships. A site near Dover has been selected as one entrance to the proposed Channel Tunnel. Dover already leads the rest as a holiday ferry port, and if passengers using the tunnel were to be added to the port trade, then the total would be enormous.

Overseas tourism means not only big business to the tour operators and the resorts, but employment and income to those working at the sea ports and airports and on planes and ships used to carry the holidaymakers.

1 Tourist operators understandably mention the good features of package tours. What are some of the disadvantages?

2 Copy the graph and add labels explaining the variations at the times indicated.

3 Make a sketch of the photograph of Dover harbour and port, and label to show features mentioned in the text and on the map.

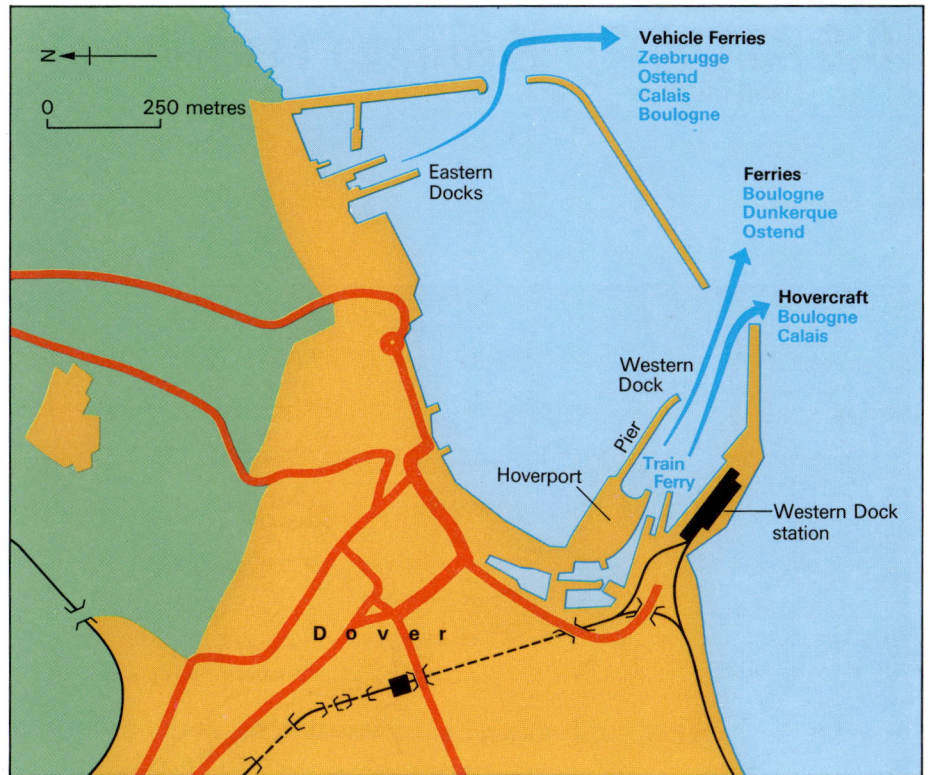

A plan of Dover harbour

View over Dover harbour

Exercise 36 Holiday areas abroad

The countries of Europe

1 Copy or trace the map of the countries of Europe. Show the percentage of British holidaymakers that visited each in 1982. Choose three colours to indicate those which showed an increase, no change and a decrease in percentage between 1971 and 1982.

2 **a)** Suggest why Spain had so many more visitors than any other European country. **b)** What have Greece and Switzerland to offer as tourist attractions? **c)** Account for the change in percentage of tourists from Britain to the USA.

3 What were the main changes in accommodation used by holidaymakers abroad between 1971 and 1980?

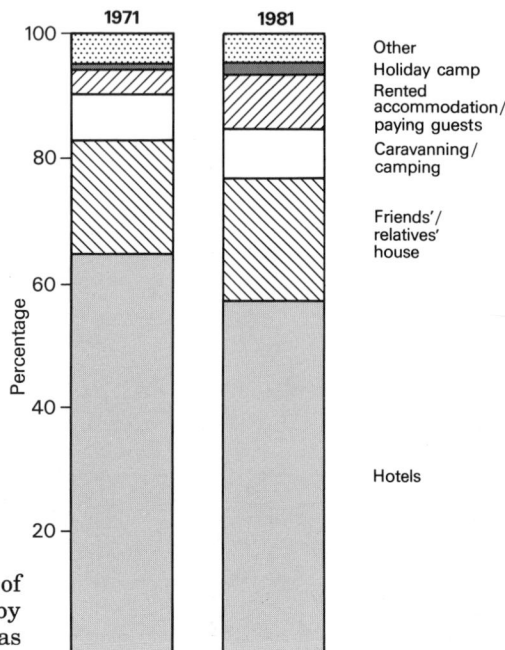

The different kinds of accommodation used by British tourists overseas

Destination of Britons on holiday abroad (adults only) %

	1971	1982
Belgium	3	1
France	10	15
West Germany	6	5
Ireland	6	4
Italy	8	7
Netherlands	3	2
Austria	7	3
Denmark	1	1
Greece	3	8
Spain	34	30
Switzerland	4	2
Rest of Europe	4	8
United States	2	5
Other countries	7	7
No one country for more than 3 nights	2	3
Total	100	100
Number taking holidays (millions)	41	47

Chapter 7 Transport and travel

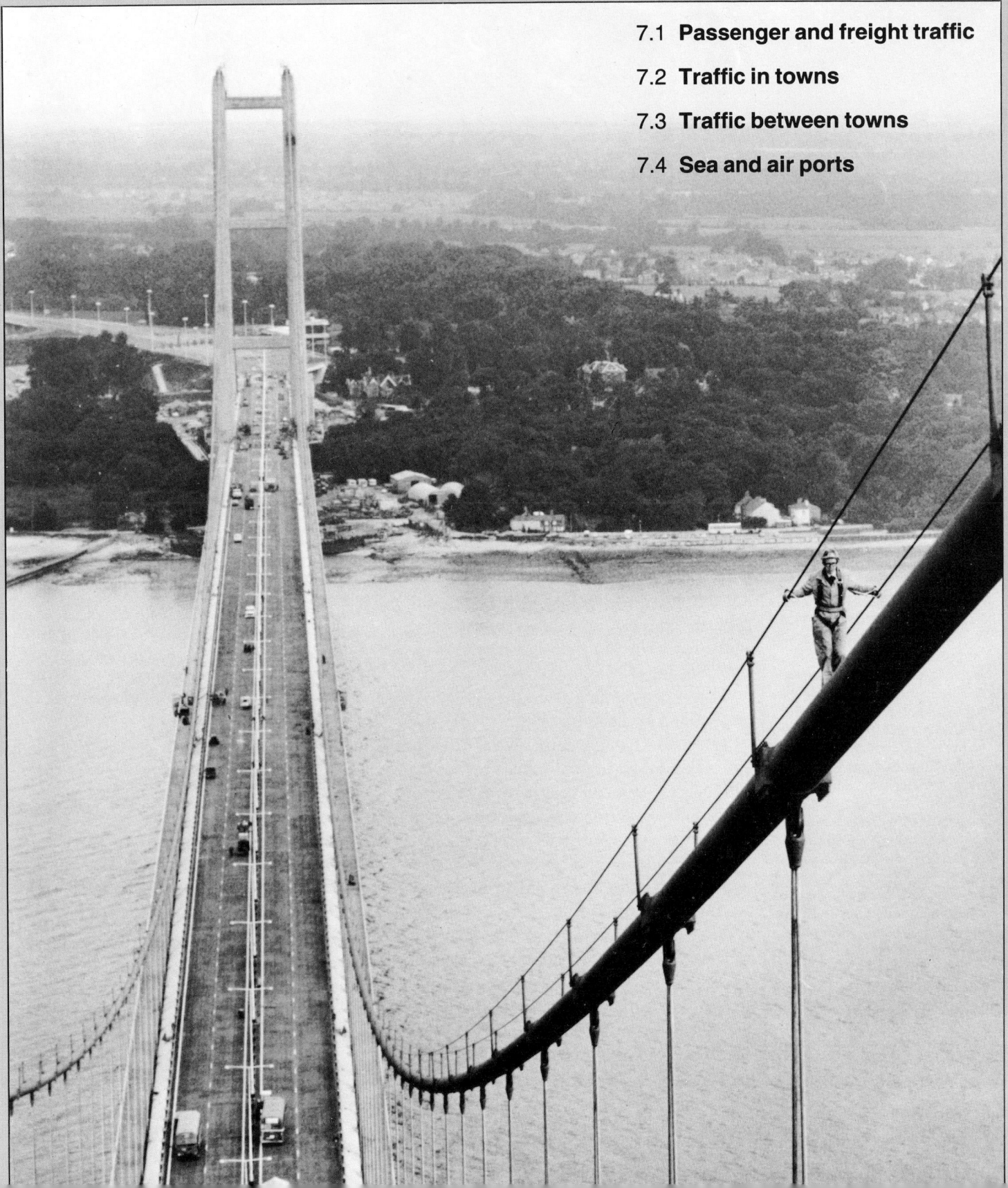

Passenger and freight traffic

At peak periods Victoria Coach Station is swamped with coaches and travellers. It is London's main coach terminal

Housewife's feet are made for walking

The housewife is still a great footslogger, according to an unpublished study by the Transport and Road Research Laboratory. Deprived of both public and private transport, she makes nearly half her journeys on foot, much more than average for the population.

She lacks the use of a car either because her husband has it, or because she cannot drive. She lacks the use of a bus because, with children, the effort and expense are too great. Housewives make up 45 per cent of women of working age, and although 65 per cent of them live in households owning one or more cars, only 31 per cent hold a driving licence.

Most housewifely journeys take place by day, a survey of more than 3000 households shows. But that is just when the car is not available.

Passenger traffic

The graph tells us two things about passenger traffic in Britain, a) the contributions of different methods of travel and b) how these and the total changed over twenty years. The unit of measurement is 'passenger kilometres', and this figure is obtained from calculating the total distance travelled by all passengers in a particular year. What is very striking is the big increase in private car passenger kilometres.

The causes of this changing pattern are varied and complicated.

The growth of car journeys is obviously linked to the growth in car ownership. Cars are used increasingly for work journeys, and there has also been a big increase in car journeys for shopping, recreation and holidays. The cost of car travel has increased a great deal with the increases in the cost of petrol, but the convenience of car travel is very powerful. Usually it means that people can go from home to destination, if not door-to-door, by car. The newspaper article is a reminder, though, that not all people have equal access to car transport. There is a danger that with the decline of public passenger traffic, those families without cars and women in families with only one car may be at an even greater disadvantage.

Cost is one of the important factors to consider in deciding whether to travel by car, train or coach. Rail fares have risen a great deal in recent years and coach services try to compete with rail and car by offering lower costs. This certainly attracts many passengers. The problem of coach travel is that it usually takes longer than a similar journey by rail or car, and on the whole there is not the same comfort and convenience. To counter this, some coaches now offer luxury travel with film or video, refreshment and toilet facilities. Speed and comfort have to be taken into account as well as the cost of the journey. Air travel is usually fastest for longer distances, but the time taken to get to and from airports can easily affect this big advantage. Perhaps the most dramatic example of passenger travel is the daily rail commuter service to and from big cities, and these present their own problems of cost and comfort.

Private car use has greatly increased over the last twenty years

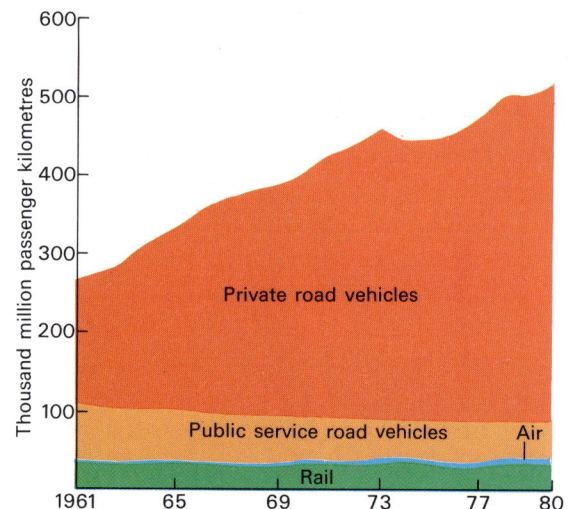

152

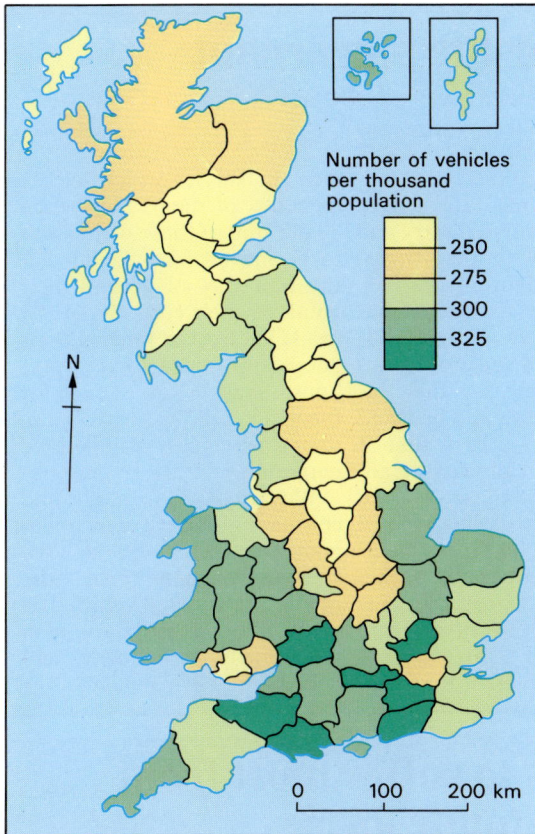

Car ownership varies considerably between different parts of Britain. It has increased rapidly, however, in all areas in recent years

Freight traffic

Marked changes have also taken place in freight traffic. The reasons are once again to do with costs, speed, and reliability. There are great differences in the nature of freight to be carried, though, and this affects the type of transport used. Under the general heading of freight come the following diverse things, a) bulk commodities like coal and ore, b) fresh foodstuffs, c) small but valuable engineering products, d) mail and packages, e) liquids such as milk and oil and f) dangerous chemicals. Designers and engineers have produced special vehicles to carry these different sorts of freight. Bulky low-value goods are carried in special trucks, lorries or barges, while liquids are often transported by pipeline. Refrigerated trucks are used to carry frozen or chilled goods. All these special facilities have to be taken into account when deciding what form of transport to use.

Who pays for the transport system?

It is sometimes argued that users should pay the actual cost of the service provided. This should cover not only wages and fuel, but also costs of maintaining or improving the service. The trouble is that if this were the case, many services would close down. A rather different view is to regard an efficient public transport system as an essential social service, and to keep even uneconomic rail and bus services operating for social reasons.

Many complicated fare arrangements exist to attract passenger and freight users. There are rail fare reductions for the elderly, for students, for season ticket holders, and for everyone at certain times of the day. As far as freight goes, road, rail, inland waterways and air all compete for business. Special terms are therefore offered to attract customers.

1 Describe the share of freight carried by different methods of transport in the early 1980s.

2 **a**) Account for the variation in car ownership per 1000 people in Britain, **b**) Which sectors of society are most dependent on public transport?

3 Where does the money come from to pay for the various transport systems?

4 Look through this book and give examples of specialised forms of freight traffic.

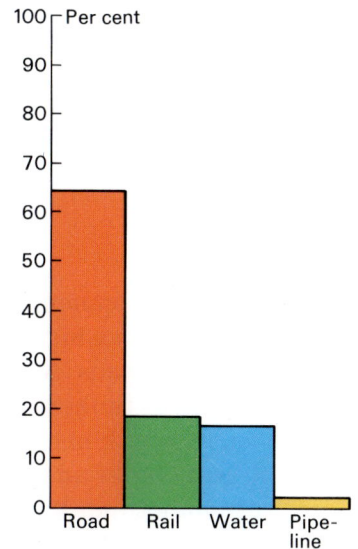

The majority of Britain's goods traffic goes by road

Rail commuters leaving London's Liverpool St. Station

Power stations are large customers for British Rail freight traffic

153

The juggernaut

One of the developments in freight traffic in recent decades has been a big increase in the amount carried on the roads. As well as the use of specialised lorries, such as tankers for carrying liquids, there has been a growth in container loads and lorry size. The largest lorries and lorry and trailer combinations are sometimes known as juggernauts (the name is based on that of a Hindu god whose idol was annually dragged along on a huge waggon, under which people are said to have thrown themselves).

Lorry owners want lorries to be large and carry big loads, in order to reduce the cost of transport. Most people would approve of this if it kept the cost of goods down. On the other hand these big lorries cause a great deal of noise and fumes, and they block other traffic in towns and on narrow roads. Their sheer weight and the vibration they cause is also blamed for the break-up of many roads, bridges and buildings. Opponents of juggernauts argue that more freight should be carried by rail and canal, and there is a continuing debate about what limits should be imposed on the length and weight of lorries, their loads, and the amount of noise and pollution they cause.

Juggernauts are nowadays a common sight on British roads

Case for the juggernaut
It is a vital servant of society

Some years ago the word 'juggernaut' became attached to the heavy articulated lorry and identified it with that frightening Hindu figure; since then an emotional campaign has been launched against this vital servant of society. In this campaign, some say that this type of vehicle should be taxed more heavily, others that it should not be allowed at all. Let us consider these ideas.

First, why does this type of vehicle exist? The road haulage industry operates within what economists call the 'perfect market.' This means that those engaged in it can only remain in business if they provide the service which society demands of them. More than 80 per cent of those with goods to be moved have found that the best way of getting their goods to their customers is by road. The cost of moving their goods to shops and warehouses must be low enough for them to sell successfully in their own highly competitive markets.

We are now a greedy and consuming society which demands everything at the cheapest possible price. The modern articulated vehicle has evolved to play its vital role in this cruelly competitive and demanding environment.

Bridges to suffer most from new 40-tonne lorries

After years of nervous hesitation, the Government has finally announced details of its proposal to raise the maximum lorry weight from 32.5 to 40 tonnes. The news was greeted with fury and sadness by environmentalists, and with pleasure and relief by industry. But the White Paper says that the effect will be to improve the environment because there will be fewer heavy lorries, and to improve the economy by saving about £150m a year.

Because the extra weight will be spread on five axles instead of four, road damage will be reduced by 5 per cent. There is one exception to that, however: long-span bridges could suffer more.

Noise levels of heavy lorries will be progressively reduced so that by 1990 the noise coming from new lorries on the road will be half this year's level, and no louder than a modern new car.

The paper accepts that 'the effect of big lorries on people and the communities through which they pass is now a matter of grave public concern. The Government is determined to tackle those environmental and social problems vigorously.'

Heavy freight, such as petrol, would benefit most. ICI stands to gain £16m a year, or 12 per cent of its transport costs.

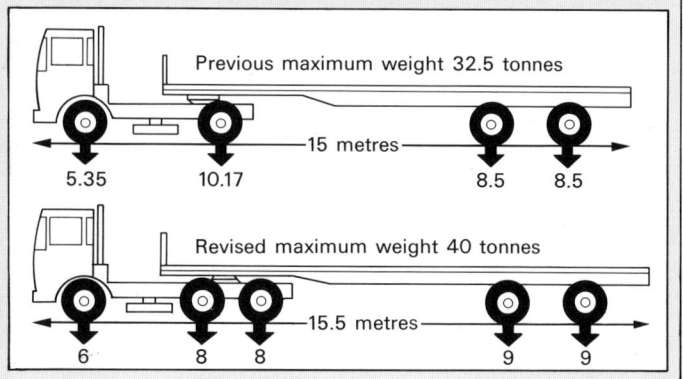

Previous maximum weight 32.5 tonnes
← 15 metres →
5.35   10.17   8.5   8.5

Revised maximum weight 40 tonnes
← 15.5 metres →
6   8   8   9   9

Exercise 37
Contrasts in road and rail travel

1 Design another advertisement that puts an opposite point of view.

2 Refer to the diagram below showing the relative times of rail and coach from City Z to 5 other towns.
a) Why is it not surprising that rail journeys are shorter than coach journeys? b) It is much quicker by rail than road from Z to C and not much quicker from Z to A. Explain.

3 Using the information in the table draw a similar diagram to show the times taken to travel by coach and rail from London to five of the other cities. Is the difference in coach and rail times always the same? If not, account for the variations.

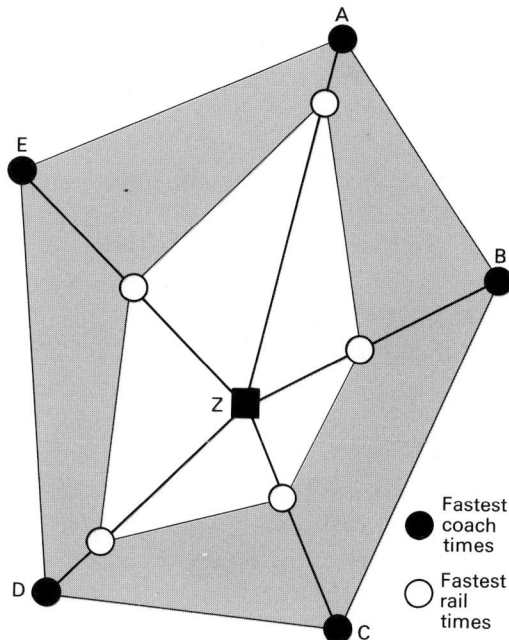

IS BURNING UP AND DOWN THE MOTORWAY BURNING UP YOUR ENERGY?

Even without accidents or hold-ups, motorway driving is a tiring and frustrating business. You daren't stop concentrating.

Admittedly, a long drive might allow you time to collect your thoughts. But then try writing them down. And if you stop for a quick bite, you just lengthen the time of your journey.

So why burn up valuable energy when you can work and relax in comfort and arrive at your meeting feeling ready to face anything? **This is the age of the train ⇒**

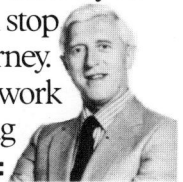

Fastest coach times ●
Fastest rail times ○

Journey times from London by coach and rail

London to	Bearing (degrees)	Distance (km)	Coach	Rail
Bradford	335	330	4 hrs	2 hrs 34 mins
Brighton	182	85	2 hrs	58 mins
Bristol	270	190	2 hrs 30 mins	1 hr 27 mins
Cardiff	270	245	3 hrs 15 mins	1 hr 43 mins
Carlisle	334	490	6 hrs	3 hrs 44 mins
Edinburgh	339	650	9 hrs	4 hrs 37 mins
Exeter	254	275	3 hrs 30 mins	2 hrs 18 mins
Glasgow	325	640	9 hrs	5 hrs 8 mins
Hull	356	330	4 hrs	2 hrs 51 mins
Leeds	339	310	3 hrs 30 mins	2 hrs 4 mins
Manchester	328	320	3 hrs 45 mins	2 hrs 29 mins
Newcastle	346	450	5 hrs 15 mins	2 hrs 58 mins
Nottingham	335	205	3 hrs 15 mins	1 hr 59 mins
Norwich	036	184	3 hrs	1 hr 50 mins
Sheffield	335	267	3 hrs 40 mins	2 hrs 30 mins
Southampton	234	125	2 hrs 15 mins	1 hr 7 mins

Traffic in towns

A variety of types of road traffic in Corporation Street, Birmingham

The main streets of many old towns are almost choked by road traffic at certain times of the day

Many older cities like Bath have had to introduce complicated one-way systems

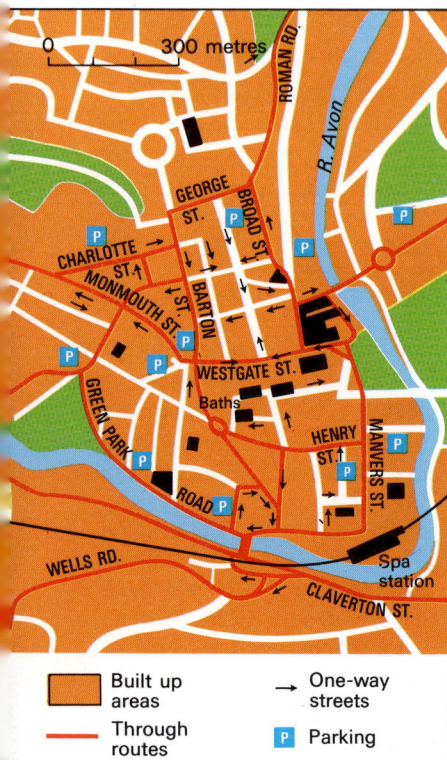

300 metres

ROMAN RD.
R. Avon
GEORGE ST.
BROAD ST.
CHARLOTTE ST.
MONMOUTH ST.
BARTON ST.
WESTGATE ST.
Baths
GREEN PARK
HENRY ST.
MANVERS ST.
ROAD
WELLS RD.
CLAVERTON ST.
Spa station

Built up areas

Through routes

→ One-way streets

P Parking

Problems of congestion

People and goods in large numbers need to move or be carried around towns and cities. Most traffic has a town as the starting point or destination of its journey. The basic difficulty in most towns is that the rail and road network is not adequate to carry all this traffic, particularly at times of heavy flow. Another very common problem is that there are not enough places for cars and lorries to park in the town when the journey is completed. Car parking problems, crowded roads and traffic jams, are the reasons why many people travel by public transport in our towns and cities.

Most people will have travelled by car or bus through a town during the evening, and will know how much easier this journey is than during the day. The twice-daily rush-hours are particularly difficult times for road travel, while commuter trains including underground trains are often packed in the early morning and late afternoon. The movement of freight traffic may be more evenly spread in time – the very early morning deliveries to the

wholesale markets have already been mentioned. But many goods can only be delivered during working hours, and vans and lorries add to the car and bus traffic. In some towns and cities traffic congestion and delay has become more than a nuisance. It has become a serious threat to efficiency and the quality of life.

Speeding the flow

Different methods have been used to try to speed traffic flow through towns. A mixture of different sorts of traffic, and an outdated road system, built in the past to serve different conditions, are two major causes of delay. One solution has been to build urban motorways directly through cities along the major routes. This certainly speeds up the flow, but it is extremely expensive. Apart from that urban motorways use large amounts of extremely valuable land, and can have a disastrous impact on the surrounding environment. The people who suffer are frequently not those who benefit from the smoother flow. Yet another problem is the congestion that occurs when the motorway ends and traffic has to flow along older main roads.

Other methods taken to speed the flow are shown on page 158.

While so many people use cars to get to work or shop, there have to be car parks. Yet land in the city centre is in great demand. The solution has been to build upwards, and the multi-storey car park is a feature of most urban centres. Parking is also controlled by the use of meters, traffic wardens, and by restricting or forbidding parking along certain sections of streets. There is plenty of evidence, however, that many parking offences go undetected and the system is not very effective. Illegal and irresponsible parking of cars can add to road congestion and traffic flow. The parking of heavy commercial lorries in quiet suburban areas is a problem for local residents, as is the use of these roads as a useful short-cut route for freight traffic.

Policies for public transport

Local authorities responsible for public transport want to provide an efficient and reliable service that is also cheap. At the same time they want it to provide enough money to both pay for and continually improve the service. Most find the task almost impossible! If fares are raised to obtain sufficient income to run the service, many people will not be able to afford it and the income will fall. If in order to be more efficient, or to cut costs, some services are reduced or abandoned, then more people will be forced to use cars. Once again the income will fall. As more cars are used, traffic flow and parking problems increase. Many people would claim anyway that a cheap and efficient public transport service is something all communities are entitled to. In the case of London and other tourist places, a good public transport system is necessary to attract visitors and tourists. So a means has to be found to pay for the service.

In 1982 the Greater London Council tried to improve its service provided by London Transport by dramatically cutting fares. This was to be paid for by an increase in the rates. There were strong arguments both for and against this policy, but eventually it was declared illegal on a point of law. The fares were then increased again to try and increase income from the users rather than the ratepayers. Many other authorities have used this method of subsidising public transport from rates. There is clearly no simple answer to the enormous task of running a city transport system.

1 Draw a graph and explain the information about travel shown in the table for **a**) two methods of travel, e.g. bus and train and **b**) two types of purchase, e.g. casual purchase and luxury goods.

2 Make a plan of a local road system that shows **a**) a one-way system, **b**) a zone of restricted parking, **c**) a car park.

3 What method of easing rush-hour traffic has not been mentioned above?

4 Argue the case for and against raising funds for transport from the local rates.

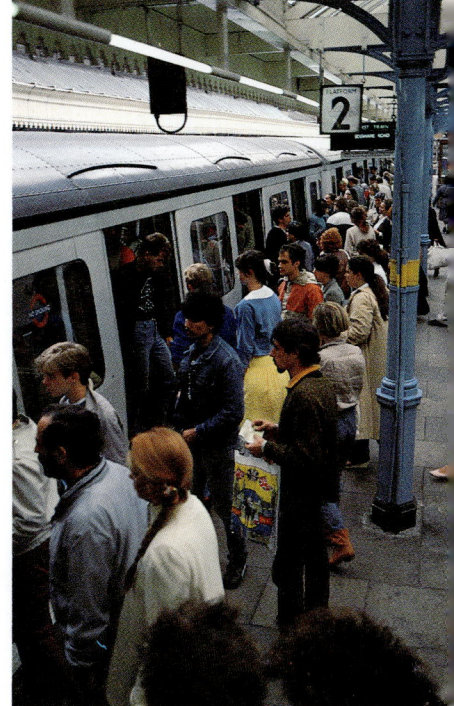

Millions of people use the London Underground each day

Urban motorways were built to speed the flow of traffic in towns

Analysis of shopping journeys by different means of transport

Commodity	Distance travelled (km)	No. of days between trips	Percentage travelling by				
			Foot	Bus	Cycle	Train	Car
Casual purchase	0.55	2.02	83.96	6.42	0.53	0.00	9.09
Regular purchase	1.11	5.49	58.94	14.74	0.53	0.00	25.79
Minor household	1.17	37.67	47.04	24.32	0.53	0.00	28.11
Minor clothing	2.08	66.81	23.78	45.41	0.00	0.00	30.81
Major purchase	3.13	164.71	10.40	44.51	0.00	4.05	41.04
Luxury goods	3.86	286.98	5.43	37.98	0.00	6.98	44.61

Speeding the traffic flow

Cycles are increasingly used for personal transport in many towns

Park-and-ride schemes are designed to keep cars out of city centres

Traffic flow can be improved by various types of control, such as the double roundabout shown here

Some of the methods of speeding up the flow of traffic in towns were mentioned on the previous pages. The solutions were based on the construction of new roads, and on laws allowing only certain routes to be followed. Another approach is to try and persuade people not to bring their cars into the town, either by charging very high prices for parking, or by making the public transport system so cheap and efficient that people prefer to use it. A few inexpensive and small-scale methods of easing the flow of traffic in towns are shown here.

The 'bendy-bus' is designed to carry lots of passengers through city streets

Exercise 38 The Tyne-Wear Metro

A train at the platform on the Tyne-Wear Metro

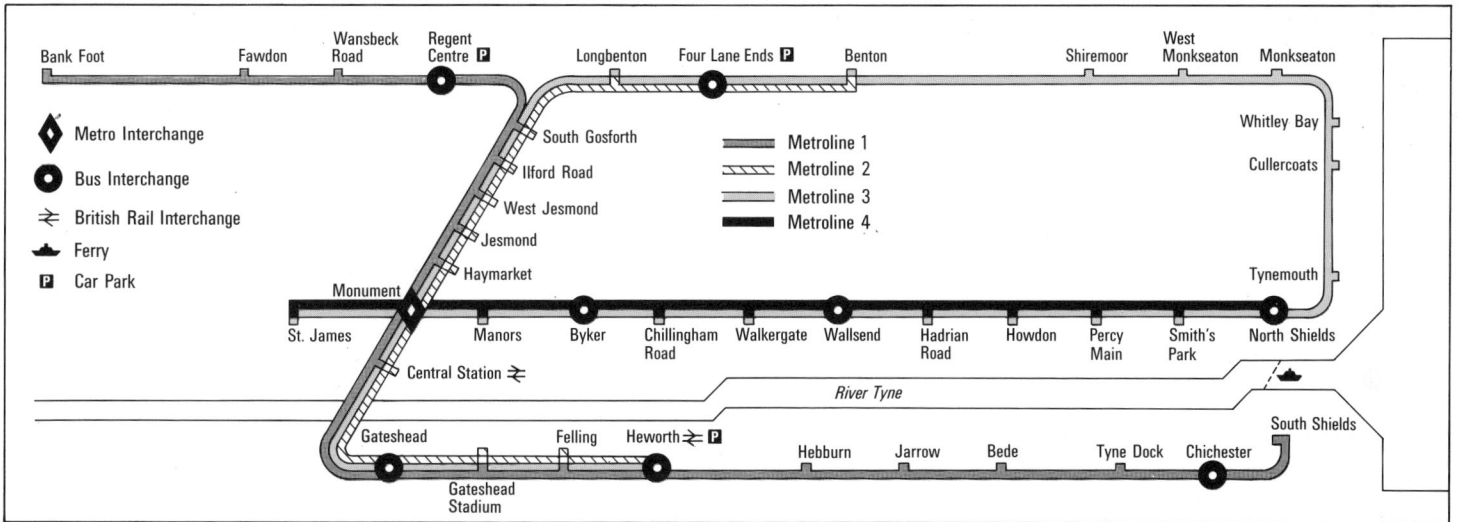

1 **a**) Which towns and cities, and which Local Authorities are served by the Tyne-Wear Metro? **b**) Which other towns or cities in Britain have an underground system?

2 **a**) What is the approximate length of the Metro? Which map must be used? **b**) Which metrolines would you use to get from Gateshead to Tynemouth and from South Shields to Wallsend?

3 What are the advantages and disadvantages of each of the maps shown?

4 Draw a simple map showing the ideal metro system for your town or area.

Metro Interchange
Bus Interchange
British Rail Interchange
Ferry
P Car Park

Metroline 1
Metroline 2
Metroline 3
Metroline 4

Bank Foot, Fawdon, Wansbeck Road, Regent Centre P, Longbenton, Four Lane Ends P, Benton, Shiremoor, West Monkseaton, Monkseaton, Whitley Bay, Cullercoats, Tynemouth

South Gosforth, Ilford Road, West Jesmond, Jesmond, Haymarket, Monument

St. James, Manors, Byker, Chillingham Road, Walkergate, Wallsend, Hadrian Road, Howdon, Percy Main, Smith's Park, North Shields

Central Station, River Tyne, South Shields

Gateshead, Felling, Heworth P, Hebburn, Jarrow, Bede, Tyne Dock, Chichester, Gateshead Stadium

The user's map of the Metro system

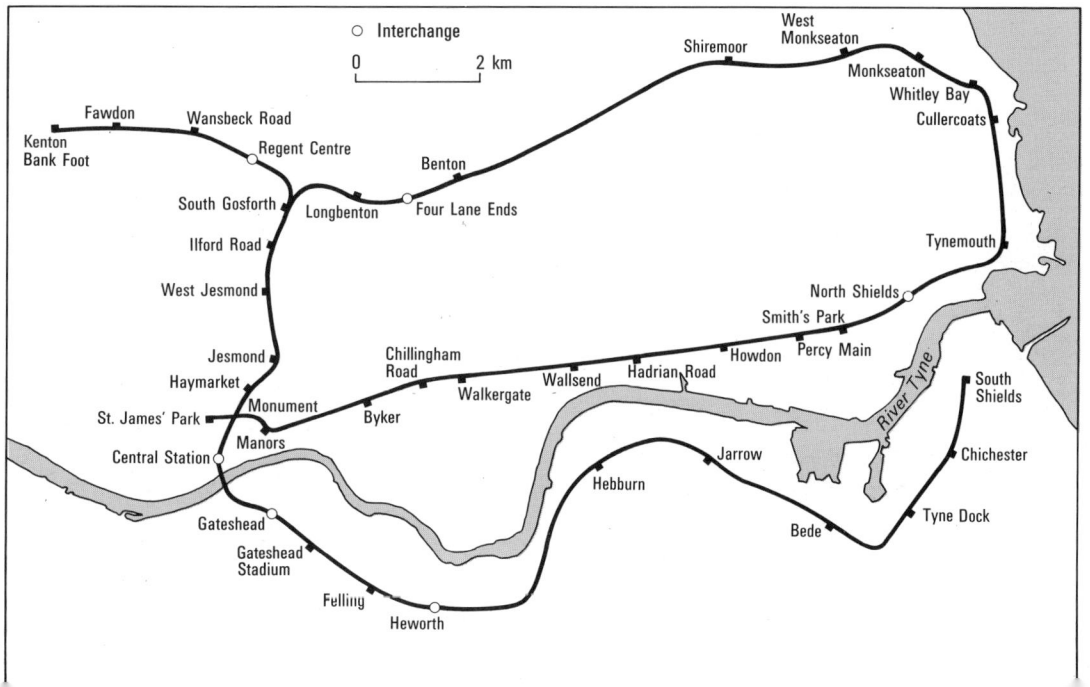

Right: A true-to-scale map of the Metro system

○ Interchange

0   2 km

Fawdon, Kenton Bank Foot, Wansbeck Road, Regent Centre, South Gosforth, Ilford Road, West Jesmond, Jesmond, Haymarket, St. James' Park, Monument, Central Station, Gateshead, Gateshead Stadium, Felling, Heworth, Byker, Chillingham Road, Walkergate, Wallsend, Hadrian Road, Hebburn, Jarrow, Bede, Tyne Dock, Chichester, South Shields, Smith's Park, Percy Main, Howdon, North Shields, Tynemouth, Cullercoats, Whitley Bay, Monkseaton, West Monkseaton, Shiremoor, Benton, Four Lane Ends, Longbenton, Manors, River Tyne

Traffic between towns

British railways

One of the striking features of transport in Britain in recent decades has been the decline in the railway network and in its services. Hundreds of kilometres of line have been taken out of service, especially in rural areas where the lines were being run at a loss. There has also been a reduction of rail services on many lines.

On the other hand there has been investment in some parts of the rail system. Many large towns are now linked by the high-speed trains on the 125 services. Some heavily used routes have already been electrified, while others are planned for the near future. There have also been considerable improvements in productivity per person, with a big reduction in the numbers of workers in the industry. Even so, British Rail continues to be run at a loss, and has to be subsidised by the Government using taxpayers' money.

The diagrams on pages 152 and 153 showed that the railway's share of passenger and freight traffic is a lot less than that of road transport. But the power and steel industries are still big users. In the early 1980s railways carried about 300 000 tonnes of coal and coke each day from the pits to power stations, industrial users and domestic retail points. They also carried about 80 000 tonnes or raw materials and

This topological map of main line routes shows the shortest time taken to reach each town from London in 1984

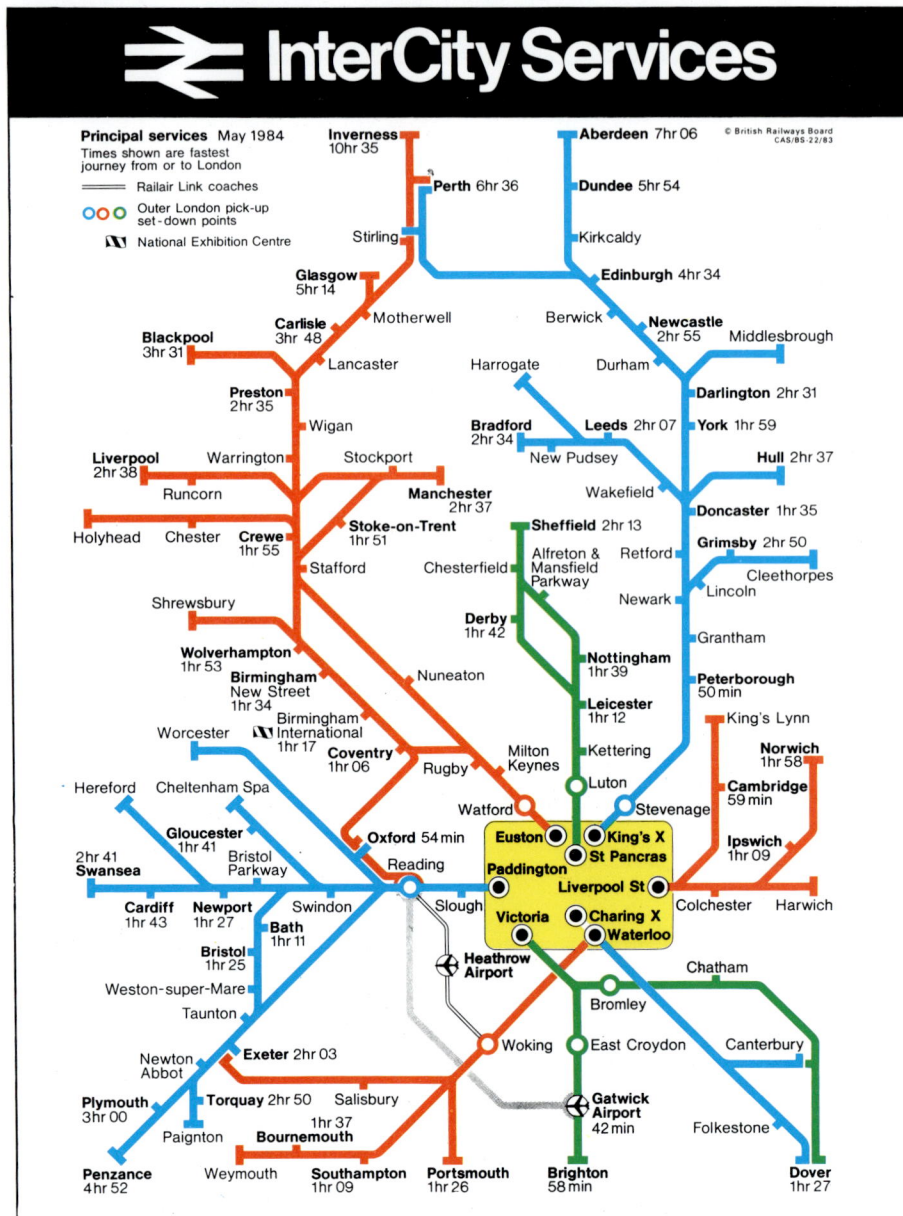

InterCity Services

Principal services May 1984
Times shown are fastest journey from or to London
— Railair Link coaches
○○○ Outer London pick-up set-down points
⊠ National Exhibition Centre

© British Railways Board
CAS/BS-22/83

The share carried by British Rail, of several classes of goods

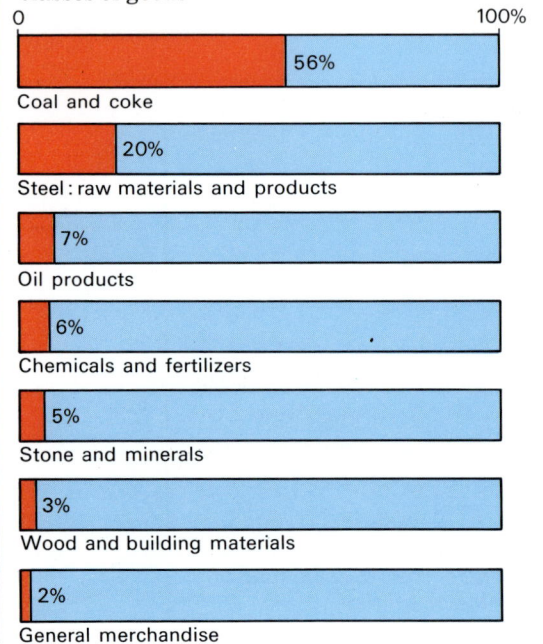

Coal and coke — 56%
Steel: raw materials and products — 20%
Oil products — 7%
Chemicals and fertilizers — 6%
Stone and minerals — 5%
Wood and building materials — 3%
General merchandise — 2%

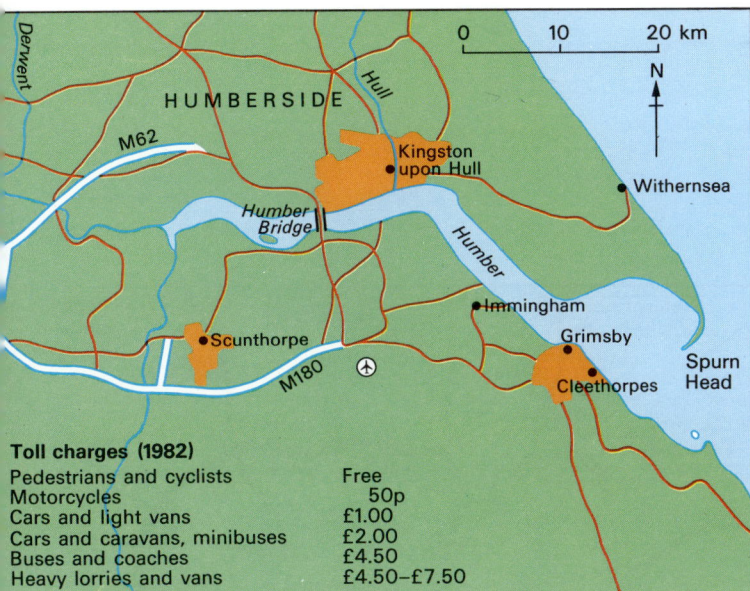

Toll charges (1982)

Pedestrians and cyclists	Free
Motorcycles	50p
Cars and light vans	£1.00
Cars and caravans, minibuses	£2.00
Buses and coaches	£4.50
Heavy lorries and vans	£4.50–£7.50

The Humber Bridge: a magnificent piece of engineering. There is disagreement as to whether the bridge was really needed, and if it was worth the great cost

Left: The location of the Humber Bridge with 1982 toll charges

products for the steel industry each day. As can be seen from the diagram, British Rail's share of other freight is quite small, and it is trying to capture some of this. As far as passengers go, the Inter-City services carry about 2 000 000 a day while there are a further 400 000 commuters each day in the London region.

The road network

At the same time as the rail network has shrunk, there has been a remarkable growth in road building. The most significant part of this has been the construction of the motorways. But the amount of traffic has increased enormously in recent decades, and so a great deal of road traffic is still carried on non-motorway roads. There is no doubt that the motorways have greatly speeded up the flow of traffic, making passenger and freight journeys much easier and quicker. The map on page 162 shows the present motorway pattern, and the photograph is a reminder that motorway construction is still going on.

Some of the road engineering has been spectacular, such as the M4/M5 Almondsbury Interchange (page 121) and the new Humber Bridge. It is also worth remembering that no transport system lasts for ever. Motorways and bridges need continual upkeep and repair. Almost every day there is a radio announcement of motorway roadworks going on somewhere or other. The Severn Bridge, built in 1965 at a cost of £8 million, is showing signs of structural weakness due to heavier-than-expected traffic. Repairs are being done, but the Government is considering building a second Severn Bridge, costing about £100 million, to link England and Wales.

Not everyone is equally enthusiastic about motorways. Some complain that they use up valuable farmland. Others argue that the 'road lobby' is too powerful, and has persuaded the Government to spend money on roads that could have been better spent on rail, canal or air transport.

1 Compare the railway map and motorway map on the next page with the one showing the main towns and cities on page 52. **a**) Which main towns are not served by easy access to motorways? **b**) which areas of Britain are served by Inter-City rail services but not motorways?

2 British Rail is a 'nationalised' industry and a 'monopoly'. What do these two words mean? What are the advantages and disadvantages of being **a**) a nationalised industry, **b**) having a monopoly?

3 What will be the affect of the decline of rail and bus services on village life?

4 Give the cases for and against the building of the Humber bridge.

Bus cuts threat to villages

The Government's proposed cuts in transport grants could sound the death knell for hundreds of English villages from which shops, schools, doctors and recreation facilities have already departed, it was claimed yesterday.

The largely elderly population of such villages depends on local buses to get them to the services in other towns or villages. The proposed cut of 25 per cent in local transport support grants in the coming financial year could be the last straw for bus services already suffering from a decline in the number of passengers and rising costs.

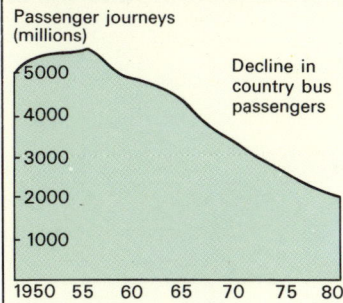

Decline in country bus passengers

A huge motorway junction for the M25 under construction

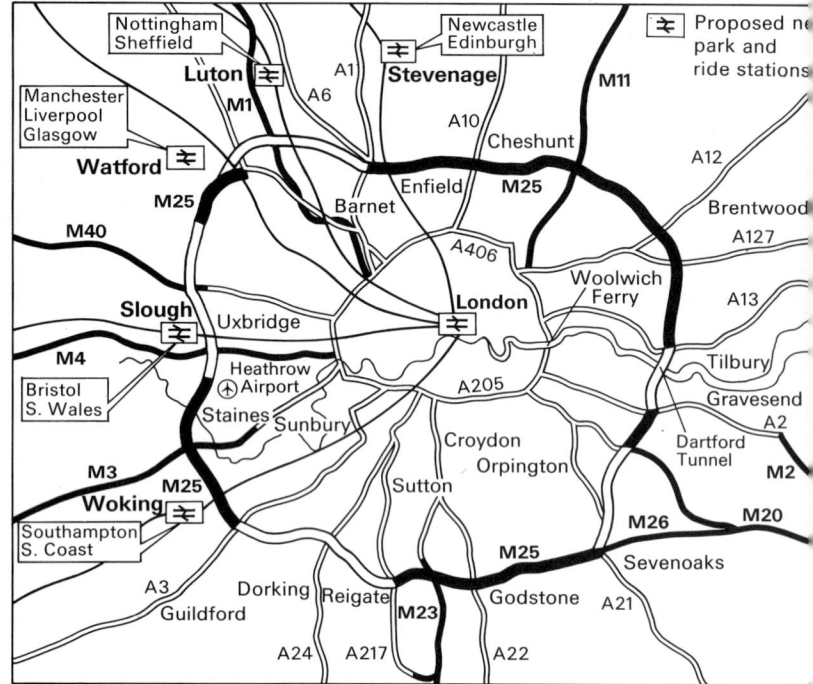

The route of the M25 encircling London

The M25 is Britain's most important new road. The map shows that this motorway encircling London at a radius of 15–20 miles from the centre, should be complete (with the exception of the Dartford Tunnel section), by mid 1986. It is expected that the motorway will attract many new industrial and commercial developments, as well as warehouses and hypermarkets, especially near the junctions with other routes radiating from London. It is also thought that British Rail's Inter-City business traffic will be affected by the new motorway, and to profit from it, BR plan to build a series of new 'park and ride' Inter-City Stations around the M25, as shown on the map.

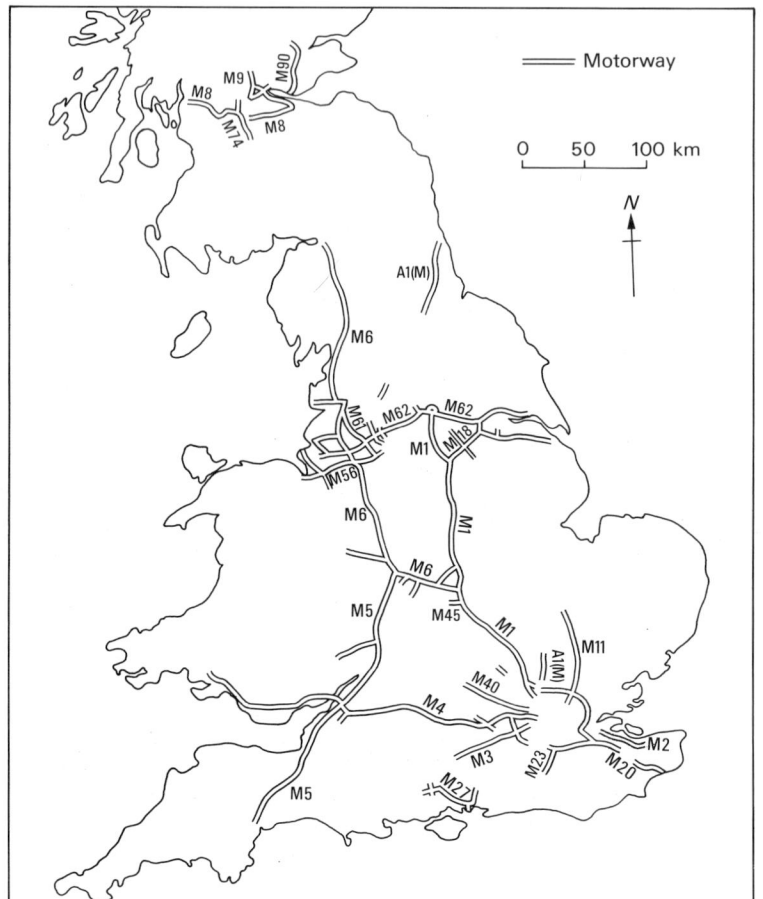

The motorway system in 1983

Exercise 39
Future plans for British Rail

1 Choose two proposals mentioned in the extract below and describe the improvements they would bring. What objections might be raised to these proposals?

2 Describe what is meant by the 'social railway'.

3 Imagine you had to choose 2 000 km to close and 2 000 km to electrify. Which would you select and why?

4 Rank the seven countries shown according to the **percentage** of line electrified. Is there any similarity with the ranking according to total length of rail network?

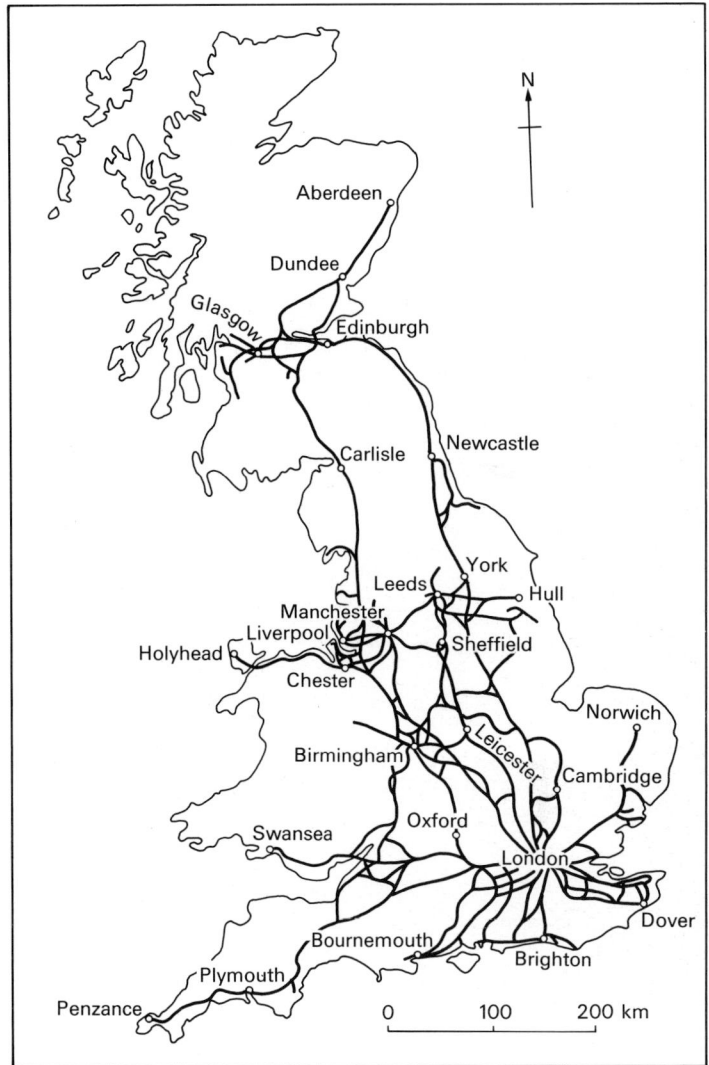

The routes BR wanted to electrify in 1982. In 1984 Government approval was given for the electrification of the East Coast route from London to Edinburgh

BR plea for £5700m modernization

A modernization plan for Britain's railways that proposes overall investment of £5700m in electrified main lines, improved commuter services, low-cost rural railways and a Channel tunnel was announced by British Rail yesterday. Investment should be raised from £306m to £567m a year until 1990, British Rail states. Without it, the railways will continue to decline and 3000 miles of track will have to close.

British Rail suggests a new contract with the Government to pay for the 'social railway', those parts that are un-economic but socially valuable, and greater private sector involvement in the commercial service, for freight, parcels, and inter-city passenger transport. The main decision, to be taken in 'weeks rather than months, and days rather than weeks', was approval for main-line electrification costing about £1000m over 20 years.

A reduction of 38000 in staff over the next five years is envisaged, with the reduced workforce earning higher real wages. Whatever productivity gains were made, extra investment funds would still be needed. Another area for investment would be improving staff working conditions, which have suffered badly in recent years.

Britain's railway system has reached a point at which the nation must choose between investment in improvement or letting the system run down.

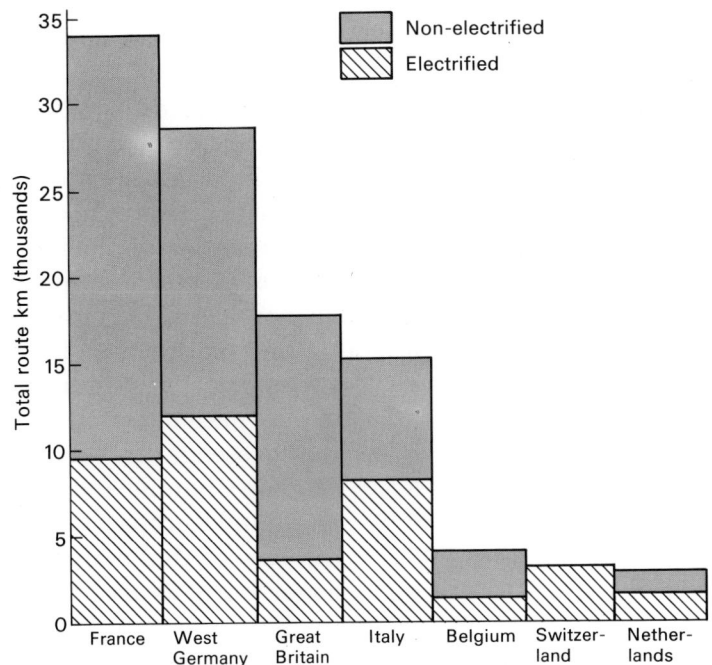

The extent to which some West European countries have electrified their railway lines

Sea and air ports

Newcastle airport. These smaller regional airports are very important locally, and play an increasing part in travel around Britain

Airports in Britain

BAA Airports
Heathrow
Gatwick
Stansted
Glasgow
Edinburgh
Aberdeen
Prestwick

Other authorities
Southend
Manchester
Shoreham
Birmingham
Blackpool
Bristol
Sunderland
Teeside
Cardiff
Coventry
Leicester
Haverfordwest
Humberside
Leeds and Bradford
Liverpool
Newcastle
Dornoch
Dundee
Glenforsa (Mull)
Benbecula Hebrides
Inverness
Islay
Kirkwall
Stornaway
Sumburgh

Other authorities cont.
Eastleigh
Hurn
Glenrothes
Skye
Whalsay Shetlan
Enniskillen
North Ronaldsay
Papa Westray
Sanday
Stronsay
Unst
Alderney
Guernsey
Jersey
Scillies

0   100 km

Cross-Channel passenger traffic 1980

	millions
Foot passengers	6.4
Excursionists	2.6
Car drivers and passengers	6.1
Coach passengers	3.1
Total sea passengers	18.2
Air passengers	2.4
Total passengers	**20.6**

Transport by air and sea

There are many sea and air ports around the coast of Britain handling passengers and freight although only a couple of dozen are of more than local importance. They vary greatly in size and type of traffic handled. A surprising amount of trade is in the coastal movement of heavy and bulky goods such as coal, oil and building materials from one part of Britain to another. Sea ports play little part in the internal movement of passengers whereas airports play an increasingly important part.

Since Britain is an island, it is not surprising that ships contribute greatly to international trade. The table shows that passenger travel across the English Channel and North Sea to mainland Europe is also very great. It can be seen that many millions of passenger journeys are made each year, and the total is expected to become much higher. Air freight is valuable for certain kinds of goods while millions of people travel overseas by air every year.

Three features of international transport by sea are worth stressing. The first is the growth of movement of bulk goods such as oil, coal and iron ore in giant supertankers or bulk carriers. These ships need deep water and special dock facilities, and this has led to the construction of a number of new specialist ports in recent decades. A second change has been the switch from handling general cargo in thousands of separate boxes, bags and packages to the use of containers. These containers, loaded with goods, can be handled by gantry crane directly into or out of ships on to dockside wharves. From here they can be as easily loaded off or on to railway trucks and lorries designed to carry containers. The whole process is fast, efficient and less demanding of labour than older methods. The third change is the introduction of roll-on/roll-off ships and facilities. This means that lorries, coaches and cars can drive directly onto or off a ship. This is an improvement on the expensive and time-consuming methods used in the past. The combination of bulk transport, containerisation and roll-on/roll-off methods have revolutionised the nature of ports and dock practice.

Ports and harbours

There are hundreds of inlets around the coast that provide the combination of deep water and shelter needed for a safe harbour and efficient port. In fact the big British ports developed in the estuaries of the Thames, Mersey, Clyde, Humber, Severn and Southampton Water. The effects of the tides were countered by building docks. Until quite recently the docks at London, Liverpool, Manchester (linked to the estuary by canal), Clydeside, Hull and Southampton were amongst the biggest general ports in the world. The past few decades have seen great changes.

The Port of London Authority has many responsibilities in the lower Thames estuary, including the management of the docks. In the past ships were handled in docks very close to the heart of London (page 114), but with the increase in size of ships and the change in methods of handling freight mentioned above, these older sections of the port became increasingly inefficient. The result is a movement of activity some 40 kilometres downstream from the City to Tilbury docks. Here all the modern methods are employed, and when working normally the turn-around of shipping takes one or two days, rather than weeks as in the older docks. Further downstream are other specialist ports for handling oil and bulk cargoes.

1 What specialist cargoes or traffic are associated with the ports of Milford Haven, Immingham, Hunterston, Hull, Southampton, Folkestone and Newhaven?

2 a) What are the advantages and disadvantages of Tilbury as the main port area for London? b) Why has there been a general decline in west coast, and growth in east and south coast trade in recent decades?

3 a) Which parts of Britain have few Local Authority airports? b) Why are there so many airports in the North of Scotland?

4 How are passengers and freight moved from the port areas?

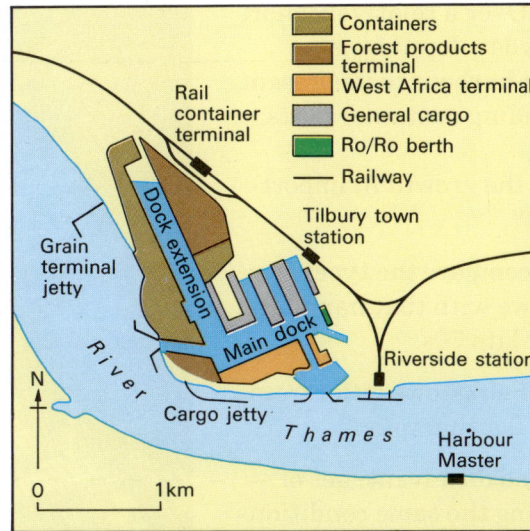

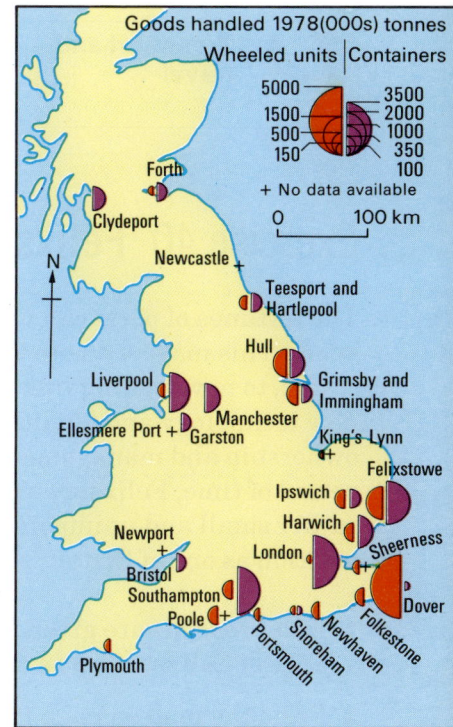

The seaports of Britain

Left: Features of Tilbury docks, in the Port of London

A view over Tilbury docks on the north bank of the Thames, about 40 km from central London

165

Exercise 40 Felixstowe Port

The fortunes of ports can vary greatly over the years. This may be due to the changing nature of traffic, to new trading links, to the introduction of new technology and facilities, or to changes in ownership and management. Over a relatively short period of time, Felixstowe has developed from a rather small and unimportant harbour to its present position as one of Britain's leading container ports.

1 What reasons are given for the growth in importance of Felixstowe as a port?

2 From the map on page 165 compare the type of freight handled at Felixstowe with that handled at London and Dover in the late 70s.

3 How does the ownership of Felixstowe differ from that of London, Bristol and Southampton?

4 What are the advantages and disadvantages of dockers in all seaports having the same conditions of service?

View over Felixstowe docks, near Ipswich, Suffolk

The Times 7 July 1981.

The port is important for its roll-on/roll-off and container trade

Felixstowe becomes top container port

Felixstowe has overtaken London as Britain's top container port. A new £32m container terminal was opened at the private enterprise port by Mr Norman Fowler, Secretary of State for Transport, yesterday. It will double Felixstowe's capacity to 750000 6 metre boxes a year compared with London's capacity of about 500000. Actual traffic this year is expected to exceed 500000 through Felixstowe compared with about 450000 through London.

Felixstowe was founded only 30 years ago by a corn merchant, but it has experienced a remarkable growth in a generally declining industry.

Helped by a good geographical position between Europe and the industrial Midlands, Felixstowe has gone from strength to strength while London declined. But another of its strengths, the fact that it is right away from other port areas and outside the dock labour scheme, is under threat and the port had its first big strike recently.

Chapter 8 Energy

Coal and coal mining

Large scale open cast mining is cheap, but it has a great impact on the environment. About 10 per cent of Britain's coal is obtained this way with three per cent of the labour force

Coal reserves

Coal is rock formed millions of years ago from the decay of trees and other vegetation as it became buried and compressed beneath later deposits. Because conditions varied from place to place in the past, coal is found in some areas but not others. The layers or seams of coal may be exposed at the surface or be at great depth. They may be thick and almost level and unbroken, or greatly folded, faulted and thin. Sometimes the seams near the surface can be obtained by open-cast mining, but in Britain most coal is obtained by drift or deep-shaft mining.

Exposed coal seams near the surface have been mined for centuries, but deposits and reserves are continually being found for the first time. The guess is that there are sufficient known deposits or 'reserves' to last for 300 years with present technology and rate of use. In view of the likely exhaustion of oil and natural gas, and anxieties about nuclear power, this is good news for Britain, assuming it is accurate. There

seems to be no immediate shortage of coal in the country, and there is probably far more not yet discovered. The question is whether it is worth the cost of mining.

The uses of coal and changing demand

The diagram shows the various sources of energy in the early 1980s, and the one on page 182 shows how these were used. The figures are always changing, but these are still roughly the same in the mid 1980s. On the other hand, they would have been greatly different, say, fifty years ago. There was no nuclear power, for example, and coal was used for steam power in railway and ship engines and vast amounts were used for domestic purposes. Nowadays coal producers have to face competition from oil, gas, nuclear and hydro-electric power, as well as from imported coal.

The two big users of coal are the electricity and steel industries. Over two-thirds of the coal sold is burned in

Sources of energy (%)

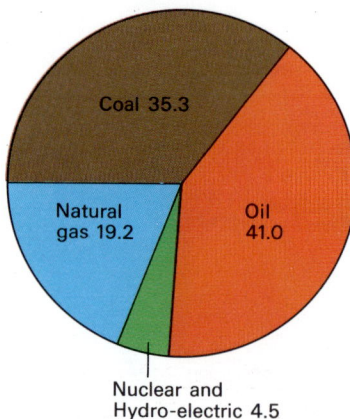

Coal 35.3
Natural gas 19.2
Oil 41.0
Nuclear and Hydro-electric 4.5

Right: Wistow pit, the first of five in the Selby field, opened in July 1983. Soon afterwards, it was producing coal at four times the national rate before floods halted production for a while

giant power stations to make electricity, while coke ovens at steelworks consume about 10 per cent. A lot of research and development is going into other uses such as improved heating techniques, converting coal to liquid fuel and into chemicals. In spite of competition, therefore, the demand should not greatly change.

If there is plenty of coal in the ground, and there are many possible uses for it, what are the problems of the coal industry? There are several answers. There has been a general falling off in demand for any sort of energy since the early part of the decade due to the economic 'recession'. Industries have been forced to cut back production or close down, and so their demand for energy has dropped. Coal has had to take its share of these cuts.

Even without this, though, the British coal industry would have been faced with severe competition. First there is the import of cheaper coal from other parts of the world (in spite of the costs of the long sea journey). Then there is competition from other forms of energy that can do the same job; electricity, for example, can be produced from oil, gas or nuclear sources. The National Coal Board (the coal industry is state-owned) plans to meet this competition in several ways. It hopes to get increased production per worker by modernising certain pits, and it wants to close down uneconomic mines and develop large, efficient ones in completely new areas. In this way it hopes to produce coal efficiently and cheaply to hold and increase its present share of the energy market. Opposition to its plans from the National Union of Mineworkers led to the 1984 strike. One of the main disagreements was over the definition of the term 'uneconomic pit'.

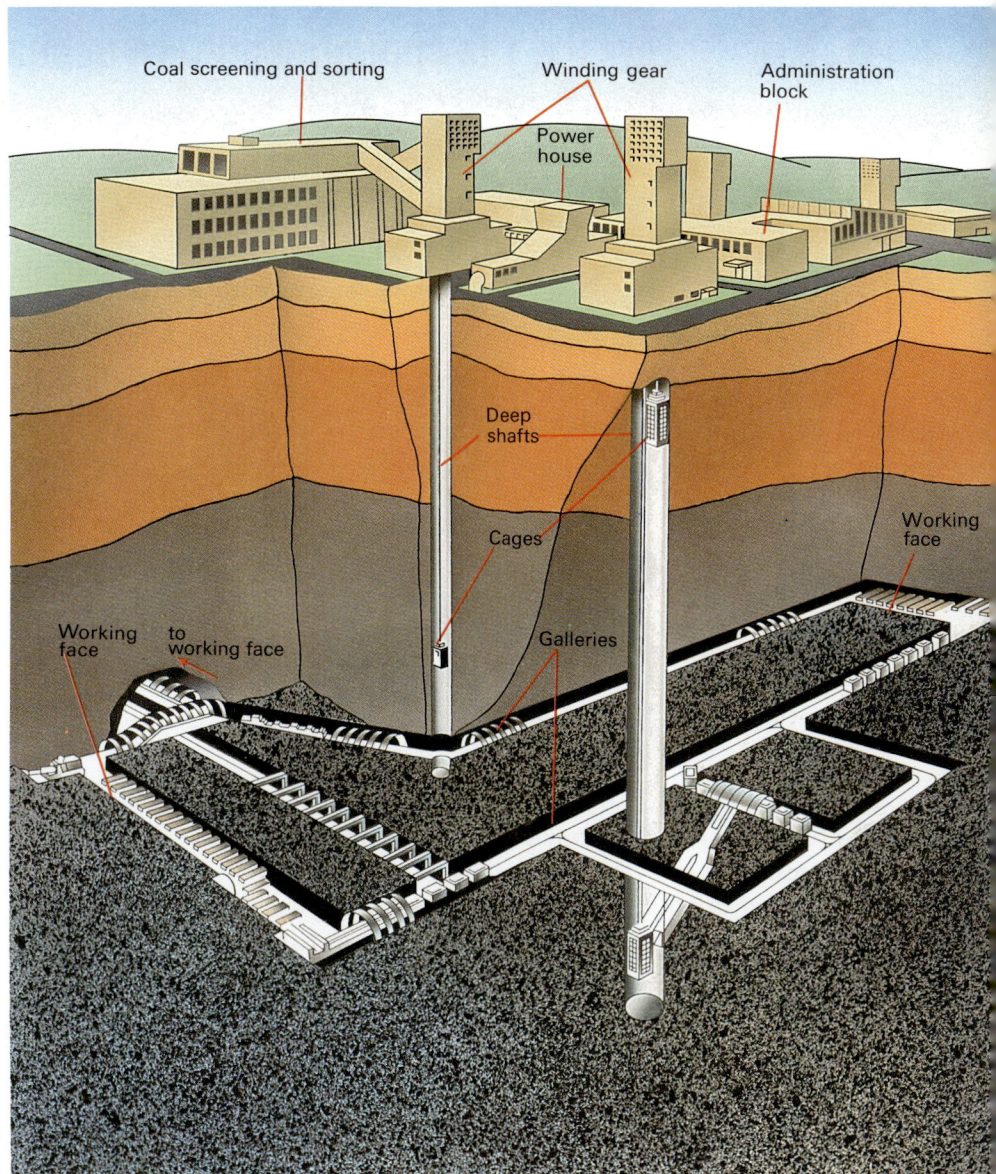

The main features of a deep-shaft mine

1 Compare the view of the new Wistow colliery with that of the old mine on page 200. Refer to the pit-head works themselves and the surrounding areas.

2 Look at the map and diagrams on page 170. Rank the regions according to a) recent output b) change in output over the period. Show if the change is a gain or a loss.

3 What may make a coalmine uneconomic and unable to produce coal as cheaply as some from the other side of the world? Why is the National Union of Mineworkers opposed to the closure of 'uneconomic' mines?

Coal is now cut by large and complicated machinery

The changing pattern of coalmining

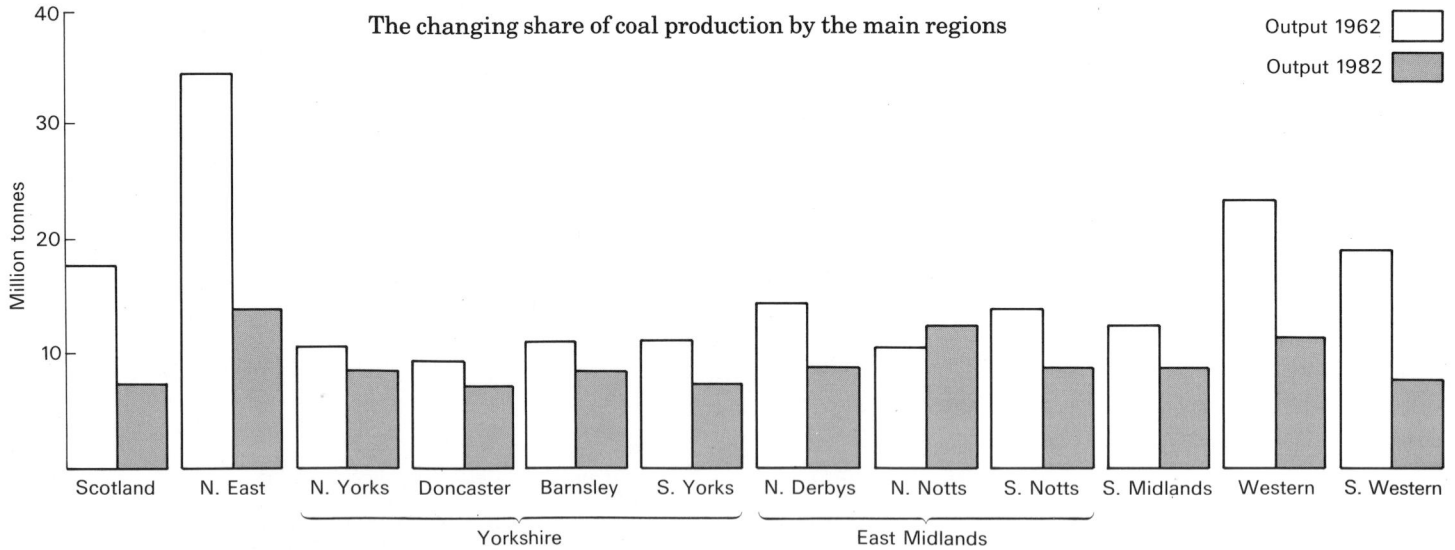

The changing share of coal production by the main regions

Output 1962 ☐
Output 1982 ▨

Million tonnes

Scotland | N. East | N. Yorks | Doncaster | Barnsley | S. Yorks | N. Derbys | N. Notts | S. Notts | S. Midlands | Western | S. Western

Yorkshire   East Midlands

Coal has for centuries been a vital source of energy to Britain. The growth of Britain into a leading world power during the Industrial Revolution was based on the availability of coal. During that time most of Britain's iron and steel-works and heavy industry were located on the coalfields. Since then there have been many changes in the demand for this fuel. At times the industry has seemed about to collapse in the face of competition from nuclear power, natural gas and oil. These fears have proved groundless however, and the coal industry today still fulfils a vital part of Britain's energy needs. It has the big advantage of very large proven reserves, and there is probably far more coal yet to be discovered. The National Coal Board wants to make production as efficient as possible, so that coal can compete with other fuels. This means the closure of some mines and a loss of jobs. Some of the changes in the coal-mining industry are shown on these pages.

The main problem of 1983 was over-production. Output was 118 million tonnes a year, but industry needed 10 per cent less than that, and the demand was getting less. As a result huge stocks of coal (a half-year production) was held in colliery yards, or with consumers such as power stations.

The N.C.B. wants to reduce output by 10 per cent. Opening new mines such as those at Selby, with large-scale production, means closing about 75 loss-making pits over a ten year period, with a decline in jobs from about 200 000 to 120 000.

Coalfields, past, present and future

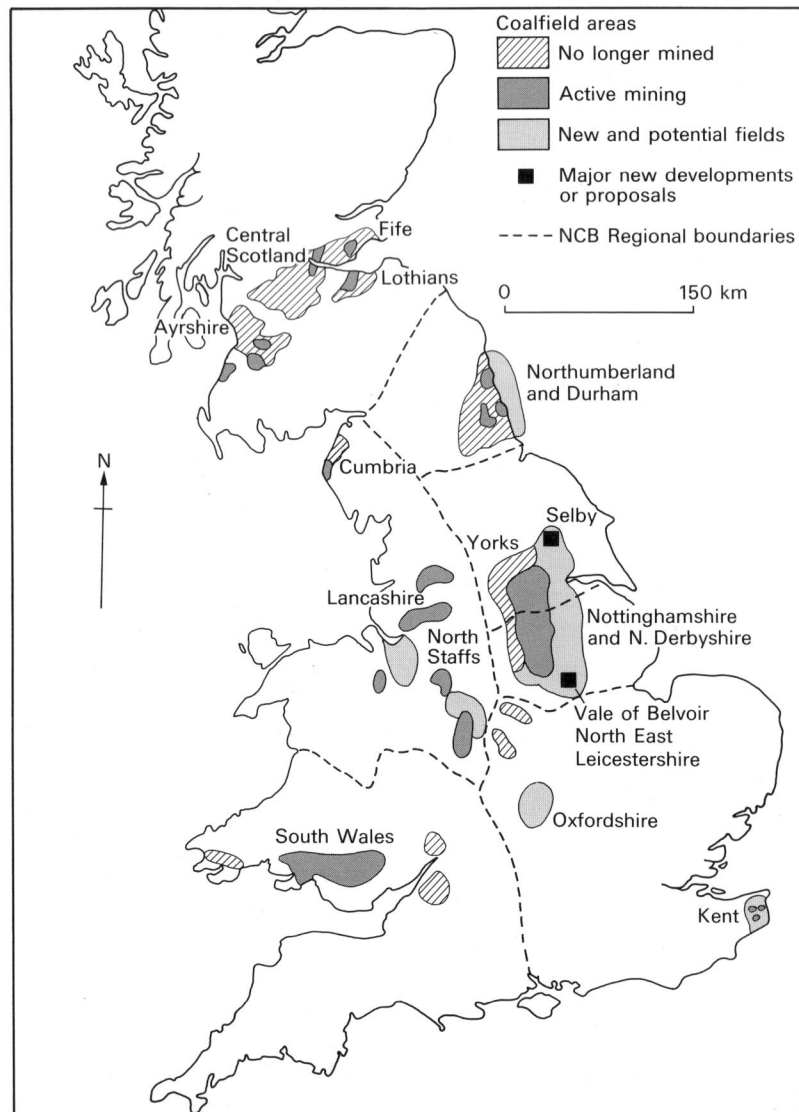

Coalfield areas
▨ No longer mined
▨ Active mining
▨ New and potential fields
■ Major new developments or proposals
- - - NCB Regional boundaries

0   150 km

Central Scotland
Fife
Lothians
Ayrshire
Northumberland and Durham
Cumbria
Selby
Yorks
Lancashire
Nottinghamshire and N. Derbyshire
North Staffs
Vale of Belvoir North East Leicestershire
Oxfordshire
South Wales
Kent

Exercise 41 Profits, losses and subsidies in the coal industry

Record £575m grants for NCB

The Government paid a record £575m in grants to the National Coal Board last year to cover the adverse effects of the economic recession, rail disputes and the climb-down over the Board's contentious pit closure plans.

Coal-face productivity increased by more than 5 per cent to a record level of more than 10 tonnes per manshift at the end of the year and the board achieved 'considerable success' in its marketing efforts. Overall sales increased by two million tonnes to 120 million tonnes despite a drop in domestic demand, thanks to a doubling of exports from 4.7 million to 9.4 million tonnes.

1 Rank all the areas, mining and opencast, according to their profitability in 1982. Are the most productive regions the most profitable?

2 What might explain a big change in profit or loss from one year to another? Which region showed the largest change, and what was it?

3 What happened to the 'output per manshift' between 1980/81 and 1981/82? What happened to profits/losses? What were some of the reasons given for the change?

4 Do you think the taxpayer should subsidise the coal industry? Give reasons for your answer.

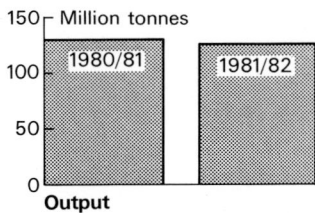

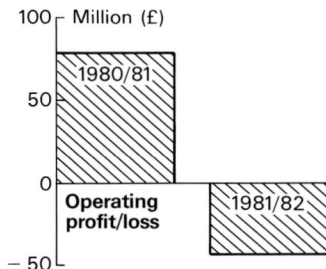

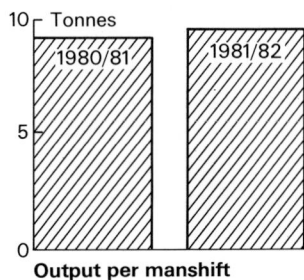

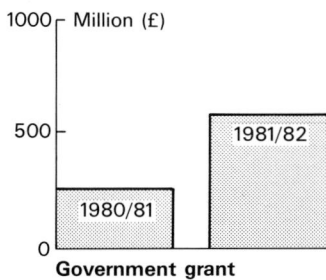

The NCB regions

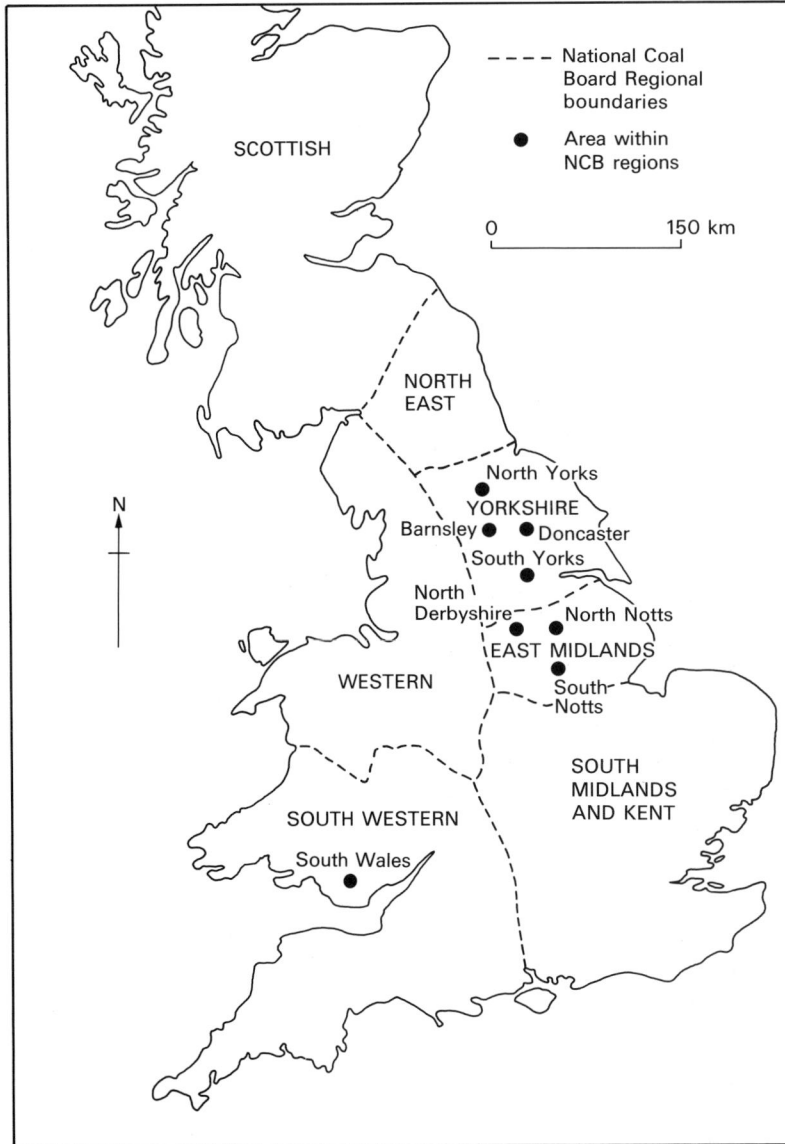

- - - - National Coal Board Regional boundaries

● Area within NCB regions

0 ————— 150 km

Mining areas: operating profit (loss) £ million		
	1981	1982
Scottish	(25.1)	(33.8)
North-East	(28.7)	(48.5)
Western	(13.3)	(9.2)
N Yorkshire	(14.8)	(20.2)
Barnsley	(9.3)	(7.2)
Doncaster	(20.2)	(17.5)
S Yorks	(8.5)	(3.5)
N Derbyshire	28.1	2.7
N Nottinghamshire	62.0	42.2
S Nottinghamshire	2.4	(18.4)
S Midlands & Kent	(10.2)	(16.8)
S Wales	(68.9)	(95.9)

Opencast regions: operating profit £ million		
	1981	1982
Scottish	29.6	34.7
North-East	32.7	31.0
North-West	8.1	9.7
Central-East	40.3	34.7
Central-West	35.1	23.6
South-Western	11.1	23.2

Oil and natural gas

Major oil and gas fields and pipelines, 1983

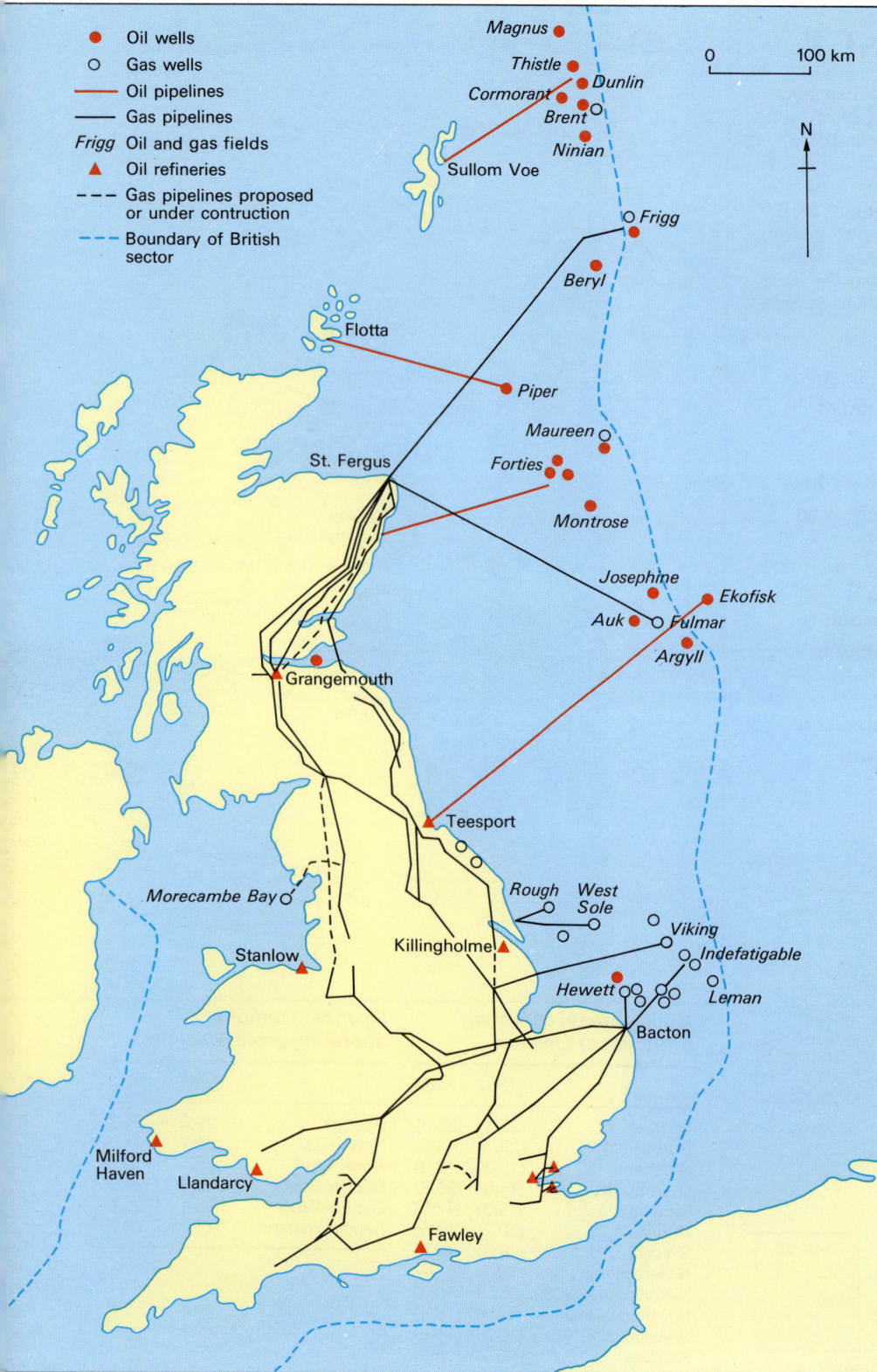

Map legend:
- ● Oil wells
- ○ Gas wells
- — Oil pipelines
- — Gas pipelines
- *Frigg* Oil and gas fields
- ▲ Oil refineries
- - - Gas pipelines proposed or under contruction
- - - Boundary of British sector

Labelled on map: Magnus, Thistle, Dunlin, Cormorant, Brent, Ninian, Sullom Voe, Frigg, Beryl, Flotta, Piper, Maureen, Forties, Montrose, St. Fergus, Josephine, Ekofisk, Auk, Fulmar, Argyll, Grangemouth, Teesport, Morecambe Bay, Rough, West Sole, Viking, Indefatigable, Stanlow, Killingholme, Hewett, Leman, Bacton, Milford Haven, Llandarcy, Fawley

0   100 km

N

Nature and uses

Petroleum (sometimes known as crude oil) and natural gas are found in certain porous rocks under particular geological conditions. Like coal they are due to the decay and action by bacteria on dead vegetation. Also like coal they are non-renewable resources. Once extracted and used they will never be replaced.

Petroleum and gas have a number of important and valuable uses. The crude oils obtained from rocks are very variable in nature, but all need 'refining' into more useable products. Outstanding among these is petrol and diesel oil used in vehicle, ships, and some aeroplane engines. At the moment there are few realistic alternatives to petrol and diesel fuel for car, lorry and bus engines, and the whole pattern of transport would be fundamentally affected if petroleum supplies failed. Oil is also used to produce electricity in power stations, but since the price of oil increased dramatically in the 1970s, it has not proved a very good competitor with coal and nuclear fuels. A third important use is in the manufacture of many chemicals, as was seen on page 92. Natural gas is more efficient and cheaper than gas made from coal, and it is widely used for domestic and industrial heating.

Sources of oil and gas

Until 1975 the vast bulk of Britain's oil had to be imported, and the first natural gas came in liquid form by tanker from North Africa. Enormous and important changes took place during the 1970s. Natural gas and oil was discovered in the rocks under the North Sea, and the United Kingdom was fortunate enough to have a great deal in its sector. After a lot of expensive exploration and test

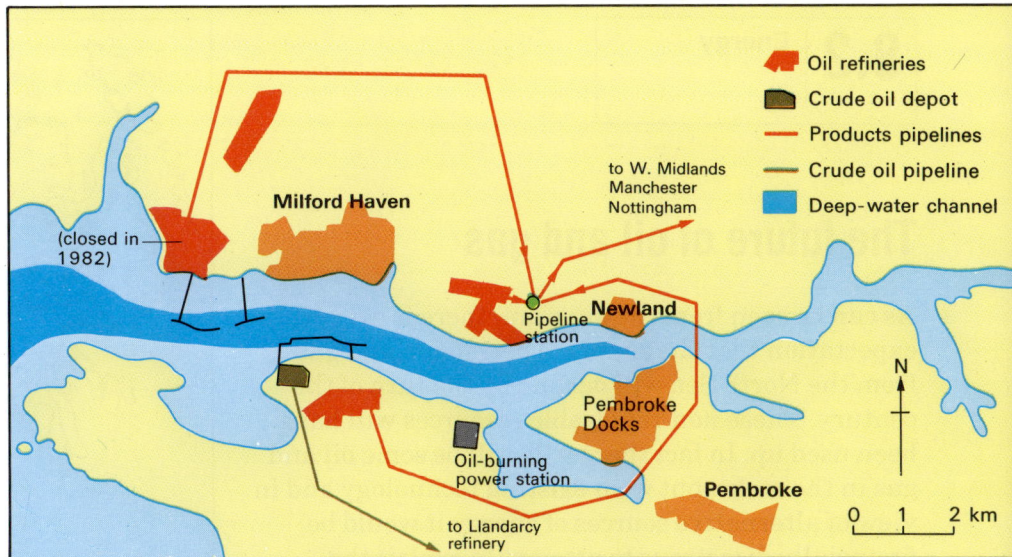

The location of refineries near Milford Haven, 1982

drilling a number of separate fields of oil were confirmed and developed off the north-east coast of Scotland and a number of gas fields further south. Because of the vast sums of money involved, most of the exploration and development was undertaken by the huge oil companies such as Shell. They make profits from their investment, and pay taxes to the government in return for this. The oil and gas is brought ashore to terminals in the Orkneys, Shetlands and the east coast of England. This is done either by pipeline in the case of the gas and some oil, or by supertankers in the case of some oil fields. The gas is fed into a grid of pipelines that cross much of Britain. The petroleum ends up in one or other of the oil refineries around the coast although some is exported. From the refineries the products are taken to the consumer by coastal vessel, road or rail tanker, or pipeline.

Oil refineries

Some idea of the appearance and work of a refinery was suggested on page 93 in the account of the ICI works at Teeside. The location of that and other refineries is shown on the map. It should be realised that while Britain exports some oil, it also imports a great deal of a quality that is needed in industry but is not found in the North Sea. Huge supertankers are needed to handle this international trade in petroleum, and this restricts the number of sites that are suitable for an oil refinery. One of the largest is at Milford Haven, where several international companies have their refineries. The photograph and map suggest what the terminal, refineries and surrounding area looks like.

1 What are the difficulties of exploiting the North Sea deposits of oil? What would be the advantages and disadvantages of exploiting large inland reserves?

2 Describe the location and site of Milford Haven. What seem to be its advantages and disadvantages as a site for oil refineries?

3 Why do some people object to licences being given to oil companies to search for and exploit 'Britain's' oil? What reasons are there in its favour?

View over Milford Haven. By 1983 it seemed that its period of prosperity was over. Esso were pulling out of the town and the Gulf Oil operation was in doubt. The recession, North Sea Oil and the reopening of the Suez Canal made the fact that Milford Haven is the deepest natural harbour in Europe less and less important

The future of oil and gas

As can be seen from the diagram, there is every expectation that the supply of petroleum and gas from the North Sea will decline by the turn of the century. These non-renewable resources will have been used up. In fact there will still be some oil and gas in the rocks, but with existing technology and in view of alternative sources of energy it would be financially disastrous to attempt to exploit the reserves. Britain and other European countries will also be short of natural gas – hence the need to import it by pipeline from the USSR. The expected exhaustion of known reserves is one reason why on-shore exploration for oil and gas is going on. In 1981 some 240 000 tonnes of on-shore oil were produced, and in the following year there were 113 licences allowing companies to search for more oil and gas on the mainland. If reserves like those under the North Sea were discovered they would be far cheaper to exploit – but the impact on the environment and local people could be damaging.

In view of the inevitable decline in North Sea oil and gas supplies thought has to be given to alternatives. This could mean greater investment in coal mining, the nuclear power industry, energy saving or alternative sources of energy. The days of cheap oil and gas have gone for ever, and the remaining known British reserves will not last very long.

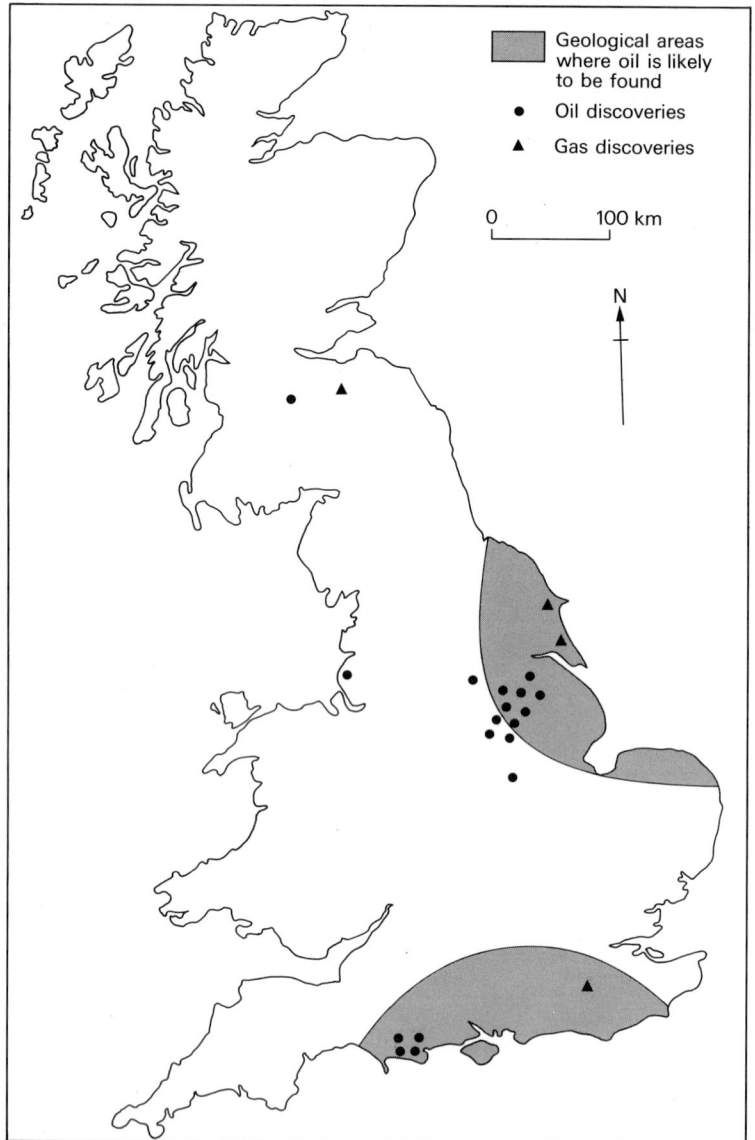

On-shore oil-bearing rocks and production areas
On-shore oil drilling has been stepped up in recent years

Exercise 42 **The oil industry**

The two graphs give various information about petroleum and its place in Britain's energy programme.

1 Calculate the estimated share of petroleum to Britain's energy needs in the year 2000. Why is it unwise to plan too precisely on such an estimate? If it proves true, where would the balance of needs be likely to come from?

2 Describe the abrupt change in the price of oil shown in the graph. What might have accounted for this? What does it tell us about the advantages of having our own sources of energy? Why should world suppliers of petroleum raise or lower their prices? What is the danger of their doing this?

3 Which were the main countries from which Britain imported petroleum in 1980? Put them in rank order.

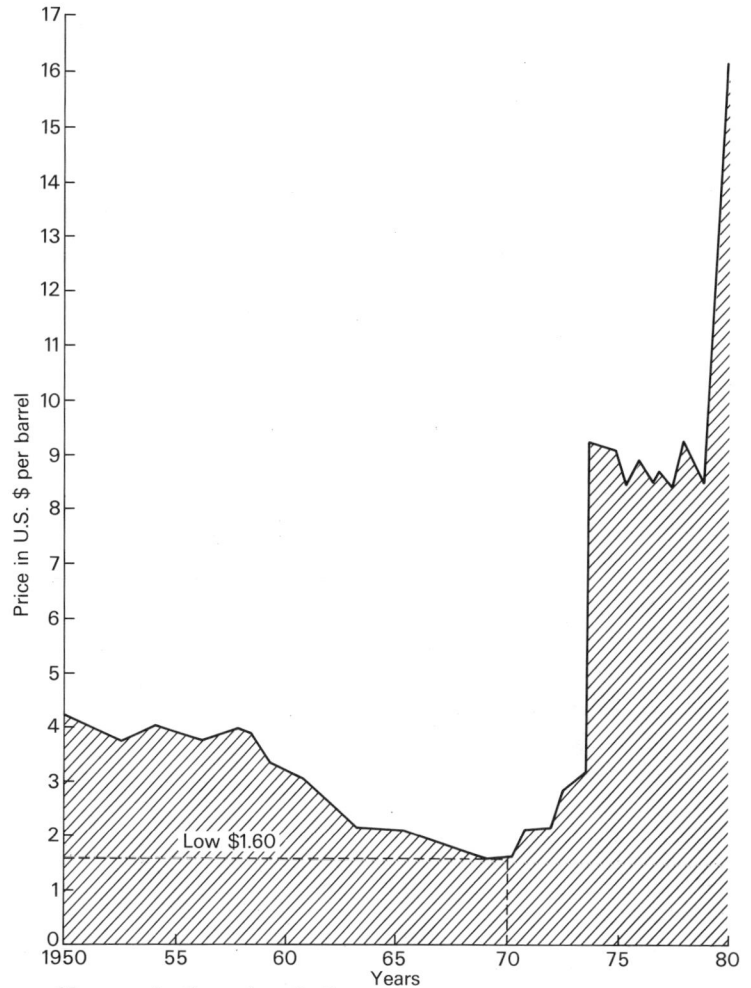

Changes in the price of oil

Changing pattern of supply and demand for oil

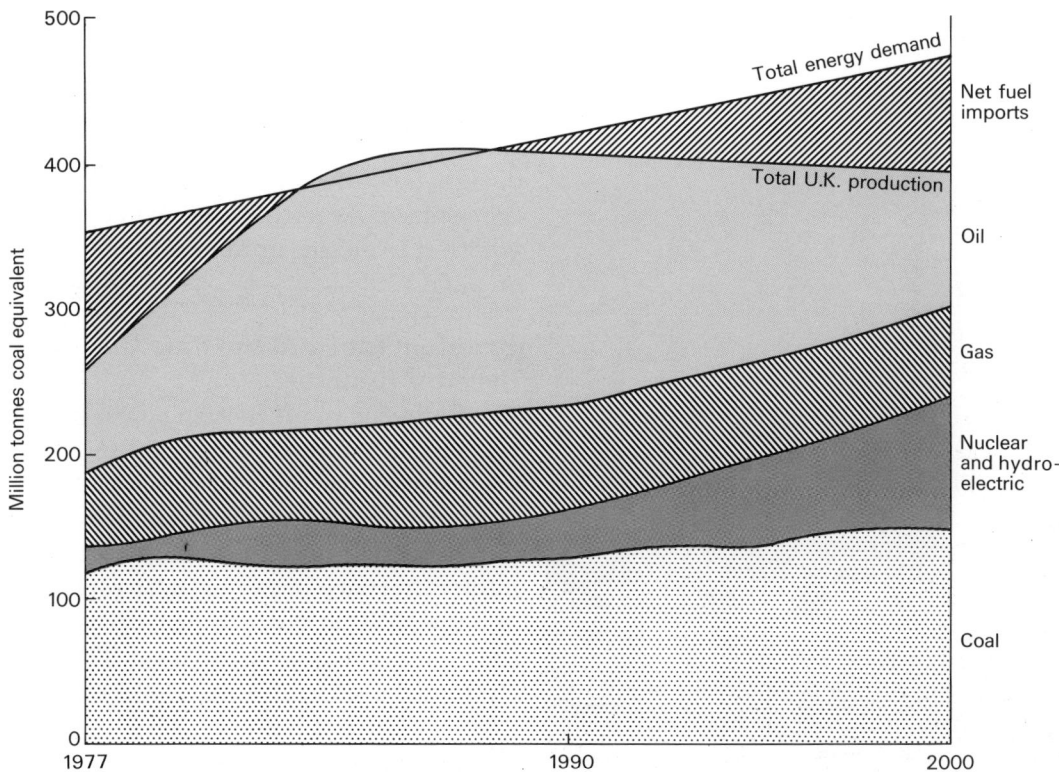

The percentage of oil imports into the UK from its major suppliers, 1980

Saudi Arabia	40.4
Nigeria	1.2
Iraq	8.5
UAE	6.9
Algeria	1.2
Kuwait	20.1
Iran	2.7
Mexico	0.7
USSR	0.6
Venezuela	2.8
Other countries	14.9

Nuclear power

Selecting nuclear power station sites

Sir, It really is nonsense to say that convenience rather than public safety has dominated the choice of nuclear power sites in Britain.

The combination of physical characteristics needed to build a power station is difficult to find in developed countries such as England and Wales. Suitable foundation conditions are essential. Unfailing supplies of large volumes of cold water, ready connection into the transmission system and acceptable environmental effects are other factors.

Yours faithfully
D. A. DAVIS, Director, Corporate Strategy Dept, Central Electricity Generating Board

Wylfa nuclear power station

The location of nuclear power stations

Nuclear power stations produced about 11 per cent of Britain's electricity in the early 1980s. The map shows their location and relative capacity; the amount of electricity they could produce when working fully. It can be seen that with the exception of Trawsfynydd, which has a pumped storage reservoir, the nuclear power stations are all on the coast. The selection of a site is a long and complicated business. When it is finally proposed, it has to be acceptable from a safety viewpoint. This is particularly important with nuclear power because of the dangers of radioactivity should there be plant failure. The Nuclear Installations Inspectorate (NII) decide whether or not a site is suitable from safety considerations. This is only one consideration, of course, as the letter suggests.

The Central Electricity Generating Board (CEGB) has to estimate what future electricity needs are likely to be, and which form of station – coal, oil or nuclear – will be most efficient and least costly. This is difficult to do, and estimates are frequently challenged and changed with time. Nevertheless decisions have to be made, and in the early 1980s the Conservative Government decided to support a programme of nuclear power stations as part of its energy policy. The aim at that time was to build ten new nuclear stations at roughly one a year between 1982 and 1992. The questions were, which type of nuclear power station and which locations and sites? The first generation of nuclear power stations built in Britain have Magnox reactors. The second generation have Advanced Gas cooled reactors (AGRs). The first of these stations produced electricity for the National Grid in 1976. Future stations may be of yet another variety, known as the Pressurised Water Reactor (PWR), it is proposed that the first of these PWRs, based on an American design, be built at Sizewell in Suffolk. Some of the issues invoved in deciding whether to do this or not are considered on page 179.

Uranium fuel and the Fast Breeder Reactor

The fuel used in all British power stations built before 1982 is uranium. Heat produced by the controlled reaction is used to make steam which then produces electricity in the generators. The main difference between these reactors and the PWR is the technical one of how the heat is controlled and used. The PWR also uses uranium as a fuel.

One of the problems of using uranium is that the raw material comes from foreign mines. This not only costs money, but also means that the country has to rely on others, and such economic dependence has its dangers. Some people are also concerned that the ores come from South Africa and Australia, amongst other countries, and they are opposed to the social and political conditions under which it is mined. Another problem is that only a small proportion of the uranium ore is actually used, and this means that there is a known limit, using present techniques, to known reserves of ore. As well as looking for new reserves, attempts have been made to use nuclear fuels more efficiently.

The power station at Dounreay in the north of Scotland is an experimental one to test the possibilities of what is called a fast-breeder reactor. It is only one quarter the size of a commercial station, but it has shown that it would be possible to use plutonium that results from the 'normal' reactions using uranium. Only a small part of natural uranium is used in existing reactors; the rest is 'waste'. In a fast breeder most of the uranium can be used, and the process actually makes more plutonium! On technical grounds alone it would be a marvellous solution to the energy problem. There are several snags, however. At the moment the cost of building a commercial reactor would be very high, and there have been no full-scale trials to prove the technical, economic and safety requirements would be met. At the moment the government will not give the go-ahead for such trials, so it would be at least 2010 before the first series of commercial fast-breeder reactors could be producing power. Another very important doubt is over the safety factors. Plutonium is a vital part of nuclear weapons, and many people are appalled at the thought of such devastating materials entering world trade on some commercial basis. The fast-breeder reactor is a good example of how technological developments have to be weighed against economic, political and moral concerns.

Nuclear waste disposal

The problem of nuclear waste disposal is dealt with in chapter 9, but here it can be said that the potentially dangerous used fuel-rods have to be treated with great care. The safe management of nuclear power involves not only the raw material during the process itself but of waste products afterwards.

1 Which were the four largest nuclear power stations in terms of capacity that were operating or under construction in the early 1980s?

2 Look at the estimates for energy needs in the year 2000 (page 175). What does it suggest? What was the estimated percentage contribution in the year 2000? How would this be provided?

3 List all the factors involved in choosing a location and site for a nuclear power station mentioned in the letter.

4 What might be some of the reasons for and against nuclear rather than coal or oil power stations, when old stations need to be replaced or when more power is needed?

The location of nuclear power stations in Britain in the early 1980s

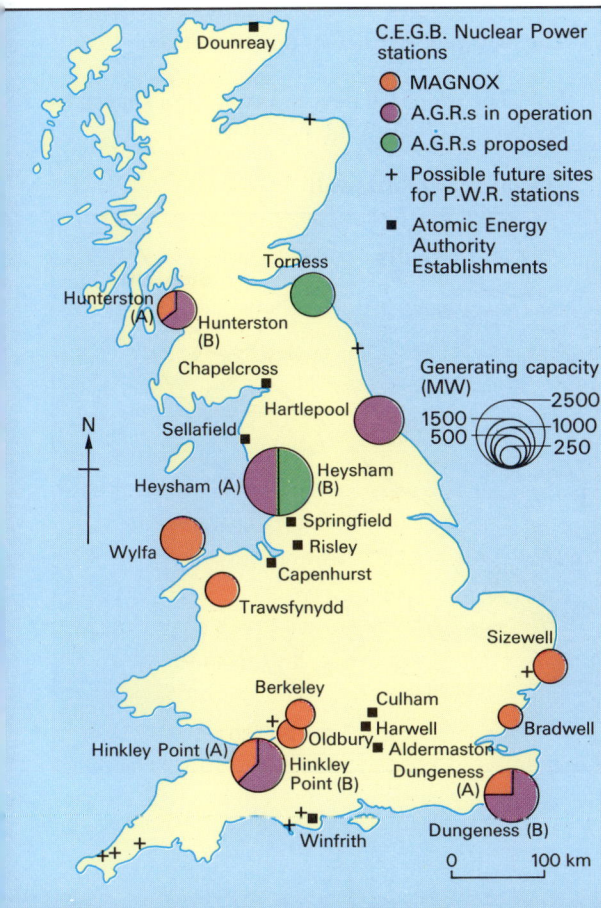

C.E.G.B. Nuclear Power stations
- MAGNOX
- A.G.R.s in operation
- A.G.R.s proposed
+ Possible future sites for P.W.R. stations
■ Atomic Energy Authority Establishments

Generating capacity (MW)
2500
1500
1000
500
250

Dounreay
Torness
Hunterston (A)
Hunterston (B)
Chapelcross
Hartlepool
Sellafield
Heysham (A)
Heysham (B)
Springfield
Risley
Wylfa
Capenhurst
Trawsfynydd
Sizewell
Berkeley
Culham
Oldbury
Harwell
Bradwell
Hinkley Point (A)
Aldermaston
Hinkley Point (B)
Dungeness (A)
Winfrith
Dungeness (B)

N

0   100 km

The heart of the nuclear power station at Oldbury-on-Severn, Gloucestershire

Sellafield (once known as Windscale) is where much nuclear waste is stored until long term decisions are made about its disposal. Special rail wagons are used to transport the waste

The Sizewell nuclear power station

Early in 1983 a public inquiry was started to consider the cases for and against building a second nuclear power station (Sizewell B) at Sizewell in Suffolk. The Central Electricity Generating Board proposes to build a pressurised water reactor (like many in the USA, but unlike existing gas-cooled reactors in Britain). This type of power station is recommended because of the need for extra power, and at a lower cost than that provided by existing stations. Many objections to the proposal have been raised. Some people challenge the need anyway for extra electricity over the next few decades, while others are anxious about safety, building and running costs, and the effect on other fuels such as coal.

It is very difficult to predict future electricity needs, but they are now thought to be less than once expected. The need for nuclear power also depends on the availability and relative costs of other fuels such as coal and oil. The decision over the Sizewell Station will probably indicate whether many other PWR nuclear power stations will be built over the next few decades.

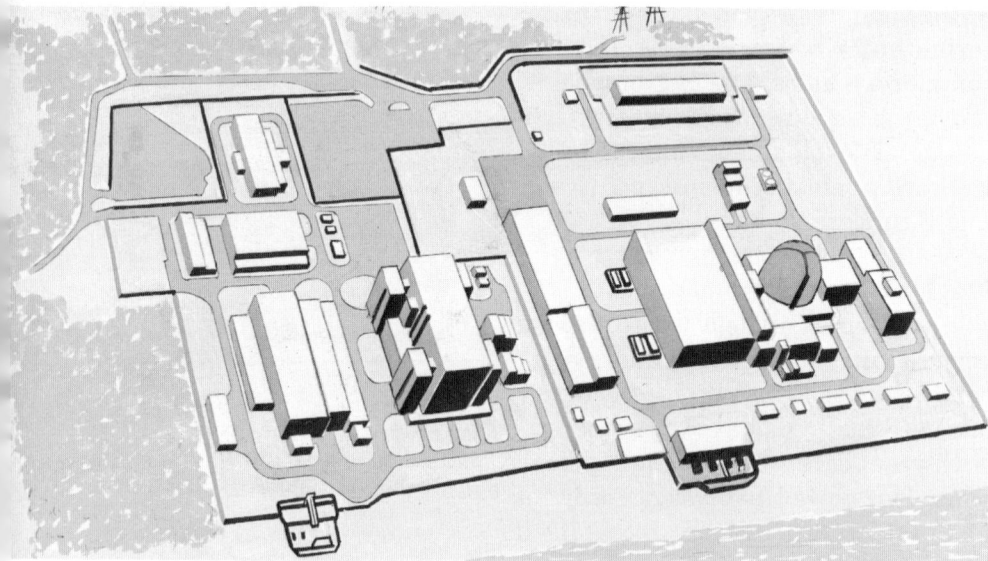

The Sizewell 'A' nuclear power station

Left: The proposed new power station shown alongside the existing 'A' station

Diagram of the fuel cycle in a PWR nuclear power station

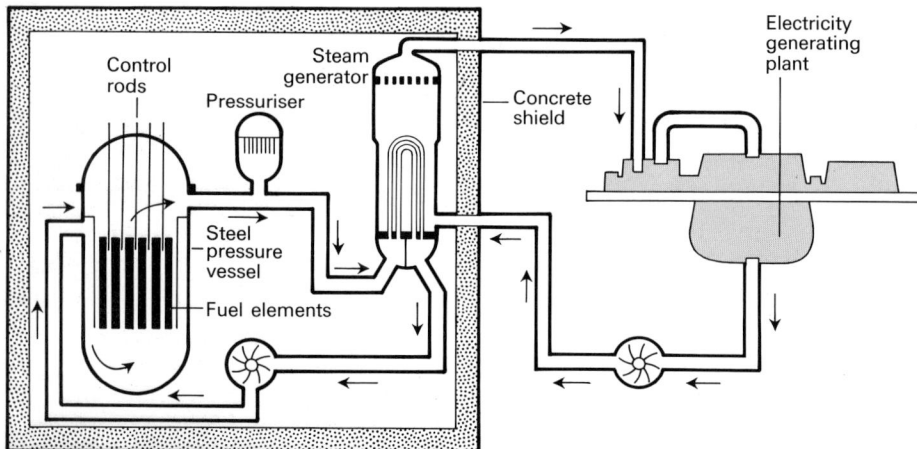

The location of Sizewell

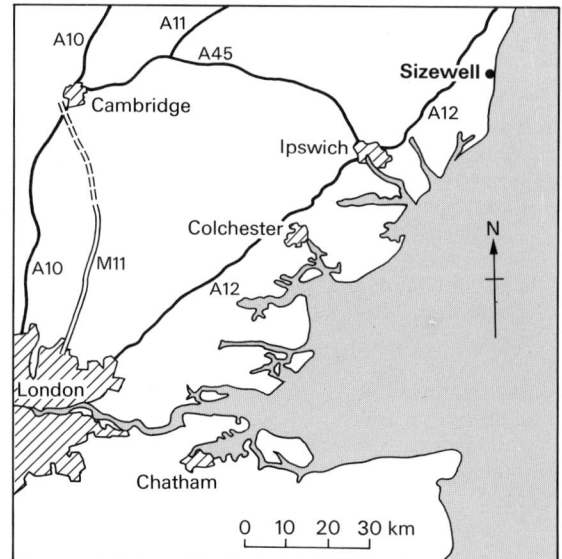

Exercise 43 **The public inquiry**

Read the three extracts.

1 For what particular safety reason did people object to the building of the new Sizewell Nuclear Power Station?

2 Why did the emphasis of the inquiry 'change' and what replaced safety as a major area of concern? What was the case of the supporters and the objectors? On this limited evidence, which do you find most convincing?

3 List the main groups who were 'supporters' and 'objectors' in the proposal. What were the objectors complaining about in the first of the preliminary meetings? Do you think it right or wrong for people to be able to object to such proposals? Give reasons for your answer.

Many people are anxious about the use of nuclear energy for power production

Board emphasizes safety of £1147m nuclear plant

The Sizewell nuclear power station in Suffolk is expected to cost £1147m and will be the prototype for future pressurized water nuclear reactors in Britain, the Central Electricity Generating Board announced yesterday.

Mr John Baker, the board member for commercial and public affairs, says the PWR is easier to build than the AGR because many more of its components are factory made, which could cut costs by nearly 15 per cent.

When the Conservatives came to power, Mrs Margaret Thatcher announced that 10 pressurized water reactors (PWR) would be built at the rate of one a year from 1984. But the decision has been criticized for safety reasons because it is the same type of reactor as that which failed at Three Mile island, Harrisburg, Pennsylvania, three years ago.

Technical details of the safety of the design form the largest part of the evidence in favour of Sizewell. Radiation risk, the effects of radiation, and radiological protection are all examined.

Battle lines drawn up for Sizewell

Supporters and objectors to proposals to build the controversial American-type nuclear power station at Sizewell on the Suffolk coast gathered at the Maltings, Snape, yesterday for the first of three preliminary meetings.

The process by which questions about the safety of the £1200m project will be examined took a back seat yesterday, when the dominant issue concerned arguments put by objectors for a public fund to enable them adequately to present their case.

The Central Electricity Generating Board has already spent £10m on preparing the way for Sizewell B. It has assembled teams of lawyers and technical experts. Other supporters of the scheme include the National Nuclear Corporation, British Nuclear Fuels and the Nuclear Installations Inspectorate.

In contrast to the nuclear industry group, objectors such as the Town and Country Planning Association, the Council for the Protection of Rural England, Friends of the Earth, the East Anglian Alliance Against Nuclear Power and the Stop Sizewell B Campaign, have, in legal terms, more modest representation.

The great nuclear debate changes course

When the new Conservative Government agreed to the CEGB's plans for a major expansion of nuclear power three years ago, there was generally little doubt that new nuclear stations could be justified on grounds of future energy need.

All that has changed. The CEGB has had to acknowledge that economic recession and falling energy demand have altered the nature of the argument. The central question now is: even before we consider the safety aspect, do we actually need Sizewell and the stream of other nuclear reactors that were scheduled to follow?

Three years ago the CEGB expected demand to grow by more than 40 per cent by the end of the century but its central projection now is that demand will grow by little more than 10 per cent.

A great deal turns therefore on the CEGB's argument that PWRs are cheaper than the alternatives and that it makes economic sense to build them, even though they are producing power that is not needed. For Sizewell, the net savings are put at between £500m and £1100m.

Alternative sources of energy

New houses have been designed to use solar energy

Right: Wind power has been used as a source of energy for centuries, but large numbers of big windmills would be needed to make a major contribution to our power supply today

Expenditure on research into alternative energy sources in the UK, 1981

	£ million
Solar	6.0
Wave	5.4
Geothermal	1.7
Tidal	1.5
Wind	0.97

*By comparison, the cost of nuclear energy research by the Atomic Energy Authority was £150 million.

Renewable and non-renewable sources

Coal, oil, natural gas and uranium are non-renewable resources. Although there are undoubtedly vast reserves yet to be discovered, let alone exploited, sooner or later they could be used up.

There are other sources that are renewable, in the sense that provided the sun goes on shining and creating energy, they will be replaced when used. Some are described below. In the longer term there is the dream of nuclear fusion – producing energy by combining elements in the air around us in a reaction similar to that of the sun.

Developments and research

The most widely developed form of renewable energy in Britain is hydro-electric power. The energy of falling water is captured in pipes leading from the upper parts of rivers or from reservoirs to turbines and generators in power stations. The fall of water turns the turbine blades, so generating electricity. The location of HEP stations is shown on the map on page 182, and the diagram gives the share of electricity produced in this way.

Solar energy – energy from the sun – might seem impossible in Britain with its particular climate. In fact careful measurement shows that the average house in Britain receives more solar energy in a year than its total annual consumption. Quite a number of houses have been designed to make best use of existing solar heating by careful choice of building materials, insulation and ventilation. Some have solar heating panels to concentrate and increase the heating effect. In other cases the solar energy is converted to electricity. None of these techniques are yet widely used.

Wind power used to be very important, but in recent centuries its relative inefficiency and unpredictability has led to its decline. But new designs with greater efficiency are beginning to make them attractive again. There are many small ones used to pump water on farms, for example, but none that produce large amounts of electricity. The CEGB believes that windmills could generate electricity competitively in lowland Britain. It remains to be seen if people would accept thousands of windmills with blades 50 metres long dotting the countryside. It would need about 1 000 mills over 800 square kilometres to generate the same output as one large nuclear station. Another possibility is to instal huge offshore windmills and transmit the power to the mainland – but the costs and problems could be enormous.

Vast amounts of heat are stored in lower layers of the earth's crust. Some of this geothermal heat is contained in water trapped below the surface. A small development has taken place in Southampton where heated water from rocks below the city is used to heat offices and shops in the city centre. Far more promising in the long run is the plan to tap heat from granite rocks at depth by pumping cold water down one hole, and gathering the steam generated by the hot rocks from another. If the second-phase trials shown in the diagram work, further deeper trials will be held. Some idea of the scope, however, is given by the estimate that it would require 120 pairs of holes 6 000 metres deep to meet about 2 per cent of the national demand for electricity – at a cost of £1 000 million.

One of the most spectacular proposals is to build a barrage and power station across the Severn Estuary near Weston-super-Mare. The barrage would cross via the islands of Steepholm and Flatholm to the Welsh coast at Laverock point, between Cardiff and Barry. The tidal range and cycle make this one of the world's most attractive sites for tidal power generation. The rising tide would flow through the sluices and 'idling' turbines. Electricity would be generated on the ebb or outflow tide. The barrage would include large locks to allow ships to enter the upper estuary. It is calculated that this version of the barrage could produce about 6 per cent of the country's energy needs, but it would cost about £5 600 million, while the local environment and social impact would be very great.

A view over the Bristol Channel where the Severn Barrage might be built

Left: A favoured proposal for the Severn Barrage

Experiments are being undertaken to see if heat can be obtained from rocks at depth

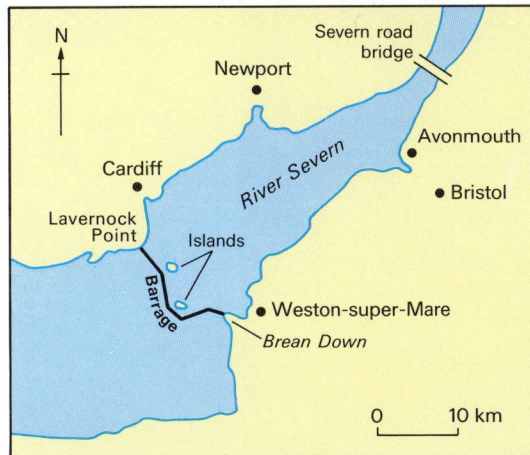

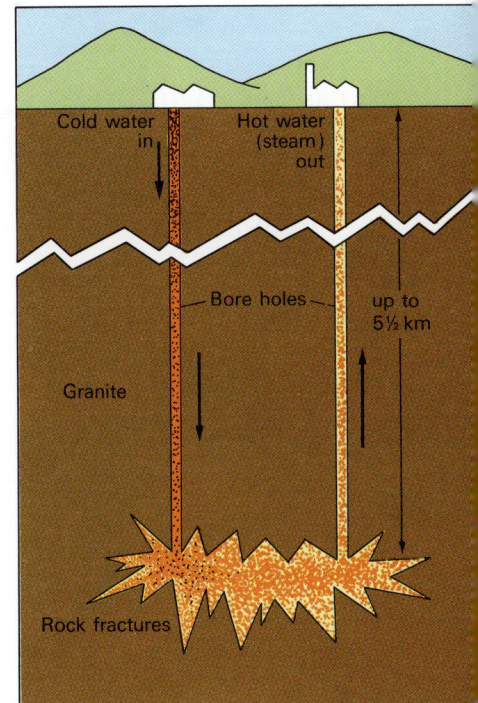

1 Sketch the area shown in the photograph of the Severn Estuary. Label with the names given and add the line of the proposed barrage. Which ports would need access to shipping? What would the environmental impact be a) during construction, b) on completion of the barrage?

2 Why is it not surprising to find experiments in deep rock geothermal energy production in Cornwall?

3 Argue the cases for and against spending lots of money at the present time on research into alternative forms of energy.

Exercise 44 **Generation of electricity**

1 Describe the main concentrations of coal-burning power stations. For two named areas suggest why they are located there.

2 Describe the location of two oil-fired stations. Name the locations and suggest reasons why they are there.

3 Describe the location of the main centres of hydro-electricity generation. Why do you think they are concentrated in these parts of Britain?

Generation of electricity in Great Britain

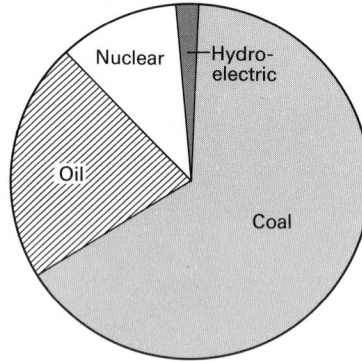

How Britain's electricity was generated, 1983

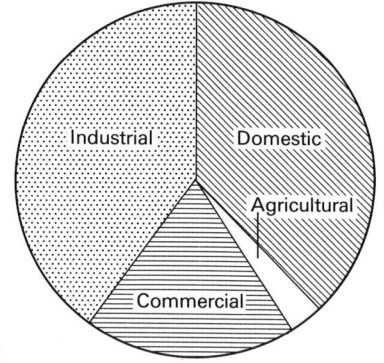

Use of electricity in Great Britain

Hydroelectric power stations make a small contribution to Britain's energy needs but can have great importance for local industry

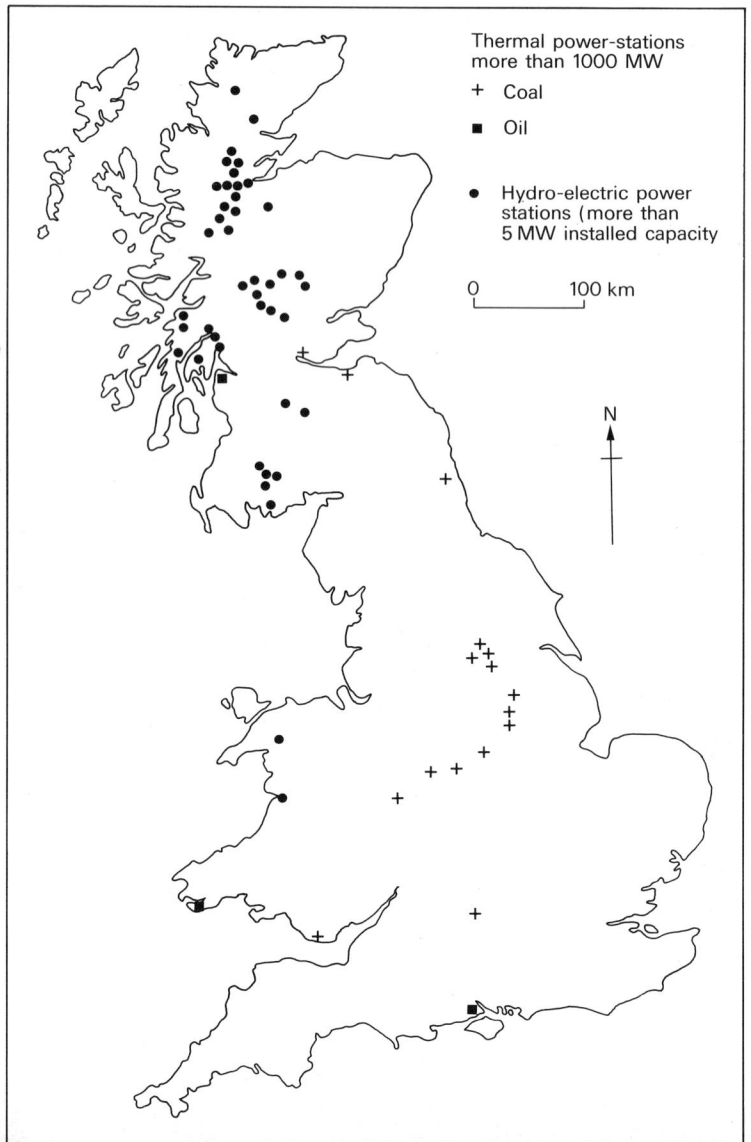

Thermal power-stations more than 1000 MW

+ Coal

■ Oil

● Hydro-electric power stations (more than 5 MW installed capacity

0   100 km

N

The location of different types of power stations, 1983

Chapter 9 Managing the environment

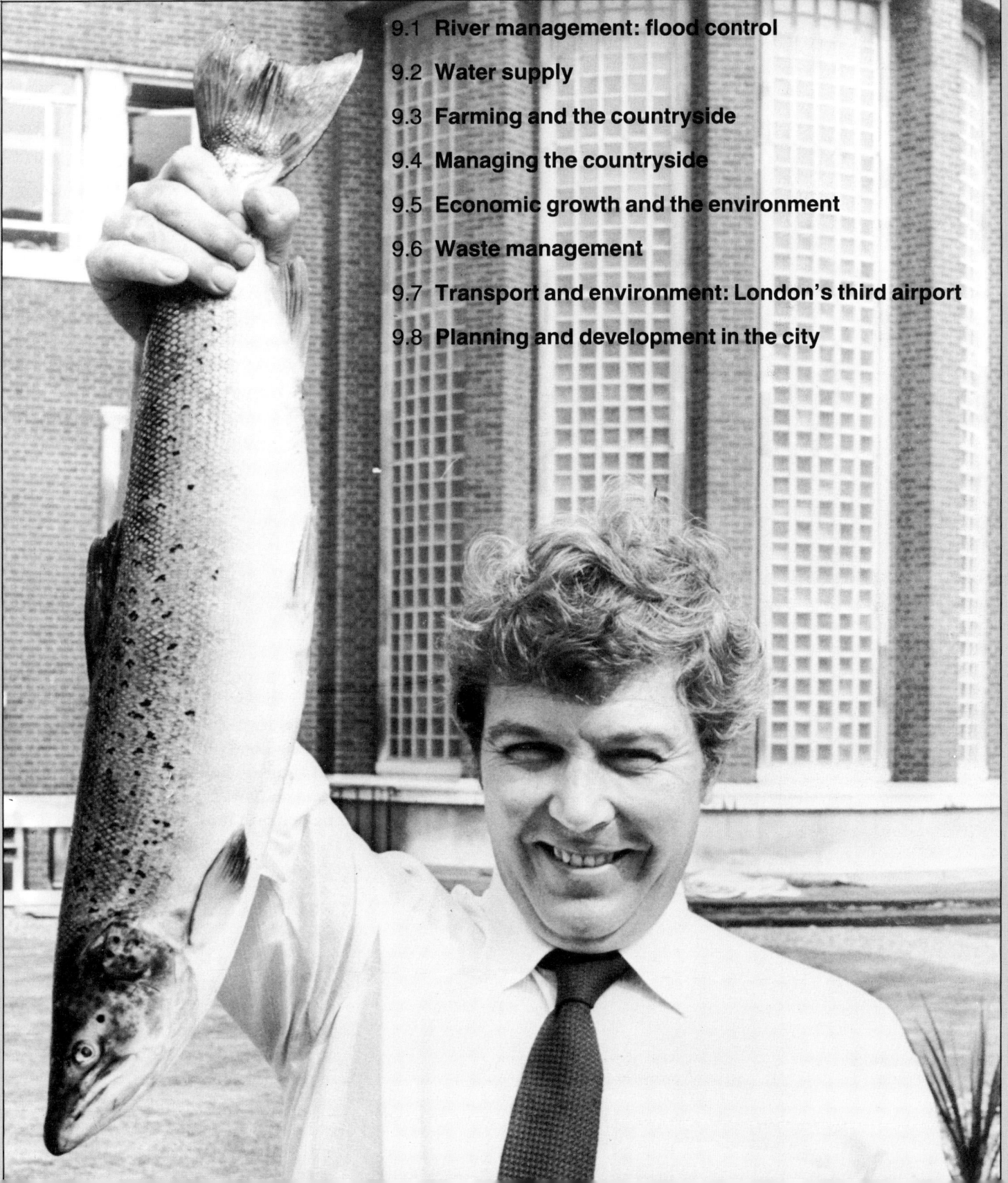

River management: flood control

Floods and flood control

Those who live away from rivers and their flood plains have little idea of the impact of river floods. On a hot summer day riverside sites seem very attractive, and give no suggestion of the hazards at certain other times of the year. River floods can be dangerous and have devastating effect on people, livestock, farmland and towns. Some of the consequences are shown in the photographs on these and the following pages. There were particularly severe floods in January 1982, and this led to many people arguing that much more money and effort should be spent on flood protection. The problem is that severe conditions may occur once every few decades, and it may not be worth all the extra expense to cater for these occasional disasters.

It will be seen that the Regional Water Authorities are responsible for drainage and flood control in their areas, as well as for the provision of water. The map shows the main drainage pattern of Britain's rivers, though because of the scale many smaller streams cannot be shown, nor the details of relief which create the small islands of higher ground that stand above the flood plains. The extract about the River Soar flood prevention scheme on page 187 also suggests that plans to drain land and control the flow of rivers are not always welcomed by everyone.

The Thames barrage

A very different type of project is the barrage built on the Thames to protect London from flooding by the river. This is the responsibility of the Greater London Council, working closely with the Port of London Authority, and built by a group of Dutch and British en-

River water carries vast amounts of silt and soil over the flooded valley floor

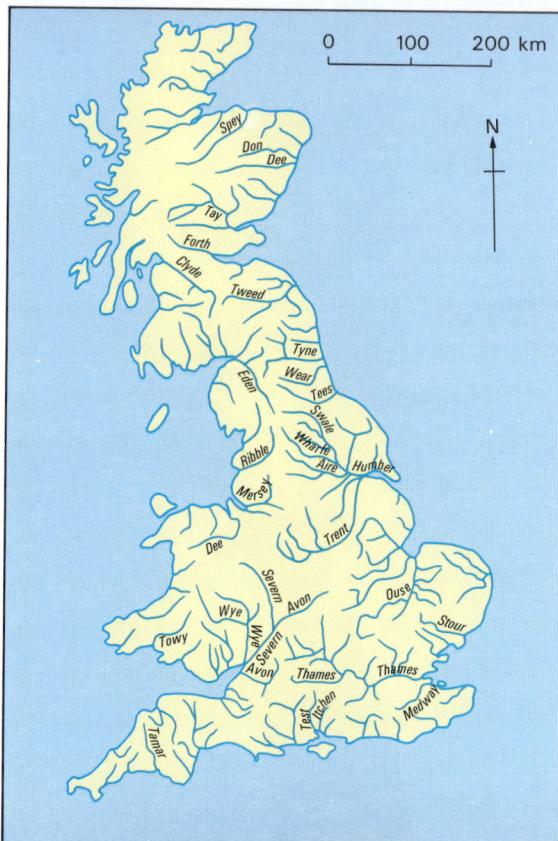

The main rivers and river basins of Britain

gineering firms. It took about eight years to build and was opened in 1984.

The map shows those parts of London liable to be flooded before the barrier was built. The danger was from very high tides coinciding with storms over the North Sea, forcing vast amounts of water up the estuary towards the city. In any case, the south-east of Britain is gradually sinking at the rate of about one foot every one hundred years, and London itself is slowly settling into the London Clay bedrock on which it is built. The tide at London Bridge, for example, is markedly higher now than a century ago. The consequences of such flooding would have been disastrous, with something like a quarter of a million homes engulfed, much of the Underground system inundated and essential services out of action for weeks. There would almost certainly have been many people drowned. The need for protection was urgent.

The project was one of the largest pieces of civil engineering ever carried out in Europe. The barrage is located at Woolwich. It consists of nine spectacular piers. Four massive gates, each weighing 3 000 tonnes, control the deep centre of the river, with smaller gates near the shallower sides. Shaped like a giant D, the gates lie snugly in gutter-like grooves on the river bed. If there is a flood alert, enormous rocker beams will rotate the gates into a vertical position, effectively shutting off London from the estuary and the sea. When the alert has passed, the gates will be opened to allow the flow of river water to the sea and also the free passage of Thames shipping.

1 Describe some of the causes and consequences of river flooding. What are some of the ways in which areas near rivers might be protected, and what prevents this happening?

2 a) Draw a sketch of the major river basin in which your home is located, naming the river and showing the location of your home area. b) Have there been any river floods in your area in recent years? Give details of the causes and consequences.

3 a) What length of riverside was liable to flooding prior to the building of the barrier? b) Why was the barrage solution preferable to building massive defences along both banks of the river? c) Why is it not surprising that Dutch companies were involved in the design and construction of the Thames barrage?

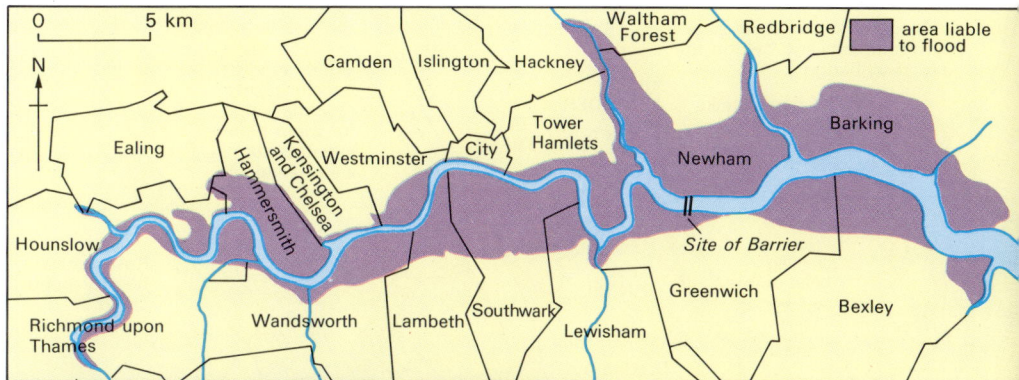

Parts of London that were liable to flooding before the Thames Barrage and strengthened river defences were built

Left and below: The Thames Barrage. These piers house the hydraulic arms that raise or lower the barrier gates. Huge steel gates normally rest flat in concrete grooves between the piers, allowing about 50 000 shipping movements a year across the barrier site

Some flooding can be controlled by the use of storm tunnels

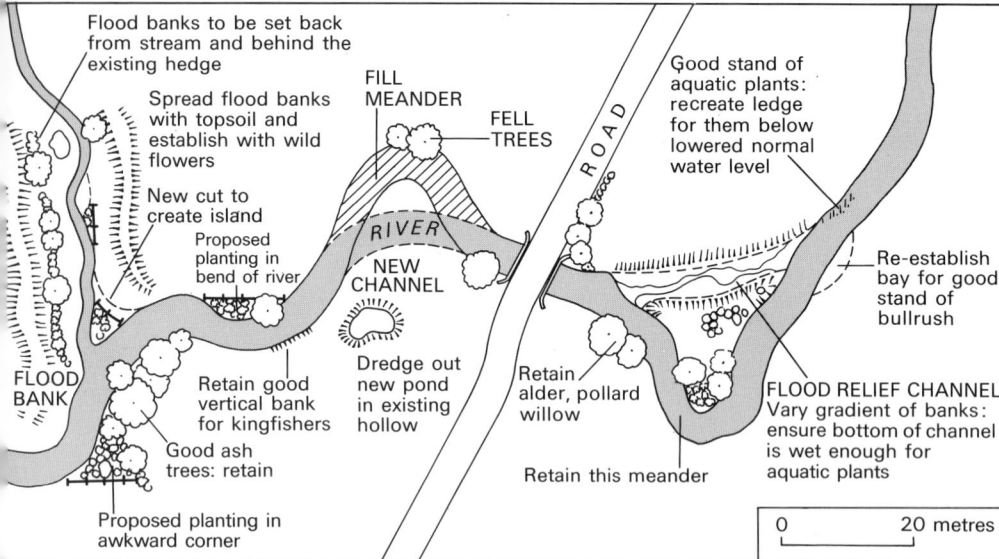

Map labels (river flood control diagram)

Flood banks to be set back from stream and behind the existing hedge

Spread flood banks with topsoil and establish with wild flowers

New cut to create island

Proposed planting in bend of river

FLOOD BANK

Retain good vertical bank for kingfishers

Good ash trees: retain

Proposed planting in awkward corner

FILL MEANDER

FELL TREES

RIVER

NEW CHANNEL

Dredge out new pond in existing hollow

Retain alder, pollard willow

Retain this meander

ROAD

Good stand of aquatic plants: recreate ledge for them below lowered normal water level

Re-establish bay for good stand of bullrush

FLOOD RELIEF CHANNEL Vary gradient of banks: ensure bottom of channel is wet enough for aquatic plants

0   20 metres

River flooding can be controlled by well-planned engineering

In the early months of 1982 many parts of Britain were affected by severe flooding. Some of the worst hit areas are shown on the map and in the photographs while explanations for the floods are given in the extract opposite.

While some places experience flooding most years, severe flooding may occur once every twenty or thirty years. This makes it difficult to know what action to take. To prevent the worst flooding would be extremely expensive, and the defences would be rarely needed. Should large sums of money be spent to prevent these very infrequent disasters? The answers that people give probably depend on how badly they and their property have suffered in the past!

Floods in a York Street in 1982

1 Read the article 'The bursting banks of British rivers'. Copy or trace the map on page 184. On it name the rivers and towns mentioned in the extract.

2 What explanation is given for the floods? Describe the types of damage or threatened damage mentioned in the article and shown in the York and Tewkesbury photographs.

3 Read the article 'Drainage plan likely to go ahead'. Add the location of the scheme to the map you drew for Question 1. What was the group which objected to the flood prevention scheme, and why did it do so?

The bursting banks of British rivers

Houses and farms at Haw Bridge between Gloucester and Tewkesbury are isolated by floodwater, as shown in this aerial photograph, after the River Severn reached its highest level for 13 years. Several other rivers burst their banks as a combination of torrential rain and a rapid thaw caused flooding all over Britain.

Farmers moved livestock to higher ground after warnings that the River Wye was ready to break its banks between Hereford and Ross-on-Wye. Flood alerts were also sounded for the Conwyl, Mawddach, Dovery and Dee in North Wales.

In Yorkshire the River Ouse was expected to be only 2 ft short of its flood level of 13 ft. The River Aire at Keighley burst its banks and homes in Otley and Ilkley were under water.

Roads in the Carlisle, Kendal and Workington areas were affected. In Northumbria the River Tyne over flowed and flooded fields. In Scotland, four roads were completely blocked by flood water.

Drainage plan likely to go ahead

Implementation of the Severn-Trent authority's £6.4m flood-prevention scheme for about twenty miles along the river Soar, near Leicester, has been made likelier by the Nature Council's decision to drop its objections. One of the strongest objectors, the Royal Society for the Protection of Birds (RSPB), criticized the basis for the scheme as a 'national scandal'.

The Soar scheme is the latest in a line of much criticized drainage proposals that include the Somerset levels. Although the Soar proposal includes flood protection for some small villages, its main component, according to the RSPB, is the draining of almost 7000 acres of farmland so they can be used for intensive crop growing.

The centre of Tewkesbury, standing on a low hill, was surrounded by flood water in 1982

Water supply

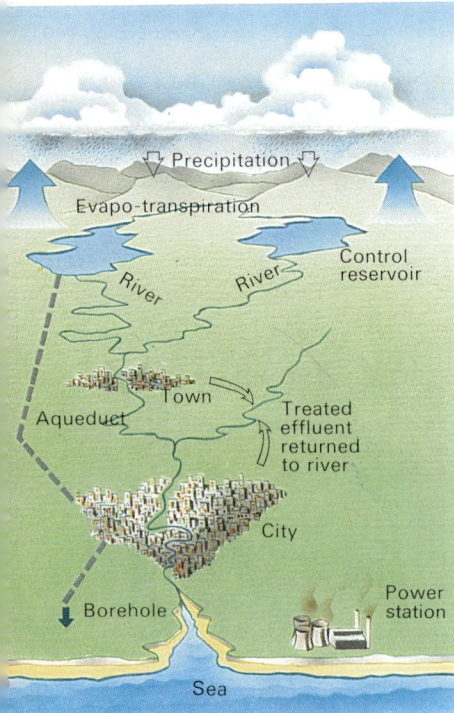

The surface and underground flow of water is part of the water cycle

Increasing demand for water

Clean and unlimited water is taken for granted in Britain. Large amounts are used each day in the home, and far greater amounts in industry and commerce. The diagram on page 191 shows some of the uses to which water is put and the average amounts used each day. It needs to be remembered that a great deal of the water used has been recycled. After being used in the home or factory it is gathered together and purified to acceptable standards in sewage or treatment plants and then made available, often through rivers, for further use. It is also worth pointing out that a great deal of water used in processes such as making power is re-used again and again, while some industrial plants near the sea abstract sea water and return it to the sea after use.

There has been a steady increase in demand for water from all users in recent decades, though now and again there may be a temporary fall for a year or so as in 1976 and 1980. Industrial consumers pay for the water they actually use, and licences have to be obtained for the extraction of water from rivers or underground sources. In all but a few areas, householders are charged a water rate, and this varies from place to place. It is often argued that there would be more careful use if the domestic supply was also metered, but the cost of conversion would be very high.

Supply of water

All water comes from rainfall in the beginning. The rain that falls on land either evaporates, flows in surface streams and rivers, or seeps underground into water-bearing rocks or aquifers. Chalk, limestone and sandstones are the sorts of rocks forming aquifers from which water can be extracted through boreholes or wells. Some river water accumulates in natural lakes, as in the Lake District, and

Keilder Water, one of the largest artificially created lakes in Europe, was built to provide water for the cities and industries of the north-east of England. A decline in demand has meant that the reservoir is unlikely to be fully used until after the year 2000

188

these are valuable reservoirs. Sea water can be used for some purposes, as mentioned above but desalination (taking the salt out of sea water) has been rejected as a means of providing water on a large scale in Britain.

Water is often extracted directly from rivers or aquifers, but nowadays a great deal is held in and obtained from reservoirs built especially for the purpose. These may be storage reservoirs, the water being led to where it is needed by aqueducts and underground pipes, or control reservoirs that are used to keep up the flow of a river to a desirable level at all times. Most large reservoirs are in mountainous and hilly parts of Britain, where rainfall is high and the relief of the land allows efficient construction of huge retaining dams. Keilder Water is the newest of these in Britain, and is one of the largest artificial bodies of water in Europe. The map is a reminder that in certain areas it is possible to build huge reservoirs in lowland areas. These reservoirs near London can also be seen on the satellite photograph on page 9. London is one of many places that also gets water from underground sources in aquifers.

One of the features of water supply is that the areas of greatest supply are often distant from the areas of greatest demand. This is why water for cities such as Birmingham, Liverpool and Manchester has to be brought long distances from reservoirs in upland areas. This raises the issue of 'ownership' of water resources, especially that which comes from Wales into England.

Water management

In the past water was provided by private companies, but in 1974 the present pattern was started. Overall control is under a National Water Council, but the actual management is in the hands of ten Regional Water Authorities. Responsibilities cover not only water supply, but also water conservation, sewage disposal, control of pollution, land drainage and land reclamation. Private water companies are responsible to these Water Authorities.

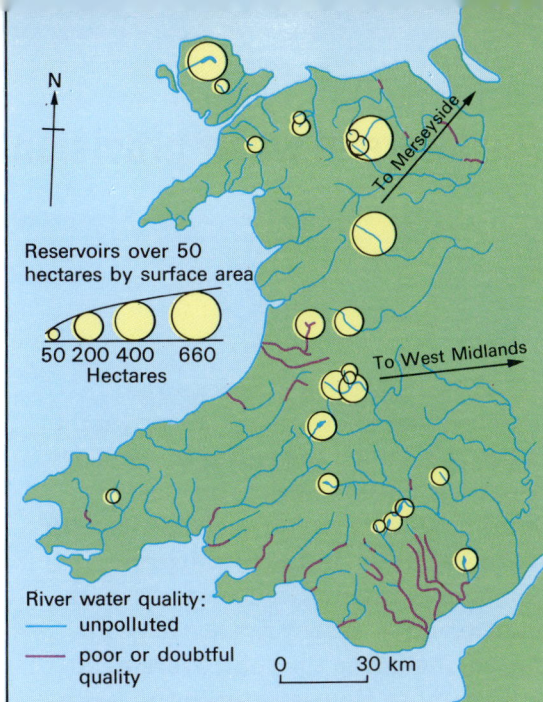

Reservoirs over 50 hectares by surface area

50 200 400 660
Hectares

River water quality:
— unpolluted
— poor or doubtful quality

0   30 km

Much water for lowland Britain is obtained from reservoirs in upland and mountain Wales

The quality of water needs to be carefully checked and controlled

1 From which upland areas do Birmingham, Sheffield, Newcastle and Manchester get their water? Name your Regional Water Authority. (page 190)

2 a) Make a sketch of Keilder Water and label to show the features of the area and its development b) What are some of the recreational possibilities provided by the water? c) What are some of the objections to the project?

3 From the map of future proposals (page 190), name two sets of river catchments that will be linked by water transfers.

4 What are some of the ways in which demand for water could be reduced?

Huge reservoirs in the Thames valley store much of the water for London's enormous demands

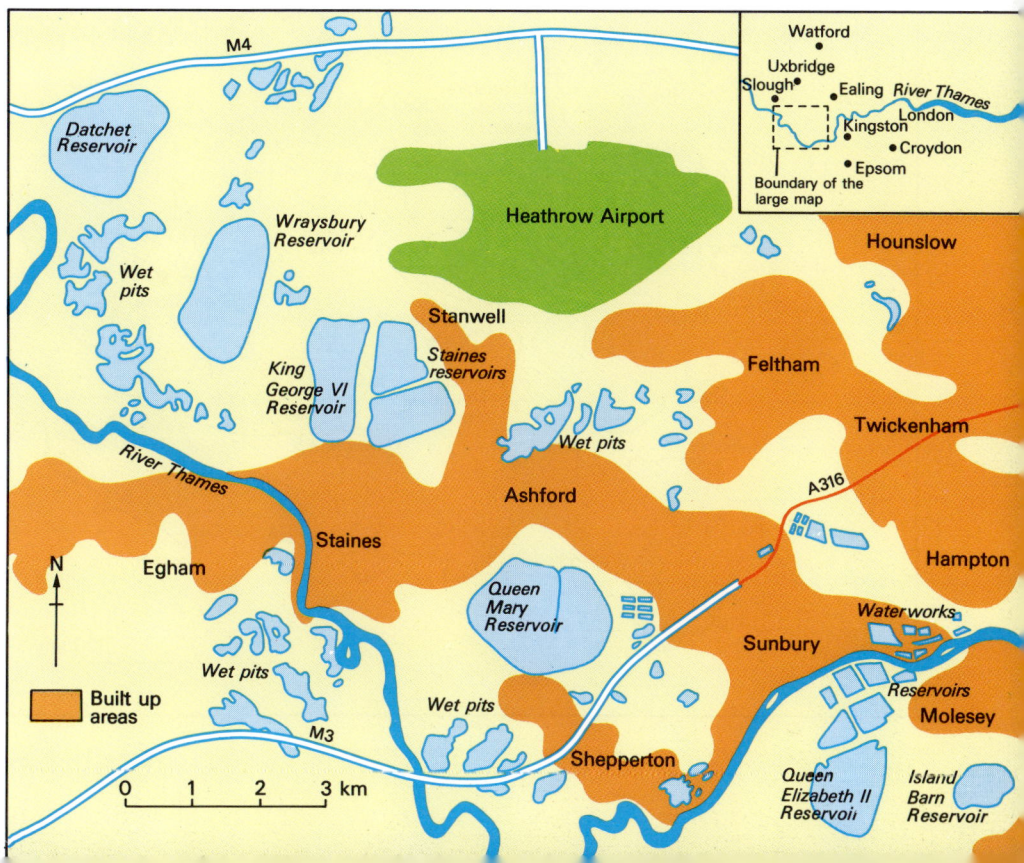

189

The future of water provision

In 1974 a long-term plan was announced that showed how water would be provided until the end of the century. Short term needs were to be met by building new reservoirs such as Keilder Water, at Aston in Derbyshire and Longdon Marsh in Gloucestershire. In addition other reservoirs are to be enlarged, including the controversial development at Haweswater in the Lake District. There will be a reservoir created in the Dee estuary, and groundwater

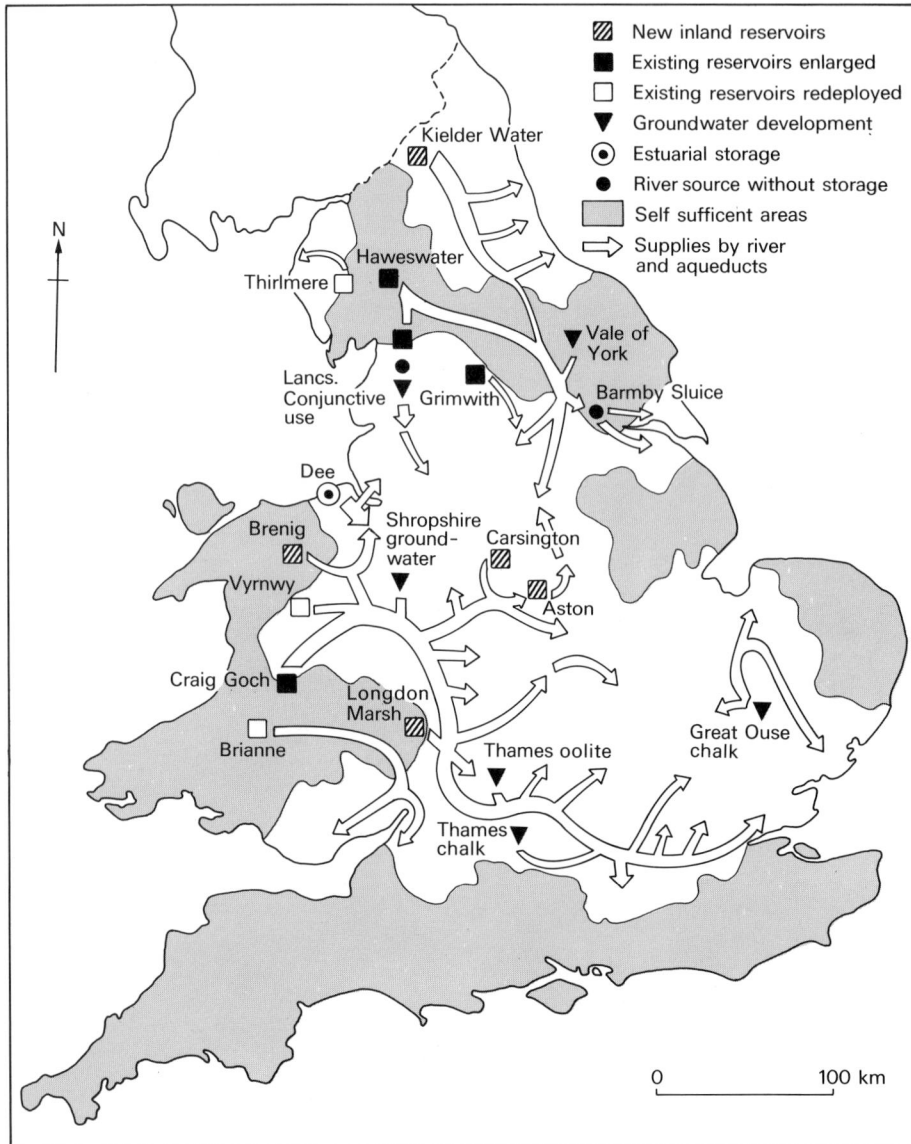

Water supply, water conservation, sewage disposal and drainage are the responsibility of the Water Authorities shown on the map

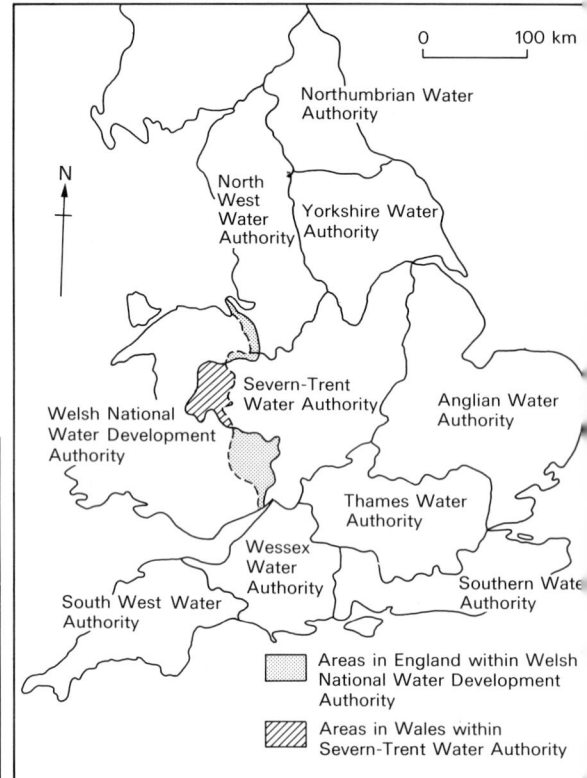

schemes will be developed in the Vale of York, Shropshire, East Anglia, and the Thames valley. Some aquifers will be used as a sort of underground reservoir, having water pumped into them during periods of excess supply. As the map shows, the plan involves a massive transfer of water from some river basins to others. These plans, of course, involve vast sums of money and there are objections to them on environmental grounds. As a result, some may never be completed.

Future water needs have to be calculated well in advance so that large engineering schemes can be completed in time

Exercise 46 Water balance in Britain

1 Draw the input and output data in two separate diagrams (ignore evaporative and saline cooling), using different colours. Add up the totals. What do you notice about them?

2 Draw a diagram to show the relative use of water by domestic and non-domestic users, based on the data provided.

3 What types of industry are likely to be using water in the evaporative cooling and saline cooling systems?

4 Convert the figure for domestic water use into percentages and show in a bar diagram.

This diagram of Britain's water balance is, of course, highly simplified

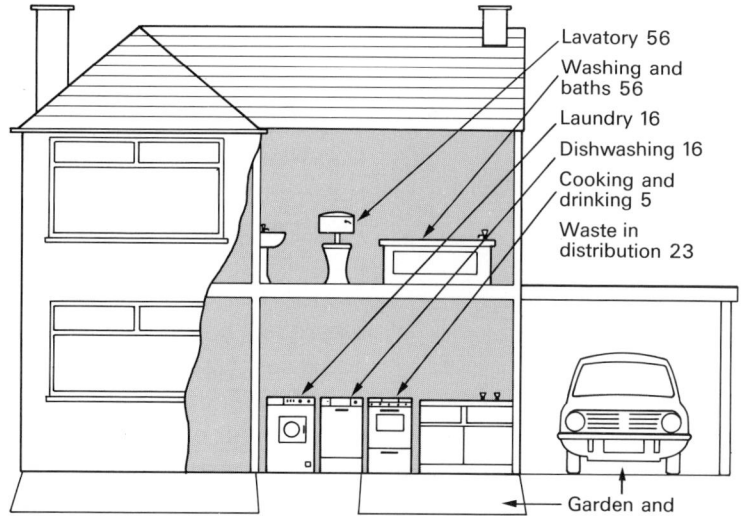

Lavatory 56
Washing and baths 56
Laundry 16
Dishwashing 16
Cooking and drinking 5
Waste in distribution 23
Garden and Car wash 5

Where the water goes in a British house (in litres per day)

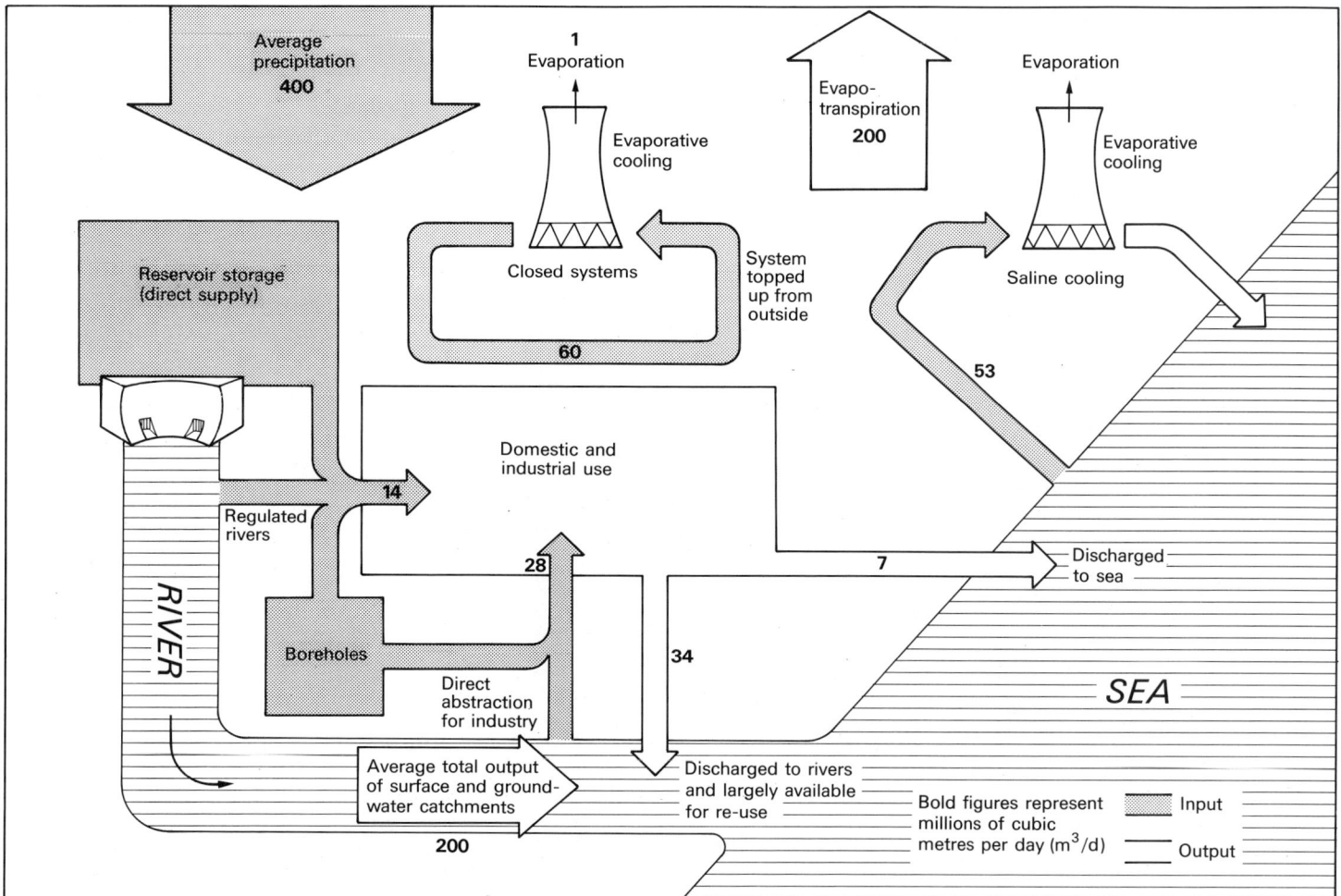

Average precipitation **400**

1 Evaporation

Evaporative cooling

Evapo-transpiration **200**

Evaporation

Evaporative cooling

Reservoir storage (direct supply)

Closed systems

System topped up from outside

Saline cooling

60

53

Domestic and industrial use

Regulated rivers

14

RIVER

28

Boreholes

Direct abstraction for industry

7

Discharged to sea

34

SEA

Average total output of surface and ground-water catchments

Discharged to rivers and largely available for re-use

200

Bold figures represent millions of cubic metres per day (m³/d)

Input
Output

Farming and the countryside

Moorland vegetation is still found in the more remote parts of Exmoor

Below: Much of Exmoor has been 'reclaimed' and used for farming and other purposes

The changing countryside

The appearance of the countryside has always been changing, and the landscape of small fields and hedgerows, woods and streams, meadows and pastures enjoyed by many people is the result of centuries of care and development by farmers. But recent changes are more dangerous and threatening. There has been an enormous loss of hedgerow trees, and thousands of kilometres of hedges, some many hundreds of years old, have been uprooted. About one-third of old woodland has been cut down and lost forever with its wildlife over the past thirty years. Ponds, bogs and marshes have been drained and rivers straightened and dredged. The heather and heath of the uplands has been ploughed up and replaced by grass fodder crops or coniferous woodland.

Quite apart from the loss of landscapes that many people find attractive and interesting, there is a further anxiety. Rare and attractive plants, butterflies, frogs and toads, birds and small animals are becoming still rarer, and in some places are in danger of extinction. These different species of plants and animals exist in close interdependence and interaction amongst themselves and with their environments. Disturbing the habitat of one species may affect the whole ecosystem. So it is not just the complete removal of hedges or woodlands that destroys plant and animal life. It is also less obvious changes such as deeper ditching, wetland drainage, excessive fertilising and the grazing of heath and moorland. To some people this may be a matter of no importance, but others think it essential to conserve some areas that show what habitats and wildlife were like in the past and which offer enjoyment to millions today.

Moorlands and wetlands

Thousands of hectares of moorland have been ploughed up in recent decades and used to graze livestock, grow fodder crops or plant coniferous trees. This has been encouraged by grants and subsidies from the taxpayer through the Ministry of Agriculture and Fisheries. Farmers argue that it is necessary to improve this 'marginal' land if they are to produce the food the nation needs. They also argue that they are the real guardians of the land. The conservationists, who include many people who are not farmers nor live in the moorland areas, claim that the countryside and its wildlife, although owned by farmers or companies, really belongs to everyone. It is too important to be used purely for commercial interests and economic gain. They argue that since farmers are supported by taxpayers' money they should all have some say in how the countryside is developed. They suggest that this may be done by buying up marginal moorland, or by persuading farmers and landowners to retain it as moorland by paying them to do so.

Another type of environment under threat of extinction is the wetland. These wetlands are the result of hundreds, perhaps thousands, of years of farming that was based on the regular winter flooding of meadowland and the harvesting of sedges. When drained they can be used for grazing animals or growing crops, which increases the farm income very considerably. The trouble is that they are also environments rich in plant and animal wildlife, some of them extremely rare. Quite a few of the 3 800 or so Sites of Special Scientific Interest (SSSI) are in these wetlands, and as such are supposed to justify some protection. Once again, though, there is often a clash between what farmers and Water Boards want and what the conservationists think should happen. The Sedgemoor areas of Somerset are just one of these wetland areas where there has been a clash. The conservationists object not only to sites being destroyed but also to farmers

The locations of Exmoor and Sedgemoor; two contrasting types of 'moor'

being paid compensation for not developing them. The farmers understandably ask 'why not?', since they would benefit from a bigger income if they developed these areas. As with the moorlands, there is not enough taxpayers' money given to The Nature Conservancy Council to buy up valuable sites, or to compensate farmers for their claimed 'loss of possible earnings'.

1 Describe and draw an annotated sketch of the farm on the margins of the moorland on Exmoor. What do you feel about the landscape? What are the arguments for and against farming these marginal moorland areas? Who are likely to be for and against it?

2 In what sense is it true that 'farmers are the true guardians of rural areas'?

3 Do you think it is sensible to a) spend taxpayers' money on Sites of Special Scientific Interest? b) give financial help to farmers who produce surpluses of crops or livestock which are then sold at a loss?

One of the larger canals used for draining Sedgemoor

There is conflict between landowners who wish to drain and use more of Sedgemoor for farming, and others who want it conserved in its 'natural' state

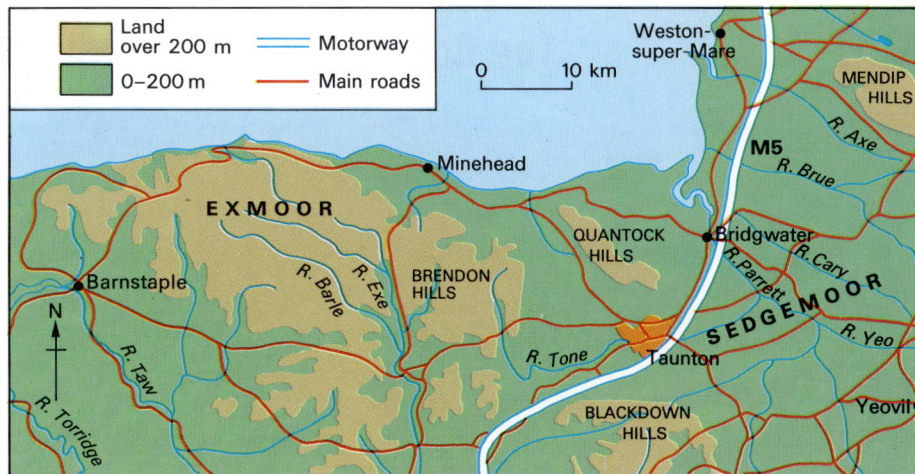

The Countryside and Wildlife Act 1981

A conservator tending a drainage channel in a wetland area

The threat to many environments and their wildlife such as those described on the last two pages led to the passing of the Countryside and Wildlife Act by Parliament in 1981. This followed months of argument and debate by people with many different viewpoints and interests. The Act states that areas of the countryside which are important either in themselves or for the survival of wildlife shall be declared 'sites of scientific interest'. The decision about which environments shall be SSSI's is decided by the Nature Conservancy Council. The Council has to tell the owner of the site, usually a farmer or group of farmers, of its decision and explain what needs to be done (or not done) to conserve its scientific interest and value. There are about 4 000 sites thought to be worth conserving in this way, and these are on properties of some 30 000 owners or tenants. There is no compulsion about the use of the land, and the Act is based on understanding and agreement between the NCC and the owners.

The main remaining 'wetland' areas of Britain

A conflict of interests

Emer Bog is a damp piece of countryside just to the north of the outer suburbs of Southampton. Next to Emer Bog lies the main part of Baddesley Common, where Mr John Burns, a local builder, bought 154 acres for £99 000 last summer.

When the family took over the land and its occupants, they wanted to run it as a business, not as a nature reserve. They were not interested in a 'management agreement' made under the *Wildlife and Countryside Act.*

Last year they became the first landowners to receive a Nature Conservation Order.

The order issued against the Burns family said they could not plough, harrow, seed, spray or irrigate their land. They may not remove any soil, peat, moss, mineral or plant, or place on the land any creature which does not already live there. Mrs Burns said: 'Either we own the land or we do not.' They have appealed against the order.

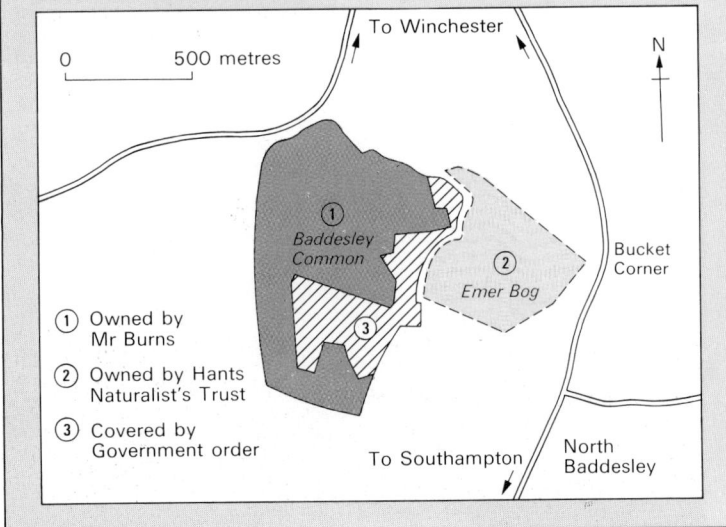

North Baddesley

0   500 metres

To Winchester

To Southampton

Bucket Corner

① *Baddesley Common*
② *Emer Bog*
③

① Owned by Mr Burns
② Owned by Hants Naturalist's Trust
③ Covered by Government order

0   100 km

N

Derwent Ings, Yorkshire ●
Idle Washes, Nottinghamshire ●
River Soar Leicestershire ●
Nene Washes ●
Nene Valley ●
Ouse Valley ●
Halvergate Marshes Norfolk
Waveney Marshes, Norfolk
Upper Cleddau, Pembrokeshire ●
Worcester/ ● Avon
Lower ● Severn
River Stort, Essex and Hertfordshire
North Kent Marshes
Somerset ● Levels
Pevensey Levels, Sussex ●
Seaton Marshes, Devon ●
Romney Marsh, Kent
Poole Harbour Marshes

Exercise 47 Farming and the countryside

Ploughing has 'destroyed nature site'

Conservationists accused the Government yesterday of failing to protect five important nature reserves. The groups said that 16 acres of an official site of special scientific interest at Ripon, North Yorkshire, had been destroyed by ploughing. They also claimed that notification of such sites by the Nature Conservancy Council, was worthless, because 'landholders exploit a loophole in the Act which allows them to destroy sites during the three month consultation period'.

The other reserves covered by the statement were Halvergate Marshes, Norfolk, Romney Marsh, East Sussex, the Berwyn Mountains, Gwynedd, and West Sedgemoor, Somerset. The Nature Conservancy Council had failed to object to a drainage proposal for part of Romney Marsh and the groups were worried about partial drainage of wetlands at West Sedgemoor.

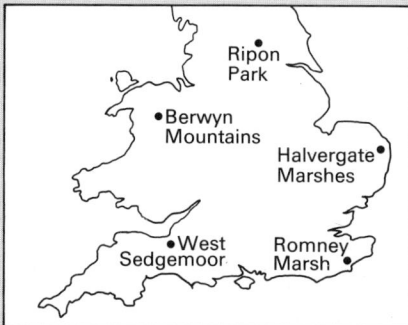

Uplands 'devastated by land use'

Large areas of Britain's national parks 'should cause us great shame as monuments to disastrously bad land use', Mr John Andrews, national conservation officer of the Royal Society for the Protection of Birds, said yesterday.

Over-frequent burning and over-stocking of sheep had devastated many upland areas in England and Wales, he said.

Farm pollution kills 20 000 Devon trout

Farmers in the South-west are being told about serious pollution caused by farm waste which has killed more than 20 000 trout on three Devon rivers in six weeks.

Two farmers have been told by the South-west Water Authority that it is considering prosecuting them. In the latest incident, 20 000 gallons of slurry escaped from a lagoon into the River Carey killing about 5 000 trout. Attempts are going on to save many more in the lower reaches of the river.

The pollution is caused when heavy rain breaks down the walls of slurry pits and causes them to overflow.

Farmers are the truly rural guardians

In swirling mist 1 200 ft up on Exmoor Mr John Pugsley led the way across a heather-covered hillside.

'Conservationists say that once you plough up moorland like this it is gone for ever', he said. 'But I remember as a young boy watching Italian prisoners of war digging potatoes off this very spot.'

Mr Pugsley farms 1 100 acres of upland which supports about 1 300 sheep and 110 beef cattle. About 650 acres of that was identified by Lord Porchester in his 1978 report on Exmoor as 'critical amenity moorland' which should be conserved in the national interest. Far from being anti-conservationists, Mr Pugsley is proud of his immaculate house and village and anxious to see the traditional Exmoor way of life survive. But he insists that if farming is to remain viable farmers must be compensated under management agreements for not putting moorland under the plough.

The rights and wrongs of straw burning became an important issue in the mid-1980s

1 Read the four extracts, and look at the photo. What are the types of damage to the countryside caused, or said to be caused, by farmers?

2 Do you think that ownership of land should entitle the owner or owners to be able to use it in any way they care to? If not, why not? If so, what are your arguments?

3 Describe any SSSIs that are near you, or that you know about. How would you find out where they are?

Managing the countryside

The National Trust gets its money from voluntary gifts. It owns large areas of attractive countryside and many historic sites

Mam Tor in the Peak National Park. Erosion is caused by thousands of people walking along the same track

Ownership, use and management

Rural land in Britain is owned by many private individuals, companies, trusts and voluntary bodies, local authorities and the government. Amongst the biggest landowners are the Royal Family, the Church and Oxford and Cambridge Universities. This land is used in many different ways – for farming, forestry, mining and quarrying, waste disposal, water supply, transport and recreation. They are also managed and their use controlled in varied ways. The owners and users often have competing and sometimes conflicting demands on the countryside, some of which were considered in the last section.

National Parks and their management

There are ten of these areas in England and Wales, their location being shown on page 199. They were selected or 'designated' because of their outstanding natural beauty. The purpose of managing them and controlling developments within their borders is to preserve the beauty of the landscapes so that everyone can enjoy them. But this has to be done with land that is frequently privately owned and farmed, or used for industrial purposes, and where many people live and have to make a living. The Parks are managed by the Local Authorities within whose areas they fall, although the Peak and Lake District Parks have their own authorities. Many local and national interest groups are represented on the boards of the Park Authorities. These groups give their expertise, but they also try to protect their own particular interests. The authorities do have some powers over development, but some argue that it is not enough. They also lack the money for major purchases of land or for development projects.

Many of the features and problems of National Parks are illustrated by these maps and photographs and data about Snowdonia and the Peak Park. As with all of them the difficult task is to resolve the conflicts between different users and what they want. It is often argued that the Park authorities do not have enough power or money to do their job properly, while others say that government policy towards farming and forestry and industrial development does a great deal to damage the recreational value and social life of people living in the Parks. In spite of all the criticisms it is likely that the areas are better cared-for than in an economic 'free-for-all' where people could do what they liked within the general law.

Other countryside managers

The Countryside Commission, originally called the National Parks Commis-

Key:
- National Park
- Limestone rock
- • Quarries

Barnsley
M1
A628
Greater Manchester
A57
Sheffield
A625
Macclesfield
Buxton
A6
Bakewell
A53
A515
Matlock
Leek
Ashbourne

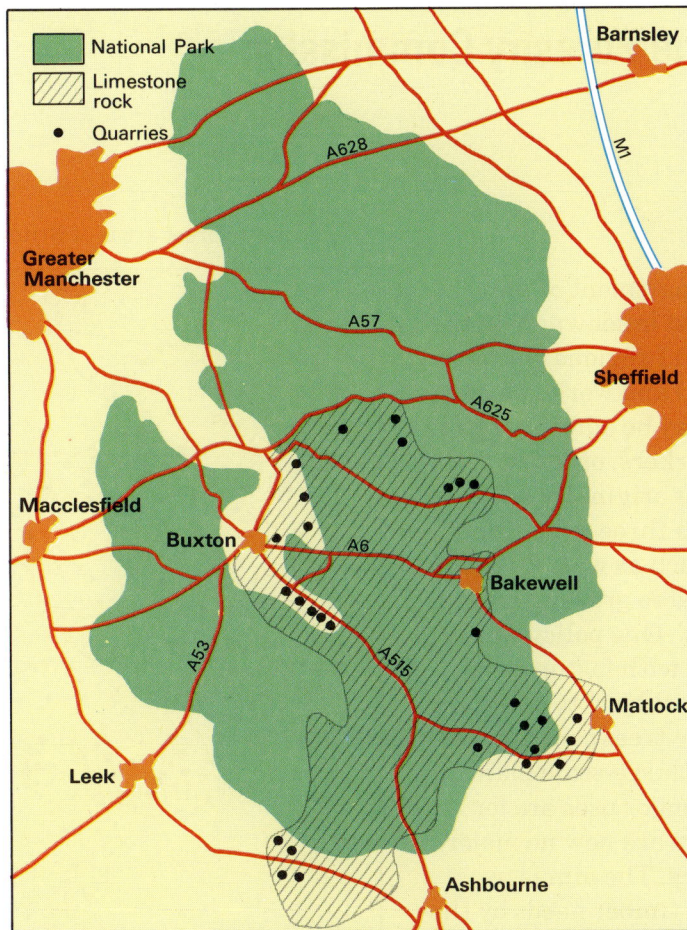

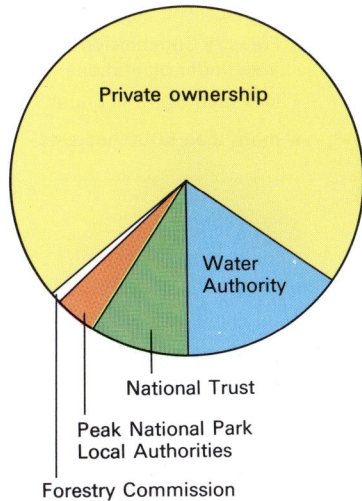

Ownership of the Peak National Park land

Private ownership
Water Authority
National Trust
Peak National Park Local Authorities
Forestry Commission

A great deal of land in the National Parks is used for farming. Edale in the Peak Park

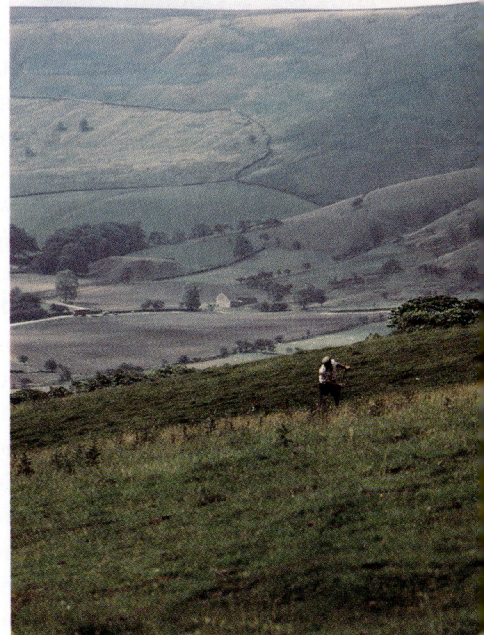

The Peak National Park can be easily reached by millions of city dwellers from the Midlands and North of England

sion, took its new name in 1968. It has responsibilities towards National Parks and Areas of Outstanding Natural Beauty (AONBs). It is financed by the Government, and can give grants and advice to Local Authorities when they want to set up Country Parks or local nature reserves. It has also been responsible for establishing the long-distance footpaths in England and Wales. The Nature Conservancy Council, since 1965 a part of the Natural Environment Research Council, was set up to provide scientific advice on the conservation and control of natural flora and fauna in Britain, and to establish and maintain nature reserves. It is also responsible for Sites of Special Scientific Interest (SSSIs), but many of these, like Nature Reserves are in private ownership.

Local Authorities, through their planning departments, also have some say in the management of countryside areas and other 'country' areas such as the so-called Green Belts. These are areas of green and open land on the margins of large towns and cities. As with other authorities, there is the continual problem of trying to reach some sort of compromise between different people wanting to use the same bit of land for different purposes. At the same time they have to look ahead to future needs of individuals and of the community as a whole.

1 From the map, graph and photographs, suggest what some of the pressures on the environment of the Peak Park might be.

2 Draw a sketch of and describe the landscape of Edale shown. What are your feelings about it? Should 'outsiders' have any say in how it is used or developed? Why, or why not?

3 Why is it easier to control house building, for example, than the extension of limestone quarrying in the Park?

4 Use an atlas to describe the location and general characteristics of the ten National Parks shown on page 199.

Most National Parks contain minerals and rocks needed by industry. These limestone quarries in the Peak Park provide jobs and wealth, but ruin the recreational value of the area

197

The Forestry Commission, a department of the Government, is one of the largest landowners in the country. Britain is divided into 11 regions or 'conservancies', and these are managed and worked by just under 8000 employees. They may be administrators, scientific researchers, forest workers, or forest craftsmen. The Commission was originally set up in 1919 with the aim of providing a three-year standing of timber for emergencies such as war. By the late 1950s this aim was switched to growing trees for 'social and economic reasons'. One policy was to replace forests of oak and beech with fast-growing conifers. The Commission is not subject to planning laws, and as land on which these trees can grow is relatively cheap, a great deal of large-scale planting of conifers took place. The two major uses are for woodpulp and sawlogs, but there are now no major saw and pulpmills in the country. The aim is to provide about 12 per cent of our timber needs by the

The main forest areas of Britain

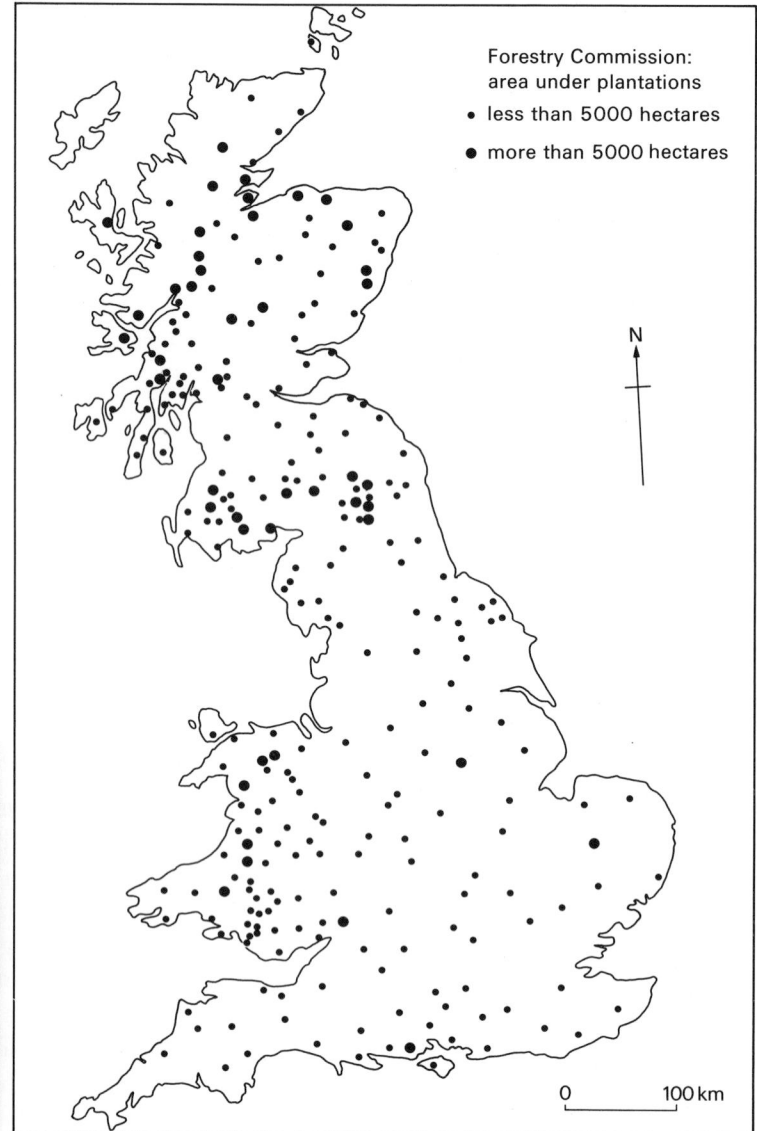

Forestry Commission: area under plantations
• less than 5000 hectares
● more than 5000 hectares

N

0   100 km

Forestry Commission land in Scotland

turn of the century. The Commission also gives grants for planting private woods, and there are also considerable tax reliefs on private planting.

The other activities of the Commission include providing picnic spots, camping sites, forest trails, and motorcycle and car rally routes for use by the general public. The map shows where the main plantations are located, and some of the larger Forest Parks that are visited by thousands of people each year. The Forestry Commission is responsible to the Minister for Agriculture and Fisheries, the Secretary of State for Wales and the Secretary of State for Scotland.

198

Exercise 48 **National Parks, AONBs and long-distance footpaths**

Explanation of terms

Areas of Outstanding Natural Beauty
These are similar to but smaller than National Parks. The Countryside Commission (a government-financed body) decides which areas shall be AONB's, but they are controlled by local authorities.

Long-distance footpaths
These have been established by the Commission to allow people to walk for long distances through areas offering a range of scenery, wildlife and history.

National Nature Reserves
These are areas of land selected by the Nature Conservancy Council (another national body) because they have important types of plants or animals or geological features. Over half are privately owned, but they are managed by the Council.

Sites of Special, Scientific Interest (SSSI)
These are areas containing rare species of plants or animals or showing features of special geological interest. The Council has to be informed of developments being planned within them, and can advise on their management. They are mostly owned by private owners who may wish to develop them for some purpose. The Nature Conservancy Council reported in 1980 that 10% of SSSI's were lost or seriously damaged.

Protected areas in England and Wales

	Number	Area	% of land surface
National Parks	10	13 600 km²	9.0
Areas of Outstanding Natural Beauty	33	14 493 km²	9.6
Heritage Coasts	33	1 084 km*	24.7*
National Nature Reserves	111	37 380 ha	0.25
Sites of Special Scientific Interest	3800	401 660 ha	2.65
Other sites of special Interest	3349	311 088 ha	2.06

*Length of coastline, as a percentage of total length.

The location of National Parks, AONBs and long distance footpaths

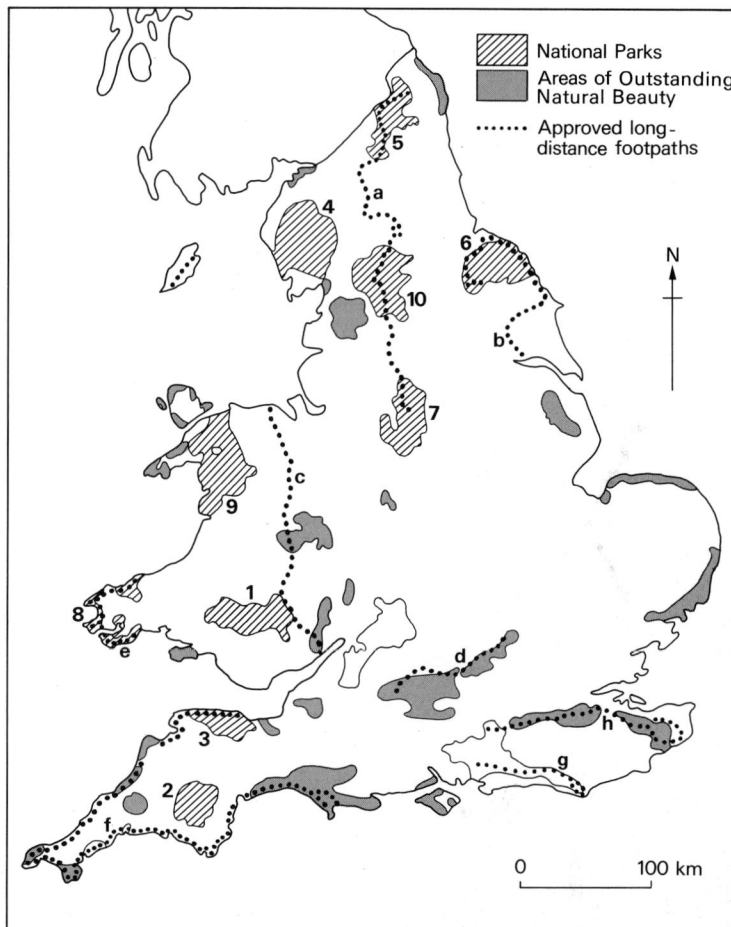

1 Which Parks are nearest and which most distant from large centres of population? Which are most likely to suffer from the impact of too many tourists and visitors? Which of the ten National Parks can you name?

2 Draw two generalised graphs that represent the changing pattern of visits to a National Park over a 24 hour period on **a**) a summer weekday **b**) a summer Sunday. Explain the difference. Draw a graph showing the likely seasonal pattern of visits over a twelve month period.

3 Write down a list of the long-distance footpaths in England and Wales. Look back through this book and give a brief description of the main landscape features of two of these long-distance footpaths.

Economic growth and the environment

A new industrial plant

'Where there's muck there's brass'

A great deal of present-day Britain shows the effects of past industrial activity. Some of it is unattractive to look at, and was probably very unpleasant to live and work in, but this was where much of the past wealth of Britain was made. The signs are still there of quarries and holes where minerals were and are being extracted. There are the industrial landscapes with their confusion of factories, waste tips, railway and canal tracks. There is the grime, the dereliction and the scarred land that are a reminder of the environmental price that was paid for economic growth. An important question is what can and should be done to reclaim these industrial wastelands. Another is whether future economic development must inevitably mean such devastation.

Mining in the Vale of Belvoir

One of the big national inquiries in the early 1980s was over the application of the National Coal Board to open three new mines in the Vale of Belvoir in Leicestershire. Proved recoverable reserves of over 500 million tonnes of coal, ideally suited to burning in power stations, lie beneath it. The area covers about 230 square kilometres of Leicestershire and adjoining Nottinghamshire and Lincolnshire in an area of mixed farming, small villages and, except in the south, little industrial development. The nearest of the huge Vale of Trent power stations is little more than 15 kilometres away.

The proposed new mines were to be at **a**) Hose, in the heart of the Vale, **b**) Saltby, another farming area but near a disused airfield and ironstone quarry,

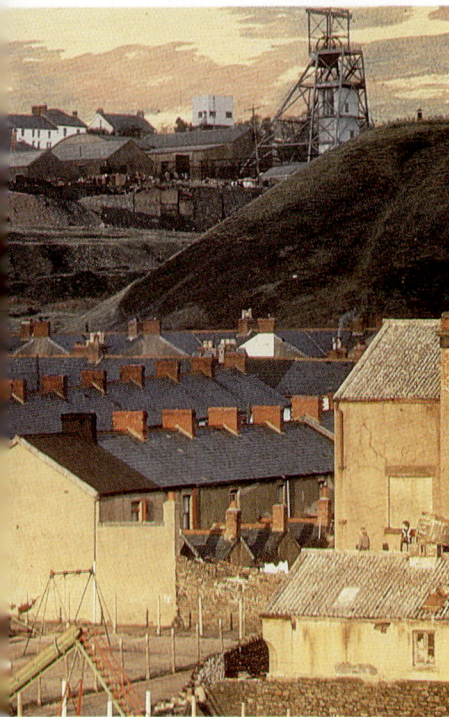

An old coal mine

Some objectors show their views very clearly

and **c**) Asfordby, near a heavy industrial works belonging to BSC. Arguments raged about whether the coal was really needed at all; a view already considered in chapter 8. In addition there was great concern about the impact of the pithead gear and slag and waste heaps on the pleasant rural landscape, and the social upheaval of some 3 000–4 000 workers coming to the area. By 1982 the Secretary of State for the Environment had decided that he was prepared to consider only the two southern pits, but not the 'environmentally unacceptable' Hose pit.

'Acid rain' and air pollution

The environmental impact of mining, quarrying and industrial development is often all too easy to see. Just as damaging may be the unseen pollution of the atmosphere caused by industrial activity. For decades there have been various forms of smoke control as well as of other industrial pollutants. A new threat became evident in the early 1980s; so-called 'acid rain'.

All rain is slightly acid as a result of carbon dioxide mixing with water in the atmosphere. This is 'natural' and has the effect of helping dissolve minerals in the soil and helping plants to grow. Acid rain is the result of sulphur and nitrogen oxides from power stations, factories and car exhausts entering the atmosphere in large amounts. These chemicals turn into sulphuric and nitric acids which fall as a corrosive rain. It has been calculated that much rainfall in North America and Europe is between three and thirty times the acidity of normal rainfall. The results have been devastating to many lakes, forests and buildings in Scandinavia and Germany in particular. One problem of control is that the pollution in the atmosphere may be carried thousands of kilometres. Much of Scandinavian acid rain is claimed to be produced by British industries, for example, and carried over the North Sea. As the extract shows, Britain itself is now suffering from the same problem, although the exact extent is not known. Acid rain

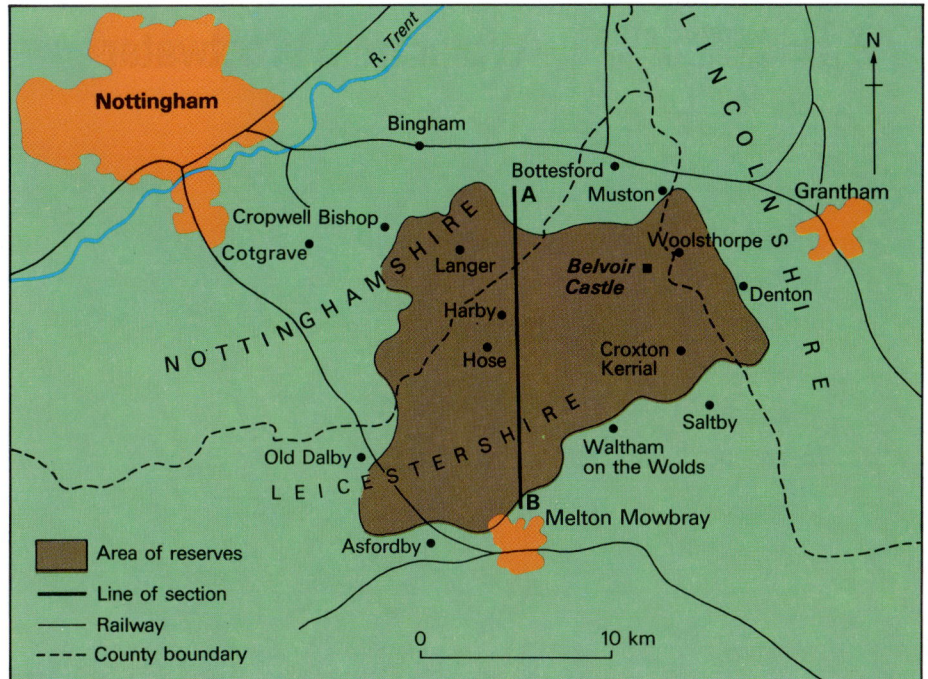

A map of the coalfield and the proposed mining area in the Vale of Belvoir

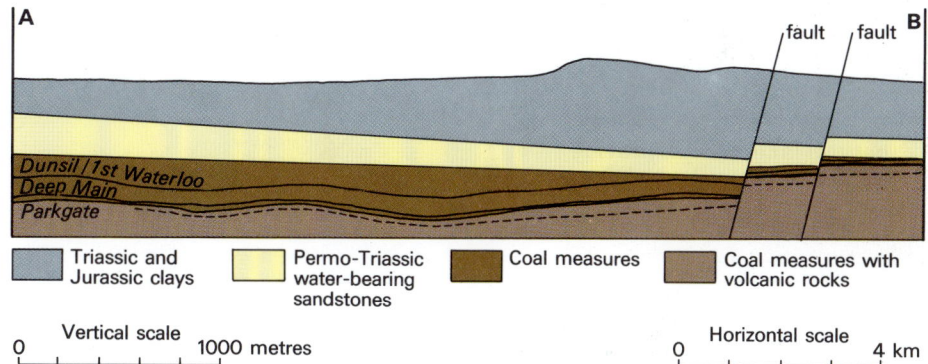

A geological cross-section through the Vale of Belvoir

and its destructive consequences is another part of the price to be paid for economic development.

1 Give examples and locations of the environmental effects of **a**) mining or quarrying, **b**) factory activities, that you know or have studied.

2 Make lists of the arguments for and against the development of the three mines in the Vale of Belvoir. Why should your view be likely to differ from that of a resident of the Vale or a miner who might otherwise be unemployed?

3 A newspaper headline in June 1982 said 'Britain moving towards acid rain disaster'. Why are such statements to be treated with caution? What is the case for and against the heading given in this extract rather than the one just quoted?

Acid rain falls over Britain

Acid rain is falling in Britain, according to a report commissioned by the Department of the Environment, and in some regions it is severe. The most acid rain was found in two sites in southern England. Overall, the most consistently high readings were taken in parts of Cumbria, the west central Highlands and southern uplands of Scotland.

'Acid rain' is created when sulphur and nitrogen oxides are released by the burning of coal and oil. The oxides are converted to sulphuric and nitric acids in the atmosphere, settling as rain, snow or minute solid particles.

201

Water from Wastwater

The Lake District

Wastwater, one of the natural lakes used to provide water for use in the North of England

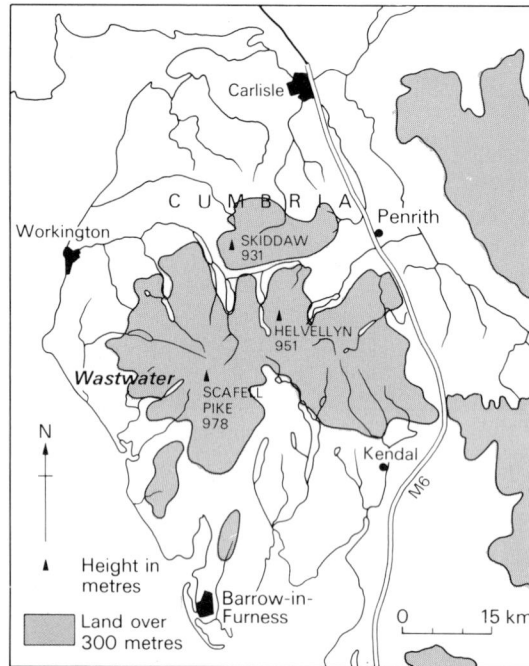

An example of a dispute over economic development was provided by the request of British Nuclear Fuels Limited to extract more water from Wastwater in the Lake District for their nuclear plant at Sellafield (the works originally called Windscale and Calder Hall) in Cumbria. These are the works where much of the contaminated waste from power stations is processed or stored. The high quality of the lake water makes it very suitable for steam raising and cooling the tanks which store these highly radioactive wastes from British and overseas power stations. Already some four million gallons were being taken each day and the proposal was to take a further 7 million gallons a day. This was to be done either by raising the level of the lake with a new weir, or simply pumping more out. The former would raise the level of the lake and drown some land, the latter would run the risk of lowering the level of the lake during times of drought to a point where the River Irt that drains the lake would no longer flow.

The lake is one of the more spectacular and attractive of those in the Lake District, as well as being in a National Park, and many people objected to the proposal. These included local residents, conservationists and the National Trust who own much of the land around the lake. In July 1982 BNFL were given a temporary licence by the Secretary of State to take out an extra 2.4 million gallons a day, with careful monitoring by the Planning Authority.

Some months later British Nuclear Fuels withdrew its application to take more water and planned to use other supplies obtainable nearby.

This example shows the complicated link between industrial growth and the environment.

Exercise 49
Economic growth and environment in Scotland

1 Look at the map of Scotland. Describe and account for **a**) the distribution of 'good' farmland, **b**) the scenic and conservation sites, **c**) the areas set aside for industrial activities.

2 From examples given in this book describe the landscape and activities at one of the identified industrial areas and one of the conservation areas.

3 Which type of industrial development in Scotland (described in chapter 4) is *not* likely to cause much environmental damage? Why is this the case?

4 Imagine you had to decide on whether or not a new manufacturing industry was to be allowed in an attractive countryside area. What sort of questions would you ask **a**) those who were for it **b**) those opposing it?

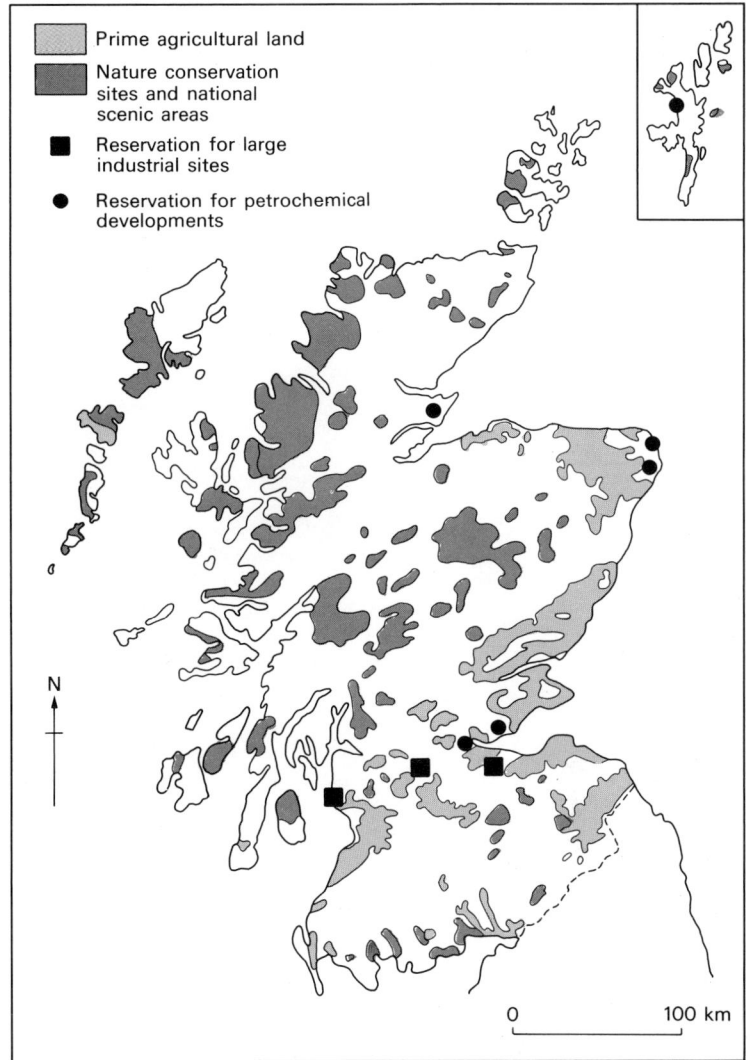

▨	Prime agricultural land
▨	Nature conservation sites and national scenic areas
■	Reservation for large industrial sites
●	Reservation for petrochemical developments

A map showing land use priority areas in Scotland

Plan for Scotland

In Scotland an attempt has been made to distinguish areas where there is a land use priority. These act as guides for developers and are not binding on any decision-making authority. But they do provide an early warning for developers, including agencies and landowners seeking to promote agriculture and forestry, as to what may be the best use of particular areas.

The danger of a map of this kind is that it may lead to people expecting things to be permitted or not permitted. It may lead to greater conflict or lead to demands by landowners for compensation if development is denied on conservation grounds. This is not the intention of the agencies involved. Rather, they want to establish aims so that the pattern of economic development fits in with the principles of conservation.

Something along these lines may well be prepared for England and Wales though this will be harder to achieve because the scope for conflict between the forces of production and conservation is much greater.

Destruction of part of Abernethy Forest in 1984 led to a great deal of protest

Waste management

Vast sums of money have to be spent to collect and dispose of rubbish and waste. In an effort to save money some local councils are now 'contracting out' the work to private waste disposal companies

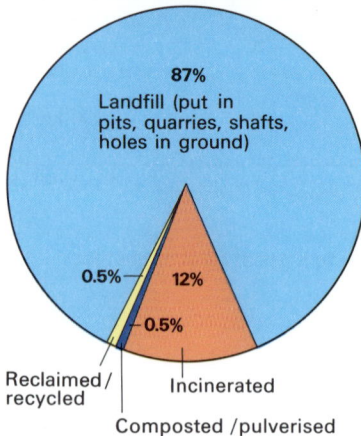

Various methods are used to dispose of waste from domestic, commercial and industrial sources

Comparative costs of rubbish disposal (London and S E England) in the early 1980s

	Cost per tonne £
Landfill	2.20
Pulverisation	8.86
Incineration	12.56
Transfer loading (excluding landfill and transport costs)	12.81

Rubbish collection and disposal

About 18 million tonnes of domestic and commercial refuse and 5 million tonnes of industrial waste are handled by local authorities in England and Wales each year. A further 15–20 million tonnes of industrial waste is disposed of by private operators. All this is apart from the large quantities of waste produced by coal mining and other extractive industries, by power stations and by sewage treatment plants. Since 1974 local authorities have been responsible for all the waste created in their areas.

The main form of rubbish disposal is to tip it directly from collecting lorries into pits or quarries known as infill or landfill sites. As tips become full the waste disposal authorities have to look for new sites, and this presents two problems. First, there are limits to the distances that collecting lorries can travel economically. Second, planners are likely to refuse permission to use sites on good farmland or where water catchment, recreation or general public interests are at risk. Direct tipping of untreated refuse is sometimes used to

reclaim derelict land, marshland and coastal areas. If only distant sites are available, the refuse from the collection lorries has to be transferred into containers to be transported by road, rail, river or canal. As the table shows, however, the costs of 'transfer loading' equipment can be high.

Another method is to reduce the bulk of the waste, and so use less tipping space. This can be done by compressing the rubbish in the tip with special vehicles, or by pulverising it in large rotating drums. The most common method used in Britain is incineration, which gives a reduction of about 80 per cent. Almost all local-authority incinerators burn raw refuse as it is delivered. A few use the heat for commercial or industrial purposes, but at the moment this is not widespread. A final method is to reclaim or 'recycle' waste for further use. Steel, glass and paper are suitable for this practice. There are strong arguments for and against recycling, the main objection being the cost, while the main supporting argument is that it helps to slow down the consumption of basic resources.

Some authorities provide tips where rubbish can be dumped by householders

Problems of waste disposal

Waste products are getting more complex and bulky. The amount of paper and plastic packaging is increasing rapidly while new materials and industrial processes create more difficult-to-handle wastes. Clean air laws and the growth of central heating have meant less refuse is burnt on the spot at home or at the workplace. Sites are also more difficult to find and to get permission to use. Each year enough quarries are created to accommodate many times the volume of British refuse, but unfortunately they tend either to be in the wrong places, or are still being used for quarrying. So they cannot easily be used for tipping as well.

Toxic wastes

A growing problem is that of dangerous and poisonous 'toxic' wastes. Growing concern about pollution by industrial wastes and the callous dumping of items such as drums of cyanide wastes led to the Disposal of Poisonous Wastes Act in 1972. Each year Britain produces about 3½ million tonnes of toxic waste which needs to be safely disposed of. Tipping sites have now to be licensed, and often there are none suitable near the producing areas. About thirty-six sites took almost 70 per cent of the toxic waste in 1981. At that time Essex had more than a third of Britain's total hazardous waste sites, and lorries brought their dangerous cargoes from as far afield as Cornwall, Wales, Northumberland and Scotland. Movement of certain wastes have to be notified to the local authority, but this is not a very efficient system.

A particular worry is co-disposing – the dumping of liquid toxic wastes and domestic rubbish. Britain's biggest tip at Pitsea in Essex has a licence to receive 160 million litres of toxic liquids over 240 hectares of domestic rubbish each year. There is a fear that such tipping is dangerous and will produce huge and dangerous chemical quagmires. The waste has to be disposed of, but there is a great deal of money involved and some operators are prepared to take risks to improve their profits.

Huge sites, such as this one at Pitsea in Essex, are used to dump dangerous 'toxic' wastes as well as domestic rubbish

Burning waste in large incinerators reduces its bulk and provides heat and useful by-products. But there is the problem of site selection. A modern 600 tonne-a-day incinerator requires 6 ha of land, 250 000 gallons of water per day and brings 400 vehicles in and out every day

1 **a**) What proportion of industrial waste is disposed of by local authorities and what by private operators? **b**) The Government is responsible for the disposal of radioactive waste. Who is responsible for domestic and toxic wastes?

2 What are the arguments for and against recycling paper and glass? Are there collections or collecting points in your area or nearby?

3 Do you think that money spent on refuse collection is justifiable? What are the arguments for and against the 'privatisation' of refuse collection?

4 What are your views about the transport of **a**) toxic wastes, **b**) nuclear wastes across the country?

Nuclear waste

£100m store for nuclear fuel planned

A plan for a long-term £100m store for spent nuclear fuel, stacked in magazines cooled by an inert gas at a national repository, was outlined yesterday by Dr John Wright, of the Central Electricity Generating Board.

The revelation that a national waste fuel dump has been considered provided more than a ripple of surprise among objectors to the Sizewell scheme. They interpret the move as a complete reversal of the arguments which the CEGB was pursuing five years ago, when it supported the building of the waste fuel reprocessing plant at Windscale, in Cumbria.

But Dr Wright said the new type of waste reprocessing plant for Windscale, a thermal oxide reprocessing plant (THORP) would have a life of only about 10 years. The bulk of the waste from the existing AGR programme and the planned PWR would be produced after that date. Reprocessing could take place only five years after PWR fuel had been removed from a reactor and three years for AGR fuel.

A very special category of waste is that produced by the use of radioactive materials in power stations, weapons manufacture, medical and industrial applications and (when it finally happens) the dismantling of old nuclear power stations. Nuclear wastes vary greatly in their effects, but at worst they can be deadly. There are different varieties of radioactive waste; gas, liquid and solid, and the materials may be 'active' for thousands of years in some cases.

Low level radioactive wastes are either disposed of at a land site in Cumbria or packed into drums and then taken by ship to be dumped in an internationally agreed area of the deep Atlantic, 500 miles out to sea. Intermediate wastes are too radioactive to be disposed of at sea. These will be solidified in concrete and disposed of deep underground in stable rock formations or in concrete lined trenches. High level wastes are a different matter. Proposals to bury such waste in deep shafts have been shelved. At the moment it is carefully stored in stainless steel tanks, biologically isolated and continually monitored. It will be finally stored as a glass compound at the British Nuclear Fuels plant at Sellafield, Cumbria for several decades. Once they have cooled and decayed sufficiently, they are disposed of deep underground. Research is also being done into ways of either burying the waste in the deep ocean sediments or in containers designed to last thousands of years on the ocean floor.

Special railway waggons are used to transport nuclear waste across Britain

Below: There are international rules about dumping waste at sea. In 1983 transport unions prevented nuclear waste being dumped in this way. There are strong disagreements about how to dispose of nuclear waste from power stations, armaments factories, hospitals, and other sources

Exercise 50 Dioxin tip in Derbyshire

An innocent-looking field of crops near the dioxin tip

The site of the tip where dioxin was dumped

1 Why was there need to dump dioxin waste in 1968? Why was there no apparent control over the dumping? Who was responsible for creating and dumping the contaminated materials?

2 Why had the dioxin disposal become a major issue so long after the event?

3 The same company that disposed of the dioxin was given permission by Derbyshire County Council to open and operate another new site for disposing toxic waste in 1978 close to the village of Morton. There have been objections about the suitability of the site for this purpose. What seem to be some of the disadvantages of the new site?

4 In view of the dangers and objections, why should permission be given for a company to operate a tip in the area? Who benefits from the existence of the tip? Who loses, or claims to lose, because of the tip?

Inquiry into dioxin tip

The site of a secret Midlands tip containing dioxin, one of the most dangerous chemicals known to man, will be identified at a public inquiry this week.

The tip is under a field in the tiny village of Stretton, south of Chesterfield, in Derbyshire. The dioxin is in an old open-cast mine working on the south side of the road between Stretton and the village of Morton. The ground is being reworked for coal by a drift mine and local people fear that the miners are getting close to the poison.

The dioxin-contaminated material was dumped after an explosion in the Coalite factory at Bolsover, Derbyshire, in 1968. One man was killed in the accident and 79 contracted chloracne, a severe skin disease. The county council says it was told that dioxin had been dumped in Derbyshire only when it talked to the company after 1976.

The Severn Trent Water Authority says that Coalite has never told where the poison is buried. In 1978 the county council granted planning permission to a small private mining company to develop a drift mine near the site. The head of the mine is only 500 yards from the field.

Coalite has declined to attend the inquiry. The inquiry has no power to force it to attend. Last June a managing director of Coalite said a small amount of dioxin was involved in the explosion and the contaminated material was buried at depth and covered over with soil. That was 'perfectly adequate' he said.

But an expert on dioxin says that the chemical does not decay fast when buried in soil, and would remain poisonous for up to 50 years.

Transport and environment: London's third airport

Heathrow is one of the largest airports in the world

International passengers preparing for a flight on Concorde

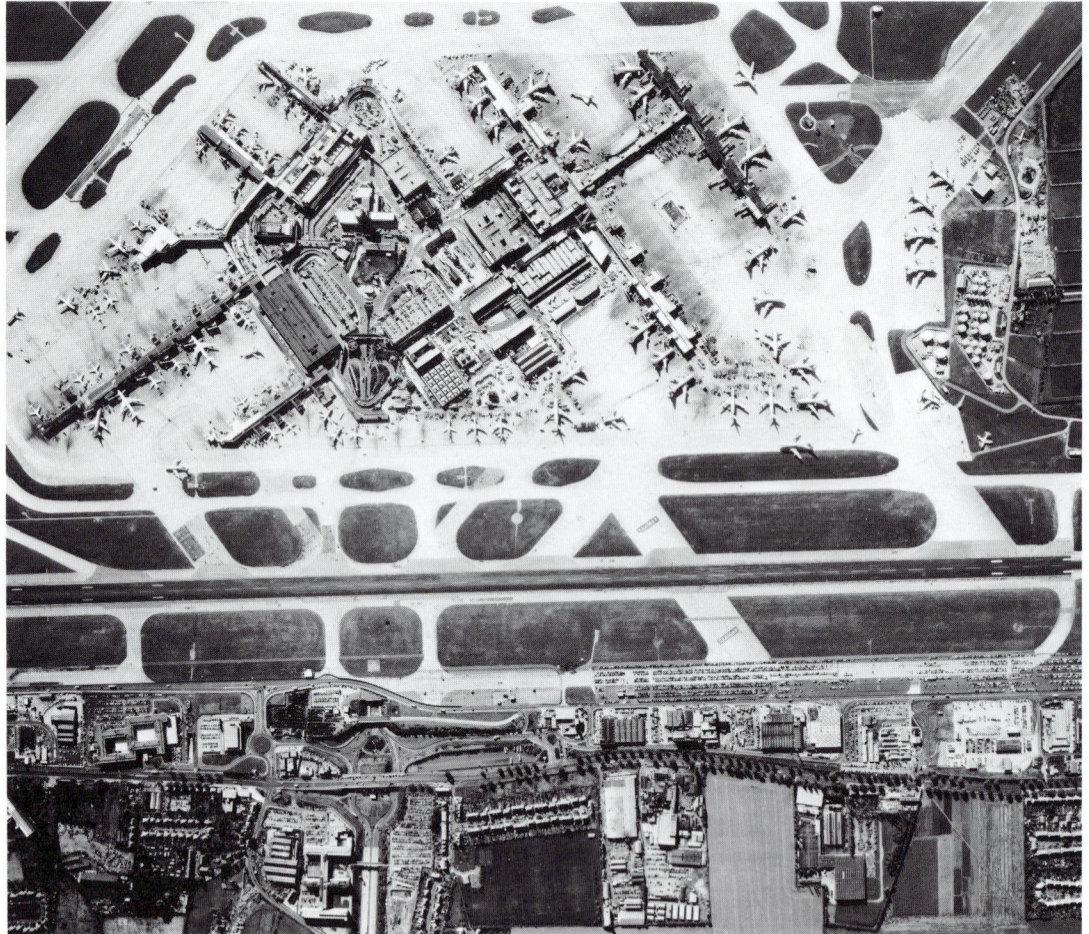

One of Heathrow's advantages is its Underground connections with London

Future needs

The name 'third' airport for London is rather misleading as there are already four airports serving the London region. They vary greatly in size and number of passengers handled, but all have grown in recent decades and look likely to go on doing so. Predictions are no more than guesses, based on as much evidence as possible, and so are likely to change with time. Even so, it has been estimated that passenger traffic should grow to about 80 million a year by 1990, with a further growth to between 100–120 million by the turn of the century. Whatever the final figures turn out to be, the demand for air travel seems bound to increase a great deal. If no plans are made to cope with this there could be the loss of valuable business for the air transport industry and the tourist industry, two important earners of money for Britain. If we accept that it is sensible to encourage rather than prevent this passenger growth (and not everyone does) the question becomes about how it should be provided. Should it be shared out between Heathrow, Gatwick and Stansted (Luton cannot expand very much more for physical reasons), or concentrated on one airport only? Some groups make a case for a completely new 'green-field' site. The Town and Country Planning Association, for example, argue that Maplin is a desirable site, on the grounds of caus-

Gatwick handles large numbers of flights each day. It is the second largest airport in Britain

ing little environmental damage while creating new jobs and economic growth in an area that badly needs it.

Proposals for the future

By the end of 1982 a decision had been made to build a second terminal at Gatwick by 1987, raising its capacity to 25 million passengers. At that time, two further proposals seemed likely to be accepted. A fourth terminal at Heathrow, already started, would be completed, raising passenger capacity to 38 millions by 1985. If the Stansted proposal were accepted, a new terminal would be built there, raising the capacity to 15 million passengers. The BAA has argued that if it were allowed to build a fifth terminal at Heathrow, raising its annual capacity to 53 million by 1990, it would not need to develop Stansted. There were many objections to this proposal, not least from residents around Heathrow, and the fact that a large sewage works would have to be moved. Longer term developments might be a second new terminal and runway at Stansted (total 50 million capacity) or a fifth terminal at Heathrow (total capacity 53 million). By then the M25 London orbital motorway (page 160) should be completed, providing a fast, convenient link between the three airports and Greater London.

1 **a**) Why is it difficult to make accurate predictions about future air passenger traffic? **b**) What arguments might there be for 'not bothering' to provide for future demands?

2 What are the main land-use needs of an airport? How can an airport affect **a**) the environment **b**) other development beyond the immediate boundaries of the airport itself?

3 Why are transport links from airport to London so important? What links exist for Heathrow and Gatwick?

The location of the main airports around London

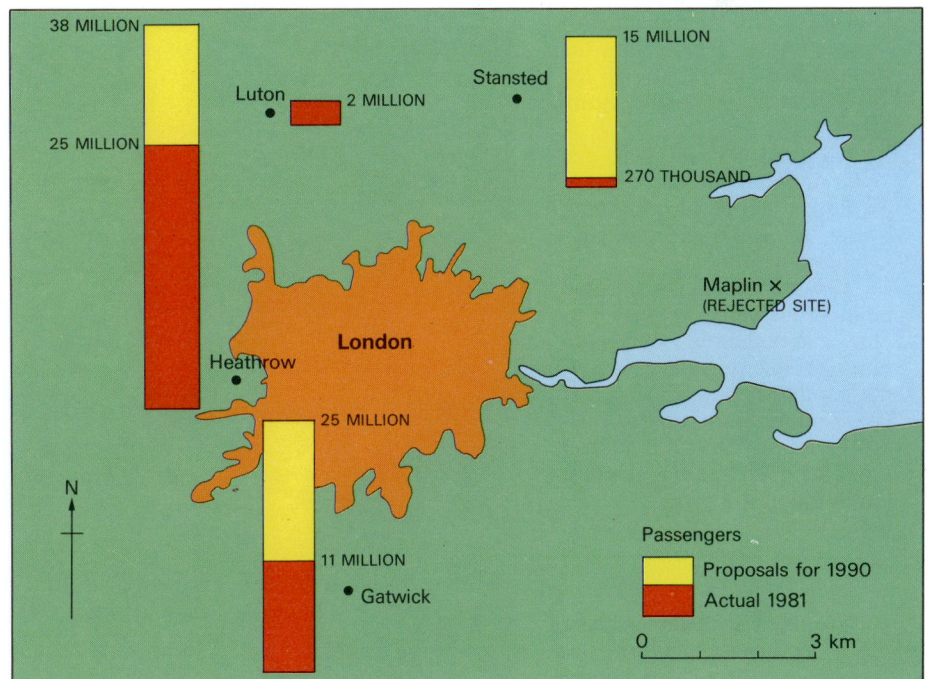

209

25 000 farm acres under threat

To most observers at the Stansted public inquiry this week, it must have seemed that the Ministry of Agriculture had dug itself a large hole and jumped feet first into it. There was a relatively minor official from a regional office trying to explain to a clearly irritated inspector why the ministry had made no assessment of the loss to agriculture of putting anything up to 25 000 acres of Hertfordshire and Essex under tarmac and concrete.

Why, he was asked, had the ministry in its evidence considered only the 3000 acres or so that might be needed for the airport itself, when everyone knew that the real issue was the massive urbanization that would follow if the project went ahead? Was it not strange that the ministry had in the past strongly opposed almost every development application in the neighbourhood, on the ground that the nation could not afford the loss of such high-quality farmland?

All this was music to the ears of the National Farmers' Union, which is furious about what it regards as ministerial spinelessness.

The union believes that the ministry is failing in one of its fundamental duties, namely to protect the dwindling supply of good farmland. It feels that past emphasis on environmental issues has obscured the fact that the land is among the best in South-east England.

There have been a number of public inquiries about the expansion of airport capacity or the building of new airports in the south-east of England. In 1981 another was started, known as the Stansted Local Inquiry. Over a year or so, and at a cost of some £110,000, an Inspector listened to the cases for and against the development of Stansted, and to alternative proposals. The British Airports Authority had applied for permission to expand passenger services at Stansted from ¼ to 15 million passengers a year by 1990. As part of the inquiry, the Inspector listened to objections and counter-proposals from many groups such as the Countryside Commission, the National Trust, the National Farmer's Union, the Ministry of Agriculture and the North-West Essex and East Hertfordshire Preservation Association that claimed to represent over 200 local groups. Local people felt that as the site had been rejected at two earlier inquiries they should not have to object again. Following the inquiry the Inspector made his recommendations but it was still left to the Government to decide what to do.

During the inquiry the people of Essex objected to the destruction, as they saw it, of an attractive part of the English countryside. Some airline operators, led by British Airways, objected to the splitting of traffic between three London airports, claiming it would add enormously to costs. The Air Transport Users Committee objected that Stansted, 30 miles from central London, was too far out. The farming lobby claimed that it would lead to the loss of good quality farmland. There were strong arguments for and against Stansted on a whole range of grounds, and the case showed the way in which economic growth can have considerable environmental and social consequences.

Stansted has been proposed as the site of a large new airport for London

Many local people have very personal reasons for objecting to a larger airport at Stansted

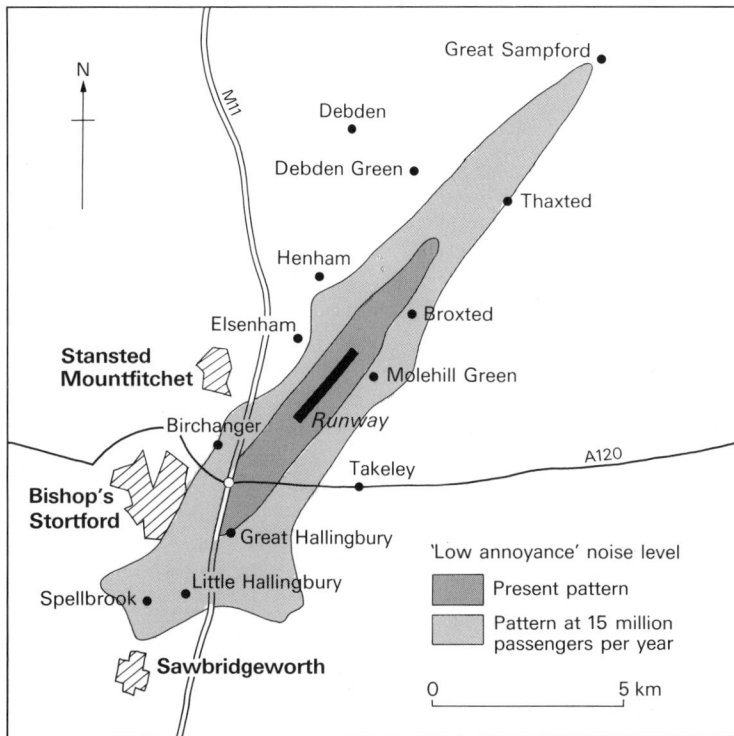

This diagram shows how the development of Stansted will widen the areas affected by the noise of aircraft movements

1 The British Airport Authority sought permission to expand Stansted airport, and one of its supporters was the Transport and General Workers' Union. What were their arguments?

2 Has there been a result to the Stansted Inquiry? What action, if any, has the Government taken?

3 From the evidence on these two pages describe four different objections to the development, in each case saying which groups were involved.

4 What would be the environmental impact of developing Stansted to accommodate 15 million passengers a year? Do you think these losses alone are justified by the other gains? Why would your answer vary according to where you live?

Stansted's impact

The area within a 15-mile radius of Stansted airport comprises mainly a pleasant, well-farmed countryside containing many beautiful villages and small market towns. To the south the area is more urbanised, but the metropolitan green belt in this sector is still well protected. Despite Harlow, and some growth at Bishop's Stortford, Stansted lies within what is probably the least spoilt and most remote area of countryside within 40 miles of London. The quality and extensiveness of the largely rural zone within which Stansted lies caused *Strategy for South-East* to identify it as one of the green sectors around London which should be carefully protected.

The British Airports Authority claims that the impact of airport development (up to 15 million passengers per annum (mppa)) would be very limited because some 70 to 80 per cent of airport-related jobs could be filled from within the sub-region without a need for any more immigration. But the BAA studies seem to allow nothing for the general growth effects of the airport.

First, whatever planners may intend, market pressures will certainly grow for the provision of more housing near to the airport. This housing cannot be confined to the use of airport workers, so there will be an additional influx of population.

Second, a series of related factors – the airport itself, the linked services, the increased labour pool, and the wider market – will stimulate further industry and commerce within the sub-region.

But apart possibly from the case of Harlow, this is the type of area which least needs the economic stimulus of a major airport. Without the airport, the area will certainly remain relatively prosperous. Airport expansion at Stansted is contrary to established regional policies and to good regional planning. A development up to 15 mppa would greatly change the character of the sub-region, and a development beyond that would transform it altogether.

Planning and development in the city

The old Covent Garden fruit and vegetable wholesale market has been converted to a new leisure use

There are very many examples of bad urban planning in Britain. Planners and local residents are often in disagreement over the results

These expensive mews houses and flats in London were converted from old stables and carriage sheds

The need for planning

As with the countryside, so with the urban areas, most proposed developments have to be approved by some authority or other. This is sometimes seen as interference, a waste of time and money and 'bureaucratic meddling'. On the other hand, what is a desirable change for some may be damaging or disastrous for others. What may be perfectly acceptable in the near future may be unacceptable in the long term. One aim of planning is to try to look ahead at different demands and wishes to decide on what should or should not be allowed to happen. The opinions of highway engineers, developers of property, industrialists, politicians and residents in the area under review must be considered.

Following the Town and Country Planning Act (1947) and later developments all Local Authorities, and the Government through the Department of Environment (DOE), became responsible for planning and controlling de-velopments. They are expected to produce a whole series of 'plans' that may include maps but also many diagrams, statistics and written statements. These are produced for some local areas and for all districts, and counties. Each Local Authority has a Planning Department and a Planning Committee of elected politicians who make the decisions based on advice from the professional planners and architects. Their decisions range from the simple and small change of use of buildings through making changes to private houses to major development projects that may involve massive demolition of areas and construction of new buildings. Applications may come from individuals concerning their own house or from giant development companies.

Conservation and planning

One particular responsibility is to protect old, beautiful or historically important and unique buildings. Such buildings may be 'listed' in one of several grades to give them some protection. Just as important is the identification of 'conservation areas' where whole groups of buildings (they are not all likely to be listed, and there may in fact be no listed buildings at all) are given some sort of protection. They are something like the SSSIs and National Parks in the Countryside, though on a much smaller scale. Even when buildings are regarded as worth preserving or conserving by some, others may disagree and want to use the site for other purposes. What to do with old 'heritage' buildings or areas when the land is needed for other purposes, whether for community needs or for private profit, is often a difficult choice. It is hardly surprising that there are different views about what should be done.

Planning, politics and pressure groups

Apart from professional planners and architects there are many other people interested in change and development in the city. Some represent (or try to represent) the interests of the local community. If the elected representatives seem not to be doing this well enough, or if it is thought they need extra support, then individuals or groups may form amenity societies or local pressure groups. Others such as the Civic Trust or Town and Country Planning Association have a national influence and may work through local groups. Property developers or industrialists or local or national government engineers may also want to influence the 'decision makers' – the planning committees at local or national level. They may all work in harmony, but as many public inquiries show, whether they are about power station sites, motorway routes, airport sites or developments in the city, the different interest and pressure groups may be violently opposed. The difficult task of the planners and decision makers involves not only looking ahead, but also trying to decide which course of action would be 'best', and best for whom!

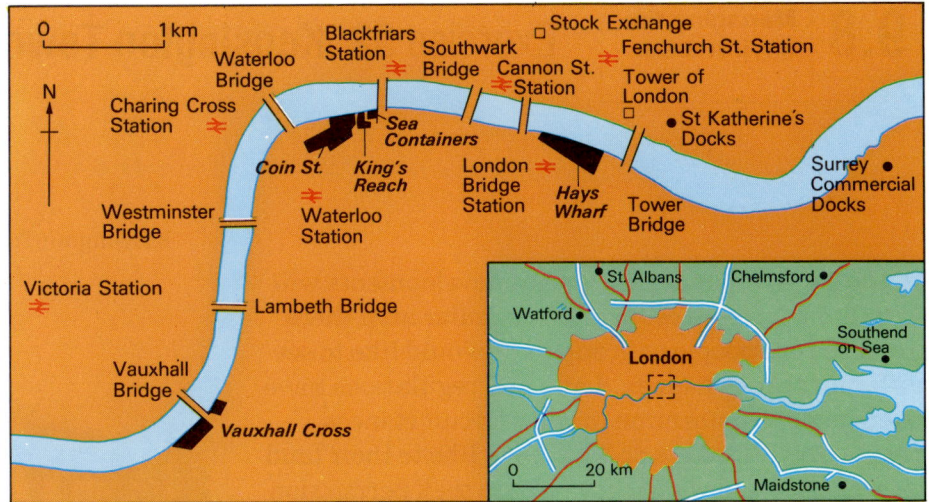

1 Give examples from your town or nearest town of a listed building, a conservation area, and an area undergoing development. For the latter say what the buildings used to be for and what the new buildings will be like and what their function will be. Who is paying for the development? Who benefits and who (if anyone) loses?

2 Name your local District/Borough and County a) Chief Planner, b) Chairman of Planning Committee. (They may not have these exact names.) Give the name of any local amenity group concerned with the urban area and development and describe any event in which it has been involved.

The 1970s and 1980s have seen enormous commercial developments along the banks of the river Thames. In 1983 developers were planning to increase London's estimated 210 m sq. ft of office space by 32 m sq. ft, and many of them were concentrating on the South Bank. Many people feel that this big increase in London's office accommodation is unnecessary

This is a model of one development proposed for the Coin Street site

213

Planning is about deciding what developments will or will not take place. In any particular area there are different people or groups who would like to see different things happen. Laws and regulations have been made to determine in what circumstances people are allowed to do what they like to their land or property, and when they have to seek permission or agreement from others. Individual owners of buildings, for example, may have to get permission from the Local Authority or from the Department of the Environment, before changing a building's appearance or use. This can lead to strong clashes of opinion, and all sorts of methods are used by different interest groups in order to achieve their ends, as the case of Kensington Town Hall shows.

Study the extract and photographs referring to the Kensington Town Hall.

1 Describe the two groups which are in conflict over the demolition of Kensington Town Hall.

2 What other people or groups might be concerned about the future of the buildings? Distinguish between **a**) professional people, **b**) politicians, **c**) other interest groups.

3 Describe the reason for the row about the new building on the site of the old Town Hall.

The old Town Hall, partly demolished

Kensington Town Hall, about 50 years ago

New battle for 'vandal' council

Kensington, the 'vandal' council which bulldozed its empty town hall to escape a conservation order has been attacked for choosing a redevelopment scheme putting money above environmental needs. Experts have accused it of rejecting the best entry in an architectural 'competition' to find a new design. The council's choice has outraged the Royal Fine Art Commission which 'deplores the short-sighted commercial approach to a site which is both prominent and environmentally sensitive'.

The Conservative run council sent in demolition workers in a secret night-time operation last June, hours before the Labour-controlled Greater London Council was to issue a protection order. In retaliation, the GLC issued a Conservation Order on the partly-destroyed premises. Because the building is 'listed' it can neither be completely knocked down nor rebuilt until a tangle of planning hearings takes place. The resultant eyesore has become a familiar sight for residents and tourists in this exclusive shopping area.

The council bowed to public criticism and called for designs for a new building on the site with the co-operation of the Royal Fine Art Commission. Five architects submitted plans and the council chose the entry from Frederick Gibbert and Partners. The Commission says however that the scheme by another partnership, Mac-Cormac, Jamieson and Prichard 'stands head and shoulders above the others'.

The almost-unprecedented anger of the Commission provoked Councillor Nicholas Freeman, leader of Kensington council, to condemn its 'abusive' language. He said: 'We have chosen the architect who would produce a scheme leading to planning consent for a building which will then enable the council to sell the site for the best possible price'.

Chapter 10 Issues for the 1980s

Economy in decline

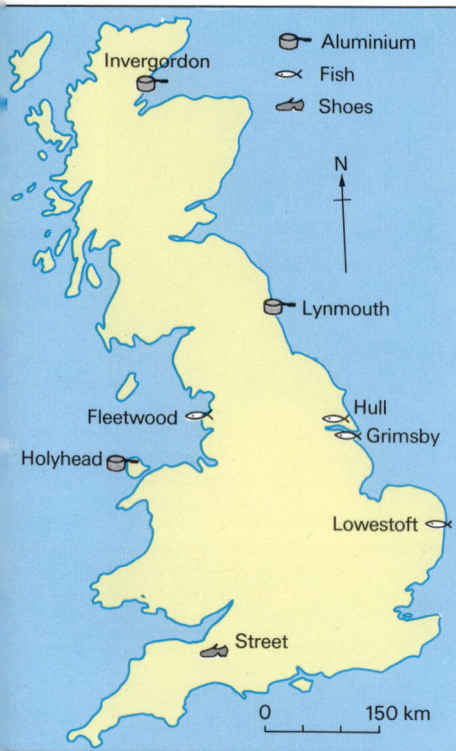

The location of the places mentioned in this Unit

One of the most worrying aspects of life in Britain in the early 1980s was the continuing decline of many industries. As the diagram shows some activities can be growing while others are suffering losses or closing down. Even within a single industry some firms may be making profits and expanding while others fail. Some of the declining and troubled industries, such as steelmaking and shipbuilding have already been discussed. A few others are described here to show the variety of reasons for the decline, and some of the consequences.

Aluminium production

The giant aluminium smelter at Invergordon was one of three built with the help of government funds in the late 1960s. Aluminium is important in the aerospace and defence equipment, and it was felt important for Britain to provide its own. It is made from alumina in large smelters that consume vast amounts of electricity. The smelters at Invergordon and Holyhead used cut-price electricity associated with the development of nuclear power stations at

Hunterston and Dungeness, while the smelter at Lynmouth uses cheaper-than-cost coal from the collieries off the Northumberland-Durham coast.

In 1981 British Aluminium, the company owning the Invergordon smelter, decided either to sell the plant to another company, or to close it down. This would involve making hundreds of skilled workers redundant. The demand for aluminium world-wide had slumped, prices were low and the plant was making a big loss. On the other side of the equation, in spite of getting cheap electricity, its costs were still too high. The combination of high electricity costs and low prices was behind the company's decision to close. During 1982 similar threats hung over the other two aluminium plants, for similar reasons. The British Aluminium decision to close the Invergordon plant was also because of the threat to other companies in the group, the majority investment being in the hands of Tube Investments (TI). The companies involved might have been able to lower their price and so increase sales and income if electricity costs could be low-

Areas of job loss and gain in the UK, 1966–80

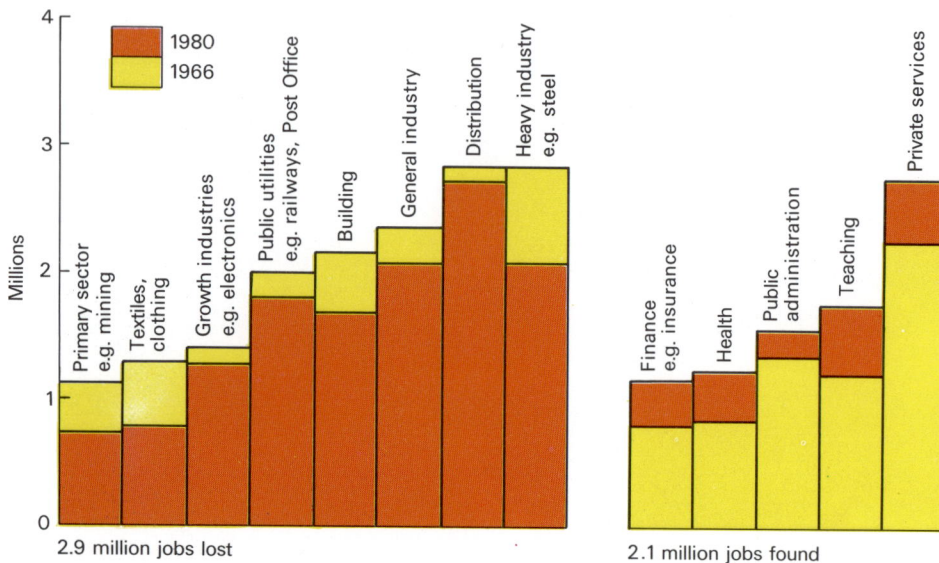

2.9 million jobs lost

2.1 million jobs found

The Invergordon aluminium smelter

ered. But the CEGB and the NCB also wanted to run their businesses economically, so that proved impossible without a huge extra government or taxpayer subsidy – £25 million per year for electricity alone at the Invergordon plant, if it was going to be profitable!

Shoemaking in Somerset

A very different sort of manufacturing industry is making shoes. One of the oldest established and best known British firms is Clarks, with a factory at Street in Somerset, that physically and economically dominates the small town. As the extract says, it suffered too during the early 1980s and had to cut its work-force. The article describes the problems of the British shoe manufacturing industry and says that if it cannot manage to be competitive it had better 'abandon making shoes the traditional way to those who do it more cheaply abroad, and concentrate on high technology methods with much lower labour costs.' Foreign competition is seen as one cause of the decline, but there are clearly other reasons as well. The impact of declining sales and cuts in production can be devastating in a one-company town like Street.

What are the causes?

These examples, here and on the next two pages, give some idea of the range of problems faced by industry. Some argue that it is mostly due to workers asking for too much money and to the power of the trades unions. Others say this is merely an excuse for bad management, the financial policies of the Government, and the greed of investors who are interested only in making profits and not in putting money back into the industries. Yet others claim it is a world economic problem, and there is little any one country can do alone, especially in the face of the international nature of much investment, control and profit. Whatever the causes, the declining performance of many branches of industry with the consequent high unemployment is a major concern in Britain in the 1980s.

A firm like Clarks is faced with the double problem of foreign competition and keeping up with changing fashions

The Clarks Shoe factory at Street in Somerset dominates the town

1 What reasons are offered for the decline of a) the Invergordon plant, b) the British shoe industry, c) the deep-sea trawling fleet at Hull (on page 218)? Add any other explanations you can think of.

2 Look at the diagram of job gains and losses. From an example given earlier in the book describe one growing and one declining industry.

3 Describe any local firm that has shown difficulties or closed down, mentioning the explanations offered and the consequences of the closure.

4 To what extent should companies in difficulty be supported by the taxpayer? Are there any that should be supported at any cost, and if so when? If profit should not decide whether an industry operates or not, what other system might work – and where would money to start and run it come from?

Why UK shoemakers are down at heel

Tomorrow, that bastion of the British footwear industry, the company founded and run for five generations by the Clark family, will announce that despite short-time working, it must still cut back its workforce.

Clarks only mirrors a worse picture in the industry at large. The British cannot compete with shoes made abroad by cheap labour, often subsidised to undercut the British producers. This applies both to the home market and to exports. The industry's workforce is now about .68000 – down 11000 over the past two years.

217

The British deep-sea fishing fleet

The reduction in trawlers at two British fishing ports, 1972–82

Hull

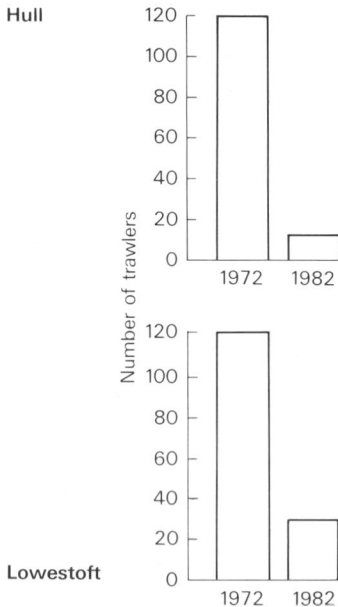

Lowestoft

The fish docks at Hull were once the scene of great activity

Market where most of the catch arrives by lorry

At 8 o'clock on a fine, bright morning the Grimsby fish market is in full swing. Although probably still the largest wholesale fish market in Britain, its pattern of trade has shown a drastic change.

Only 10 years ago, nearly three quarters of all the fish sold on Humberside was caught locally. Last year only 12 000 tons of wet fish were landed at Grimsby. The other 74 000 tons which passed through the market came overland by lorry from other British ports, or were imported from countries such as Iceland and Norway.

The biggest blow to the Humber fishing industry was the loss of the distant water fishing grounds off Iceland and Newfoundland. Since then much of the so-called middle water trawling has also proved unprofitable.

British fishing has experienced a dramatic change in recent decades, with the virtual disappearance of its long-distance, deep-water trawler fleet. In January 1982 two modern freezer-trawlers were sold to a New Zealand Company complete with crews of 60 fishermen and a small management team. Soon after, another Hull company, J Marr & Sons, sold three big deep-sea trawlers to Iceland, and later withdrew its eight ships from Fleetwood.

These sales were seen as the virtual end of the British trawler fleet which a few years earlier had been the largest in Europe. During the past decade over 1 300 smaller, new inshore and middle-water ships have joined the British fleet, but at the same time over a hundred of the large distant-water boats, mainly from Hull, have either been transferred to work on the North Sea oil rigs, sold overseas or scrapped. There has been a decline of shore-based port work, and the trawler ports have experienced an increase in unemployment with few alternative jobs available.

The government has been unwilling to give financial support to the trawler industry. It has preferred to support the inshore and middle-distance fleets. This is linked to the fact that long, drawn-out negotiations with other EEC countries about fishing rights are going on. The British fleet has suffered badly from the loss of rights to fish in distant fishing grounds within 200 mile limits of other countries, by having to keep to quotas, by high costs of fuel for the ships, and by competition from other fishing fleets that sell their produce in Britain.

Exercise 53
Industries at risk in Scotland

The Ninian Central Oil Platform is towed out to its site in the North Sea

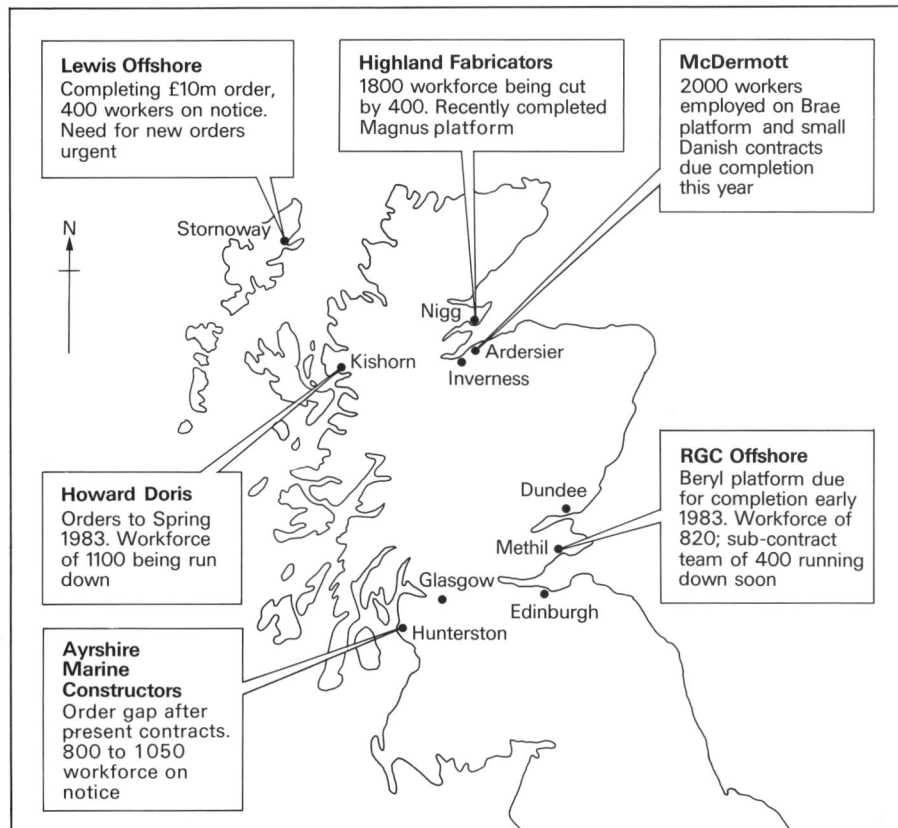

Lewis Offshore
Completing £10m order, 400 workers on notice. Need for new orders urgent

Highland Fabricators
1800 workforce being cut by 400. Recently completed Magnus platform

McDermott
2000 workers employed on Brae platform and small Danish contracts due completion this year

Howard Doris
Orders to Spring 1983. Workforce of 1100 being run down

RGC Offshore
Beryl platform due for completion early 1983. Workforce of 820; sub-contract team of 400 running down soon

Ayrshire Marine Constructors
Order gap after present contracts. 800 to 1050 workforce on notice

Important steel fabricating sites threatened with job losses in 1982

Has the North Sea bubble finally burst?

Industry is reconciling itself to hard times as North Sea activity, for so long the shooting star of the limping British economy, slows to a virtual standstill.

It is now almost two years since the last big platform construction project – the Hutton Field development – was given the go-ahead. And in the past few months a series of projects that might have been expected to provide much-needed orders have been postponed.

Hopes for new orders in the immediate future rest largely on development work by three groups: British Gas will be placing orders soon for hardware for its Morecambe Bay gasfield in the Irish Sea and its Rough field modifications; British National Oil Corporation has begun placing orders for its Beatrice field. Total/Elf is expected to make a decision on Alwyn North soon.

This could mean ten platforms at most ordered this year, and perhaps seven (including three for the Indefatigable and Leman gas fields) in 1983. But most would be small compared to existing North Sea structures.

1 Study the map and describe the locations of the manufacturing industries referred to. Account for this pattern of location and for the nature of the sites that are needed.

2 What are the reasons for the likely decline of activity in these industries?

3 What are the likely consequences of any decline? What should the companies or the local and national Governments do about it, if anything?

4 What other Scottish industries can you name that have experienced a decline in recent years?

Unemployment

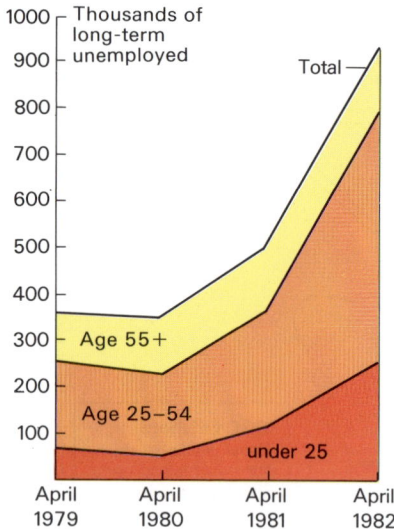

The rise in long-term unemployment affects all age groups

Dramatic growth

The graphs and maps show that during the early 1980s there was a frightening rise in unemployment. By the middle of 1982 over 30 000 jobs were being lost each month in manufacturing alone, with over 100 000 going in August. Between 1979 and 1982 this meant that one in five manufacturing jobs had disappeared – over 1.4 million – and the steel industry, for example, shed one third of its workforce. By the middle of 1984 there were between 3 and 3¼ million people unemployed, over one in seven of the labour force in Britain.

It is important to see that unemployment could well be the result of increased efficiency and a booming economy. Revolutionary changes in working methods, such as using the new microchip technology for automation, would result in a loss of jobs. The introduction of new working practices has resulted in British Rail wanting to cut its workforce from about 170 000 to 130 000 between 1981 and 1985. The increased production and wealth being created in these ways could have been used to help the unemployed immediately, and to prepare for a change in society where the idea of full-time employment for all was considered possible. But, as we have seen, the unemployment during the early 1980s was accompanied by a drastic decline in economic output, a fall in production and some enormous losses of trade and income. The new growth of unemployment affected most parts of the country and sections of the workforce, and vast sums of public money were being spent (or wasted, some would say) on paying unemployment benefits or creating training and temporary jobs.

Contrasts in unemployment

The three British Isles maps are a reminder that the pattern of unemployment has changed, as well as the amount. At one time unemployment was restricted to areas with older declining industries such as shipbuilding, textile manufacturing and steelmaking. It was particularly marked in the

There are still differences in the rate of unemployment from place to place, but few areas are completely unaffected

I've been Unemployed for so long - I've forgotten what I'm unemployed at ...

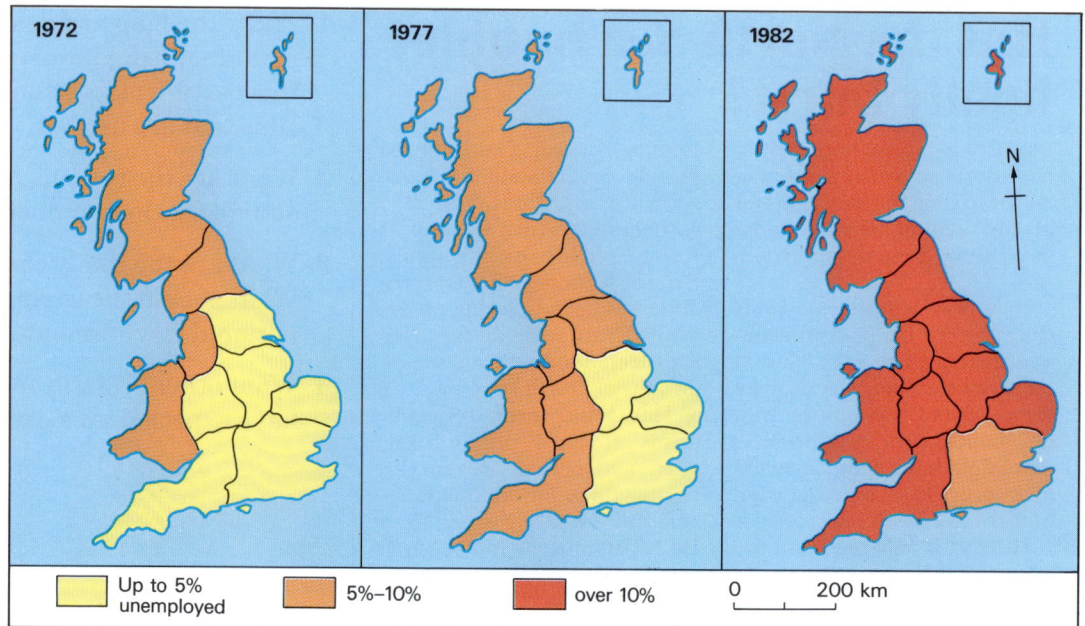

One of the causes of unemployment is increased automation

One disastrous result of recent events is the difficulty young people have of finding a job at all

north of England and the Glasgow region. The maps show that although regional variations still persist, unemployment now affects most parts of the country. The map of the northern region on page 223 is a reminder, though, that even in regions of high unemployment there can be considerable variations from place to place. This will depend on the traditional nature of employment in the area. It will also depend on whether employers have decided to operate in the region on economic grounds or whether the government has deliberately supported some jobs there by grants or subsidies.

Unemployment statistics are quite complicated. The official figures refer only to registered unemployed. The number of people actually not working who wish to be, and who could if jobs were available, is much higher than the official totals.

The graphs show that there are variations according to age and sex, as well as place. Although the number of women unemployed is lower than that of men, it has to be remembered that there are fewer women in employment anyway. In fact, many women suffer worse than men, partly as a result of being in part-time employment. If the principle of 'last in – first out' were observed, it is claimed that far fewer women would be made redundant. As will be seen in a later section, the number of unemployed black men and women is way above the average, suggesting discrimination against them

too. Another important distinction to make is between temporary, short-term unemployment, and more harmful long-term unemployment.

1 List the explanations suggested for unemployment given above. Add others you may think of. With which do you agree? With which do you disagree? Give your reasons.

2 a) Name any works or factories in your area that have had to close down or employ fewer people. b) Name any new large employers that have started in your area, if any.

3 Give your reasons for the causes, and the consequences of unemployment.

4 What are the arguments for and against a) part-time working, b) compulsory early retirement, c) compulsory job sharing?

Duration of unemployment, broken down into age groups

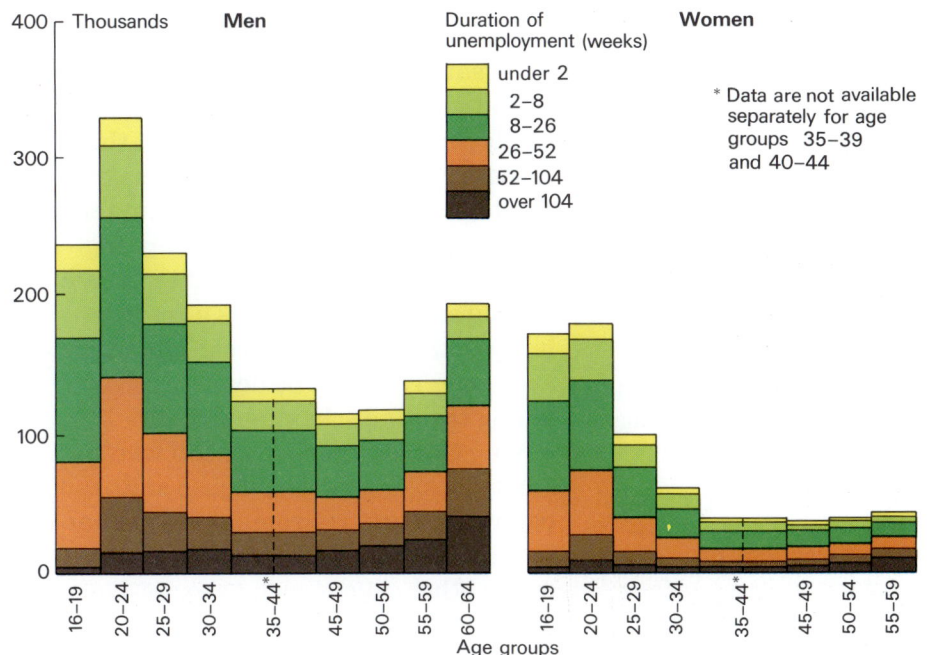

Duration of unemployment (weeks)
- under 2
- 2–8
- 8–26
- 26–52
- 52–104
- over 104

* Data are not available separately for age groups 35–39 and 40–44

221

Proposed remedies for unemployment

Completely new methods of education, training and production are needed to meet new conditions. Wilmot Jeremiah and Richard Helyer

Training for new technology

Wilmot Jeremiah left school with two CSEs and, like so many other black youngsters, was destined for the dole. A passing interest in gadgetry led him to the two-year-old Notting Dale Technology Centre in West London. After a year's training in micro-electronics and computers along with 30 other youngsters, Wilmot has stayed on to develop and make sophisticated micro-processor products for sale to industry.

Notting Dale training schemes concentrate on four main areas – microelectronics; the electronic office (word processors and Prestel); computer programming; and prototype development. The centre has about 15 of its own computers. 'Most of those who come here have never had anything to do with a computer before,' says the Director, Chris Webb.

A few Notting Dale pupils, like Wilmot, stay on its research and development unit, and the others try to get jobs or go on to further education.

The reactions of young people to the causes and results of unemployment was the task of a survey made in 1981. The results showed that boredom as much as making ends meet was a major problem. There is no doubt that the experience of unemployment, especially when it seems never-ending, is demoralising and often financially disastrous. It is evident that with a few exceptions, the majority of people would like to have a job and do something rewarding in terms of income and personal satisfaction.

Quite obviously, the remedies for unemployment will depend on what the causes really are, and there is disagreement about this. If unemployment for some is inevitable, through changing technologies or international economic pressures, then society has a responsibility to try to share the costs amongst everyone. This may be done by providing training schemes (though having trained people by itself won't create jobs) or by encouraging and paying for early retirement or job-sharing schemes. But if unemployment is due to other causes such as excessive demands for wages, unwillingness to

move to find jobs, mismanagement, inadequate investment or wrong government policies, then these need to be corrected. Effort and money should be spent on the diseases, not the symptoms. Once again, though, there are different views. One political group argues that unemployment is necessary to 'slim down' overmanned industries. With little or no increase in wages, the industries will then be more competitive, begin to pick up orders and production and wealth will increase again. Others feel this is unjust and one-sided, and that money from the taxpayer should be deliberately put into projects such as electrification of railways and housing construction to create jobs. Yet others feel that everyone is at the mercy of 'international capital' and the whole system needs to changed. Whatever the explanations offered, over three million men and women in Britain were unemployed by the middle of 1984. Quite apart from the personal hardship this caused, it was a disastrous waste of skill and resources.

Various training schemes have been funded by the government for school leavers without jobs

Exercise 54 **Regional variations in unemployment in Britain, 1982**

Regional unemployment seasonally adjusted (excluding school leavers)

	Number (thousands)	% of all employees
S-East	702.6	9.3
E Anglia	72.3	10.2
S-West	178.0	10.7
W Midlands	340.2	14.9
E Midlands	176.7	11.0
York and Humberside	270.7	13.1
N-West	425.7	15.1
North	215.2	16.2
Wales	166.8	15.7
Scotland	321.2	14.4
Great Britain	2869.4	12.3

1 Draw a map of the regions of Britain (see page 60 for help) and construct a statistical map showing the information given in the table.

2 Account for the regional variations within Britain.

3 The map of the northern region shows the percentage of male unemployed (it is slightly different for female unemployment, but broadly the same). Describe and account for the local differences of male unemployment in the northern region.

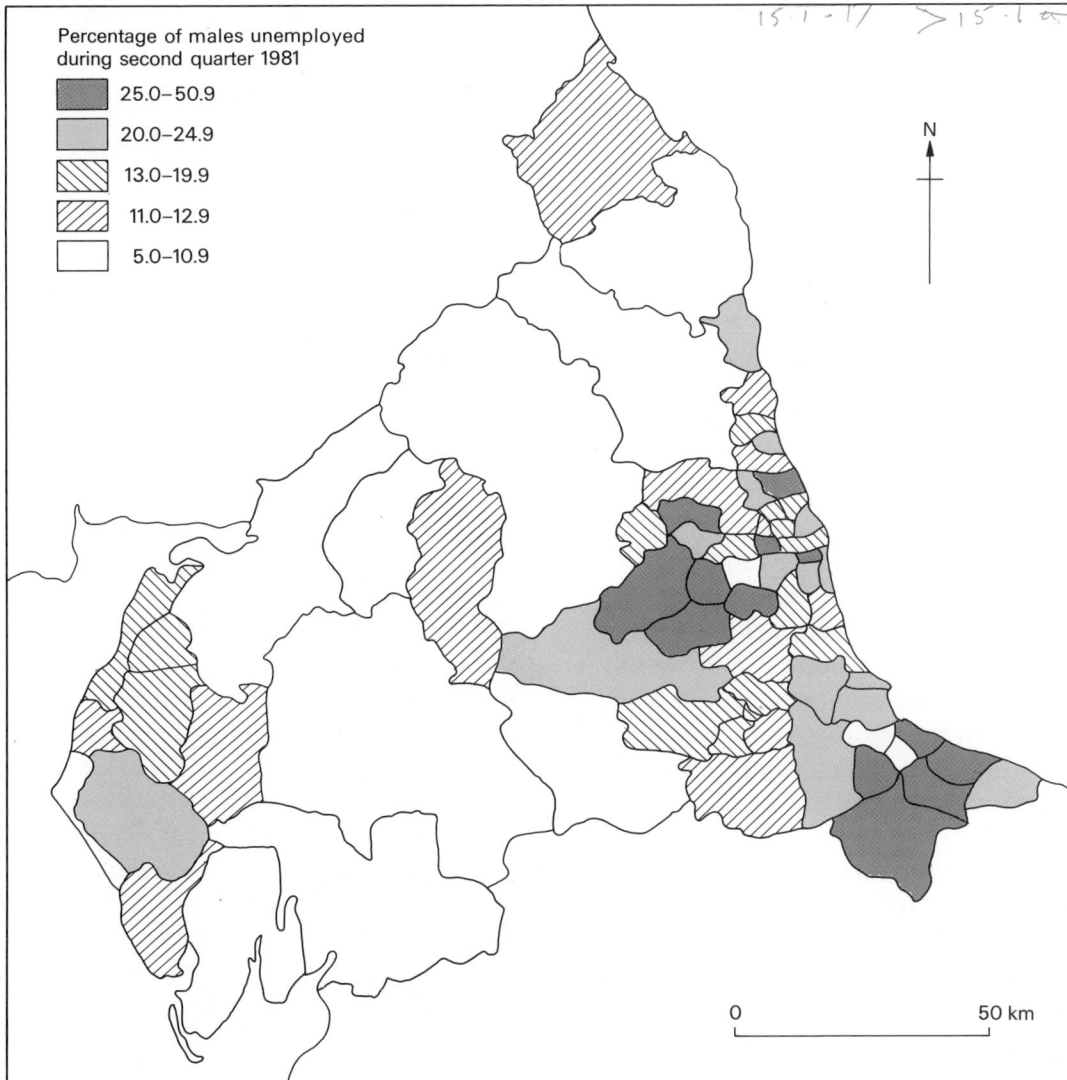

Percentage of males unemployed during second quarter 1981

- 25.0–50.9
- 20.0–24.9
- 13.0–19.9
- 11.0–12.9
- 5.0–10.9

N

0   50 km

This map of Northern England shows that there is a lot of variation in the amount of unemployment within, as well as between, regions

223

Racial discrimination and racial justice

These photographs show some of the signs of racial prejudice

Roots of prejudice

A recent article in *The Times* (10 August) suggested that prejudice increased with the size of the ethnic minority group. In reply, a correspondent wrote the following:

'There is no such connection. In August 1911, the Jewish community of South Wales were subjected to a reign of terror which it was beyond the ability of the police to control; yet the Jews formed but a minute proportion of the total population. At the same time every Chinese laundry in Cardiff was attacked; the Chinese proportion in that city was even more minute.

Prejudice against ethnic minorities is the product of ignorance and malevolence and nothing else.

Background

Some of the facts about the different cultural groups in Britain were given in Chapter 2. The point was made that Britain has a long tradition of receiving immigrants and helping those who have had to leave their homelands. Many millions of people, over the centuries, have settled happily in Britain and contributed to its development. There have also been many examples of racial intolerance and racial discrimination, and this remains an unpleasant feature of life in this country. In terms of the definitions quoted on page 69, Britain is still a long way from being a truly multicultural society.

Racial intolerance and discrimination

Extreme forms of racial intolerance are clear to see in the verbal and physical abuse and violence experienced by some men and women from ethnic minority groups. This takes the form of offensive graffitti, organised marches with a clear racist message, destruction of property, physical assaults on individuals and outright expressions of contempt and dislike. The number of people engaged in these open and deliberate actions may be few, but their impact on individuals and groups is degrading, threatening and dangerous.

Discrimination takes many forms. There can be what is described as 'official' discrimination, such as is claimed for some immigration laws. Any government is able to propose and pass laws about who may or may not enter the country, and who may or may not settle here and take British citizenship. There is a great deal of dispute about whether various governments have been racist, in discriminating against immigrants purely on grounds of race and colour. Some claim for instance, that families wanting to be together in this country are subjected to unfair restrictions because they are black. Others argue that such immigration control is sensible if the country is to preserve its past customs and traditions (see page 69), and if the 'rights' of others are to be protected.

There is another less obvious form of discrimination practised against ethnic minority groups. It is true that blacks, and young blacks in particular, have a much higher rate of unemployment than the average. In many cases it seems that blacks are refused jobs, not because they lack ability or qualifications, but on grounds of colour. Similar examples of discrimination are often found in housing, education, and treatment by police.

Beneath racial hatred and discrimination lie very basic emotions, and it is sometimes difficult to understand the reasons for them. The article suggests one reason may be ignorance. Others may argue that their views and behaviour stem from their own experiences. It is always hard to decide to what extent racial prejudice and bias come from people's direct experience, and how much they are the result of propaganda, or the influence of parents and friends. Certainly, ignorance plays a large part in it, and people are often unaware of the full significance of what they say and do in this sensitive area.

Racial justice

The official body set up to deal with racial matters is the Commission for Racial Equality (CRE). The tasks of its few permanent members are to enforce the law, undertake research and to promote racial harmony. So far its success has been limited by indifference, suspicion and downright opposition from people of all groups. It has not been able to undertake many prosecutions against people or firms breaking the racial laws, for example.

The Government could do a lot to get rid of discrimination. Central and Local government and the State corporations between them employ about seven million people, roughly one third of the workforce. The public sector is also the biggest purchaser of goods and services

provided by the private sector. If they agreed to practise and enforce in their own training, employment and promotion the legal requirements and terms already written into their suppliers' contracts, then they would have a big impact on racial discrimination.

Such actions really need the goodwill and backing of the majority of the population, and while there are many examples of friendly relations and mutual help between people from different groups, it is not everywhere the case. Some minority groups, mostly black, have started to form their own organisations to back their claims for their rights in society. These legal and peaceful groups have arisen since the angry and violent outbursts in many cities in 1981 and 1982. In the end an improvement in racial harmony will have to be based on both the rigid enforcement of the law and changes in the attitudes of people of many different ethnic and cultural groups. Fear, intolerance and hatred will have to be replaced by trust, acceptance and a refusal to judge and value people purely on their ethnic background or colour of their skin.

1 List the *examples* of racial discrimination mentioned on these pages. Add any other examples you know of.

2 Give some of the *reasons* stated why some people discriminate against others. What do you think about the reasons given?

3 Have you, or any friends, ever been discriminated against? What was the reason? How did you or they feel about it?

Jewish tombstones in London, desecrated and daubed with slogans saying 'Hitler should have finished the job' or '6 million was not enough' make a nonsense of the neo-Nazi attempt to whitewash Nazism.

Many people suggest that relations between the police and the ethnic minorities could be improved

Overcoming racial discrimination

There are complex reasons why some people show prejudice against others of different age, sex, social group, religion, colour or culture. They are usually related to feelings of suspicion and fear based on ignorance or limited experience, and due to social changes which seem very threatening. The previous pages were a reminder that such fear and prejudice can lead to discrimination, hostility and violence. Racial prejudice and discrimination are not simply a matter of white versus black, since many black people and white people live together in harmony, and there is plenty of evidence of racial tension within the racial groups. Nevertheless, in Britain racial prejudice shows most clearly in discrimination against black people.

Progress towards a genuine multi-cultural Britain will have to be based on the rigid enforcement of the law. More important in the long run, however, will be a change of attitude between people in the various ethnic and cultural groups. Fear, intolerance and hatred will have to be replaced by trust, acceptance, and a refusal to judge and value people purely on their ethnic background or by the colour of their skin.

In some fields, such as music and sport, there is little racial prejudice. This group is UB40

What the Scarman report recommended

Lord Scarman's report included suggestions for central government, local authorities, the Commission for Racial Equality and the media. But the bulk of the recommendations affected the police. Of these the most important were:

The introduction of an independent element into the police complaints procedure.

A statutory framework for police-community consultation.

An urgent study of ways to recruit more police from ethnic minorities.

Scientific ways of detecting racial prejudice in police applicants should be vigorously pursued.

Existing law should be used to ban 'racist' marches in sensitive areas. If this proves inpracticable, the Public Order Act 1936 should be amended.

Among Scarman's more general suggestions were calls for:

A better co-ordinated and directed attack by the government on inner-city problems.

Local authorities to review their housing policies to eliminate possible discrimination and provide better education for ethnic minorities.

The government to give a lead in ethnic minority education. Areas of special need included the provision of facilities for under-fives and training teachers in the cultural backgrounds and needs of minority groups.

The media to examine its coverage of major social disorders.

Nim Sandhu came to Coventry from India 20 years ago and has built up a business worth more than £500 000. He finds little racist reaction within his community

Left: The Scarman report suggested ways of improving relations between the police and ethnic minority groups

Exercise 55
Attitudes to race in Britain

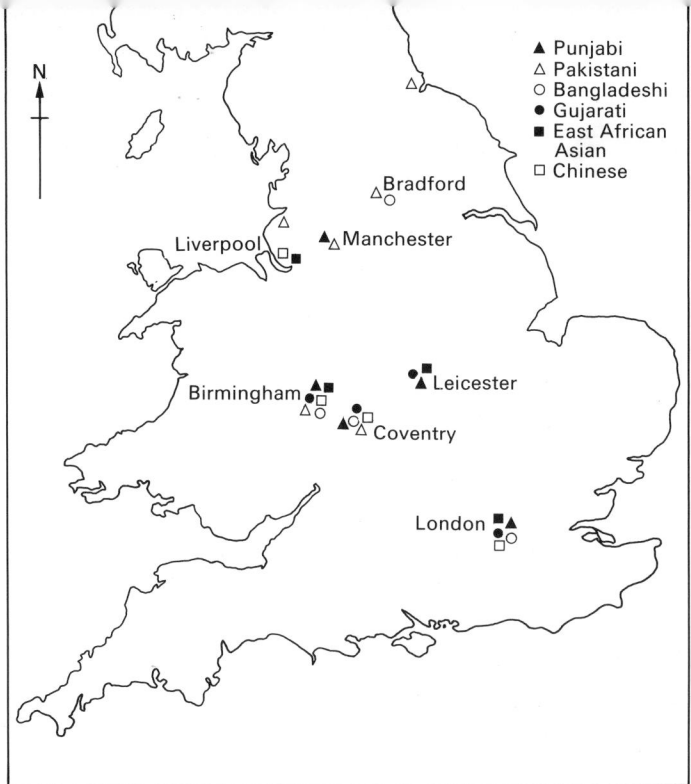

'Asian Links' was a series of broadcasts on BBC Radio 4 in the summer of 1982 in which Asians who have settled in Britain talked about their social, cultural and historical links with places from which they came. The following extract is from a discussion between members of these four communities.

The speakers are *Towyn Mason*, an ex-BBC Correspondent from Pakistan; *Indarjit Singh*, Editor of 'Sikh Courier', from Punjab, India, and West London; *Mohammed Ajeeb*, from Mirpos district, Pakistan, and Bradford; *Tasadduq Ahmed*, from Sylhet district, Bangladesh, and East London; and *Mira Trivedi*, from Gujarat, India, and Leicester.

Towyn Mason: Now, as these links weaken, as you say, how do you see the future in, say, the next ten, twenty, fifty years? Do you see what you might call British Asian communities, British Punjabis, Bangladeshis and so on, in rather the way that English people who migrated to Australia or Canada in the past have taken with them their Anglo-Saxon characteristics but they've developed in certain ways and they're now Australians and Canadians of English background? Do you see something like that happening here?

Mohammed Ajeeb: I think it depends on the political climate in this country. If people like Enoch Powell continue to make statements which can create a tremendous amount of insecurity and apprehension among minority communities, then obviously I think that they will tend to cling together, and they will tend to become more and more united, and they will tend to shield themselves against all these pressures.

Tasadduq Ahmed: I tend to look at it from a different point of view. At present, because of the national situation in which we are living, our blackness is a liability to some of us. But looking fifty years hence that blackness is going to be an asset, in the sense that the world that we are moving in, not Britain the small island, but the bigger world in which we are now learning to live, two thirds of the population of that world is going to be black, and therefore in that context our blackness will not be a liability but an asset.

Indarjit Singh: I'd like to differ slightly. I hope, looking twenty years to the future, that the colour of the skin is neither an asset nor a liability. It's a hope. I'm not sure how far it will go, but it shouldn't be either.

Mira Trivedi: I don't know whether this word 'Asians' will be abolished, because even after fifty years I think they will still be calling us Asians. I call myself British Gujarati, and perhaps this is how one should introduce oneself, because we are living here, this is our home, we've got British passports. So I would call myself a British citizen, but British Gujarati-speaking citizen…

Tasadduq Ahmed: We'll be British by origin but I think we'll go onwards to world citizenship.

1 **a)** Which four Asian ethnic minority groups are represented in this extract? **b)** Name four countries where English people form an ethnic minority group.

2 How can minority communities be made to feel "a tremendous amount of insecurity and apprehension"? If you were (or are) a member of an ethnic minority group feeling "insecurity and apprehension", how would you react?

3 What is meant when one speaker says "looking fifty years hence … blackness is going to be an asset"? Do you agree that in fifty years time two thirds of the world population will be black?

4 Do you think that the hopes of Indarjit Singh and Tasadduq Ahmed are likely to have been realized? Do you share their hopes or not?

Northern Ireland

Ireland is divided into two parts, the Irish Republic, and Northern Ireland, a part of the United Kingdom

Below: British troops are stationed in Northern Ireland to help prevent violence between those who want to remain part of the UK and those who want a united Ireland. *Right*: Murals like this are common

The partition of Ireland

It may seem strange to see from a map of Ireland that it is divided between two countries, The Irish Republic and Northern Ireland, which is a province of The United Kingdom. The boundary between these two neighbouring states is patrolled by two armies and police forces. They are not there to confront each other, but to share in the control of a conflict based on Northern Ireland. News items all too frequently describe violent incidents in the province or in England that are a result of the conflict.

The boundary was first established in 1921, but its origins go back to the 17th century. At that time much of Ireland was controlled from Britain, and during the century many Scottish farming families were 'planted' or settled in the northern part of Ireland known as Ulster. They were Protestant by religion and so had a different religious and cultural background to the Catholic Irish. The Irish people quite understandably resented being ruled from London, and finally fighting broke out

between them and the British army. As a result of the uprising the Irish people gained their independence and formed their own state with its government in Dublin. Because there were so many Protestants in the north who refused to belong to this new state, it was agreed between the British and Irish Governments that the island would be partitioned and a provisional boundary drawn.

The idea in drawing the boundary was to ensure that a Protestant majority existed, although as the map shows there were many non-Catholics in the new Irish state, with many Catholics in the six counties that made up the new Northern Ireland. They were concentrated in certain areas, but in the province as a whole were in a minority. Although it was proposed to make some adjustments the border was finally agreed in 1925. It came into being in an atmosphere of general dissatisfaction and distrust, and many thought it was only a temporary arrangement. It is 412 kilometres long,

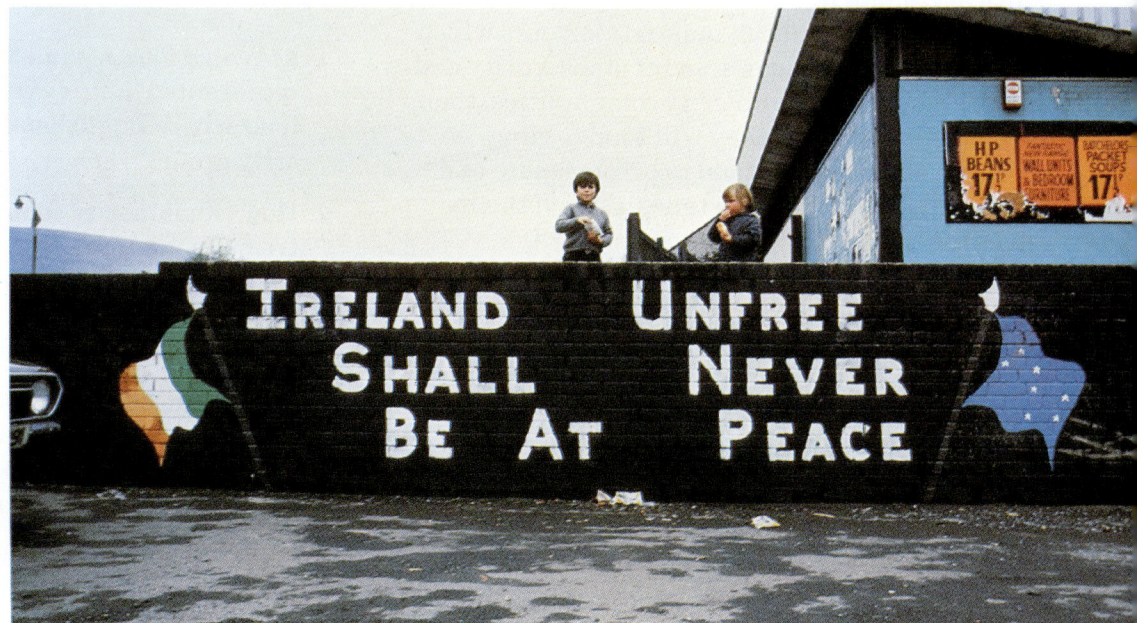

and cuts through many farms, houses, settlements and about 180 roads. Some towns such as Londonderry were separated from their natural and economic region or hinterland. The partition was a compromise that has never been accepted by many people.

Catholics and Protestants

The conflict between Catholics and Protestants that originated in the past came to a critical point with the partition of Ireland. The Catholics claimed in the years that followed that they had not received fair economic and social treatment over things like jobs, housing, social care and education. Since they could never gain power through democratic elections, they felt their position would never improve, and this caused great bitterness and resentment.

Apart from this it was, and is, the strongly held belief of many Catholic people both in the Irish Republic and Northern Ireland that the two areas should be united under one government in Dublin. Quite understandably the Protestants of Northern Ireland feel just as strongly that they wish to remain a part of the United Kingdom. They refuse to accept the possibility of being a minority in a Catholic country. While many efforts have been made to find a peaceful and political settlement acceptable to everyone, none has succeeded. In the meantime some have turned to physical violence to try to resolve the issue. The IRA in particular has become associated with bombings and shootings, while the equivalent Protestant groups have used similar violent means to ensure that their needs and interests will be protected. The suspicion and hostility continues, with extremists from several groups determined to get their way by force if necessary, and the UK government prepared to use the army to prevent this. The late 1980s will inevitably see further attempts, both political and violent, to find a solution to this difficult and long-lasting issue.

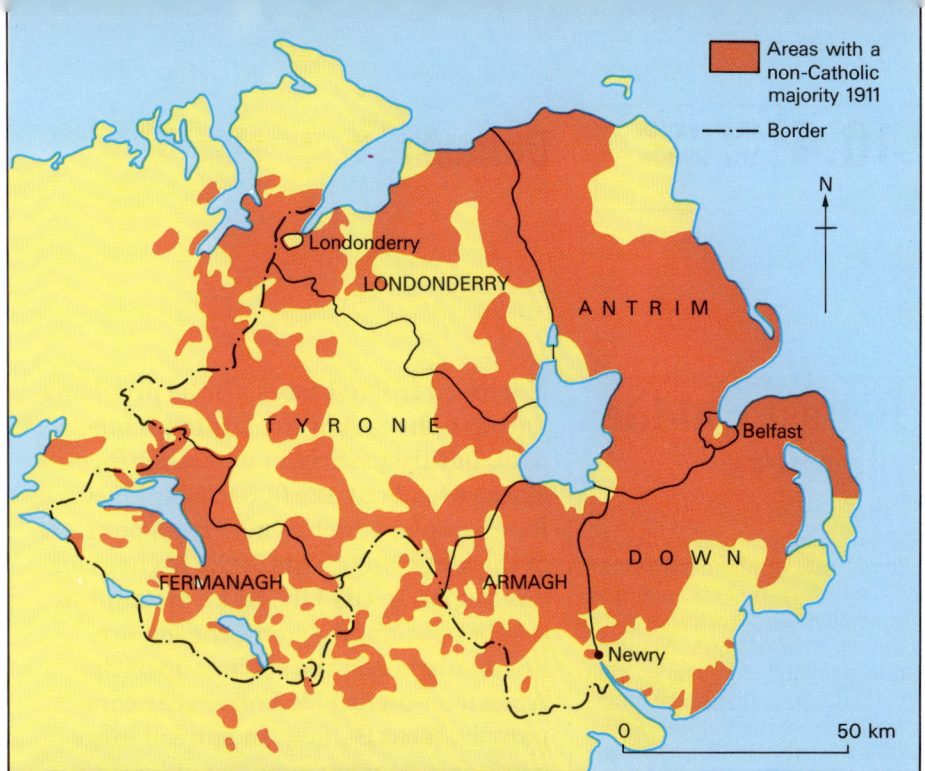

Areas with a non-Catholic majority 1911

— · — Border

This map shows those parts of Ulster with a non-Catholic majority earlier this century, before Ireland was divided

Some villages like this were divided in two when the official boundary was drawn between Ulster and the Irish Republic

Protestants march once a year to celebrate a centuries-old victory over the Catholics

1 What are some of the ways in which day-to-day life in Northern Ireland reflects the conflict due to partition? What news items have recently described events in Northern Ireland related to the conflict?

2 What other areas do you know of that have been partitioned? What was the reason, which groups were involved, who made the decisions, and was there a peaceful solution?

3 List the arguments for and against unification of Ireland from the point of view of a) an Ulster Protestant, b) an Ulster Catholic, c) a person in the Irish Republic, d) a person in England, Scotland or Wales. Why is it difficult in each case to say what the opinion and attitude would be?

Shipbuilding is a traditional key industry in Belfast

Belfast's hidden planners

Cities are shaped by largely unpredictable forces, despite the efforts of planners. For all its statutory powers, planning is relatively powerless to stop the face of Britain changing dramatically in ways that sometimes horrify planners and the public alike. Cities decay, suburbs sprawl, the countryside is spoiled. The public sometimes blames the planners, who promise to do better next time. Despite the tendency of our divided society to form enclaves of rich and poor, black and white, most planners have hopes of playing a part in the development of harmonious, balanced communities.

The situation is different in Belfast. There, what is being reflected in bricks and mortar and concrete is a bitterly divided society. What should Belfast's planners do? Should they use their position and skills to create a harmonious community? Or should they accept the existence of fear and hatred between Protestants and Catholics, and the active presence of the Army and police, and merely do what they can to accommodate a state of permanent tension? If the latter, will they not be helping to ensure that Belfast will never be at peace with itself? Do they have any real choice in the matter? Belfast's planners may not be discussing these questions publicly, but they can not avoid them in their work.

Northern Ireland faces all the problems found in the rest of the United Kingdom, but frequently in a harsher form. There are about 125 000 unemployed, for example, which is nearly 25 per cent of the workforce. This is the highest for any region in the UK. In an attempt to create new employment, the government subsidised the setting up of the American-owned De Lorean car company in West Belfast. In spite of large sums of taxpayers' money paid out to support it, many jobs were lost when the company failed. Also in Belfast is the Harland and Wolff shipyard, situated in the Protestant area. In 1982 it employed about 7 000 people, but falling orders posed a threat to about 1 000 jobs. In the previous seventeen years over £200 million of public money had been spent to support this state owned company; it needs this government help to compete with other shipbuilders around the world. Other job losses have occurred in the synthetic fibres industries, with several large factories clos-

ing down, and in the aircraft, missile and textile machinery industries. There have been a few areas of growth as in the Short Brothers aircraft company. Over 600 workers were employed in their factory in 1982, with further plans for expansion to 1 000. But, even more than in the rest of the United Kingdom, Northern Ireland has to cope with economic problems and high unemployment.

After a riot. The flats in the background are a religious ghetto. Keeping the communities apart has become an unfortunate part of the planner's job

Exercise 56 Catholic and Protestant in Northern Ireland

The Distribution of Roman Catholics and Protestants in Northern Ireland

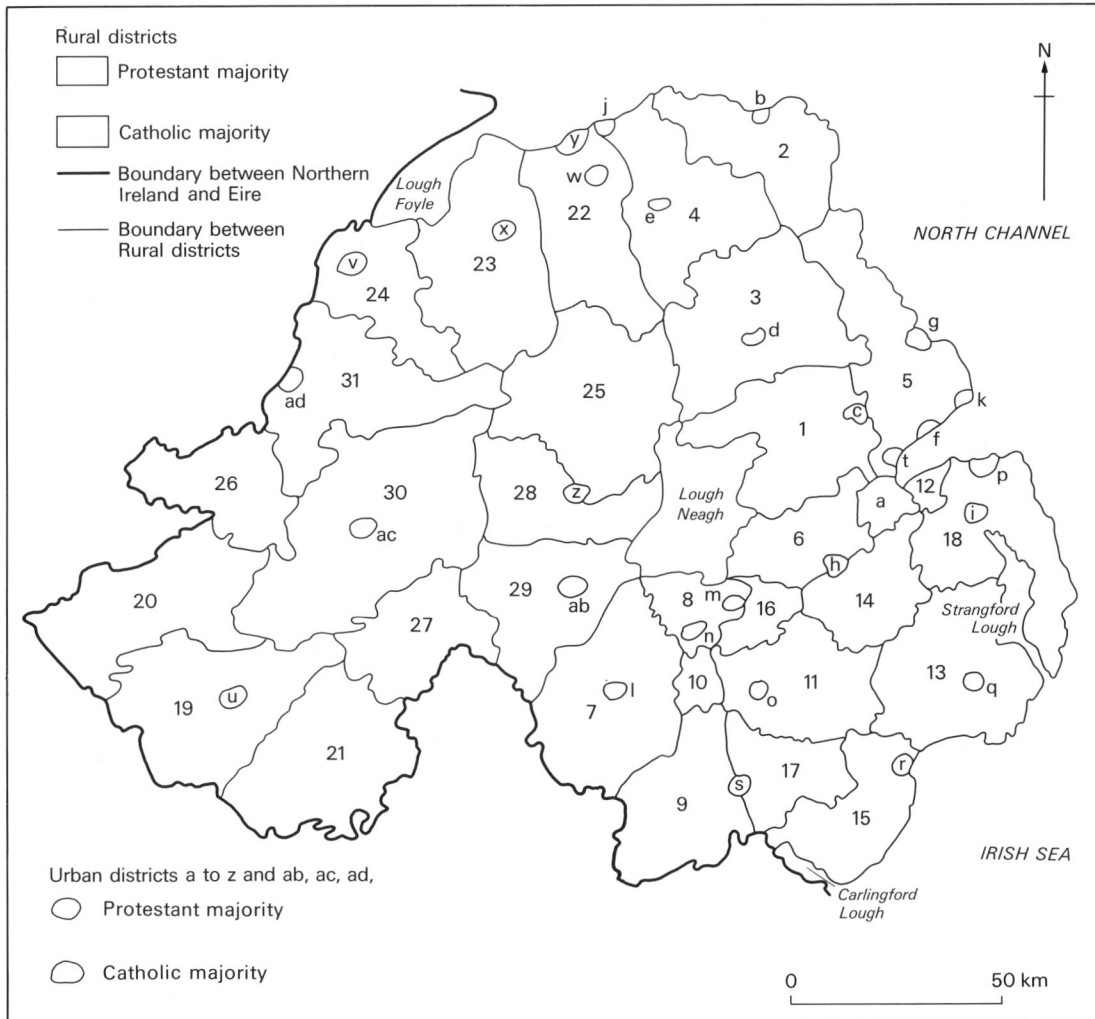

Rural districts

☐ Protestant majority

☐ Catholic majority

— Boundary between Northern Ireland and Eire

— Boundary between Rural districts

Urban districts a to z and ab, ac, ad,

⬭ Protestant majority

⬭ Catholic majority

Lough Foyle

NORTH CHANNEL

Lough Neagh

Strangford Lough

IRISH SEA

Carlingford Lough

0   50 km

Rural District	Roman Catholics %
1 Antrim	20
2 Ballycastle	53
3 Ballymena	17
4 Ballymoney	22
5 Larne	19
6 Lisburn	40
7 Armagh	44
8 Lurgan	40
9 Newry (1)	73
10 Tandragee	15
11 Banbridge	27
12 Castlereagh	10
13 East Down	51
14 Hillsborough	9
15 Kilkeel	56
16 Moira	20
17 Newry (2)	78
18 North Down	16
19 Enniskillen	49
20 Irvinestown	52
21 Linaskea	59
22 Coleraine	26
23 Limavady	53
24 Londonderry	77
25 Magherafelt	55
26 Castlederg	49
27 Clogher	51
28 Cookstown	55
29 Dungannon	52
30 Omagh	60
31 Strabane	48

Urban District	Roman Catholics %
(a) Belfast	27
(b) Ballcastle	63
(c) Ballclare	6
(d) Ballymena	21
(e) Ballmoney	25
(f) Carrickfergus	14
(g) Larne	25
(h) Lisburn	18
(i) Newtonards	11
(j) Portrush	18
(k) Whitehead	14
(l) Armagh	58
(m) Lurgan	46
(n) Portadown	24
(o) Banbridge	30
(p) Bangor	9
(q) Downpatrick	73
(r) Newcastle	47
(s) Newry	84
(t) Newtonabbey	19
(u) Enniskillen	52
(v) Londonderry	67
(w) Coleraine	23
(x) Limarady	37
(y) Portstewart	23
(z) Cookstown	38
(ab) Dungannon	51
(ac) Omagh	62
(ad) Strabane	78

1 Draw or trace the map of Northern Ireland.

2 Shade in the districts with a Catholic majority in one colour or hatching and those with a Protestant majority in another. Describe the pattern.

3 Why does the pattern of distribution make partition by religious belief very difficult – even if it were thought desirable and could be accepted by both groups?

231

Inner city

View of the inner city, Liverpool

Buildings in inner city areas often show changes of use. This residential building became a factory and is now derelict

Inner city: decline and deprivation

The older large towns and cities in Britain have many features in common. This is partly due to their long history and the economic, social and political forces that have shaped them. Several references have been made to the central areas where the settlement usually started and that are now centres for business, administration, commerce and entertainment. Immediately around the fringes there tends to be a zone quite distinct in appearance and character from the CBD and also from the outer suburbs and the new private and local authority estates. These zones are known as the inner city areas.

Housing

Much of the housing in the inner cities was built in the eighteenth and nineteenth centuries. Not surprisingly, much is small and inadequate by today's standards, and a great deal is in poor physical shape. The density of this housing is also very high. The response of some local authorities has been to demolish large areas, rehouse the residents on newer estates elsewhere, and redevelop the sites. A few decades ago it was the practice to redevelop with huge high-rise blocks of flats, but the problems some people found in living in them has led to a widespread change of policy. Nowadays either low-rise development or the repair of old houses is more in favour, since these seem to combine the necessary high density with conditions that residents prefer. Even so, much housing in the inner city area remains either old and worn out, or bleak and unattractive. A great deal is owned by the local authority or rented from private landlords, and home ownership is relatively low. Some accommodation in the inner cities is privately owned, or is rented as luxury flats. This 'gentrified' housing with access to the central city is quite unlike the more usual inner city housing in design and cost. Few inner city residents can afford to buy or rent such property.

Apart from housing, the general environment of inner cities often shows a great deal of dereliction and decay. This is due partly to housing clearance, with

Houses like these are a health hazard

empty sites awaiting redevelopment, and partly to the closure of factories, warehouses and their surrounding lorry parks and grounds. The widespread construction of urban motorways with their massive flyovers and road junctions has also made the inner city less and less hospitable. A great deal of money needs to be found to provide attractive alternatives.

High unemployment

Many people feel that the crucial problem is that of unemployment. The early 1980s saw a massive increase in unemployment, and people in the inner city areas suffered badly, especially younger people. There has been a virtual collapse of traditional industries. As more and more docks, warehouses and factories have closed down completely or the work transferred elsewhere, the inner cities have become 'economic ghost towns', relics of previous industrial growth. The high rates of unemployment add to the difficulties of inner city residents, especially since they often lack the mobility to travel long distances to work elsewhere.

As those people who can have moved elsewhere to find jobs, the less economically mobile such as the old, the poor and the unemployed remain. This leads in turn to shops closing and a deterioration of social services and school provision, especially in times of economic 'cuts'. Another feature of inner cities is the concentration of black and Asian

families. This is partly due to difficulties of finding homes and jobs elsewhere, partly to the understandable wish of most people to live near others with similar attitudes and expectations. Whatever the reasons, the attitude or suspicions between some black residents and the local police adds further tensions to life in the inner city.

Many other parts of cities and the country have their problems, but the Secretary of State for the Environment felt the need to say in 1982 that unless there was some help for and improvement to the quality of life in the inner cities there might well be a collapse of community life and a breakdown of public order. There are many good features to life in the inner city, but the stress felt by some residents began to show in the outbreak of riots in 1981 and 1982. The future of the inner cities is an important issue for the 1980s.

1 Look back to the illustration of St Pauls, Bristol (page 45) and at the pictures on these pages, and pages 236–7. What do they say about features and life in inner city areas?

2 a) Why might it be uneconomic for a firm to locate in an inner city area? b) If it were uneconomic, should financial help be given to encourage jobs to be made available? If so, where should the funds come from?

3 Describe three reasons why many inner city residents are less mobile than the average for the country.

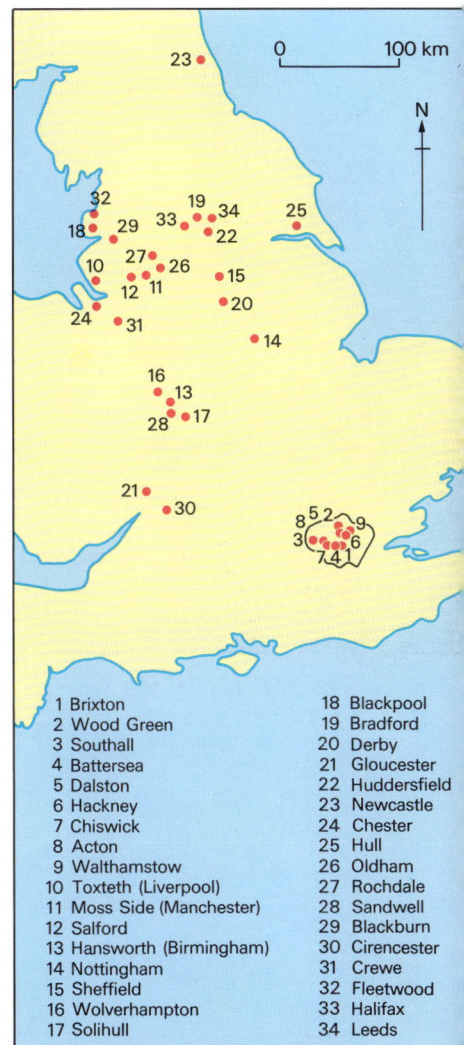

1 Brixton	18 Blackpool
2 Wood Green	19 Bradford
3 Southall	20 Derby
4 Battersea	21 Gloucester
5 Dalston	22 Huddersfield
6 Hackney	23 Newcastle
7 Chiswick	24 Chester
8 Acton	25 Hull
9 Walthamstow	26 Oldham
10 Toxteth (Liverpool)	27 Rochdale
11 Moss Side (Manchester)	28 Sandwell
12 Salford	29 Blackburn
13 Hansworth (Birmingham)	30 Cirencester
14 Nottingham	31 Crewe
15 Sheffield	32 Fleetwood
16 Wolverhampton	33 Halifax
17 Solihull	34 Leeds

There was an outbreak of rioting in many inner city areas in 1981/82

Inner city areas can become bleak and derelict while they await redevelopment

233

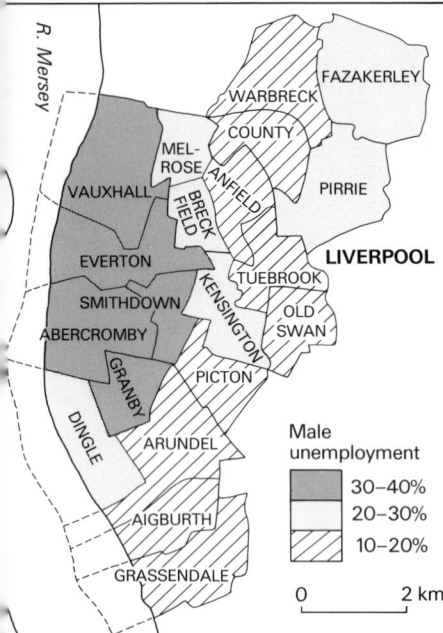

Male unemployment

- 30–40%
- 20–30%
- 10–20%

0   2 km

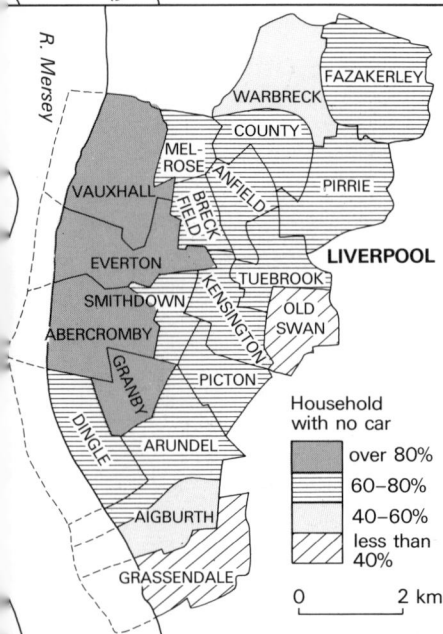

Household with no car

- over 80%
- 60–80%
- 40–60%
- less than 40%

0   2 km

These maps show some of the social and economic features of inner Liverpool

The Liverpool Garden Festival project has been built on the site of a once-thriving dock

The signs of deprivation in housing, social services, employment, mobility and the environment are clear to see, but people disagree about their causes and the most sensible ways of improving things. Neither local authorities or voluntary agencies, nor residents on their own, seem to be able to make any significant improvement. Various governments have tried to give help in different ways, usually by providing money in some form or other. The Merseyside Development Corporation, for example, has tried to revitalise the area of derelict dockland alongside parts of the Mersey. The area is not well located for much of industry, and they cannot fill existing sites. But the MDC hope to attract new jobs to the area as well as provide greater security of tenure to the small industrial and commercial users of dock premises. Residents from the nearby inner city zone hope that they too may benefit from improvements such as access to riverside walks and better public transport. In 1982 the government launched a programme to attract private industry to the inner city, by offering financial support to any project or development relating to housing, jobs, or recreation.

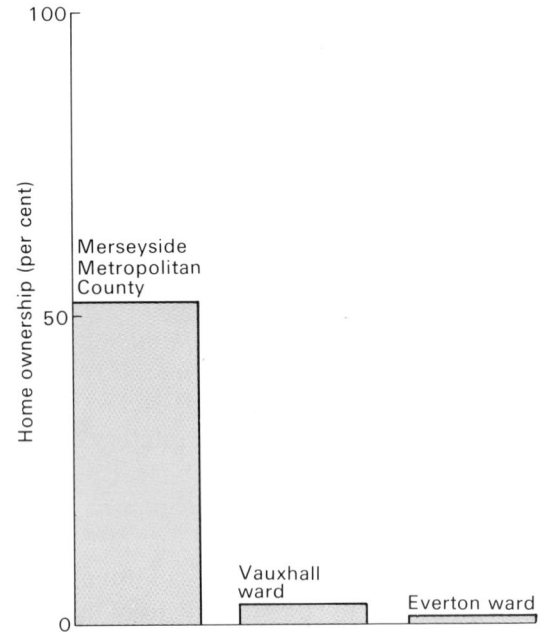

This graph shows how few people own their own homes in the Vauxhall and Everton areas of Liverpool, compared with the whole of Merseyside

Critics of this Urban Development Grant argue that such private development supported by government funds does not do enough to help or involve the local community, nor take account of overall needs. Nor can it do much to remove wider social and racial inequalities that loom so large in the inner city.

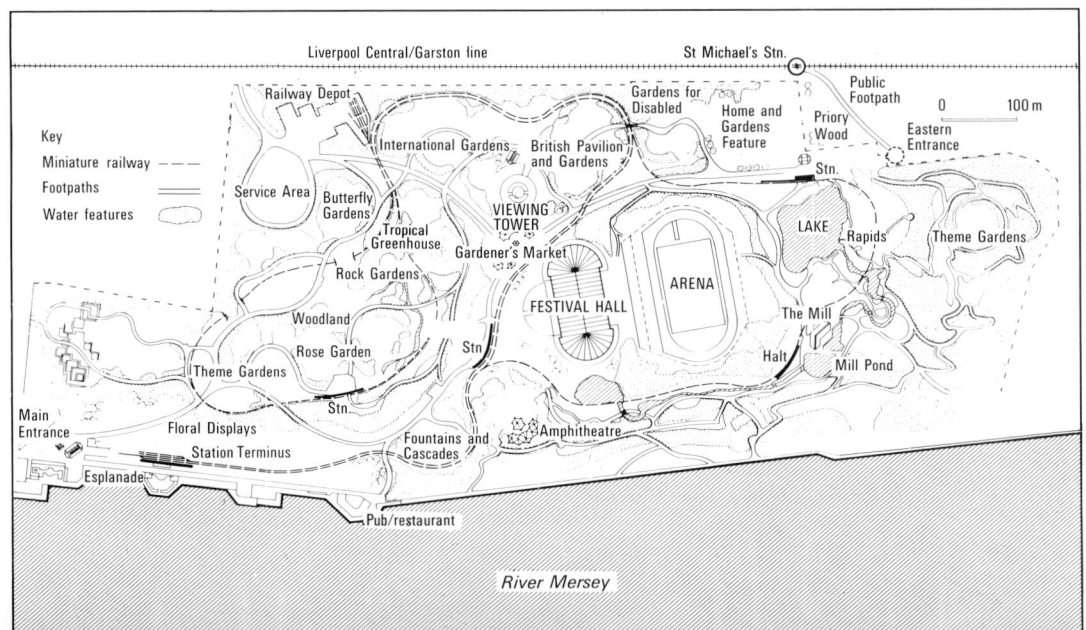

234

Sombre anniversary for Toxteth

Last year shops were burnt and looted. The police fired CS gas for the first time in an English city and were themselves attacked in unprecedented violence. On one night alone 450 officers were treated for injuries, and doctors reported considerable numbers of local people hurt. Petrol bombs were thrown: cars were burnt and whole streets devastated in outbreaks of violence which lasted throughout July. Perhaps surprisingly, only one person died.

The difference from last year's trouble is that this year the culprits appear to be children. The police have made a few arrests, of 10- and 12-year-olds as opposed to youths and men in last year's conflict.

The police have made progress since the events of last July, it is claimed. Public consultation meetings in line with Lord Scarman's recommendations have been set up and committees of police, local authority representatives at district and county level, and residents meet regularly.

Mr Wally Brown, chairman of Merseyside Community Relations Council, is not convinced that much progress has been made. The police liaison committees, he says, are not manned by the people who criticized the police last year. He is not happy that enough has been done by the Government in Liverpool 8, in spite of Mr Heseltine's appointment as 'Minister for Merseyside'. In short, while more than 60 per cent of black youths are unemployed and on the street in the district, trouble will never be far away.

The Islington area of Liverpool 7

1 Describe the particular site and location of Liverpool's inner city area.

2 From the data provided on these two pages describe the ways in which inner city Liverpool shows many of the features characteristic of inner city areas in general.

3 Argue the case for and against money being used for a large project such as the Liverpool Garden Festival.

Above: A news extract from 1982. *Below:* Liverpool takes pride in its two great football teams

Housing and homelessness

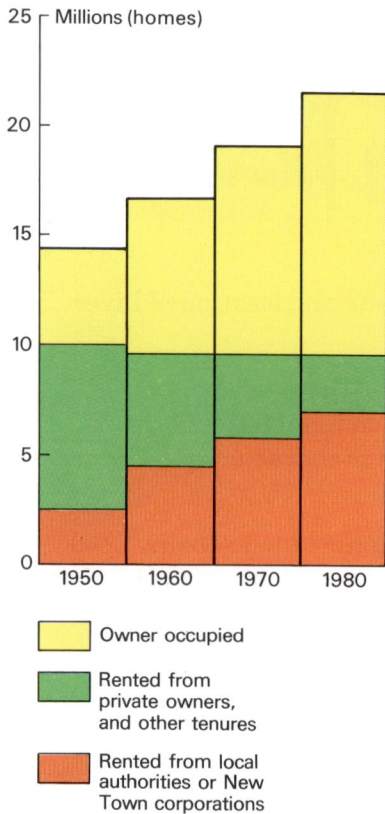

The number and proportion of people owning their own homes has risen greatly in the last 30 years

Legend:
- Owner occupied
- Rented from private owners, and other tenures
- Rented from local authorities or New Town corporations

Tenure, owning or renting

Few things affect people more than the nature and quality of their homes. The diagram shows how the tenure of housing (whether it is owned or rented, and if rented, from whom) has changed in recent decades. It illustrates two trends that have been going on throughout the century, a) an increase in owner-occupancy and renting from local authorities and b) a decline in the renting of furnished or unfurnished accommodation from private landlords. It is surprising to discover that about seventy years ago as many as ninety per cent of families rented their homes from private owners, that only nine per cent were owner-occupiers and that as few as one per cent rented their homes from a local authority. During the 1970s and early 1980s both Labour and Conservative Governments encouraged the sale of local authority housing, using different degrees of persuasion. As a result the proportion of owner-occupancy increased. During the decade there was also an increase in the number of hous-ing associations and cooperatives, but there is still very little of this type of shared ownership. The map on page 238 shows that the proportion of types of tenure varies considerably from region to region.

Housing construction

Taking the country as a whole, there was an increase in the number of dwellings available between 1971 and 1981, while the number of households fell. That suggests that there should not be a real housing problem, but many think otherwise. One worrying feature was the dramatic fall in the number of new houses being built in the late 1970s and early 1980s. In 1967, for example, about 400 000 new houses had been started, but by 1981 this had fallen to 135 000, of which only about a quarter were local authority dwellings. This drop in the number of new houses being constructed might not have mattered a great deal, but there are two problems that could make it disastrous for many people.

Above: Poor housing in the East End, the sort of conditions in which many migrants, such as these Bengalis have to live.
Right: The 'piggeries' in Liverpool. Much recent housing is of poor quality

Church Row, Hampstead. Housing such as this is beyond the means of all but a few families in Britain

Terraced houses in Durham. In recent years the trend has been to retain and improve older, solidly built properties such as these

Housing need

Most people would regard a decent home, with adequate space and amenities, as a high priority in their needs. Yet very many live in homes that are overcrowded, lacking in basic amenities or in serious need of repair. This may sometimes be due to the carelessness or laziness of the people who live in them, but in the majority of cases there is very little the occupants can do, no matter how hard they try. In most cases they can't afford either to move somewhere more suitable. Local authorities estimated in the early 1980s that there were some 547 000 unfit dwellings in England alone, another 1 035 000 dwellings lacking one or more basic amenity and a further 1 736 000 which needed major repairs although they were technically fit for human habitation. Apart from this there were those who were actually homeless. There were over 50 000 statutory homeless families in England alone in 1981 that had to be taken into bed and breakfast hotels, hostels or short-life dwellings. Although the housing stock may be adequate at the national level, when looked at locally or through the experience of many individuals and families, there is clearly the need for something better. The real questions, as seen by Des Wilson, a past Director of the voluntary organisation 'Shelter', are, a) is the provision of houses in the right place (that is where people have to live and work), b) is it of the right quality (that is of a standard fit for human habitation), c) is it of the right price (that is at a price a family can afford without being driven deeper into debt or poverty) and d) is it secure (that is to say that they do not fear eviction onto the streets)?

1 Take a survey of housing tenure of families represented in your class or school. Is this the same as the proportion for the Region in which you live? (page 238)

2 What are the advantages and disadvantages of owner-occupancy? How do most people manage to pay for the very high cost of houses?

3 Why could both statements in the extract on the right be correct and seem to disagree at the same time?

Two views of housing in Britain, 1981

'Very few households in the regions suffered deficiencies in their accommodation. In England as a whole, accommodation is deficient for just under 5 per cent of households, but in Scotland the figure is 9 per cent . . . Wales, the North West, Yorkshire, Humberside and the East Midlands still have around 5–6 per cent of households with only an outside WC . . .'
Regional trends 1981. HMSO. Central Statistical Office

'A vast number of families in Britain are inadequately housed. They are homeless in that they are not living in conditions conducive to a decent family life; overcrowded, often with parents and children sharing one bedroom; living in conditions officially unfit for human habitation; living with friends or relatives in a situation of strain and tension.'
Des Wilson, former Director of 'Shelter'

Exercise 58 **Tenure of housing**

1 Describe which parts of Britain have: **a**) the highest and the lowest proportions of owner-occupied housing, **b**) the highest proportion of privately rented accommodation, **c**) the highest and the lowest proportion of local authority rented housing.

2 Try to explain why the type of tenure should differ in this way from place to place in Britain.

3 What do you think are the advantages and disadvantages of **a**) owning or buying your own home **b**) renting from the local council **c**) renting from a private landlord?

Types of tenure in the United Kingdom %

| Region | Owner occupied | Rented | |
		Local Authority	Private
North	46	41	13
Yorks. and Humberside	55	33	12
East Midlands	58	29	13
East Anglia	59	26	15
South-East/Greater London	49	31	20
Remainder of South East	63	24	13
South-West	64	22	14
West Midlands	57	33	10
North-West	59	31	10
Scotland	36	54	10
Wales	59	29	12

Differences in the types of tenure in the various regions of Britain

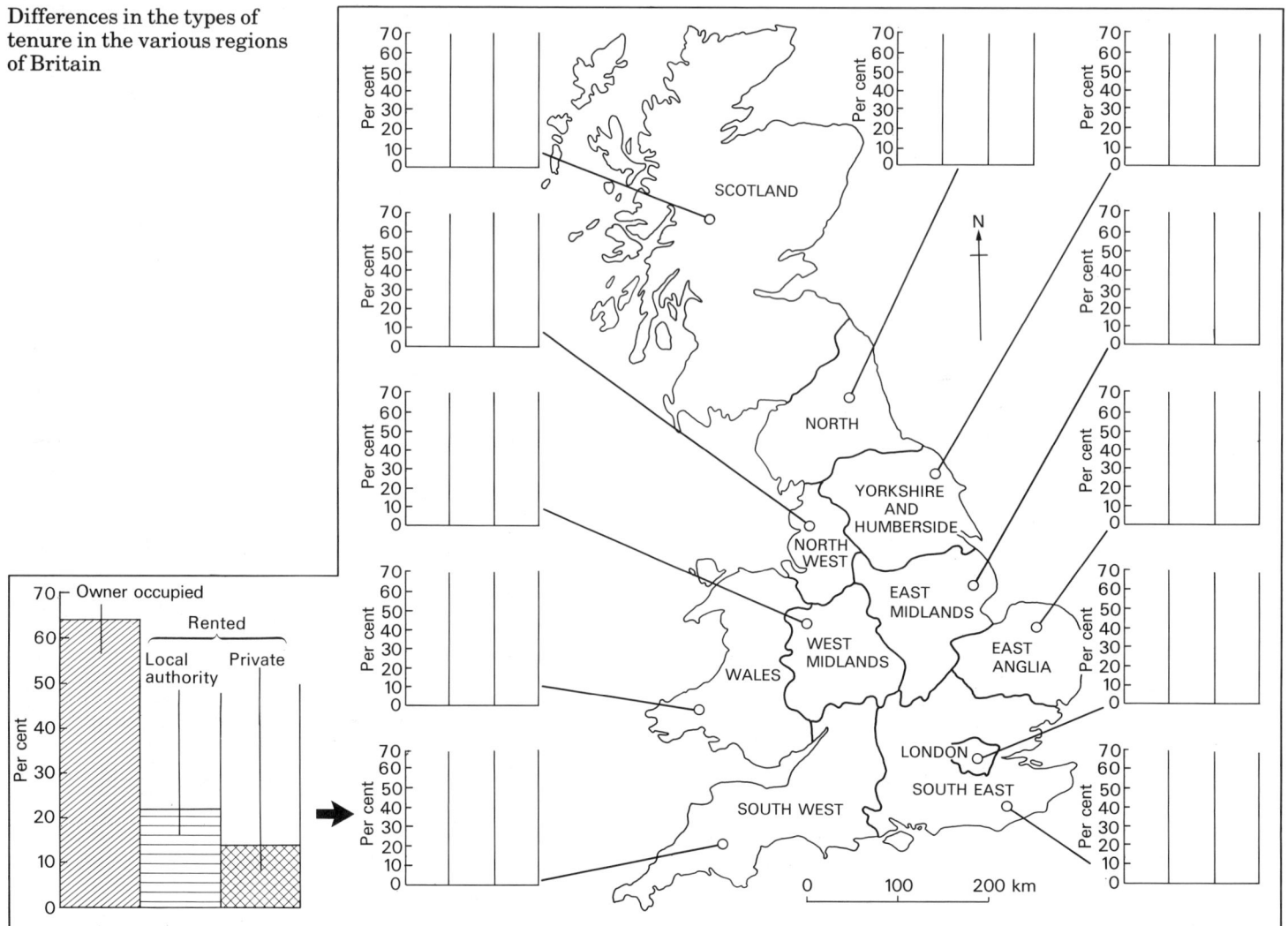

Chapter 11 Contrasts in Britain

Regional contrasts: the North-west and the Home Counties

Lancashire and surrounding areas

Some contrasts between North-West and South-East England early 1980s

	Lancs.	Surrey
Persons per sq km (1982)	451.9	603.9
Population (1982)	1384.1	1013.9
Over retiring age (%)	19.9	18.2
Live births (per 1000 pop)	12.7	10.7
Deaths (per 1000 pop)	13.9	10.8
Perinatal mortality rate (per 100 live births)	12.9	10.8
Population projections: (% change in 1981–1991)	3.6	0.3
Employment (%):		
Agriculture, forestry, fishing	1.5	1.4
Metal manufacture, engineering, etc.	20.2	16.5
Other manufacturing	16.2	5.2
Construction, distribution, transport	27.3	33.4
Mining, quarrying, electricity, water	1.4	2.1
Other services	32.3	41.4
Unemployment rate (July 1981)	13.0	6.0
Earnings (average gross weekly, full time) 1983		
Man over 21 (£)	151.0	176.1
Woman 18 and over (£)	102.8	112.4
Education: Pupils aged 16 staying beyond leaving age (% 1982)	20	46
Housing:		
Owned by local authority (%) 1981	19.0	18.0
Average domestic rates (1982/83)	148.0	281.0
Owning or buying house (%)	71.7	68.7
Renting from local authority (%)	19.8	19
Below bedroom standard (%)	5.2	2.8
Car and Van Licences (per 1000 pop.) 1979	282	358
Commercial/industrial floorspace (%)		
Industrial	62	37
Warehouses	20	29
Commercial offices	4	13

Area contrasts in Britain

A great many examples have been given of the landscape, settlements, types of work and ways of life around Britain. Although they are within one country, ruled by one government and with a few exceptions speak one language, there are considerable differences between the places and peoples of the different regions. Indeed it is this very diversity that often strikes visitors to Britain. It is the particular combination of landscape, past history, present activities and social characteristics that give the special 'feel' to various places or regions.

Some of the contrasts can be seen by comparing the two counties of Lancashire and Surrey. Lancashire, in 'the north', occupies the area between the Pennine moorlands and the sea, and between the northern outskirts of Merseyside and Greater Manchester and the Lake District. It has an economic past based on coal mining, textile and chemical manufacturing and a wide range of engineering. Surrey lies to the south-west of Greater London,

Surrey and surrounding areas

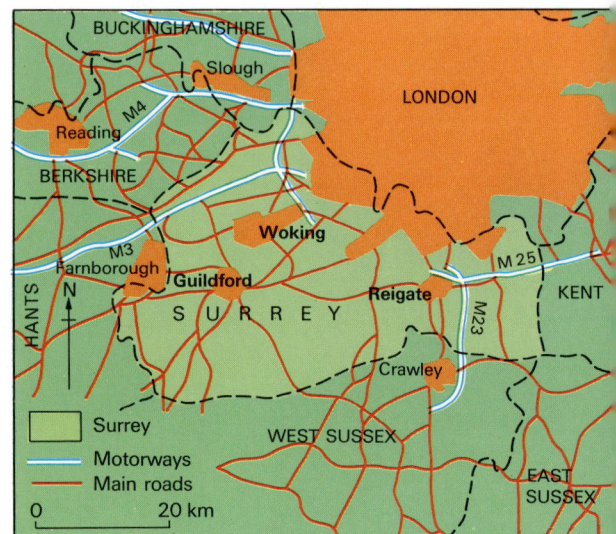

and extends from the outer margins of the Greater London conurbation, across the claylands and chalk hills of the North Downs and the Weald. It shows few signs of mining or heavy industry. Its main character comes from the farming landscape and the villages and towns that once served as market centres. These are now much more concerned however, with providing homes for commuters to London and workers in light industries and the service industries. In many ways the mill towns of Lancashire and the commuter and 'stockbroker' villages of Surrey represent the contrast that many people have in their minds of the 'hard' north, where wealth is created, and the 'soft' south where the more favoured and leisurely live.

Real places and their images

Pictures, maps and statistics like these are just one way in which people gain an impression or image of other places. Other powerful means are through TV and films and, of course, through travel. One of the difficulties is that it is impossible to show or describe all aspects of a small town, let alone a county. So an author or film maker makes a selection of things to show or describe. The result is that the reader or viewer gets only a part of the picture of a place and its people – the one selected by someone else! That is why descriptions and pictures should be read and viewed with caution. The same is true of statistics. It has been said that 'there are lies, damned lies and statistics'. Most

people will have heard two people giving different opinions and views based on the same statistics or information. While it is necessary and convenient to get information and explanations about parts of Britain from secondary sources (such as this book), their limitations should be realised.

When certain views about places and people are repeated again and again they result in what are called 'stereotypes'. Many cartoons, jokes (about the Irish) and TV films (such as the very popular 'Coronation Street') present stereotypes that may be based on a few people, places or events in the actual world, but are far from being wholly real or true. This may not matter, although some groups understandably object to being laughed at or presented in a false light. Our views about places and people can affect our behaviour, and may encourage or discourage us from wanting to live and work in certain places, or take holidays there. This is why many firms or local authorities or towns use advertisements to create a 'good image' of their locality.

1 Select four of the characteristics that are markedly different in Lancashire and Surrey. Comment on these differences. What do they suggest about the two counties?

2 Compare the pictures above, and those on page 243. What do they suggest about differences between the north and south of England. Why should they be used carefully for this purpose?

3 Describe two TV series that give an image of the contrasting parts of Britain.

Left: Pigeon fancier, Northern England

Above: Afghan fanciers, Southern England

Much housing in Britain shows no sign of which part of the country it is in. Guess where these houses are found! (Answer: 53°25′N, 2°38′W)

241

Images of North and South: voting patterns

Political maps of Lancashire and Merseyside (*below*) and of Surrey and South-West London (*bottom*)

It is often said that the way people vote says a great deal about their life style, living standards and hopes for the future. In many people's minds 'the North' is seen as largely Labour and 'the South East and Suburbs' as Conservative. The maps show the voting pattern in 1983.

The Conservative dominance in Surrey and the other suburbs is clear to see. Surprisingly, in view of the image, the Lancashire results show a large Conservative support. A few Lancashire towns had a Labour majority as did most parts of Liverpool within the Merseyside Metropolitan County.

When one looks at the 'hard-core' Conservative areas the traditional 'Home Counties' image of Surrey is clearly shown, as well as the non-urban parts of Lancashire and Merseyside. Similarly the 'hard-core' Labour areas of the inner and industrial city stand out with their big majorities.

Voting patterns change, of course, and these maps reflect people's view in the early 1980s. They need to be compared with past and with local elections.

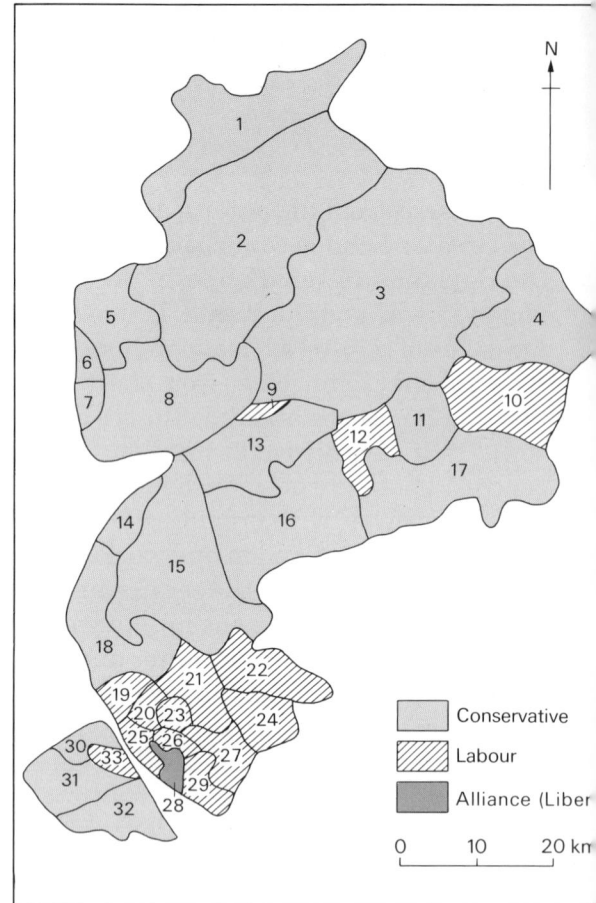

Contrasts in voting patterns

Lancs. & Merseyside (with % majority)

1 Morecambe and Lunesdale C 31.4	18 Crosby C 5.3
2 Lancaster C 25.4	19 Bootle L 21.4
3 Ribble Valley C 41.4	20 Liverpool, Walton L 27.6
4 Pendle C 11.9	21 Knowsley North L 44.5
5 Wyre C 31.5	22 St. Helens North L 17.5
6 Blackpool North C 25.2	23 Liverpool West Derby L 27.0
7 Blackpool South C 25.9	24 St. Helens South L 19.8
8 Fylde C 38.6	25 Liverpool Riverside L 45.2
9 Preston L 15.0	26 Liverpool Broadgreen L 8.3
10 Burnley L 1.5	27 Knowsley South L 24.6
11 Hyndburn C 21.0	28 Liverpool Mossley Hill Lib. 9.1
12 Blackburn L 5.4	29 Liverpool Garston L 8.7
13 South Ribble C 22.5	30 Wallasey C 13.5
14 Southport C 9.9	31 Wirral W C 33.5
15 Lancashire West C 12.5	32 Wirral S C 30.0
16 Chorley C 17.8	33 Birkenhead L 20.7
17 Rossendale and Darwen C 15.3	

Surrey (with % majority)

34 Hayes and Harlington C 10.4	48 Spelthorne C 26.3
35 Ealing, Southall L 21.8	49 Surbiton C 26.1
36 Hammersmith L 6.0	50 Sutton C 21.9
37 Kensington C 16.4	51 Carshalton and Wallington C 21.7
38 Chelsea C 39.8	52 Epsom and Ewell C 33.8
39 Fulham C 12.2	53 Surrey North West C 38.2
40 Brentford and Isleworth C 18.2	54 Chertsey and Walton C 30.9
41 Feltham and Heston C 3.9	55 Esher C 35.2
42 Richmond and Barnes C 0.2	56 Woking C 28.9
43 Putney C 10.7	57 Guildford C 21.7
44 Twickenham C 9.6	58 Mole Valley C 30.2
45 Kingston upon Thames C 21.7	59 Reigate C 32.2
46 Wimbledon C 24.9	60 Surrey East C 35.6
47 Mitcham and Morden C 13.9	61 Surrey SW C 27.6

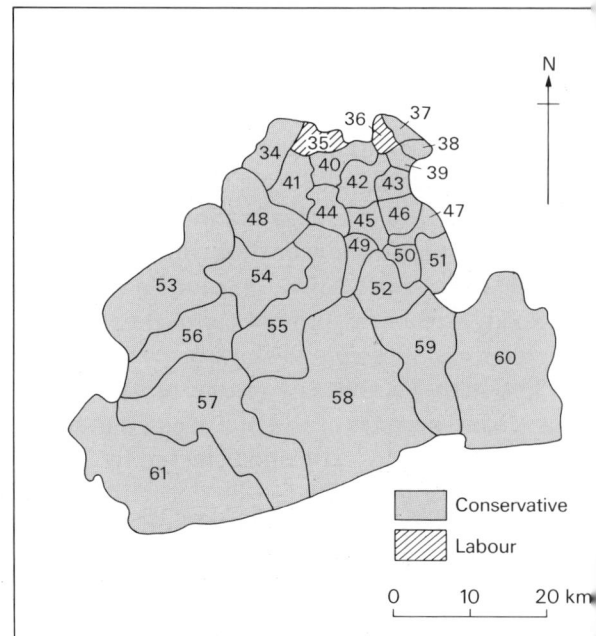

Exercise 59 **Images of Britain**

This map shows the places that were thought by a group of school pupils in Newcastle to be desirable or undesirable places to live. High scores (such as the '90' for Devon) were places they favoured and low scores (such as the '10' for Glasgow) were places they for the less desirable ones. Why do you think the map was drawn 'upside down'?

1 Draw an outline of Britain from the map. Shade in one colour those areas that had a score of 70 or more (most desirable) and those that had a score of 40 or below (least desirable).

2 Describe the desirable areas and say why you think the pupils chose them as such. Do the same for the less desirable ones. Why do you think the map was drawn upside down?

3 Choose two places over which you would disagree with the Newcastle opinions, saying what you like or dislike about them. Are you more likely to be 'right' than anyone else? Say why, if you think you are, and suggest why the pupils in Newcastle held a different opinion to yours.

4 In what ways might a map showing how people voted tell one something about the place and the people who live there? What are the dangers in basing too much on this evidence?

A map of Newcastle pupils' views (or 'perceptions') about Britain

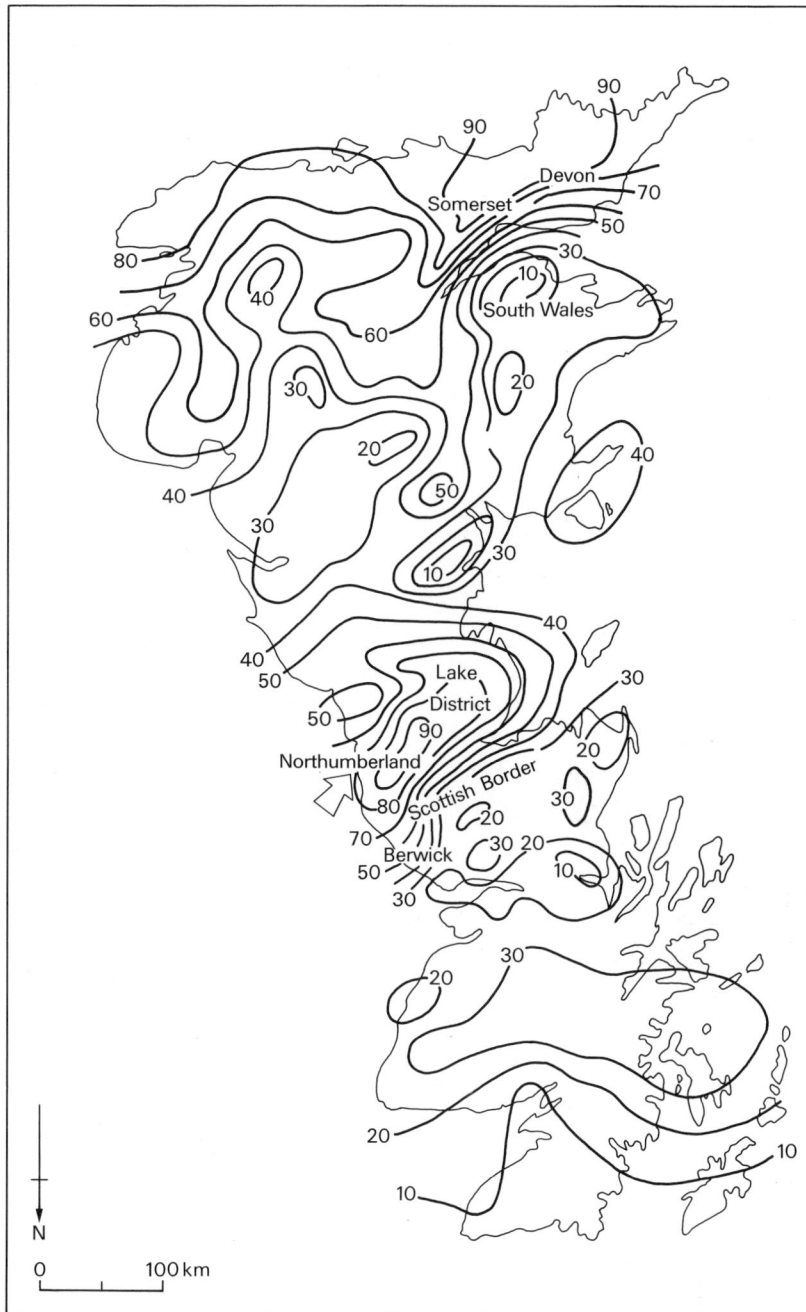

A working men's club, North of England

A pie shop, South-East England

243

Contrasts in Inner London: The City and the East End

The City is dominated by offices and banks

The streets in the East End are quite unlike those in the nearby City

The Smithfield Trust

Marc Dorfman of the Town and Country Planning Association is secretary to the Smithfield Trust. He sees Smithfield's complicated problems in the context of London's other declining inner area communities. 'The pleas by the diminishing number of residents and small businesses that such areas should not be lost to new traffic schemes and creeping office developments are often treated with patronising contempt by local authorities,' he says.

The Smithfield Trust has a serious and urgent task. It is conducting a survey to determine the size, type and location of all vacant floorspace in the area; to identify buildings and sites suitable for development (particularly residential); and to build up a picture of what is going on throughout the area.

Change in the area

There is no clear boundary to the area considered here, but it consists of parts of The City of London and adjoining boroughs of Islington and Tower Hamlets. Something about its townscapes and functions were described in Chapter 2. A glance at the map on page 56 shows that this was about the eastern limit of the built-up area in 1572. The locations of 'The Towre' and 'The Spital Fields' can be recognised on the map opposite. The following centuries saw an expansion of the urban area and the open fields became covered with houses, warehouses, factories, docks, and all the various services such as shops, schools and hospitals. Other important elements in the townscape were roads and railways, including main-line terminals such as Liverpool Street and Fenchurch Street, canals linking the docks to inland Britain, and at a later stage, the Underground stations. Just inside the City boundaries stood the banks and offices that made this the financial centre of not just Britain, but the whole world. Along the riverside the once-famous London, East India, West India, Millwall and Royal Docks were constructed. This was the part of London known as the 'East End', and here are well known districts such as Stepney, Bow, Spitalfields, Limehouse and Millwall.

Change in the City

Recent decades have seen many changes. In the city there has been a remarkable series of new developments. Large and impressive high-rise commercial blocks dominate the skyline and dwarf the older buildings such as St Paul's Cathedral, the Guildhall, the Stock Exchange and the Bank of England. Further east, much of the area was bombed during the last war, and soon afterwards a great deal of residential land was cleared and redeveloped. Local authority estates of high-rise flats mingle with rehabilitated terrace houses and newer low-rise developments. Wholesale markets of national importance such as Smithfield meat market have closed down, and the bacon, sausage and offal factories linked to it. As in other inner city areas, most of the small factories have been closed down and warehouses either lie derelict or have been put to different uses. The docks themselves have been closed down, and have been either filled in, redeveloped as recreational centres or are still awaiting redevelopment. It is often difficult to know how to use such areas whose traditional functions have been lost.

Change beyond the City

Immediately to the north and east of the Barbican, one is back among the old narrow streets of Spitalfields and the post-war estates of flats, schools, shops and offices. Street markets are still held in between some of the older terraced rows, in sharp contrast to the Barbican centre nearby. The variety in the scale, the architectural style and age of buildings, is very great for such a small area, as is the range of activities and peoples.

It is also an example of the conflicts in needs and possibilities of various people in the inner city areas. The wants and needs of the local residents, the local authority planners, the visitors, the tenants of the new flats and commercial and industrial developers are often in conflict with each other. The ability and power of the different groups to bring about change also varies. One impor-

tant key to the future of such places is the greater combined involvement of local groups in suggesting what they would like to be done. But there are many reasons why this may not be possible. The City and Spitalfields is a good example of the changes and contrast found in many inner city zones of Britain's cities.

1 Describe the locations of the City, the Blackwall Tunnel, the Barbican, and Fleet Street (national newspapers).

2 Measure the stretch of the River Thames shown on the map. Name a place that is the same distance from your school.

3 Choose four words or phrases that describe your reaction to a) the street in the City b) the street in the East End.

4 Draw a skyline sketch based on the photograph above. Label with as many townscape features as you can. Add a title.

The Barbican skyline

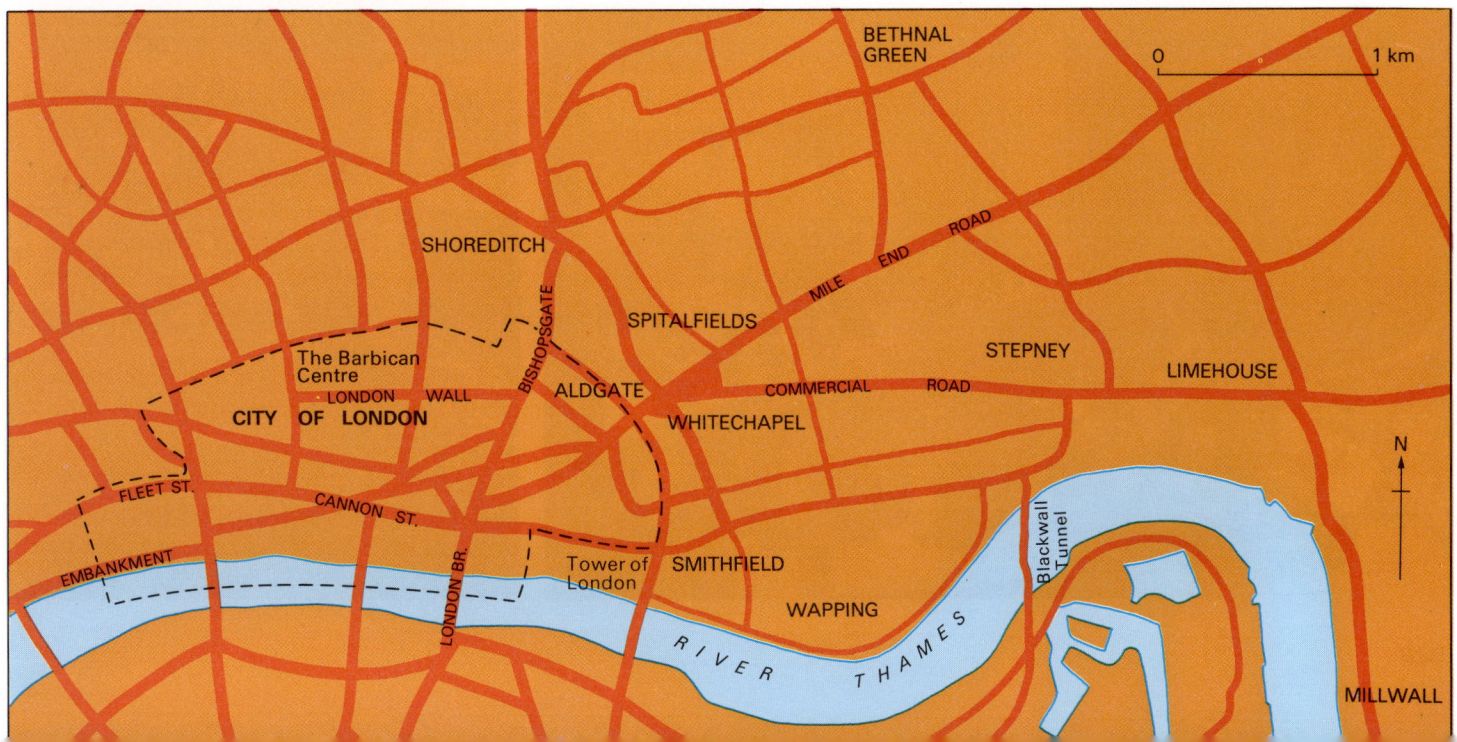

The location of the City and Spitalfields

The Barbican

Perhaps the most remarkable example of large-scale development is that known as the Barbican. It consists of a number of spectacular high-rise residential blocks, low-rise flats, office accommodation and a huge leisure and recreational complex of theatres, cinemas, galleries, gardens, restaurants and landscaped pedestrian terraces, water pools and grass. The Barbican is set in the middle of the older area and the new architecture mingles with older structures like churches and commercial developments. It is an attractive and exciting townscape in the middle of an ancient part of London.

Some views of the heart of the Barbican development, the Centre for Arts

Exercise 60 **Poplar and Millwall**

1 Draw an outline sketch of the river. Mark on your map as many different types of 'land use' as you can recognise, showing these in a key. With the help of the map on page 244, add a scale line.

2 The area shown has experienced great changes in recent years. Describe some of these changes and try to explain why they have occurred.

3 Suggest some possible future uses for an area such as this. What might make your plans difficult to carry out?

The Isle of Dogs. All the docks in this meander of the Thames have now been closed down

Contrasts in living standards

Contrasts in wealth

There are very considerable differences of wealth in Britain, although there may not be the great extremes of wealth and poverty found in some parts of the world. These may be seen in the variety of housing, cars and other material possessions and from the sorts of recreation and leisure that can be taken. It may also be reflected in the existence of fee-paying schools and private medical schemes.

Wealth is gained in several ways. For the majority of people it is through earned income. As the illustrations show there can be enormous differences in gross income, and the net income, after taxes have been taken and allowances added, remains very different. We have already seen that well over three million men and women were unemployed in 1984, and their income was provided by the state out of taxes. Many individuals and families receive other grants and benefits, although a remarkable number are never claimed for some reason or other. A big question is how much different jobs are worth, and how they should be assessed.

Quite apart from earned income, many people acquire wealth from unearned sources. They may have proper-

Some families have earned, made or inherited enough wealth to live in large houses set in beautiful grounds

These miners' wives live in small terraced houses

Right: This map shows variations in 'levels of living'. This index is based on unemployment, overcrowding, infant mortality and housing quality

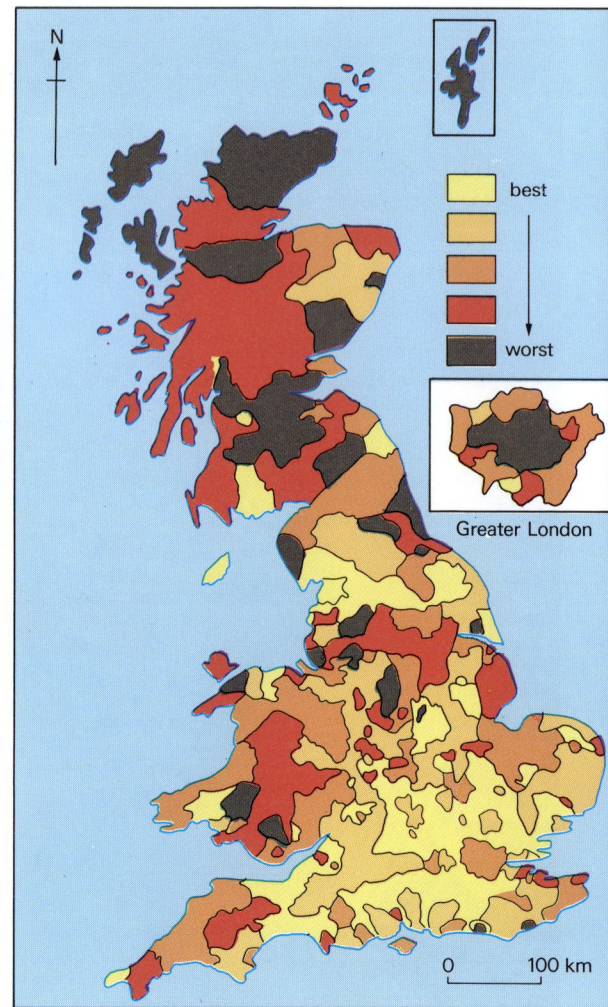

N

best
worst

Greater London

0   100 km

ty from which they get rent, or money invested in stocks or shares, for example. Others make money by buying and selling property. It is sometimes argued that this is 'earned' in the sense that it is business, and that risks have been taken and skill shown in knowing when to buy and sell and about planning procedures and legal matters. There is also inherited wealth, which often takes the form of estates or houses and their contents. This is wealth being handed down from one generation to the next. This private wealth, is different from the wealth owned by large companies or institutions such as the Church. Taxes have to be paid on such wealth, and the upkeep of some properties is very great. Nevertheless the vast majority of those who inherit wealth rarely suffer the poverty known to the unemployed or lowest paid.

Regional contrasts in need and provision

Quite apart from the unemployed and poor, there are young people, elderly and sick or injured who need support and care. If they have sufficient wealth, then they may be able to pay for their needs. Very many cannot do this, however. At the beginning of 1984, for example, there were more than a million children in families dependent on supplementary benefit, mostly due to unemployment. There were also nearly nine million men and women over retirement age. The majority of these had worked hard all their lives, but were unable to save enough to keep themselves without any support. All these people – the retired, the sick, the young and the unemployed – frequently need help from society at large. This is provided out of contributions paid by working people and out of taxes, as well as by direct payments. For very many people the amount and quality of support by the state makes the difference between a tolerable life and misery.

The map of 'levels of living' is made up from information about unemployment, infant mortality, overcrowding and housing quality. The one on 'expen-

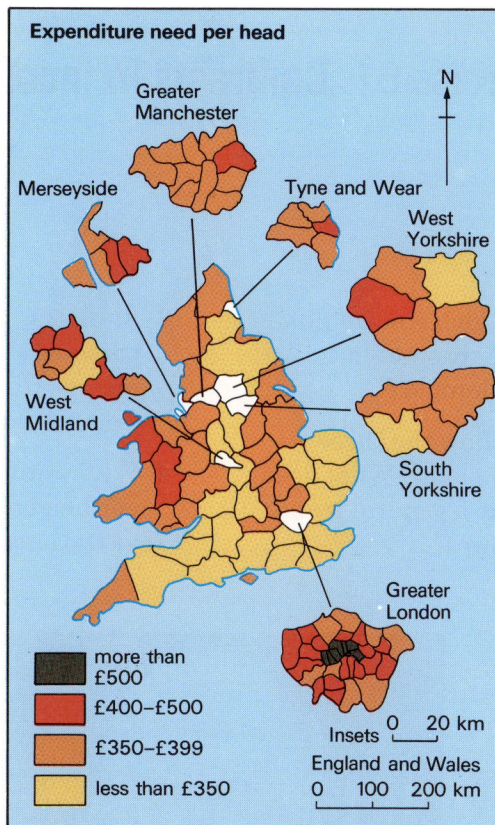

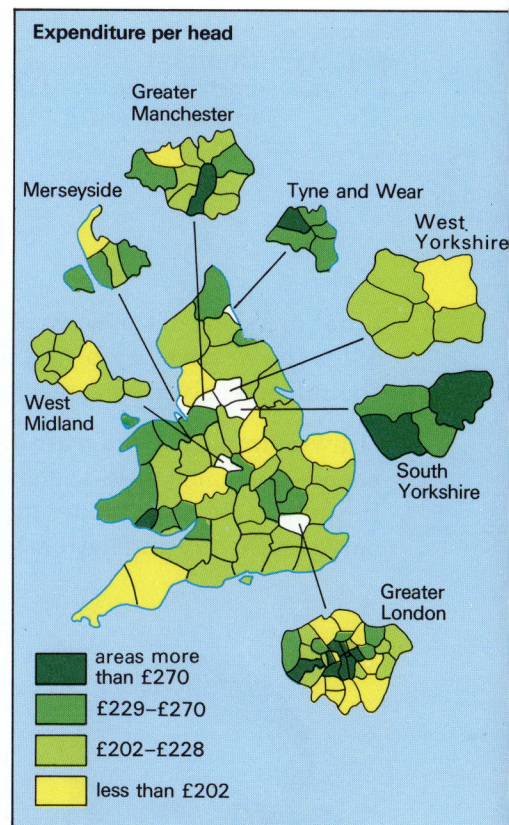

Expenditure need per head

Greater Manchester
Merseyside
Tyne and Wear
West Yorkshire
West Midland
South Yorkshire
Greater London

more than £500
£400–£500
£350–£399
less than £350

Insets 0   20 km
England and Wales
0   100   200 km

Expenditure per head

Greater Manchester
Merseyside
Tyne and Wear
West Yorkshire
West Midland
South Yorkshire
Greater London

areas more than £270
£229–£270
£202–£228
less than £202

Maps of differing local authority 'need' and 'provision' in 1980/81. The difference between expenditure and assessed need is made up by the Government in the form of Rate Support Grants. In order to control spending the government reduced or withdrew grants to certain local authorities in 1984 in the face of strong protest

diture needs' is based on such things as the number of pupils of school age, the number of old age pensioners and sixty-seven other factors. From the two maps it is clear that conditions vary from one place to another. Some local authority houses and estates are better than others, for example, while some authorities spend more on education and social services than others. There is also a difference between the number of hospital beds and doctors per person from one Health Region to another.

1 From the map of 'levels of living' name two places with a high and two with a low grading on the four-point scale. Describe the sort of environment and type of work done in the four places.

2 Argue the case for and against individuals and companies being allowed to make and keep large profits from the buying and selling of property.

3 Where does your area lie in the map of 'levels of living', 'expenditure needs' and 'provision'? Do you think this accurately gives the picture in your area?

Great wealth can be made from the buying and selling of property and land

Councillors hit out at GLC ex-leader's £1½m land deal

A series of deals which ended in a local council paying Sir Horace Cutler – former Tory leader of the Greater London Council – £35000 an acre for land which it had originally agreed to buy at £1000 an acre, is creating an increasingly bitter political storm. The deals involving the 72-acre Southwood Farm – which Cutler bought through two of his companies for £24000 in the 1950s and '60s – have caused controversy for years. Between 1973 to 1979, the Cutler companies sold the farm piece by piece to Rushmoor Council for £1600000. Most of the land was used for playing fields and a golf course.

Exercise 61 Contrasts in income

1 What are some of the ways in which you would judge the worth of a job, and the income that should be received by someone doing it?

2 Draw a simple bar diagram to show the three people's incomes in 1983 shown below. What does the article claim is happening as a general trend between the top and bottom groups?

3 Rank the regions of Britain according to a) personal disposable income, b) percentage of income from rent, dividends and net interest. Comment on the pattern.

4 Why would a map of the average personal income per head not show the same pattern as one showing variations in standards of living (page 248)?

Chief Executive of BOC: salary £579 000 a year

Lord Chief Justice: salary £75 000 a year

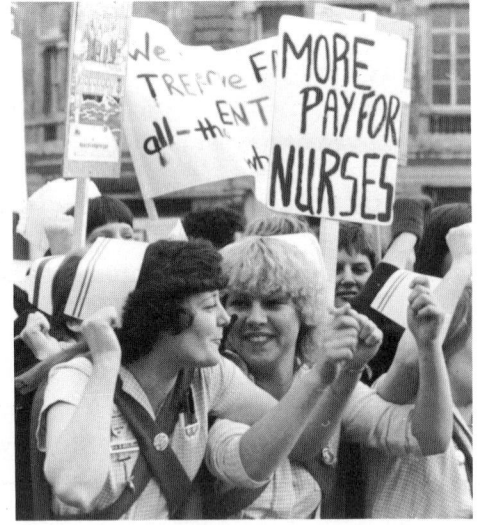

Nurse: salary £3 500 a year

The rich get richer, the poor get poorer

The distribution of income in Britain is becoming more un-equal, according to the Government's own figures. The main reason is the rise in unemployment. This, together with an increasing number of pensioners, means that the bottom 40 per cent of British households are getting a di-minishing share of total income, while the top 40 per cent are getting a rising share.

The source of people's incomes by region, 1983

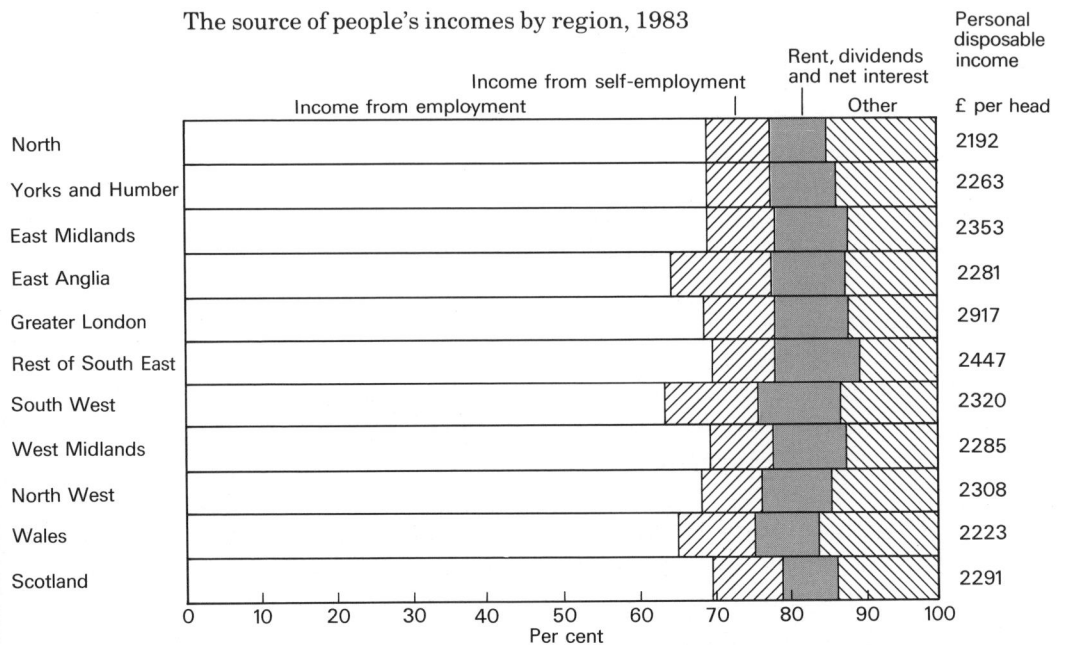

Region	Personal disposable income £ per head
North	2192
Yorks and Humber	2263
East Midlands	2353
East Anglia	2281
Greater London	2917
Rest of South East	2447
South West	2320
West Midlands	2285
North West	2308
Wales	2223
Scotland	2291

Chapter 12 **Britain and the world**

Britain and world trade

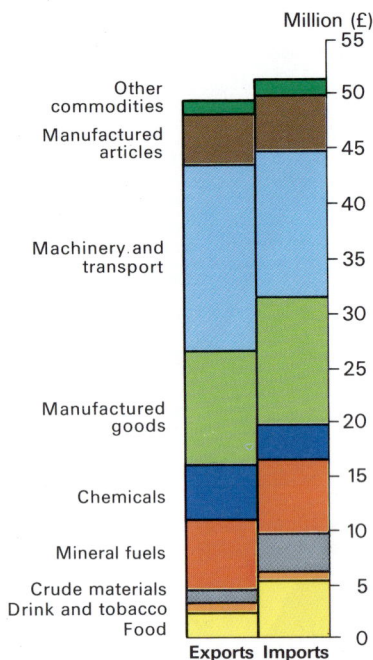

Million (£)

UK exports and imports 1980

Caithness glass. Many British exports are of high quality craft products.

International trade

Trade is an important feature of modern economic activity, and there are very few countries that are not dependent on the buying and selling of goods and services. Britain has always relied on international trade, and in the past it depended on the import of large amounts of food and raw materials for its factories, and the export of manufactured products. More recently this pattern has become more varied, with many manufactured goods being imported and increased British sources of energy such as oil and gas. Britain also nowadays sells food and primary raw materials and resources to other countries, as the table shows. It may seem strange to both import and export the same types of goods, but they vary so much in type, quality and cost that it can make a lot of sense to do so. It has to be remembered that the volume and value of imports and exports change all the time, and that on the whole it is better for a country to earn more from exports than it pays out for imports. But as the diagram on page 255 shows, the total 'balance of payments' takes into account 'invisible' earnings and costs as well as visible trade.

The pattern of exports

The graph opposite shows that Britain's share of world manufacturing exports fell during the late 1970s. In 1960, some fifteen years before the first data shown on the graph, the share of exports was almost twice as great. It has become increasingly difficult for Britain to export and sell goods abroad. Many explanations are offered for the decline.

In the past Britain had a world-wide Empire that provided not only cheap raw materials and foods, but also a market for exports. As the colonies gained their independence they often chose to trade with other states, and Britain had to compete in the world market with other producers. One reason given for the loss of some markets, particularly in steel, cars, ships and textiles, is the higher costs of British goods. This is sometimes said to be due to demands for high wages, or to inefficiency, but others would argue it is due to poor management or not enough investment in new equipment. It is also the case that prices can be greatly increased with a change in the value of the British pound compared with the money of importing countries. This is outside the control of manufacturers,

HOLSTEN BRAUEREI HAMBURG
HOLSTEN DISTRIBUTORS LIMITED

Some Gern beer is imported b container

Britain's top twenty trading partners in 1982

Exports to	% total exports	Imports from	% total imports
1 USA	13.4	1 West Germany	13.0
2 West Germany	9.7	2 USA	11.7
3 Netherlands	8.4	3 Netherlands	7.8
4 France	8.1	4 France	7.5
5 Irish Republic	5.2	5 Belgium	5.0
6 Belgium/Luxembourg	4.2	6 Italy	4.8
7 Italy	3.6	7 Japan	4.6
8 Sweden	3.5	8 Norway	3.6
9 Saudi Arabia	2.5	9 Irish Republic	3.5
10 Switzerland	2.3	10 Sweden	2.9
11 Nigeria	2.2	11 Switzerland	2.9
12 South Africa	2.2	12 Canada	2.6
13 Denmark	2.0	13 Saudi Arabia	2.6
14 Australia	1.9	14 Denmark	2.3
15 Norway	1.7	15 Spain	1.7
16 Spain	1.6	16 Finland	1.5
17 Canada	1.5	17 South Africa	1.4
18 Japan	1.2	18 USSR	1.2
19 Finland	0.9	19 New Zealand	1.0
20 Portugal	0.8	20 Australia	0.9

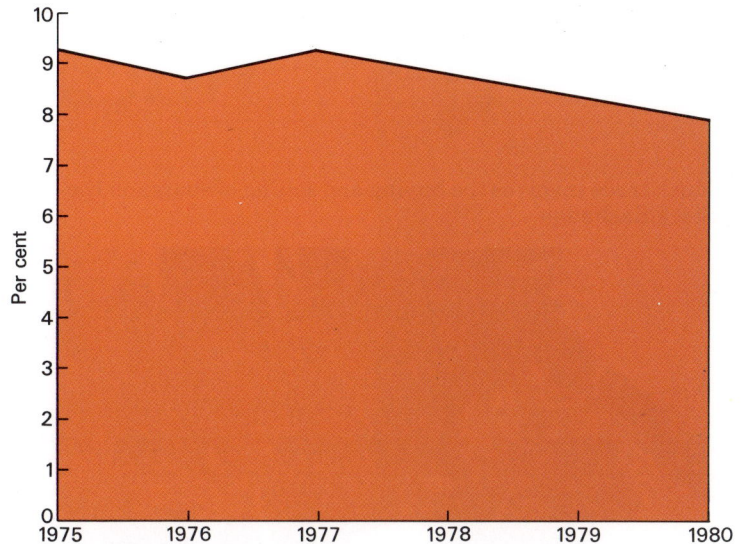

Britain's share of world manufacturing exports

but it can greatly increase the buying price of goods being sold abroad. Other explanations put forward are late delivery and poor quality, or just bad marketing and selling methods. Whatever the reasons, many sectors of British industry are finding it harder to sell against foreign competition.

There are many other reasons why selling is difficult. In the middle of 1982, for example, the sale of British steel to the USA was threatened by a decision of the American government to set a limit on imported steel to protect its own steel-making companies. The USA also tried to prevent Britain and other European countries selling steel pipes and turbines to the USSR for a huge gas pipeline. By threatening the British manufacturers the USA hoped to put political pressure on the USSR. These are just two of the complex ways in which exports can be affected.

Imports into Britain

Understandably, consumers want to buy the best that they can afford, and they normally welcome the greater variety and lower prices that foreign goods can provide. Unfortunately, this foreign trade can have a damaging effect on British manufacturers, and in extreme cases can lead to the closure of firms, and greater unemployment. The government can influence the volume

and value of foreign imports and foreign competition, by limiting the amount imported by means of a quota system, or by asking for higher import duties and taxes, so that the products become too expensive to buy. The difficulty is in striking a balance between helping the consumer who wants good products as cheaply as possible, and helping industry to make profits and provide jobs, thus improving the economic output of the country. It could result in less competition, less variety and higher prices.

1 a) Put the three largest types of import and export into rank order. b) For each category describe or name one British product that is exported. c) Describe four foreign products that are available in your local shops.

2 Imagine you were advising a manufacturing company about sales. List the things affecting costs the company can influence and those that the company can do little or nothing about.

3 a) Apart from cost, what influences a consumer to buy one product rather than another?
   b) What are the risks to a government of 'protecting' its own producers by making it difficult or impossible for foreign goods or services to be sold?

4 Why is a healthy balance of payments, with income greater than expenses, *not* necessarily a sign of a strong economy? Give examples from Britain in 1984.

All the items in this electronics shop window have been imported

253

Much trade involves the buying and selling of shares on the Stock Exchange

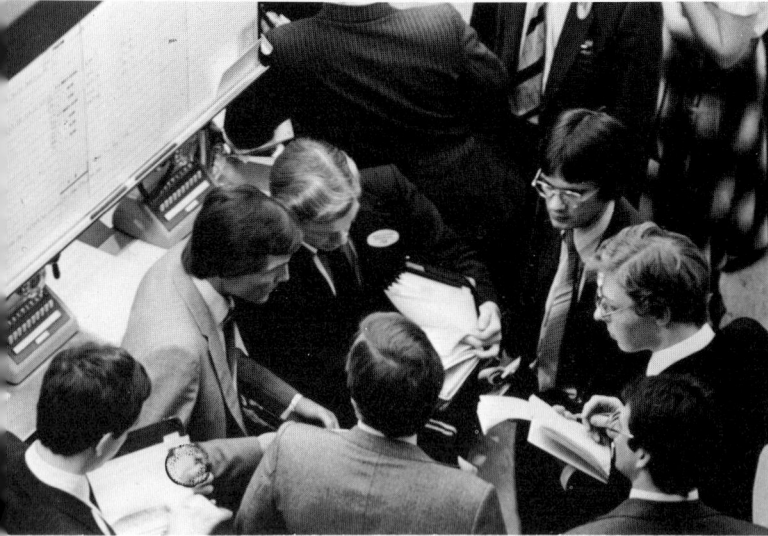

Spending by foreign tourists in Britain is one source of invisible earnings

The products described on page 253 are all actual products, and are known as 'visible' trade. There are also 'invisible' imports and exports. Whenever foreign money is spent in Britain by tourists or investors, or is received in payment for financial help, or in exchange for insurance or some kind of consultancy service, then it forms a part of invisible trade. Britain earns a lot of such trade, and in the early 1980s it was the world's largest net earner of invisible income.

(Net means the result of adding invisible earnings to invisible costs. In the case of Britain far more is earned than spent.) Not all types of invisible trade are increasing. In some areas Britain is now spending more than it earns, but overall invisible earnings are increasing. When invisible and visible trade figures for exports and imports were added together in 1981, Britain had a balance of payments surplus.

An example showing different ways of investing British money overseas

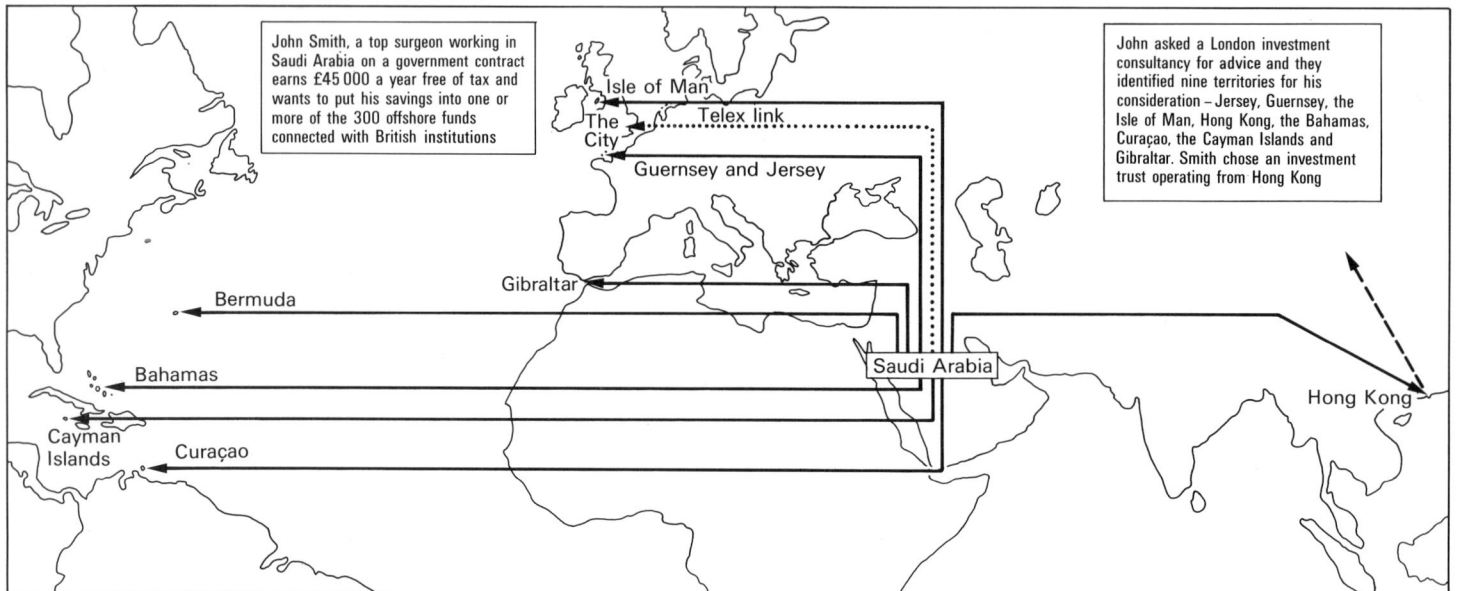

John Smith, a top surgeon working in Saudi Arabia on a government contract earns £45 000 a year free of tax and wants to put his savings into one or more of the 300 offshore funds connected with British institutions

John asked a London investment consultancy for advice and they identified nine territories for his consideration – Jersey, Guernsey, the Isle of Man, Hong Kong, the Bahamas, Curaçao, the Cayman Islands and Gibraltar. Smith chose an investment trust operating from Hong Kong

Exercise 62
Britain's balance of payments

1 What type of industry is illustrated in the advertisement? Why is it **a**) important, **b**) difficult for British manufacturers to sell such products to other countries?

2 Describe the changes in balance of payment between 1971 and 1981.

3 In very general terms, how is the balance of payments worked out?

4 Give two examples of each of the following:
   a) UK visible imports;
   b) UK invisible imports;
   c) UK visible exports;
   d) UK invisible exports.

British skill and experience used in Bahrein earns foreign money

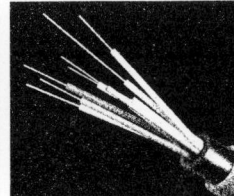

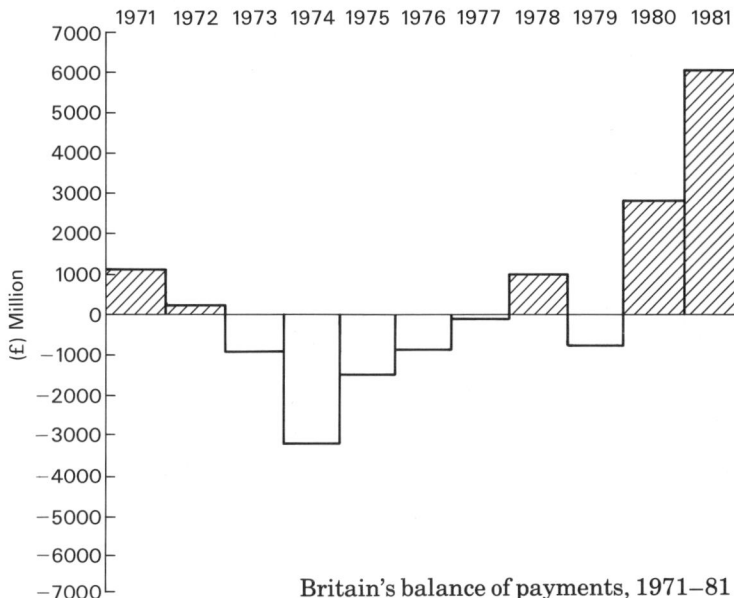

Britain's balance of payments, 1971–81

Britain and the EEC

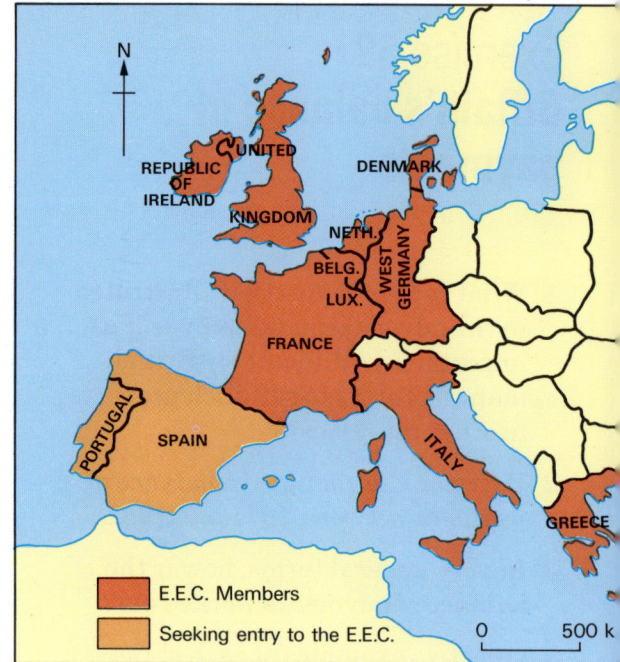

Member states of the EEC in 1983

The European Economic Community

The EEC was established in 1957 when Belgium, France, West Germany, Italy, Luxembourg and the Netherlands signed the treaty that laid down the terms for cooperation. The United Kingdom, together with Denmark and Ireland, joined in 1973, and the tenth member, Greece, in 1981. Spain and Portugal have also started discussions about joining the community.

The EEC is run by four main bodies, and their offices are based in Brussels and Luxembourg. The final decisions on most proposals are made by the Council of Ministers. Each member state sends a representative to the regular meetings, but votes on certain issues are weighted according to the size of the populations of the ten countries. The European Parliament in Strasbourg is quite different. Its members are elected by voters in the individual countries, and the UK has 81 seats in the Parliament. It has the job of debating issues, guided by the civil servants in the Commission, and making recommendations to the Council of Ministers. It also has the important task of approving or rejecting the budget each year.

Decisions are made by the Council of Ministers and the Parliament.

The ten countries also nominate members of the Commission. Six of the smaller states have one commissioner, while the four largest, which includes the UK, have two. These 14 Commissioners are responsible for such things as agriculture, fishing, employment and regional aid throughout the whole community, and are not supposed to represent just their own countries' interests. Together with their staffs, they maintain the day-to-day running of the EEC, and advise the Parliament on what needs doing and what should be controlled, changed or stopped. The fourth body is the European Court of Justice.

The EEC Council of Ministers in session

Member states of the EEC, 1983

Country	Population (millions)	GDP (US$ per capita)	% GDP from agriculture	% employed in farming	% foreign workers	% wealth from manufacturing
Belgium	10	11 260	2	3.4	6.6	30
Denmark	5	12 925	5	9.3	2.0	20
France	53	10 720	5	10.9	10.9	30
West Germany	62	12 419	2	7.1	10.3	38
Ireland	3	4412	17	23.8	0.3	25
Italy	56	5686	7	15.5	0.4	36
Luxembourg	0.3	9723	3	3.4	35.0	33
Netherlands	14	10 624	4	6.5	3.0	29
United Kingdom	56	7192	2	2.7	7.3	31
Greece	9.2	4093	14	3.4	—	19

This has ten judges, one from each country. Their job is to settle disputes over community laws between members of the EEC, and their judgement is binding on all member countries.

Benefits and costs of membership

The Community was formed for a variety of reasons, but the main ones were to provide mutual help by sharing resources and wealth. The basic idea was that each country should pay money into the fund according to its size and wealth, and there has been considerable disagreement about what makes a fair contribution from each of the ten countries. This money was then to be spent to help any country or group where the need was great. The ultimate aim is to have many regulations and laws in common, and to have common policies about such things as agriculture and fishing. So far a great deal of the income has been spent on agriculture and in trying to introduce a common agricultural policy. Many people feel that this has benefited those members with a large farming industry or with many agricultural workers, but has penalised the others. They would like to see less of the budget spent on agriculture and more on other forms of help.

Trade

One of the major changes caused by membership is related to trade. Normally a country controls its trade by having quotas or limits on the amount of goods it imports, and taxes or tariffs to encourage or discourage certain products. The aim of the EEC is to have no trade boundaries and barriers, but have the whole market of some 270 million people available to producers in all the member states. In the end this could lead to lower prices for the consumer, but while adjustments are being made it can lead to higher prices and strong competition for some producers. Attempts have been made to adopt common trade policies towards other producers, and an effort has been made to 'rationalise' and make more efficient the steel industry in the EEC so that it

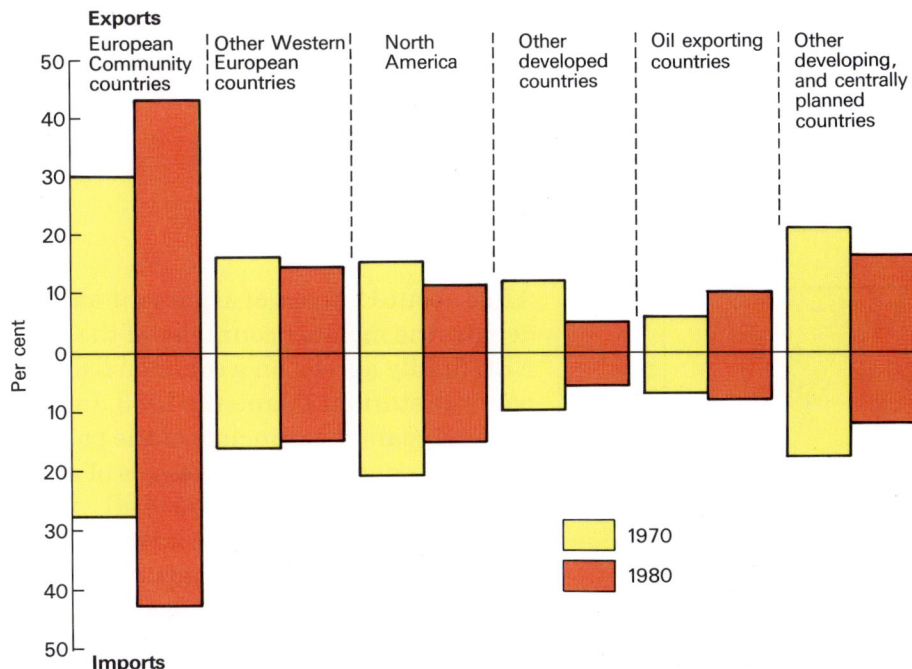

Britain's changing trade pattern since joining the EEC

can face competition from elsewhere. Although production has fallen, steelworks have closed and jobs have been lost, the damage would have been greater without some collaboration and agreement within the framework of the EEC. Overall, the effect on the UK has been to greatly increase trade with other EEC countries, at the expense of older trade links with countries such as New Zealand and Australia.

Employment

People within the Community are free to seek jobs in any of the ten countries. This is supposed to be on equal terms with nationals in the country concerned. Work permits are not required, and there is no loss of social security rights. With unemployment rising, there has not been the free movement of workers that there might have been in a growing economy.

1 Give examples of how British farmers, consumers and manufacturers have been affected by membership of the EEC.

2 What are the advantages and disadvantages of becoming part of a 'common market' of some 270 million people?

3 Who is your Euro-MP? What are the different attitudes of the main UK political parties to membership of the EEC?

4 Comment on the costs and benefits of Britain's EEC membership.

What Britain puts in the EEC

1 A share of running costs.

2 Free access for other EEC countries to Britain's market of 56 million people.

3 Free access for other EEC citizens to British jobs.

4 Agreement to accept EEC regulations and laws.

What Britain gets out of the EEC

1 A share of loans for grants from EEC funds for required developments.

2 Free access to the EEC market of over 200 million people.

3 Free access for British workers to jobs anywhere in the EEC.

4 Economic and political protection provided by belonging to a larger group.

257

The EEC and the British fishing industry

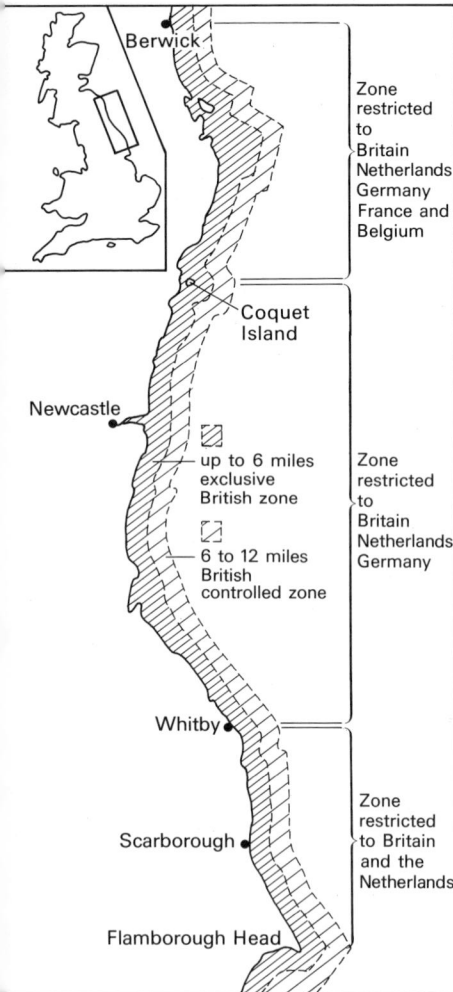

One example of EEC fishing regulations

Map labels:
- Berwick
- Zone restricted to Britain Netherlands Germany France and Belgium
- Coquet Island
- Newcastle
- up to 6 miles exclusive British zone
- 6 to 12 miles British controlled zone
- Zone restricted to Britain Netherlands Germany
- Whitby
- Scarborough
- Zone restricted to Britain and the Netherlands
- Flamborough Head

After about 12 years of argument and debate, the member countries of the EEC finally agreed on a common fishing policy to start on 1 January 1983. In the earliest years the principle of the policy had been equal access for vessels of all member states to the waters of all member states. This would have very badly hit some countries, particularly Britain, which argues that over 60% of the fishing stocks are in what were traditionally British waters. The British fishermen felt it unjust that foreign vessels could fish these once-British waters. Their industry had already suffered a dramatic decline with the loss of fishing rights off Iceland and Norway (decline of jobs, page 218), and many firms had switched from deep-sea trawling to these North Sea and coastal waters.

As a result of negotiations Britain was awarded 37% of the catch of the seven most important fish species in the common EEC waters – far less than the 60% they claimed. They have absolutely exclusive rights to fish in a six

How the fish in EEC waters, traditionally once regarded as British, are shared between different EEC countries

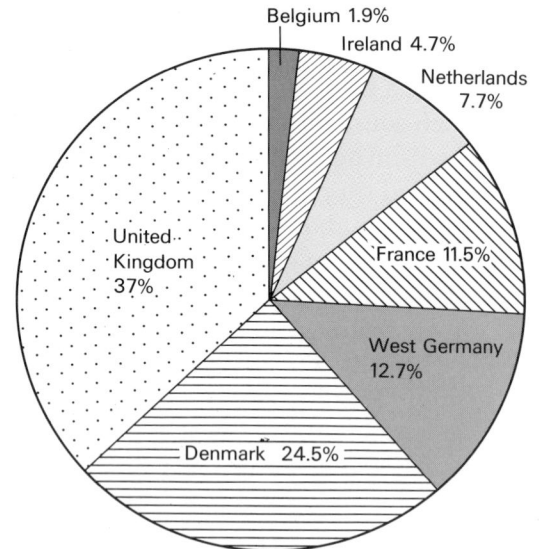

Pie chart labels:
- Belgium 1.9%
- Ireland 4.7%
- Netherlands 7.7%
- France 11.5%
- West Germany 12.7%
- Denmark 24.5%
- United Kingdom 37%

mile zone, and control and special preference in the six–twelve mile zone. The details are very complicated as the example of herring catching shows.

The British fishing industry has suffered badly as a result of the EEC agreement – an example of how membership may bring losses to some and gains to other people within the country.

The future of British fisherman such as this man in Pittenween in Scotland is very much influenced by EEC fishing regulations

Exercise 63 **Population in the EEC**

Population density in the EEC

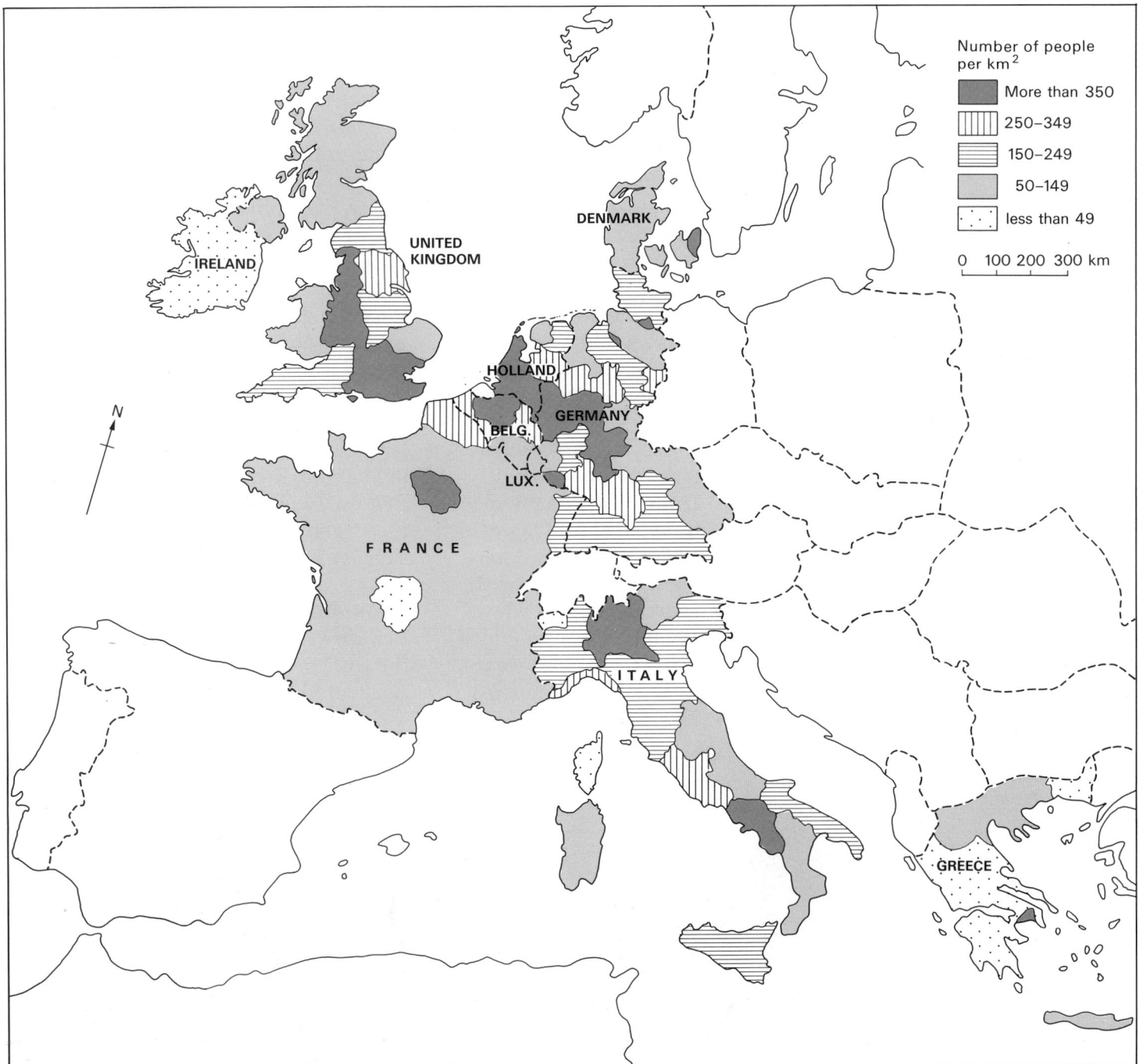

Number of people per km²

- More than 350
- 250–349
- 150–249
- 50–149
- less than 49

0 100 200 300 km

IRELAND

UNITED KINGDOM

DENMARK

HOLLAND

BELG.

GERMANY

LUX.

FRANCE

ITALY

GREECE

1 Describe and account for the pattern of population density in the UK and one other country of the EEC.

2 Rank the countries of the EEC according to their density of population.

3 Draw a graph to compare density of population with a) percentage of workforce in agriculture, b) GDP. Is there any correlation or link between density of population and either of the other features?

Britain and international relations

British troops recaptured the Falklands from Argentinian occupation in 1982, but their future ownership and control remain in doubt

Different nations have different views of the world. These maps show Britain's military and trade perspectives of the rest of the world

Military relations

Britain's history, like that of most older countries, has been marked regularly by periods of war with other states. As recently as 1982 differences with Argentina over the ownership and future of the Falkland Islands in the south Atlantic ocean led to bitter and violent conflict. Earlier in the century, the United Kingdom had been involved in conflicts in Korea, Malaysia, Palestine and South Africa as well as in two vast and destructive world wars in 1914–18 and 1939–45. Many lives were lost and huge sums of money spent on these wars.

Countries who are only concerned with defending their territories will still maintain armies, navies and an air force, often at great expense. They also try to improve their security by entering into treaties and agreements with other states who are friendly or who fear the same threats, real or imagined. In the early 1980s the two main rival groups were the communist countries, headed by the USSR, and the western capitalist countries headed by the USA. The situation was more complicated than this, since there were strong differences and dislikes between some communist countries and between some western ones. There were also many states, particularly the 'developing' countries of Latin America, Africa and South-East Asia who did not want to get politically involved with either of the main groups. They were called 'non-aligned' countries, and were often helped by both groups to try and gain their support. There were also many regional conflicts, such as between Israel and the Arabs, and civil wars as in Morocco, Ethiopia and El Salvador. Britain was only indirectly involved in these, giving arms, resources or moral support, but not actually fighting.

Economic relations

Britain's trade with the world and with the EEC in particular has already been considered. The way in which the econ-

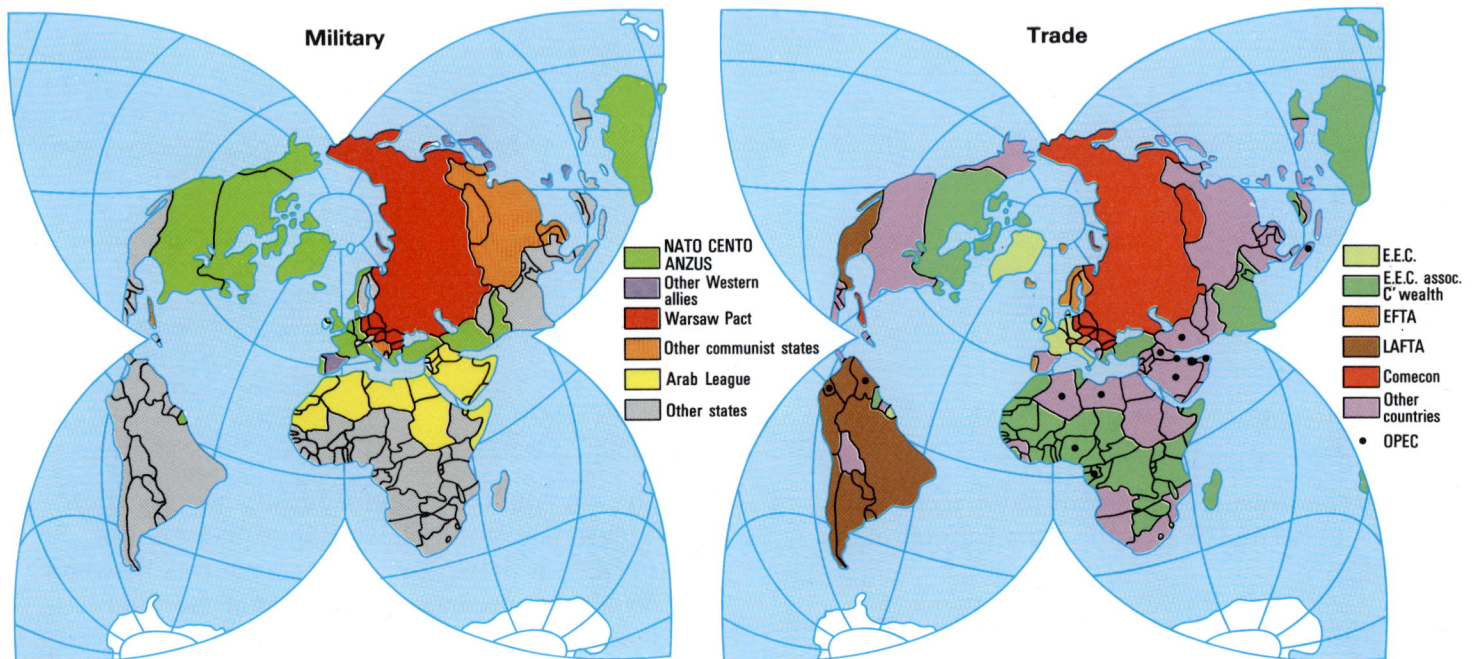

Military

- NATO CENTO ANZUS
- Other Western allies
- Warsaw Pact
- Other communist states
- Arab League
- Other states

Trade

- E.E.C.
- E.E.C. assoc. C' wealth
- EFTA
- LAFTA
- Comecon
- Other countries
- • OPEC

omic activity, even of large groups, can be influenced by politics was well illustrated in 1982. Several manufacturers in Europe wanted to sell pipelines and equipment to the USSR for its huge gas pipeline network leading from Siberia into Europe. The USA used all its economic power to prevent this happening because of its political suspicion and fear of the USSR. The decision of Britain to support its firms placed a strain on relationships with the USA, who determined to penalise them for their action. Trade relationships are often bound up with political ones in confusing ways. At the very same time that the USA was protesting about this, it was selling grain to the USSR!

Social and cultural relationships

The map of economic groupings refers to countries associated with the EEC and the Commonwealth.

People from different states may wish to share ideas of a cultural or a scientific nature, to join together for sporting events, to exchange students or specialist workers, and so on. With enormous improvements in communications, with instant television coming from most parts of the world, relationships are bound to be affected. Britain once had great power, both politically and economically. Those days are now past, but the influence of British people can be seen – for good and bad – all round the world. Britain remains relatively wealthy by world standards, and is capable of having influence on world affairs.

1 a) What are some of the arguments for and against belonging to NATO or any other military group? b) What are the arguments for and against Britain having its own nuclear weapons?

2 What is the case for Britain being a member of the United Nations? Why is that international organisation sometimes said to be fairly powerless?

3 Argue the case for or against Britain giving a larger share of its wealth to poorer states. Should there be any conditions attached to giving aid?

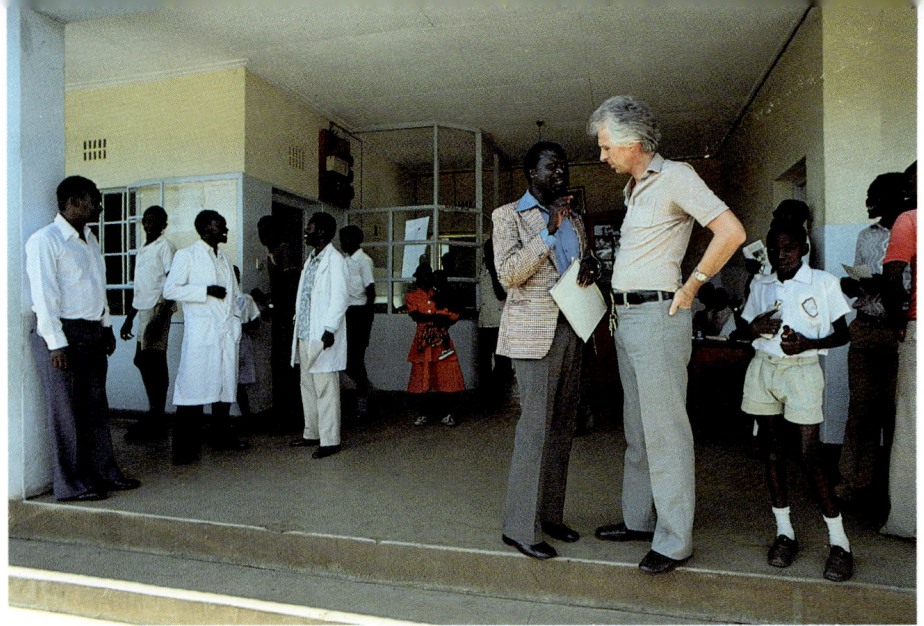

This medical expert in Kenya is one example of British aid to developing countries

Average living standards vary enormously from nation to nation, and within each country

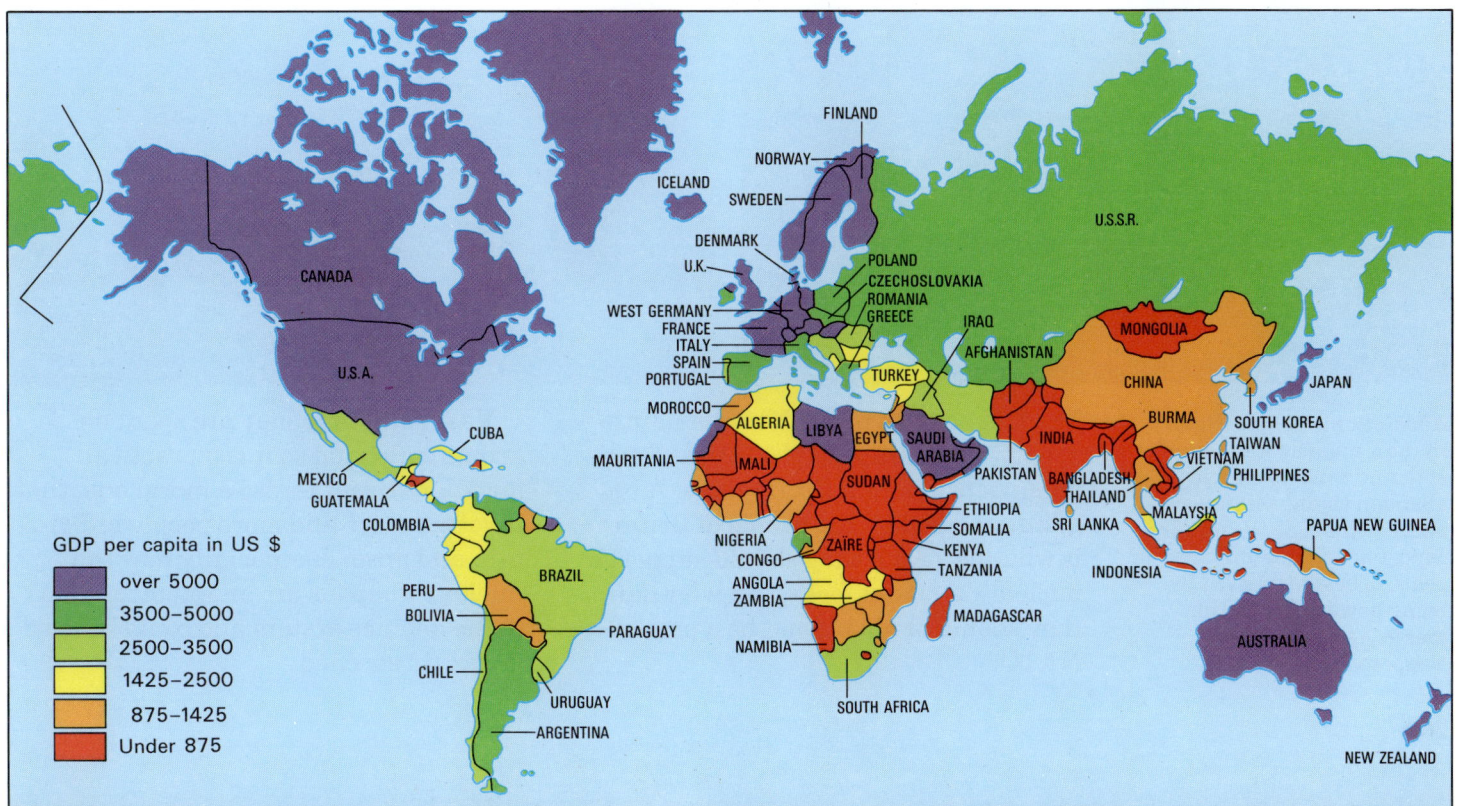

GDP per capita in US $

- over 5000
- 3500–5000
- 2500–3500
- 1425–2500
- 875–1425
- Under 875

The military balance in Europe

It is difficult for nations to agree on what weapons each is entitled to have, while there is no real trust between them

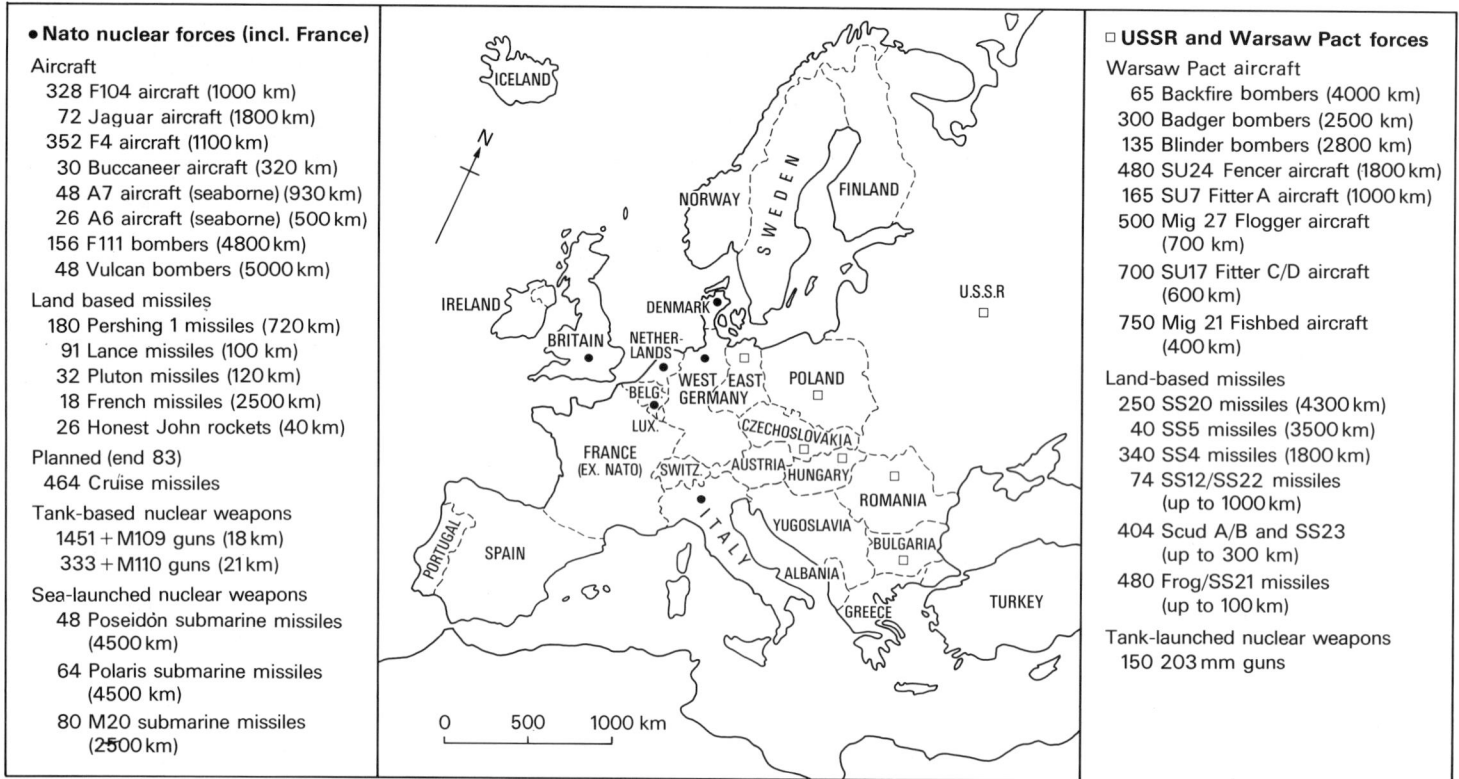

● Nato nuclear forces (incl. France)

Aircraft
- 328 F104 aircraft (1000 km)
- 72 Jaguar aircraft (1800 km)
- 352 F4 aircraft (1100 km)
- 30 Buccaneer aircraft (320 km)
- 48 A7 aircraft (seaborne) (930 km)
- 26 A6 aircraft (seaborne) (500 km)
- 156 F111 bombers (4800 km)
- 48 Vulcan bombers (5000 km)

Land based missiles
- 180 Pershing 1 missiles (720 km)
- 91 Lance missiles (100 km)
- 32 Pluton missiles (120 km)
- 18 French missiles (2500 km)
- 26 Honest John rockets (40 km)

Planned (end 83)
- 464 Cruise missiles

Tank-based nuclear weapons
- 1451 + M109 guns (18 km)
- 333 + M110 guns (21 km)

Sea-launched nuclear weapons
- 48 Poseidon submarine missiles (4500 km)
- 64 Polaris submarine missiles (4500 km)
- 80 M20 submarine missiles (2500 km)

□ USSR and Warsaw Pact forces

Warsaw Pact aircraft
- 65 Backfire bombers (4000 km)
- 300 Badger bombers (2500 km)
- 135 Blinder bombers (2800 km)
- 480 SU24 Fencer aircraft (1800 km)
- 165 SU7 Fitter A aircraft (1000 km)
- 500 Mig 27 Flogger aircraft (700 km)
- 700 SU17 Fitter C/D aircraft (600 km)
- 750 Mig 21 Fishbed aircraft (400 km)

Land-based missiles
- 250 SS20 missiles (4300 km)
- 40 SS5 missiles (3500 km)
- 340 SS4 missiles (1800 km)
- 74 SS12/SS22 missiles (up to 1000 km)
- 404 Scud A/B and SS23 (up to 300 km)
- 480 Frog/SS21 missiles (up to 100 km)

Tank-launched nuclear weapons
- 150 203 mm guns

0   500   1000 km

Above: Some people argue that all nuclear weapons are evil, and that we should abandon them, whatever other nations do. *Right*: The opposing argument is that peace is best preserved by being powerful, and that means having nuclear weapons

The UK belongs to the North Atlantic Treaty Organisation (NATO), and contributes to a joint military force. A big question faced by the people of Britain is whether or not they should support a nuclear deterrent force, and whether they should or should not be a part of NATO.

Vast sums of money are spent on armaments, and so it is a practical question. But it is also a moral one, that involves more and more people in Britain and abroad, especially now that nuclear weapons are an important part of the defence system and could be used if war threatened.

Exercise 64 The Commonwealth

A meeting of the Queen with her Commonwealth Prime Ministers

The Commonwealth is a group of countries once a part of the British Empire. When they gained their independence most of them chose to remain in what was then called the British Commonwealth. The change of name is an indication that it is an association of equals, who meet every two years to discuss world affairs and matters of interest to them as a group. The Commonwealth is often accused of being without influence and power, but it does contain about a quarter of the world's population drawn from all parts of the world. They meet voluntarily for mutual support. It is one of the few international groups where states from the 'developed' and 'developing' areas of the world can share views in this way. These meetings of Commonwealth ministers are a reminder that relationships can be for reasons other than military or economic.

1 Name a member of the Commonwealth in each of the continents. It used to be said that 'the sun never sets on the British Empire'. Explain what this meant.

2 What are the advantages of belonging to a large group such as the Commonwealth? Why do some consider it a waste of time, effort and money?

3 What are the signs in the mid 1980s of Britain's past influence around the world? In what ways do you think that other people have gained or lost through their past contacts with Britain?

Member countries of the Commonwealth are situated in all parts of the globe

The countries of the Commonwealth

1 Canada 23 million
2 Britain 56 million
3 Cyprus 560 000
4 Malta 300 000
5 Bermuda 218 000
6 Jamaica 2 million
7 Barbados 254 000
8 Grenada 110 000
9 Trinidad and Tobago 1.1 million
10 Guyana 830 000
11 The Gambia 495 000
12 Western Samoa 151 000
13 Tonga 90 000
14 Sierra Leone 3 million
15 Ghana 9 million
16 Nigeria 79 million
17 Tanzania 14.5 million
18 Zambia 4.5 million
19 Botswana 675 000
20 India 604 million
21 Bangladesh 71 million
22 Sri Lanka 14 million
23 Malaysia 12 million
24 Singapore 2.2 million
25 Papua/New Guinea 2.8 million
26 Nauru 7 500
27 Kenya 12 million
28 Fiji 559 000
29 Australia 14 million
30 New Zealand 3 million
31 Seychelles 60 000
32 Uganda 11 million
33 Mauritius 881 000
34 Malawi 5 million
35 Swaziland 530 000
36 Lesotho 1 million

Great Britain

Scale: 1:2,200,000

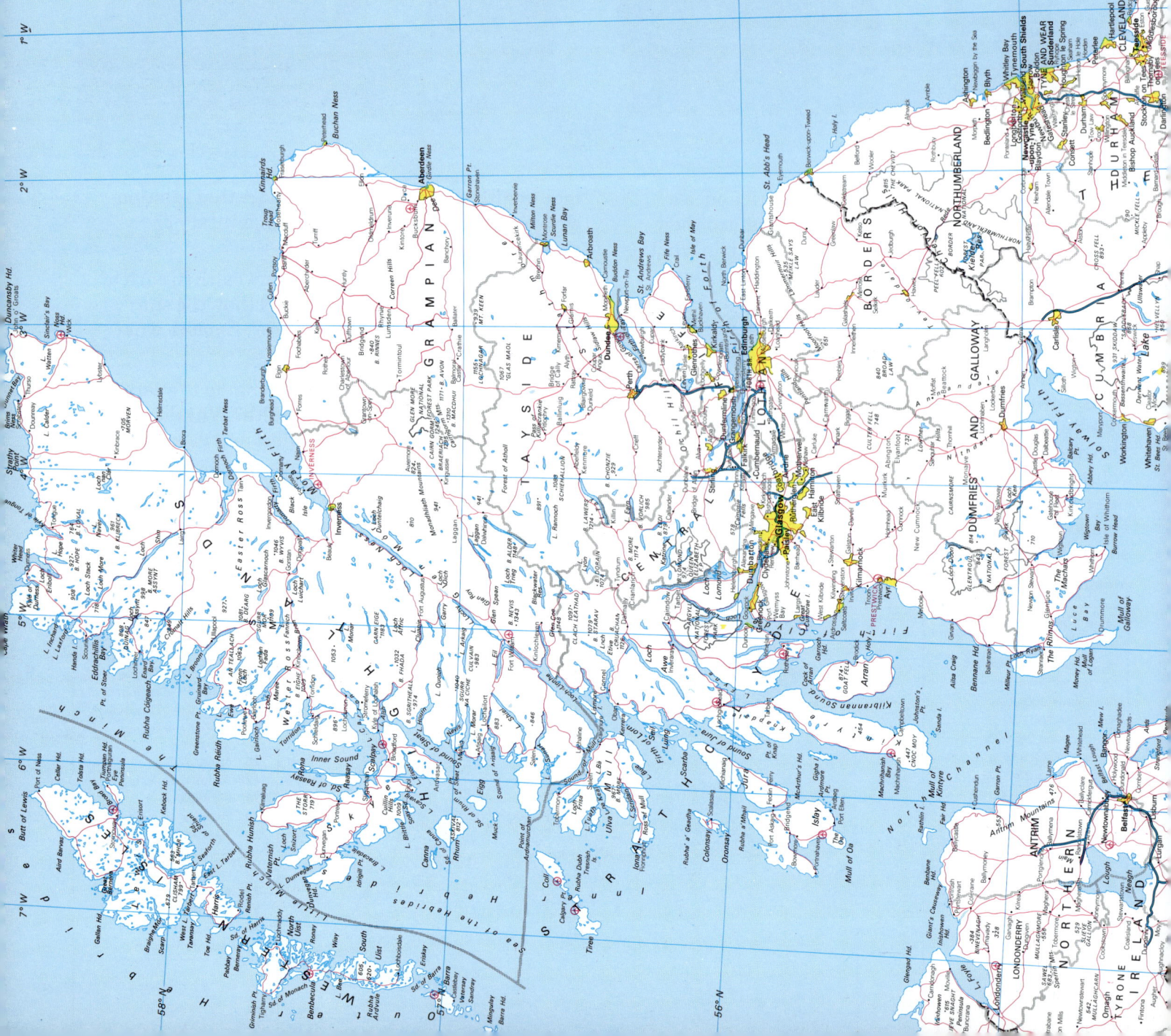

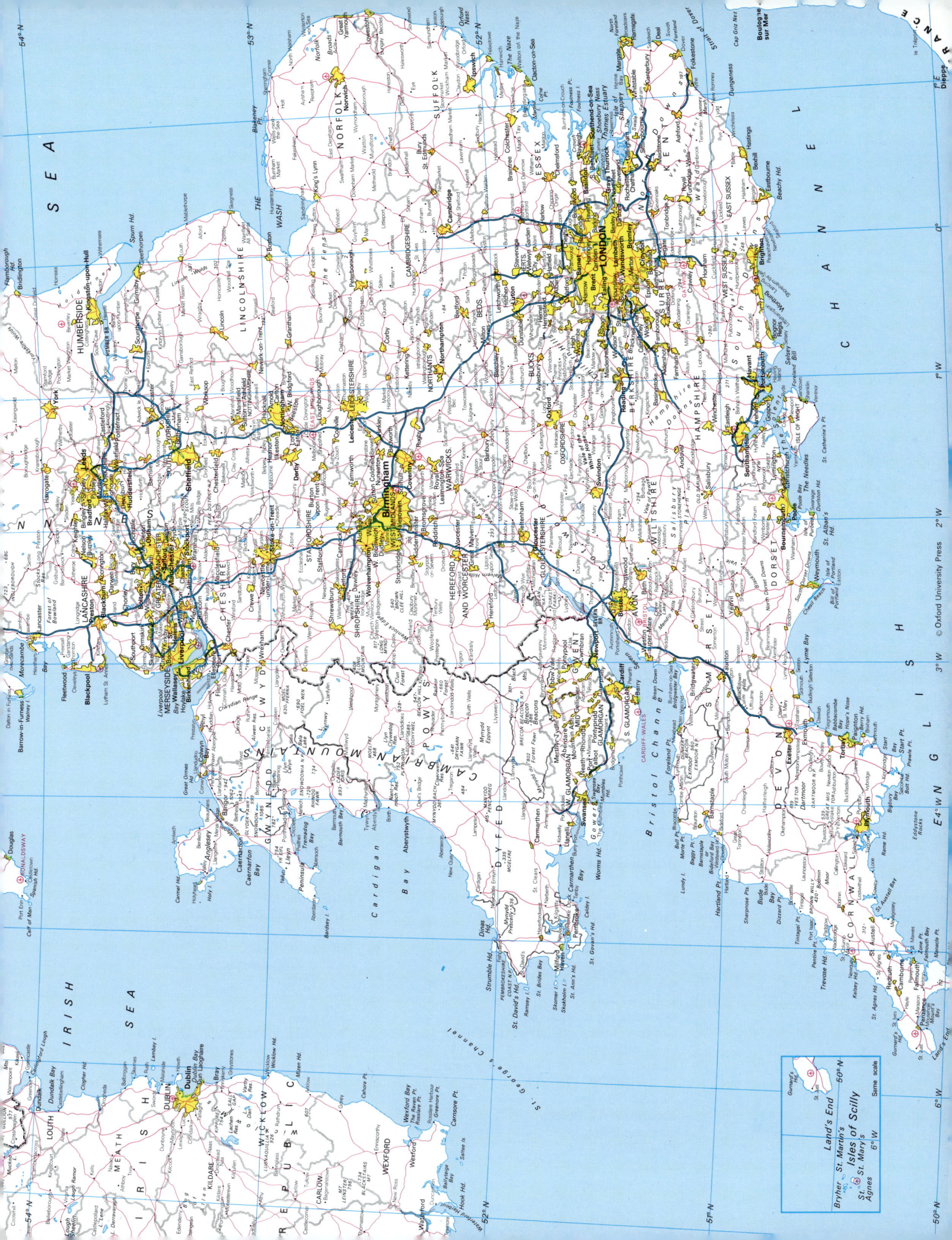

Index

Place index